Innovation, Technology, and Knowledge Management

Series editor:

Elias G. Carayannis
George Washington University
Washington, DC, USA

More information about this series at http://www.springer.com/series/8124

Nicholas Kalaitzandonakes • Elias G. Carayannis
Evangelos Grigoroudis • Stelios Rozakis
Editors

From Agriscience to Agribusiness

Theories, Policies and Practices in
Technology Transfer and Commercialization

 Springer

Editors
Nicholas Kalaitzandonakes
Department of Agricultural and Applied
Economics
University of Missouri
Columbia, MO, USA

Elias G. Carayannis
Department of Information Systems and
Technology Management
GWU School of Business
Washington, DC, USA

Evangelos Grigoroudis
School of Production Engineering &
Management
Technical University of Crete
Chania, Crete, Greece

Stelios Rozakis
Institute of Soil Science and Plant
Cultivation
IUNG-PIB
Pulawy, Poland

ISSN 2197-5698   ISSN 2197-5701   (electronic)
Innovation, Technology, and Knowledge Management
ISBN 978-3-319-67957-0   ISBN 978-3-319-67958-7   (eBook)
https://doi.org/10.1007/978-3-319-67958-7

Library of Congress Control Number: 2017955375

Printed on acid-free paper

This Springer imprint is published by Springer Nature
The registered company is Springer International Publishing AG
The registered company address is: Gewerbestrasse 11, 6330 Cham, Switzerland

Series Foreword

The Springer book series *Innovation, Technology, and Knowledge Management* was launched in March 2008 as a forum and intellectual, scholarly "podium" for global/local, transdisciplinary, transsectoral, public–private, and leading/"bleeding"-edge ideas, theories, and perspectives on these topics.

The book series is accompanied by the Springer *Journal of the Knowledge Economy*, which was launched in 2009 with the same editorial leadership.

The series showcases provocative views that diverge from the current "conventional wisdom," that are properly grounded in theory and practice, and that consider the concepts of *robust competitiveness*,[1] *sustainable entrepreneurship*,[2] and *democratic capitalism*[3] central to its philosophy and objectives. More specifically, the aim of this series is to highlight emerging research and practice at the dynamic intersection of these fields, where individuals, organizations, industries, regions, and nations are harnessing creativity and invention to achieve and sustain growth.

---

[1] We define *sustainable entrepreneurship* as the creation of viable, profitable, and scalable firms. Such firms engender the formation of self-replicating and mutually enhancing innovation networks and knowledge clusters (innovation ecosystems), leading toward robust competitiveness (E.G. Carayannis, *International Journal of Innovation and Regional Development* 1(3), 235–254, 2009).

[2] We understand *robust competitiveness* to be a state of economic being and becoming that avails systematic and defensible "unfair advantages" to the entities that are part of the economy. Such competitiveness is built on mutually complementary and reinforcing low-, medium-, and hightechnology and public and private sector entities (government agencies, private firms, universities, and nongovernmental organizations) (E.G. Carayannis, *International Journal of Innovation and Regional Development* 1(3), 235–254. 2009).

[3] The concepts of *robust competitiveness* and *sustainable entrepreneurship* are pillars of a regime that we call *democratic capitalism* (as opposed to "popular or casino capitalism"), in which real opportunities for education and economic prosperity are available to all, especially—but not only—younger people. These are the direct derivative of a collection of top-down policies as well as bottom-up initiatives (including strong research and development policies and funding, but going beyond these to include the development of innovation networks and knowledge clusters across regions and sectors) (E.G. Carayannis and A. Kaloudis, *Japan Economic Currents*, pp. 6–10, January 2009).

Books that are part of the series explore the impact of innovation at the "macro" (economies, markets), "meso" (industries, firms), and "micro" levels (teams, individuals), drawing from such related disciplines as finance, organizational psychology, research and development, science policy, information systems, and strategy, with the underlying theme that for innovation to be useful, it must involve the sharing and application of knowledge.

Some of the key anchoring concepts of the series are outlined in the figure below and the definitions that follow (all definitions are from E.G. Carayannis and D.F.J. Campbell, *International Journal of Technology Management*, 46, 3–4, 2009).

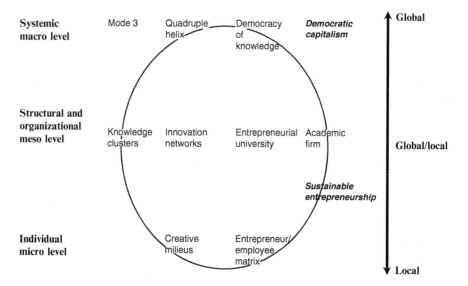

Conceptual profile of the series *Innovation, Technology, and Knowledge Management*:

- The "Mode 3" Systems Approach for Knowledge Creation, Diffusion, and Use: "Mode 3" is a multilateral, multinodal, multimodal, and multilevel systems approach to the conceptualization, design, and management of real and virtual, "knowledge-stock" and "knowledge-flow," modalities that catalyze, accelerate, and support the creation, diffusion, sharing, absorption, and use of cospecialized knowledge assets. "Mode 3" is based on a system-theoretic perspective of socio-economic, political, technological, and cultural trends and conditions that shape the coevolution of knowledge with the "knowledge-based and knowledge-driven, global/local economy and society."

- Quadruple Helix: Quadruple helix, in this context, means to add to the triple helix of government, university, and industry a "fourth helix" that we identify as the "media-based and culture-based public." This fourth helix associates with "media," "creative industries," "culture," "values," "lifestyles," "art," and perhaps also the notion of the "creative class."

- Innovation Networks: Innovation networks are real and virtual infrastructures and infratechnologies that serve to nurture creativity, trigger invention, and catalyze innovation in a public and/or private domain context (for instance, government–university–industry public–private research and technology development coopetitive partnerships).
- Knowledge Clusters: Knowledge clusters are agglomerations of cospecialized, mutually complementary, and reinforcing knowledge assets in the form of "knowledge stocks" and "knowledge flows" that exhibit self-organizing, learning-driven, dynamically adaptive competences and trends in the context of an open systems perspective.
- Twenty-First-Century Innovation Ecosystem: A twenty-first-century innovation ecosystem is a multilevel, multimodal, multinodal, and multiagent system of systems. The constituent systems consist of innovation metanetworks (networks of innovation networks and knowledge clusters) and knowledge metaclusters (clusters of innovation networks and knowledge clusters) as building blocks and organized in a self-referential or chaotic fractal knowledge and innovation architecture (Carayannis 2001), which in turn constitute agglomerations of human, social, intellectual, and financial capital stocks and flows as well as cultural and technological artifacts and modalities, continually coevolving, cospecializing, and cooperating. These innovation networks and knowledge clusters also form, reform, and dissolve within diverse institutional, political, technological, and socioeconomic domains, including government, university, industry, and nongovernmental organizations and involving information and communication technologies, biotechnologies, advanced materials, nanotechnologies, and next-generation energy technologies.

Who is this book series published for? The book series addresses a diversity of audiences in different settings:

1. *Academic communities*: Academic communities worldwide represent a core group of readers. This follows from the theoretical/conceptual interest of the book series to influence academic discourses in the fields of knowledge, also carried by the claim of a certain saturation of academia with the current concepts and the postulate of a window of opportunity for new or at least additional concepts.
2. Thus, it represents a key challenge for the series to exercise a certain impact on discourses in academia. In principle, all academic communities that are interested in knowledge (knowledge and innovation) could be tackled by the book series. The interdisciplinary (transdisciplinary) nature of the book series underscores that the scope of the book series is not limited a priori to a specific basket of disciplines. From a radical viewpoint, one could create the hypothesis that there is no discipline where knowledge is of no importance.
3. *Decision-makers—private/academic entrepreneurs and public (governmental, subgovernmental) actors*: Two different groups of decision-makers are being addressed simultaneously: (1) private entrepreneurs (firms, commercial firms, academic firms) and academic entrepreneurs (universities), interested in

optimizing knowledge management and in developing heterogeneously composed knowledge-based research networks, and (2) public (governmental, subgovernmental) actors that are interested in optimizing and further developing
their policies and policy strategies that target knowledge and innovation. One
purpose of public *knowledge and innovation policy* is to enhance the performance and competitiveness of advanced economies.

4. *Decision-makers in general*: Decision-makers are systematically being supplied
   with crucial information, for how to optimize knowledge-referring and knowl-
   edge-enhancing decision-making. The nature of this "crucial information" is
   conceptual as well as empirical (case study-based). Empirical information highlights practical examples and points toward practical solutions (perhaps remedies); conceptual information offers the advantage of further-driving and
   further-carrying tools of understanding. Different groups of addressed decision-
   makers could be decision-makers in private firms and multinational corporations, responsible for the knowledge portfolio of companies; knowledge and
   knowledge management consultants; globalization experts, focusing on the
   internationalization of research and development, science and technology, and
   innovation; experts in university/business research networks; and political scientists, economists, and business professionals.

5. *Interested global readership*: Finally, the Springer book series addresses a whole
   global readership, composed of members who are generally interested in knowledge and innovation. The global readership could partially coincide with the
   communities as described above ("academic communities," "decision-makers"),
   but could also refer to other constituencies and groups.

Washington, DC, USA   Elias G. Carayannis

Contents

About the Authors

Sherzod B. Akhundjanov is assistant professor in the Department of Applied Economics at Utah State University. His research interests broadly lie in applied microeconomics, industrial organization, and econometrics and statistics, with a focus on environment and natural resources, product attributes and safety, and statistical process control and power law analysis. His research has appeared in various economics and statistics journals. At Utah State he teaches classes in econometrics at both the undergraduate and graduate levels. He holds an MS in statistics and a PhD in economics from Washington State University.

Julian M. Alston is a distinguished professor in the Department of Agricultural and Resource Economics and the director of the Robert Mondavi Institute Center for Wine Economics at the University of California, Davis. Among other honors and distinctions, he is a fellow of the Agricultural and Applied Economics Association and an honorary life member of the International Association of Agricultural Economists. He is an agricultural economist known for his work on the economics of agricultural and food policy. His recent projects have emphasized science and technology policy and the economics of agricultural innovation; food and nutrition policy and the global challenges of poverty, malnutrition, and obesity; and wine economics. He has published hundreds of research articles, chapters, and books on these subjects, most recently *The Effects of Farm and Food Policy on Obesity in the United States* in 2017 with Abigail Okrent.

Eliseu Alves is an agronomist and holds a PhD in agricultural economics from Purdue University. He started his career in rural extension service and is the former head of the Planning and Evaluation Division of Minas Gerais Agricultural Extension Agency (ICAR and then Emater-MG). He was part of the team that in 1972 designed and planned Embrapa for the Brazilian Government. He is a former executive director and president of Embrapa. Dr. Alves is also a former president of Codevasf, the Brazilian Federal Agency targeting irrigation projects in Brazil's semiarid region. In 1989, he was Brazil's national secretary for irrigation. Dr. Alves has been acting as an advisor to Embrapa's presidents since 1990. Also since 1990, he has advised several international development agencies and national governments on themes such as agricultural research, development, and policy.

Robert S. Andrade is a PhD candidate in applied economics at the University of Minnesota and a research fellow in impact and strategic studies with the International Center for Tropical Agriculture (CIAT). He graduated from Virginia Tech with an MSc in agricultural and applied economics and received his degree in economics from the Pontificia Universidad Catolica del Ecuador. He worked at the International Science and Technology Practice and Policy (InSTePP) center as a research assistant for 5 years. Prior to that, he worked in CIAT for 3 years as an impact assessment researcher and at the National Agricultural Research Institute of Ecuador (INIAP) for 6 years as an agricultural economics researcher. His primary research interests lie in evaluating the economic returns to agricultural innovation. He is currently working on reassessing the evidence of economic returns to research in Latin American countries and assessing the economic impacts of R&D.

Steven T. Buccola is emeritus professor in the Department of Applied Economics at Oregon State University. He was assistant professor of agricultural economics at Virginia Tech and visiting associate professor at Michigan State University, where he lectured at the University of Zimbabwe. From 1999 to 2000, he was a visiting scholar at Harvard University and Lady Davis fellow at the Hebrew University of Jerusalem. He was chair of the Oregon State University Graduate Faculty of Economics and later director of its graduate program in applied economics. Dr. Buccola is a fellow and former president of the Agricultural and Applied Economics Association and has been the editor of the *American Journal of Agricultural Economics*. He has also served on the editorial boards of four other professional journals. His research has focused on the economics of cooperatives, risk, productivity, science, and technology.

Elias G. Carayannis is full professor of science, technology, innovation, and entrepreneurship, as well as cofounder and codirector of the Global and Entrepreneurial Finance Research Institute (GEFRI) and director of research on science, technology, innovation, and entrepreneurship, European Union Research Center (EURC), at the School of Business of the George Washington University in Washington, D.C. Dr. Carayannis' teaching and research activities focus on the areas of strategic government-university-industry R&D partnerships, technology road-mapping, technology transfer and commercialization, international science and technology policy, technological entrepreneurship, and regional economic development. Dr. Carayannis has several publications in both academic and practitioner journals, including *IEEE Transactions on Engineering Management, Research Policy, Journal of R&D Management, Journal of Engineering and Technology Management, International Journal of Technology Management, Technovation, Journal of Technology Transfer, Engineering Management Journal, Growth and Change: A Journal of Urban and Regional Policy, Review of Regional Studies, International Journal of Global Energy Issues, International Journal of Environment and Pollution, Le Progres Technique,* and *Focus on Change*

Management. He has also published more than 40 books to date on science, technology, innovation, and entrepreneurship with Springer, CRC Press, Praeger/Greenwood, Palgrave/MacMillan, and Edward Elgar and has several more projects under contract.

Odysseas Cartalos earned a PhD in chemical engineering and a habilitation (qualification to professorship) from the Grenoble Institute of Technology (Grenoble INP), France. He spent the first 10 years of his career as research manager in the oil and gas industry and then moved to consulting, where he worked on projects in ICT, energy, education, and employment. He has held numerous assignments for the European Parliament, the European Commission, and other institutions and government bodies. He was particularly involved in the design and implementation of European and national development initiatives. He is currently working in the areas of innovation and research, with special interest in technology transfer. He is also active in studies and projects dealing with small business competitiveness and innovative business models.

Connie Chan-Kang is research associate with the International Science and Technology Practice and Policy (InSTePP) center in the Department of Applied Economics at the University of Minnesota. Since joining InSTePP, she has contributed to various research projects on agricultural productivity measurement and analysis and on the economic evaluation of agricultural R&D. She is also responsible for the development and maintenance of several large databases, including a long-run series of global crop production, area, and yield; historical series on US agricultural production and prices by commodity; global public agricultural R&D investments; and historical series on US public agricultural R&D expenditures. She received an MSc degree in agricultural economics from Oregon State University. Prior to joining InSTePP, Connie worked as a research analyst at the International Food Policy Research Institute (IFPRI) in Washington, D.C.

Matthew Clancy is a research economist with the Economic Research Service of the US Department of Agriculture (USDA). His work centers on the economics of innovation, especially as it relates to patenting, agriculture, and the environment. He obtained his PhD from Iowa State University and an MSc from the London School of Economics. He is a cowinner of the 2016 Agricultural and Applied Economics Association Outstanding Doctoral Dissertation Award and the Center for Agriculture and Rural Development Best Dissertation Award. His work has been published in various journals including *Research Policy*, *Applied Economic Perspectives and Policy*, and the *American Journal of Agricultural Economics*.

Steven P. Dehmer is a research investigator and health economist at the HealthPartners Institute in Minneapolis, MN, and a fellow at the International Science and Technology Practice and Policy (InSTePP) center at the University of Minnesota. His research and interest areas include the economics of disease prevention, with an emphasis on cardiovascular disease, diabetes, and obesity; the impact of health technologies on individual behavior; health and science policy; and the social determinants of health. He led the development of the HealthPartners

Institute ModelHealth™: CVD microsimulation model. This model is used in cost-effectiveness analyses for multiple clinical trials supported by the National Institutes of Health and health policy analyses for the Centers for Disease Control and Prevention. He also contributed analytic support to the 2016 US Preventive Services Task Force recommendation on aspirin and the 2017 update of the National Commission on Prevention Priorities ranking of clinical preventive services.

Mark Edge is director of collaborations for developing countries for Monsanto Corp. He leads Monsanto's collaborations with public-private partnership projects to improve food security and rural livelihood among smallholder maize producers in sub-Saharan Africa. The Water Efficient Maize for Africa (WEMA) project is the signature project he leads. The WEMA project develops new drought-tolerant and insect pest-protected maize hybrids and provides the technology royalty-free. It helps build technical capacity in Africa to use conventional and molecular breeding as well as biotechnology. Mark has held multiple roles at Monsanto; most recently, he was the DroughtGard Hybrids marketing lead. Prior to that he has been the Europe and Africa marketing lead, the global cotton product manager, and the director of trait marketing at Corn States. His background before joining Monsanto includes experience in biotech research, many aspects of managing seed business development, and the grain export business. He has a BS from Iowa State University, an MS in genetics from the University of California at Davis, and an MBA from Drake University.

Keith O. Fuglie is branch chief and research economist in the economics of technological change and science policy with the Economic Research Service, US Department of Agriculture in Washington, D.C. In 2012 he was recognized with the USDA Secretary's Honor Award for Professional Service, and in 2014 he received the Bruce Gardner Memorial Prize for Applied Policy Analysis from the Agricultural and Applied Economics Association. In 1997–1998 he served as senior staff economist on the White House Council of Economic Advisers. He also spent 10 years with the International Potato Center (CIP) stationed in Indonesia and Tunisia, where he headed CIP's social science research program and was regional director for CIP in Asia. He received an MS and PhD in agricultural and applied economics from the University of Minnesota and a BA from Concordia College, Moorhead, Minnesota.

R. Karina Gallardo is an associate professor/extension specialist in the School of Economic Sciences and at the Research and Extension Center of Washington State University in Puyallup. She holds a BS in food science from the Universidad Nacional Agraria La Molina, an MS in agricultural economics from Mississippi State University, and a PhD in agricultural economics from Oklahoma State University. Her primary research and outreach program goal is to enhance value-added agribusiness opportunities for specialty crops in Washington State. As such, her areas of research are focused on consumer demand analysis and economics of technological change. More specifically, she is conducting research assessing consumer preferences for fresh fruit quality and understanding the profitability and various other factors affecting growers' adoption of new technologies, such as new cultivars, improved pest management systems, and labor-enhancing mechanisms.

Etleva Gjonça is a PhD candidate in law and economics at Erasmus University Rotterdam. During her doctoral studies, she has been a visiting scholar with the Department of Economics at the University of Bologna and the Institute of Law and Economics at University of Hamburg. She received her MSc degrees from the University of Nebraska-Lincoln and CIHEAM-Chania. Her research fields of interest include the economics of competition law, empirical industrial organization, economics of intellectual property, and applied microeconomics.

Evangelos Grigoroudis is professor of management of quality processes in the School of Production Engineering and Management of the Technical University of Crete, Greece. He has received distinctions from the Hellenic Operational Research Society, the Academy of Business and Administrative Sciences, the World Automation Congress, the Foundation of Ioannis and Vasileia Karayianni, the Technical University of Crete, and the State Scholarships Foundation of Greece. He has coauthored/coedited more than 17 books in operational research, service quality measurement, entrepreneurship, and corporate strategy and has published more than 200 articles in scientific journal, books, and conference proceedings. He is associate editor and editorial board member of several scientific journals.

Martin Grueber is a principal and research director at TEConomy Partners, LLC, an international research and strategic planning firm specializing in science and technology-based economic development, public policy, and impact assessment. Prior to cofounding TEConomy Partners, Martin was a research leader with the Technology Partnership Practice at the Battelle Memorial Institute. He holds an MA in geography and a BS in social science both from Michigan State University.

Paul W. Heisey is an economist in the Structure, Technology, and Productivity Branch of the Resource and Rural Economics Division of the USDA Economic Research Service (ERS). He received his PhD in agricultural economics from the University of Wisconsin-Madison. His work focuses on agricultural science policy, in particular public and private sector agricultural research and development, intellectual property, and genetic resources. Previously, he worked for the International Maize and Wheat Improvement Center (CIMMYT) in Pakistan, Malawi, and Mexico, where his research concentrated on impact assessment and the economics of technical change in cereals. This included work on varietal development and diffusion, seed systems, and fertilizer use in developing countries.

Sebastian Hoenen is a PhD candidate at Wageningen University and Research. In his dissertation he studies how the main actors in the knowledge economy including entrepreneurial firms, academic scientists, and universities attract resources or react to policy changes that allow them to innovate, advance science, and boost economic growth. The first part of his doctoral work has a strong entrepreneurial finance component and studies mechanisms that mitigate information asymmetries between funders and entrepreneurs. The second part of his doctoral work studies the acquisition of research funding for academics. The part of his doctoral work that has been published has received several awards and has appeared in top field journal publications. In 2018 Sebastian Hoenen will be a postdoctoral researcher at the Rotterdam School of Management.

Wallace E. Huffman is C.F. Curtiss distinguished professor of agriculture and life sciences and professor of economics at Iowa State University. His areas of research include economics of human capital, agricultural household models, agricultural productivity and R&D management, adoption and acceptance of new technologies and food products, experimental economics, and applied econometrics. He has published five books, including *Science for Agriculture: A Long-Term Perspective*, and hundreds of journal articles and book chapters. He has received four Quality of Research Discovery Awards, one Quality of Communication Award, and one Publication of Enduring Quality Award from the Agricultural and Applied Economics Association. Also, he is a fellow of the Agriculture and Applied Economics Association. He received his BS degree in production agriculture from Iowa State University and PhD in economics from the University of Chicago.

Terrance M. Hurley is Austin A. Dowell professor of applied economics at the University of Minnesota. He received his PhD in economics from Iowa State University in 1995. His primary research interests include the profitability, risk, and regulation of emerging agricultural technologies. The technologies that have received most of his attention are genetically engineered plant-incorporated protectants (e.g., Bt corn and cotton) and herbicide-tolerant (e.g., Roundup Ready® soybean) seed varieties, though he has also worked on precision nutrient management and crop protection and the evaluation of the rates of return to agricultural research and development. His research has resulted in invitations to serve on advisory and organizing panels for the US Environmental Protection Agency and National Research Council of the National Academy of Sciences. He has served as a coeditor for the Agricultural and Applied Economics Association's *Applied Economics Perspectives and Policy* journal and *American Journal of Agricultural Economics.*

Nicholas Kalaitzandonakes is Frank Miller professor of agricultural and applied economics and director of the Food Equation Institute at the University of Missouri. His research, teaching, and outreach focus on the economics and policy of agrifood innovation, especially biotechnology. He has published articles and books on the economic and environmental impacts of agrifood innovation, the impacts of innovation on the structure of the agrifood supply chain, on innovation entrepreneurship and industrial development, on the interplay of agrifood innovation and regulation, and other topics. He is the editor of *AgBioForum* and has been an editorial board member for several academic journals. Through an active outreach program, Dr. Kalaitzandonakes advises governments, international organizations, nonprofits, and Fortune 500 firms on the economics and strategy of agrifood innovation. He has also been a board member of startups, venture capital firms, and national research centers involved in the life sciences.

Christos Kolympiris is associate professor in innovation and entrepreneurship with the School of Management at the University of Bath. His research areas are at the intersection of technology innovation management, entrepreneurship, and the economics of science and technology. Within these fields, he has developed two main research programs. The first examines how physical, financial, and intellectual capital affects the creation, location, and performance of entrepreneurial firms in high-technology industries like biotechnology. The second analyzes how the main actors in the knowledge economy, including entrepreneurial firms, academic scientists, and universities, attract resources that allow them to innovate, advance science, and boost economic growth. His work has been published in leading innovation and entrepreneurship journals. He received his PhD from the University of Missouri and was assistant professor at Wageningen University in the Netherlands.

Alexandros Koutsouris is the head of the Unit of Agricultural Extension, Rural Systems, and Rural Sociology in the Department of Agricultural Economics and Rural Development at the Agricultural University of Athens. He has a strong general background in sustainable rural development with emphasis on participatory methods and is a specialist in agricultural extension and agricultural education and training. He is currently president of the steering committees of the International Farming Systems Association-European Group (IFSA) and European Seminar on Extension Education (ESEE), associate editor of *The Journal of Agricultural Education & Extension*, and an invited expert for the Strategic Working Group AKIS4 of the EU Standing Committee on Agricultural Research. He has also served as president of the Hellenic Agricultural Organization (IELGO DIMITRA) and of the Hellenic Association of Agricultural Economists (ETAGRO), has ongoing participation in several EU research and collaboration projects, is a World Bank consultant for development communication, and was an FAO resource person for the FAO WPW Expert Meeting on Gender and Rural Development in 2002 and 2003.

Denis T. Kyetere is the executive director of the African Agricultural Technology Foundation (AATF). Previously, he was the director general of Uganda's National Agricultural Research Organization (NARO). He also served as chairperson of the Forum for Agricultural Research in Africa (FARA), the Association for Strengthening Agricultural Research in Eastern and Central Africa (ASARECA), the Eastern and Central Africa Maize and Wheat Research Network (ECAMAW), and the Coffee Research Network (CORNET). Denis holds a PhD from the Ohio State University; an MSc both in genetics and plant breeding from the University of Wales, Aberystwyth College, UK; and a BSc (Hons) in botany and zoology from Makerere University, Uganda.

Kyuseon Lee is a PhD candidate in the Department of Applied Economics at the University of Minnesota. Her research is primarily focused on the economics of R&D, with particular attention to private R&D investment in the US food and agricultural sectors, and the nature of research collaboration, especially among research teams in the life sciences. Her research interests also extend into the fields of industrial organization and applied microeconomics. Originally from South Korea, she received a BA in economics from the Department of Agricultural Economics and Rural Development at Seoul National University and a master's degree in public policy from Duke University. Prior to her study at the University of Minnesota, she interned at the McKinsey Global Institute and worked as an assistant economist at the Korea Development Bank.

William Lesser is Susan Eckert Lynch professor in science and business of the Charles H. Dyson School of Applied Economics and Management at Cornell University. His research focuses on the implications of agricultural biotechnology products on production costs and the size, structure, and geographic distribution of farming. He particularly concentrates on the costs, benefits, and structural implications of intellectual property, particularly patents, for plants, seed, and animals. His analyses include comparisons between the USA, Europe, and developing countries.

Alexandre Magnier is program director with the Food Equation Institute at the University of Missouri. His research focuses on the behavior of producers, R&D firms, consumers, and other stakeholders in the agrifood chain toward agricultural and food innovations, especially biotechnology. In his most recent research, he uses experimental economics to analyze consumer preferences for various product attributes and food innovations as well as producer willingness to participate in segregated and value-added agricultural production programs. He graduated from l'Ecole Superieure d'Agriculture in France and obtained an MS and a PhD in agricultural and applied economics from the University of Missouri.

Geraldo B. Martha Jr is coordinator of the scientific cooperation program in the USA for the Brazilian Agricultural Research Corporation (Embrapa, Labex-USA) and has been a researcher at Embrapa since 2001. He received his PhD in agronomy from the University of São Paulo, with postdoctoral training in economics at the University of Brasilia. He is the former coordinator general of Embrapa Strategic Intelligence System (Agropensa) and has served as the deputy head for Strategic Studies at Embrapa Studies and Training. He is a former member of Embrapa's Strategy Management Committee and of the Commission for Sustainable Development in Agriculture of the Brazilian Ministry of Agriculture, Livestock and Food Supply and was coordinator of the research group on land use dynamics and Cerrado Regional Development.

Kingstone Mashingaidze is senior research manager of the Grain Crops Institute of the Agricultural Research Council (ARC) in Potchefstroom, South Africa. He has a PhD in plant breeding and genetics from Michigan State University. His expertise includes crop breeding, transgenics, crop physiology, agricultural biotechnology, seed science and technology, and public-private partnerships. He joined the ARC in 2004 as a senior researcher in maize breeding after spending 15 years as a senior lecturer at the University of Zimbabwe and Africa University. He has extensive experience in maize breeding for stress tolerance and has been the principal investigator for the Water Efficient Maize for Africa (WEMA), Improved Maize for African

Soils (IMAS), and Stress Tolerant Maize for Africa (STMA) international public-private partnership projects.

Jill J. McCluskey is distinguished professor of sustainability and associate director of the School of Economic Sciences at Washington State University. Her research focuses on product quality and reputation, sustainable labeling, and consumer preferences. An award-winning researcher, she has published over 100 journal articles, many of which are highly cited. She has received significant research funding from NSF and USDA, among other sources. She has served as major professor to 35 PhD graduates, many of whom are faculty at major research universities; some have won national best dissertation awards. She served as president of the Agricultural and Applied Economics Association in 2015–2016. She has established data-sharing agreements with industry partners. She has served on editorial boards and as guest editor for several academic journals. Starting in 2017, she joined the Board on Agricultural and Natural Resources of the National Academies of Sciences. She received her PhD from the University of California, Berkeley.

Stephen N. Mugo is principal scientist and maize breeder in CIMMYT's Global Maize Program. He is also the current CIMMYT project leader of the Water Efficient Maize for Africa (WEMA) project in five countries in Eastern and Southern Africa. He has led several other bilateral and multilateral maize improvement projects since joining CIMMYT. He led the Insect Resistant Maize for Africa (IRMA) project, as well as the Strengthening Seed Systems project in Kenya and Uganda. He is the CIMMYT-Africa Regional Representative (CRR) in Kenya and CIMMYT-Kenya Country Representative (CCR). He manages the CIMMYT Kenya Office ICRAF Campus, Nairobi, Kenya, and provides administrative and liaison oversight of the CIMMYT offices in Addis Ababa, Ethiopia, and Harare, Zimbabwe. He holds a BS in agriculture from the University of Nairobi, an MS in agronomy from the University of Missouri, and a PhD in plant breeding and genetics from Cornell University. He has published extensively in peer-reviewed journals and has several book chapters.

Sylvester O. Oikeh coordinates operational management and monitors the implementation of activities for the Water Efficient Maize for Africa (WEMA) project across eight public and private sector organizations in five African countries. Prior to that, he worked in the Africa Rice Centre for five years as principal scientist, soil fertility agronomist, and project leader. He developed four integrated soil fertility management packages and two farmer handbooks to support the deployment of NERICA (New Rice for Africa) rice. Also, he held various positions at the International Institute of Tropical Agriculture (IITA) for over 10 years. As a postdoctoral fellow at Cornell University, he established for the first time the link between enhanced iron and zinc in corn kernels and improvement in human nutrition using an in vitro technique. He has over 70 publications in major scientific journals, proceedings, book chapters, books, and monographs.

Onno Omta is professor of business administration and head of the Department of Management Studies at Wageningen University and Research . He earned his PhD from the University of Groningen with a thesis on the management of innovation in the pharmaceutical industry. He has published numerous articles in leading scientific and professional journals. He was the author or coauthor of a number of papers with Best Paper Awards presented at academic conferences and papers with Paper of the Year Awards published in scientific journals. As a fellow of the International Food and Agribusiness Management Association (IFAMA), he stands in close contact with major international agrifood companies.

Philip G. Pardey is professor of science and technology policy in the Department of Applied Economics at the University of Minnesota. He is also director of global research strategy for the College of Food, Agricultural and Natural Resource Sciences and the Minnesota Agricultural Experiment Station and director of the International Science and Technology Practice and Policy (InSTePP) center. He is a fellow of the American Association for the Advancement of Science (AAAS) and the American Agricultural Economics Association, distinguished fellow and past president of the Australian Agricultural and Resource Economics Society, and distinguished life member of the International Association of Agricultural Economists. Philip's research deals with spatial agricultural productivity, innovation and R&D impacts, and the economic, policy, and intellectual property aspects of genetic resources and the biosciences. He is author of more than 360 books, articles, and papers.

Peter W.B. Phillips is distinguished professor in the Johnson Shoyama Graduate School of Public Policy (JSGS) at the University of Saskatchewan. He earned his PhD at the London School of Economics (LSE) and practiced for 13 years as a professional economist in industry and government. At the University of Saskatchewan, he was the Van Vliet research professor, created and held an NSERC-SSHRC chair in managing technological change, was director of the virtual College of Biotechnology, was founding director of the JSGS, and is founding director of the Centre for the Study of Science and Innovation Policy (CSIP). He has had appointments at the LSE, the Organization for Economic Cooperation and Development (OECD), the European University Institute in Florence, the University of Edinburgh, and the University of Western Australia. He was a founding member of the Canadian Biotechnology Advisory Committee and was on the boards of CAPI, Pharmalytics, and Ag-West Bio Inc. He has held over 15 peer review grants worth more than $200 million and is author or editor of 15 books, more than 60 journal articles, and over 55 book chapters.

Lin Qin is manager of data science at comScore, Inc. in Portland, Oregon, where she is leading a data science team to develop automated analytical tools for validating and measuring massive TV viewership data and precisely quantify audience behavior. Prior to that, she received her PhD in applied economics from Oregon State University. Her doctoral dissertation "The Economics of a Research Program: Knowledge Production, Cost, and Technical Efficiency" was selected as the Outstanding Doctoral Dissertation awarded by the Agricultural and Applied Economics Association in 2013. She also holds a master's degree in statistics from

Oregon State University. Born and raised in Sichuan, China, she earned her BA in risk management and insurance and LLB in law at the Southwestern University of Finance and Economics.

Xudong Rao is assistant professor in the Business Economics Group at Wageningen University and Research. He obtained his PhD from the Department of Applied Economics at the University of Minnesota, where he remains affiliated as a fellow with the International Science and Technology Practice and Policy (InSTePP) center. His research deals with the productivity effects and economic payoffs of agricultural R&D investments; decision-making with regard to technology adoption and the risk management and performance of farms, agribusiness firms, and the overall agricultural sector; and food and agricultural policy. His work on those topics has been published in journals such as the *American Journal of Agricultural Economics* and *Food Policy*. He and his coauthors won the Quality of Research Discovery Award from the Australian Agricultural and Resource Economics Society in 2015.

Bradley J. Rickard is Ruth and William Morgan associate professor in the Charles H. Dyson School of Applied Economics and Management at Cornell University. He earned a PhD in agricultural and resource economics from the University of California, Davis. He has published widely in the area of food and agricultural economics, with a specific interest in addressing contemporary marketing and policy issues in specialty crop markets. Recent work has examined consumer response to changes in nutrition and health information, food labeling practices, and promotional efforts and the role of information on food waste patterns, agricultural policy reform, and the introduction of new technologies. His research has been highlighted by various media outlets including *The Economist*, *Freakonomics*, *National Public Radio*, *The Wall Street Journal*, *Washington Post*, and *Wine Spectator.*

Stelios Rozakis holds the ERA chair in strategies for development of the bioeconomy in Poland at the Institute of Soil Science and Plant Cultivation, Pulawy, Poland. He is also associate professor at the Technical University of Crete. He earned his PhD in agricultural economics from the Agricultural University of Athens. He was previously a faculty member at the Agricultural University of Athens and a researcher with the Public Economics Unit at INRA, France. He works in operations research and policy analysis applied to agriculture, energy, and the environment. He has published over 30 papers in peer-reviewed journals and is an editorial board member of several international academic journals. His responsibilities beyond teaching and research have included the direction of the MBA in agribusiness and the entrepreneurship and innovation program at the Agricultural University of Athens.

Steven R. Shafer is the chief scientific officer (CSO) of the Soil Health Institute (SHI). He received BS and MS degrees from the Ohio State University and a PhD from North Carolina State University, all in plant pathology. He began his career with the US Department of Agriculture as a scientist with the Agricultural Research Service (ARS). His research focused on interactions among plants, microorganisms, and soils. He held numerous positions in USDA over his 32-year career, ultimately as ARS' associate administrator for national programs and the national leader for planning, prioritizing, and budgeting ARS' comprehensive research programs before joining SHI in 2016. The institute's mission is to safeguard and enhance the vitality and productivity of the soil and make it the cornerstone of land management decisions. Dr. Shafer establishes priorities, strategy, and implementation for institute research programs that advance soil health science and lead to useful results.

Joseph Simkins is a senior economist at TEConomy Partners, LLC, an international research and strategic planning firm specializing in science and technology-based economic development, public policy, and impact assessment. Prior to TEConomy Partners, he was senior economist with the Technology Partnership Practice at the Battelle Memorial Institute. He holds an MA in applied microeconomics from the University of North Carolina, Greensboro, and a BA in economics from the University of North Carolina, Chapel Hill.

Stephen Smith is affiliate professor and visiting scientist in the Departments of Agronomy and Seed Science at Iowa State University. He recently completed a 35-year career providing technical support to secure DuPont Pioneer's intellectual property rights and publishing on the important role of plant genetic resources in plant breeding and agriculture. He holds a BSc from the University of London and an MSc in conservation of plant genetic resources and a PhD in evolution of maize from the University of Birmingham, UK. He was awarded the Henry A. Wallace Award for Revolution in Agriculture and DuPont's highest scientific recognition, the Lavoisier Medal for Scientific Achievement. He has served on intellectual property committees of the American Seed Trade Association (ASTA) and the International Seed Federation (ISF), which he chairs. He is a fellow of the Crop Science Society of America and in 2017 was made an honorary member of ASTA in recognition of his services.

Stuart J. Smyth is assistant professor in the Department of Agriculture and Resource Economics at the University of Saskatchewan, where he holds the industry research chair in agrifood innovation. His research focuses on sustainability, agriculture, innovation, and food; he publishes a weekly blog on these topics at www.SAIFood.ca. Recent publications include *Biotechnology Regulation and Trade*, coauthored with William Kerr and Peter Phillips and published by Springer in 2017; *The Coexistence of Genetically Modified, Organic and Conventional Foods*, coedited with Nicholas Kalaitzandonakes, Peter Phillips, and Justus Wesseler and published by Springer in 2016; and the *Handbook on Agriculture, Biotechnology and Development*, coedited with Peter Phillips and David Castle and published by Edward Elgar in 2014. In the summer of 2015, he was part of a large group of scientists at the University of Saskatchewan who received $37 million targeted toward designing crops that will improve global food security.

Michael S. Strauss was the peer review program coordinator at the USDA-ARS Office of Scientific Quality Review until his retirement in December 2017. He studied developmental biology at the University of California, where he focused on floral physiology. He later addressed the biology of taro, *Colocasia esculenta*, in Hawaii and the South Pacific while on the faculty of Northeastern University. In 1986 he came to the Congressional Office of Technology Assessment for a ground-breaking assessment of biological diversity. He subsequently moved to the National Academy of Sciences to direct the Committee on Managing Global Genetic Resources, then spent a decade overseeing the program of the scientifically diverse annual meeting of the American Association for the Advancement of Science (AAAS), and later oversaw the USDA-ARS Office of Scientific Quality Review. He is a research associate of the Missouri Botanical Garden, a fellow of AAAS, and member of the Crop Science and Agronomy Societies.

Alexander N. Svoronos has a BA in mathematics and economics from Oberlin College and an MSc and PhD in operations research from Stanford University. He has extensive experience in consumer credit, where he developed and managed the development of statistical models for major financial institutions, first at Fair Isaac Co. as production manager of the international division, then at Chase Manhattan Bank where he served as vice president in consumer credit risk management, and later at 1st Financial Bank where he was senior vice president in credit risk management. He was also cofounder and president of Austin Logistics Inc., where he continued to develop and manage the development of statistical models for major financial institutions and also designed and supported software utilizing both statistical and optimization techniques, predominantly aimed at improving the efficiency of the clients' marketing and collections operations.

Simon Tripp is a principal and senior director at TEConomy Partners, LLC, an international research and strategic planning firm specializing in science and technology-based economic development, public policy, and impact assessment. Prior to cofounding TEConomy Partners, Simon was senior director of the Technology Partnership Practice at the Battelle Memorial Institute. He holds an MA in geography from West Virginia University and a BA (Hons) in geography from Portsmouth Polytechnic.

Albert I. Ugochukwu is a postdoctoral fellow in the Centre for the Study of Science and Innovation Policy (CSIP) of the Johnson Shoyama Graduate School of Public Policy at the University of Saskatchewan. His research has focused on agri-business entrepreneurship, agro-industry development, food safety, rural development, value chains, technology adoption and commercialization, international trade, monitoring, and evaluation. He earned his PhD at the University of Saskatchewan and has more than 15 peer-reviewed journal articles. He has participated in various agriculture-related research projects funded by academic institutions, the US Agency for International Development (USAID), the World Bank, the Rockefeller Foundation, and Genome Canada and has consulted for the International Institute of Tropical Agriculture (IITA), Agriculture and Agri-Food Canada, USAID, and the International Development Group (IDG).

Emiel Wubben is associate professor of strategic management at Wageningen University and Research. He has a PhD in economics from the Tinbergen Institute of Erasmus University. His prime interest is in strategic management, with a keen interest in the question of how to realize the transition toward a sustainable bio-based, circular economy, in particular the trade-offs therein between the visible hand of management and authorities versus the invisible hand of markets and trade systems. He both was a winner and supervised a winner of a PhD thesis award and has won several recognitions. Earlier, he was assistant professor at the Rotterdam School of Management. He is responsible for core courses in advanced management and marketing and advanced business strategies. In recent years he has been very active in realizing MSc-level specialization courses in bio-based business, circular economy, Climate KIC CSA Booster, and several MOOCs in the same area and in developing and launching an integral MSc program in bio-based sciences.

Alyssa Yetter is a PhD candidate in sociology in the Department of Sociology and Criminology at the Pennsylvania State University. Her research focuses on the relationship between inequality and crime with an emphasis on quantitative research methodologies. She holds an MA in criminology from the Pennsylvania State University and a BA in sociology and anthropology from Denison University.

Dylan Yetter is a research analyst at TEConomy Partners, LLC, an international research and strategic planning firm specializing in science and technology-based economic development, public policy, and impact assessment. He holds an MA in sociology and demography from the Pennsylvania State University and a BA (Hons) in political science and sociology from the State University of New York at Fredonia.

Amalia (Emie) Yiannaka is professor of agricultural economics at the University of Nebraska-Lincoln. She received her PhD degree from the Department of Agricultural and Resource Economics at the University of Saskatchewan, Canada. She has served as an associate editor for the *Journal of Agricultural and Resource Economics* and the *Journal of Agricultural and Food Industrial Organization*. She has been a distinguished expert for the Hellenic Quality Assurance and Accreditation Agency for Higher Education, serving as an external evaluator of academic departments. Her research interests include the study of intellectual property rights, the economics of food innovations, consumer preferences for food technologies, and agricultural and food industrial organization.

Kenneth A. Zahringer is senior research associate with the Food Equation Institute at the University of Missouri. He earned a BA in anthropology from the University of Missouri, his MA in applied social research from West Virginia University, and an MS in economics and PhD in applied economics from the University of Missouri. His primary area of research is the adoption of innovations in agriculture, including uncertainty in the valuation of patented innovations and the market effects of delayed adoption. His work has appeared in peer-reviewed journals such as the *Journal of Technology Transfer* and *Industrial and Corporate Change*, as well as book chapters and research reports.

Introduction: Innovation and Technology Transfer in Agriculture

Nicholas Kalaitzandonakes, Elias G. Carayannis, Evangelos Grigoroudis, and Stelios Rozakis

Abstract Innovation has been an integral part of agriculture since its earliest days, when humans first began to make the shift from foraging to food production. It was only during the twentieth century, though, that private and public systems of formal research and development of innovations became common. With that came the need for formal systems to research, develop, and transfer technology from centers of discovery to end users. Continuing improvements in global food security, environmental sustainability, and economic development in the face of continuing population growth and climate change will require ongoing innovation and durable growth in agricultural productivity. Thus, a clear understanding on how to nurture innovation, from concept through development and all the way to the end user, is vital to our future. In this book we present a comprehensive treatment of the complex processes involved in the development and transfer of agricultural innovation.

Innovation has been an integral part of agriculture since its earliest days, when humans first began to make the shift from foraging to food production. It was only during the twentieth century, though, that private and public systems of formal research and development of innovations became common. With that came the need for formal systems to research, develop, and transfer technology from centers of discovery to end users. Continuing improvements in global food security, environmental sustainability, and economic development in the face of continuing population growth and climate change will require ongoing innovation and durable growth in agricultural productivity. Thus, a clear understanding on how to nurture

N. Kalaitzandonakes (✉)
Department of Agricultural and Applied Economics, University of Missouri,
Columbia, MO, USA
e-mail: KalaitzandonakesN@missouri.edu

E.G. Carayannis
George Washington University, Washington, DC, USA

E. Grigoroudis
School of Production Engineering & Management, Technical University of Crete,
Chania, Crete, Greece

S. Rozakis
Institute of Soil Science and Plant Cultivation, IUNG-PIB, Pulawy, Poland

© Springer International Publishing AG 2018
N. Kalaitzandonakes et al. (eds.), *From Agriscience to Agribusiness*, Innovation,
Technology, and Knowledge Management, https://doi.org/10.1007/978-3-319-67958-7_1

1

innovation, from concept through development and all the way to the end user, is vital to our future. In this book we present a comprehensive treatment of the complex processes involved in the development and transfer of agricultural innovation.

The time and material resources available to individual farmers for innovation was always limited, however. As civilization progressed, though, wealthier members of society saw opportunities in agricultural innovation and were able to take advantage of them. Some of the earliest achievements in this direction in Europe were "physic gardens," predecessors of today's botanic gardens and centers of investigation into medicinal plants. They were also among the first examples of university agricultural research; the first physic garden was established in 1543 at the University of Pisa. The practice soon spread throughout the rest of Europe. During the colonial period, national governments, most notably in Spain, France, and England, established botanic gardens to evaluate potential new crops brought back from their tropical colonies. During the eighteenth century, these governments also set up botanic gardens in their colonies to adapt tropical crops from other areas to local conditions (BGCI 2017). Private innovation efforts in both methods and machinery continued through the seventeenth and eighteenth centuries as well, and both public and private innovators went to considerable lengths to promote their ideas and inventions to individual farmers (e.g., Sayre 2010).

These early research programs anticipated our modern concept of agricultural research and development (R&D), which dates back only to the nineteenth century. During this era such noteworthy innovators as Thomas Edison, Henry Ford, and John D. Rockefeller instituted the practice of devoting specific shares of their firms' revenues to ongoing applied research aimed at the improvement of existing and the development of new products and industrial processes. The practice of applied research, itself a valuable innovation, soon spread to universities, augmenting their traditional roles of teaching and basic scientific investigation. Government agencies also established research laboratories, perhaps the first being the Department of Agriculture (USDA). The range of research performed or supported by the federal government steadily increased over the years, in step with the general scope of government activities. These two systems of public and private R&D have evolved separately and together, as has the nature of their interactions (Mowery et al. 2001). Innovation systems in countries around the world have gone through similar patterns of evolution, each in their own institutional environment. One outcome of these different histories is variation in the efficiency of innovation systems, which is a factor in the current state and future potential of individual national innovation systems (Carayannis et al. 2016).

A few of the contributions to this volume examine the current state of public and private sector agricultural R&D and trends that are under way. *Pardey et al.* look at changing patterns of public agricultural R&D worldwide. Using the University of Minnesota's InSTePP database, they describe trends in public R&D spending, noting significant differences between high- and middle-income countries, and in the relative amounts of public and private R&D spending in those same countries. *Fuglie, Clancy, and Heisey* focus on how the balance of public and private R&D spending in the USA has changed since 1990. *Kalaitzandonakes and Zahringer* discuss the emerging private R&D model in the global agricultural input sector, the factors that have shaped it, and the structural changes that enabled it. *Phillips* reviews the development of a completely new crop and market in Canada and chronicles the operation of a modern public-private R&D and technology transfer partnership.

The Institutional Environment, Incentives for Innovation, and Technology Transfer

Public policy has played a crucial role in shifting the division of labor of the private and public sectors in agricultural innovation through changes in the underlying incentives. Laws on intellectual property rights (IPR) have been particularly important. The debate over university patent policies started in earnest in the post-World War I era. The 1920s and 1930s saw an increase in public-private research collaboration to the point that many in the scientific community began to discuss how best to ensure the efficient exploitation of research results, to the benefit of society as a whole. The lines in the debate were quite clearly drawn. Many in the university community believed that universities, as public institutions, had the obligation to make all the products of their research freely available and that this was at least a sufficient, and perhaps even an optimal, means of technology transfer. Others maintained that private firms would be unwilling to expend significant resources developing university research results into viable products without the ability to protect their future returns with patents (Mowery and Sampat 2001). The question was seen as important enough that in 1933 the American Association for the Advancement of Science convened a special committee to address it. The final report came out in favor of university patenting, for a variety of reasons, but not unequivocally so. It also recognized the potential for holdup of subsequent research by overly broad patents, especially in the fields of medicine and research methods (Rossman et al. 1934).

During the interwar period, university patenting increased somewhat but remained quite rare. Major research universities, as well as many land-grant institutions, were at the front of the trend. Depression-era funding shortfalls led other universities to investigate patenting more seriously, as license revenues became more of an attraction. They still faced political and public opinion repercussions from potential participation in commercial enterprise, though, and generally lacked the expertise to effectively manage even a small patent portfolio. In order to deal with this situation, it became common for universities to assign their patents to a third party for management. Many institutions retained the services of the Research Corporation, a private firm founded by former faculty expressly for the purpose of technology transfer from universities to the private sector. Still, as late as 1950, most US universities had no patent policy, and some of those that did discouraged or prohibited faculty patenting (Mowery and Sampat 2001).

Patent laws and attitudes toward patenting are important parts of the institutional environment surrounding agricultural R&D. While this is perhaps a more contentious subject in the public sector, patents and patent transactions produce strong incentives for actors in the private sector as well. Another group of contributors look at the impact of this and other aspects of the institutional environment on R&D and technology transfer. *Smith and Kurtz* recount the history of yield increases in US corn production since the middle of the nineteenth century. They identify three types of factors that contributed to the adoption of hybrid cultivars and the resulting dramatic yield increase: genetics, agronomy, and policy, in particular policy concerning IPR. Some researchers have noted that IPR laws can inhibit as well as promote technology transfer. The concern is that excessive property rights assertions, such as patent thickets, can lead to the formation of an anticommons. *Lesser* examines evidence for and against the existence of an anticommons in agricultural R&D, specifically as it concerns the products of biotechnology. He investigates infringement issues in commercial use, research, and charitable product development. *Gjonca and Yiannaka* discuss how the characteristics of patents held by private firms might influence whether and how often those firms were merged, acquired, or spun off. Using a database of over 6000 private sector patents granted from 1976 to 2000, they relate measures of breadth of claims, value, enforceability, and patent holder nationality to patent ownership changes. On the other hand, *Tripp, Simkins, Yetter, and Yetter* look into the public production of patented innovations, specifically by land-grant universities that received research funding from the National Institute of Food and Agriculture (NIFA) at USDA. In separate analyses of samples of over 24,000 patents and nearly 4000 plant variety protection certificates, they assess the influence of university research and patenting on follow-on innovation and characterize differences between universities and private firms as to which subject areas and crop varieties were the objects of research and patenting. *Kalaitzandonakes, Magnier, and Kolympiris* also review private sector patenting activity in the Ag biotech and seed sectors from 1980 on and evaluate whether there are discernible patterns of strategic patenting that could limit competition. They also analyze how such IPRs have been shared across firms through licensing and cross-licensing agreements in the agricultural input sector over a 25-year period. They then evaluate how patenting and licensing agreements among firms in this sector affected the introduction of new products during this time.

Production and licensing of patents may be the most measurable technology transfer flow in the agricultural innovation system, but it is not the only one. Perkmann et al. (2013) found other forms of knowledge and technology transfer, such as collaborative research, consulting, and informal relationships among researchers, to be much more common than producing and licensing intellectual property. Their review indicated that three to four times as many university researchers engaged in such one-on-one activities, which they collectively termed "engagement," than in patenting or creating spinoff firms. Engagement is most popular with high-achieving, more senior faculty, and such relationships may provide academics with resources unavailable at their home institutions. Private firms place a high value on academic engagement as well, as it gives them access to expertise that may be otherwise hard to come by. Finally, they found that the century-old debate described earlier still has influence in academic attitudes; most faculty members view engagement as an extension of and compatible with traditional academic roles, but see patenting and commercialization as a different sort of activity. Engagement is thus a very important mode of technology and knowledge transfer but is difficult to study as much of it occurs in forms that are not easily recorded and quantified.

Academic publications are one form of knowledge and technology transfer that can readily be analyzed. In recognition of the important role played by land-grant universities in agricultural R&D and technology transfer, *Tripp, Grueber, Yetter, and*

Yetter assess the knowledge output, in the form of peer-reviewed journal articles, which resulted from NIFA-funded projects at land-grant universities and evaluate how such outputs were paired with resources from other pools for continuing research.

Formalizing University Technology Transfer

Beginning in the 1950s, increased federal research funding led to more R&D activities at many universities. As the greater volume of research produced more potentially patentable inventions, interest in patenting also grew. The pace of federal funding accelerated again in the 1960s and shifted to more basic research, especially in the biomedical disciplines. As research activity and the flow of patentable inventions continued to grow, more and more schools found it practical to manage their own patent portfolios, founding technology transfer offices (TTOs) and hiring professional staff (Mowery and Sampat 2001). Increased federal funding also meant that federal government policies became increasingly important in the technology transfer arena, not only for government labs but also for supported research in universities and private firms. By 1960, it was becoming clear that federal policy was probably inhibiting public-to-private technology transfer. There was no comprehensive policy concerning the patenting of inventions resulting from government-sponsored research. Each agency had its own rules; some operated under statutory restrictions on what could be patented, while others had more discretion. Around 1965, some agencies, notably the Department of Health, Education, and Welfare (HEW) and the National Institutes of Health (NIH), started to make it easier for universities to patent and license their inventions, but not all agencies made those changes. Throughout the 1960s and 1970s, the debate on patenting the products of federally funded research continued, finally culminating in the passage of the Bayh-Dole Act in 1980. This Act granted substantial rights to recipients of federal funds to patent and license inventions resulting from that research and made federal policy broadly and explicitly supportive of public-private technology transfer. Thus Bayh-Dole was the culmination of a decades-long process of institutionalizing university patenting (Berman 2008). University patenting is now a common practice, so much so that recent studies indicate that the former pioneers, land-grant universities, no longer seem to play a disproportionately large role in generating patentable innovations (Friedman and Silberman 2003).

At the same time that legislative and policy changes in the USA were encouraging more university patenting, other countries were making similar modifications to promote university technology transfer. The resulting widespread increase in technology transfer made the role of TTOs steadily more important (Grimaldi et al. 2011). More recently, the concept of academic entrepreneurship has become broader, no longer restricted to patenting and licensing intellectual property but encompassing activities such as faculty startup firms and curriculum changes, among others (Kolympiris et al. 2015). The role of the TTO has expanded congruently, from patent portfolio management to more general support of entrepreneurial activity (Siegel and Wright 2015). In this collection several authors examine the TTO operations and performance as well as the factors that contribute to their success. *Smyth* studies the performance of Canadian university TTOs. He describes much of the relevant history of how different research frameworks and changes in public policy affected university technology transfer in Canada. *Hoenen, Kolympiris, Wubben, and Omta* give a detailed account of the development of the technology transfer system at Wageningen University and Research. They identify several factors that have contributed to a successful program at one of the leading agricultural universities in Europe, describing the impact of formal policies, the cultural environment of the university, and the general, regional promotion of private R&D activities. *Cartalos, Svoronos, and Carayannis* review the operations of the TTO at the Agricultural University of Athens. This program is a good example of the expanding concept of TTO duties. This TTO provides a broad range of business support services not only to university researchers but also to licensees of university IP. Recognizing that one hallmark of TTO operations is that they must make decisions regarding innovations whose true potential is unknown, they also develop a model for optimal choices of services and projects TTOs can support. Along that same line, *Zahringer, Kolympiris, and Kalaitzandonakes* explore how the technology life cycle can influence the potential market value of university inventions as well as their optimal commercialization and technology transfer strategies.

Transferring Agricultural Innovation to Producer Fields

Much of public and private agricultural R&D is focused on the development of improved agricultural inputs and production practices. Thus for agricultural innovations to be useful, they must be passed along to agricultural producers. Universities have become significant centers of innovation over the last 150 years or so. Through the mid-1800s, American universities saw themselves as primarily teaching institutions. In creating land-grant colleges with the Morrill Act of 1862, the Congress sought to extend that mission beyond the traditional urban, upper-class clientele to rural and working-class Americans, emphasizing agriculture and the mechanical arts. It soon became clear that the educational mission of the land-grant schools would suffer without a quality research program to feed it. Therefore, in 1887, Congress passed the Hatch Act, establishing state agricultural experiment stations (SAES) in all states (Cash 2001). Quality education supported by research strengthened agricultural innovation, but it was not enough; most university students did not study agriculture, and only some of those that did returned to the family farm. Without a formal technology transfer program, there was a growing knowledge gap between academic researchers and the farmers they meant to serve. The US Congress supplied such a system by establishing a cooperative extension service in every state through the Smith-Lever Act in 1914. Finally, the land-grant system of agricultural research with results made freely available to all practitioners through teaching and extension was firmly in place (McDowell 2001). Variations of such public agricultural innovation systems based on research, teaching, and extension services were established in other countries as well with varying levels of funding support and organizational effectiveness.

Extension continues to be a major path for technology transfer from university researchers to producers. *Koutsouris* reviews extension research and practice and takes issue with the standard diffusion theory and linear transfer models, going on to describe several newer paradigms that emphasize two-way communication and the ties between research and practice. He charts out in detail the changes in the literature and organizational strategies as scholars developed more complex and realistic models of technology transfer.

Availability of improved inputs and production practices, whether from the private or the public sector, is not the same as use and adoption. The adoption and decision-making processes of agricultural producers are an essential part of the technology transfer process. Modern adoption paradigms are largely based on the diffusion of innovation (DOI) theory of Rogers (2003), who postulated that individuals are heterogeneous in their willingness to adopt and are normally distributed along that continuum. Early versions of this model looked only at adopter characteristics and thus had a strong pro-adoption bias, implicitly assuming that all innovations were worth adopting. Suri (2011) pointed out that adoption, from the DOI perspective, focused primarily on user learning as the main determinant, neglecting user interaction with both the transfer agent and the innovation. Later extensions took into account characteristics of the technology and its impact on users (Meade and Islam 2006). Recent models are more comprehensive and less linear, emphasizing the impact of innovations and the roles of policy, social institutions, and infrastructure in adoption (Doss 2006). *Ugochuckwu and Phillips* focus on the end user of agricultural innovation in their comprehensive review of the adoption and diffusion literature and also describe the contributions and drawbacks of DOI theory. They use studies of the adoption of a range of specific technologies to describe the variety of theoretical and practical approaches and the different factors identified as impacting adoption.

When farmers decide whether to adopt an innovation, they must consider factors that do not apply to more conventional industrial pursuits. There are some important production conditions over which farmers have minimal control, notably weather, pests, and diseases. This production risk is heterogeneous across producers and regions and sometimes even across individual farms. Farmers are likewise heterogeneous in their risk preferences. Thus risk management is a major and variable concern in all producers' decision-making. Farmers, then, do not consider only the effect of an innovation on average yield but also on yield and cost variability (Koundouri et al. 2006). The adoption decision, then, can be as much a risk management tactic as an income-increasing one. Producers are also heterogeneous in the costs they bear and the benefits they enjoy from adopting agricultural innovations, especially in developing countries. For instance, Suri (2011) showed how variable infrastructure quality and other social conditions can dramatically affect fixed costs of adoption of new crop varieties in Africa. Such costs can be considerable in some cases, making the adoption of otherwise highly attractive innovations uneconomical.

Two of the chapters in this volume address some of the practical aspects of moving agricultural innovations into actual field use. *Akhundjanov, Gallardo, McCluskey, and Rickard* investigate how contract terms can either promote or inhibit the transfer and use of technological innovations covered by IPRs. Using game theory and an experimental auction, they examine how contract exclusivity, payment structure, and time duration affect producer willingness to adopt a hypothetical new apple variety developed at a land-grant university. Technology transfer to developing countries is key to future increases in global productivity and food security; *Edge, Oikeh, Kyetere, Mugo, and Mashingaidze* describe the history of a large technology transfer project in Africa. Water Efficient Maize for Africa (WEMA) began in 2008 to develop and encourage adoption of drought-tolerant hybrid corn. They identify a number of factors that can contribute to the success of large public-private partnerships of the sort. They go on to discuss further challenges that may accompany the possible future introduction of transgenic varieties.

Benefits from Agricultural Research and Innovation

Return to research investments is a topic of continuing interest and an important part of assessing the effectiveness of research programs. The benefits of research and innovation can be evaluated from different perspectives. *Shafer and Strauss* offer a practical view of how public agricultural R&D affects us all, as they describe the many areas of USDA-sponsored research and the impact it has had on American diet. *Martha and Alves* shift the view internationally, as they discuss the public agricultural research system in Brazil. They describe the government's comprehensive program for agricultural modernization, of which research support is but one part. They go into detail about the multiple activities of Embrapa, the government-owned research firm that is the major player in agricultural innovation in Brazil, and give some measures of returns to Brazilian research investments. In order to facilitate a greater understanding of the subject, some of our authors identify and analyze alternative definitions, measures, and models related to calculating estimates of monetary returns to research expenditures. *Huffman* identifies potential definition and measurement problems that can lead to inaccurate estimates of returns to research if not taken into consideration. *Qin and Buccola* discuss the measurement of knowledge production. They construct two measures based on Bayesian reasoning that potentially express knowledge production in a way that could be directly comparable across different R&D projects. They go on to demonstrate how those measures might be used in explaining research productivity and assessing the relative contribution of various characteristics of research programs.

We see, then, that technology transfer is a complex process and a complicated research area. As Bozeman (2000, 627) quipped, "In the study of technology transfer, the neophyte and the veteran researcher are easily distinguished. The neophyte is the one who is not confused." Agricultural research takes place in universities, government, and private laboratories and experiment stations. Some technology and knowledge are embodied in specific, explicitly traded products or processes, and some are shared through more informal means. Some innovations are released into the public domain, and some are protected through IPRs and other means. Some reach producers by way of the cooperative extension system, and some come as products marketed by private firms. What is clear is that modern agricultural productivity is a direct result of technological progress in improved genetics, manufactured and other inputs, and agronomic practices. Further improvement in productivity will be essential to increasing food production, possibly as much as a 70% increase by 2050, to keep up with a continually increasing world population (Meyers and Kalaitzandonakes 2012). Thus a clear understanding of the transfer process, in all its complexity, and how to improve it is crucial to our future. Contributions in this volume present a comprehensive treatment of the complex processes involved in the development and transfer of agricultural innovation. Toward this end, our concluding chapter offers a synthesis of lessons learned from the various contributors.

References

Berman, E.P. 2008. Why Did Universities Start Patenting? *Social Studies of Science* 38 (6): 835–871. https://doi.org/10.1177/0306312708098605.

BGCI. 2017. The History of Botanic Gardens. Botanic Gardens Conservation International. Retrieved 22 May 2017, from https://www.bgci.org/resources/history/.

Bogaard, A. 2004. The Nature of Early Farming in Central and South-East Europe. *Documenta Praehistorica* 31: 49–58.

Bozeman, B. 2000. Technology Transfer and Public Policy: A Review of Research and Theory. *Research Policy* 29 (4–5): 627–655. https://doi.org/10.1016/S0048-7333(99)00093-1.

Carayannis, E.G., E. Grigoroudis, and Y. Goletsis. 2016. A Multilevel and Multistage Efficiency Evaluation of Innovation Systems: A Multiobjective DEA Approach. *Expert Systems with Applications* 62: 63–80. https://doi.org/10.1016/j.eswa.2016.06.017.

Cash, D.W. 2001. In Order to Aid in Diffusing Useful and Practical Information: Agricultural Extension and Boundary Organizations. *Science, Technology, & Human Values* 26 (4): 431–453. http://www.jstor.org/stable/690163.

Doss, C.R. 2006. Analyzing Technology Adoption Using Microstudies: Limitations, Challenges, and Opportunities for Improvement. *Agricultural Economics* 34 (3): 207–219. https://doi.org/10.1111/j.1574-0864.2006.00119.x.

Friedman, J., and J. Silberman. 2003. University Technology Transfer: Do Incentives, Management, and Location Matter? *The Journal of Technology Transfer* 28 (1): 17–30. https://doi.org/10.1023/a:1021674618658.

Fuller, D.Q., R.G. Allaby, and C. Stevens. 2010. Domestication as Innovation: The Entanglement of Techniques, Technology and Chance in the Domestication of Cereal Crops. *World Archaeology* 42 (1): 13–28. https://doi.org/10.1080/00438240903429680.

Fussell, G. 1966. Ploughs and Ploughing before 1800. *Agricultural History* 40 (3): 177–186.

Grimaldi, R., M. Kenney, D.S. Siegel, and M. Wright. 2011. 30 Years after Bayh–Dole: Reassessing Academic Entrepreneurship. *Research Policy* 40 (8): 1045–1057. https://doi.org/10.1016/j.respol.2011.04.005.

Kolympiris, C., N. Kalaitzandonakes, and D. Miller. 2015. Location Choice of Academic Entrepreneurs: Evidence from the US Biotechnology Industry. *Journal of Business Venturing* 30 (2): 227–254.

Koundouri, P., C. Nauges, and V. Tzouvelekas. 2006. Technology Adoption under Production Uncertainty: Theory and Application to Irrigation Technology. *American Journal of Agricultural Economics* 88 (3): 657–670. https://doi.org/10.1111/j.1467-8276.2006.00886.x.

McDowell, G.R. 2001. *Land-Grant Universities and Extension into the 21st Century: Renegotiating or Abandoning a Social Contract.* Ames, IA: Iowa State University Press.

Meade, N., and T. Islam. 2006. Modelling and Forecasting the Diffusion of Innovation – a 25-Year Review. *International Journal of Forecasting* 22 (3): 519–545. https://doi.org/10.1016/j.ijforecast.2006.01.005.

Meyers, W.H., and N. Kalaitzandonakes. 2012. World Population Growth and Food Supply. In *The Role of Technology in a Sustainable Food Supply*, ed. J.S. Popp, M.D. Matlock, M.M. Jahn, and N.P. Kemper, 1–16. New York: Cambridge University Press.

Mowery, D.C., R.R. Nelson, B.N. Sampat, and A.A. Ziedonis. 2001. The Growth of Patenting and Licensing by US Universities: An Assessment of the Effects of the Bayh–Dole Act of 1980. *Research Policy* 30 (1): 99–119. https://doi.org/10.1016/S0048-7333(99)00100-6.

Mowery, D.C., and B.N. Sampat. 2001. University Patents and Patent Policy Debates in the USA, 1925–1980. *Industrial and Corporate Change* 10 (3): 781–814. https://doi.org/10.1093/icc/10.3.781.

Perkmann, M., V. Tartari, M. McKelvey, E. Autio, A. Broström, P. D'Este, R. Fini, A. Geuna, R. Grimaldi, A. Hughes, S. Krabel, M. Kitson, P. Llerena, F. Lissoni, A. Salter, and M. Sobrero. 2013. Academic Engagement and Commercialisation: A Review of the Literature on University–Industry Relations. *Research Policy* 42 (2): 423–442. https://doi.org/10.1016/j.respol.2012.09.007.

Rogers, E.M. 2003. *Diffusion of Innovations.* New York: Free Press.

Rossman, J., F.G. Cottrell, A.W. Hull, and A.F. Woods. 1934. The Protection by Patents of Scientific Discoveries. *Science* 79 (Supplement(1)): 1–40.

Sayre, L.B. 2010. The Pre-History of Soil Science: Jethro Tull, the Invention of the Seed Drill, and the Foundations of Modern Agriculture. *Physics and Chemistry of the Earth, Parts A/B/C* 35 (15): 851–859.

Siegel, D.S., and M. Wright. 2015. Academic Entrepreneurship: Time for a Rethink? *British Journal of Management* 26 (4): 582–595. https://doi.org/10.1111/1467-8551.12116.

Suri, T. 2011. Selection and Comparative Advantage in Technology Adoption. *Econometrica* 79 (1): 159–209.

Part I
R&D Spending and Agricultural Innovation: Organization and Emerging Trends

The Shifting Structure of Agricultural R&D: Worldwide Investment Patterns and Payoffs

Philip G. Pardey, Julian M. Alston, Connie Chan-Kang, Terrance M. Hurley, Robert S. Andrade, Steven P. Dehmer, Kyuseon Lee, and Xudong Rao

Abstract The future path and pace of agricultural productivity growth areinextricably intertwined with investments in food and agricultural research and development (R&D). Looking back over half a century of evidence, we find that the lay of the global food and agricultural R&D land is changing, with indications that we are in the midst of an historic transition. The more notable trends are as follows: (1) for the first time in modern history (in purchasing power parity, PPP, terms), the middle-income countries now outspend the rich countries in terms of public-sector investments in food and agricultural R&D; (2) the shifting public shares reflect a continuing decline in the rate of growth of food and agricultural R&D spending by the rich countries, along with a generally sustained and substantial growth in spending by the middle-income countries (especially China, India, and Brazil); (3) in PPP terms, China now spends more than the United States on both public- and private-sector food and agricultural R&D; (4) the global share of food and agricultural R&D being conducted by the private sector has increased, especially in the high- and rapidly growing middle-income countries; and (5) the low-income countries are losing ground and account for an exceptionally small share of global spending. The mean and median values of the reported rates of return to food and agricultural R&D based on the IRR are high and remain so, with no signs of a diminution in the payoffs to more recent (compared with earlier) investments in R&D. But the available evidence on the returns to food and agricultural R&D is not fully representative of the institutional (i.e., public versus private), locational, or commodity orientation of the research and the agricultural sector itself.

P.G. Pardey (✉) • C. Chan-Kang • T.M. Hurley • K. Lee
University of Minnesota, Minneapolis, MN, USA
e-mail: ppardey@umn.edu

J.M. Alston
University of California, Davis, CA, USA

R.S. Andrade
International Center for Tropical Agriculture (CIAT), Cali, Colombia

S.P. Dehmer
Health Partners Institute, Minneapolis, MN, USA

X. Rao
Wageningen University and Research, Wageningen, Netherlands

© Springer International Publishing AG 2018   13
N. Kalaitzandonakes et al. (eds.), *From Agriscience to Agribusiness*, Innovation,
Technology, and Knowledge Management, https://doi.org/10.1007/978-3-319-67958-7_2

Introduction

The food and agricultural sciences have changed markedly over the past half century. Conventional crop and livestock breeding methods are now enabled by ever-more sophisticated gene editing and computational biology techniques. Complementary advances in the measurement and sensor sciences are opening up entirely new opportunities for understanding the phenotypic outcomes of genetic-by-environment interactions, including those that encompass the complex microbiomes that coexist with all agricultural plants and animals. New materials, engineering, robotic, and data sciences are transforming the way in-ground, on-ground, and remote-sensed information is captured and used on experimental plots, farmers' fields, and agricultural landscapes more broadly. Similarly, revolutionary integration of data and findings from the food production, processing, nutritional, and medical sciences are reshaping the links between on- and post-farm technologies, with profound consequences for the nutritional and other quality attributes of the food we eat. In parallel with these changes in the science itself, the investment and institutional realities of the R&D (research and development) systems supporting food and agriculture have also changed markedly in terms of the total amount of R&D, who pays for and performs that research, and where in the world the research is carried out.

In this chapter, we summarize key trends in the global investment landscape for food and agricultural R&D over the past half century. We also draw on a recently updated and expanded set of worldwide data on the returns to food and agricultural research to describe and interpret the economic payoffs to R&D. This discussion draws heavily on projects undertaken over the past several years (and in some cases, decades) compiling data and developing measures of agricultural science and its consequences around the world, including efforts to develop the methods and metrics for those measures.

Measuring R&D and Its Impacts: Facts and Factology

Just like the data used in the social sciences more generally, the data used to inform our understanding of the investments in and the returns to food and agricultural R&D are difficult to come by and require care in their use. In his Fellows lecture to the American Agricultural Economics Association, Gardner (1992) discussed the importance of data creation and of having econometricians, policy analysts, and other data users know how the data they use were created:

> Agricultural economists and other social scientists tend to take data as facts... The problem is the data are not facts. Facts are what is really there. Data are quantitative representation of facts, which statistical workers and economists concoct (p. 1074). . . I call the study of how primary statistical information is made into economic data "factology." The neglect of factology risks scientific ruin. (p. 1067)

Measuring R&D Investments

Compiling data on food and agricultural R&D entails a host of analytical choices that affect our measured assessment of the underlying R&D realities (Pardey et al. 2016). In addition to dealing with the more obvious but nonetheless still difficult problems associated with inconsistent, incomplete, and missing data, we must confront a host of subtle measurement issues that can have not-so-subtle measurement consequences. For example, the changing scientific landscape blurs the measurement boundaries as to what distinguishes "food and agricultural R&D" from the rest of research.

The R&D spending data reported and discussed here measure R&D spending on a by-performer basis.[1] As a practical matter, this measure of spending includes research conducted by government agencies that typically fall under the administrative jurisdiction of ministries of agriculture, food, forestry, and (sometimes) fisheries, the food- and agriculture-related parts of university research, and research conducted by firms deemed to have food and agricultural interests according to SIC (Standard Industrial Classification), or similar, codes. But potential measurement problems can arise, even in the case of food and agricultural firms, notably for firms that include business segments outside food and agriculture. For example, while pharmaceutical companies (such as Pfizer and Elanco-Lilly) focus most of their research on human health, many have business segments that involve veterinary medicine or food safety research of relevance for a measure of "food and agricultural R&D." Likewise, while much of the R&D conducted by chemical companies (e.g., Bayer, BASF, and DuPont) is focused on industrial business segments outside agriculture, they also conduct R&D on pesticides, herbicides, and other chemicals used by agriculture. These segment shares also change over time—Monsanto was once principally a nonagricultural chemical company and is now an entirely agriculturally focused life science company—meaning decisions must be made as to how to parse the R&D spending totals reported by such firms between their agricultural and nonagricultural business segments.[2]

The R&D estimates summarized and discussed here are based on version 3.5 of the University of Minnesota's InSTePP (International Science and Technology Practice and Policy) global food and agricultural R&D series.[3] These country, regional, and worldwide estimates of domestic public spending on food and agricultural R&D (agPERD) represent a completely revised, updated, and historically expanded set of estimates compared with previous versions of the InSTePP series. They also represent the most comprehensive estimates of global food and agricultural R&D presently available. They include data for 156 countries for

---

[1] R&D series are denominated sometimes on a "by-purpose" basis and, in some instances, according to the source of funding rather than the agency conducting or spending the funds. See OECD (2002 and 2007) for more details.

[2] Of course a host of other measurement matters remain to be resolved, such as accounting for inflation (or, more specifically, the changing price of R&D inputs), standardizing currency units of measurement among countries (and over time), and so on.

[3] See Pardey et al. (2016) for complete details on data construction and data sources.

over half a century, spanning the years 1960–2011 (plus a satellite account of 28 countries from the former Soviet Union and Eastern Europe for more recent years). The global estimates of privately performed food and agricultural R&D (agBERD) are entirely new. They encompass expenditure estimates of privately performed food- and agriculture-related R&D in the United States developed from firm-specific data for 408 companies from three business sectors, specifically "agriculture and chemicals," "machinery," plus "food processing, beverages, and tobacco." Country-level data and various statistical interpolation and extrapolation methods were used to develop the private R&D spending estimates for the remaining 155 countries spanning the period 1980–2011. The R&D data were generally compiled in nominal local currency units, deflated to base year 2009 using country-specific implicit GDP deflators, and then converted to 2009 PPP dollars using base year purchasing power parity (PPP) estimates, both sourced from the World Bank.[4]

Measuring R&D Impacts

Formal assessments of the returns to investments in R&D typically report payoffs in terms of conventional summary statistics such as the net present value of benefits (NPV), the benefit-cost ratio (BCR), or the internal rate of return (IRR), computed using methods that are described in various books and manuals on capital budgeting and benefit-cost analysis (e.g., Barry and Ellinger 2011) including some specifically developed for those engaged in evaluating research investments (e.g., Alston et al. 1995).[5] While the IRR is the predominant metric used to summarize evidence on the payoff to agricultural R&D, recent work by economists has shown that using IRRs for this purpose is problematic. Alston et al. (2011) pointed to a conceptual flaw in the method, the implausibly high values that are typically obtained as a result, and the questionable implications of these values. For example, a dollar invested at an annual rate of return of 50% per year would be worth in excess of US$11 million after 35 years and US$600 million after 50 years.[6] The implausibly high estimated values are driven in large part by two implicit assumptions used in the IRR calculation. First, the calculation assumes that the beneficiaries (i.e., farmers and consumers) can reinvest their benefits at the same rate of return (i.e., the computed IRR).

---

[4] Here, "rich countries" are synonymous with high-income countries. Countries are classified into income classes according to the World Bank (2015) data and income classifications. High-income countries are those with 2013 GNI (gross national income) per capita of $12,746 or more; upper middle-income countries had 2013 GNI per capita between $4126 and $12,745; lower middle-income countries had 2013 GNI per capita between $1046 and $4125; and low-income countries had 2013 GNI per capita less than or equal to $1045.

[5] The IRR is the interest rate that equates the present value of benefits from an investment to the present value of its costs. The BCR is the ratio of the present value of benefits from an investment to the present value of its costs.

[6] These concerns were noted earlier by Alston et al. (2000).

Second, the cost of the investment over time is discounted at the same rate (i.e., the computed IRR). These two assumptions are generally questionable and are empirically problematic when an investment is highly profitable, as is typically true for investments in agricultural R&D.

To avert these problems, Alston et al. (2011) suggested using a BCR or a modified internal rate of return (MIRR) instead of the IRR. In computing the MIRR, the analyst chooses values for the rate of discount for research costs and the rate of return to reinvested research benefits (as well as the time period from the inception of R&D costs to the termination of benefits associated with that research) (Rao et al. 2017b). If more reasonable assumptions are made about rates of discount for research costs and rates of return to reinvested research benefits, the computed MIRR will be much smaller than the conventional IRR in typical situations with high payoffs to agricultural R&D, and typically much more plausible, as demonstrated for the United States by Alston et al. (2011) and Andersen and Song (2013).

Hurley et al. (2014a, b) developed a method for using information reported in previous studies to recalibrate a subset (270) of the previous IRR estimates using the MIRR. With this recalibration, Hurley et al. (2014a, Table 1) report a mean MIRR of 13.6% per year, much lower than the mean corresponding IRR of 67.9% per year; likewise, the median is reduced from 39.0% per year for the IRR to 9.8% per year for the MIRR.[7] The range of estimates is correspondingly compressed in going from the IRR to the MIRR. The interquartile range of the MIRRs is much smaller, just 15% of the corresponding range for the IRRs. The minimum MIRR is −2.0% per year, below the corresponding IRR of 7.4% per year, and the maximum MIRR is 107.0% per year, well below the corresponding IRR estimate of 1736% per year.

As Rao et al. (2017b, p. 1) observed:

Critiques of using the IRR to measure the value of an investment date back to Griliches's seminal paper (e.g., Hirshleifer 1958) and continue to the present (e.g., Hurley et al. 2014a, b, 2017). Similarly, defenses of the utility of the IRR date back to Griliches's seminal paper (e.g., Bailey 1959) and continue to the present. (Oehmke 2017).

Why is this so? Hurley et al. (2017) show that both the BCR and MIRR provide measures that can be used to compare the relative profitability of alternative investments, provided consistent discounting assumptions are used in the calculations. However, the potential to construct comparable BCRs and IRRs with consistent assumptions does not exist except under restrictive conditions that are often violated in the agricultural R&D literature (e.g., when project costs and returns span multiple years). This is one reason why Alston et al. (2000, 2011) and Hurley et al. (2014a, b, 2017) prefer the BCR or MIRR over the IRR. Another is the implausibly high rate of return to research implied by the

---

[7] In more recent work, Rao et al. (2017b) were able to recalibrate 2165 of the published IRR estimates, resulting in a median MIRR of 17.0% per year (conditional on a research lag length of 30 years and a discount rate of 5% per year), well less than the corresponding 39.0% per year median IRR.

IRR when incorrectly compared with the opportunity cost of funds such as the rate of return to private equity—as we have often observed in policy discussions.

The Shifting Structure of R&D

Global gross domestic public and private expenditures on R&D directed to food and agriculture (agGERD) totaled $69.3 billion (2009 PPP dollars) in 2011, around 5.0% of the overall $1397 billion invested worldwide in all forms of R&D that year.[8] This implies a 2.8% annual rate of growth in inflation-adjusted agGERD since 1980, when public and private spending on food and agricultural R&D was $27.38 billion (Fig. 1).

The Economic Geography of Global Agricultural R&D

Around 47.3% of the world's 2011 expenditure on *publicly* performed domestic food and agricultural R&D (agPERD) took place in rich countries, with the United States and Japan accounting for 24.4% and 19.2%, respectively, of that rich country total (Fig. 2).[9] Even more of the world's expenditure on *business* (or domestic, privately performed) food and agricultural R&D (agBERD) took place in the rich countries (63.9% in 2011), of which the respective US and Japanese shares were 38.3% and 18.4%.

The middle-income countries accounted for 49.8% of global agPERD and 35.5% of agBERD in 2011. China and Brazil combined accounted for 55.5% of the upper-middle income agPERD and 85.6% of the respective agBERD share. India dominated the share of agricultural R&D performed by lower-middle income countries, accounting for 52.5% of the respective agPERD and 67.8% of the agBERD totals. Starkly, this means that in 2011 just 2.9% of the world's agPERD and a miniscule 0.5% of the world's agBERD were performed in low-income countries, home to an

---

[8] Dehmer et al. (2017) report total global gross domestic expenditures on R&D (GERD) of $1492 billion (2009 PPP$) for 2011 GERD (inclusive of countries from the former Soviet Union and Eastern Europe, FSU&EE). The $1397 billion in total science spending quoted and the time series of agGERD estimates reported in this paper exclude estimates of R&D spending by countries of the former Soviet Union and Eastern Europe. In a set of "satellite accounts," InSTePP estimates (with less confidence compared with the rest-of-world estimates) that in 2011 the 28 countries that make up this group spent $1.9 billion on agGERD. Unless otherwise stated, all dollar-denominated R&D estimates in this chapter are expressed in base year 2009 purchasing power parity (PPP) dollars.

[9] Spending by the international agricultural research centers that constitute the CGIAR totaled $668.4 million (2009 prices) in 2011, such that public (including national or "domestic" and international) plus private spending totaled $69.9 billion in 2011 (Fig. 2).

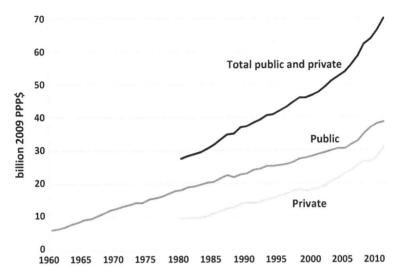

Fig. 1 Food and agricultural R&D spending (domestic and international) worldwide, 1960–2011 (*Source:* InSTePP R&D Accounts, version 3.5. *Notes:* Countries from the Former Soviet Union and Eastern Europe are excluded from the time series because of limited data; the public agricultural R&D series includes 130 countries; the private agricultural and food R&D series includes 128 countries as there were no data available for Guam and US Virgin Islands. Public series includes domestic as well as CGIAR (international) spending)

estimated 26.3% (265.6 million) of the world's population living below the poverty line that year.

Looking back over half a century, our new data show we are in the midst of an historic transition. The rich countries' share of global public investments in food and agricultural R&D continues to fall. The rate of growth in rich country agPERD peaked in the 1960s and 1970s and has fallen since then, with an inflation-adjusted growth rate averaging just 0.8% per year from 2000 to 2011. In more recent years (and especially since 2002), historically important agricultural research countries including the United States, the United Kingdom, and Australia began cutting back on (inflation-adjusted) public spending on food and agricultural R&D. In contrast, growth in inflation-adjusted public agricultural R&D spending accelerated to 5.8% per year from 2000 to 2011 for the middle-income countries, compared with an average of 3.8% per year for the period 1960–2000 (versus 3.5% per year for the rich countries). The low-income countries increased their public agricultural R&D spending by about 2.6% per year since 1960, but that growth failed to keep pace with growth elsewhere in the world, such that their share of the global public total has shrunk over the past half century (4.2% in 1960 to 2.9% in 2011).

Collectively, the middle-income countries began outspending the rich countries on agPERD in 2010 if spending is measured in purchasing power parity (PPP) terms. By this measure, China had risen to the top of the global agPERD rankings by 2011, while India had moved up the global rankings, and Brazil maintained a high ranking over the past half century (Table 1). These three middle-income countries are now

Fig. 2 Public and private food and agricultural R&D by income group, 2011. Panel A: Public (domestic and international) $38.8 billion (2009 PPP$). Panel B: Private $31.1 billion (2009 PPP$) (*Source:* InSTePP R&D Accounts, version 3.5. *Notes:* Countries are classified into income classes in line with World Development Indicators 2015 report's schema (available at https://openknowledge.worldbank.org/handle/10986/21634). See footnote 4 for income classification details)

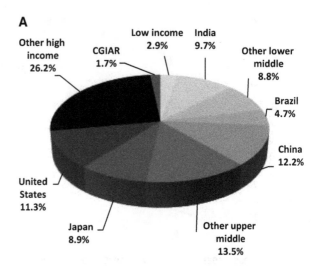

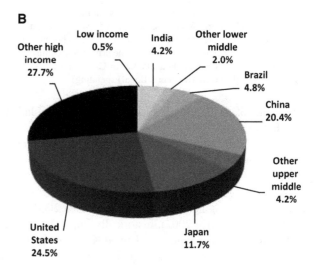

firmly entrenched among the top ten agPERD countries in the world, pushing aside countries such as the United Kingdom and Australia that were in the top ten in 1960.[10]

The 2011 agPERD relativities of the United States and China are particularly noteworthy, with China outspending the United States. Part of these changing US-China relativities reflect a substantially more rapid (and sustained) real rate of growth of agPERD in China versus the United States over recent decades. The

---

[10] The current status and future prospects for agricultural R&D funding in Brazil are conditioned by (1) the 40% reduction in overall R&D funding during 2013–2016 as a consequence of reduced public spending and (2) the prospects of a freeze on overall federal government spending for the next two decades (Angelo 2016).

Table 1 Top ten countries in public food and agricultural R&D, 1960 and 2011

Country	Rank PPP (2011) 1960	2011	Market exchange rate (2011) Rel. to China	Amount	Share	PPP (2011) Rel. to China	Amount	Share
	(1)	(2)	(3)	(4)	(5)	(6)	(7)	(8)
			(China =100)	*(billion 2009 US$)*	*(%)*	*(China =100)*	*(billion 2009 PPP$)*	*(%)*
China	5	1	100.0	2.2	7.8	100.0	4.7	12.4
United States	1	2	202.4	4.4	15.9	93.2	4.4	11.5
India	7	3	47.2	1.0	3.7	79.8	3.8	9.9
Japan	9	4	196.5	4.3	15.4	73.4	3.5	9.1
Brazil	3	5	55.4	1.2	4.4	38.9	1.8	4.8
Germany	2	6	61.2	1.3	4.8	25.2	1.2	3.1
France	14	7	59.3	1.3	4.7	22.9	1.1	2.8
Canada	8	8	48.8	1.1	3.8	21.3	1.0	2.6
Italy	16	9	49.2	1.1	3.9	21.0	1.0	2.6
S. Korea	20	10	28.5	0.6	2.2	20.4	1.0	2.5
Top 10				18.5	66.6		23.4	61.5
Top 20				23.0	82.8		30.1	78.9
Bottom 100				3.0	10.9		4.5	11.9

Source: InSTePP R&D Accounts, version 3.5; implicit GDP deflator data from United Nations Statistics Division (2013) and World Bank (2015); market exchange rate data from United Nations Statistics Division (2013); PPP (purchasing power parity) conversion factor from World Bank (2015)

Notes: Columns 1 and 2 are rankings of each county's agPERD (expressed in 2009 PPPs) for years 1960 and 2011, respectively. Columns 3, 4, and 5 relate to 2011 agPERD expressed in 2009 US dollars using market exchange rates. Columns 6, 7, and 8 relate to 2011 agPERD expressed in 2009 PPP dollars using purchasing power parities. In descending rank order, the top ten countries in 1960 (using PPPs for the currency conversions) were the United States, Germany, Brazil, the United Kingdom, China, South Africa, India, Canada, Japan, and Australia

inflation-adjusted rate of growth in agPERD spending in China averaged 8.1% per year since 1980 (and 15.1% per year since 2002), compared with just 1.7% per year for the United States, where inflation-adjusted agPERD spending has actually shrunk since 2002.[11]

---

[11] Cross-country relativities reflect a currency conversion issue. Using purchasing power parities to adjust for differences in prices across countries is common, but has well-known issues. Namely, while the goal is to account for differences in the unit costs of scientific staff and other R&D inputs across countries, the PPP conversion factors reflect price differences for a standard basket of goods and services related to GDP rather than a targeted basket of goods and services related to R&D costs. For example, using market exchange rates for the currency conversions has the United States outspending China in 2011 with US$4.40 billion of agPERD in the United States versus US$2.18 billion for China (Table 1).

Table 2 Private and public food and agricultural R&D, 1980 and 2011

	Private (AgBERD)				Public (AgPERD)			
	1980		2011		1980		2011	
Income class	Total	Per capita	Total	Per capita	Total	Per capita	Total	Per capita
	(million 2009 PPP$)	*(2009 PPP$)*	*(million 2009 PPP$)*	*(2009 PPP$)*	*(million 2009 PPP$)*	*(2009 PPP$)*	*(million 2009 PPP$)*	*(2009 PPP$)*
Low income	63	0.18	165	0.22	593	1.73	1112	1.51
Lower middle	402	0.31	1919	0.81	2377	1.85	7179	3.04
Upper middle	1096	0.74	9146	4.12	3997	2.69	11,816	5.32
High income	7992	9.75	19,899	19.58	10,863	13.25	18,022	17.73
Total	9553	2.43	31,129	4.91	17,830	4.53	38,129	6.02

Source: InSTePP R&D Accounts, version 3.5. Population data from the United Nations (2013)
Notes: See Figs. 1 and 2. Countries are classified into income classes according to the World Development Indicators 2015 report (available at https://openknowledge.worldbank.org/handle/10986/21634) data and income classifications

While the rank order of the top spending countries has been shaken up, the dramatic divide between rich and poor country public spending on food and agricultural R&D persists and in some key dimensions is widening. In 1980, for every dollar of agGERD spent in low-income countries, $28.80 was spent in the high-income countries. Four decades later, every dollar of food and agricultural R&D spending in the low-income countries was matched by $29.70 of R&D spending by the high-income countries (Table 2). The agPERD spending gap is even more striking when expressed per capita. In 1980, the rich countries invested $13.25 per person on public food and agricultural R&D compared with $1.73 per person among the poor countries on average; by 2011, the spending gap had widened to $17.73 per person by rich countries versus just $1.51 per person by the poor countries.

The rich country-poor country gap is even more pronounced when it comes to private-sector spending on food and agricultural R&D (Table 2). In 2011, for every dollar of agBERD spent in the low-income countries, $120.80 of agBERD was spent in the high-income countries. Moreover, in 2011 in the rich countries the ratio of agBERD to agPERD was 1.10, while the corresponding ratio in the low-income countries was 0.15. Hence the private share of food and agricultural R&D spending was much higher in rich relative to poor countries.

The Privatization of R&D

Not only is the public food and agricultural R&D landscape changing, so too is the global geography of privately performed food and agricultural R&D. Here, too, the middle-income countries (notably China, Brazil, and India) are gaining ground on the rich countries in terms of both their share of global agBERD (15.7% in 1980 increasing to 35.5% in 2011) and their combined spending on agBERD expressed as a share of global agGERD, which increased from 5.5% in 1980 to 16.0% in 2011. The recent rapid growth in investment in private food and agricultural R&D in China—especially research carried out by state-owned agribusinesses such as CNDAC (China National Agricultural Development Corporation) and COFCO (China National Cereals, Oils and Foodstuffs Corporation) but also privately listed companies such as the WH Group, the Yili Group, and the China Yurun Food Group—means that China now also outspends the United States in private food and agricultural R&D. This shifting global balance reflects two reinforcing developments: (1) the accelerating growth of domestic private R&D capacity in (at least some and generally the larger) middle-income countries directed to crop genetics, farm machinery, food processing, and other relevant business segments and (2) the relatively recent offshoring of R&D endeavors into rapidly growing middle-income countries by multinational firms headquartered in the rich countries. The low-income countries continue to account for a miniscule share of the world's private food and agricultural R&D: just 0.5% in 2011.

The broadly shifting global geography of publicly versus privately performed food and agricultural R&D stems from changes in the underlying structure of the food and agricultural economies across countries and the political economy in which those sectors are positioned. We might tend to think of private food and agricultural R&D spending—such as by companies like Monsanto, Pioneer-DuPont, Syngenta, John Deere, and BASF—as being archetypal investments in research on agricultural chemicals, crop breeding, and machinery. Important as those companies and areas of innovation are research targeted to the food, beverages, and tobacco subsector—involving companies such as PepsiCo, Kraft-Heinz, Nestle, General Mills, and Philip Morris—accounted for 43.9% of the rich country private food and agricultural R&D total in 2011 (Fig. 3). Typically, people in more-developed countries—i.e., those with higher per capita incomes—consume a larger share of their food away from home, and an increasing share of food consumption expenditure is on processed foods (Fabiosa 2012). For these post-farm, consumption-oriented reasons, one might expect relatively more of the world's private food-oriented research to be conducted in the richer countries, where the appropriable returns from those investments are likely to be higher. Likewise, farmers in more-developed countries tend to use the purchased inputs arising from private R&D more intensively than do farmers in poorer regions of the world, and this also incentivizes more private participation in farm-oriented agricultural R&D in richer countries.

Rich countries can differ markedly in the emphasis and orientation of their private food and agricultural R&D investments. For example, in Ireland and Portugal, food, beverages, and tobacco R&D accounted for more than 80% of their private

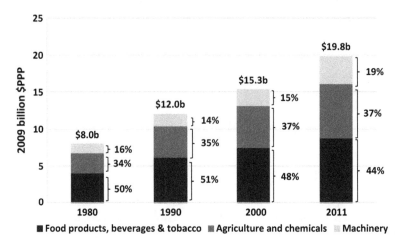

Fig. 3 Private food and agricultural R&D in the rich countries (*Source:* InSTePP R&D Accounts, version 3.5. *Note:* Includes 26 high-income countries for which we have sector-specific agBERD data)

food and agricultural R&D totals in 2011; in contrast, in Sweden, Germany, and Austria, about two-thirds of private agricultural R&D was focused on machinery, agriculture (including crop breeding), and chemicals.

The Intensity of R&D

Over the past 50 years, the high-income group has progressed steadily toward an ever-more research-intensive mode of agricultural production. Compared with an average of just 0.61 cents for every hundred dollars of agricultural output (here measured as agGDP) in 1960, these countries invested an average of $3.40 into public agricultural R&D per hundred dollars of agricultural output in 2011. R&D intensity has increased in spite of a slowdown in the rate of growth of agricultural R&D spending, an indication of an even more pronounced slowdown in the rate of growth of agricultural output in these countries.

Ruttan (1982) had the notion that as productivity increases, a larger share of R&D spending is directed toward preserving the gains in the face of pressures from changes in climate, reductions in the amount and quality of soil and water and other natural inputs used in agriculture, and increased pest and disease pressures that all act to undermine the productivity promoting effects of past research. Because many rich countries rank highly in terms of crop yields and other agricultural productivity indicators, their increasing research intensities may indicate a shift in the supply-side orientation of their research toward research that maintains past productivity gains. The increasing intensities may also reflect an Engel effect in the demand (expressed through political processes) for R&D outputs, whereby, as per capita incomes rise, increasing shares of food and agricultural R&D are directed toward more income elastic concerns such as the environment, food safety, and health, giving rise to growth in R&D spending that is not reflected in corresponding growth in agricultural output or productivity.

In contrast with the high-income countries, the intensity with which the Asia and Pacific region invests in public agricultural R&D has grown much more modestly: from 0.2% of agGDP in 1960 to 0.4% in 2011. Although this region has sustained growth in agPERD at a comparatively rapid pace—averaging 5.0% per year since 1960—agricultural output (i.e., agGDP) also grew reasonably rapidly (3.7% per year). Thus, even though the growth in spending on agPERD outpaced the corresponding growth in the value of output, the growth rate differentials were comparatively modest such that the region's research intensity only inched up over time, although increasingly so after the mid-1990s. In sub-Saharan Africa, public research intensities have been slipping, especially during the past couple of decades, with 19 of the 44 countries (43%) in sub-Saharan Africa in the InSTePP series having lower research intensities in 2011 than they had in 1980.

The product of the intensity ratio and agGDP exactly equals agGERD; we exploit this identity via a logarithmic decomposition to derive the portion of agGERD growth associated with growth in the food and agricultural economy (i.e., increases in agricultural gross domestic product, agGDP) and the portion associated with intensification of research spending (i.e., increases in food and agricultural R&D spending relative to agGDP). Based on this decomposition, over the period 1980–2011, 7.4% of the growth in global agGERD is associated with an increase in the intensity of investment in food and agricultural R&D. Most (92.6%) of the global growth in agGERD is associated with the change in agGDP. These estimates are for the world as a whole, but the relative importance of the two sources of R&D growth varies markedly from country to country and region to region. For example, among most of the rich countries (and for that group of countries as a whole), increases in agGERD spending were entirely attributable to increasing the intensity of R&D investment (given that for many of these countries, agGDP actually shrunk). In contrast, for the low- and middle-income groups of countries, the increase in agGERD was largely associated with an expanding agricultural economy, with agGDP growth accounting for all of the growth in the low-income countries and 83.8% in the middle-income countries.

The Returns to R&D

Public and private R&D for food and agriculture matters: the amounts invested are large and growing, and the consequences for the world are significant. Here we review and assess the evidence of the payoffs to that investment and examine how well the reported returns-to-research evidence represents (1) the structure of the investments in science supporting the food and agricultural sectors and (2) the economic structure of the sectors themselves. We do this by quantifying the concordance between the balance of focus and emphasis of the returns-to-research estimates and both (1) the balance of the R&D spending (across countries and between public and private) and (2) the geographical-cum-commodity characteristics of global agricultural production.

Overview of the Evidence

Prior compilations of the returns-to-research evidence include studies by Evenson et al. (1979) who reviewed 23 studies, Echeverría (1990) whose compilation included 124 studies (and about 256 estimates), Alston et al. (2000) who analyzed 292 studies reporting 2306 rate-of-return estimates, and Evenson (2001) who tabulated 260 studies and 566 estimates. Here we summarize evidence from the latest (version 3.0) compilation of the InSTePP returns-to-research database, which includes 3426 rate-of-return estimates from 492 separate studies published between 1958 and 2015.[12] Nearly all studies of the rates of return to food and agricultural R&D report either an IRR or a BCR. In his seminal study, Griliches (1958) reported both, though he expressed a preference for the BCR. This advice appears to have eluded most subsequent researchers: 94% of the compiled studies report IRRs, with only 34% reporting BCRs and one in four reporting both.

Figure 4, Panel A, shows the distribution of IRRs and other common descriptive statistics for the full sample and a decomposition into two subsamples: one that consists of 388 evaluations drawn from three recent US studies (i.e., Alston et al. 2011; Plastina and Fulginiti 2012; and Wang et al. 2012) and one that consists of the remaining evaluations. The average IRR for the full sample (dark plot, Fig. 4, Panel A) is 59.5% per year, which lies between the average of 24.5% per year for the recent US evaluations (medium gray plot, Fig. 4, Panel A) and 65.6% per year for the remaining evaluations (light gray plot, Fig. 4, Panel A). A Kolmogorov-Smirnov test rejects the hypothesis that the two subsamples are drawn from the same distribution.

Given the skewedness of these distributions, the median (37.3% per year) provides a more robust measure of the centrality of the full sample estimates. The minimum is a dismal 100% per year, while the maximum is an incredible 5645% per year. Three-quarters of these IRRs exceed 22.5% per year, while one-quarter exceed 62.0% per year. The BCR estimates plotted in Fig. 4, Panel B are also positively skewed, with a mean of 26.7 and a median value of 12.0, although the preponderance (75%) of the reported BCRs are less than 31 and 62% are less than or equal to 20.

The distributions in Fig. 4 reflect many different types of evaluations conducted in many different contexts. Some of the overall dispersion in estimates appears to reflect variation in returns according to the type and commodity focus of the R&D. To explore this observation, Table 3 provides two sets of summary measures

---

[12] We use the term "evaluation" to refer to a particular model parameterization or design giving rise to a stream of benefits and a stream of costs that could give rise to multiple alternative "estimates" of summary statistics, depending on other assumptions. A single evaluation (of a particular technology) within a given study may report either an estimate of an IRR, of a BCR, or both. Version 3.0 of the InSTePP returns-to-research database includes 2827 evaluations, and it is shares of evaluations (not estimates) that are mostly reported throughout this chapter.

A

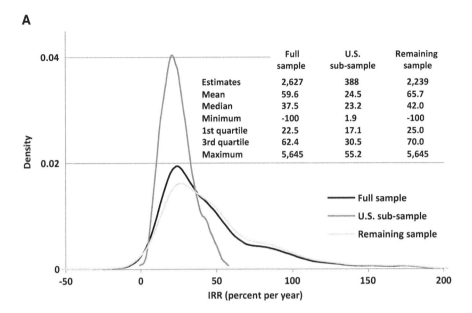

	Full sample	U.S. sub-sample	Remaining sample
Estimates	2,627	388	2,239
Mean	59.6	24.5	65.7
Median	37.5	23.2	42.0
Minimum	-100	1.9	-100
1st quartile	22.5	17.1	25.0
3rd quartile	62.4	30.5	70.0
Maximum	5,645	55.2	5,645

B

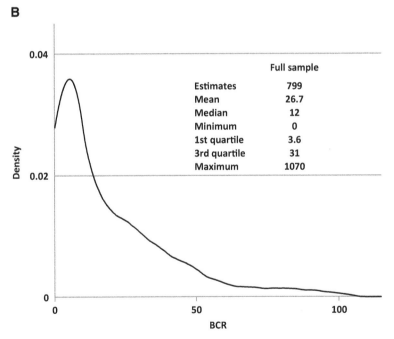

	Full sample
Estimates	799
Mean	26.7
Median	12
Minimum	0
1st quartile	3.6
3rd quartile	31
Maximum	1070

Fig. 4 Distributions of rate-of-return estimates. Panel A. Internal rate-of-return distributions. Panel B. Benefit-cost ratio distribution (*Source*: InSTePP returns-to-research database version 3.0. *Notes*: Vertical axis represents relative frequency. Panel A truncates the plotted distribution at −50 and 200 for display purposes. Descriptive statistics are reported for the "full sample" of 2630 IRR evaluations, a "US sample" (Wang et al. 2012), and a "remaining subsample" that is the full sample net of the US sample. Panel B truncates the plotted distribution at 0 and 110, again for display purposes only)

Table 3 Attributes of the reported internal rate-of-return estimates

	Complete dataset					Dataset trimmed to include IRRs ≤60%				
	Central tendency					Central tendency				
Variables	Number of Est.	Number of Pubs.	Mean	Median	Standard Deviation	Number of Est.	Number of Pubs.	Mean	Median	Standard Deviation
	(1) (count)	(2)	(3) (percent per year)	(4)	(5)	(6) (count)	(7)	(8) (percent per year)	(9)	(10)
Type of R&D										
R&D	976	183	69.2	40.0	249.4	675	152	30.0	29.3	16.2
Extension	20	10	72.2	46.0	79.1	13	9	30.7	32.0	17.5
Research and extension	1616	288	53.8	35.0	70.1	1234	254	29.7	28.1	15.0
Unspecified	15	9	52.5	29.0	45.3	11	7	28.6	24.0	13.9
Commodity orientation										
All agriculture	825	82	47.5	28.1	79.4	698	77	27.0	25.2	13.5
Natural resources including forestry	36	11	43.9	38.7	30.6	26	10	28.1	27.6	17.0
Crop total	1375	303	54.2	41.0	68.0	972	258	31.2	31.0	16.4
Livestock total	230	51	121.7	53.4	484.0	131	41	32.1	30.7	16.2
Geographical orientation										
United States	986	80	63.0	31.8	242.4	786	71	28.0	26.2	13.7
United States (excluding three*)	598	77	88.0	43.8	308.7	389	68	31.5	33.1	15.6
Other developed	409	81	72.9	49.3	129.6	246	71	29.6	25.5	15.6
Asia & Pacific	332	61	76.6	52.0	81.9	188	45	36.7	37.7	13.3
Latin America and Caribbean	407	120	45.2	39.3	27.8	315	105	33.1	31.0	13.6

	Complete dataset					Dataset trimmed to include IRRs ≤60%				
	Central tendency					Central tendency				
Variables	Number of Est.	Number of Pubs.	Mean	Median	Standard Deviation	Number of Est.	Number of Pubs.	Mean	Median	Standard Deviation
	(1)	(2)	(3)	(4)	(5)	(6)	(7)	(8)	(9)	(10)
	(count)		(percent per year)			(count)		(percent per year)		
Sub-Saharan Africa	300	83	42.0	35.0	40.9	234	71	26.0	27.4	21.7
Multinational	134	40	46.0	34.0	70.1	122	38	30.9	31.5	15.2
Global	59	19	34.5	30.3	18.9	52	15	29.2	28.0	12.4
Type of performer										
Public only	1965	389	57.5	40.0	74.7	1373	334	30.4	29.0	15.7
Private only	80	13	55.5	54.0	40.3	51	13	32.4	28.0	15.5
Public and private	314	34	33.7	29.2	28.3	298	33	28.6	28.3	13.1
Others	268	29	106.7	32.5	460.9	211	26	27.2	26.0	16.2
All studies	2627	461	59.6	37.5	161.9	1933	402	29.8	28.6	15.4
All studies (excluding three*)	2239	458	65.7	42.0	174.6	1545	399	31.2	30.7	16.2

Source: Author's estimates based on InSTePP returns-to-research database version 3.0. Table reports only IRR evaluations, excluding 632 BCR evaluations

Notes: Studies grouped according to FAO commodity classification standards at www.fao.org/waicent/faoinfo/economic/faodef/faodefe.htm; cereals include barley, maize, millet, rice, sorghum/millet, and wheat; fruit, vegetables, and nuts include apple, banana, beans, cashew nuts, chilies, citrus, cole crops, cucurbit, fruit/nut, guava, leafy vegetables, mango, melon, onion, pineapple, plantain, stone fruits, and tomato; poultry include poultry; other livestock include beef, dairy, dairy and beef, goat, sheep, sheep/goats, buffalo, cattle, other livestock, pork, and swine; natural resources include forestry and natural resources; all agriculture include all agriculture; multinational includes evaluations of investments that span several countries; and global includes evaluations that encompass a large number of countries (typically spanning multiple continents). Descriptive statistics are reported for the full sample of 2630 IRR evaluations, including 388 US estimates reported by just three studies, Alston et al. (2011), Plastina and Fulginiti (2012), and Wang et al. (2012), which are omitted from the data in lines designated with an asterisk

that characterize the distribution of the reported IRRs, including measures of the central tendency of these distributions (specifically, their mean and median values) and indications of the dispersion of the estimates (specifically, their standard deviation) stratified by the type and commodity focus of the R&D. One set of summary statistics (left half of Table 3) is for the full set of 2627 IRR estimates taken from 461 published studies. The other (right half of Table 3) is a trimmed dataset of 1933 IRR estimates from 402 studies, which excludes IRRs that exceeded 60% per year.

Consider first the summary statistics for the full sample (on the left half of Table 3). In column 3, the conditional means of the IRRs vary somewhat among the subclassifications, at first blush suggesting important differences in returns depending on the type of R&D, its orientation (by commodity or geographic region), or the type of performer. However, within each category the dispersion of the estimates is large (in each case the standard deviation is of a similar magnitude to the respective mean) such that it is challenging to draw inferences about differences among categories. Furthermore, in every instance the mean (column 3) is larger (and in some cases substantially so) than the corresponding median (column 4), indicative of IRR distributions that are (substantially) positively skewed for the individual subcategories as well as for the complete set of estimates in Fig. 4. This skewness that contributes to the dispersion of the estimates within each category also adds to the difficulty in discriminating among the categories to draw inferences. The signal-to-noise ratio is low in these data.

As noted above, very high IRRs strain credibility, and as discussed by Alston et al. (2000) in a similar context, various sources of conscious or unconscious bias, as well as attribution errors and other mistakes by analysts, could account for erroneously high IRRs, justifying a skeptical view of the very large estimates. What might we do about it? We opted to set aside the observations from the extreme right tail of every distribution to see what we could learn about the evidence in the more credible range of reported IRRs. Conscious that this is an arbitrary rule, we set aside all estimates with IRRs greater than 60% per year. In the trimmed dataset (right half of Table 3), as would be expected, both the means and the medians (columns 8 and 9) are reduced, and the difference between each mean and its corresponding median narrows substantially, indicating that the trimmed IRR distributions are more symmetric about their respective means. By the same token, the dispersion is much reduced such that the means and medians are now large relative to their respective standard errors and we can make more confident statements about the general evidence that the rate of return to agricultural R&D is high (within the subset of studies reporting IRRs at the lower end of the range, below 60% per year).

However, the differences in the mean (and median) IRRs among the various subcategories summarized in Table 3 are almost entirely eliminated in the trimmed sample. The apparent differences among the categories in their payoffs to research (on average) as indicated by the full sample are attributable to differences among categories in the extreme right tail of the distribution (in the estimates of IRRs exceeding 60% per year) which we are inclined to discount. In short, the available evidence does not permit us to draw clear inferences concerning differences in the average rates of return among categories of R&D identified in the rows of Table 3.

Composition and Representativeness of the Evidence

The preponderance (88%) of the evaluation evidence in the database pertains to research carried out by public agencies (including either state or national government or international organizations, along with universities) (Fig. 5). Just over half (54%) of the reported evaluations for publicly performed R&D involve research done jointly (say by a government agency in collaboration with a university, a private company, or an international agency), while universities are involved in 34% of the reported evaluations. Around 14% cover joint public and private research, while 15% of the estimates refer to privately performed R&D.

Around 38% of the evaluations refer to research performed by federal or state agencies (including land grant universities) in the United States. Among regions, institutions from Asia-Pacific, Latin America and the Caribbean, and sub-Saharan Africa account for 12%, 15%, and 11% of the evaluations, respectively (Fig. 6). The evaluations are evenly split between more- and less-developed countries, although among the less-developed countries just eight (specifically, and in descending order of evaluation counts, Brazil, India, Pakistan, Colombia, the Philippines, Uganda, and Zambia) account for just over half (specifically 51.7%) of all the developing country evaluations.

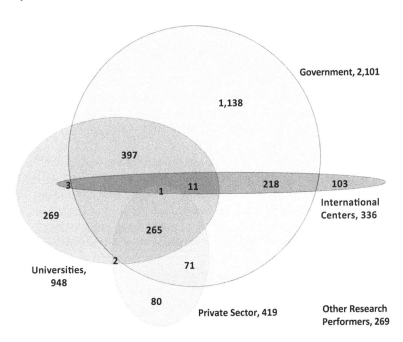

Fig. 5 Numbers of evaluations, by category of research performer (*Source*: InSTePP returns-to-research database version 3.0, including all 2829 evaluations. *Notes*: Elliptical overlaps indicate jointly performed R&D. For example, 948 evaluations pertain to university research of which 269 involved no partners, 3 involved joint research with international centers, and 397 were joint with government agencies)

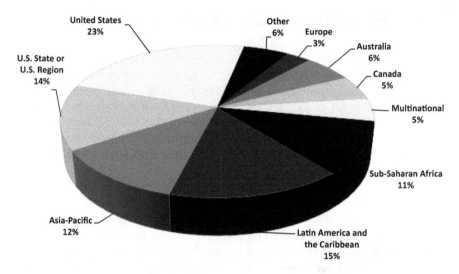

Fig. 6 Shares of evaluations, classified by location of research being evaluated (*Source*: InSTePP returns-to-research database version 3.0, including all 2827 evaluations. *Notes*: Countries are grouped according to FAO regional classifications (FAO 2016). "Other" includes evaluations for "other developed" countries, West Asia and North Africa, and "global" studies. "Multinational" includes observations that span multiple countries and, perhaps, multiple regions)

Cereal crop research makes up almost one-quarter of the evaluations, with maize and wheat research getting the most attention followed by sorghum and millet (Fig. 7). Assessments of aggregate investment in "all agriculture" account for nearly one-third of the evaluations, followed by livestock which constitutes only 9% of the studies. A small number of assessments of natural resources, forestry, and joint crop and livestock research are also represented in the InSTePP database.

To assess how well the evaluation evidence represents the science and the sector it serves, Table 4 summarizes the congruence between the reported returns-to-research evaluations vis-à-vis selected indicators of R&D spending and the value of agricultural production. Table 4 reveals how well the evaluations comport with (1) research spending, stratified by institution (i.e., public versus private performer) and location (i.e., countries within which the evaluated research was undertaken, stratified by average per capita income), and (2) agricultural production value, stratified by the commodity composition of production. Column 1 reports the total food and agricultural R&D spending (summed over the period 1961–2011 for public R&D and 1980–2011 for private R&D) and the total value of agricultural production (summed over the period 1961–2011). Column 2 reports the share of each subcategory in the respective R&D spending and value of production totals. Columns 3 and 4 are similar sums and shares of the research evaluation estimates once they have been parsed into the respective subcategories. Column 5 is a congruence ratio: the ratio of the categorical evaluation share (column 4) to the corresponding indicator share (column 2). A congruency value of 1.0 indicates that the balance of reported

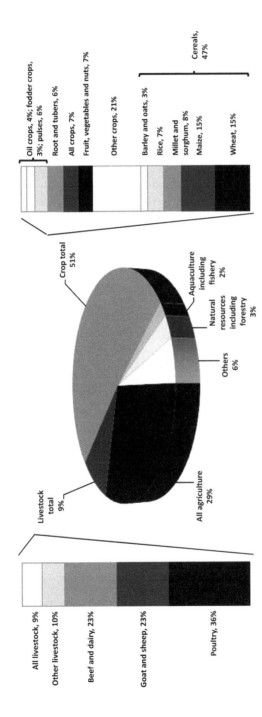

Fig. 7 Shares of evaluations, classified by commodity category (*Source*: InSTePP returns-to-research database version 3.0, including all 2829 evaluations. *Notes*: Commodities are grouped into categories according to FAO classifications (FAO 2015) (see notes to Table 1 for details). The stacked bars report commodity shares within the respective livestock total and crop total categories)

Table 4 Representativeness of the estimates

	Indicator		Estimates		Congruence
	Amount	Shares	Count	Shares	Relative shares
	(1)	(2)	(3)	(4)	(5) = (4) / (2)
Research spending	(bln 2009 PPP$)	(percent)	(number)	(percent)	
By performer					
Public	840.8	60.1	3050	89.0	1.5
Private	557.7	39.9	462	13.5	0.3
(CGIAR	14.3	na	385	na	na)
By per capita income group					
High income	927.0	66.3	1987	61.7	0.9
Upper-middle income	287.9	20.6	575	17.8	0.9
Lower-middle income	155.3	11.1	482	15.0	1.3
Low income	28.2	2.0	179	5.6	2.8
Ag production (by value)	(bln 2004–06 Int'l $)	(percent)	(number)	(percent)	
Maize	4048	4.9	256	7.5	1.5
Wheat	3752	4.6	265	7.7	1.7
Rice	9249	11.3	140	4.1	0.4
Other cereals	1780	2.2	174	5.1	2.3
Fruit, vegetables, and nuts	18,193	22.2	154	4.5	0.2
Poultry	6041	7.4	128	3.7	0.5
Other livestock	22,390	27.4	204	6.0	0.2
Natural resources (including forestry)			94	2.7	
Other commodities not define above	16,380	20.0	2011	58.7	2.9

Source: InSTePP returns-to-research database version 3.0, including all 3426 estimates; InSTePP R&D Accounts, version 3.5; World Bank (2015)

Notes: Indicator used under the heading "Resources spending" is the total of public and private food and agricultural R&D for the period 1980–2011. Indicator used under the heading "Ag production by value" is the total of gross value of agricultural production for the period 1960–2013. Agricultural R&D and gross value of production data exclude EE&FSU countries. Estimates include the respective summed total number of estimates for the period (i.e., publication date) 1958–2015. A total of 3050 public estimates were published. The table also includes accumulated CGIAR spending and estimate totals for the period 1980–2011 (between brackets), but these do not form part of the congruence calculations or the respective indicator and estimate shares

evaluation evidence is in line with the corresponding value share of research spending or value of agricultural production.

During the period beginning in 1980 for which InSTePP reports both public and private spending on food and agricultural R&D, the public sector spent $840.8 billion (60.1% of the total) while the private sector spent $557.7 billion (39.9%)

(Table 4). The CGIAR centers account for about 10% of the evaluations (and around 18% of the studies) even though CGIAR spending ($14.3 billion from 1980 to 2011) accounted for just 1.01% of the corresponding CGIAR plus domestic public and private sector spending. Thus looking at the congruency of R&D spending, it is clear that public (both domestic and international) R&D is substantially overrepresented in the evaluation evidence, whereas private R&D is heavily underrepresented given the public-private structure of R&D. In terms of the economic geography of R&D spending vis-à-vis R&D evaluation estimates, while the high and upper middle-income countries accounted for comparatively large shares (61.7% and 17.8%, respectively) of all the evaluation estimates, their respective shares of global R&D spending were even larger such that these regions of the world are slightly underrepresented (relative to R&D spending) in the evaluation evidence. In contrast, the lower middle- and low-income regions of the world are overrepresented in the evaluation evidence relative to their disproportionately small shares of global R&D.

These congruency findings suggest a "CGIAR effect" and, relatedly, a "funding effect" is in play. Publicly performed food and agricultural research is evaluated much more intensively than its private counterpart, and international R&D is subject to substantially more economic scrutiny than is national R&D performed by universities and government research agencies. Our sample includes 2.5 estimates of the economic consequences for every billion dollars of national R&D spending (averaging 3.6 estimates for every billion dollars of public research, but just 0.83 estimates for every billion spent on private R&D). The corresponding evaluation intensity of the dollars directed to the international agricultural R&D carried out by the centers that constitute the CGIAR is much higher: 26.9 estimates for every billion dollars of CGIAR spending.

This implies various political economy processes may be at play, whereby the form and source of funding for particular types of research influence the demand for (and thus supply of) research evaluation evidence. In particular it seems reasonable to suppose that appropriability of benefits matters. If funders are less certain that benefits from their research investments will be appropriable by the relevant constituency, they can be expected to pay more attention generally to seeking to justify that research spending and to allocate a greater share of the research funds to evaluation—even to the point of requiring evaluation as a condition on funding support, as in the case of the Australian Rural R&D Corporation framework. Sometimes research funders have particular purposes in mind that give rise to enhanced interest in evaluation. In the CGIAR, for example, a donor who provides funds for crop varietal research might be expected to press for evidence that those funds are used to support research that provides demonstrable benefits to the targeted groups. Similarly, on the other side of these transactions, those who conduct research may be interested in evaluation for both their own management purposes (i.e., internally) and for shoring up support from research funding agencies. In our own experience, the demands for R&D evaluation from within research agencies in government and in universities are never greater than when funding is threatened or shrinking. This political economy context has implications for the total investment in evaluation and its connection to funding cycles, as well as the types of evaluations that are undertaken and the forms of evidence compiled. We can speculate that spending on evaluation could increase with either increases in funding (evaluation is affordable and useful for management) or contractions of funding (defensive evaluations), but it seems likely that the evaluation intensity of agricultural R&D will have a countercyclical relationship with research funding.

Turning to the commodity structure of production (by value), the three crop categories, wheat, corn, and other cereals (including sorghum, millet, barley, and oats), are overrepresented in the evaluation evidence relative to their respective shares of the values of production. Conversely, several other categories are underrepresented, including rice, fruits, vegetables and nuts, and livestock (including poultry). We can speculate loosely about why this is so. Relevant considerations include the costs and benefits of a particular evaluation project. On the benefit side, the returns to research (and thus the economic stakes for an evaluation of it) turn on the scale of the relevant industry, the applicability of the particular R&D-induced technological innovation to it, and the likely timing and extent of technology adoption. On the cost side, following the pioneering work by Griliches (1957, 1958) and a few others—e.g., see the compilation and discussion of the (early) Australian evaluation efforts by Alston and Pardey (2016)—the modeling framework for evaluating returns to improvement in varieties of annual crops was well established and easy to implement, but less so for other types of production. Consequently, for food and feed grains that were grown on a large scale and where particular innovations were widely applicable, the possibilities for evaluators were accordingly abundant. In contrast, modeling innovations in livestock and perennial crops is much harder, and modeling innovations in horticulture is less rewarding because the relevant scale of adoption is smaller. These characteristics do not account for the underrepresentation of rice in the InSTePP version 3.0 returns-to-research compilation. Another consideration is where in the world those evaluations were being undertaken and by whom. Among countries, a few are heavily overrepresented in the evaluation evidence, notable among them being the United States, Canada, Australia, New Zealand, and the United Kingdom. While some of these countries grow some rice, they are much more significant producers of wheat, corn, and other cereals.

Conclusion

The contours of the global geography for food and agricultural R&D spending are presently being reshaped in historically momentous ways. The gradual retreat of the rich countries from their historically dominant position as providers of the global public goods emanating from public investments in food and agricultural R&D is clearly evident, as is the rise in R&D spending (and associated innovation capacity) of the middle-income group of countries. Meanwhile, the large gap in public R&D spending (especially in per capita terms) between the low-income countries and the rest of the world continues to widen as many of the national research agencies in these low-income countries continue to struggle. The other notable trend has been an increase in the private performance of food and agricultural R&D. Once largely limited to the rich countries, these new data reveal an increase in privately performed food and agricultural R&D in the middle-income countries, mainly centered in the agriculturally large and rapidly growing countries of China, India, and Brazil.

The economic evidence on the payoffs to these R&D investments continues to grow, albeit at a slower pace than the rate of growth in the R&D spending itself. The wide dispersion in the reported rates of return makes it difficult to discern meaningful patterns in the evidence. Some of this dispersion comes from the use of the IRR, which yields an artificially inflated perspective on the payoff to the investment compared with the MIRR. Nonetheless, the mean and median values of the reported rates of return to food and agricultural R&D based on the IRR are high regardless of the type of research, commodity focus, performer, or time period of the research—and this remains so even when we set aside the large number of estimates that strain credulity for at least some of us (IRRs greater than 60% per year). Moreover, the evidence supports the view that the returns to food and agricultural R&D remain as high as they ever have been, with no signs of a diminution in the payoffs to more recent compared with earlier investments in R&D (Rao et al. 2017a).

The evaluation evidence does not fully reflect the compositional structure of R&D spending (in terms of the public versus private and the economic geography of the research performers) or the commodity orientation of agriculture (by value). This lack of congruence could limit the types of conclusions that can be drawn from the published evaluation evidence—the average of IRRs among an unrepresentative sample may differ from the average for the whole, making it hard to make confident statements about the overall returns to the investment—if it were not for two features of the evidence. First, a goodly number (952 of 3426 or 28%) of the estimates pertain to an "all-of-agriculture" aggregate with high rates of return, indicating a persistent underinvestment in food and agricultural R&D relative to the socially optimal amount of investment. Second, when we set aside the very high estimates (IRRs >60% per year) in the trimmed sample, the mean and median IRRs are close together for any particular category and very similar among categories (mean IRRs ranging from 26.0% to 36.7% per year, mostly around 30% per year), with a relatively narrow dispersion around the mean. This trimmed sample provides a very conservative picture of the statistical and economic significance of the returns to investment in agricultural R&D as represented by the IRR, and it is strongly favorable about the overall picture while not allowing us to distinguish statistically among categories of R&D.

References

Alston, J.M., M.A. Andersen, J.S. James, and P.G. Pardey. 2011. The Economic Returns to U.S. Public Agricultural Research. *American Journal of Agricultural Economics* 93 (5): 1257–1277.

Alston, J.M., M.C. Marra, P.G. Pardey, and T.J. Wyatt. 2000. *A Meta-Analysis of Rates of Return to Agricultural R&D: Ex Pede Herculem?* Washington D.C.: IFPRI Research Report No 557.

Alston, J.M., G.W. Norton, and P.G. Pardey. 1995. *Science Under Scarcity: Principles and Practice for Agricultural Research Evaluation and Priority Setting*. Ithaca: Cornell University Press.

Alston, J.M., and P.G. Pardey. 2016. Antipodean Agricultural and Resource Economics at 60: Agricultural Innovation. *Australian Journal of Agricultural and Resource Economics* 60 (4): 554–568.

Andersen, M.A., and W. Song. 2013. The Economic impact of public agricultural research and development in the United States. *Agricultural Economics* 44 (3): 287–295.

Angelo, C. 2016. Brazil's Scientists Fight Funding Freeze: Proposed Law Could Restrict Research Spending for 20 Years. *Nature* 439: 480.

Barry, P., and P. Ellinger. 2011. *Financial Management in Agriculture*. Seventh ed. New York: Prentice-Hall.

Bailey, M.J. 1959. Formal Criteria for Investment Decisions. *Journal of Political Economy* 67 (5): 476–488.

Dehmer, S.P., P.G. Pardey, and J.M. Beddow. 2017 (in process). Reshuffling the Global R&D Deck, 1980–2013. InSTePP Working Paper. St Paul: International Science and Technology Practice and Policy (InSTePP) center.

Echeverría, R.G. 1990. Assessing the Impact of Agricultural Research. In *Methods for Diagnosing Research System Constraints and Assessing the Impact of Agricultural Research*, ed. R.G. Echeverria. The Hague: International Service for National Agricultural Research (ISNAR).

Evenson, R.E. 2001. Economic Impacts of Agricultural Research and Extension. In *Handbook of Agricultural Economics, Volume 1A. Agricultural Production*, ed. B. Gardner and G. Rausser. Amsterdam: Elsevier Science.

Evenson, R.E., P.E. Waggoner, and V.W. Ruttan. September 1979. Economic Benefits from Research: An example from Agriculture. *Science* 205 (4411): 1101–1107.

Fabiosa, J. 2012. Globalization and Trends in World Food Consumption. In *The Oxford Handbook of the Economics of Food Consumption and Policy*, ed. J. Lusk, J. Roosen, and J.F. Shogren. Oxford: Oxford University Press.

FAO. 2015. *FAOSTAT database. Food and Agricultural Commodities Production/Commodities by Regions, Africa*. Food and Agriculture Organization of the United Nations, Rome. Available at: http://faostat3.fao.org/browse/rankings/commodities_by_regions/E. Accessed January 1, 2015.

———. 2016. *FAOSTAT Country classifications. Food and Agriculture Organization of the United Nations*, Rome. Available at: http://faostat.fao.org/site/371/default.aspx. Accessed May 2016.

Gardner, B.L. 1992. How the Data we Make Can Unmake Us: Annals of Factology. *American Journal of Agricultural Economics* 74 (5): 1066–1075.

Griliches, Z. 1958. Research Costs and Social Returns: Hybrid Corn and Related Innovations. *Journal of Political Economy* 66 (5): 419–431.

Hirshleifer, J. 1958. On the Theory of Optimal Investment Decision. *Journal of Political Economy* 66 (4): 329–352.

Hurley, T.M., X. Rao, and P.G. Pardey. 2014a. Re-examining the Reported Rates of Return to Food and Agricultural Research and Development. *American Journal of Agricultural Economics* 96: 1492–1504.

———. 2014b. AJAE Appendix for Reexamining the Reported Rates of Return to Food and Agricultural Research and Development. Supporting online material, May 3, 2014. Available at http://ajae.oxfordjournals.org/content/early2014/05/31/ajae.aau047/suppl/DC1

———. 2017. Re-examining the Reported Rates of Return to Food and Agricultural Research and Development—Reply. *American Journal of Agricultural Economics* 96 (5): 1492–1504.

OECD. (Organization for Economic Cooperation and Development). 2007. *Revised Field of Science and Technology (FOS) Classification in the Frascati Manual.* Paris: Organisation for Economic Cooperation and Development. Available at: http://www.oecd.org/innovation/inno/38235147.pdf

——— (Organization for Economic Cooperation and Development). 2002. *Frascati Manual: Proposed Standard Practice for Surveys on Research and Experimental Development.* Paris: Organisation for Economic Cooperation and Development.

Oehmke, J. 2017. Re-examining the Reported Rates of Return to Food and Agricultural Research and Development: Comment. *American Journal of Agricultural Economics* 99 (3): 818–826.

Plastina, A.S., and L.E. Fulginiti. 2012. Rates of Return to Public Agricultural Research in 48 US States. *Journal of Productivity Analysis* 37: 95–113.

Pardey, P.G., C. Chan-Kang, J.M. Beddow, and S.M. Dehmer. 2016. InSTePP International Innovation Accounts: Research and Development Spending, Version 3.5 (Food and Agricultural R&D Series)-Documentation. St. Paul, MN: International Science and Technology Practice and Policy (InSTePP). Available at http://www.instepp.umn.edu/products/documentation-instepp-international-innovation-accounts-research-and-development-spending

Rao, X., T.M. Hurley, and P.G. Pardey. 2017a. Are Agricultural R&D Returns Declining and Development Dependent?" InSTePP and Department of Applied Economics Staff Paper. St. Paul: International Science and Technology Practice and Policy (InSTePP) center and the Department of Applied Economics, University of Minnesota.

———. 2017b. Recalibrating the Reported Returns to Agricultural R&D: What if We All Heeded Griliches? InSTePP and Department of Applied Economics Staff Paper. St. Paul: International Science and Technology Practice and Policy (InSTePP) center and the Department of Applied Economics, University of Minnesota.

Ruttan, V. 1982. *Agricultural Research Policy.* Minneapolis: University of Minnesota Press.

United Nations Statistics Division. *UN National Accounts Main Aggregates Database* (United Nations, 2013., Accessed at http://unstats.un.org/unsd/snaama/introduction.asp).

United Nations, Department of Economic and Social Affairs, Population Division. 2013. *World Population Prospects: The 2012 Revision.* New York: United Nations. Data downloaded October 29, 2013 from http://www.un.org/en/development/desa/population/

Wang, S.L., E.V. Ball, L.E. Fulginiti and A.S. Plastina. *Benefits of Public R&D in U.S. Agriculture: Spill-ins, Extension and Roads*, Selected Paper from International Association of Agricultural Economists Triennial meeting, Foz do Iguaçu, Brazil 18–24 August, 2012. Available at http://ageconsearch.umn.edu/handle/126368

World Bank. *World Development Indicators* 2015 Washington D.C.: World Bank (available at https://openknowledge.worldbank.org/handle/10986/21634).

Zvi Griliches. (1957). Hybrid corn: An exploration in the economics of technological change. PhD Dissertation. Department of Economics, Chicago: University of Chicago.

Private-Sector Research and Development

Keith O. Fuglie, Matthew Clancy, and Paul W. Heisey

Abstract Over the past several decades, the private sector has assumed a larger role in research and development (R&D) for food and agriculture. Private companies fund nearly all food processing R&D and perform a growing share of production-oriented R&D for agriculture. The willingness of private companies to invest in agricultural R&D has been influenced by policies toward intellectual property rights, regulations, and antitrust. As private R&D capacity in food and agriculture has grown, so have institutional partnerships for public-private research collaboration. An important implication for public science policy is whether public R&D complements or competes with private R&D. This chapter reviews these developments and the major forces driving them.

Introduction

The phenomenal rise in food and agricultural productivity over the past century, which substantially reduced the price of food despite the rapid growth of world population, can be largely attributed to society's investment in agricultural research and development (R&D). This R&D produced the new knowledge and technologies that made farming and food processing more efficient, safer, and more nutritious. Historically, because of the dominance of small firms (farms) in agriculture and the absence of intellectual property protection for biological inventions, the public sector was the main source of formal R&D for agriculture. The private sector concentrated its agricultural R&D on improving farm machinery and after World War II on developing agricultural chemicals for crop nutrition and protection and veterinary pharmaceuticals for animal health and nutrition. The private sector also developed significant R&D capacity in food manufacturing, including the processing, storage, and transport of food and agricultural commodities and the development of new and

---

The views expressed in this chapter are the authors' own and should not be attributed to the USDA or ERS.

K.O. Fuglie (✉) • M. Clancy • P.W. Heisey
USDA Economic Research Service, Washington, DC, USA
e-mail: kfuglie@ers.usda.gov

© Springer International Publishing AG 2018   41
N. Kalaitzandonakes et al. (eds.), *From Agriscience to Agribusiness*, Innovation,
Technology, and Knowledge Management, https://doi.org/10.1007/978-3-319-67958-7_3

diverse food products. While farmers have engaged in crop and livestock breeding for millennia, the emergence of formal R&D divisions in private companies for these activities is a more recent phenomenon. Commercial crop breeding got its start in the United States in the 1920s with the application of hybrid seed technology to corn. This technology provided a means to protect intellectual property in seed, because farmers could not reproduce the genetic combinations that produced high yield simply by saving seed from the harvest. But the emergence of multinational corporations making multibillion dollar R&D investments in agriculture awaited the last decades of the twentieth century. In the United States and other industrialized countries, the private sector has now become the leading investor in agricultural R&D. Its role as a provider of improved agricultural technology for farmers in developing countries is also growing.

This chapter describes the rise in private food and agricultural R&D and how this is shaping the overall food and agricultural research system, with a focus on the United States. In the next section, we describe the changing volume, composition, and structure of public and private agricultural R&D. In section three we then discuss how public policies influence the amount and direction of private R&D. We give specific attention to intellectual property rights, regulatory regimes, and competition policy. We also review the evidence on whether public R&D complements or "crowds out" private R&D in food and agriculture. Section four describes new and evolving institutional structures for public and private cooperation in applied research. The last section summarizes major findings and has some suggestions for future research on the economics of private agricultural R&D.

The Structure of the Food and Agriculture R&D System

Globally, it appears the private-sector share of food and agricultural R&D has been rising in recent decades, although estimates of that share have varied widely (Bientema et al. 2012; Pardey et al. 2015). Not only has it been difficult to measure the level of private R&D, but what gets counted in these estimates is often inconsistent or incomplete. For example, national surveys of business R&D typically classify "private agricultural R&D" as R&D by business firms that primarily produce agricultural commodities. While this may include R&D by seed companies, it excludes agriculturally related R&D by firms in the chemical, pharmaceutical, and machinery sectors. Rarely do national statistical sources report private R&D by sector of intended use (Pray and Fuglie 2015). Furthermore, many national and global estimates group private R&D by food companies together with R&D by agricultural companies, even though most R&D in the food sector has little relevance for production agriculture (Fuglie et al. 2011).

Drawing on a survey of several hundred firms in seven agricultural input industries,[1] Fuglie et al. (2011) provided the first comprehensive estimate of global

---

[1] These input industries consist of crop seed and biotechnology, agricultural pesticides, fertilizers, animal breeding, animal health, animal feed, and farm machinery.

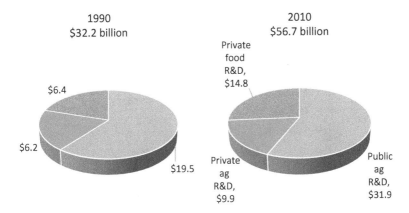

1990
$32.2 billion

2010
$56.7 billion

Private
food
R&D,
$14.8

$6.4

$6.2

$19.5

Private
ag
R&D,
$9.9

Public
ag
R&D,
$31.9

Fig. 1 Global spending on public and private food and agricultural R&D Figures in constant 2005 PPP$, billions (Sources: Public R&D in developing countries from Agricultural Science and Technology Indicators, public R&D spending in developed countries from Heisey and Fuglie (forthcoming), and private R&D from Fuglie (2016))

private R&D intended for agriculture over 1994–2010, and these were recently extended to cover 1990–2014 (Fuglie 2016). These studies found that agricultural R&D by the business sector more than tripled over this period, from $5.06 billion in 1990 to $15.3 billion in 2014.

Using these updated figures for private R&D together with estimates of public R&D, Fig. 1 compares public and private spending on food and agricultural R&D in 1990 and 2010. Total global spending on food and agricultural R&D increased by 78% in constant dollars, from $32.2 billion to $56.7 billion. The private share of the total increased from 39% to 44% over these two decades, although much of this growth was in R&D by the food sector. Private R&D oriented toward agriculture appears to have grown at about the same pace as public agricultural R&D. The recent estimates by Fuglie (2016) show that private agricultural R&D remained flat from the 1990s to about 2002 and then grew rapidly after that point. In constant dollars, global private agricultural R&D spending nearly doubled between 2002 and 2013. Farm machinery and crop R&D were the fastest growing components of private agricultural R&D spending during this period.

Turning to the United States, for which longer time series data are available, recent trends indicate a dramatic change in the importance of the private sector as a source of R&D for agriculture. Since 2010, private R&D spending by agricultural input industries (for crop seeds and chemicals, animal health, breeding and nutrition, and farm machinery) has exceeded total spending by the Federal-State system on agricultural research (Fig. 2). In constant 2005 dollars (where nominal spending is adjusted by a cost-of-research price index), agricultural R&D by the public sector peaked at about $4.9 billion in 2002 and then declined to $3.6 billion by 2013. Private-sector agricultural R&D, on the other hand, continued to grow during these years, and by 2013, the private sector was spending nearly $2 billion more in agricultural research than the public sector. Growth in private R&D was especially pronounced in the crop seed and biotechnology sector, which emerged as a significant

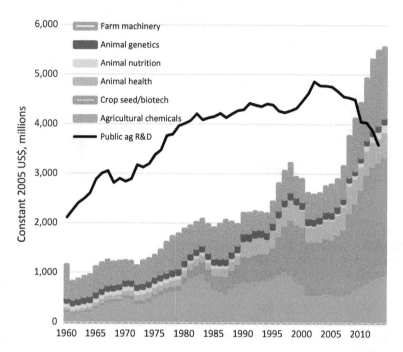

Fig. 2 Composition of private agricultural R&D spending in the United States. Annual spending adjusted for inflation by a cost-of-research price index (Sources: Private R&D spending from Fuglie (2016); public R&D spending and the cost of research price index from USDA ERS)

R&D-based industry in the 1990s. By 2014, more than 40% of total private agricultural R&D in the United States was oriented toward crop genetic improvement and trait development.

To understand the implications of these trends for food and agricultural innovation, it is useful to have a picture of who funds, and who performs, this R&D. In 2013 (the latest year for which comprehensive estimates are available), federal, state, and private institutions funded and performed roughly $16.3 billion worth of R&D for food and agriculture in the United States (Fig. 3). Of this total, the majority was funded and performed by the private sector. The Federal government, through the USDA and other federal agencies, funded approximately $2.8 billion of this R&D. Of this amount, about $1.5 billion worth of federally funded research was performed by USDA intramural research agencies. State institutions – land grant universities (LGUs), state agricultural experiment stations (SAES), and other cooperating institutions – received $3.1 billion from all sources, including $1.3 billion in federal monies, for agricultural R&D. About two-thirds of the federal support for LGUs was channeled through the USDA and the rest from other federal agencies. State institutions received another $1.1 billion from state governments and $0.7 billion from nongovernment sources for research. Nongovernment sources include

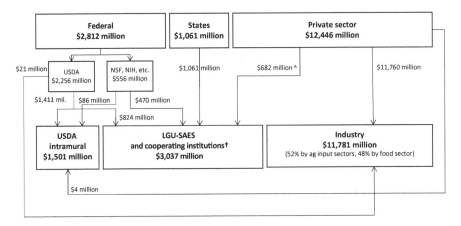

Fig. 3 Funders and performers of food and agricultural research in the US in 2013 (Source: OECD (2016)) Notes: (†LGU-SAES and cooperating institutions: The 1862 and 1890 land grant universities and state agricultural experiment stations. Cooperating institutions include veterinary schools, forestry schools, and other US colleges and universities receiving agricultural research funding from the USDA). (^Private-sector contributions to LGU-SAES ($682 million) consist of (1) research grants and contracts from private companies; (2) research grants from farm commodity groups, philanthropic foundations, individuals, and other organizations; and (3) revenue and fees from the sale of products, services, and technology licenses)

producer assessments,[2] private companies, nonprofit foundations, and earnings from licensing fees and product sales. Research performed at USDA, LGU-SAES, and cooperating institutions is mostly oriented toward agriculture but also includes research on forestry, natural resources, food and nutrition, economics and statistics, and rural development.

Food and agricultural research performed by the private sector is financed almost entirely by for-profit companies and includes firms from several industries. Of the estimated $11.8 billion in food and agricultural R&D performed by these firms in 2013, just under half was by the food manufacturing industry (composed of firms that process raw agricultural commodities into food and feed products). Research by these firms was heavily oriented to new product development or manufacturing process improvements. Only a small part of the R&D performed by the food manufacturing sector was for agricultural technology. The other part of private R&D was to develop improved inputs for use on farms. This agriculturally oriented R&D was performed by crop seed and livestock genetic companies as well as a range of manu-

---

[2] Federal and state legislation provides for mandatory or voluntary producer assessments ("check-offs"), subject to majority support from participants, to be leveed and used to support research and market promotion for specific agricultural commodities. The principal federal authorizing legislation for producer assessments is the Commodity Promotion, Research and Information Act of 1996. Most funds raised through assessments are used for generic advertising. PCAST (2012) estimated that in 2009, 18 federally authorized check-off programs contributed $132 million to support public agricultural research in the United States.

facturing industries (chemical, machinery, biotechnology, and pharmaceutical). In addition to the for-profit sector, some agricultural research is conducted by private, nonprofit institutes funded primarily through charitable or government grants (these form a very small part of the system in terms of funds involved and are not shown in Fig. 3).

Despite the recent growth in private R&D, total funding for agricultural R&D in the United States is not exceptional when compared with the size of the sector. In 2011, total public and private R&D spending for agriculture was equivalent to 2.3% the value of farm sales. For the food manufacturing sector, business R&D spending was even lower, at less than 1% of gross sales. For the US economy as a whole, public and private R&D spending was 2.6% of US GDP, and for research intensive industries like information technology and pharmaceuticals, research spending exceeded 15% of industry sales (OECD 2016).

Public Policy and Incentives for Private R&D

Profit maximizing firms invest in R&D up to the point where the marginal cost of research equals its expected marginal revenue, appropriately adjusted for risk and the time lag between when costs are accrued and revenue realized. Dasgupta and Stiglitz (1980) posit three main factors that influence the returns to private research: *the size of the market* for a new technology, the *R&D costs* of developing the new technology (which is a function of the state of applied science, the cost of R&D inputs, and the time and cost for regulatory approvals), and the degree of *appropriability* (the share of total economic benefits of the new technology that the innovating firm can capture).

Public policies have an important influence on all of these factors. Public investments in research can expand technological opportunities available for private R&D to commercialize, although public R&D that competes directly as an alternative supplier of farm inputs can crowd out private R&D. Regulatory protocols affect the cost and time of bringing new agricultural inputs to the market place, while intellectual property rights (IPRs) and market concentration can affect appropriability. In this section of the chapter, we review the economics literature on how these policies – IPR, regulations, antitrust, and public agricultural R&D – have affected incentives for private agricultural R&D.

Intellectual Property Rights for Biological Innovations

Whereas public R&D can justify the cost of research by pointing to society-wide benefits, the costs of private R&D must be outweighed by the benefit to the performing firm alone. Private firms employ a number of approaches to maintain exclusive control over their discoveries. The menu of options available, especially for plants

Table 1 Intellectual property rights for agricultural innovations in the United States

Type	Year available	Length of protection	Eligibility criteria	Limitations
Trade secrecy	Grew out of common law beginning in 1837	Indefinite	Economically valuable information not generally known Firms make reasonable efforts to maintain secrecy	Reverse engineering is not protected Independent invention is not protected State-level enabling legislation is not uniform across country
Plant patents	1930	20 years	Asexual plants At least one distinguishing characteristic Nonobvious Not sold or released in United States more than 1 year prior to application	Tubers are not eligible
Plant variety certificates	1970 (with 1994 amendments)	25 years for trees and vines 20 years otherwise	Sexually reproducing plants and tubers New Distinct Uniform Stable	Farmers may save seeds that result from growing for reuse (but not resale) Researchers may use for breeding and other bona fide research
Utility patents	1790 (extended to plants and animals in 1980)	20 years	-"Anything made by man under the sun" Novel Useful Nonobvious	Must disclose invention so that someone skilled in the relevant arts can replicate

Source: OECD (2016)

and animals, has expanded considerably over time, concurrent with the rise in private agricultural R&D as a share of all agricultural R&D (Table 1).

The use of *trade secrets* has played an important role in protecting intellectual property in agriculture. So long as firms make a reasonable effort to maintain the secrecy of an economically valuable discovery, the law forbids rivals to discover the product by certain prohibited means (e.g., corporate espionage). Notably, independent invention and reverse engineering do not fall under these prohibited means, which has tended to make trade secrets applicable only in some technological domains. In agriculture, hybrid seeds are particularly amenable to trade secrecy protection, because replicating the performance of the seed in future generations is nearly impossible without the parent lines, which are held privately by the firm.

However, commercial production of hybrid seed or breeding stock has been economically viable for only a few commodities (corn, sorghum, some vegetable species, and in animal breeding, poultry, and pigs), and private R&D in breeding initially focused on these commodities. Trade secrecy protection is based on state level, rather than federal legislation. Although 48 states have adopted a version of the Uniform Trade Secrets Act, state-level modifications to the act, as well as state-level differences in interpretation of the act by courts, mean there is some variation in trade secrecy protection across the country.

Newly discovered asexually reproducing plants (excluding food tuber crops like potatoes) have been eligible for *plant patents* since the Plant Patent Act of 1930. To be eligible for a plant patent, a plant must differ from known related plants by at least one distinguishing characteristic, must not have been sold or released in the United States more than 1 year prior to the date of the application, and must be nonobvious to one skilled in the art at the time of invention. A plant patent gives the assignee the right to exclude others from asexually reproducing, selling, or using the patented plant for a period of 20 years. At that point, the plant becomes part of the public domain.

Protection for newly discovered varieties of sexually reproducing plants, and food tubers, was extended by the Plant Variety Protection Act of 1970 and its 1994 amendments, which established a system of *plant variety certificates*. Plants must be new, distinct, uniform, and stable in order to receive a certificate, and breeders must provide a seed sample to a public seed bank. Upon being granted the certificate, the plant has protection from resale and commercial use for 20 years (25 years for trees and vines). There are two important exceptions to the protections provided by plant variety certificates. Most important is the saved seed exemption, which allows farmers to retain and use (but not sell) the seed that results from growing the protected plant. Second is the research exemption, which allows use of the protected plant for breeding and other bona fide research. These exemptions mean plant variety certificates provide a weaker form of intellectual property rights than standard utility patents. The United States is a member of the 1991 UPOV convention, which established harmonized plant breeder rights among member countries.

Utility patents (hereafter patents) have a much longer heritage, being established in the United States in 1790. Originally, five categories of subject matter were patentable: machines, compositions of matter, articles of manufacture, processes, and improvements in each of the preceding. Discoveries that are novel, nonobvious, and useful are eligible for patent protection which entails a 20-year right to exclude others from commercial exploitation of the innovation. In exchange, the patent holder must disclose the invention, providing enough information for someone skilled in the relevant arts to replicate it.

The understanding of what subject matter is eligible for patent protection has changed over time. Until 1980, plants and animals were viewed as products of nature and therefore *not* eligible for patent protection. Nonetheless, patents remained an important incentive for agricultural innovation in other agricultural input sectors, such as farm machinery and chemical pesticides. Patent rights were extended to plants via the Supreme Court case *Diamond vs. Chakrabarty* (1980) which established multicellular living plants, and animals are not excluded from patent protection, a decision that was reaffirmed by internal rulings by the US Patent and Trademark Office, *ex parte Hibberd* (1985) for plants and *ex parte Allen* (1987) for animals. Now, the same new crop variety may obtain a plant variety certificate and a utility patent. Plants protected by utility patents do not have saved seed or research exemptions, and so they offer a more stringent form of intellectual property rights. There is widespread use of patents for transgenic crops.

In sum, over the twentieth century, biological inventions intended for agriculture were finally extended intellectual property rights (IPR) protection, after a long period of ineligibility. Asexual plants (excluding food tubers) were the first to receive protection in 1930 under the Plant Patent Act. Sexually reproducing plants (and tubers) received a weaker form of IPR (plant variety protection certificates) in 1970, with the Plant Variety Protection Act. A decade later, the Supreme Court case ruled multicellular living plants and animals were eligible for the stronger utility patents that had protected most other forms of US innovation since 1790 (Diamond vs. Chakrabarty 1980).

At each of the above junctures, three questions can be asked. First, how much did the extension of property rights actually increase the ability of firms to appropriate the value of their innovations? Second, how are innovation inputs affected? Third, how are innovation outputs impacted? A simple model of innovation would imply stronger IPR that leads to more value per innovation, which leads to more investment in innovation, which leads to more innovations. But efforts to assess the impact of stronger IPRs on innovation in general have proven inconclusive (see Cohen 2010 for a summary). Alas, this simple model may not hold in agriculture either due to the influence potential confounding dynamics discussed below.

Plant Patents

The 1930 Plant Patent Act provides the first such opportunity to examine these questions. Plant patents do appear to be valuable to breeders. Drew et al. (2015) conducted a hedonic price analysis on ornamental plants for the years 2005–2007. Ornamental plants account for more than 75% of plant patents (Pardey et al. 2013), but not all horticultural plants are patented (only 19% of plants in Drew et al.'s sample). Drew et al. found on average a plant patent is associated with a 23.5% price premium (although the exact premium varies widely by species). Moreover, the patent premium declines over time by an average of 0.3% per year.

While this is suggestive that plant patents help firms appropriate the value of their innovations, it is difficult to say whether they have spurred new R&D in plant breeding. There is little published work on whether plant patents induce innovation. An exception is Moser and Rhode (2011), who examine the impact of the Plant Patent Act on the American rose, which accounted for nearly half of all plant patents between 1931 and 1970. On the one hand, the number of patents for roses grew rapidly after the Act's passage, in tandem with the emergence of a large commercial growing sector. This suggests the Plant Patent Act provided the IPR infrastructure

necessary for a private growing sector to emerge. However, Moser and Rhode ultimately conclude that plant patents played a secondary role in explaining the rise of
the industry. The rate of new rose registrations with the American Rose Society
actually fell after plant patents were introduced. Moreover, the impact of the Plant
Patent act is difficult to disentangle from the effects of World War II, which simultaneously curtailed rose imports from Europe (which remained the dominant source
of new rose varieties through 1970) and provided grounds for American growers to
expropriate patents held by European countries at war with the United States.

Plant Variety Protection Certificates

The 1970 Plant Variety Protection Act has been studied much more intensively. In
contrast to plant patents, the saved seed and research exemptions of PVPCs may
severely limit the value of the certificates. Other breeding companies are permitted
to use the genetic stock of a high-yielding plant with a PVPC to develop a slightly
different but equally high-yielding plant, thus dissipating sales of the original high-
yielding variety (Janis and Kesan 2002). For example, Lesser (1994) describes a
soybean plant granted a PVPC in 1991 that differed from a parent only in the color
of its flowers (white instead of purple). Moreover, enforcement of PVPCs is costly,
because firms must enforce their own rights (Hayes et al. 2009).

There is ample evidence that PVPCs are not very valuable to firms. A hedonic
price analysis on New York soybeans in 1992 shows that a PVPC is associated with
just a 2.3% price premium for the protected plant, substantially less than associated
with plant patents (Lesser 1994). Alston and Venner (2002) also show no apparent
effect of the PVP Act on wheat seed prices over the period 1954–1994. In Canada,
plant breeders' rights (which are very similar to PVPCs) were surrendered or
revoked in half of a sample of 105 Canola plants, implying companies did not find
them worth maintaining (Carew and Devadoss 2003). Finally, it does not appear that
PVPCs are frequently litigated, which might be expected if they conferred substantial market power. Janis and Kesan (2002) report that Pioneer – which holds a large
number of PVPCs – engaged in no license infringement lawsuits based solely on
PVPCs, during 1997–2001. Over the same period, Pioneer initiated 15 patent lawsuits and was sued 11 times for patent infringement. All that said, it is important not
to overstate the case. Clearly PVPCs have some value. After all, they are still sought
by many firms every year.

Several studies have shown that the enactment of the PVP Act led to an increase
in R&D spending for crops eligible for the new protection. Perrin et al. (1983) and
Butler and Marion (1985) each surveyed a large set of seed breeding companies on
their R&D activities around the time of the Act's passage. We would anticipate
PVPCs to have no impact on plants ineligible for PVPC protection such as hybrid
corn (PVPC protection for first-generation hybrids was only available following the
1994 amendment to the Act). And indeed, although corn R&D by seed companies
rose rapidly over 1960–1979, there does not appear to be any discontinuity in spending levels around the time the Act was enacted. Soybeans, in contrast, are not hybrid

varieties, and the appropriability of soybean varieties likely increased with the Act's passage. Indeed, there was a rapid increase in R&D spending for soybeans, as well as the number of active breeding programs, right around the passage of the Act in 1970 (some surveyed firms explicitly stated they started breeding programs in response the PVP Act passage). There is also evidence, less strong, for a surge in R&D for cereals around the time of the Act's passage, although Alston and Venner (2002) point out wheat R&D subsequently stagnated. Malla et al. (2004) and Malla and Gray (2000) provide similar evidence for a Canadian context. There, the passage of a very similar form of PVPCs in 1990 appears to have stimulated private R&D in the canola industry.

The evidence that the PVP Act improved research outputs is weaker. Perrin et al. (1983) and Babcock and Foster (1991) were unable to detect a statistically significant shift in soybean and tobacco yields, respectively, around 1970, when the Act was passed, despite apparent increases in private soybean R&D spending and the dominance of the private sector in tobacco breeding. Carew and Devadoss (2003) detect a positive impact of plant breeders' rights on Canadian canola yields in some specifications, but this effect disappears when time fixed effects are included. Nasseem et al. (2005) do find a net positive effect of PVPCs on US cotton yields, when they allow for a trend break in yield growth in 1982.

There is mixed evidence again for the impact of the PVP Act on wheat yields. Alston and Venner (2002) find no evidence of higher wheat yields for varieties with PVPCs, but Kolady and Lesser (2009), who are able to control several omitted factors by comparing wheat yields in each year with the yield of a reference plant, find PVPCs are indicative of higher yields for one of the two wheat varieties they consider. Hayes et al. (2009), summarizing earlier studies, note that the yield of European wheat grown under controlled conditions increased faster than US yields. They argue this is at least consistent with more wheat R&D being induced by various institutional arrangements that tend to make PVPCs more valuable in Europe. Finally, Thomson (2015) introduces a sophisticated model of farmer wheat variety choice and measures the impact in Australia of a shift from publicly supported breeding to a private system reliant on a form of plant variety protection. He finds the rate of yield improvement *worsened* after switching to a private system.

Utility Patents

While sexual and asexual plants were both eligible for IPRs after 1970, the IPRs available to sexually reproducing plants were significantly weaker than that available to asexual plants. This changed in 1980, when Diamond vs. Chakrabarty (1980) ruled plants and animals cannot be excluded from utility patent protection, a decision reaffirmed and clarified by ex parte Hibberd (1985) and ex parte Allen (1987). Utility patents provide 20 years of excludability to the assignee, with no exemptions for researchers or farmers, so long as the patented innovation is novel, useful, and nonobvious. Internationally, in 1995, the WTO's Trade-Related Aspects of Intellectual Property Agreement also came into force, requiring plants to be protected by patents or another sui generis system (e.g., PVPCs) in all signatory countries.

Multiple research strands indicate utility patents are very important in agricultural biotechnology, if not agriculture more generally. Squicciarini et al. (2013) showed the quality of a patent is correlated with the number of citations made to it, the dispersion of technology fields to which these citations belong, the number of claims made by the patent, and the number of jurisdictions where the patent is in force. By these metrics, Lippoldt (2015) shows agricultural patents relating to biocides, foods, and animal husbandry are lower quality, while Schneider (2011) shows plant biotechnology patents are high quality (when compared to the typical patent).

An alternative method of assessing value relies on patent challenges. Patents in the European Union may be challenged within 9 months of being granted if the challenger believes the granted patent is not novel, useful, or nonobvious. Because it is costly to challenge patents, they are most likely to be challenged when they actually cordon off valuable territory in technological space. Schneider (2011) documents that plant biotechnology patents are challenged in this manner at a rate nearly twice the typical patent.

The high level of technology fees and royalties in the global seed market (up to 50% for cotton, Fuglie et al. 2011) also hints at the importance of patents in this sphere, since IPRs are crucial for negotiating royalties and license fees. Finally, the high value of agricultural biotechnology patents is consistent with surveys of businesses. Cohen (2010) documents the extensive literature on the value of utility patents, which generally finds they are most valuable to medical, health, and chemical industries. While agricultural biotechnology is not a sector broken out in the studies Cohen summarizes, it draws on a similar scientific basis and is subject to regulatory oversight in the same way.

There is little in the way of attempts to measure how discrete changes in utility patent law impacted agricultural firm R&D decisions or firm R&D outputs. Perhaps the closest is Lippoldt (2015), which shows an index of patent strength is positively correlated with more agricultural patents across 41 countries. There is, however, strong evidence that R&D by the agricultural biotechnology sector is yielding many measurable outputs. For one, agricultural biotechnology patents have grown rapidly since 1980. For every 1000 granted patents, the number of agricultural biotechnology patents has grown from 1.5 in 1980 to 3.1 in 1990 to 8.2 in 2000 (USDA Economic Research Service 2004 and United States Patent and Trademark Office 2016). Lippoldt (2015) also shows the number of agricultural patents granted in a country is correlated with various measures of agricultural productivity including domestic value added in agricultural exports, cereal crop yields, and agricultural equipment imports, although not total factor productivity growth in agriculture (moreover, it should be noted that Lippoldt is not measuring biotechnology patents). Finally, using data on field trials, Nolan and Santos (2012) show biotechnology has contributed substantially to corn yields over the period 1997–2009. A rough calculation indicates genetic modification technology may have boosted corn yield gains by 40–50% compared to what they would have been without genetic engineering.

Summary

There are a host of rival factors that may potentially complicate a simple model where stronger IPRs lead to more investment in R&D and therefore more innovation. In agriculture, confounding dynamics include the role of the public sector, the stochastic nature of R&D, variation in technological opportunity, the proper measurement of innovation quality, changes in the marketplace, the effects of IPR on knowledge spillovers and market concentration, and the political economy underlying changes to IPRs. Not discounting the importance of these other factors, the evidence from plant IPR extensions appears to broadly support the above model.

Across the three IPR extensions considered, it appears PVPCs may have some modest impact on the ability of firms to appropriate the value of their new innovations, while plant and utility patents increase appropriability substantially more. Nonetheless, even the weak increase in appropriability associated with PVPCs did induce more R&D spending in eligible crops. However, the modest impact on R&D did not generally translate into significant R&D outputs, perhaps for some of the reasons discussed above. For the stronger IPRs associated with plant and utility patents, new industries such as the commercial rose and agricultural biotechnology sectors emerged in the wake of better IPRs. While the value of patents in these industries is consistent with them playing an important role in these industries, it is not clear how much patents actually contributed to their development, especially in the rose industry. The case is probably strongest for agricultural biotechnology, which seems to rely heavily on the kind of licensing that is facilitated by IPRs.

Market Concentration, Competition, and Antitrust Policy

As agricultural input sectors have become important sources of new technologies for farmers, significant structural changes in these input industries have occurred. Through mergers and acquisitions (M&As), market concentration increased. By 2009, more than half of global sales of crop seed, agricultural chemicals, veterinary pharmaceuticals, and farm machinery were estimated to have been produced by the four leading firms in each of these sectors (Fuglie et al. 2011). There was also horizontal integration, with several large agricultural chemical companies acquiring significant presence in the seed sector. Growing concentration, particularly in the seed sector, raised concerns about the exercise of market power in the pricing of agricultural inputs and in the range of technological options available to farmers and consumers.

Economic assessments of whether large firms are able to exercise market power – defined as the ability to charge prices for their products above marginal costs – are complicated by the IPR held over many of the products sold by these companies. As described in the previous section, IPRs provide limited monopolies to the developers of new technologies. With IPR, innovators can legally exercise market power – limiting a product's supply and charging more for it than its marginal cost of production – in order to earn a return on past investments in R&D. Merely the presence of market power in the pricing of agricultural inputs is insufficient evidence that antitrust laws have been violated or that social welfare has been reduced. If profits from the exercise of market power incentivize R&D in an industry, the long-term welfare gains from greater innovation could well offset the short-term welfare losses from higher input prices (indeed, the entire IP system is premised on the assumption that this is generally the case). Nonetheless, even with IPR, antitrust laws prohibit certain forms of behavior, such as exclusive licensing, exclusive dealing, and tying arrangements in which a firm may grant a license to one product under the condition that the licensee purchase another product (Moschini 2010).

To assess the impact of concentration in an R&D intensive industry like crop seed, studies have attempted to gauge whether increased concentration resulted in more, or less, R&D investment by the industry or whether firm profits have been excessive relative to their R&D spending. Schimmelpfennig et al. (2004) found that as the number of companies conducting field trials with GM crops declined, the total number of GM field trials (relative to seed sales) also declined. They concluded that less competition reduced R&D investment by the seed industry. However, other factors, such as learning-by-doing as the industry gained experience with GM crop development, may also have led companies to reduce GM field trials, without necessarily reducing their R&D spending or rate of crop improvement. Kalaitzandonakes et al. (2010) compared industry profits due to price markups for seed to industry R&D spending on crop breeding and genetic improvement in the United States during 1997–2008. Although their estimates of R&D spending are only approximate, their results suggest that industry profits did not fully cover R&D spending until 2007. Moreover, Magnier et al. (2010) found that product life cycles in the US seed industry appeared to be shortening, implying an accelerated rate of crop improvement. Finally, Fuglie et al. (2011), using new estimates of market concentration and R&D spending by the seed, agricultural chemical, veterinary pharmaceutical, and farm machinery industries worldwide over 1994–2010, found no major change in the research intensities (R&D spending as a percentage of industry sales) of these industries despite significant increases in market concentration (measured by the Herfindahl Index and four- and eight-firm concentration ratios) in these industries over this period (Table 2).

Other studies have investigated the underlying motivations behind M&A in agricultural input industries that led to increased concentration. As biotechnology began to be applied to crop improvement, changes in seed industry structure were motivated by a need to combine complementary technology assets, including core germplasm, GM traits, and biotechnology research tools (Graff et al. 2003). Marco and Rausser (2008) found that M&A activity in the seed industry was partly in response to overlapping patent rights in new plant biotechnologies and high transaction costs in negotiating cross-licensing agreements. In a review of factors affecting M&A activity in agricultural input industries, Fuglie et al. (2011) found motivations to be specific to each industry. The emergence of biotechnology and the need to acquire complementary technology assets affected the structure of both the crop seed and animal breeding industries. In the animal health industry, increased concentration

Table 2 Global market concentration and research intensity in agricultural input industries

Year	Herfindahl Index	4-firm concentration ratio	8-firm concentration ratio	Industry R&D intensity
		Share of global market (%)		R&D/sales (%)
Crop protection chemicals				
1994	398	28.5	50.1	7.0
2000	645	41.0	62.6	6.8
2009	937	53.0	74.8	6.4
Crop seed				
1994	169	21.1	29.0	7.5
2000	359	33.0	43.7	12.7
2009	727	46.2	54.3	11.2
Animal health				
1994	510	32.4	57.4	8.6
2000	657	41.8	67.4	8.5
2009	827	50.6	72.0	8.6
Farm machinery				
1994	264	28.1	40.9	1.9
2000	353	32.8	44.7	2.3
2009	791	50.1	61.4	2.7

Source: Fuglie et al. (2011)

was largely an outcome of M&A among parent pharmaceutical firms and motivated by developments within the much larger market for human pharmaceuticals. Consolidation in the farm machinery industry was one consequence of a farm-sector recession in the 1980s, when farms significantly reduced purchases of new machinery in response to rising farm debt. In the agricultural chemical industry, when new regulations mandated greater health and safety testing of new and existing chemical products, many companies with limited R&D capacity sold their assets rather than invest in the technological capacity to meet these requirements (see Ollinger and Fernandez-Cornejo 1998 and section below on regulation).

Another concern that has been expressed about rising concentration in input industries is that it could limit technological choices by farmers and consumers. With only a few companies accounting for most R&D spending in these industries worldwide, critical decisions about the kinds of technologies to develop (e.g., GM or non-GM varieties), for what crops and for what production environments, may rest with a relatively small number of corporate boards. Importantly, if the large fixed costs of establishing effective R&D programs serve as a barrier to entry for new firms in these industries, then high concentration could stifle innovation. Byerlee and Fischer (2002) noted that the great majority of GM applications to agriculture focused on only a few crops (mainly corn, soybean, and cotton) and just two traits (herbicide tolerance and insect resistance conferred by the *Bt* gene). However, it is unlikely that concentration in the seed industry explains these patterns of GM crop development. For example, Naylor et al. (2004) argue that the public sector has also been guilty of neglecting biotechnology development for "orphan crops" (which they define as crops that receive little scientific focus relative to their importance for food security in the world's poorest regions). Rather, lack of consumer acceptance, absence of regulatory frameworks, poorly defined or enforced IPR, and the small size of potential markets seem to be the major constraints to broader R&D investment in crop biotechnology (Byerlee and Fischer 2002, Alston et al. 2006).

One indicator of whether an industry remains open to new technological opportunities and innovations is its ability to attract venture capital for start-up companies. Venture capital is especially attracted to technologies that, if successful, could potentially transform an industry (Gompers and Lerner 1999). Fuglie et al. (2011) traced entrants and exits of 77 small agricultural biotechnology start-up companies between 1979 and 2010. Most of these start-ups exited after just a few years, either through bankruptcy or, if their technologies demonstrated proof of concept, through acquisition by a larger company who then incorporated the technology into their R&D portfolio. The study found that despite frequent exits, the number of active companies grew and then remained roughly constant at between 30 and 40 each year after 1998. While the number of new entrants appeared to diminish after the world financial crisis of 2007, Fuglie (2016) reported a surge in new venture capital financing for food and agricultural innovations in 2014 and 2015. While funding of new start-ups in agricultural biotechnology continued to be significant, a large share of the increase in venture capital was for applications of new information and communication technologies to food and agriculture (e.g., e-commerce food marketing and precision farming).

The 2014–2015 downturn in commodity prices and pressure from activist investors appear to have renewed interest in further consolidation among leading agricultural input companies, particularly in the seed-biotechnology-chemical sector. In December 2015, Dow Chemical and DuPont announced their merger; in February 2016, Syngenta accepted an acquisition offer from ChemChina; and in May 2016, Bayer proposed to buy Monsanto. Together, these actions could raise the four-firm concentration ratio in global seed and agricultural chemical markets substantially. While previous rounds of M&A activity were strongly motivated by the need to obtain complementary technology capabilities, one major factor driving the current round of mergers appears to be a desire to reduce costs through elimination of redundancies in company operations, including R&D. This raises the prospect that concentration may reach a point where it negatively affects the amount and diversity of R&D in these industries.

Regulation and Private Agricultural R&D

Governments regulate the introduction of new food and agricultural technologies to assure the health and safety of people and the environment and to achieve other social goals. Over time, as new scientific evidence accumulates or due to pressures from industry or consumers, regulations may change. Regulations impose costs on new product development and influence incentives for the amount and direction of private R&D. Regulations may also affect market structure by giving a competitive advantage to firms that have greater financial and technical capacities to meet regulatory requirements.

In the United States, the 1972 and 1978 amendments to the Federal Insecticide, Fungicide, and Rodenticide Act (FIFRA) imposed stricter health and safety requirements on agricultural pesticides. FIFRA required manufacturers to collect and submit data evaluating the chronic and acute toxicity effects of new and existing pesticides and to establish dosage and use limits. The Environmental Protection Agency (EPA) was responsible for reviewing the data and approving any new pesticides for manufacture and sale. Existing pesticides not meeting these requirements were withdrawn from the market. In an assessment of how FIFRA affected innovation in the pesticide industry, Ollinger and Fernandez-Cornejo (1995) found that while FIFRA encouraged firms to develop less toxic pesticides, it also raised the costs of new pesticide development. This discouraged firms from developing new pesticides for minor crop markets. In a subsequent paper, Ollinger and Fernandez-Cornejo (1998) found that the higher "sunk costs" of regulation contributed to consolidation in the pesticide industry, leading to fewer, larger firms and encouraged foreign firms to expand in the US market. Surveys sponsored by the pesticide industry claim that the cost of bringing a new pesticide to market has continued to rise, exceeding $280 million by 2010 (Phillips McDougall 2016). Fuglie et al. (2011) found that new pesticide registrations in the United States fell significantly following the 1970's amendments to FIFRA. As Fig. 2 showed, R&D spending by the US pesticide industry has not grown in real terms since in the mid-1980s, although this also reflects slow growth in demand for pesticides due in part to the development of biotechnology substitutes for pest control (Fuglie et al. 2011).

The emergence of agricultural biotechnology in the 1980s led governments to develop new regulatory protocols for this technology. In the United States, Federal agencies drew upon existing legislative authority to establish in 1986 the Coordinated Framework for Regulation of Biotechnology Products. Under the Framework, the EPA, the US Department of Agriculture (USDA), and the Food and Drug Administration (FDA) shared responsibility for regulating the testing and approval of agricultural biotechnologies (Cowan 2015). EPA uses its FIFRA authority to regulate biotechnology-derived plant or microbes that exhibit pesticide properties. The USDA, using its authority under the Federal Plant Pest Act of 1957 (which was superseded by the Plant Protection Act of 2000), reviews applications for the field testing of biotechnology-derived applications which may contain or produce potential agricultural pests harmful to agriculture or forestry. Under the 1938 Federal Food, Drug, and Cosmetic Act (FFDCA), the FDA regulates the safety of foods for human consumption.

Economic studies on the effects of biotechnology regulations on private R&D have shown, first, that they impose large fixed cost on genetically modified (GM) crop development and, second, that this has likely led private companies to focus agricultural biotechnology R&D on large markets. Kalaitzandonakes et al. (2007) estimate that the cost of fulfilling EPA, USDA, and FDA regulatory requirements was between $6.2 and $15.4 million per GM event. Industry assessments have been even higher. From a survey of the six leading agricultural biotechnology companies, Phillips McDougall (2011) estimated that the total cost of discovery, development, and bringing to market a plant biotechnology trait averaged $136 million, of which $17.9 million was to meet regulatory science requirements and another $17.2 million for registration and regulatory affair costs (the first component includes the cost of the field, greenhouse, and laboratory tests to confirm food, feed, and environmental safety, and the second component includes the cost to prepare, submit, and manage submissions to the regulatory agencies of multiple countries for cultivation and import approvals).

Another cost element is the extent to which meeting regulatory requirements may delay product commercialization. The Phillips McDougall (2011) survey estimated that development activities related to regulation took 7–9 years to complete. However, as these activities are generally conducted concurrently with breeding and wide-area testing, it is not clear whether regulatory protocols, where they have been established, have substantially delayed GM crop commercialization. However, regulatory uncertainty – whether or when protocols will be established or significantly changed – has very likely been an impediment to the commercialization of agricultural biotechnology and may have negatively affected private R&D investment decisions.

The high fixed cost of GM crop development and commercialization partly explains why most private R&D investments in GM crops have focused on crops offering large seed markets like corn, soybean, and cotton. A larger market allows fixed development costs to be spread more widely. In contrast, relatively little private R&D has been directed toward GM development for horticulture. With its diversity of fruit, vegetable, and ornamental species, seed markets for particular GM events would be relatively small. Incentives for private R&D for GM horticulture have also been constrained by consumer resistance and, to some extent, greater technical complexity in GM modification for desired traits for these crops (Alston et al. 2006).

Similar to agricultural chemicals and GM crops, new veterinary pharmaceuticals and vaccines require regulatory review. In the United States, the 1913 Virus-Serum-Toxin Act gives the USDA responsibility for approving new animal vaccines and other biological products, while the FDA handles regulatory review of animal pharmaceuticals, including antibiotics, under the authority of the FFDCA. Pesticide use on livestock is regulated by the EPA, as specified in FIFRA. Similar to agricultural chemicals and GM traits, industry surveys point to large and rising costs of meeting regulatory requirements (International Federation for Animal Health 2011). Uncertainty regarding future regulations, particular governing antibiotic use in animals, is cited by industry as a disincentive to invest in R&D to develop new veterinary pharmaceuticals and biologicals. However, there is a general lack of economic research to objectively assess the implications of regulations on R&D and technological development in animal health.

Public and Private Agricultural R&D: Crowding out or Complementary?

One view of public-private roles in science and technology is that they are complementary: publicly funded science expands the set of new technological opportunities available for private business to develop and commercialize. In this way, public R&D raises the marginal returns to private R&D and therefore stimulates more private R&D investment. However, when both public and private R&D are focused on applied applications in an economic sector, their activities may be duplicative. If public R&D produces technologies that directly compete with technologies from the private sector, the increased competition could reduce what the private firms could charge for their technologies. Facing lower returns to its R&D investments, private R&D spending could be "crowded out" by public R&D.

Empirical studies have sought to test these views of public and private R&D in agriculture by (1) comparing the nature and kind of R&D each sector undertakes to see how similar or different they may be and (2) using econometric models to test whether R&D spending in one sector influences R&D spending in the other. King et al. (2012) split public and private food and agricultural R&D spending in the United States into eight subsectors (food, crops, livestock, farm machinery, natural resources, etc.) and showed that for most of these subsectors, either public or private R&D was dominant (Fig. 4). Nearly all R&D on food and farm machinery were private, while the public sector was the main provider of R&D for a number of socially important issues like environment and natural resources, food nutrition and safety, economics and statistics, and community development. The public sector also dominated animal R&D except for animal health product development. The important exception appeared to be crop research, where each sector spent significant amounts on R&D.

Focusing on crop breeding, Frey (1996) conducted a near-complete 1994 census of public and private plant breeders to make detailed comparisons of their time allocation across commodities and where their work was situated along the basic-applied R&D spectrum. He found that even though the private sector employed nearly twice as many plant breeders (1499) as the public sector (706), 80% of private-sector breeders were concentrated on applied cultivar development (Fig. 5).[3]

---

[3] More current plant breeding information is not as complete as that provided by Frey (1996). However it is likely that the number of public breeders working on applied cultivar development has declined since Frey's study. Traxler et al. (2005) found a reduction in the number of state agricultural experiment station *plant breeders* working on cultivar development between 1994 and 2001. Carter et al. (2014) estimated the number of *public-sector breeding programs focusing on cultivar development* declined by about one-third between 1993 and 2013. Recently Sylak-Glassman et al. (2016) found that since 2001, state-level public institutions decreased the number of plant breeders working on cultivar development for ten crops or classes of crops, including corn, soybeans, pasture and forage crops, and tomatoes, in most cases even after accounting for nonresponse bias. Only for a few crops, notably several fruit crops and beans, did the number of public-sector plant breeders engaged in cultivar development appear to increase. Overall, they reported 71 instances of the cessation of public sector cultivar development programs between 2005 and 2015.

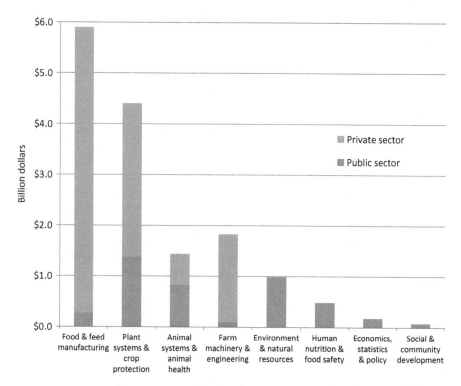

Fig. 4 Composition of US public and private food and agricultural R&D by subsector in 2013 (Source: OECD (2016))

More basic, upstream research on germplasm enhancement and basic plant breeding tools were emphasized by public-sector plant breeders. Private crop breeding was also more concentrated on a narrow set of commodities: nearly half (48%) of private breeding was allocated to just three crops (corn, soybean, and cotton), while the share of public breeding to these crops was just 17%. The differences in the nature and focus of public and private crop improvement research are further evidence of complementarity.

Econometric analysis to examine behavioral interactions between public and private agricultural R&D draws its conceptual framework from a broader literature that asks if public R&D complements or substitutes for private R&D (David et al. 2000, Toole 2007). Complementarity takes place when public R&D investments stimulate additional private R&D investments. Substitution takes place when private firms have reduced their own investment relative to a situation without public funding. In regression analyses, finding a positive and significant effect of public R&D on private R&D is taken as evidence of a complementary relationship, whereas a negative and significant coefficient indicates substitution.

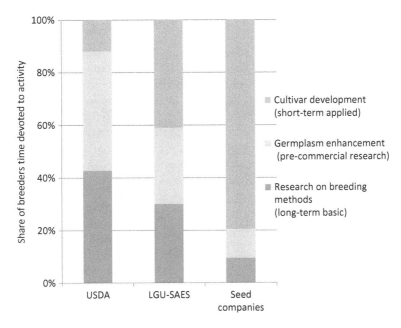

Fig. 5 Allocation of public and private plant breeding among basic, pre-commercial and applied research activities in the United States (Source: Frey (1996))

Most of the econometric studies of public-private interaction in agricultural R&D focus on the United States and generally find evidence of complementarity. Applying a regression model to Frey's (1996) data on public and private plant breeding investment on 84 commodities, Fuglie and Walker (2001) found that commodities with higher levels of public basic research (basic breeding and germplasm enhancement), after controlling for market size and other factors, were associated with higher private applied R&D (cultivar development), while higher public applied research (cultivar development) was associated with less private applied R&D. Toole and King (2011) analyzed agricultural patenting by companies in the Chemical and Allied Products Industry and found that public agricultural research performed in universities stimulated (and thereby complemented) private invention at the firm level. Using the Standard and Poor's Compustat database for the period 1991–2003, Wang et al. (2009) estimated an elasticity of private agricultural R&D with respect to public life sciences research of 0.65 (i.e., a 1% increase in public research leads to a 0.65% increase in private R&D). Tokgoz (2006), using national aggregate R&D expenditure data, found that public basic life sciences research had a positive and significant elasticity of 0.69 on private agricultural R&D but found no significant relationship between public applied life sciences research and private agricultural R&D. Using agricultural R&D data extended to more recent years and disaggregated into components, Tokgoz and Fuglie (2013) found that public agricultural R&D stimulated private "land-saving" R&D, but not private "labor-saving"

R&D. Their elasticity estimates for private land-saving R&D ranged from 0.61 to 0.97.

Wang et al. (2013) separated private R&D into crop and livestock components. Using a vector autoregression (VAR) model and data covering 1970–2009, they found that a shock (exogenous spending increase) to public crop research caused private crop research to rise, but no significant interactions were found between public and private livestock research. Wang et al. (2013) also found that a shock to private applied crop research caused public applied crop research to fall. These results suggest the public sector responded to the changing market and institutional environment by reallocating its research portfolio in a way that avoided direct competition with the private sector. Evidence of short-run substitution between public and private sources of funding of bioscience at US universities was found by Buccola et al. (2009). Based on a national survey of US academic bioscience researchers in 2003–2004, Buccola, Erwin, and Yang found that individual scientists tended to specialize in their sources of research funding and that an increase in private funding led to a decrease in public funding (and vice versa) for that scientist. This could cause crowding out in funding sources in the short run but would not likely affect the system level in the longer run given entry and exit possibilities of new scientists or scientists from related fields.

International evidence on public-private research interactions in agricultural research is relatively sparse and the findings more mixed. In a study of agricultural R&D investment in China, Hu et al. (2011) found private agricultural R&D spending increased with public investment in basic research but decreased with public investment in development research. However, Alfranca and Huffman (2001), using data from seven European Union countries over 1984–1995, found significant crowding out (substitution) between public and private agricultural research spending.

Public-Private Collaboration in R&D

Stronger incentives and greater capacity for research in the private sector can change the portfolio allocation of publicly funded research and create new opportunities for public-private research collaboration and knowledge transfer. Public research may focus more on upstream, fundamental science, leaving more applied research and market development to the private sector. But to efficiently transform advances in fundamental science into commercial opportunities may require closer collaboration between public and private institutions.

In the United States, new laws and regulations were put in place in the 1980s and 1990s to encourage the transfer of knowledge and technology between public research laboratories and private firms. These laws affected ownership rights to new technologies developed with government funds and established mechanisms for direct research collaboration between public and private-sector scientists. The primary goal was to increase the economic impacts of public R&D by moving public

Table 3 Major US legislation encouraging public-private collaboration in research and technology transfer

Year	Legislation	Action
1980	Stevenson-Wydler Technology Innovation Act	Encouraged government laboratories to increase cooperation with the private sector. Each major government laboratory was directed to create an Office of Research and Technology Applications to facilitate transfer to private companies
1980	Bayh-Dole act	Authorized government agencies to grant exclusive licenses to government-owned patents and allowed universities to own patents on research developed with government funds
1981	Economic Recovery Tax Act	Established tax credits for R&D grants to universities for basic research
1982	Small Business Innovation Development Act	Established the SBIR program. The program requires a minimum percentage of each federal agency's extramural R&D budget to be allocated to small businesses
1986	Federal Technology Transfer Act	Authorized government research laboratories to enter into CRADA with private companies

Source: Adapted from Schacht (2012)

research findings that have commercial applications rapidly into the marketplace (Fuglie et al. 1996).

The Changing Environment for Public-Private Research and Technology Transfer

The development of new policies and institutions for public-private research and knowledge transfer in the United States has been incremental. Congress has enacted successive pieces of legislation aimed at creating new institutions for technology transfer between the public and private sectors and periodically has introduced modifications to improve or strengthen them. Some of the major technology transfer legislation that has affected the food and agricultural sector are listed in Table 3.

One of the first major changes dealt with patent policy. While universities and public institutions had for some time possessed the right to seek patents, the federal government assumed ownership of any invention resulting from federally funded research. Discoveries described in patents are often far from commercial viability, however, and without exclusive licenses, companies may be unwilling to make the investments necessary to commercialize them. Responding to this constraint, the Bayh-Dole Act (the Patent and Trademark Act Amendments of 1980)[4] gave institutions "certainty of title" for inventions resulting from research funded by the federal government. The legislation allowed universities, nonprofit organizations, and other

---

[4] US laws are often referenced by the names of their principal sponsors as well as by their official title. In addition, they are designated a specific number (e.g., Public Law 96–517 in the case of the Bayh-Dole Act).

institutions receiving government funding for research to obtain, own, and license the patents on any invention they discovered. It also expanded the right of federal laboratories to issue licenses for patents of their inventions. Previously, federal laboratories had been able to grant only nonexclusive or open licenses, but the Bayh-Dole Act allowed them to grant exclusive licenses as well. These changes to patent policy were designed to encourage scientists at universities and other public institutions to seek more patents and to provide private companies with incentives to work with these patents.

Other legislation sought to promote greater research collaboration between government laboratories and private companies. The 1980 Stevenson-Wydler Technology Innovation Act mandated that each federal agency develop specific mechanisms for disseminating government innovations. Prior to this Act, technology transfer activities by federal agencies had been voluntary, and each agency had used its own discretion for disseminating information on new research discoveries and technology. Further incentives were provided in the 1986 Technology Transfer Act. This Act spelled out conditions under which federal laboratories could work directly with researchers employed by private companies. The Act provided for formal agreements, known as Cooperative Research and Development Agreements (CRADAs), to specify the responsibilities and resource commitments of each research partner and their rights to intellectual property developed through the agreement. Further legislation in 1991 (the National Defense Authorization Act) and 1995 (the National Technology Transfer and Advancement Act) clarified the rules regarding patent licensing and royalty sharing for inventions developed in CRADAs.

Other initiatives encouraged government agencies to provide direct research grants to the private sector. The Small Business Innovation Act of 1982 required federal agencies to earmark a portion of extramural research funds to small companies (i.e., companies with 500 or fewer employees) through the Small Business Innovation Research (SBIR) program. The 1981 Economic Recovery Tax Act provided tax credits for research grants given by companies to universities. Other legislation sought to encourage research cooperation among firms within industries. The 1984 Cooperative Research Act provided incentives for private research consortia by providing some antitrust exemptions and liability limits on companies collaborating on pre-commercial R&D.

Models of R&D Collaboration

The legislation described above governs the exchange of knowledge and resources between public and private collaborating institutions and, in general terms, states how rights to new inventions are to be owned and benefits shared. Figure 6 presents a stylized model of the various mechanisms available to government research agencies for cooperating with the private sector and other nongovernment institutions.

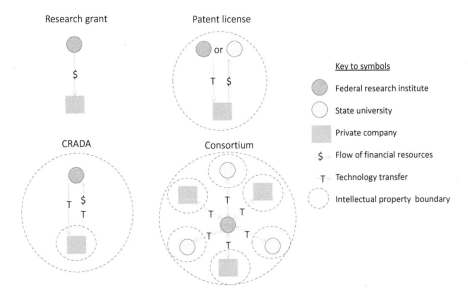

Fig. 6 Models of public-private research collaboration (Source: Fuglie and Toole (2014))

The research grant model. The simplest mechanism for collaborative research is for the government to fund private in-house research. In this model there is no formal research collaboration between a government lab and the nongovernment partner, and the grant recipient has sole ownership over any patentable technology. This type of arrangement characterizes the SBIR program. Often, government R&D grants are targeted toward projects of high government priority. In 2000, the US Department of Agriculture and Department of Energy combined a portion of their SBIR resources to form the Biofuel Research and Development Initiative (BRDI). The BRDI provided research grants to companies for biofuel-related "plant science research" and "biorefinery demonstration and deployment" projects, as well as feasibility studies on next-generation biofuels (Fuglie et al. 2011).

The patent licensing model. Here, a public research institution develops and patents a technology and then assigns the rights to use the patented technology to nongovernment institutions or private companies. The rights may be exclusive, partially exclusive, or nonexclusive (Heisey et al. 2006). Exclusive patent licenses are awarded when they are deemed necessary to promote private commercialization – for example, when a company must make significant investments in product and market development or when substantial commercial risk is involved. Patent licenses usually include a royalty payment that returns either a fixed fee or a percentage of revenues to the public institution that owns the patent.

The CRADA joint-venture model. A CRADA typically involves a government laboratory collaborating with one company to develop a technology for a specific commercial application. Both parties commit in-house resources to R&D, and the nongovernment collaborator may provide the government laboratory with some research funds. Government laboratories may provide personnel, equipment, and laboratory privileges, but not financial resources, to a nongovernment partner. Patents resulting from a CRADA may be jointly owned, and the nongovernment partner has the first right to negotiate an exclusive license. Some data also may not be publicly disclosed for a certain period of time (Day-Rubenstein and Fuglie 2000). The first CRADA established by a federal agency following the passage of the 1986 Technology Transfer Act was between the USDA and Embrex, Inc., which led to the commercialization of a method for vaccinating poultry against disease before they hatch.

The research consortium is a somewhat more complex model. Unlike a CRADA, which involves only one private and one public partner, a consortium brings together several private companies to undertake joint research and may also include public-sector partners. Consortium members contribute resources for the research, which is usually pre-commercial, and have the first rights to technologies developed by the consortium. Companies can protect spin-off technologies through trade secrets or new exclusive patents. Research consortia have proven useful for increasing support for research that is considered to be long term and high risk and for research to develop common standards in an industry. Additional applied and adaptive research is often required, however, to develop and disseminate technology to end users like farmers. Thus, a consortium often relies on the in-house research capacity of its members to develop specific applications from the more generic results of consortium-sponsored research.

Figure 7 shows the growth in the use of public-private technology transfer instruments by the USDA since the mid-1980s. One of the first Federal agencies to initiate a CRADA with a private firm, by 2012 the USDA's Agricultural Research Service (ARS) was participating in 257 active CRADAs. It had another 384 active patents licensed to private firms. The USDA's SBIR program is managed by the agency's extramural funding agency, the National Institute for Food and Agriculture (NIFA). In 2012, NIFA awarded 88 SBIR grants which totaled $16.8 million to private firms, about 2.5% of the USDA's total extramural research expenditure.

There has been only limited research on the effects of these new institutional arrangements for public-private research on the rate and direction of innovations for food and agriculture. From an examination of 366 USDA CRADA agreements during 1986 and 1995, Day-Rubenstein and Fuglie (2000) found that the private-sector partners contributed 64 percent of the total R&D resources tied to the CRADAs, though most of this was in the form of in-house R&D by the firm rather than cash transfers to ARS. They also found that topical areas addressed by these CRADAs may have been slightly skewed in favor of public-sector priorities like environmental protection and food nutrition. Heisey et al. (2006) found that patent licensing by ARS was instrumental in increasing private investment to commercialize USDA research discoveries but brought in only limited licensing revenue to the agency. Knudson et al. (2000) obtained a similar result from a survey of state agricultural experiment stations – that patent licensing was used primarily as an inducement for private companies to commercialize experiment station inventions rather than as a source of revenue to support public research. To our knowledge the effects of

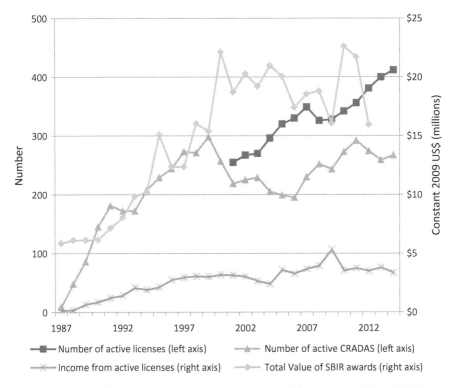

Fig. 7 Growth in public-private research collaboration by the USDA (Source: OECD (2016))

USDA's SBIR grants have not been assessed, although studies on the impact of the SBIR program across the Federal government as a whole have given mixed results (Fuglie and Toole 2014).

Conclusions and Areas for Future Research

Private agribusiness is playing an increasingly important role as a source of innovations for food and agriculture. In the United States, while private companies have long dominated R&D spending in the food sector, their R&D spending now surpasses public R&D for agriculture as well. Private agricultural R&D encompasses a range of technologies, from improved crop seeds and animal breeds, new chemicals and pharmaceuticals for pest and disease control, better farm machinery, and new products and formulations for crop and animal nutrition. Over the last few decades, private R&D spending has grown most rapidly for crop breeding and biotechnology trait development.

Public policies have a major influence on the growth and direction of private food and agriculture R&D. Public R&D investments can stimulate private R&D by opening up new technological opportunities for private firms to commercialize. Scientific advances in molecular biology and genetic engineering, for example, gave rise to private R&D in agricultural biotechnology. However, public R&D can also "crowd out" private R&D if it competes directly as a supplier of new technologies. Most evidence, however, suggests that public and private agricultural R&D have been complementary, at least in the United States. Evidence also points to contributions from broader (public) life science research to applied (private) agricultural research.

Other policies that influence private R&D incentives include provision and enforcement of intellectual property rights, the regulatory regimes governing the introduction of new technologies, and antitrust or competitiveness policies. Affirming the patentability of biological inventions increased the willingness of private firms to investment in crop breeding and biotechnology trait development. The evidence is less clear for plant breeders' rights, however, as the farmer and research exemptions dilute their exclusionary power. While the establishment of regulatory protocols for new chemical, biological, and pharmaceutical technologies for agriculture has helped to assuage (but not eliminate) consumer concerns about the health and safety of these technologies, obtaining approvals can impose significant costs and delays on technology development. These costs reduce incentives for private R&D and may discourage investment in technologies that serve relatively small markets but can help direct technology development in socially beneficial directions. Antitrust (competitiveness) policy has thus far not been an impediment to the growing market concentration in agricultural input industries, and M&A activity may enable firms to acquire complementary technology assets, particularly for crop biotechnology. However, a new round of M&As among major agricultural chemical and seed firms proposed in 2015–2020 appears likely to involve closer antitrust scrutiny. Since a significant motivation behind these M&As appears to be cost reduction, if approved they could negatively affect R&D spending by this industry.

The growing R&D capacity in the private sector creates new opportunities for public-private collaboration in technology development and knowledge transfer. In the United States, a number of institutional mechanisms have been established to facilitate collaborative research between public laboratories and private firms. These instruments appear to have helped speed up commercialization of research findings from public laboratories, although licensing technologies to the private sector has generally not been a significant source of new funding for public research.

This review suggests a number of areas where we believe additional economics research could be particularly useful for science and technology policy:

- One way to view the rise of private agricultural R&D is that it represents, indirectly, a gradual shift in the burden of financing R&D from general tax revenues to technology fees (input price markups) paid by farmers for agricultural inputs. What has this implied for the incidence of welfare costs and benefits from technical change in agriculture? How has this affected the stability of R&D funding and the responsive of agricultural R&D to evolving market demands? How do these outcomes compare with more direct measures to fund public R&D through producer levees such as commodity checkoffs?

- What are the short-term and long-term effects of rising concentration and market power in agricultural input industries? Does it raise prices farmers pay for inputs above the market power conferred through IPR? How has concentration affected the amount and diversity of private R&D? Is there a point where concentration reduces incentives to invest in private R&D?

- Overlapping patent claims and high transactions costs of cross-licensing technologies have been identified as behind much of the merger and acquisition activity in the crop seed-biotechnology industry. But in recent years, cross-licensing of proprietary technologies over crop germplasm and biotechnology traits has become widespread in this industry. What institutional, legal, or economic factors enabled the use of cross-licensing to grow? How has it affected market competition and pricing behavior in the industry?

- Empirical evidence seems to suggest that public R&D is a valuable contributor to private R&D because it expands the set of technological opportunities available for commercial development. If so, why haven't private firms been willing to provide more support for public R&D, either individually or jointly through research consortia? What are the institutional barriers preventing the private sector from jointly financing pre-commercial R&D by public institutions?

- How effective are new institutional mechanisms for public-private collaboration in agricultural research? Have they significantly affected the rate of innovation and productivity growth? Has this collaboration generated broad welfare benefits to consumers and technology spillovers to other firms, or has it primarily benefitted participating firms?

- Have instruments of science policy (IPR, regulation, public R&D, technology transfer, R&D subsidies, etc.) influenced the direction of private R&D in socially desirable ways? For example, have they provided more environmentally friendly technologies or healthy and safer foods? Have they been able to encourage technology development for more diverse markets (horticulture, organic, local foods, nutritious traits, small farms)?

References

Agricultural Science and Technology Indicators. 2016. *On-Line Database*. Washington, DC: International Food Policy Research Institute.

Alfranca, O., and W. Huffman. 2001. Impact of Institutions and Public Research on Private Agricultural Research. *Agricultural Economics* 25: 191–198.

Alston, J., K. Bradford, and N. Kalaitzandonakes. 2006. The Economics of Horticultural Biotechnology. *Journal Crop Improvement* 18: 413–431.

Alston, J., and R. Venner. 2002. The Effects of the US Plant Variety Protection Act on Wheat Genetic Improvement. *Research Policy* 31: 527–542.

Babcock, B., and W. Foster. 1991. Measuring the Potential Contribution of Plant Breeding to Crop Yields: Flue-cured Tobacco, 1954-87. *American Journal of Agricultural Economics* 73: 850–859.

Bientema, N., G.S. Stads, K. Fuglie, and P. Heisey. 2012. *ASTI Global Assessment of Agricultural R&D Spending*. Washington, DC: International Food Policy Research Institute.

Buccola, S., D. Erwin, and H. Yang. 2009. Research Choice and Finance in University Bioscience. S. *The Econometrics Journal* 75: 1238–1255.

Butler, L., and B. Marion. 1985. The Impacts of Patent Protection on the U.S. Seed Industry and Public Plant Breeding. In *North Central Regional Research Publication 304*. Madison, WI: University of Wisconsin-Madison.

Byerlee, D., and K. Fischer. 2002. Accessing Modern Science: Policy and Institutional Options for Agricultural Biotechnology in Developing Countries. *World Development* 30: 931–948.

Carew, R., and S. Devadoss. 2003. Quantifying the Contribution of Plant Breeders' Rights and Transgenic Varieties to Canola Yields: Evidence from Manitoba. *Canadian Journal of Agricultural Economics* 51: 371–395.

Carter, T.E., Jr., W.F. Tracy, T.R. Sinclair, T.G. Isleib, and R. Joost. 2014. What is the State of Public Cultivar Development? In *Proceedings of the 2014 Summit on Seeds and Breeds for 21ˢᵗ Century Agriculture, Washington, D.C., March 5–7, 2014*, ed. W.F. Tracy and M. Sligh. Pittsboro, NC: Rural Advancement Foundation International.

Cohen, W. 2010. Fifty years of Empirical Studies of Innovative Activity and Performance. In *Handbook of Economics of Innovation*, ed. B. Hall and N. Rosenberg, vol. 1, 129–213. Amsterdam: Alsevier.

Cowan, T. 2015. *Agricultural Biotechnology: Background, Regulation, and Policy Issues*. CRS Report 7–5700, Congressional Research Service, United States Congress, July 20.

Dasgupta, P., and J. Stiglitz. 1980. Industrial Structure and the Nature of Innovative Activity. *The Econometrics Journal* 90: 266–293.

David, P., B. Hall, and A. Toole. 2000. Is Public R&D a Complement or Substitute for Private R&D? A Review of the Econometric Evidence. *Research Policy* 29: 497–529.

Day-Rubenstein, K., and K. Fuglie. 2000. The CRADA Model for Public-private Collaboration in Agricultural Research. In *Public-Private Collaboration in Agricultural Research*, ed. K. Fuglie and D. Schimmelpfennig, 155–174. Ames: Iowa State University Press.

Drew, J., C. Yue, N. Anderson, and P. Pardey. 2015. Premiums and Discounts for Plant Patents and Trademarks Used on Ornamental Plant Cultivars: a Hedonic Price Analysis. *Hortscience* 50 (6): 879–887.

Frey, K. 1996. National Plant Breeding Study. In *Special Report 98, Iowa Agriculture and Home Economics Experiment Station*. Ames/Iowa: Iowa State University.

Fuglie, K. 2016. The Growing Role of the Private Sector in Agricultural Research and Development World-wide. *Global Food Security* 10: 29–38.

Fuglie, K., N. Ballenger, K. Day, C. Klotz, M. Ollinger, J. Reilly, U. Vasavada, and J. Yee. 1996. *Agricultural Research and Development: Public and Private Investments Under Alternative Markets and Institutions. Agricultural Economics Report 735*. Washington, DC: Economic Research Service, U.S. Department of Agriculture.

Fuglie, K., P. Heisey, J. King, C. Pray, K. Day-Rubenstein, D. Schimmelpfennig, S.L. Wang, and R. Karmarkar-Deshmukh. 2011. *Research Investments and Market Structure in the Food Processing, Agriculture Input and Biofuel Industries Worldwide. Economic Research Report 130*. Washington, DC: Economic Research Service, U.S. Department of Agriculture.

Fuglie, K., and A. Toole. 2014. The Evolving Institutional Structure of Public and Private Agricultural Research. *American Journal of Agricultural Economics* 96 (3): 862–883.

Fuglie, K., and T. Walker. 2001. Economic Incentives and Resource Allocation in U.S. Public and Private Plant Breeding. *Journal of Agricultural and Applied Economics* 33: 459–473.

Gompers, P., and L. Lerner. 1999. *The Venture Capital Cycle*. Cambridge, MA: MIT Press.

Graff, G., G. Rausser, and A. Small. 2003. Agricultural Biotechnology's Complementary Intellectual Assets. *The Review of Economics and Statistics* 85: 349–363.

Hayes, D., S. Lence, and S. Goggi. 2009. Impact of Intellectual Property Rights in the Seed Sector on Crop Yield Growth and Social Welfare: a Case Study Approach. *AgBioforum* 12 (2): 155–171.

Heisey, P., and K. Fuglie. 2016. *Agricultural Research Investment and Policy Reform in High Income Countries. Economic Information Bulletin. Economic Research Service*. Washington, DC: U.S. Department of Agriculture (forthcoming).

Heisey, P., J. King, K. Day-Rubenstein, and R. Shoemaker. 2006. *Government Patenting and Technology Transfer. Economic Research Report 16. Economic Research Service*. Washington, DC: U.S. Department of Agriculture.

Hu, R., Q. Liang, C. Pray, J. Huang, and Y. Jin. 2011. Privatization, public R&D policy, and private R&D investment in China's Agriculture. *Journal of Agricultural and Resource Economics* 36: 416–432.

International Federation for Animal Health. 2011. *IFAH global benchmarking survey 2011. International Federation for Animal Health*. Paris: France, October.

Janis, M., and J. Kesan. 2002. U.S. Plant Variety Protection: Sound and Fury...? *Houston Law Review* 39: 727.

Kalaitzandonakes, N., J. Alston, and K. Bradford. 2007. Compliance Costs for Regulatory Approval of New Biotech Crops. *Nature Biotechnology* 25: 509–511.

Kalaitzandonakes, N., A. Magnier, and D. Miller. 2010. A Worrisome Crop? Is there Market Power in the U.S. Seed Industry. *Regulation* 33: 20–26.

King, J., A. Toole, and K. Fuglie. 2012. *The Complementary Roles of the Public and Private Sectors in U.S. Agricultural Research and Development. Economic Brief No. 19*. Washington, DC: Economic Research Service, U.S. Department of Agriculture.

Knudson, M., R. Lower, and R. Jones. 2000. State Agricultural Experiment Stations and Intellectual Property Rights. In *Public-Private Collaboration in Agricultural Research*, ed. K. Fuglie and D. Schimmelpfennig, 199–218. Ames: Iowa State University Press.

Koladi, D., and W. Lesser. 2009. But are they Meritorious? Genetic Productivity Gains Under Plant Intellectual Property Rights. *Journal of Agricultural Economics* 60: 62–79.

Lesser, W. 1994. Valuation of Plant Variety Protection Certificates. *Review of Agricultural Economics* 16 (2): 231–238.

Lippoldt, D. 2015. Innovation and the experience with agricultural patents since 1990: food for thought. Food, Agriculture and Fisheries Paper No. 73. Organisation for Economic Cooperation and Development, Paris, France.

Magnier, A., N. Kalaitzandonakes, and D. Miller. 2010. Product Life Cycles and Innovation in the US Seed Corn Industry. *International Food and Agribusiness Review* 13: 17–36.

Malla, S., and R. Gray. 2000. An Analytical and Empirical Analysis of the Private Biotech R&D Incentives. Selected Paper. Annual Conference of the Agricultural and Applied Economics Association, Tampa, FL.

Malla, S., R. Gray, and P. Phillips. 2004. Gains to Research in the Presence of Intellectual Property Rights and Research Subsidies. *Review of Agricultural Economics* 26 (1): 63–81.

Marco, A., and G. Rausser. 2008. The Role of Patents Rights in Mergers: Consolidation in Plant Biotechnology. *American Journal of Agricultural Economics* 90: 133–151.

Moschini, G. 2010. Competition Issues in the Seed Industry and the Role of Intellectual Property. *Choices* 25: 1–14.

Moser, P., and P. Rhode. 2011. Did Plant Patents Create the American Rose? NBER Working Paper 16983.

Naseem, A., J. Oehmke, and D. Schimmelpfennig. 2005. Does Plant Variety Intellectual Property Protection Improve Farm Productivity? Evidence from Cotton Varieties. *AgBioforum* 8: 100–107.

Naylor, R., W. Falcon, R. Goodman, M. Jahn, T. Sengooba, H. Tefera, and R. Nelson. 2004. Biotechnology in the Developing World: as Case for Increased Investments in Orphan Crops. *Food Policy* 29: 15–44.

Nolan, E., and P. Santos. 2012. The Contribution of Genetic Modification to Changes in Corn Yield in the United States. *American Journal of Agricultural Economics* 94 (5): 1171–1188.

OECD. 2016. Innovation, Agricultural Productivity and Sustainability in the United States. Discussion Paper TAD/CA/APM/WP(2016)15. Trade and Agriculture Directorate, Organisation for Economic Cooperation and Development (OECD), Paris, France.

Ollinger, M., and J. Fernandez-Cornejo. 1995. *Regulation, Innovation, and Market Structure in the U.S. Pesticide Industry, Agricultural Economics Report No. 719. Economic Research Service.* Washington, DC: U.S. Department of Agriculture.

———. 1998. Sunk Costs and Regulation in the U.S. Pesticide Industry. *International Journal of Industrial Organization* 16: 139–168.

Pardey, P., B. Koo, J. Drew, J. Horwich, and C. Nottenburg. 2013. The Evolving Landscape of Plant Varietal Rights in the United States, 1930-2008. *Nature Biotechnology* 31: 25–30.

Pardey, P., C. Chan-Kang, J. Beddow, and S. Dehmer. 2015. Long-run and Global R&D Funding Trajectories: the U.S. Farm Bill in a Changing Context. *American Journal of Agricultural Economics* 97: 1312–1323.

PCAST. 2012. Report to the President on Agricultural Preparedness and the Agricultural Research Enterprise. President's Council of Advisors on Science and Technology (PCAST). Executive Office of the President, Washington, DC, December.

Perrin, R., K. Kunnings, and L. Ihnen. 1983. *Some Effects of the U.S. Plant Variety Protection Act of 1970. Research Report No. 46, Department of Economics and Business Economics.* Raleigh: North Carolina State University.

Phillips McDougall. 2016. The Cost of New Agrochemical Product Discovery, Development and Registration in 1995, 2000, 2005–8 and 2010 to 2014. R&D expenditure in 2014 and expectations for 2019. A Consultancy Study for CropLife International, CropLife America and the European crop Protection Association. Phillips McDougall, Midlothian, United Kingdom, January.

———. 2011. The cost and time in the discovery, development and authorization of a new plant biotechnology derived trait. Consultancy Study for Crop Life International. Phillips McDougall, Midlothian, United Kingdom, September.

Pray, C., and K. Fuglie. 2015. Agricultural Research by the Private Sector. *Annual Review of Resource Economics* 7: 399–424.

Schacht, W. 2012. *Industrial Competitiveness and Technological Advancement: Debate over Government Policy. CRS Report for Congress 7–5700.* Washington, DC: Congressional Research Service.

Schimmelpfennig, D., C. Pray, and M. Brennan. 2004. The Impact of Seed Industry Concentration on Innovation: a Study of US Biotech Market Leaders. *Agricultural Economics* 30: 157–167.

Schneider, C. 2011. The Battle for Patent Rights in Plant Biotechnology: Evidence from Opposition Fillings. *Journal of Technology Transfer* 36: 565–579.

Squicciarini, M., H. Dernis, and C. Criscuolo. 2013. Measuring patent quality: indicators of technological and economic value. Science, Technology and Industry Working Paper No. 2013/03. Organization for Economic Cooperation and Development, Paris, France.

Sylak-Glassman, E.J., C.T. Clavin, E.A. Klein, R.M. Whelan, A.E. Ressler, and M.S. Hindman. 2016. *Examination of Plant Breeding at U.S. Academic Institutions and Private Companies in 2015.* IDA Paper P-5331. Washington, D.C. Institute for Defense Analyses (IDA) Science and Technology Policy Institute.

Thomson, R. 2015. The Yield of Plant Variety Protection. *American Journal of Agricultural Economics* 97 (3): 762–785.

Tokgoz, S. 2006. Private Agricultural R&D in the United States. *Journal of Agricultural and Resource Economics* 31: 212–238.

Tokgoz S, and K. Fuglie. 2013. Public Policy, Induced Innovation, and Private Research: The case of Agriculture. Selected Paper. Annual Conference of the Agricultural and Applied Economics Association, Washington, DC.

Toole, A. 2007. Does Public Scientific Research Complement Private Investment in Research and Development in the Pharmaceutical Industry? *The Journal of Law and Economics* 50: 81–104.

Toole, A., and J. King. 2011. Industry-science Connections in Agriculture: Do Public Science Collaborations and knowledge Flows Contribute to firm-level Agricultural Research Productivity? Discussion Paper No. 11–064. Centre for European Economic Research (ZEW), Mannheim, Germany.

Traxler, G., A.K.A. Acquaye, K. Frey, and A.M. Thro. 2005. Public Sector Plant Breeding Resources in the U.S.: Study Results for the year 2001. http://nifa.usda.gov/resource/national-plant-breeding-study.

USDA Economic Research Service. 2012. *ERS Web Data Product: Agricultural Research Funding in the Public and Private Sectors*. Washington, DC: U.S. Department of Agriculture. Available at http://www.ers.usda.gov/data-products/agricultural-research-funding-in-the-public-andprivate-sectors.aspx.

———. 2004. *Agricultural biotechnology intellectual property* [database]. Washington, DC: USDA ERS. Available at http://www.ers.usda.gov/Data/AgBiotechIP/.

United States Patent and Trademark Office. 2016. *U.S. Patent Statistics Chart: Calendar Years 1963–2015*. Arlington, VA. Available at http://www.uspto.gov/web/offices/ac/ido/oeip/taf/us_stat.htm/.

Wang, C.Y., Y. Xia, and S. Buccola. 2009. Public Investment and Industry Incentives in Life-Science Research. *American Journal of Agricultural Economics* 91: 374–388.

Wang, S.L., P. Heisey, W. Huffman, and K. Fuglie. 2013. Public R&D, Private R&D, and U.S. Agricultural Productivity Growth: Dynamic and Long-run Relationships. *American Journal of Agricultural Economics* 95: 1287–1293.

Structural Change and Innovation in the Global Agricultural Input Sector

Nicholas Kalaitzandonakes and Kenneth A. Zahringer

Abstract Recent proposed mergers and acquisitions (M&As) in the agricultural input industry, especially among developers of crop protection products, seeds, and biotechnology, have attracted much attention. Vertical and horizontal consolidation in this sector has been ongoing, however, and such restructuring both makes possible and is driven by technical innovation. In this chapter, we review the emerging innovation and business model in the agricultural input sector and discuss the factors that have enabled it.

Introduction

Over the past 2 years, proposed mergers and acquisitions (M&As) in the agricultural input industry, especially among developers of crop protection products, seeds, and biotechnologies, have attracted much attention. The media has chronicled advances among members of the so-called Big Six in great detail.[1] Much of the activity began in May 2015, when Monsanto announced that it had made an acquisition offer to Syngenta (Sutherland 2015). Syngenta's directors and stockholders were reportedly not eager to pursue the deal, some of them citing concerns about antitrust regulatory hurdles. Even though Monsanto subsequently increased their bid and included a breakup fee in the offer, in case regulators did block the acquisition, Syngenta was not won over, and Monsanto ultimately dropped the offer in August of that year (Gara 2015).

Just a few months later, Dow and DuPont announced that they had agreed on a merger-of-equals plan to combine the two firms. Subsequently, within 2 years, the merged firm DowDuPont would split into three separate firms, specializing in agricultural inputs, industrial materials, and specialty products, respectively (Harwell 2015). The proposed merger came under intense regulatory scrutiny, especially in the European Union (EU) but also in the USA (Kosman 2017). On March 27, 2017,

---

[1] BASF, Bayer, Dow, DuPont, Monsanto, and Syngenta are often referred to as the "Big Six."

N. Kalaitzandonakes (✉) • K.A. Zahringer
Department of Agricultural and Applied Economics, University of Missouri, Columbia, MO, USA
e-mail: KalaitzandonakesN@missouri.edu

© Springer International Publishing AG 2018

N. Kalaitzandonakes et al. (eds.), *From Agriscience to Agribusiness*, Innovation, Technology, and Knowledge Management, https://doi.org/10.1007/978-3-319-67958-7_4

75

the EU Commission announced that it would allow the merger to proceed under the condition that DuPont's entire crop protection R&D platform as well as other assets be divested.

Even though their initial plans did not work out, Monsanto and Syngenta were not out of the acquisition market. In early 2016, the China National Chemical Corporation, known as ChemChina, made an offer to acquire Syngenta. Although US regulators soon approved the deal (Bray 2016b), the acquisition came under more intensive scrutiny by EU antitrust officials (Bray 2016a). After few changes to the original proposal, the deal was approved by US and EU regulators in April, 2017 (Petroff 2017). About a year after Monsanto walked away from its Syngenta offer, it became the target of an acquisition bid by another Big Six firm, Bayer, in an offer announced in September, 2016 (Harwell 2016). Antitrust regulators in different parts of the world have been closely examining the potential consequences of this proposed acquisition (Varinsky 2017).

All three proposed M&As have been slow to consummate, but they have been cheered by investors. Industry observers expect all of them to close, even if some divestments become necessary. Still, opposing views have continued to come in from various stakeholders. On March 17, 2017, the Congressional Record included a letter from US Senator Grassley to the President of the US summarizing the main points of the opposing view, stating that "the mergers of these international agrochemical and seed giants will significantly reduce competition and innovation in the agricultural sector, and will cause irreparable harm to the American farmer via increased input costs" (pp. S 1775).

Given these considerations, important questions remain: What drives the recent interest of firms to merge and consolidate? How are such structural changes related to innovation and what might be the level of innovation in the agricultural input sector in the future if such structural changes were consummated? In order to answer these questions, in this chapter we first analyze the market environment and the strategic intent of the key players that are driving the current cycle of reorganization and consolidation in the global agricultural input industries. Since the potential outcomes of the M&A actions are uncertain, we explore scenarios of alternative futures and discuss their implications for R&D spending and innovation in the biotechnology, seed, and crop protection industries.

The rest of the chapter is organized as follows: In order to provide historical context in the relationship between structural change and innovation in the agricultural input sector, in the next section we review the factors that initiated the vertical integration and consolidation of the US biotechnology and seed industries almost 20 years ago and examine the realized impacts. Following that, we review a new round of structural changes underway in the biotechnology, seed, and crop protection industries and the factors that have triggered them. As we discuss, innovation induced by both challenges and opportunities has given rise to the structural changes and has been enabled by them. Along the way, the agricultural input sector has begun to pursue a new and expansive innovation model which we subsequently discuss in some detail. Because many of the structural changes are ongoing and the possible outcomes are uncertain, we next examine potential structural futures and their implications for innovation in the agricultural input industry and beyond. In the final section, we summarize and conclude.

The Restructuring of the Seed, Biotech, and Crop Protection Industries: Some Historical Context

Understanding the structural evolution of the USA and global seed, biotech, and crop protection industries and its relationship to innovation in these industries requires historical context. Since the emergence of a commercial seed industry in the USA over 150 years ago, assets have changed hands frequently. Until the late 1960s, assets in the seed industry were primarily traded among seed firms. Starting in the 1970s, however, multinational petrochemical and pharmaceutical firms became the primary acquirers. Much of this activity has been traced to the introduction of the Plant Variety Protection Act of 1970, which promised to increase returns from plant research and attracted R&D-minded multinationals (Kalaitzandonakes and Bjornson 1997). However, this wave of M&As had little subsequent discernible impact on the structure of the seed industry because the petrochemical and pharmaceutical multinationals mainly acquired and merged small- and medium-size regional seed firms, which lost market share over time (Kalaitzandonakes et al. 2010). Both independent market leaders (e.g., Pioneer, DeKalb) and smaller regional and local seed firms maintained their market positions despite the significant capital resources of the multinational entrants.

At that time, only a few large seed firms maintained extensive breeding efforts and developed proprietary varieties. A few foundation seed firms and some universities also developed and broadly licensed proprietary varieties to a large number of small regional and local seed firms. In turn, these regional seed firms scaled up and distributed a small number of licensed varieties within limited geographic regions and remained competitive through superior local market knowledge and by avoiding the excessive inventory costs that frequently hampered national seed firms (Kalaitzandonakes et al. 2010).

By the early 1990s, many of the multinational firms that led the M&A activity in the previous two decades had divested their seed assets and exited the industry. A handful of multinationals with significant investments in biotechnology and crop protection, however, maintained or expanded their presence in the US seed industry. Indeed, since the advent of agricultural biotechnology research in the mid-1970s, superior seed genetics (germplasm) were recognized as an essential complementary asset for delivering biotechnology traits. For the commercial introduction of a new biotechnology product to be successful, the intellectual property, the biotechnology know-how, and the seed germplasm base had to be coordinated. This need for coordination led to a wave of strategic vertical M&As that changed the structure of the seed, biotechnology, and crop protection industries in the late 1990s.

Strategies to vertically integrate seed and biotechnology assets were as old as the agricultural biotechnology industry itself. Early biotechnology startups, like Agrigenetics, began to acquire regional seed firms in 1975 in order to finance biotechnology research and deliver products to the market. Other leading biotechnology startups (e.g., Celgene, Biotechnica International, and Mycogen) had similar strategies and acquired a number of small- and medium-size seed firms in the 1980s and 1990s (e.g., Kalaitzandonakes 1997; Kalaitzandonakes and Bjornson 1997). It was not, however, until Monsanto and DuPont began their acquisitions that the structure of the seed industry changed. They acquired the two largest independent seed firms, DeKalb and Pioneer, respectively, and kicked off a round of M&As that vertically integrated the biotechnology and seed industries. Dow, Syngenta, Aventis, and AgrEvo (later merged into Bayer) all entered into a number of M&As of seed firms in the last 15 years.

The Impacts of Structural Change on the Global Input Sector

The M&As that drove the restructuring of the USA and global seed industry in the 1990s and the 2000s were vertical in nature and sought to accelerate the commercialization of biotechnology innovations in agriculture. Because all of the multinational biotechnology firms that led the M&As in the seed industry also had significant presence in the crop protection industry, a close integration of these three industries occurred during this time. With the benefit of historical perspective and a number of published studies, we now have a better understanding of the impacts these structural changes had on innovation, new product development, and the competitiveness of agricultural producers.

First, it is now clear that an R&D-minded, vertically integrated industry emerged from the restructuring. Annual spending in the research and development of new biotechnology traits and seed germplasm grew from just over $1 billion in 2000 to more than $4.4 billion in 2015 (Fig. 1). For comparison, the global seed industry was spending less than $300 million on R&D prior to 1996. Indeed, R&D investment in biotechnology traits and seed germplasm development outpaced investment in the development of crop protection products, but both types of R&D investment increased in the last 15 years. In particular, R&D spending for crop protection products increased from almost $1.9 billion in 2000 to $3.3 billion in 2015 (Fig. 1).

Second, the increased R&D spending in the biotechnology and seed industries has generally translated into greater product variety and choice for agricultural producers. For instance, the number of hybrids and varieties sold (Brookes and Barfoot 2015) in the US corn and soybean seed markets more than doubled over the last 15 years (e.g., Magnier et al. 2010). Similarly, a large number of novel biotechnology traits conferring insect resistance, herbicide tolerance, and other useful traits to corn, soybeans, cotton, rapeseed, and other crops were introduced and broadly adopted by agricultural producers in 28 countries over the same period (James 2015).

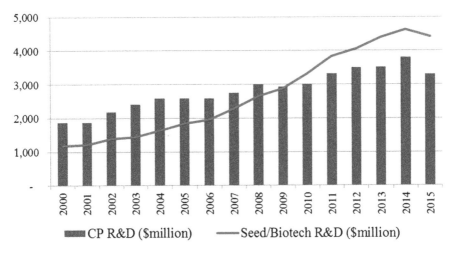

Fig. 1 R&D spending on crop protection, seeds, and biotechnology traits, 2000–2015 (Source: Company data, Phillips McDougal, GfK, Author calculations)

Third, the new seed genetics and biotechnology traits developed through the increased R&D spending in the biotechnology and seed industries led to improved agricultural productivity and farmer profitability (e.g., Qaim 2009; Carpenter and Gianessi 2010; Klümper and Qaim 2014). Economists have estimated the annual economic benefits from new biotechnology traits and seed genetics that were commercialized during this period to be in billions of dollars, with the largest share going to agricultural producers (Falck-Zepeda et al. 2000; Konduru et al. 2008; Alston et al. 2014; Brookes and Barfoot 2015).

Recent Structural Changes in the Crop Protection, Biotechnology, and Seed Industries and their Causes

Successful commercialization of biotechnology innovations as well as improved economics in the global agricultural economy drove the growth of the biotechnology, seed, and crop protection industries in the last 15 years. The global sales of the vertically integrated biotechnology and seed industry grew by $20 billion during this period, from less than $17 billion in 2000 to more than $37 billion in 2015. More than 90% of the sales growth came from the commercialization of novel biotechnology traits. Sales of crop protection products also increased, though at a slower rate – from $28 billion in 2000 to an estimated $51 billion in 2015 (Fig. 2).

During this period of strong growth, however, the integrated biotechnology, seed, and crop protection industries faced some unique challenges and opportunities. On the one hand, a worsening regulatory environment for crop protection and new biotechnology products added costs and delays to R&D, while increased pest

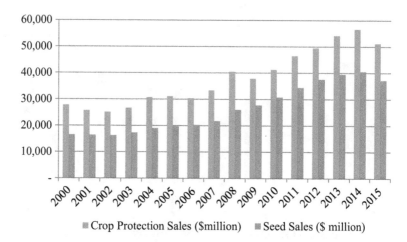

Fig. 2 Global crop protection, biotechnology, and seed sales, 2000–2015 (Source: Data from Phillips McDougal, GfK, and companies; author calculations)

resistance hastened the depreciation rate of the existing crop protection products and biotechnology traits. On the other hand, the emergence of fundamental new discoveries and technical developments (e.g., gene editing and digital agriculture tools) enabled expanded innovation and accelerated new product development in biotechnology, seeds, and crop protection. These challenges and opportunities have shaped the future business model of these industries and have kicked off another round of structural change. As we discuss below, the recent M&A announcements among the Big Six should be understood as part of this latest round of restructuring and consolidation.

A Worsening Regulatory Environment and New Product Development

In recent years, regulatory requirements for crop protection products have become increasingly more stringent, with added demands on environmental, nontarget, and toxicological product profiles. As a result, crop protection firms have had to spend more money and time in their search for new active ingredients that provide improved efficacy and selectivity while at the same time meeting more stringent regulatory requirements. In practice, this has meant screening more molecules in order to find a marketable new active ingredient; carrying out more toxicology, safety, and environmental chemistry tests, both in the greenhouse and in the field; and submitting more voluminous dossiers for regulatory approval and registration. In turn, the average R&D costs for bringing a new crop protection product to the market have increased by more than 50% in the last 15 years – from $181 million in 2000 to $287 million in 2010–2014. This is, in large part, due to the tripling of

Table 1 Average R&D spending for new crop protection product, $ million

	1995	2000	2005–2008	2010–2014
Research	72	94	85	107
Development	65	76	146	147
Registration	13	11	25	33
Total costs	150	181	256	287

Source: Phillips McDougall (2016)

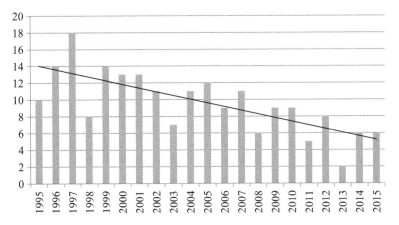

Fig. 3 New product introductions for crop protection, 2000–2015 (Source: Phillips McDougal, various years)

development costs associated with an increased number of field trials and safety assessments and the more than doubling of registration costs (Table 1). The time required to get a new crop protection product approved and on the market has also increased – from 8 to more than 11 years.

Because of the higher average R&D costs, and despite a significant increase in the total R&D spending, the number of new product introductions, with new active ingredients, continued to decline in the crop protection industry over the 2000–2015 period (Fig. 3).

Increasingly stringent regulations, especially in the EU, have also pushed firms to discontinue the sale of a large number of existing crop protection products as reregistration could not be achieved. The combination of deregistration of existing chemistries and the slowdown in new product introductions has left the crop protection industry with a smaller product portfolio and a smaller cohort of proprietary, patent-protected products. In 2015, more than 60% of the crop protection market was composed of generics, up from 36% a decade earlier (Table 2). As such, over the last 15 years, the global market for crop protection products has experienced significant competitive price pressure.

Increased regulatory costs and delays have also been experienced in the development of new biotechnology traits. Regulatory costs for the approval of a new biotechnology event in the mid-2000 were estimated to be $7.5–$15 million

Table 2 Share of proprietary and generic crop protection products

Chemistry/AI	1995	2005	2015
Proprietary	34.9%	29.9%	19.5%
Proprietary off patent	34.9%	34.1%	19.6%
Generic	30.2%	36.0%	60.9%
	100.0%	100.0%	100.0%

Source: Philips and McDougal, various issues

(Kalaitzandonakes et al. 2007). Preliminary estimates of regulatory costs for the approval of new biotechnology events during the 2014–2015 period suggest that such costs have almost doubled (author unpublished data and estimates). Similarly, the amount of time for the regulatory review and approval of new biotechnology events has increased in almost every jurisdiction. For the moment, regulatory cost increases and delays have not visibly affected the rate of submissions of new biotechnology events, which has remained constant during the last 10 years (though it has declined since the previous decade).[2] Some studies have estimated that regulatory delays alone can substantially diminish the economic value of new biotechnology traits (e.g., Kalaitzandonakes et al. 2015). It is therefore possible that in the absence of higher regulatory costs and delays, the rate of new biotechnology trait introductions could have been higher than the one realized.

Pest Resistance Buildup and New Product Development

The biotechnology and crop protection industries have also faced worsening pest resistance[3] to many of their products over the last 15 years. Across the globe, an increasing number of insect pests, weeds, and pathogens have been reported as demonstrating resistance to various chemistries (Fig. 4).

Pest resistance to commonly used pesticides is not a new issue. Early reports of resistant insects and weeds both date from the early twentieth century (Retzinger and Mallory-Smith 1997; Sparks and Nauen 2015). What does seem to be new, though, is the number of resistant species and the rate at which newly resistant species are appearing, particularly among weeds and pathogens. A number of factors contribute to the development of resistance, including the reproductive biology and ecology of the pest and the frequency and intensity of pesticide application (Whalon et al. 2008). Resistance is most closely associated with the intensive and exclusive use of one pesticide or a small group of pesticides with the same or similar modes

---

[2] The estimated rate of submission of new biotechnology events is based on data from USDA APHIS.

[3] Pest resistance is defined as a "genetically based decrease in susceptibility to a pesticide" (Tabashnik et al. 2014).

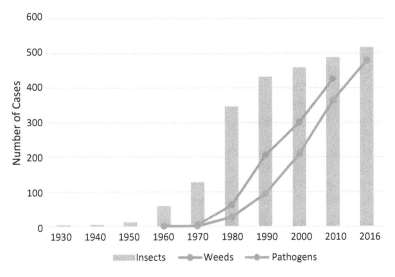

Fig. 4 Pest resistance buildup over time (Source: Data from FRAC, APR database, and Weedscience.org; Author calculations)

of action. Such a pattern of use places pest populations under extreme, focused selection pressure that greatly increases the probability of resistance (Powles 2008).

Global adoption of insect-resistant (IR) and herbicide-tolerant (HT) biotechnology crop varieties, along with sustained use of the herbicides associated with HT crops, mainly glyphosate, has also placed significant selective pressure on many pests, resulting in increasing pesticide resistance. Worsening resistance to glyphosate has been documented in various studies (e.g., Tabashnik et al. 2014; Heap 2015). Insect resistance to biotech IR crops has also been documented in a few occasions. In 2005, one species of insect pests of cotton or corn had populations reported to be sufficiently resistant to a Bt protein so as to significantly reduce its effectiveness in pest control. In 2012, it was reported that five pest species had developed significant resistance to four different Bt toxins (Tabashnik et al. 2013).[4]

The reduced efficacy of existing biotechnology traits and chemistries in the face of increased pest resistance limits the size of the effective product portfolio and the potential income stream of the biotechnology and crop protection industries. In response, these industries sought to slow down pest resistance to existing products and to develop new ones with novel modes of action. The crop protection industry has faced the most significant challenges and has made the biggest adjustments. In the last 15 years, firms in the crop protection industry, especially those who spend

---

[4] Insect resistance is managed by two main strategies: Newer biotechnology cultivars have groups of multiple Bt traits, known as pyramids, among which cross-resistance is rare, making it highly unlikely that pest species will develop resistance to all members of the pyramid. Farmers also plant refuges of non-Bt crops that will harbor populations of susceptible pests, diluting the genetic influence of resistant individuals in future generations. Natural refuges of non-Bt plants other than the target crop can also serve this function but are generally less effective (Jin et al. 2015).

significant sums on R&D,[5] progressively directed more resources toward the development of:

- New product formulations that combine multiple existing chemistries in order to improve product efficacy and protect from pest resistance buildup through the use of multiple modes of action.
- New seed treatments in order to improve delivery of an effective bundle of multiple crop protection products, applied at low rates and with improved application convenience.
- New biologic products[6] in order to reduce the regulatory burden of bringing new products to the market and develop new modes of action. Particular attention has been paid to the development of biologicals that can be used in combination with synthetics, especially in seed treatments.

R&D Portfolio Changes

A number of firm strategies have been put to work in order to enable the above portfolio and R&D adjustments in the crop protection, seed, and biotechnology industries. More specifically:

First, a large number of licensing and marketing agreements as well as strategic research collaborations were put in place across the whole crop protection industry in order to allow the broad use of available chemistries in proprietary formulations and in seed treatments. For instance, determining which foliar pesticides may be used as seed treatments requires significant R&D effort. As such, Dow AgroSciences and Syngenta established a long-term agreement so that Dow's active ingredients could be screened by Syngenta for use in new seed treatments. Similarly, Monsanto came into the seed treatment business in 2011 through collaborations with some 25 firms which provided access to synthetic active ingredients and biologicals.

Second, significant R&D effort was expended in order to expand the market scope and efficiency of seed treatments. Technical advances from such R&D efforts include:

- New product formulations with expanded functionality (e.g., moving from a single fungicide application for early-season seed protection to the use of multiple active ingredients that provide insect, disease, and nematode protection and can stimulate growth for up to 45 days)

---

[5] It is important to note that Syngenta, Bayer, BASF, Dow, and DuPont represent almost 80% of the total annual R&D budget and the bulk of spending in the discovery of new active ingredients in the crop protection industry.

[6] Biologics are crop protection products based on microorganisms, biochemicals produced from biological sources, microbials, and other similar sources.

- The ability to combine biologicals and synthetics in seed treatments (e.g., Bayer's initial use of the Votivo biological seed treatment that disrupts nematode feeding along with the synthetic Poncho, in 2011)
- Various improvements in the use of spray and other application equipment (e.g., improvements in the flow of seeds through treater equipment, flow through standard grower planters, etc.)
- The ability to apply overtreatments at a retailer location or at the farm in order to enhance the scope of seed treatments according to local needs
- The development of polymers and coatings that improve product effectiveness and usability

Based on such adjustments in the R&D portfolio of key firms, particularly the Big Six, sales of seed treatments have grown fast. The market was valued at $2.65 billion in 2011, $3.6 billion in 2013, and between $4 and $5.6 billion in 2016. Bayer, Syngenta, Monsanto, and BASF are the most significant suppliers with some 80% share of the seed treatment market.

Third, a large number of research strategic alliances have been put in place between the Big Six and a number of startups and other firms that specialize in the development of biologicals in order to accelerate innovation in this area (Table 3).

Fourth, a number of specialists and startups with R&D in biologicals have been acquired, mostly by the Big Six, and their research assets have been internalized and integrated into the firms' R&D portfolios (Table 4). For instance, through the acquisition of specialist Backer Underwood for $1 billion, BASF formed the core of its biologicals unit in 2012. Accelerated product development has led to increased sales in biologicals in recent years. As a category, biologicals were valued at $2.25 billion in 2015 and are projected to grow to $4.5 billion by 2023.

Table 3 Selected agreements among firms with R&D in biologicals

Year	Firm 1	Firm 2	Type of agreement
2010	Bayer	Heads UP Plant	Research agreement – Seedling
2011	FMC	Chr. Hansen Biologicals	Commercialization agreement
2011	Bayer	Koppert biological	Commercialization agreement
2011	Syngenta	Pasteuria	Research agreement
2013	Syngenta	Isagro	Commercialization agreement
2013	Monsanto	Novozymes	Joint venture – Research
2013	Monsanto	SGI	Research agreement
2014	Syngenta	Stockton	Distribution agreement
2014	Monsanto	Preceres	Joint venture – Research agreement
2014	Syngenta	AgBiome	Research agreement, investment
2015	Dow	Radiant genomics	Research agreement
2015	Dow	Synthace	Research agreement
2016	Monsanto	Second genome	Research agreement
2016	Dow	TeselaGen	Research agreement

Source: Author

Table 4 Selected M&As of firms with R&D in biologicals

Year	Firm 1	Firm 2	Type of agreement
2009	Bayer	AgroGreen	Acquisition of assets
2011	Syngenta	Marrone bio innovations	Equity investment
2012	Syngenta	Pasteuria	Acquisition
2012	Syngenta	DevGen	Acquisition
2012	BASF	Becker underwood	Acquisition
2012	Bayer	AgraQuest	Acquisition
2013	Bayer	Prophyta	Acquisition
2013	FMC	Center for Agr and Env sol	Acquisition
2013	Monsanto	Agradis	Acquisition
2013	Monsanto	Rosetta green	Acquisition
2014	Bayer	Biagro	Acquisition
2014	Bayer	Belchim crop protection	Acquisition
2014	Monsanto	Preceres	Firm establishment
2015	DuPont	Taxon biosciences	Acquisition

Source: Author

Discoveries and New Market Opportunities

In addition to making investments in response to regulatory and pest resistance challenges, the Big Six (and others) has also made large R&D investments in areas of opportunity. Fundamental innovations, such as digital agriculture and genome editing, have created such opportunities.

Precision agriculture (PA) technologies, first commercialized in the 1990s, are widely regarded as having the potential to make farming much more efficient and productive. With PA, producers have the ability to manage crop inputs on a fine scale instead of treating each field, or their entire holding, as one homogeneous unit. By tailoring the use of inputs to within-field variation, precision agriculture can minimize waste, and thus costs, as well as increase overall yields, thereby enhancing farm profitability while also granting environmental benefits. More recent developments include on-the-go monitors; stationary plant canopy, soil, and atmospheric sensors; and remote imaging sensors carried by drones, aircraft, and satellites that provide additional information inputs for more efficient scouting and even more targeted management.

This increasing number of sensors has multiplied the volume and variety of data available about each agricultural field, and their increasing sophistication speeds the movement of data from collection to analysis to use. Large datasets covering multiple years and a wide geographical area enable scientists to uncover more subtle relationships among variables with a higher degree of confidence. Exploiting "big data" capabilities means that agronomic input performance can be optimized by matching genetics with local growing environments and farm practices.

Progress in hardware, software, analytics, and data provides producers with continually improving ways to visualize and use agricultural data in ways that directly enhance their management decision making. For instance, Internet connectivity, cloud storage, a variety of mobile devices, and other communications capabilities can tie together sensors, variable rate implements, and computing assets to optimize farm management.

Because PA, big data, and digital agriculture have significant synergies with input performance research, biotechnology, seed, and crop protection firms and especially the "Big Five" (the Big Six minus BASF) have made large investments, both internally and through strategic alliances and acquisitions, in this area. DuPont and Monsanto have the most advanced positions.

DuPont (through its Pioneer subsidiary) has developed its Encirca platform – a suite of decision tools that combine soil mapping, local weather, various crop models, and other data that seek to optimize the choice of cultivar as well as seeding populations and seeding rates; create planting prescriptions; track crop performance; manage phosphorous, potassium, and other nutrients; and make real-time adjustments as weather and growing conditions change. DuPont acquired the firm MapShots, a software development company with crop management planning tools and GIS/PA functionality, to add to its digital agriculture platform.

Monsanto has also made significant investments starting with its Integrated Farming System (IFS) program in 2010 which provided field- and zone-level decision support to growers on seed genetics and agronomic management. Through aggressive internal research expansion and several acquisitions, Monsanto has expanded its PA/digital agriculture platform significantly in recent years adding hardware, software, data, and analytics capabilities. It acquired Precision Planting for more than $200 million in 2012, Climate Corp for $930 million in 2013, the soil analysis specialist Solum in 2013, and startup 640 Labs in 2014; the firm has also made a number of investments in other startups.

Syngenta, Bayer, and others have also made acquisitions and investments in a number of digital agriculture specialists in the last several years. For instance, since 2012, Syngenta has made investments in digital agriculture, robotics, and satellite imagery startups including the firms S4, Phytech, Blue River Tech, Planet, and Agworld Pty. Bayer has similarly made investments in Zoner, proPlant, and Agrar.

The Emerging R&D and Business Model of the Agricultural Input Industry

From the description of the recent firm strategies above, it should be clear that several multinational firms in the agricultural input industry have secured a significant presence in the crop protection, biotechnology, and seed industries and have adopted an R&D and business model which brings together multiple product platforms (biologicals, synthetics, germplasm, biotechnology traits, data and analytics, etc.) in order to produce technology bundles that can maximize yields and cost efficiencies in crop production. Multiple chemistries and biologicals can be combined by the

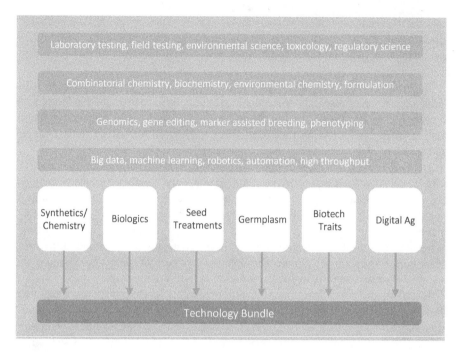

Fig. 5 The integrated technology platform (ITP) R&D model

manufacturer or the distributor in a seed treatment to protect from insects, nematodes, and other pests while enhancing fertility and nutrient availability. Growers or distributors can further "customize" seed defenses through localized overtreatments appropriate to local environments. These seed treatments can be combined with superior genetics that have been developed for native resistance to other pathogens or modified with biotechnology traits that can assist with limited moisture, insect resistance, and weed control through selected herbicide tolerance. Digital agriculture and precision farming can ensure compatibility with soil and the larger environment and can inform the optimal variety choice and seed populations. In effect, this expansive R&D business model calls for the integrated use of multiple vertical technology platforms in the development of technology bundles with maximum yield and cost-efficiency potential (Fig. 5).

Synergies are derived by coordinating the development of technology bundles rather than individual technologies alone. The model therefore calls for maximizing the collective performance of the various technology platforms at minimum development and implementation costs. Synergies may also be possible in the various capabilities and knowledge domains that are needed for the practical implementation of the various technology platforms (e.g., genomics, genome editing, marker-assisted breeding, biochemistry, combinatorial chemistry, robotics, automation, artificial intelligence and machine learning, laboratory and field testing, regulatory science, etc.). These capabilities may use common tools and may be employed across technology platforms.

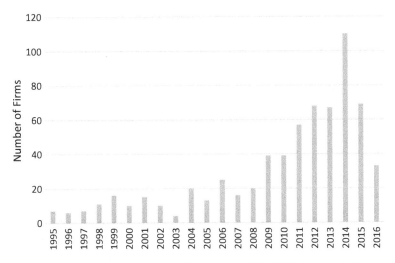

Fig. 6 Entry of VC funded firms in the agrifood sector, 1995–2016 (Source: Author data and calculations)

The success of this R&D and business model depends on its ability to deliver input innovation with maximum performance in the field through superior bundles but also through its efficiency and cost effectiveness in delivering more input innovation per R&D dollar spent. Given the increasing technology performance transparency it promotes at the field and farm level through its digital agriculture and PA tools, it is a maximum performance in a grower's field that will drive economic value and competitive position for the technology suppliers that have adopted it.

Innovation in the Agricultural Input Industry and Firm Entry

While key multinationals have led the development and implementation of the integrated technology platform (ITP) model described above, a large number of other firms have embraced its possibilities. Indeed, M&As and corporate investments in biotechnology, biologics, digital agriculture, and other startups have prompted the interest of entrepreneurs as well as of venture capitalists, private equity firms, and other investors. As a result, there has been a significant uptick in new firm creation and firm entry since 2009. In 2014, when the largest number of new firms entered the agrifood sector, there were more than 110 startups that received funding from institutional investors; most of them specialized in digital agriculture, biotechnology, and biologicals (Fig. 6).

It is expected that this large number of specialists will support the development of the ITP model described above. Some might contribute as parts of research and product development networks through contracts or strategic alliances. Others might be acquired and added to the core capacity of larger entities. Yet others might grow to become independent competitors in the development of product bundles or bundle components. Still others might fail altogether. Whatever their fate, the large population of new entrants suggests more innovation should be expected in the agricultural input industries in the years to come.

R&D Investment and the Influence of the Agricultural Commodity Cycle

The heightened firm entry as well as the increased R&D investments and associated portfolio adjustments made by incumbents in the crop protection, biotechnology, and seed industries in the last 15 years have been enabled by an unprecedented growth in global crop agriculture – a golden era of sorts. For instance, the global farm-level value of corn, soybeans, cotton, and rapeseed grew by more than 300% within just over 10 years – from $116 billion in 2000/2001 to almost $490 billion in 2012/2013. Crop yields, crop acreage, crop supplies, as well as crop prices all grew as the increase in demand for agricultural commodities outpaced supply expansion (Fig. 7).

This increased farm revenue spurred demand for yield-increasing inputs and accelerated the adoption of biotech crops and the use of crop protection products. As such, the revenue of the crop protection, biotechnology, and seed industries grew in parallel. For instance, as Fig. 8 illustrates, global spending on crop protection products, biotechnology traits, and seeds by corn, soybean, cotton, and canola/rapeseed producers grew from an estimated $17 billion in 2000 to $49 billion in 2014 – almost 200%. Given that these four crops account for 70% of global farmer spending

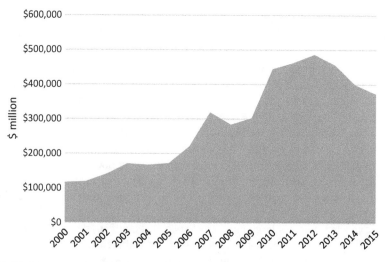

Fig. 7 World crop receipts for corn, soybeans, cotton, and canola, 2000–2015 (Source: USDA data, Author Calculations)

in seeds and just over 30% in crop protection products, they give an accurate depiction of the close link between farm revenue and spending in these inputs.

Crop revenues, however, peaked in 2012/2013 and have since declined by almost 25%, though they still remain well above historical levels. Spending on crop protection, biotechnology, and seeds has also followed the downward trend, though with a short lag. In turn, following the downward trend in industry sales, R&D spending in crop protection, biotechnology, and seeds declined in 2015 for the first time in the last 15 years (see Fig. 8).

Given the close link between crop sales, input sales, and R&D spending in the biotechnology, seed, and crop protection industries, understanding the direction and pace of agricultural commodity cycles becomes essential. Based on our estimates and forecasts, global sales of seeds and crop protection products likely declined slightly in 2016 and will likely decline somewhat in 2017 before they begin to recover in 2018, reaching levels similar to those of 2014 5 years later (Fig. 9). This downturn in revenue confronts the expansive vision of the ITP model in the biotechnology, seed, and crop protection industries. Growing revenue and R&D spending are required to finance the ITP model; in the face of continuing market weakness, consolidation appears to have become a primary strategy among the top firms in the agricultural input sector that are pursuing this innovation model.

Given the above considerations, the underlying economics of the global agricultural sector and the fate of the proposed M&As (as well as other factors) should be expected to shape the future R&D model of the biotechnology, seed, and crop protection industries, at least in the short run. Since structural changes are still ongoing and since there are policy uncertainties (e.g., the decisions of antitrust authorities) and market uncertainties (which influence the direction and pace of the commodity cycle, etc.), we might explore possible scenarios of structural futures in the agricul-

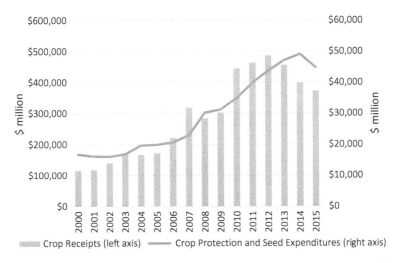

Fig. 8 Receipts and expenditures in crop protection and seeds for selected key crops (Source: Author calculations)

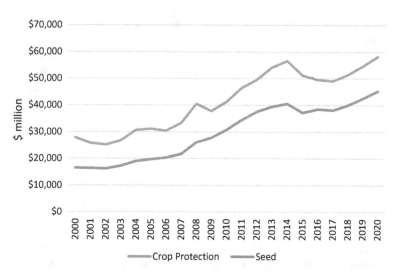

Fig. 9 Global crop protection and seed sales: history and forecasts (Source: Author calculations and forecasts; underlying crop revenue forecasts WAEES and FAPRI, 2017)

tural input industry and draw conclusions about their potential impacts on the firm strategies, R&D spending, industry structure (e.g., entry, M&As, strategic alliances), innovation, and the competitiveness of growers.

Industry Scenarios of Structural Change and Innovation

Future scenarios can be constructed by envisioning discrete potential outcomes in the decisions of the antitrust authorities (they allow the proposed M&As or not) and in the direction of the commodity cycle (return to growth or worsening recession).[7] Such representative potential futures can be illustrated in a 2X2 matrix as in Table 5, and their conditioning effects can be examined in some detail based on the analysis presented above.

---

[7] There are of course other external factors of consequence. However, the agricultural commodity cycle and the fate of the pending M&As are the most impactful in the short run, so we focus on them for our scenario analysis.

Table 5 Scenario analysis through key drivers

	Agricultural growth	Agricultural recession
M&As allowed	SCENARIO 1	SCENARIO 2
M&As not allowed	SCENARIO 3	SCENARIO 4

Scenario 1: Proposed M&As are Allowed and the Agricultural Economy Grows

A world where the agricultural economy recovers from its current levels and grows again would spur producer spending in agricultural inputs and hence growth in the revenue base of the biotechnology, seed, and crop protection industries. Increased revenue in these industries would support higher R&D spending. A world where the proposed M&As are allowed by antitrust authorities would also support higher R&D spending, as the increased scale and scope of the consolidated firms would enable the pursuit of the more expansive ITP model. As a result, R&D would increase among key players and overall (Table 6).

Pursuit of the ITP model would call for more research alliances among integrated firms, large specialists, and various startups as numerous technical capabilities and solutions would need to be brought to bear in the development of new technology bundles. Entry of new firms would likely increase from current levels as the potential for R&D outsourcing to startups and other specialized firms would expand and M&As of startups would provide opportunities for investor "exits." Increased entry is also supported by the growth in the industry revenue base.

Increased R&D efficiency and spending, a greater number of technology alliances, and increased entry of new firms all imply greater amounts of innovation in crop protection, biotechnology traits, germplasm, digital agriculture, and other technologies. More input innovation leads to economic gains from higher yields and lower costs in crop production, and agricultural producers can capture a share of

Table 6 Summary of impacts in scenario analysis

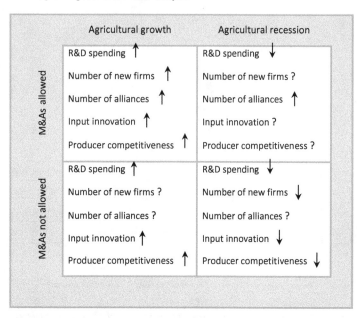

these economic gains. Producers would therefore gain in competitiveness and profitability under this scenario.[8]

Scenario 2: Proposed M&As are Allowed and the Agricultural Economy Contracts

A world where the agricultural economy continues to contract from its current levels would lead to reductions in agricultural input spending and hence further contraction in the revenue of the biotechnology, seed, and crop protection industries. Lower revenues in these industries would lead to reduced R&D spending. A world where the proposed M&As are allowed by antitrust authorities, however, would support higher R&D spending at the firm level, as increased scale and scope in the consolidated firms would enable the pursuit of the more expansive ITP model. R&D spending would therefore increase among some firms, but the overall industry R&D spending would likely decline, at least in the short run (Table 6).

---

[8] Producers also benefit from innovation performance transparency in their fields. Yields, costs, and the economic parameters for input innovations produced in the future should be progressively more measurable through the digital agriculture tools which are currently being developed. This increased performance transparency should allow better valuation of benefits and costs for input innovations.

Pursuit of the ITP model by some key firms would encourage more research alliances among integrated firms, large specialists, and various startups as numerous technical capabilities and solutions must be brought to bear in the development of new technology bundles. Whether entry of new firms would increase or decrease from current levels is uncertain. Potential for R&D outsourcing to startups is supported by the ITP model, but M&As of startups would likely become less lucrative as a contraction in the industry revenue base would limit future opportunities for new firms.

While overall R&D spending in the biotechnology, seed, and crop protection industries would decrease, at least in the short run, successful implementation of the ITP model by leading firms could yield efficiency gains in R&D and could lead to greater amounts of input innovation per R&D dollar spent. As a result, the net impact on input innovation across the three industries is uncertain.

Since the direction of input innovation drives the economic gains from higher yields and lower costs in crop production, some of which are captured by agricultural producers, it is uncertain whether producer competitiveness and profitability improves or worsens under this scenario.

Scenario 3: Proposed M&As are not Allowed and the Agricultural Economy Recovers

A world where the agricultural economy recovers from its current levels and grows would spur producer spending in agricultural inputs and growth in the revenue base of the biotechnology, seed, and crop protection industries. Increased revenue in these industries would support higher R&D spending. A world where the proposed M&As are not allowed by antitrust authorities, however, would lead to lower R&D spending as the scale and scope that are currently considered necessary to support of the more expansive ITP model would not be immediately possible. Overall, R&D spending across the biotechnology, seed, and crop protection industries would likely increase from current levels (Table 6).

As firms could choose to scale back parts of ITP model, they could internalize some of the research and development and limit research alliances with other firms. The expanded industry R&D spending, however, could support some alliances as well as M&As of startups and specialists. Whether alliances or entry of new firms would increase or decrease from their current levels is therefore uncertain in this scenario.

Since the overall R&D spending in the biotechnology, seed, and crop protection industries would tend to increase, the level of input innovation would also increase from its current levels. This increase in innovation, however, would likely be less than in scenario 1 since the ITP would not be fully implemented and associated efficiency gains in the R&D process may not be realized. As a result, agricultural producer competitiveness and profitability would improve but at levels lower than those in scenario 1.

Scenario 4: Proposed M&As are not Allowed and the Agricultural Economy Contracts

A further decline in the agricultural economy from its current levels would lead to reductions in agricultural input spending from current levels and hence further contraction in the revenue of the biotechnology, seed, and crop protection industries. Lower revenues in these industries would lead to reduced R&D spending. A world where the proposed M&As are not allowed by antitrust authorities would also lead to lower R&D spending as the scale and scope that are currently considered necessary to support the more expansive ITP model would not be immediately possible and some portions of this R&D model may need to be scaled back. As a result, R&D spending would decrease among key players and overall (Table 6).

Research alliances among integrated firms, large specialists, and various startups could increase in order to reduce R&D expenses or could decrease as some R&D projects would be shelved in cost cutting measures and some parts of the ITP are scaled back. As such, it is unclear whether research alliances under this state of the world would increase or decrease from their current levels. Entry of new firms would decrease from its current level as M&As of startups would become less lucrative, parts of the ITP are scaled back, and a contraction in the industry revenue base would limit future opportunities for new firms.

Declining R&D spending and a potential departure from the full implementation of the ITP, along with reduced entry of new firms in the biotechnology, seed, crop protection, digital agriculture, and related industries, all imply less input innovation. Lower input innovation implies diminished opportunities for associated economic gains. Unrealized gains in competitiveness and profitability from foregone input innovation would leave agricultural producers worse off in the long run.

Summary and Concluding Comments

In this chapter we have described two cycles of structural change in the biotechnology, seed, and crop protection industries. In the late 1990s, biotechnology firms vertically integrated into the seed industry in order to acquire advanced germplasm as a delivery mechanism for biotechnology traits. Many of the firms that led the M&As in the seed industry also owned assets in the crop protection industry. This cycle of consolidation produced an integrated, research-minded sector that spent copiously on R&D over the last 15 years. Of course, not all biotechnology, seed, or crop protection firms spend significant resources in R&D, and not all have a presence in all three industries. There is a large number of specialized firms in each of the biotechnology, seed, and crop protection industries, many of which have limited R&D capacity. Still, the top firms, and certainly the "Big Six," do emphasize R&D and stake their market positions on such investments.

Increased R&D spending in the biotechnology, seed, and crop protection industries over the last 15 years was supported by an unprecedented expansion in the global agricultural economy. In turn, high R&D spending in these industries produced innovations which increased yields and created cost efficiencies in crop production. Key challenges (increasing regulatory costs and delays in the approvals of new crop protection products and biotechnology traits, regulatory restrictions for crop protection product reregistration, and increasing pest resistance to crop protection and biotechnology traits) as well as opportunities (fundamental innovations in digital agriculture, gene editing, and other technology platforms) also confronted these three industries in recent years. Through these challenges and opportunities, firms with large R&D assets in biotechnology, seeds, and crop protection, and especially the Big Five, began to envision and implement a new R&D model – one where multiple pest control and yield-increasing input technologies could be coordinated and integrated into comprehensive input innovation bundles.

In effect, coordination of multiple technology platforms in the development of such innovation bundles could reduce the regulatory burden by focusing on less regulated solutions, when available (e.g., biologics, conventional genetic traits); extend the productive life of existing technologies through pyramiding to slow pest resistance buildup (e.g., multiple chemistries in seed treatments or reinforcing stacked biotechnology traits); choose the best solutions among technologies that could substitute for one another (e.g., chemistries, biologics, or biotechnology traits targeting the same pests); coordinate the development of complementary technologies to maximize their value (e.g., new herbicides and herbicide-tolerant traits); and optimize the efficacy of input technologies through improved field placement, scouting, and integrated management through "big data," advanced analytics, and other digital agricultural technologies.

Coordination of multiple technology platforms to produce innovation bundles could, in principle, make spending in R&D more efficient by leveraging synergistic research skills and assets, reducing duplication in product development, and producing more robust and efficacious technology solutions for agricultural producers. Of course, such an expansive and complex integrated research model, requiring coordination across multiple technical platforms with uncertain outcomes and timelines, is not without risks. If successful, however, this R&D and innovation model could produce more agricultural input innovation per R&D dollar spent.

Investments and market strategies implemented by the "Big Five" and others in the past few years indicate that the ITP model of R&D has been embraced in earnest. Indeed, these key firms have made large investments in the development of seed treatments, biologicals, and digital agricultural technologies, while they have reinforced their positions through increased R&D spending and investments in biotechnology, seeds, and chemistry. They have also sought to consolidate through the recently announced M&As. Presumably the integrated innovation model calls for a much higher level of R&D spending that cannot be currently supported by the existing level of firm sales.

The commodity down cycle which began in 2013 appears to have accelerated the perceived need for consolidation among the Big Five as the organic revenue growth necessary to finance the expanding R&D model was not expected, due to the declining agricultural commodity prices and input demand. As such, the recently announced M&As among the Big Five should be understood as one more step toward the implementation of the ITP model pursued in the biotechnology, seed, and crop protection industries.

To the extent that coordination and integration across the different technology platforms as in Fig. 5 can produce more innovation per R&D dollar spent, the ITP model will be implemented irrespective of external conditions. Still, key external factors, such as the antitrust allowances of the proposed M&As and the duration of the ongoing agricultural commodity cycle, can have significant conditioning effects in the short term. These effects were examined through scenario analysis. What the scenario analysis presented above clarifies is that policy choices matter and that industry structure and innovation will continue to be inextricably tied to each other in the agricultural input sector.

References

Alston, J.M., N. Kalaitzandonakes, and J. Kruse. 2014. The Size and Distribution of the Benefits from the Adoption of Biotech Soybean Varieties. In *Handbook on Agriculture, Biotechnology, and Development*, ed. S.J. Smyth, P.W.B. Phillips, and D. Castle, 728–751. Cheltenham: Edward Elgar.

Bray, C. 2016a. Syngenta Warns of Delay in Takeover by ChemChina, 25 October 2016. from https://www.nytimes.com/2016/10/26/business/dealbook/syngenta-chemchina-delay.html?_r=0

———. 2016b. U.S. Regulator Signs Off on ChemChina-Syngenta Deal. The New York Times, 22 August 2016. from https://www.nytimes.com/2016/08/23/business/dealbook/us-china-chemchina-syngenta-merger.html

Brookes, G., and P. Barfoot. 2015. Global Income and Production Impacts of Using GM Crop Technology 1996–2013. *GM Crops and Food* 6 (1): 13–46. https://doi.org/10.1080/2164569 8.2015.1022310.

Carpenter, J.E., and L.P. Gianessi. 2010. Economic Impact of Glyphosate-Resistant Weeds. In *Glyphosate Resistance in Crops and Weeds : History, Development, and Management*, ed. V.K. Nandula, 297–312. Hoboken: John Wiley & Sons.

Falck-Zepeda, J.B., G. Traxler, and R.G. Nelson. 2000. Surplus Distribution from the Introduction of a Biotechnology Innovation. *American Journal of Agricultural Economics* 82 (2): 360–369.

Gara, A. 2015. *Monsanto Drops $46.5b Bid for Syngenta, Paving Way for Stock Buyback Amid Market Rout*. Forbes: 26 August 2015: from https://www.forbes.com/sites/antoinegara/2015/08/26/monsanto-drops-46-5-billion-offer-for-syngenta-stock-buyback-double-earnings-market-rout/#703b2bdd5a1a

Harwell, D. 2015. Dow and DuPont, Two of America's Oldest Giants, to Merge in Jaw-Dropping Megadeal. The Washington Post, 11 December 2015. from https://www.washingtonpost.com/news/business/wp/2015/12/11/dow-and-dupont-two-of-americas-oldest-giants-to-merge-in-job-dropping-megadeal/?utm_term=.09d6fe021e31

———. 2016. Bayer and Monsanto to Merge in Mega-Deal That Could Reshape World's Food Supply. *The Washington Post*, 14 September 2016. from https://www.washingtonpost.com/news/business/wp/2016/09/14/bayer-and-monsanto-merge-in-mega-deal-aimed-at-domi-worlds-food-supply/?utm_term=.b9545baa6cf9

Heap, I. 2015. *The International Survey of Herbicide Resistant Weeds*. Retrieved 27 January 2015, from http://www.weedscience.com/summary/home.aspx

James, C. 2015. *Global Status of Commercialized Biotech/GM Crops: 2015*. Ithaca, NY, ISAAA. Available at http://www.isaaa.org/purchasepublications/itemdescription.asp?ItemTyp e=BRIEFS&Control=IB051-2015. ISAAA Brief No. 51.

Jin, L., H. Zhang, Y. Lu, Y. Yang, K. Wu, B.E. Tabashnik, and Y. Wu. 2015. Large-Scale Test of the Natural Refuge Strategy for Delaying Insect Resistance to Transgenic Bt Crops. *Nature Biotechnology* 33 (2): 169–174. https://doi.org/10.1038/nbt.3100.

Kalaitzandonakes, N. 1997. Mycogen: Building a Seed Company for the Twenty-First Century. *Review of Agricultural Economics* 19 (2): 453–462.

Kalaitzandonakes, N., J.M. Alston, and K.J. Bradford. 2007. Compliance Costs for Regulatory Approval of New Biotech Crops. *Nature Biotechnology* 25 (5): 509–511.

Kalaitzandonakes, N., and B. Bjornson. 1997. Vertical and Horizontal Coordination in the Agro-Biotechnology Industry: Evidence and Implications. *Journal of Agricultural and Applied Economics* 29 (1): 129–139.

Kalaitzandonakes, N., D.J. Miller, and A. Magnier. 2010. A Worrisome Crop? Is There Market Power in the US Seed Industry? *Regulation* 33 (4): 20–26.

Kalaitzandonakes, N., K.A. Zahringer, and J. Kruse. 2015. The Economic Impacts of Regulatory Delays on Trade and Innovation. *Journal of World Trade* 49 (6): 1011–1046.

Klümper, W., and M. Qaim. 2014. A Meta-Analysis of the Impacts of Genetically Modified Crops. *PLoS One* 9 (11): e111629. https://doi.org/10.1371/journal.pone.0111629.

Konduru, S., J. Kruse, and N. Kalaitzandonakes. 2008. The Global Economic Impacts of Roundup Ready Soybeans. In *Genetics and Genomics of Soybean*, ed. G. Staceyp, vol. 2, 375–395. New York: Springer.

Kosman, J. 2017. DuPont-Dow Merger Faces Stiff EU Resistance. New York Post, 15 January 2017. from http://nypost.com/2017/01/15/dupont-dow-merger-faces-stiff-eu-resistance/

Magnier, A., N. Kalaitzandonakes, and D.J. Miller. 2010. Product Life Cycles and Innovation in the US Seed Corn Industry. *International Food and Agribusiness. Management Review* 13 (3): 17–36.

McDougall, Phillips. 2016. Agriservice Report: Products Section, 2015 Market.

Petroff, A. 2017. *China Gets Green Light for Biggest-Ever Foreign Acquisition*. CNN Money. Retrieved 29 June 2017, from http://money.cnn.com/2017/04/05/investing/syngenta-chem-china-takeover-acquisition/index.html

Powles, S.B. 2008. Evolved Glyphosate-Resistant Weeds around the World: Lessons to Be Learnt. *Pest Management Science* 64 (4): 360–365.

Qaim, M. 2009. The Economics of Genetically Modified Crops. *Annuual Review of Resource Economics* 1 (1): 665–694.

Retzinger, E.J., and C. Mallory-Smith. 1997. Classification of Herbicides by Site of Action for Weed Resistance Management Strategies. *Weed Technology* 11 (2): 384–393.

Sparks, T.C., and R. Nauen. 2015. Irac: Mode of Action Classification and Insecticide Resistance Management. *Pesticide Biochemistry and Physiology* 121: 122–128. https://doi.org/10.1016/j.pestbp.2014.11.014.

Sutherland, B. 2015. *Monsanto, Syngenta in Mega-Merger Talks*. FarmOnline National: 4 May 2015: from http://www.farmonline.com.au/story/3378746/monsanto-syngenta-in-mega-merger-talks/

Tabashnik, B.E., T. Brevault, and Y. Carriere. 2013. Insect Resistance to Bt Crops: Lessons from the First Billion Acres. *Nature Biotechnology* 31 (6): 510–521. https://doi.org/10.1038/nbt.2597.

Tabashnik, B.E., D. Mota-Sanchez, M.E. Whalon, R.M. Hollingworth, and Y. Carrière. 2014. Defining Terms for Proactive Management of Resistance to bt Crops and Pesticides. *Journal of Economic Entomology* 107 (2): 496–507. https://doi.org/10.1603/EC13458.

Varinsky, D. 2017. *Trump Could Approve a Giant Merger That's Scaring American Farmers*. Business Insider: 5 February 2017: from http://www.businessinsider.com/bayer-monsanto-merger-trump-farmers-worried-2017-2

Whalon, M.E., D. Mota-Sanchez, and R.M. Hollingworth. 2008. Analysis of Global Pesticide Resistance in Arthropods. In *Global Pesticide Resistance in Arthropods*, ed. M.E. Whalon, D. Mota-Sanchez, and R.M. Hollingworth. Wallingford: CAB International.

Private-Public R&D in the Development of the Canola Industry in Canada

Peter W.B. Phillips

Abstract Canola has emerged as one of the world's largest and most important edible oil crops through a mix of government action, private investment, farmer organization, and industry engagement. For the most part, the key activities have been led by or undertaken in Canada, not traditionally viewed as one of the agrifood innovation powerhouses. In many ways, this case represents the best of adoption theory in practice. Purposeful research partnerships and teams led to innovative product attributes that needed regulatory approval, then farmer acceptance, industry adaptation, and consumer demand. This has involved a nested set of investment and engagement processes that over the past 40 years have variously brought forth new varieties with improved agronomic and nutritional properties, new biotechnology traits, and a range of industrial and pharmaceutical attributes, all while maintaining both a role for producers in the research system and significant competition in the research, seed, marketing, and food processing sectors. Along the way, the industry has had to develop a range of new systems, including industry-managed identity-preserving production and marketing systems and strict segregation structures.

Introduction

Economic theory says that in a world of perfect information and limited market power, individual producers would be able to select new technologies and cultivars from a range of options based on one's individual knowledge of the current and future impacts of the options. In effect, this involves an objective evaluation of the farm-level benefits and costs of each choice. The challenge to the theory is that

P.W.B. Phillips (✉)
University of Saskatchewan, Saskatoon, SK, Canada
e-mail: peter.phillips@usask.ca

© Springer International Publishing AG 2018   101
N. Kalaitzandonakes et al. (eds.), *From Agriscience to Agribusiness*, Innovation,
Technology, and Knowledge Management, https://doi.org/10.1007/978-3-319-67958-7_5

information is far from perfect and the options do not emerge organically but are purposefully constructed and marketed by owners or interested intermediaries. In this context, theory needs to be combined with strategy and practice to understand the complex interplay of a range of imperfectly known objective factors and a dynamic landscape of motivated actors.

Canola, the third most important edible oil crop in the world behind corn and palm, has had an extensive experience of developing, testing, and using a range of adoption strategies and models. It is a globally competitive oilseed crop that has adapted and adopted new technologies and traits to address rapidly differentiating demands. The product has gone through four different technological transformations. In the early 1960s, competitive rapeseed varieties were developed, and the related oilseed industry was created. In the 1970s, the rapeseed stock was entirely replaced by new canola-quality seeds that had better nutritional profiles, albeit initially with measurably lower yields. In the mid-1990s, transgenic, herbicide-tolerant varieties were introduced. Finally, in the past 10–15 years, new oil profile seeds have been introduced for differentiated food and industrial markets. Each new introduction triggered different strategies and different practices. Examining those experiences offers an important addition to the theoretically rich explanation of how farm-level decision makers interact with the industry to select new technologies. This chapter examines those four transformations through the lens of adoption efforts and impacts.

Four Stages of Industrial Development

Each stage of industrial development has generated a step adjustment in the productive capacity of the canola industry (Fig. 1). In the first two decades of development, starting during the Second World War, rapeseed gained a toehold in the Western Canadian agrifood landscape but was largely a novelty crop, with less than a 1% market share. The transformation of rapeseed into canola, by the proactive removal of erucic acid and glucosinolates from the seed and the confirmation of its status as a healthy oil, led to a global expansion of the market. Production in Canada rose to an average of almost 6 million acres annually or about 4.5% of the total available acreage. The advent of transgenic technologies and the development of herbicide-tolerant and hybrid varieties caused an almost tripling of the Canadian production area. Over the past 20 years, the industry has planted on average about 15 million acres or about 11.5% of the available acreage. In the past few years, production has exceeded 20 million tonnes, using about 15% of the available farmland. Most recently, there has been a move to differentiate the types of oilseeds produced, with a range of different industrial and food grade oils being developed and produced under closed-loop contract systems. Some estimate that more than 1 million acres are now planted to differentiated oilseeds. Each of these transformations was facilitated by a different model of marketing and production.

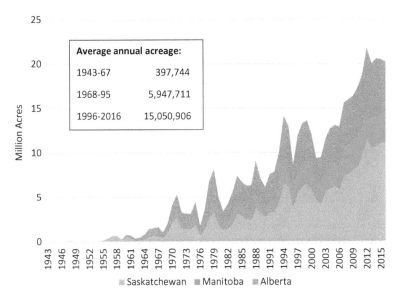

Fig. 1 Canola area planted in Western Canada (Source: Statistics Canada. Table 001–0017—estimated areas, yield, production, average farm price, and total farm value of principal field crops, in imperial units, annual (Accessed: January 6, 2017))

Looking simply at the rate of adoption of new seeds, we observe that use of new varieties usually starts slowly but accelerates rapidly, at times significantly changing the market shares of seed developers. Few private varieties existed as recently as 1985. As the number of new private varieties grew, the market share of private seed companies rose dramatically. The public sector ceased producing commercial varieties in the late 1990s, so that now the entire market is composed of private, proprietary varieties. Production records tell us quite a bit about the adoption process. In the first instance, we can see that from 1960 to 1995, the average number of active varieties rose sharply. In the early days of public breeding, we might see one new variety approved and released every year or so. Now more than 30 new varieties are approved and commercialized by an array of seed companies annually. One result is that both the maximum and minimum market shares per variety have diminished. As the rate of introduction of new varieties rose, the average age and the expected average economic life of the variety declined. Putting these two trends together, one can see that the adoption phase of each individual innovation has shortened significantly, with an expected economic life of about 3 years, down from an average of as much as 14 years in the earlier decades (Table 1).

Moreover, we can observe that the peak market share for each variety is reached much faster for the new varieties than previously. In the 1954–1984 period, the peak market share (20% for *B. napus* and 43% for *B. rapa* varieties) was reached either

Table 1 The evolution of the canola seed industry

Year	Number of active varieties	Weighted average age	Average market share
1960	4	13.9	25.0
1965	6	9.5	16.7
1970	7	6.1	14.3
1975	8	3.4	12.5
1980	8	4.6	12.5
1985	9	2.8	11.1
1990	16	5.2	6.3
1995	48	3.9	2.1
1996	50	3.6	2.0

Source: Phillips and Khachatourian (2001)
Note: the average age is the number of years since introduction for each variety weighted by the market share for that variety in that year.

Table 2 Adoption rates for new varieties

	B. napus		B. rapa	
	Lag between introduction and peak market share(years)	Average maximum market share (%)	Lag between introduction and peak market share (years)	Average maximum market share (%)
1954–1984	3.5	19.9	3.9	43.2
1985–1992	2.5	5.4	3.5	13.1
1993–1995	1.5	1.2	1.4	3.1

Source: Phillips and Khachatourian (2001)

in the third or fourth season after introduction. As innovation accelerated, the average peak market share dropped sharply; by the 1990s the average peak was less than 5%. The drop in the peak market share occurred more rapidly for *B. napus* as the product was subject to earlier and more intensive research effort. At the same time, the average lag between introduction of the variety and its peak market share narrowed to less than 2 years from almost four seasons in the earlier period (Table 2).

The evidence suggests canola has been an innovation-led product, with basic and applied research and development setting the pace for commercial development, which has correspondingly radically shortened the economic and commercial life of each variety, intensifying the adoption process.

1943–1967

Canada historically lacked an indigenous crop that could produce edible oils. While some maize has always been produced in Central Canada, most of that crop was used for feed, necessitating the import of edible oils. In the 1940s, a group of public sector scientists, in collaboration with the oil processing industry, took a few imported crop lines and converted them into viable competitive seeds for cultivation in the Prairie region of Canada. During 1943–1967, research funding came almost exclusively from the public sector, research was undertaken in public labs or universities, and the resulting product was released into the public domain through a network of pedigreed seed growers. New technologies and new varieties were released for use without any restrictions. The first years of rapeseed research were characterized by general research into the agronomics of rapeseed and its properties as an edible oil and animal feed. The small return from this early research (in terms of yield and improved oil and meal content) was dispersed between growers and all other social groups. Producers only captured a small portion of the returns, which limited adoption.

Adoption during this period was rather patchy. Initially a mix of early adopting farmers begged and borrowed seeds to try and then shared their seeds, agronomic experience, and advice through informal farmer networks. Over time the Federal Department of Agriculture developed an extensive network of research and demonstration farms and stations that tested new varieties and technologies; the Universities of Alberta, Saskatchewan, and Manitoba had Agricultural Colleges that contributed research, training, and extension to farmers; and the provinces each had extension services that supported the translation of the information to producers. The grain trade became interested in this crop, but for the most part, it was viewed as a niche crop of interest to a narrow subset of farmers. The lack of ready markets and limited grain handling capacity restricted growth. Farmers responded accordingly, testing and producing on only modest acreages.

The first stage ended auspiciously, with the development of standards for rapeseed oil in 1965 through the Edible Oil Institute. Samples of oil from the then four Western crushers were examined in six refiners' laboratories. Specifications for free fatty acids, moisture and impurities, flash point, refined bleached color, green color in crude oil, refining loss, and phosphatide content were approved and published by the Canadian Government Specification Board (McLeod 1974). The industry looked set to grow.

1968–1994

The late 1960s brought a fundamental change in the development of the sector. The slow but steady development by the public sector of rapeseed as an oil crop had reached a threshold where more investment in both product development and in market structures (e.g., extension, foreign market development) was required, but no single institution, public or private, had the means or incentive to undertake the work alone. The industry faced a true holdup problem, with the benefits of any individual's investments likely being shared with a wide variety of free riders.

Necessity became the mother of invention. The absence of adequate individual incentives or an effective institution to develop the industry further spurred a collective response, culminating in the creation of the Rapeseed Association of Canada (RAC). Established in 1967 to serve as an umbrella organization for the groups that had a stake in the Canadian canola industry, the RAC played an increasingly significant role in the development of the industry over the next two decades. The Rapeseed Association, as a nonprofit organization, was effective in mobilizing a relatively small amount of financial resources from industry and government, which came to leverage and direct a large volume of activity in support of industry development. At the beginning, 70% of the Association's budget came from crushers and exporters through a voluntary $0.50 per tonne levy on rapeseed exports and seed crushed domestically. In conjunction with the Association, the Federal Department of Industry, Trade, and Commerce set up the $1.25 million Rapeseed Utilization Assistance Program, funded by the federal department but administered by the research committee of the Association (McLeod 1974).

The first order of business for the RAC was to develop new varieties with lower levels of erucic acid and glucosinolates. By 1968 researchers in industry and government had bred Oro, the first low erucic acid *B. napus* variety, and in 1971 Span, the first *B. rapa* variety, was released. The timing was fortuitous as in 1970 a team of European scientists released a study that showed that high erucic acid rapeseed oil consumption by young animals caused a short-term fat buildup around the heart and kidney, which appeared to cause long-term muscle lesions of the heart. In response, both Japanese and European buyers signaled uncertainty about continuing to use Canadian rapeseed. The new association was instrumental in resolving the problem. While their financial contribution was small (only about 2.5% vs 80% from government and 17% from industry), the RAC was instrumental in signaling industry and farmer interest to the universities and in targeting efforts on specific research priorities. During the 1967–1973 period, about 95% of the technologies and all of the new varieties came from public labs, and the results were released without restriction to producers.

The Association also took the lead in market development, extension, and public relations, in an effort to more firmly position rapeseed in the market. Given the problems with high erucic acid rapeseed oil identified at the 1970 conference, it was vital for the Canadian industry to adopt as quickly as possible low erucic acid varieties. Due to the extensive efforts of AAFC and the Association, the changeover to low erucic acid varieties was 86% complete by 1973 and 95% complete by 1974 (NRC, 1992:54). Given that the Association did not engage in actual market transactions or handling of the product and did not take a position on the marketing system, it was able to act as a credible voice in the market. Without the efforts of the Association, many believe it would have been highly unlikely that any of the firms or actors in the sector would have been able to put together the necessary package of programs both to push rapeseed research forward at that critical juncture and to lay the groundwork for expanding production and export markets. The market development problems were simply too large.

A small but significant development in this period was the effort by growers to form separate provincial associations to mobilize producers to have a say in the development of the sector. These associations in Saskatchewan in 1969, Manitoba in the late 1960s, and Alberta in the early 1970s started small, with limited funds coming from producer membership fees. Their primary purpose when they started was to focus on extension, agronomy, and policy development, in order to accelerate development of the sector.

A major watershed in the industry came in 1974, when Agriculture Canada registered Tower, the first *B. napus* variety with both low erucic acid and low glucosinolates, but the new varieties yielded about 15% below the earlier cultivars. Although public research continued to work to lower the levels of erucic acid and glucosinolates, the push was to improve yields and extend the effective planting range for canola. While public breeding remained dominant, the private sector began to invest in new breeding technologies.

In 1978, the Rapeseed Association took what may have been the most astute and fundamental step in developing the market for the new product, registering the name "canola" as the registered trademark for rapeseed varieties with low erucic acid (5% or less) and low glucosinolate content (3 milligrams per gram or less). With continuing research through the following 8 years, the levels of erucic acid and glucosinolates continued to drop, so that in 1986, the canola trademark was amended to restrict the designation to rapeseed varieties with less than 2% erucic acid and less than 30 micromoles of glucosinolates per gram (DuPont et al. 1989).

The Rapeseed Association of Canada formally completed its shift to the new product when it changed its name in 1980 to the Canola Council of Canada, acknowledging the development and acceptance of canola varieties. Throughout this period, the Council worked with researchers and marketers to position canola as a premium human oil. The Council funded extensive research into the health impacts of canola, with a successful outcome. By 1984 a number of health studies showed that consumption of canola oil, which was low in saturated fats, provided significant health benefits compared to consumption of palm coconut and corn oils (Gray and Malla 1998). These results, plus longitudinal food safety studies, contributed to the evidence that the US FDA used to grant canola "generally regarded as safe" (GRAS) status in 1986.

With market demand assured, the provincial growers' associations intensified their extension efforts to increase the rate of adoption of the new crop and to steadily improve the quality of the product. In Saskatchewan, for example, the provincial Canola Growers Association began the "Grow with Canola" program, which provided an extensive set of agronomic services, including basic varietal, agronomic, and fertility information and demonstration test plots that were harvested with standard farm equipment. Many participants in the sector credit such programs with the rapid expansion of canola in the Prairies. Without such a rapid take-up, the export market growth would have been severely limited and further investment curtailed.

The institutions of the 1970s worked well for the 1980s but, by increasing market size and attracting the attention of large private actors, sowed the seeds for change in the 1990s. A series of technological breakthroughs in US universities related to genetic modification made commercial investment more attractive. Calgene's breakthrough patent on the *Agrobacterium* transformation technology for *Brassica* ultimately led the way to intensive investment and research by private companies. By the early 1980s, private companies had positioned themselves to dominate varietal development in the following period. The first few private varieties were released in this period, heralding a new market configuration.

Post-1995 Commodity Production

The current stage of development is dominated by private actors. The ascendancy of the private sector was assured in 1990, with the adoption of plant breeders' rights in Canada, the decisions to extend patent rights for genes, technologies, and, in some limited ways, whole plants and the development of new canola hybrids. Together, these developments strengthened private control over intellectual property in the breeding and seed business, removing one of the main impediments to private investment.

By 1990, the playing field for development had changed dramatically. Although producers in the three Prairie provinces and Ontario introduced checkoffs to raise funds for more extensive farmer-directed programming and research, their efforts came too late to offset the move to a privately driven research sector. The public sector research agencies for the most part refocused their efforts to complement rather than to compete with private efforts.

The combination of new proprietary technologies, patented genes, and hybrid technologies greatly increased private interest and investment in canola. The most dramatic change was the introduction of large agrochemical companies into the plant genetics industry. AgrEvo, Dow, Monsanto, and Zeneca, for example, entered canola breeding on a significant scale. The very large capital base and international networks of these companies introduced a whole new level of capacity in canola breeding. These multinationals vertically integrated much of the plant breeding and herbicide production intracompany, along with contracts with producers, in an effort to capture the economic value of these new technologies. In 2017, virtually all of the seed sold is subject to some form of contract, regulatory, or rights claim. Almost every breeder uses plant breeders' rights; most use proprietary technology, such as a gene or transformation technology, that is patented; the bulk of the seed is hybrid; and much of the acreage is subject to some form of production contract that can involve the purchase of seed, chemicals, and inoculants, as well as financing and delivery options, among other variables.

After 1988 the provincial associations began to implement producer checkoffs, each using different provincial enabling legislations to collect the funds. Each established a grower checkoff of $0.50/tonne, with about half of the resources directed to research and half to extension and market development. Meanwhile, the Canola Council of Canada expanded its programming to include an extensive extension program, in 1998, involving sites in the Peace River country, three in Alberta, three in Saskatchewan, and two in Manitoba. In addition, the Council collaborated with the Minnesota Canola Council on sites in the USA. This activity was largely coordinated with the continuing extension programs in Alberta, Saskatchewan, and Manitoba, but in competition with an increasing effort by private companies to use extension as part of their marketing programs. With the development of private seeds that had specific agronomic requirements, private companies saw both a need to provide greater information directly to farmers and value in doing so. Most of the larger private seed developers report that since 1993 they have undertaken demonstration seed trials in competition with the cooperative system. The private companies assert that their private trials, which tend to be head-to-head competitions in larger plots (10–20 hectares), are more likely to influence farmer's seed purchases than the smaller plot trials run by the CCC. Some companies have even declined to participate in the Council program, while others participate but supplement that activity with their own private trials. Most of the companies market their seeds using the results of their own trials. Increasingly, given the proprietary nature of the seed and input packages on the market, it is becoming difficult for farmers to get unbiased agronomic advice. Once a producer has decided to purchase a seed with these novel traits, they are often forced to take the related agronomic advice, simply because extension agents from the Canola Council, the provincial canola growers' associations, and the provincial agriculture departments often do not have access to the full and timely information required to give appropriate advice.

Product Differentiation After 2000

Since 2000, private industry has invested heavily in developing and commercializing a variety of novel oils. Canola seed actually has the capacity to produce about a dozen different oil profiles, each with a specific set of properties. A first target was to amplify the erucic content in rapeseed to make what is now called a high erucic acid rapeseed (HEAR), which is sold as an industrial lubricant. Other oil profiles are valuable for the food and baking industry. An increasing number of novel oil varieties have been developed and released since 2000. By some estimates, up to 1 million acres (or about 5% of total canola acreage) is directed to these oils. Each of these novel products has been released under some form of managed production and marketing relationship, either because of the need to isolate the novel product from the commodity food chain to ensure safety (e.g., HEAR varieties) or to ensure purity of the product to secure price premiums in processed oil markets (Smyth et al. 2004).

Specific Adoption Strategies

Segregation Systems for HEAR Varieties: 1982–Date

Ever since the development of rapeseed low in erucic acid and glucosinolates—trademarked as canola in Canada and called double zero or oilseed rape in Europe—there has been an effort to sustain some production of high erucic acid rapeseed (HEAR) for industrial applications where that particular oil has beneficial properties. Conventional rapeseed before canola had about 30–40% erucic acid content, which was not high enough to be valued for industrial applications but too high for safe human consumption. After low erucic acid varieties were developed, the University of Manitoba developed a rapeseed breeding program to increase the level of erucic acid to 55%. The first HEAR variety was commercialized in 1982 in conjunction with CanAmera Foods, a regional oilseed crusher. HEAR varieties are used as biodiesel feedstock, in the nondigestible synthetic fat olestra, as coating for fish feed, as a slip agent for plastic film manufacture, as a stabilizer in peanut butter, and as a plasticizer in perfumes, nylons, and lubricants (McVetty 2009). In the past decade, the volume of acreage under production contracts for HEAR varieties is estimated at a maximum 2% of the overall canola area, or about 400,000 acres (Statistics Canada 2009).

In Canada, the industry segregated HEAR production to prevent the industrial oils from entering supply chains that have products destined for human consumption. Contract registration, mandated at the time of varietal registration by the Canadian Food Inspection Agency (CFIA), specifies conditions for segregating the crop in the field and the supply chain (http://www.inspection.gc.ca/english/plaveg/variet/proced/regproe.shtml#a43). Seed companies are required to sign production contracts with producers who are required to follow specific containment strategies. Under contract registration, regulators from the CFIA have the right to inspect all HEAR fields to ensure compliance with segregation requirements.

HEAR producers incur a number of costs (Phillips and Smyth 2004). Producers are required to plant buffer zones (5 meters) and harvest the portion of the crop that falls in the isolation area separately and sell it as animal feed, thus losing the opportunity of premiums for an estimated 1.13% of the yield from a standard 160 acre production contract. There is also additional paperwork required with the production of HEAR. Producers have to complete post-seeding surveys and map all fields under production. Producers are required to purchase pedigreed seed on an annual basis and deliver all of their production under the contract. Producers are also required to bin all HEAR separately from other crops, using visually distinguishable coded grain confetti provided by the processor; this frequently leads to underutilized on-farm storage.

Genetically Modified Herbicide-Tolerant Canola in 1995–1996

In March 1995, the Canadian and US governments approved two genetically modified herbicide-tolerant varieties of canola (AgrEvo's HCN92 marketed as LibertyLink™ and Monsanto's GT73, sold as Roundup Ready™). The new varieties were initially commercialized in Canada before approval in Japan or the European Union (EU). Those two markets absorbed almost 50% of the total Canadian production in 3 years immediately before the introduction of GM canola (Smyth and Phillips 2001). Both AgrEvo and Monsanto accepted that if these varieties were comingled in the export system, then Canadian canola would be shut out of export markets. In response, the firms agreed to release materials only if they were approved in the "key canola markets," defined as Canada, Japan, the USA, and Mexico by the Expert Committee for Canola of the Pest Management Review Agency.

The industry ultimately chose to self-regulate the commercialization of GM canola. The product proponents worked with the CCC, the wholesale sector, crushers, the provincial canola development commissions, and federal regulators and policy officials to construct an identity-preserved production and marketing (IPPM) system to identity-preserve and deliver GMHT canola only to the North American market. Monsanto had two separate systems—one with the Saskatchewan Wheat Pool, Alberta Wheat Pool, and Manitoba Pool Elevators and the other with Limagrain and Cargill—while AgrEvo worked exclusively through the three pool elevator companies. In 1997 Monsanto added two additional IPPM systems for Roundup Ready™ *B. rapa* varieties. Each of these systems involved an agreement between the research company, a breeder, a grain merchant, farmers, truckers, and an oilseed crusher. The objective of the IPPM systems was to differentiate HT canola from traditional canola marketing channels. This meant that the HT canola could not touch any part of the export handling system, including elevators, rail cars, and port terminals. The 1996 production was delivered to Canadian oilseed crushing plants that had markets for the oil and meal in Canada and the USA, where regulatory approval had been granted. In each case, the grain merchant acted as the operating agent for the system, managing the supply chain from seed multiplication to processing.

In 1997 the IPPM systems for GMHT varieties were wound down, as Japan approved GMHT canola. Cost estimates for two of the five IPPM systems suggest that transaction costs for IPPM systems are quite high (Smyth and Phillips 2001). There were five main areas where additional costs were incurred: by the producer ($1/tonne), during transportation ($6.50–$13/tonne), by the processor ($3–$5/tonne), in administration ($4–$5/tonne), and through opportunity costs ($15–$20/tonne). In total, the two IPPM systems were estimated to cost between $33 and $41/tonne. Based on the acreage involved, it is estimated that the IPPM systems adopted in 1995–1996 cost between $2.8 million and $3.5 million for the AgrEvo system and $750,000 and $930,000 for the Monsanto systems. As noted, all the stakeholders in the IPPM process shared the costs. The producers assumed both the identified on-farm costs and some increased transportation costs and did not receive any formal price premium; in some cases, their production contracts called for delivery when the spot prices were relatively unattractive, which some viewed as a further cost. The grain companies assumed the dead freight costs, a portion of the freight inefficiency, and part of the administration cost, which were at least partly compensated through their normal operating margins. The crushers picked up most of the incremental crushing costs. The remaining costs (opportunity cost, administration, and other subsidies) were paid by Monsanto and AgrEvo, based on the acreage they had under cultivation. In Monsanto's case, they expensed this additional cost to research and development costs related to the development of the technology.

The total cost of the IPPM systems amounted to about 12% to 15% of the average farm gate price, which could not be fully justified simply based on the immediate benefits of the technology. Most studies calculate that in those years, farmers gained upward of $10/acre or $5/tonne from the new technologies, which would have compensated most farmers for only some of their added costs. The grain merchants and processors saw this as a market development effort. While the margins on the small volumes involved in the IPPM systems did not compensate for the added costs, the industry gained in the long run, as adoption of GMHT varieties accelerated. Smyth and Phillips (2001) estimate that the two companies accelerated adoption by at least 1 year, which was estimated to have increase the net present value in 1995 by more than C$100 million.

The main result was the rapid and virtually total adoption of HT canola by 2007. A survey conducted in 2007 revealed that the new technology generated between C$1.063 billion and C$1.192 billion net direct and indirect benefits for producers over 2005–2007 period, partly due to lower input costs and partly from better weed control (Gusta et al. 2011). The survey also identified significant environmental benefits, as producers removed summer fallow as part of their crop rotations. The adoption of HT canola varieties, combined with new conservation tillage practices, allowed farmers to extend the number of years that they could go without having to till a field. In 1999, 89% of canola acres were heavily tilled; by 2007 64% of producers used zero or minimum tillage (Smyth et al. 2011a). There have also been significant changes in herbicide usage. Comparing 1995 and 2006, the toxicity of agro-herbicides applied to canola decreased 53%, with a decrease of 1.3 million kg of active chemical ingredient applied (Smyth et al. 2011b). The cumulative environmental impact per hectare (EI/ha) of the top five herbicides used dropped by 37% in the first decade of adoption.

While the industry no longer operates a full-scale IPPM system for trade purposes, some of the cooperation among the Canadian actors remains. One aspect that requires continued vigilance is maintaining market acceptance of the germplasm in use in Canada. As biotechnology firms de-register GM varieties in Canada that are no longer part of their commercial programs, it is important to ensure that shipments to foreign markets do not contain de-registered varieties. The CCC, on behalf of the industry, has an "export-ready" program that involves an annual education and advocacy campaign to encourage farmers to replace outdated seed to ensure market acceptance (CCC 2011).

Organic and Novel Canola Production: 1990–Date

Like most segments of the food industry, the canola sector has contested both the organic and differentiated foods markets with some success. The two systems have similar objectives but different structures and motivations (Smyth and Phillips 2002; Phillips and Smyth 2002).

The organic sector involves a three-step adoption process. First, the organic industry developed a range of standards to guide production and marketing. Then, farm operators need to make up-front investments to secure certification that they conform to the appropriate standards through a third-party audit; this process normally takes about three growing seasons. Then the farmer can choose from among a select range of seeds and production methods approved as organic. Litigation about the coexistence of organic production and GM crops in 2003 revealed the nature of the industry at that time. In brief, the evidence showed that while between 720 and 1250 of the 51,000 producers in the province over the preceding decade were certified and producing organic crops, only 76 individual producers could be identified as having ever grown certified organic canola in 1990–2001. Only 23 producers grew organic canola for more than 1 year in 1990–2001, and there were fewer than 20 sustained organic canola producers. Only 14,074 acres were planted over the 12 years considered in the court evidence, equal to an annual average of only 1170 acres (compared to the average of 5 million canola acres in the period). The range of canola planted by any producer in any single year ranged from a low of 5 acres to a high of 1370 acres. One producer was reported to have cultivated 2010 acres in the period, equal to 15% of the total organic canola area (Phillips 2003a, b). The evidence produced in the discovery process suggested that a number of factors inhibited organic adoption. Industry observers reported that widespread adoption of GM canola varieties in Western Canada made it more difficult to find isolated fields, which is a strategy organic producers use to manage coexistence. The fact that canola is generally regarded as a weedy crop compounded the difficulties; as a small seeded crop, canola tends to have a lot of weed seed admixtures, causing extensive downgrading and price discounts. Without effective weed management options, organic canola was less competitive than other organic crop opportunities. The high transportation and handling costs to access offshore markets, like the EU, especially when compared with East European competitors, and the lack of any sustained price premiums worked to limit adoption to a narrow set of producers. Drawing lessons from such a small sample is problematic.

Meanwhile there has been a sustained effort to develop and introduce new varieties with specific output traits that may have differential value in parts of the supply chain. This involves varieties with improved oil content, higher than the average of 40% by volume of seed, or with different profiles of oils (e.g., specialty fatty acids normally found in the composite oil in canola). Some novel oils, such as low linolenic oils that are more stable in fryers, only have value at the processing level, while others, such as high oleic oils, have health attributes that can be marketed to consumers. Cargill and Dow AgroSciences have a range of novel oils they produce under contract with Western Canadian canola producers. All of these oils are managed by private firms in closed-loop channels that facilitate delivery of an assured quality by managing production from the development of pedigreed seed to the processed product. Generally, these systems offer producer contracts which specify the inputs to be used, impose compulsory delivery, provide producer premiums, and sometimes provide a producer storage subsidy for late-season deliveries and for restrictions on other canola crops on adjacent fields. There are few substantive differences between how these voluntary identity-preserving production systems are organized and segregation systems mandated by the regulatory system.

Adoption in Theory and Practice

The Canadian canola industry has been challenged to develop and adopt a range of innovative products, including conventional, organic, GM, and industrial crops all in the same space. Theory suggests farmers can and do make comparative choices of technologies and varieties based on individual evaluations of the partial value each factor contributes to their profit. But producers in the canola sector have seldom had opportunities to make such unaided choices. Instead, governments, industry associations, and various supply chain actors have bundled together information and agronomic advice with an array of inputs and market opportunities, making it next to impossible for farmers to make explicit, discrete decisions about specific technologies and varieties. In this context, the evolution and development of the sector exhibit significant path dependence, as key organizations invest in pursuing their interests. Some assert the restricted choices of farmers has disadvantaged farmers, but the evidence suggests farmers have realized significant benefits, perhaps not from adoption of every innovation but from the sustained flow of innovative technologies and varieties that have created a $26.7 billion industry (LMC International 2016).

References

Canola Council of Canada. 2011. Are you export ready? Available at: http://www.canolacouncil.org/crop-production/are-you-export-ready/. Accessed 25 Apr 2013.

Dupont, J., P.J. White, K.M. Johnston, H.A. Heggtveit, B.E. McDonald, S.M. Grundy, and A. Bonanome. 1989. Food Safety and Health Effects of Canola oil. *Journal of the American College of Nutrition* 8(5): 360–375.

Gray, R., and S. Malla. 1998. The evaluation of the economic and external health benefits from canola research. In *Returns to Agricultural Research*, ed. J. Alston and P. Pardey.

Gusta, M., S. Smyth, K. Belcher, P. Phillips, and D. Castle. 2011. Economic Benefits of Genetically-modified Herbicide-tolerant Canola for Producers. *AgBioforum* 14 (1): 1–13.

LMC International. 2016. *The Economic Impact of Canola on the Canadian Economy*. Oxford: LMC International. Available at: https://www.canolacouncil.org/media/584356/lmc_canola_10-year_impact_study_-_canada_final_dec_2016.pdf. Accessed 29 Oct 2017.

McLeod, A. 1974. *The story of rapeseed in Western Canada*. Regina: Saskatchewan Wheat Pool.

McVetty, P. 2009. High Erucic Acid Rapeseed (HEAR) Cultivar Development at the University of Manitoba: An Update. Presentation to the Plant Bio-Oils Workshop, Saskatoon, 25–26 Feb. Available at: http://agwest.sk.ca/events/plantbio-oils09/plant-bio-industrial-oils-09_presentations.htm. Accessed 25 Apr 2013.

NRC. 1992. *From Rapeseed to Canola: the Billion Dollar Success Story*. Saskatoon: National Research Council.

Phillips, P. 2003a. Affidavit of Peter WB Phillips, QB NO. 67 of 2002, Court of Queen's Bench for Saskatchewan Between Larry Hoffman, LB Hoffman Farms Inc., and Dale Beaudoin (Plaintiffs) v. Monsanto Canada Inc. and Aventis CropScience Canada Holdings Inc. (Defendants) brought under the Class Actions Act. September.

———. 2003b. Affidavit of Peter WB Phillips, QB NO. 67 of 2002, Court of Queen's Bench for Saskatchewan Between Larry Hoffman, LB Hoffman Farms Inc., and Dale Beaudoin (Plaintiffs) v. Monsanto Canada Inc. and Aventis CropScience Canada Holdings Inc. (Defendants) brought under the Class Actions Act. November.

Phillips, P., and G. Khachatourians. 2001. *The Biotechnology Revolution in Global Agriculture: Invention, Innovation and Investment in the Canola Sector*. Wallingford: CABI.

Phillips, P., and S. Smyth. 2004. Managing the value of new-trait varieties in the canola supply chain in Canada. *Supply Chain Management* 9 (4): 313–322.

Smyth, S., and P. Phillips. 2001. Competitors Co-operating: Establishing a Supply Chain to Manage Genetically Modified Canola. *International Food and Agribusiness Management Review* 4: 51–66.

———. 2002. Product differentiation alternatives: Identity preservation, segregation, and traceability. *AgBioforum* 5 (2): 30–42.

Smyth, S., P. Phillips, W. Kerr, and G. Khachatourians. 2004. *Regulating the Liabilities of Agricultural Biotechnology*. Wallingford: CABI Publishing.

Smyth, S., M. Gusta, K. Belcher, P. Phillips, and D. Castle. 2011a. Environmental Impacts from Herbicide Tolerant Canola Production in Western Canada. *Agricultural Systems* 104: 403–410.

———. 2011b. Changes in Herbicide Use Following the Adoption of HR Canola in Western Canada. *Weed Technology* 25 (3): 492–500.

Statistics Canada. 2009. Canola: A Canadian Success Story. http://www.statcan.gc.ca/pub/96-325-x/2007000/article/10778-eng.htm.

Part II
Institutional Incentives for Agricultural Innovation

Why Do US Corn Yields Increase?
The Contributions of Genetics, Agronomy,
and Policy Instruments

Stephen Smith and Brad Kurtz

Abstract Much of the future quality of life will depend upon improved abilities to sustainably increase agricultural production while maintaining ecosystem services and supporting conservation of natural diversity. Some lessons for the future reside in an improved understanding of the factors that have contributed to increased agricultural productivity during recent past decades. Using US maize production as an example, we demonstrate the critical contributions of plant breeding using native maize germplasm and improved agronomic practices. We outline the policy instruments that condition successful plant breeding through determining access to plant genetic resources and by providing economic incentives for investment and innovation through intellectual property. Maximum progress in improving global agricultural production can only be made when potentially contradictory policies are implemented in a balanced fashion.

Introduction

The future of humankind depends fundamentally upon the ability of farmers to sustainably produce sufficient nutritious food. Historically, challenges to avoid the Malthusian prediction (Malthus 1798) that the demands of a growing population growth would outrun agricultural supply have been avoided by taking more land into production, by technological innovation leading to increased production per unit area, and by reductions in population growth either through choice or by decree (Food and Agriculture Organization of the United Nations [FAO] 2014).

A previous version of this chapter was published under the same title in AgBioForum 18(3):297–302.

S. Smith (✉)
Iowa State University, Ames, Iowa, USA
e-mail: jscsmith@iastate.edu

B. Kurtz
ADAMD, LLC, Bradenton, Florida, USA

However, challenges to maintain a sufficient and equitable supply of food and raw materials from agriculture eclipse those encountered previously. The global population is predicted to grow by more than 33% (or 2.3 billion) from 2009 to 2050 from the current level of approximately 7 billion (FAO 2009). Global food demand is predicted to double by 2050 (Tilman et al. 2011). Most good arable land is already in cultivation, so agricultural production must increase to counter a declining per capita supply of arable land. Further extension of global arable area would include taking more ecologically fragile land into cultivation and compromise environmental services provided by natural ecosystems, rivers, and forests (Foley et al. 2011). Agriculture should also contribute to an improved environmental footprint by reducing soil erosion and nutrient runoff. Crops need to remain resilient in the face of competition from weeds and persistent attacks by pest and disease organisms. And crop production must be maintained in the face of unpredictable and possibly more extreme weather.

Elucidating the factors that have contributed to increased agricultural production is the first step to understanding the elements needed to sustain future increases in agricultural production. Chief among these is the more effective use of a broader base of plant genetic resources made possible through innovative plant breeding, underpinned by improved knowledge of the genetic basis of plant physiology. We then introduce the international instruments that are in place to guide policy. We identify areas in which implementation of policies causes overreach and disruption of individual policies. We argue that the overarching public need to improve agricultural production via plant breeding is restricted when individual policies are implemented in an imbalanced manner.

US Maize Production: Disentangling the Contributing Factors to Production and Productivity

The history of US maize production can be split into three phases (Fig. 1). First, from 1866 to 1920, increased production occurred by taking more land into cultivation. Second, from 1940 to 1970, maize production further increased (Fig. 1) even as the land area used for maize cultivation shrank. Third, from the late 1980s to today, there have been increasing production and increasing area under maize cultivation. US area planted to maize in 2013 represented the highest figure since 1936, when an estimated 41.7 million ha (103 million acres) were planted (US Department of Agriculture [USDA], National Agricultural Statistics Service [NASS], US Department of Agriculture (USDA), National Agricultural Statistics Service (NASS) 2013).

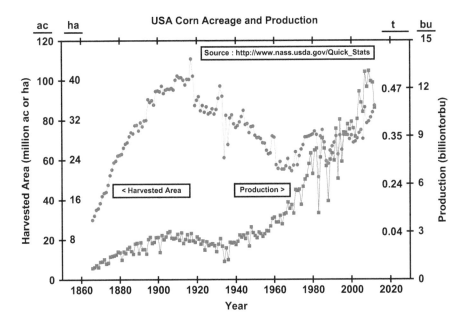

Fig. 1 US corn harvested area and production, 1865–2013 (Source: http:/www.nass.usda.gov/ Quick_Stats. Reprinted with permission from Smith et al. 2014)

What Are the Factors that Have Contributed to Increasing Productivity?

Productivity is production per unit land area, i.e., yield. Examination of US maize yields from 1866 to 2011 (Fig. 2) explains the annual dynamics and interactions of land area harvested and total production (Fig. 1). From 1866 to the 1930s, maize yields approached stagnation, increasing at 3 kg/ha/yr (0.05 bu/ac/yr; Fig. 2). During the late 1930s through to the 1980s, yield increases allowed total production to increase even as land area harvested declined. From 1990 to 2011, both yields and land area harvested increased leading to record levels of US annual maize production. Factors contributing to yield must then be examined to provide a more complete understanding of their quantitative (percent contributions) and qualitative (do they interact?) aspects.

What Are the Factors that Contribute to Yield?

It is a well-established biological fact that phenotypic appearance is a result of *genotype × environmental effects*. Likewise, *genotype × environment* interactions determine yield. With regard to crop yields, numerous factors can be included

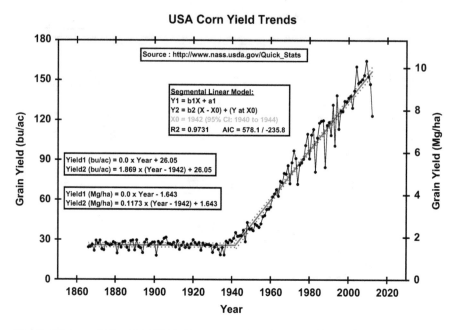

Fig. 2 US corn yields, 1865–2013 (Source: http:/www.nass.usda.gov/Quick_Stats. Reprinted with permission from Smith et al. (2014))

under the definition of "environment." These include weather, soil type, pests, diseases, and farm management practices; choice of weed, insect, and pest control methods; planting density; tillage type; planting date; and amount and dates of fertilizer applications.

How to Disentangle the Contributions of These Components to Yield

The crucial first step is to experimentally isolate and measure the genetic effects, i.e., the contribution made by plant breeders (genetic gain). Genetic effects can be extracted using sophisticated statistical analyses from yield data provided sufficient check varieties are present among a set of varieties that represent a time series of varieties according to their initial release and availability on farms. A more precise measure of genetic gain can be obtained using specially designed progress evaluation trials. Here, a series of varieties with different release dates are planted in the same environmental and farm management conditions over a series of locations and years. This is the experimental design adopted in the study reported here. Field conditions were akin to those of the target production environment (central Corn Belt) and were nonirrigated. As an additional component, we planted the hybrids at three planting rates to be comparable with current practice (high) and those employed in previous decades (medium and low). The chronological time series of hybrid release dates spanned 1930–2011. We also conducted an experiment to measure the effect on yield of adding resistance to the European corn borer (ECB) via the presence of the protein *Cry1Ab* produced by a gene extracted from the bacterium *Bacillus thuringiensis* and inserted into the maize genome by genetic engineering. For the later experiment, we used 15 pairs of hybrids grown at 3739 locations per year in 24 US states and 2 Canadian provinces over 7 years. For each pair of hybrids, the only difference was the presence or absence of the *Cry1Ab*-producing gene.

Results

The oldest hybrids performed best at low planting densities, medium-age hybrids performed best at moderate planting densities, and hybrids released since 1990 performed best at high planting densities. It is therefore most appropriate to compare yields for each hybrid when planted at its optimum planting density. These results are shown in Fig. 3. The rate of genetic gain during the period of 1930–2011 was 87.6 kg/ha/yr. (1.4 bu./ac/yr). For a subset of single-cross hybrids—which are more representative of the type of hybrid grown today and during the past five decades—the rate of genetic gain was 92 kg/ha/yr (1.5 bu/ac/yr). US maize breeders have selected for plants with greater stress resistances imposed by higher planting densities. Adaptation to those stresses includes change in leaf canopy architecture to maximize light interception and an improved ability to mine soil water and nutrients. Additional data showed more recent hybrids had reduced the flow of photosynthates to the male tassel, presumably thereby repartitioning photosynthates to the female ear, which is the site of grain production. More recently developed hybrids expressed more resistance to certain diseases and insects and were better able to retain a vertical stand.

Resistance to attack by ECB provided a mean yield advantage of 5.3% (range 2.0–5.8%). It is important to understand that ECB resistance did not increase the potential genetic gain. All potential genetic gain was generated via improvement of the native maize germplasm. Insect resistance contributed to protecting that genetic potential. During the era of single-cross hybrids, USDA data showed the rate of production gain on Iowa farms was 123 kg/ha/yr. Consequently, the contribution of genetic gain to yield gains on Iowa farms during this period was 92/123 (75%). Farm management practices accounted for the remaining 25% of yield improvement. The maximum yield that could conceivably be generated using most recently released maize hybrids and maximum input management practices was indicated by data from yield contest trials conducted under the auspices of the National Corn Growers Association. Potential yields under nonirrigated conditions were 18,599 kg/ha with a rate of yield gain of 193 kg/ha/yr. In contrast, mean maize yields on Iowa farms was 11,741 kg/ha. A vital question is how much of the yield gap of 18,599–11,741 = 6858 kg/ha can be reduced economically? The answer varies with many factors, including weather, management practices, price of fertilizer, and grain prices.

Hybrid BLUP (at the optimum density)

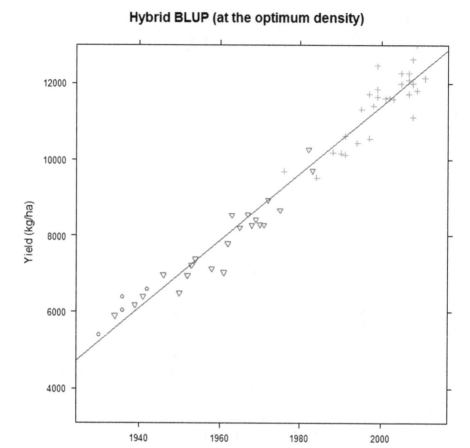

Fig. 3 Yields (Best Linear Unbiased Predictor) of Pioneer corn hybrids grown in the same environment at their individual optimum planting density (blue circles = low; inverted red triangles = moderate; green + = high) (Note: Reprinted with permission from Smith et al. 2014)

Changes in Genetic Constitution of Hybrids as a Result of Plant Breeding Associated with Genetic Gain: Genetic Diversity Change in Time

Tracking back hybrids in their pedigrees to founder parental sources enables one portrayal of change in genetic makeup as a result of plant breeding (i.e., a change in the underlying genetics that underpin genetic gain). Figure 4 shows the average founder constitution of current DuPont Pioneer maize hybrids used in the central Corn Belt. In comparison, farmers in this region in the decades before the 1930s were largely growing Reid Yellow Dent—a genetic source which now only contributes 24% of the genetic background—thus exemplifying the integration of different

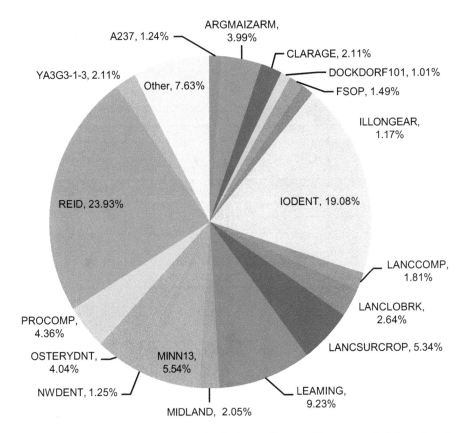

Fig. 4 Mean landrace or founder contribution by pedigree to Pioneer corn hybrids released 2000–2009 (Note: Reprinted with permission from Smith et al. (2014). Most farmer landrace saved-seed varieties cultivated in central Iowa during the late nineteenth century and 1900–1930 were Reid Yellow Dent which now represents only 24% of the pedigree background, showing an increase in genetic diversity)

genetic diversity, primarily at least during the past 2000–3500 years, from other regions that are now within the borders of the United States. Figure 5 shows genetic change in time of chromosomal segments due to plant breeding.

Valuation of Increased Productivity

Comparing the land required to produce the 2013 US level of corn production using the hybrids and management practices of earlier eras is illustrative of both the economic and environmental importance of improving productivity. For example, if the entire state of Iowa was planted with corn—including land that is now under concrete or under water—then it would require 2.4 Iowa states to produce the entire

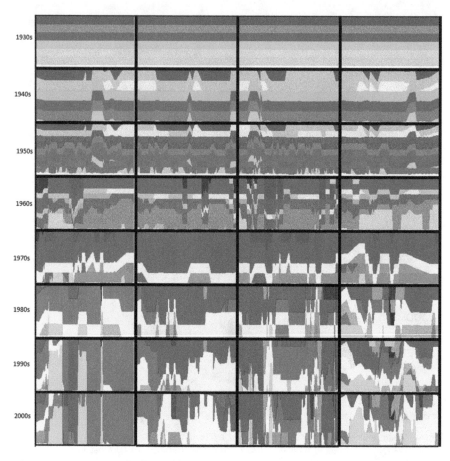

Fig. 5 Change in decadal genetic diversity of corn hybrids from the 1930s to the 2000s (Note: Reprinted with permission from Smith et al. (2014). Comparison of four of the ten diploid chromosomes. Changes in color denote different genetic segments along each of the four chromosomes (horizontal) tracked by molecular markers and DNA sequence. Note the huge changes during the 1960s and 1970s, with changes continuing during subsequent decades)

2013 US corn crop using 2013 genetics and farm management practices. If maize hybrids and farm management practices of the 1980s were used, then it would require 3.6 Iowas. And if maize hybrids and farm management practices from the 1930s were used, it would require 14.5 Iowas. There is also an increased environmental valuation of increased productivity as genetic inputs replace chemical inputs; these include providing insect or disease resistance, having a requirement for less use of fuel for cultivation, contributing to soil conservation, or making more effective use of fertilizer or water resources. As contributions from chemical inputs plateau or decline, then there will be an increased dependence upon productivity gains and in contributing to a cleaner environment through the use of plant genetic resources via plant breeding.

Access to and Use of a Range of Genetic Diversity: The Policy Arena

Access to a useful range of genetic resources and an increased ability to effectively utilize those resources in plant breeding will be ever more critical components of helping to achieve a more sustainable, environmentally friendly, and productive agriculture system. Critical policy areas that come into play in helping to promote more effective agriculture as a result of plant breeding are those dealing with terms of access to germplasm and the ability to obtain intellectual property protection (IPP). International treaties can be, and usually are, modified on a country and regional basis. This leads to a highly complex international landscape for IPP and access and benefit sharing (ABS) with regard to plant genetic resources for food and agriculture.

Four treaties are the most relevant in this respect. First, the World Intellectual Property Organization (WIPO), a specialty agency of the United Nations, was created in 1967 with the goal "to encourage creative activity, to promote the protection of intellectual property throughout the world" (WIPO 1967). WIPO has 188 member states.[1] The Patent Cooperation Treaty (PCT)[2] is an international patent law treaty, signed in 1970, that provides a unified procedure for filing patent applications in 148 countries. WIPO and the PCT seek to incentivize innovation primarily through the grant of patents, trademarks, and industrial designs to eligible subject matter. A primary incentive is to make information about an invention public via a patent in exchange for an exclusive right for a temporal period. WIPO members also examine how to protect traditional knowledge and folklore related to genetic resources.

Second, the International Union for the Protection of New Varieties of Plants (UPOV) was established as an intergovernmental organization in 1961 and revised in 1972, 1978, and 1991. UPOV provides specialist or "sui generis" intellectual property rights for plant breeders who develop varieties that are distinct, uniform, and stable. UPOV's mission is to provide and promote an effective system of plant variety protection (PVP), with the aim of encouraging the development of new varieties of plants for the benefit of society—provided breeders have exclusive rights to sell their variety. However, unlike patents, PVP does not restrict unlicensed further breeding of a protected commercialized variety. However, if the new variety is determined to be essentially derived (UPOV of 1991) from the initial variety, then the owner of the initial variety retains ownership of the essentially derived variety. As of June 10, 2014, there were 72 UPOV members.[3]

Third, the Convention on Biological Diversity (CBD) was opened for signature at the Earth Summit in Rio de Janeiro in 1992 and entered into force in December 1993. The CBD seeks to achieve the conservation and sustainable use of biological diversity coupled with the fair and equitable sharing of the benefits arising out of the utilization of genetic resources. There are 195 parties to the CBD.

---

[1] See http://www.wipo.int/members/en

[2] See http://www.wipo.int/pct/en

[3] For the full list, please see http://www.upov.int/export/sites/upov/members/en/pdf/pub423.pdf

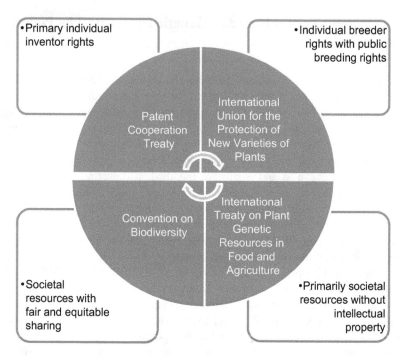

Fig. 6 The four treaties that impact access to plant genetic resources and finance, risk-taking, innovation in research, and product development with regard to plant breeding (Note: Two treaties (Patent Cooperation and the International Union for the Protection of New Varieties of Plants) are designed to incentivize investment in innovation, and two (The Convention on Biological Diversity and the International Treaty on Plant Genetic Resources for Food and Agriculture) are designed to conserve and facilitate use of genetic resources while respecting and supporting society)

Fourth, the International Treaty on Plant Genetic Resources for Food and Agriculture (ITPGRFA) recognizes the contribution of farmers to the diversity of crops that feed the world. It establishes a global multilateral system to provide farmers, plant breeders, and scientists with access to plant genetic materials and seeks to ensure that recipients share benefits they derive from the use of these genetic materials with the countries from which they were sourced. The CBD (from December 1993) brought the jurisdiction of genetic resources under national sovereignty. The treaty was developed as a comprehensive international agreement in harmony with the CBD because of the special and distinctive nature of agricultural genetic resources, including thousands of years of pedigree histories crossing countries and continents and because of their international importance for global food security. The ITPGRFA entered into force in June 2004 and currently has 193 contracting parties.[4]

These four treaties are presented in Fig. 6 in such a way to emphasize both the nature of their individual and collective or complementary underlying public policies. Two treaties (WIPO with PCT and UPOV) are designed to incentivize

---

[4] See the list of parties at http://www.planttreaty.org/list_of_countries

investment in innovation, whereas the other two treaties (CBD and ITPGRFA) are designed to protect societal resources. Collectively, each of the four treaties has the public policy of increasing social welfare, albeit through some degree of competing interests. Consequently, unbalanced implementation may lead to a loss in overall social welfare that an otherwise more balanced implementation could have supported. For example, an encroachment of CBD onto the ITPGRFA could result in reduced access to germplasm for further breeding and thus have a net negative effect on increasing agricultural productivity. Achieving a balanced approach can lead to the protection of societal resources while incentivizing the innovation required to increase crop yields. These treaties can be viewed as a matrix according to their policy goals (Fig. 6).

Ideally, policy goals should be individually and collectively directed toward achieving the common public goal of improving global agricultural production, i.e., working complementarily and synergistically. However, overall opportunities are lost when implementation of one treaty expands and overreaches, thereby stifling the positive goals of another treaty. For example, implementation of biodiversity laws by some countries has reduced or halted international flows of germplasm and undermined the policy goals of UPOV to allow further breeding with commercialized varieties. Likewise, overreach of patent protection can reduce short-term spread of newly developed germplasm. Or a lack of effective legal instruments to provide time-limited IP can result in greater dependence upon the use of trade secrets, which undermines dissemination and use of new knowledge or germplasm. We understand at least some of the complexities and political challenges in raising the common global good above national or more parochial interests. Nonetheless, given the crucial importance of plant breeding and agriculture to improving lives and livelihoods while also contributing to improved environmental health and ecosystem sustainability, we consider it important that the greater global and public good be always kept in mind as the ultimate goal to achieve.

Acknowledgments Figures 1, 2, 3, 4, and 5 are reprinted with permission from Smith et al. (2014).

References

Food and Agriculture Organization of the United Nations (FAO). 2009. *How to feed the world 2050: Global agriculture toward 2050*. High-level expert forum hosted by FAO's Office of the Director, Agricultural Development Economics Division, October 12–13, Rome. Available at: http://www.fao.org/fileadmin/templates/wsfs/docs/Issues_papers/HLEF2050_Global_Agriculture.pdf

FAO. 2014. *FAOSTAT Production Data [database]*. Rome: Author. Available on the World Wide Web: http://faostat3.fao.org/faostat-gateway/go/to/browse/Q/*/E.

Foley, J.A., N. Ramankutty, K.A. Brauman, E.S. Cassidy, J.S. Gerber, M. Johnston, et al. 2011. Solutions for a Cultivated Planet. *Nature* 478 (7369): 337–342.

Malthus, T.R. 1798. *An Essay on the Principle of Population, as it Affects The Future Improvement of Society with Remarks on the Speculations of Mr. Godwin, M. Condorcet, and Other Writers*. Oxford: Oxford Worlds Classic Reprint.

Smith, S., M. Cooper, J. Gogerty, C. Loffler, D. Borcherding, and K. Wright. 2014. Maize. In *Yield Gains in Major U.S. Field Crops: CSSA Special Publication 33* (Chapter 6), ed. S. Smith, B. Diers, J. Specht, and B. Carver, 125–172. Madison: Crop Science Society of America (CSSA).

Tilman, D., C. Balzer, J. Hill, and B.L. Befort. 2011. Global Food Demand and The Sustainable Intensification of Agriculture. *Proceedings of the National Academy of Sciences USA* 108 (50): 20260–20264.

US Department of Agriculture (USDA), National Agricultural Statistics Service (NASS). 2013. *Corn, Sorghum, Barley, and Oats: Planted Area, Harvested Acreage, Production, Yield, and Farm Price [database]*. Washington, DC: Author.

World Intellectual Property Organization (WIPO). 1967. *Convention Establishing The World Intellectual Property Organization*. Geneva: Author. Available on the World Wide Web: http://www.wipo.int/treaties/en/text.jsp?file_id=283854.

Whither the Research Anticommons?

William Lesser

Abstract Fifteen years ago, the "tragedy of the anticommons" article warned that excessive patenting of biotech products and research methods could deter rather than stimulate invention, but little evidence was offered. Here, subsequent changes in patent law, public research support, and surveys of researchers are summarized. Results indicate the anticipated anticommons has not materialized significantly, and while ongoing monitoring is warranted, declining public research funding may necessitate more patenting to stimulate private investment.

Introduction

Nearly 16 years ago, Heller and Eisenberg (1998) published in *Science* a highly influential article (more than 2000 citations) warning of the accelerated use of biotech patents stifling subsequent developments rather than incentivizing them as intended. Their analysis focused particularly on biomedical research, but the issues are general to biotech research applications, including agricultural and veterinary medicinal. They used the term "tragedy of the anticommons" in contrast with the "tragedy of the commons," which popularized the observation that common property resources are overexploited because no one has a preservation incentive (Hardin 1968). While the "commons" concept argues for privatization, Heller and Eisenberg (1998, p. 698) cautioned that overprivatization creates fragmented ownership and high transaction costs—an anticommons. "Privatization can solve one tragedy but cause another."

The anticommons potential is of ongoing significance because of the cumulative nature of scientific research. Reductions in access to past developments diminish current and all future research productivity. Economists explain those reductions in terms of transactions costs: more and potentially overlapping patents increase the costs of negotiating access, which causes further declines in output. That point is

---

W. Lesser (✉)
Cornell University, Ithaca, NY, USA
e-mail: whl1@cornell.edu

N. Kalaitzandonakes et al. (eds.), *From Agriscience to Agribusiness*, Innovation, Technology, and Knowledge Management, https://doi.org/10.1007/978-3-319-67958-7_7

well documented at a theoretical level. Less well documented is the empirical question: if more patents increase transaction costs for researchers, do they indeed cause an anticommons? This article summarizes the available evidence.

An example of a potential "anticommons" is the materials required for the development of "Golden Rice," a genetically engineered rice that produces beta-carotene as a source of vitamin A for those with deficient diets, primarily in developing countries. Because severe shortages of vitamin A can lead to blindness, the development was greeted with great excitement. As a step in the commercialization process, the Rockefeller Foundation commissioned a "freedom-to-operate" (FTO) review of the product to determine what and from whom permission needed to be secured to avoid legal culpability.

The FTO review identified up to 44 patents covering the completed Golden Rice product. But because patents are national, the actual number varies from country to country, from a low of zero (Bangladesh) to around 40 in the United States and most of the European Union. There is considerable judgment required in determining which patents actually apply to Golden Rice and whether to consider applications or only granted patents. The patent numbers referred to here are on the conservative side—what the authors refer to as a "wide net"—so that it is possible the core patent rights (which would need to be negotiated) would be smaller in number. There are additional so-called technical (or tangible) property rights which must be negotiated as well. The number for Golden Rice was calculated to be at least 15 of these, primarily material transfer agreements for biological materials (Kryder et al. 2000).

This number of potential pieces of intellectual and technical property indeed suggests a formidable negotiating process to secure rights for commercializing Golden Rice. And that is before the ongoing changes typical in corporate licensing arrangements. At a more aggregate level, Jenson and Murray (2005) evaluated the number of human genes that were patented. They determined that nearly 20% of human genes were explicitly claimed, or 4382 of 23,688 genes in the National Center for Biotechnology Information database at the time of writing. This number of patented genes is less than reported in prior studies, according to the authors, because only genes claimed in the patents were counted, not those merely disclosed. The 4000+ patented genes had 1156 owners; about two thirds of these were private firms. Two genes had up to 20 patents claiming various form and use rights, but more than 3000 (68%) only had a single rights holder. For the 144 genes with five or more rights holders (3%), there is a real potential of a costly licensing process to secure access, but less so for the great majority. Unsurprisingly, the heavily patented genes are associated with human health and diseases, making them particularly important research targets.

Heller and Eisenberg's cautionary note now has great practical significance as the Supreme Court recently decided on two related cases. In *Association for Molecular Pathology v. Myriad Genetics* (2013),[1] Verrilli, representing the Solicitor General's Office, observed, "But allowing a patent on [natural genes] would effec-

---

[1] 133 S. Ct. 2107, 2111 (2013).

tively preempt anyone else from using that gene itself for any medical or scientific basis."[2] Myriad Genetics had patented two isolated genes—referred to as BRCA1 and BRCA2—associated with an elevated risk for developing breast and uterine cancer and utilized in diagnostic testing. The unanimous June 2013 decision bans patents on naturally occurring DNA segments ("isolated DNA") as products of nature while permitting them for complementary DNA (cDNA), which is not naturally occurring. As part of their ruling, the justices quoted a lower court decision that allowing patents for isolated DNA would create a "considerable danger" that "patents would 'tie up' the use of such tools and thereby 'inhibit future innovation premised upon them' (p. 2116)." Indeed, the patent validity case was brought by a researcher who used a different diagnostic lab to perform the genetic testing but ceased after receiving a warning letter from Myriad Genetics. Note should be made though that the plaintiff was involved with commercial use of Myriad's invention, not research access. Indeed, in its court filings, Myriad pledged to grant open research access to its then-patented genes, balking only at use by fee-charging labs.

Concerns over patents "preempting" subsequent research were also emphasized in *Mayo Collaborative Services v. Prometheus Laboratories* (2012, p. 1294)[3] which related to a method for determining drug dosages. The Supreme Court noted that "… the grant of patents that tie up [a law of nature] will inhibit future innovation premised upon them […] or otherwise forecloses more future invention than the underlying discovery could reasonably justify." Like Heller and Eisenberg (1998), the justices apparently saw a potential anticommons in biomedical research and constrained it by invalidating the Prometheus patents, narrowing the field of patentable inventions.

However, while the Supreme Court was categorical in asserting an anticommons effect, Heller and Eisenberg (1998) were circumspect. They identified the *potential* for patents to create an anticommons, using the conditionals "may/can/likely/potential/might" more than 40 times. The intent here 15+ years later is to examine the evidence for or against any actual patent-based anticommons in biomedical research. Evidence must be multifaceted, as the authors identify multiple components under their heading of a biomedical anticommons:

- Privatization of "upstream" research previously public
- Multiple patents incorporated in a single product/research program
- Patents on components, not just complete products
- Long delays in examining patents, allowing possible overestimates of patent scope
- Licensing issues, including stacking and reach through licenses
- Heterogeneous interests and conflicting agendas of multiple patent owners, compounding licensing issues

We begin with changes/reforms to the patent system itself.

---

[2] Oral arguments before the US Supreme Court, April 15, 2013, transcript p. 25.
[3] 132 S. Ct. 1289 (2012).

Changes in Patent Practices

In addition to the recent Supreme Court patent decisions noted above, other limitations on patenting had been applied to gene components, particularly expressed sequence tags (ESTs). In *In re Fisher*[4] (2005), the US Court of Appeals for the Federal Circuit ruled ESTs lacked "specific and substantial utility"—that the disclosed uses "were generally applicable to any EST" and hence unpatentable.

Going back further in time to when living organisms became patentable, the US Patent and Trademark Office (USPTO) began to require deposits of the material if necessary to assure availability to the public to satisfy the disclosure requirement. Under patent law:

> "Every patent must contain a written description of the invention sufficient to enable a person skilled in the art to which the invention pertains to make and use the invention. Where the invention involves a biological material and words alone cannot sufficiently describe how to make and use the invention in a reproducible manner, access to the biological material may be necessary for the satisfaction of the statutory requirements for patentability under 35 U.S.C. Section 112." (USPTO 2014).

That is, the disclosure requirement of patent law mandates the invention be publicly available, including through access to a sample if a written disclosure is deemed inadequate. This is an oft-overlooked component of the concept of patents, providing an incentive not only to invest in an inventive activity but also to make the invention public rather than holding it in secrecy.

Prof. Potrykus, coinventor of Golden Rice, recognized the importance of disclosure despite the frustrations caused by private ownership:

> "At that time [of commercialization] I was much tempted to join those who radically fought patenting. Fortunately I did a bit further thinking and became aware that 'Golden Rice' development was only possible because there was patenting. Much of the technology I had been using was publicly known because the inventors could protect their right. Much of it would have remained secret if this had been the case." (Potrykus 2011).

So while patenting encumbers use of an invention during its pendency, it fosters public availability, as interested parties have access once the patent expires. This aspect of the patent system—the provision of an incentive to make an invention public—is often overlooked.

Currently, most US patent applications are published 18 months following first application worldwide (America Invents Act 2011),[5] which means that applications are no longer secret during the full multiyear examination period. Concurrently, the United States joined the rest of the world under the "first-to-file" system, which recognizes the first filer as the inventor (America Invents Act 2011). Gone is the ownership uncertainty under the previous "first-to-invent" system and its complex "interference" proceedings.

---

[4] 421 F. 3d 1365, (2005).

[5] Amendment 35 UCS. HR 1249, Leahy-Smith America Invents Act PL 112-29, September 16, 2011.

Sometimes time itself has a mitigating effect on patents; they lapse due to end of term or failure to pay the requisite maintenance fees. This factor is particularly relevant for key "upstream" inventions, which have a disproportionate effect on subsequent research. And so it is with the basic plant transformation technology patents—the "gene gun" (#6004287) and *Agrobacterium tumefaciens* (#4658082). Both are now in the public domain, although some improvements remain under patent. This kind of broad pioneering patent grant is unlikely to be repeated in the biotech field due to an attribute of the US patent system which treats a patent as the right of an inventor. It is thus the responsibility of the USPTO (the assigned examiner) to document why a patent should be withheld, typically meaning the application is either nonnovel and/or nonobvious (35 USC 102–103). What happens in new fields of endeavor—as biotechnology was in the 1980s—is that most applications by definition are nonobvious. To document lack of novelty, the examiner must identify a publication or use or related patent, which destroys the novelty. Again, in new fields of research, there are limited numbers of such documents so lack of novelty is difficult to establish. The consequence is broad patent grants. The situation, though, is self-correcting since time provides more evidence for examiners to reject or narrow patent grants.

Thus, over multiple years, the scope of patentable inventions applicable to biotech research has been curtailed and the process simplified and made more transparent. All limit the anticommons potential.

Privatization of Research

Many observers have decried—as do Heller and Eisenberg (1998)—the privatization of research, placing many important discoveries and tools in private hands. However the public domain had shown itself not to engender use of many publicly supported inventions. The major justification for the Bayh-Dole Act (Pub. L. 96–517), which allows publicly supported inventions to be owned by nonprofit (research) institutions and small businesses, was a recognition that few such inventions were ever commercialized (Cook-Deegan and Heaney 2010). Most institutional inventions are at an early stage and require significant additional investment for which the absence of patents is a disincentive (Nelsen 2007).

An example of the kinds of privatization issues raised is exemplified by the 7-year skirmish between the National Institutes of Health (NIH) and Burroughs Wellcome to the rights for AZT, the first effective treatment for AIDS. AZT was initially developed as a cancer drug by the National Cancer Institute and, according to some accounts, identified as effective against AIDS by researchers at Duke University. A partnership between the NIH and Burroughs Wellcome, however, led to Burroughs Wellcome receiving six patents for the production and use of AZT, initially pricing the drug at $7000–$10,000 annually per patient. Due to pushback by the government, two 20% price reductions were instituted in 1987 and 1989, but lawsuits by firms seeking to overturn the patents for lack of inventorship by

Burroughs Wellcome—asserting that the NIH and Duke researchers were the true inventors—were eventually unsuccessful. The drug subsequently reached $1 billion in yearly sales (Yarchoan 2012).

The Bayh-Dole Act allows the federal agency providing the funding underlying the research leading to the patented invention to grant additional licenses if the initial licensee refuses a reasonable request. These so-called "march-in" rights, a form of compulsory license, may be utilized if the granting agency determines the "action is necessary to alleviate health or safety needs" and is "necessary to meet requirements for public use specified by Federal regulations" (35 USC 203). While potentially very powerful, the practical effect of this authority has been scant. An example of the constraints to application was the technical difficulties experienced in 2009–2011 by Genzyme in producing Fabrazyme, a medication for suffers of Fabry disease. Fabry is a rare genetic disease with varied symptoms and is potentially fatal. The manufacturing (contamination) problems necessitated dose reductions of two thirds followed by a return of symptoms in patients and a petition to the NIH, the research funding agency, to exercise its march-in authority to enhance the supply of the medication (Johnson 2010).

The NIH's decision though was negative, primarily because of the time delays for alternative supplier(s) to receive regulatory approval as well as marketing authority under the Orphan Drug Act (Cassedy and Love 2014). But the NIH did require the Mount Shasta School of Medicine—the patent holder—along with Genzyme to provide monthly reports while committing itself to reconsider licensing if a third-party request was submitted. Additionally, the US Food and Drug Administration (FDA) allowed Shire PLC to give Replagal away for free pending US approval of the substitute drug. Replagal had been approved in Europe as a treatment for Fabry disease for more than a decade. During the Fabrazyme shortage, the FDA encouraged Shire to apply for regulatory approval in the United States, but eventually decided to require some additional clinical trials for Replagal, which led to Shire dropping its application (Kelley 2012).

These two examples, AZT and Fabrazyme, hinge more on drug pricing and availability than research access, but of course the evident strength of the private patent rights would extend to controlling research access, were that the issue. What the examples do indicate is that access and use of biomedical inventions is controlled by other legislation in addition to patent rights. In particular, FDA safety and efficacy testing and other laws like the Orphan Drug Act effectively control access and use, along with patent rights. Patents for sure limit access, but often if they evaporated, use rights would still be restricted by other legislation. Fully rectifying the research access situation would require more than changing the patent statutes.

While an issue not identified by Heller and Eisenberg (1998), concerns have arisen regarding so-called defensive patenting. In the current context, this is an effort by public research entities to patent genes and other gene-related materials so as to prevent private-sector control. The consequence can be duplicative and wasteful of research spending, as has been identified in the quest for control of the SARS virus. "The race to patent the SARS virus seems to be an inefficient means of allocating resources….It will also be difficult to resolve the competing claims between the various parties..." (Rimmer 2004, p. 372). Economists have studied the "winner-take-all" aspect of patenting for decades with no definitive conclusions. On the one hand, patent races can be wasteful of resources compared to cooperative research; on the other hand, they tend to hasten the identification of solutions (see a brief literature review in Jensen (2009)).

And then there is the recent emergence of "patent assertion entities," better known colloquially as "patent trolls." The troll "business model focuses not on developing or commercializing patented inventions but on buying and asserting patents..." (Yeh 2013, p. ii). While the trolls' patent claims are typically weak—they lose 92% of infringement cases—they prevail in private settlements by setting royalty demands below litigation costs, thus making a settlement a clear business decision (Yeh 2013). To date, patent trolls have focused on the IT sector, which has its own acute patent thicket issues, but biomedical patents could be a future target.

A final consideration of the public vs. private research issue is the ongoing reduction in public research support. The NIH budget for human genome research (National Human Genome Research Institute) has been flat for the past decade, while the total budget declined slightly, both in real terms (NIH n.d.). The sharp annual budget increases of the 1990s are over; maintaining research support for the foreseeable future depends increasingly on private monies, which often require incentives like patent rights.

Evidence of the Existence of an Anticommons

Actual evidence of an anticommons is the most telling factor; however, empirical studies are few. Hall and Harhoff (2012) cite a study of how the Cetus Corporation's use of intellectual property led to reductions in research and development. However, another quoted study found such practices "had little impact thus far due to the work-arounds adopted by university researchers: taking out licenses, inventing around, using informal research exemption, and developing available research tools" (Hall and Harhoff 2012, p. 557). Even the Golden Rice example cited above had a positive outcome. The inventors teamed up with the International Rice Research Institute (IRRI), a public research organization, and Syngenta, a private firm, to improve on the original Golden Rice product. Syngenta then negotiated a free humanitarian use license with the owners of the intellectual and technical property, while commercial users are required to pay royalties (IRRI n.d.).

One semi-documented example is that of Chiron, the patent holder for the hepatitis C virus (HCV). Gilead Sciences is on record for dropping work on a hepatitis C drug after it was sued for infringement because it was unwilling to pay Chiron's high initial licensing fees. Gilead and other small- to medium-sized companies did license the patents following a 2004 reduction in upfront licensing fees (although the post-commercialization royalty rate was increased). The high initial rates had not deterred larger drug firms from licensing the patents, as 15 had done (Gillene 2004).

Williams (2010) completed a systematic study of the privatization effect of gene ownership by comparing research on genes sequenced under the Human Genome Project, which had data publicly released within 24 hours, with those privately held by Celera for the 2001–2003 period, after which the ownership entered the public domain. By comparing the Celera and public research and commercialization outcomes over the entire sequencing period as well as the post-Celera privatization period, and making adjustments for the possibility the Celera-sequenced genes had inherently less scientific/commercial value, the author concludes Celera's brief ownership "led to reductions in subsequent scientific research and product development on the order of 20–30%" (Williams 2010, p. 1). These are very strong empirical findings, all the more so because Celera's ownership was brief, raising the possibility (not explored in the study) that longer-term ownership would have suppressed research to an even greater extent.

While strong, the results have several caveats. One is that Celera's ownership was based not on patents—which was the focus of Heller and Eisenberg's (1998) concerns—but instead was based on "contract law-based IP." Second, the analysis is based during the biotech boom, when the demand for prompt access to data and ownership rights could justify the willingness of major private firms to pay $5–$15 million annually for access to materials they knew would be entering the public domain in a few years. At a minimum, the uniqueness of the situation makes it more difficult to generalize the results. The author explains the outcome as a result of transaction costs, including the uncertainties over Celera's attempts to patent the genes it had sequenced and the conditions of granting free access to academic researchers for "noncommercial" research. And because Celera used a different sequencing technique from the public-sector researchers, Celera's involvement is often credited with speeding up the entire sequencing process. These are limited examples; more useful evidence is surveys of researchers' experiences.

Cho et al. (2003) surveyed 127 directors of clinical genetic testing services, concluding that "virtually all laboratory directors felt that patents have had a negative effect on all aspects of clinical testing, except on the quality of testing" (p. 5). The ability to conduct research decreased modestly. However, it is important to recognize that the respondents (all but one) were involved in genetic testing for clinical (fee based) rather than research purposes. It is unsurprising that patent holders prevented that group from using patented technologies with no charge and thwarted the development of alternative tests.

Walsh et al. (2003) contacted 70 attorneys, business managers, and scientists from universities and pharmaceutical and biotechnology firms for in-depth personal interviews. Their focus was the more extreme forms of access restriction. They first addressed the sheer number of patents potentially burdening research, a factor identified by Heller and Eisenberg (1998) when citing 100 patents termed "adrenergic receptor." Respondents, however, saw matters differently. Only a "small number" of licenses were found to be required—13 in the final analysis. Generally complicated cases involved 6–12 key patents, but the "more typical number was zero" (p. 294). Jenson and Murray (2005) though found that "some genes have up to 20 patents asserting rights to various gene uses and manifestations" (p. 239) suggesting additional FTO issues for researchers.

Next assessed were research tools (upstream inventions). This too was a problem area identified by Heller and Eisenberg (1998), who cited the Cetus and OncoMouse patents. Walsh et al. (2003), however, found "almost no evidence of such [negotiation] breakdowns that led to a project's cessation" (p. 298). Nor was royalty stacking found to be a practical barrier, and while the royalty burden could at times become "onerous," "the research always went forward" (p. 300). Reasons for this outcome include discounts for university and government researchers (Walsh et al. 2003) as well as various negotiation strategies. Those include establishing a "ceiling" (as well as a "floor" for individual components) for combined royalties along with the choice of a lump-sum payment or use of a patent pool or employing field-of-use licenses (Shotwell 2007). The Federal Trade Commission (2009) subsequently concluded that concerns about the patenting of research tools potentially obstructing commercialization of new products have yet to materialize.

For universities and other nonprofits, there is the option of infringement. Generally, if the work does not involve fees (such as for clinical tests), infringements are largely ignored; some may receive a cease-and-desist notification, but that is rare and frequently ignored as well. Myriad, for example, allowed tests so long as fees were not charged (Walsh et al. 2003).

Walsh et al. (2007) subsequently interviewed 507 academic biomedical researchers with similar results. That is, patents in the field do not regularly prevent researchers from access to the knowledge inputs for their research. None of the researchers interviewed abandoned a research project due to impediments from patents; few noted delays. However, nearly 20% indicated that requests for materials or data had been denied. The cause was not patents per se but rather scientific competition, a history of business activity, and the time and effort needed to fulfill requests, among others.

Also in 2007, Hansen et al. (2007) sought answers on the same topics from the membership rolls of the American Association for the Advancement of Science. A total of 2117 responses were received from a random sample of US-based members, with an overall response rate of 27%. Sample weights were varied according to the interest in a scientist member's area of research, with 34% of respondents in the biological sciences. Of particular relevance here, the researchers explored access to research technologies protected by intellectual property rights. Those technologies included research tools.

For all respondents, including academic respondents, industry was the major source of new technologies. Among the biological scientists, research tools constituted the majority of new acquisitions. For academics the dominant exchange mechanism used was a material transfer agreement (MTA), while industry scientists relied largely on licensing. Most transfers within academia were completed within 1 month; industry required 6 or more months for completion. Two thirds of respondents reported no difficulties with technology acquisition, but when difficulties appeared, they were more likely to come from academia than industry. When problems occurred, they resulted most often in delays (37%) and project modification (32%), with only 11% of projects needing to be abandoned. For all respondents, there was no increase in the amount of licensing required post-2002 compared to the prior period.

In 2002, the Organization for the Economic Co-operation and Development (OECD) conducted an international workshop on just these topics. Conclusions included the following:

- The transaction costs of negotiating arrangements within the complexity or overlapping patent claims are real and should not be ignored.
- The available evidence does not suggest a systematic breakdown in the licensing of genetic inventions.
- Evidence of fragmented patent rights, blocking patents, uncertainty, and abuses of the patent monopoly positions appear anecdotal and are not supported by existing economic studies.
- In specific areas, there is evidence of problems associated with the numbers and breadth of gene patents, although the exact cause of those problems has not been fully identified.
- FTO is not unduly impeded (OECD 2002).

Adelman and DeAngelis (2007, p.1729) examined 50,000+ biotech patents over the period of 1990–2004 for trends in numbers and ownership. They concluded that "the lack of concentrated control, the rising number of patent applications, and the continuous influx of new patent owners suggest that overall biotechnology innovation is not being impaired by the growth in patents issued each year."

Holman (2007) approached the issue from the perspective of human gene patents that had been litigated. The author carefully notes that infringement actions are not the sole measure of negative effects of patents—the payment of royalties would be an obvious one—but nonetheless provide an objective measure of the degree to which patent rights are asserted. Four categories of human gene patents are identified: (1) recombinant production of human therapeutic proteins, (2) research tools, (3) genetic testing products and services, and (4) gene therapy. Of the 4270 gene patents previously identified, only 18 were found to have been involved in six infringement actions. This is a litigation rate of 0.4%, far below the 1%–2% for all patents. Of the six actions, four were settled privately, one dismissed for lack of standing by the plaintiff, and one determined to be non-infringing. That is, not a single human gene patent had been determined by the courts to have been infringing. Access to research tools is of particular relevance to researchers, and all but seven infringement actions were identified in this manner. Citing a relationship between the level of litigation frequency and non-litigation impact, the author "find[s] that the impact of human gene patent litigation has been relatively modest [which] suggests that non-litigation impact is not as extensive as commonly perceived" (p. 359).

When considering gene patenting in particular, two additional anticommons-related issues arise: (1) does the uniqueness of a gene prevent "patenting around" it, creating a "double monopoly," and (2) do patents on genes prevent the sequencing of an individual's genome, a promising new field? Huys et al. (2009) examined 118 US patents selected using key words and classifications for 22 genetic-based diseases. The analysis involved scrutinizing by knowledgeable researchers to establish the necessity of having access to the technology for carrying out a diagnosis. Three levels of blockage were established—easily circumvented, circumvention requires a substantial investment, and nearly impossible to circumvent ("blocking claims").

Only 3% of the gene patents were considered to be "blocking"—too few to constitute a patent thicket. Conversely, 30% of the method claims were categorized as blocking, enough to constitute a thicket. Overall, the authors concluded that "the present analysis and accompanying observations do not point to the existence of a wide patent thicket in genetic diagnostic testing. Rather, they highlight a problem of lack of transparency and clarity, leading to legal uncertainty" (Huys et al. 2009, p. 909). The recent Supreme Court decision in *Myriad*, which invalidated patents for isolated genes (see above), will largely obviate this issue going forward. In addition, existing gene patents may possibly be revoked.

Conclusions

While the trend in the privatization of biotechnology research is far from ideal, the anticipated anticommons has not materialized significantly. Simply stated, that emperor is scantily clad. Contributing factors mitigating the anticommons potential are changes in patent-granting practices, use by firms of nonexclusive licenses for research tools, and the facility of simple material transfer agreements used by academic researchers. In many cases, industry and academics developed "working solutions" under which research access is facilitated for noncommercial purposes. "The fact of the matter is that academic researchers who are not engaged in research for commercial use are not affected by the existence of a patent. Biotech companies do not sue researchers who are conducting research for purely academic purposes" (Feldbaum 2002, p. 1).

Certainly there are, and have been, holdups and disruptions over access to materials, just not to the extent initially feared. These observations, though, are about the past, and "though fears that gene patents could stifle research have not been borne out, for the most part, commentators are now raising questions about how the many existing gene patents might be used in the future" (Cook-Deegan 2008, p. 71). So what can be done? Two legislative remedies were attempted in the 2000s. One—the Genomic Research and Diagnostic Accessibility Act of 2002—was a "limited exemption from liability for certain uses of patented genetic sequences and genetic sequence information in the context of basic research and genetic diagnostic information" (Holman 2007, p. 295). The bill was not acted on by Congress and was not reintroduced when the introducing representative left office. The second would bar the patenting of any nucleotide sequence, or its functions or correlations, or the naturally occurring products it specifies (the Genomic Research and Accessibility Act of 2007). This language is very broad and ambiguous, potentially encompassing all inventions involving polynucleotides (Holman 2007). The bill never made it out of committee. Congressional action to control patent trolls has met a similar fate. Following a yearlong effort, the process was declared all but dead when patent reform was withdrawn from the Senate Judiciary Committee's agenda in May 2014

(Wyatt 2014). These experiences strongly suggest any legislative remedy is off the table for the foreseeable future.

Another possible "remedy" is to be more specific about defining the issue, at least as it applies to patent numbers and ownership. From their assessment of 50,000 patents in the biotechnology complex, Adelman and DeAngelis (2007, p. 1729) were able to say that their analysis "also reveals the many pitfalls of seeking to resolve this question at a synoptic level using simple metrics. In this sense, both the advocates of the anticommons theory and enthusiasts of patent characteristics err by oversimplifying the multidimensional character of patent dynamics." Further, commentators on the anticommons oftentimes mix the issues of the commercialization of products incorporating patented genes and testing methods with the effect of patents on research access. For example, the patent and related rights issues surrounding Golden Rice related to commercial use, not research access, did not restrict product development (see above). Both topics are worthy of discussion, but they are not the same issue and should not be conflated. And the issue with Celera's IP of certain human gene sequences (see above) was based on contract, not patent, law. The consequences of the two may be similar, but a policy remedy would require an entirely different approach.

And then it is important not to raise the level of rhetoric, as Michael Crichton did in a *New York Times* op-ed (2007):

> "YOU, or someone you love, may die because of a gene patent that should never have been granted in the first place. Sound far-fetched? Unfortunately, it's only too real. Gene patents are now used to halt research, prevent medical testing, and keep vital information from you and your doctor. Gene patents slow the pace of medical advance on deadly diseases."

Such words do not advance the level of debate on a complex subject. But the concerned have a passionate audience; why else would the citations to the Heller and Eisenberg (1998) article continue to grow when there is so little empirical support for their cautionary note?

So where does that leave the state of affairs of the anticommons? Basically it is where it was in 1998; there "may/can/likely/potentially/might" be a problem (Heller and Eisenberg 1998). But critically, the likelihood has lessened due to time, changes in patent practice, and the largely successful efforts by industry and academia to reach workable solutions while ongoing declines in public research funding will accelerate the need for patent-focused private funding. Nonetheless, the potential remains and must be monitored, which is best done by more systematic empirical studies. Policy should not be based on anecdotal evidence, especially when that policy is made by the Supreme Court.

References

Adelman, D.E., and K.L. DeAngelis. 2007. Patent metrics: The mismeasure of innovation in the biotech patent debate (Arizona Legal Studies Discussion Paper No. 06–10). Tucson, AZ: The University of Arizona Rogers College of Law.

Cassedy, C., and J. Love. 2014. *Timeline for Fabrazyme, Replagal*. Washington, DC: Knowledge Ecology International. Available on the World Wide Web: http://keionline.org/sites/default/files/Replagal_Fabrazyme_Timeline.pdf.

Cho, M.K., S. Illangasekare, M.A. Weaver, D.G.B. Leonard, and J.F. Merz. 2003. Effects of Patents and Licenses on the Provision of Clinical Genetic Testing Services. *Journal of Molecular Diagnostics* 5: 3–8.

Cook-Deegan, R., and C. Heaney. 2010. Patents in genomics and human genetics. *Annual Review of Genomics and Human Genetics* 11: 383–425.

Cook-Deegan, R. 2008. Gene patents. In *From Birth to Death and Bench to Clinic: The Hastings Center Bioethics Briefing Book for Journalists, Policymakers, and Campaigns (Chapter 15)*, ed. M. Crowley. The Hastings Center: Garrison, NY. Available on the World Wide Web: http://www.thehastingscenter.org/uploadedFiles/Publications/Briefing_Book/gene%20patents%20chapter.pdf.

Crichton, M. 2007. Patenting Life (Op-Ed). *The New York Times*.

Federal Trade Commission. 2009. *Emerging Health Care Issues: Follow-on Biologic Drug Competition (FTC Report)*. Washington, DC: Federal Trade Commission.

Feldbaum, C.B. 2002. *Letter to the Honorable Lynn Rivers*. Washington, DC: Biotechnology Industry Organization. Available on the World Wide Web: http://www.bio.org/sites/default/files/rivers.pdf.

Gillene, D. 2004. Chiron relaxes patent licenses. *Los Angeles Times*.

Hall, B.H., and D. Harhoff. 2012. *Recent Research on the Economics of Patents (Working Paper 17773)*. Washington, DC: National Bureau of Economic Research.

Hansen, S.A., M.R. Kisielewski, and J.L. Asher. 2007. *Intellectual Property Experiences in the United States Scientific Community: A Report by the Project on Science and Intellectual Property in the Public Interest*. Washington, DC, American Association for the Advancement of Science.:Available at http://astro.berkeley.edu/~kalas/ethics/documents/intellectual_property/SIPPI_US_IP_Survey.pdf.

Hardin, G. 1968. The Tragedy of the Commons. *Science* 162: 1243–1248.

Heller, M.A., and R.S. Eisenberg. 1998. Can Patents Deter Innovation? The Anticommons in Biomedical Research. *Science* 280: 698–701.

Holman, C.M. 2007. The Impact of Human Gene Patents on Innovation and Access: A Survey of Human Gene Patent Litigation. *UMKC Law Review* 76: 295–361.

Huys, I., N. Berthels, G. Matthijs, and G. Van Overwalle. 2009. Legal Uncertainty in the Area of Genetic Diagnostic Testing. *Nature Biotechnology* 27: 903–909.

International Rice Research Institute (IRRI). n.d. *Are Private Companies Involved in the Golden Rice Project?* [website]. Los Baños, Philippines. Available on the World Wide Web: http://irri.org/golden-rice/faqs/are-private-companies-involved-in-the-golden-rice-project.

Jensen, R.A. 2009. Patent races. In *The New Palgrave Dictionary of Economics*, ed. S.N. Durlauf and L.E. Blume. Basingstoke, Hampshire, UK: Palgrave Macmillan.

Jenson, K., and F. Murray. 2005. The Intellectual Property Landscape of the Human Genome. *Science* 310: 239–240.

Johnson, J. 2010. *Petition to use Authority under the Bayh-Dole Act to Promote Access to Fabryzyme (Agalsidase Beta), an Invention Supported by and Licensed by the National Institutes of Health under Grant No. DK-34045*. Concordia, MO: Fabry Support and Information Group. Available on the World Wide Web: http://www.genomicslawreport.com/wp-content/uploads/2011/01/Fabrazyme-Bayh-Dole-Petition.pdf.

Kelley, T. 2012. Shire Drops after Pulling U.S. Application for Replagal. *Bloomberg*. Available on the World Wide Web: http://www.bloomberg.com/news/print/2012-03-15/shire-drops-after-pulling-u-s-application-for-replagal.html.

Kryder, R.D., S.P. Kowalski, and A.F. Krattiger. 2000. *The Intellectual and Technical Property Components of Pro-vitamin A Rice (Golden Rice): A Preliminary Freedom-to-Operate Review (ISAAA Issue Brief No. 20–1000)*. Ithaca, NY: International Service for the Acquisition of Agri-biotech Applications (ISAAA).

National Institutes of Health (NIH). n.d. *NIH Almanac*. Bethesda, MD: National Institutes of Health.

Nelsen, L. 2007. Evaluating Inventions From Research Institutions. In *Intellectual Property Management in Health and Agricultural Innovation: A Handbook of Best Practices*, ed. A. Krattiger et al., 795–804. Oxford, UK: Centre for the Management of Intellectual Property in Health Research and Development (MIHR) and Public Intellectual Property Resource for Agriculture (PIPRA).

Organization for the Economic Co-operation and Development (OECD). 2002. *Genetic Inventions, Intellectual Property Rights and Licensing Practices: Evidence and Policies (Workshop Report)*. Paris: Organisation for Economic Co-operation and Development. Available on the World Wide Web: http://www.oecd.org/science/sci-tech/2491084.pdf.

Potrykus, I. 2011. The 'Golden Rice' tale. *AgBioWorld*. Available on the World Wide Web: http://www.agbioworld.org/biotech-info/topics/goldenrice/tale.html.

Rimmer, M. 2004. The Race to Patent the SARS Virus: The TRIPS Agreement and Access to Essential Medicines. *Melbourne Journal of International Law* 5 (2): 335–374.

Shotwell, S.L. 2007. Field-of-Use Licensing. In *Intellectual Property Management in Health and Agricultural Innovation: A Handbook of Best Practices*, ed. A. Krattiger et al., 1113–1120. Oxford: MIHR and PIPRA.

US Patent and Trademark Office (USPTO). 2014. *Manual of Patent Examining Procedure* (Section 2404). USPTO: Alexandria, VA. Available at www.uspto.gov/web/offices/pac/mpep/

Walsh, J.P., A. Arora, and W.M. Cohen. 2003. Effects of Research Tool Patents and Licensing on Biomedical Innovation. In *Patents in the Knowledge-Based Economy*, ed. W.M. Cohen and S.A. Merrill. Washington, DC: National Research Council, National Academies Press.

Walsh, J.P., W.M. Cohen, and C. Cho. 2007. Where Excludability Matters: Material versus Intellectual Property in Academic Biomedical Research. *Research Policy* 36: 1184–1203.

Williams, H.L. 2010. Intellectual Property Rights and Innovation: Evidence from Human Genome. *Journal of Political Economics* 121 (1): 1–27.

Wyatt, E. 2014. Legislation to Protect Against 'Patent Trolls' is Shelved (Business Day section). *The New York Times*.

Yarchoan, M. 2012. The History of Zidovudine (AZT): Partnership and Conflict. *ScribD 4*.

Yeh, B.T. 2013. *An Overview of the 'Patent Trolls' Debate*. Washington, DC: Congressional Research Service. Available on the World Wide Web: http://fas.org/sgp/crs/misc/R42668.pdf.

Patent Characteristics and Patent Ownership Change in Agricultural Biotechnology

Etleva Gjonça and Amalia Yiannaka

Abstract We examine the effect of various patent characteristics on changes in patent ownership that occurred due to mergers, acquisitions, and spin-offs in the agricultural biotechnology industry in the 1980s and 1990s. Our goal is to shed light on the role certain patent qualities may play in the transfer of knowledge and technology that takes place through merger and acquisition activity. Specifically, we empirically measure the effect of patent value, scope/breadth, strength, and the nationality of the patent owner on the occurrence and frequency of patent ownership change in the agricultural biotechnology sector during the 1980s and 1990s. We find that the greater the patent breadth and the less valuable and "weaker" the patent, the greater the likelihood and frequency of patent ownership change. Also, the nature of patent ownership affects patent ownership change, with patents owned by multiple owners of different nationalities most likely to change hands.

Introduction

Patents are often viewed as the strongest form of intellectual property protection.[1] The rationale for granting patents is to stimulate innovative activity through the disclosure of technical information and to encourage investment in innovation through a temporary monopoly that prevents others from commercially benefiting from the innovator's

---

[1] A patent provides its owner exclusive rights over a claimed invention and is granted by the Patent Office of a country or group of countries (e.g., the European Patent Office) on the basis of a patent application. The exclusive right provides a legal right to the patent owner to exclude others from making, using, offering for sale, selling, or importing the patented invention without the owner's permission for a period of up to 20 years from the date that the application for patent was filed. In return, the owner is required to disclose the claimed invention to the public.

E. Gjonça
University of Bologna, Bologna, Italy

Erasmus University, Rotterdam, Netherlands

University of Hamburg, Hamburg, Germany

A. Yiannaka (✉)
University of Nebraska, Lincoln, NE, USA
e-mail: ayiannaka2@unl.edu

© Springer International Publishing AG 2018
N. Kalaitzandonakes et al. (eds.), *From Agriscience to Agribusiness*, Innovation, Technology, and Knowledge Management, https://doi.org/10.1007/978-3-319-67958-7_8

research. Patents have promoted new technologies and boosted the development of many industries through the provision of much-needed incentives for innovation. A case in point is biotechnology in general, and agricultural biotechnology in particular, which experienced tremendous growth following the Diamond vs. Chakrabarty Supreme Court ruling in 1980 that allowed the patenting of living organisms.

Starting in the mid-1980s and up until the early 2000s, the number of biotechnology (including agricultural biotechnology) patent applications to, and patents granted by, the United States Patent and Trademark Office (USPTO) grew exponentially (Adelman and DeAngelis 2007; Graff et al. 2003). The rapid growth in biotechnology patenting led to claims that it would impede innovation, thus leading to anti-commons problems. Empirical studies, including a comprehensive study by Adelman and DeAngelis (2007) that examined more than 52,000 biotechnology patents issued by the USPTO during the period 1990–2004, provide no support for the anti-commons theory in biotechnology. Adelman and DeAngelis (2007) showed that biotechnology patent applications kept increasing in the mid-2000s even though the number of patents granted by the USPTO started falling due to the introduction of more stringent standards, new entrants continued entering in the biotechnology sector, and ownership of biotechnology patents was diffuse, with the number of entities obtaining biotechnology patents continuously increasing during their study period.

During this period of growth for biotechnology patents, the agricultural biotechnology industry experienced consolidation and restructuring. Joint ventures, contracts, licensing arrangements, mergers, acquisitions, and strategic alliances increased and led to greater cooperation among firms.[2] There is little dispute that a firm's intellectual property plays an important role in changes in its ownership structure. This is especially true when this intellectual property is protected by a patent, as opposed to being kept a trade secret, in which case all relevant knowledge has to be disclosed, thus making it easier for competitors and/or complementors to evaluate its scope and value.[3] Schimmelpfennig, King, and Naseem (2003) showed that the acquisition of intellectual property is an important motivator for mergers and acquisitions, as significant as physical capital, while Graff et al. (2003) found that firms tend to acquire complementary intellectual property. Rausser (1999) drew attention to the fact that a major motivation behind the mergers and acquisitions in the agricultural biotechnology industry in the 1980s and 1990s was, according to industry insiders, control over patent rights. To investigate this claim, Marco and Rausser (2008) empirically examined the role patent rights played in the consolidation of the agricultural biotechnology industry, using patents as explanatory variables for mergers, acquisitions, and spin-offs. Specifically, the study examined how

---

[2] In 1998, five firms (AstraZeneca, DuPont, Monsanto, Novartis, and Aventis) accounted for nearly two-thirds of the global pesticide market (60%), almost one-quarter (23%) of the commercial seed market, and almost all of the transgenic seed market (Johnson and Melkonyan 2003).

[3] As an example, in August 1996, Plant Genetic Systems (PGS) was purchased by AgrEvro for $730 million, while its prior market capitalization was only $30 million. According to AgrEvro, $700 million of the purchase price was assigned to the valuation of the patent-protected trait technologies owned by PGS (Marco and Rausser 2008).

patent enforceability, which was captured by various patent characteristics, affects the likelihood of consolidation and found that it is an important factor and that firms that hold strongly protected patents are more likely to engage in acquisitions than firms that hold weakly protected patents.

Not all patents are equally attractive, however, to firms that could potentially desire to control the technology and knowledge that they protect. The commercial and strategic value of a patent depends not only on the nature of the innovation the patent protects but, critically, on patent characteristics such as the scope/breadth of the patent that, to a large extent, determine the patent's legal strength (e.g., the extent to which a patent can survive a validity challenge) and consequently the effective life of the patent.[4] As an example, a broad patent makes it harder for competitors to enter the market with non-infringing innovations, which may increase the incentive to acquire the firm that holds them. At the same time, a broad patent is more likely to be legally challenged and infringed and less likely to survive a direct or indirect validity challenge; these factors affect the value the patent confers to its owner (Yiannaka and Fulton 2006) and may influence their decision to transfer ownership.

Given that in addition to patents and other intellectual property rights, complex financial and often unobservable strategic factors influence a firm's decision to merge or acquire, we cannot directly measure the effect of patent characteristics on a firm's incentive to merge or acquire. In this study, we try to gain insights on the role certain patent qualities may play in the transfer of knowledge and technology that takes place through mergers and acquisitions by examining what type of patents was more likely to change hands in the agricultural biotechnology industry in the 1980s and 1990s when the change of ownership was the result of mergers, acquisitions, and spin-offs.

Specifically, using a dataset of 6223 private-sector agricultural biotechnology patents issued between 1976 and 2000 by the USPTO, we investigate whether and how patent characteristics that are used as proxies for patent value, patent scope/breadth, and patent strength, as well as the nature of patent ownership, influenced the occurrence and frequency of patent ownership change that resulted from mergers, acquisitions, and spin-offs in the agricultural biotechnology sector during the 1980s and 1990s. Our results show that the greater the breadth of a patent and the less valuable and the "weaker" a patent, the greater the likelihood and frequency of patent ownership change. In addition, we find that patents owned by multiple owners of different nationalities were more likely to change hands.

Our results may be of interest to innovators/"original" patent holders and patent examiners, as they both determine a number of patent characteristics during the patent-granting process, the former in their patent applications (e.g., patent claims and backward citations) and the latter when they request amendments (to patent claims and citations) and make patent classification assignments.[5]

---

[4] See Yiannaka and Fulton (2006) for a detailed discussion of the critical importance of patent scope/breadth in determining the value of a patent to the innovator.

[5] For a detailed discussion of the patentee's role in shaping the scope of patent protection, see Yiannaka and Fulton (2006).

Our study builds on a rich literature that uses patent characteristics to study innovation, technical change, optimal patent design and policy, and, more recently, merger and acquisition activity. This literature recognizes that, unlike patent counts which, when used alone, are uninformative of the nature and/or value of the innovation protected by the patent, patent characteristics can convey useful information.

Patent characteristics such as patent length (i.e., the statutory life of a patent) and patent breadth/scope (i.e., the technological territory protected by the patent) have been used in the study of optimal patent design (Gallini 1992; Gilbert and Shapiro 1990; Hopenhayn and Mitchell 2001; Takalo 2001), patenting and licensing behavior (Green and Schotchmer 1995; Yiannaka and Fulton 2006), the R&D process, and the pace of future innovations (Denicolo 1996; Matutes et al. 1996; O'Donoghue et al. 1998). A few empirical studies have tried to "quantify" the scope/breadth of a patent. These studies have used the number of patent claims, the international patent classification (IPC) assignments,[6] and backward citations[7] as patent breadth indicators (Harhoff and Reitzig 2004; Lanjouw and Shankerman 2001; Lerner 1994). Similarly, a number of studies have tried to estimate the value of a patent. These studies show that the number of forward citations (i.e., citations a patent receives from subsequent patents) is a good proxy for patent value (Hall et al. 2005; Jaffe et al. 1993; Trajtenberg 1990).

The impact of certain patent characteristics and patenting patterns on the consolidation of the agricultural biotechnology industry has been considered more recently. King and Schimmelpfennig (2005) used backward and forward patent citations to capture patent quality and measure whether the quality of patents is affected by merger and acquisition activity. They compared the number of backward and forward citations for an average patent held by every parent and their subsidiaries. Their results indicate that both types of citations are higher for the parent firms than for their subsidiaries. Brennan et al. (2005) empirically examined merger and acquisition activity by comparing the number of patents held by the top four firms (Monsanto, Pioneer, Novartis, and DuPont) before and after mergers or acquisitions took place. They showed that the number of patents held by these firms significantly increased after mergers and acquisitions. The study also examines the performance and concentration of the innovation market in the plant agricultural biotechnology industry. Assuming that market power is related to market share—where market share is defined as the proportion of patents owned or field trials conducted by a firm—they found an increase in the concentration in the innovation market, as measured by the share of the top four firms, with Monsanto being the major force behind the increase. Marco and Rausser (2008) used the average annual forward patent citations, the proportion of backward citations that are self-citations, the number of four-digit IPCs, the age of the patent at the time of litigation and negotiation, and the technology field of the patent as proxies for patent enforceability. They estimated

---

[6] The IPC classification consists of nine-digit classes of different technologies assigned by the patent examiner to each patent during the patent examination process.

[7] Backward citations are the number of prior patents and other relevant references that constitute the prior art cited in a patent.

the effect of patent enforceability on the rate at which firms acquire and showed that patent enforceability is significantly and negatively related to merger activity, therefore suggesting that firms that hold weakly protected patents are more likely to engage in acquisitions than firms that hold strongly protected patents. Finally, Schimmelpfennig and King (2006) showed that the highest-quality patents (measured by forward citations) are less likely to change hands in the agricultural biotechnology sector.

Our study adds to the above literature by examining the impact of various patent characteristics that are used as proxies for patent breadth/scope, patent value, and patent strength on the occurrence and frequency of patent ownership change that resulted from mergers, acquisitions, and spin-offs in the agricultural biotechnology sector during the 1980s and 1990s. The study discusses in detail and provides a justification for the patent characteristics that we use as proxies for the patent qualities considered in our analysis. The patent dataset and the variables used in the analysis are described first, followed by the results of the empirical models and the study's conclusions.

Data Description

Data Source

Our dataset was obtained from the Agricultural Biotechnology Intellectual Property (ABIP) database, which is made available by the Economic Research Service (ERS) of the US Department of Agriculture (USDA ERS 2006). The ABIP database provides information for US and non-US utility patents on inventions in agricultural biotechnology issued between 1976 and 2000, including information about the ownership of these patents, whether patents are held by the public or private sector, and changes in patent ownership due to firm mergers, acquisitions, and spin-offs between 1988 and 2002.[8] The database is fully searchable and accessible online[9] and has been used in a number of studies that examine the consolidation of the agricultural biotechnology sector (e.g., Brennan et al. 2005; King and Schimmelpfennig 2005; Marco and Rausser 2008; Schimmelpfennig and King 2006). Our dataset consists of 6223 private-sector US and non-US agricultural biotechnology patents that were issued by the USPTO between 1976 and 2000 and includes information on the number of patent claims, the assigned IPC codes, nationality of the patent

---

[8] In the database, patents are categorized according to a technology classification system, which includes plant technologies, patented organisms, non-plant, metabolic pathways and biological processes in plants, metabolic pathways and biological processes in animals, protection and nutrition, and biological control of plants and animals, pharmaceuticals, genetic transformation, metabolic pathways and biological processes, DNA scale, and genomics (Schimmelpfennig and King 2006).

[9] See http://webarchives.cdlib.org/sw1m04028n/http://www.ers.usda.gov/data/AgBiotechIP/. The website provides detailed information on the nature of the data and the way it was generated.

holder, forward and backward citations, and references to the non-patent literature for each patent, as well as changes in patent ownership due to firm mergers, acquisitions, and spin-offs between 1988 and 2002.

Variables

In what follows, we describe the independent and dependent variables that are used in our analysis and provide a justification for the patent characteristics that we use as proxies for patent breadth, value, and strength.

Ownership Change

Ownership change during the period of our study resulted from mergers, acquisitions, and spin-offs. Schimmelpfennig and King (2006) and King and Schimmelpfennig (2005) utilized ownership change information provided by the ABIP database to examine mergers, acquisitions, and the flows of agricultural biotechnology intellectual property. In this article, we employ a dummy variable to capture the occurrence of patent ownership change (whether the patent changed hands or not) and a variable that has a natural order to capture the frequency of patent ownership change (the number of times a patent has changed hands). In the dataset, 57.37% of all patents did not change hands, 33.92% changed hands once, 8.07% changed hands twice, and 0.64% changed hands three times.

Number of Total Claims

Patent claims are an important feature of a patent since they define the technological territory protected by the patent. In the patent literature, a positive relationship between the number of patent claims and patent breadth is assumed (Matutes et al. 1996; Merges and Nelson 1990; Miller and Davis 1990). The number of patent claims has been used as an indicator of patent breadth in a number of patent studies. As an example, the number of total claims is used as a proxy for patent breadth in Lanjouw and Shankerman (2001), who examined the determinants of patent litigation, and in Harhoff and Reitzig (2004), who examined the determinants of opposition activity. In line with the above studies, we use the number of total claims as a proxy for patent breadth and seek to examine whether they play a role in patent ownership change.

International Patent Classification (IPC) Assignments

During the USPTO examination, each patent is assigned by the patent examiner to a nine-digit category of the IPC system. Lerner (1994) suggested that IPC classification reflects the economic importance of new inventions and employed the IPC assignments as a proxy for patent scope. According to Lerner (1994), there is a positive relationship between the number of IPC classes and subclasses assigned to a patent and the breadth of the patent; the greater the number of IPC classes and subclasses assigned to the patent, the greater is the breadth of the patent. Lanjouw and Shankerman (2001) used the number of IPC assignments as another proxy for patent breadth (in addition to patent claims) to examine patent litigation patterns and found that patents with many IPC assignments are less likely to be litigated. Harhoff and Reitzig (2004) utilized the number of IPC assignments as another proxy for patent breadth to examine the likelihood of patent opposition. In this article, the count of the number of four-digit IPC subclasses to which a patent is assigned is used as another proxy for patent breadth as in Lerner (1994), Lanjouw and Shankerman (2001), and Harhoff and Reitzig (2004).

References to Prior Patents (Backward Citations)

Backward citations are the number of prior patents cited in a patent. Like claims, the citations define the property rights of the patentee. Harhoff and Reitzig (2004) employed backward citations to capture the likelihood of patent opposition, while Lanjouw and Shankerman (2001) examined the effect of backward citations in litigation activity as failure to cite relevant patents is grounds for having the patent invalidated.[10]

For our analysis, we count the overall number of backward citations listed in the patent and use them in two ways—as another proxy for patent breadth and as a proxy for how prone the patent is to litigation and invalidation (i.e., patent strength). As suggested by Trajtenberg (1990, p. 174) "[patent citations] represent a limitation on the scope of the property rights established by a patent's claim." Thus, according to Trajtenberg, there is a negative relationship between the number of backward citations and the breadth of patent protection as the greater is the number of studies/patents cited as prior art in any given patent, the smaller is the technological territory over which claims can be made by that patent. On the other hand, as suggested by Lanjouw and Shankerman (2001), the smaller the number of backward citations, the greater the risk that the innovator failed to reference the relevant literature and, thus, the greater the risk of patent litigation and invalidation. Thus, when deciding on the number of backward citations to be included in the patent, the innovator faces a trade-off; a small

---

[10] Backward citations have been used in a number of studies, such as Jaffe et al. (1993), who examined the impact of citations to previous patents in the geographical localization of the technological activity; Jaffe and Trajtenberg (1996), who used backward citations to analyze the process by which existing knowledge is transferred over time to different locations; and Jaffe and Trajtenberg (1999), who measured knowledge flows based on the information revealed by backward citations.

number of backward citations suggest greater patent breadth but also greater likelihood of patent litigation and invalidation and, consequently, a "weaker" patent.

References to Non-patent Literature

Scientific knowledge is referenced by patentees, while patent examiners search for relevant references in the scientific literature, since results from published research can be used to confirm the state of the art against which the application has to be evaluated. Harhoff and Reitzig (2004) used references to non-patent literature as an indicator of patent value—where the larger the number of these references, the higher the patent value—and suggested that patents with a large number of references to non-patent literature would face a higher likelihood of opposition. However, as was discussed in the case of backward citations, failure to cite prior art may lead to patent invalidation, which in turn implies that the greater is the number of references to non-patent literature, the greater is the likelihood of patent invalidation. In addition, when the references involve various scientific fields, a greater number of references may indicate a broader patent. In this article, we want to examine whether and how the number of references to non-patent literature affects the incidence and frequency of ownership change. Given the lack of consensus in the literature as to what this variable could capture, we will be cautious when interpreting its potential effect on the incidence and frequency of ownership change.

Citations Received from Succeeding Patents (Forward Citations)

Citations received by a patent from future patents are indicative of its contribution to the state of the art. Forward citations have been widely used in the patent literature. For example, Lanjouw and Shankerman (2001) used forward citations as an indicator of patent value to investigate its relationship with litigation activity and find that more valuable patents (i.e., patents with more forward citations) are more likely to be litigated. Schimmelpfennig and King (2006) viewed forward citations as a measure of patent quality and employed them to analyze the diffusion of knowledge among different technology classifications in the agricultural biotechnology industry. King and Schimmelpfennig (2005) used forward citations as an indicator of patent quality to examine whether the quality of patents was affected by merger and acquisition activity. Similar to the above studies, we use forward citations as a measure of patent value and examine their effect on the incidence and frequency of patent ownership change.

Patent Ownership

The patent holder may be an individual, a firm, a nonprofit organization, or a group of individuals and firms. The nationality of patent ownership is that of the assignee, or otherwise it is the nationality of the inventor. We create dummy variables to account for patent owners from the USA, Europe, Canada, Japan, Australia, and New Zealand and group the remaining ones as patent owners from the rest of the world (RoW). In addition, we create a dummy variable to account for patents owned by owners of different nationalities. The effect of these variables on changes in patent ownership is examined.

Descriptive Statistics and Empirical Results

Descriptive Statistics

The empirical analysis is based on data covering private sector US and non-US patents in the agricultural biotechnology industry that were granted by the USPTO between 1976 and 2000. The complete dataset contains 6223 US and non-US patents and includes information on patent claims, assigned IPC codes, the nationality of the patent holder, forward and backward citations, and references to the non-patent literature for each patent.

Summary statistics for the patents in our sample are given in Table 1. The patents have, on average, 1.894 IPC classifications. Independent claims range from 1 to 69, while dependent claims range from 0 to 184 with an average of 13.45 total claims per patent. Forward citations range from 0 to 549 citations per patent, with an average of about 7.381 citations per patent; citations to prior patents range from 0 to 196 at an average of about 6.768 citations per patent; citations to non-patent literature range from 0 to 535, while total backward citations (i.e., patent and non-patent literature) range from 0 to 731 with an average of 21 citations per patent. American nationals own the largest share of patents with 62.1%, followed by Europeans who own 24%, Japanese who own 10.6%, Canadians who own 1%, Australian and New Zealanders

Table 1 Descriptive statistics for the agricultural biotechnology patents ($N = 6223$)

Variable	Mean	S.D.	Minimum	Maximum
Number of IPC assignments	1.894	0.778	1	7
Number of independent claims	2.885	2.797	1	69
Number of dependent claims	13.45	13.315	0	184
Number of total claims	16.338	14.425	1	196
Number of backward citations	6.768	9.938	0	196
Number of references to non-patent literature	14.283	23.669	0	535
Number of total backward citations	21.051	30.579	0	731
Number of forward citations	7.381	17.222	0	549
Owner from the USA	0.621	0.485	0	1
Owner from Europe	0.240	0.427	0	1
Owner from Canada	0.010	0.099	0	1
Owner from Japan	0.106	0.308	0	1
Owner from Australia and New Zealand	0.008	0.087	0	1
Owner from the rest of the world (RoW)	0.006	0.077	0	1
Owner from multiple countries	0.007	0.085	0	1

who own 0.8%, and owners from other countries who own 0.6% of the patents granted. Meanwhile, only 0.7% of the patents have owners from more than one country.

Tables 2, 3, and 4 show the relationships between the incidence of ownership change and three of the exogenous variables—namely, backward citations, forward citations, and references to the non-patent literature, respectively. To assess these relationships, we use the Pearson's chi-square test, which is commonly used to assess independence between paired observations of two variables. The null hypothesis holds that there is no relationship between the incidence of ownership change and backward citations (Table 2), forward citations (Table 3), and references to the non-patent literature (Table 4).[11] The three tables present data on the univariate distribution of the exogenous variables as well as data on the bivariate relationship

Table 2 Backward citations and incidence of ownership change

Number of backward citations	Number of patents	% of total patents	Incidence of ownership change: all patents	Incidence of change: US owners		Incidence of change: European owners		Incidence of change: patents of other owners	
				Patents	Mean	Patents	Mean	Patents	Mean
0	820	13.18	0.494	574	0.540	147	0.605	99	0.606
1–5	2977	47.84	0.429	1793	0.539	738	0.343	446	0.13
6–10	1216	19.54	0.365	665	0.451	338	0.325	213	0.159
11–15	560	9.00	0.418	357	0.440	139	0.446	64	0.234
>15	650	10.45	0.457	479	0.474	135	0.444	36	0.278
Total	6223	100.00	0.427	3868	0.507	1497	0.383	858	0.143
p-value			(0.000)		(0.000)		(0.000)		(0.000)

Note: The p-value refers to a Pearson test of the hypothesis that there is no relationship between the number of backward citations and the incidence of ownership change

Table 3 Forward citations and incidence of ownership change

Number of forward citations	Number of patents	% of total patents	Incidence of ownership change: all patents	Incidence of change: US owners		Incidence of change: European owners		Incidence of change: patents of other owners	
				Patents	Mean	Patents	Mean	Patents	Mean
0	1457	23.40	0.463	820	0.572	407	0.415	230	0.156
1–5	2898	46.60	0.418	1681	0.508	768	0.392	449	0.125
6–10	788	12.70	0.410	508	0.482	181	0.343	99	0.162
11–15	358	5.70	0.388	262	0.439	59	0.305	37	0.162
>15	722	11.60	0.429	597	0.464	82	0.293	43	0.203
Total	6223	100.00	0.427	3868	0.507	1497	0.383	858	0.143
p-value			(0.000)		(0.000)		(0.000)		(0.000)

Note: The p-value refers to a Pearson test of the hypothesis that there is no relationship between the number of forward citations and the incidence of ownership change

---

[11] The results of the Pearson's chi-square test are evaluated by reference to the chi-square distribution.

Table 4 References to the non-patent literature and incidence of ownership change

Number of references to the non-patent literature	Number of patents	% of total patents	Incidence of ownership change: All patents	Incidence of change: US owners		Incidence of change: European owners		Incidence of change: patents of other owners	
				Patents	Mean	Patents	Mean	Patents	Mean
0	921	14.80	0.321	503	0.384	291	0.302	127	0.118
1–5	1696	27.25	0.353	864	0.471	481	0.319	351	0.108
6–10	1054	16.94	0.398	591	0.486	267	0.4	196	0.133
11–15	694	11.15	0.484	465	0.540	142	0.451	87	0.241
>15	1858	29.86	0.541	1445	0.569	316	0.509	97	0.237
Total	6223	100.00	0.427	3868	0.507	1497	0.383	858	0.143
p-value			(0.000)		(0.000)		(0.000)		(0.000)

Note: The p-value refers to a Pearson test of the hypothesis that there is no relationship between the number of references to the non-patent literature and the incidence of ownership change within the indicated group of patents

between these variables and the incidence of ownership change. These statistics are presented for the total number of patents in our sample and, separately, based on patent ownership for US patent owners, European patent owners, and patent owners from the rest of the countries, which are grouped together.

According to Table 2, backward citations are highly correlated with the likelihood of ownership change both in the overall sample of backward citations and in each of the subgroups. The group of patents that did not receive backward citations changed ownership in 49.4% of all cases. This is the group with the highest probability that a patent will change hands. For the same class, European patents and patents with owners from the rest of the countries have changed their ownership more than US patents (60.5% and 60.6% compared to 54%, respectively). However, within each of the subgroups of European patents, US patents, and patents with owners from the rest of the countries, there is no clear trend of how the number of backward citations affects the incidence of ownership change. For example, in the subgroup of the US patent owners, patents with no backward citations have the greatest probability of changing hands (54%), followed by patents that received 1–5 backward citation (53.9% of all the cases). While in the subgroup of European patents, the group of patents that does not receive backward citations changed ownership in 60.5% of all cases. The second group with the highest probability of ownership change is the group of patents that received 11–15 backward citations.

Table 3 shows that there is a significant relationship between forward citations and the incidence of ownership change. This is true for the subgroups of US patents, European patents, and patents from the rest of the countries. Again, the patents that do not receive any citations (i.e., 57.2% of US patents, 41.5% of European patents) are the ones whose ownership changed more often. Meanwhile, the patents of other owners that received 6–15 forward citations changed their ownership more often (16.2% of each subgroup of 6–10 citations and 11–15 citations).

Table 4 represents the relationship between the incidence of ownership change and references to the non-patent literature. In the overall sample as well as in the subgroups of patents, we find a significant relationship between the incidence of ownership change and references to the non-patent literature. Evidence shows that as the number of references increases, the occurrence of ownership change increases too in the overall sample and for the US- and European-owned patents (no clear trend exists for patents with owners from the rest of the countries). Thus, patents with more than 15 citations to the non-patent literature changed hands more than other patents—54.1% in the overall sample, 56.9% for patents of US owners, and 50.9% for patents of European owners.

Table 5 provides a general view of the correlation between all independent variables. There are a few coefficients that indicate strong correlations between certain variables. For example, the number of total backward citations and the number of reference to non-patent literature have a correlation coefficient of 0.863. Also, the number of total backward citations and the number of backward patent citations have a correlation coefficient of 0.665. The explanation for these coefficients is that the number of total backward citations is comprised of the number of references to the non-patent literature and the number of backward patent citations. A positive relationship (0.955) exists between the number of dependent claims and number of total claims, since the dependent claims are included in the number of total claims.

Empirical Results

Ownership Change

A probit regression was employed to explore how the set of the following covariates affect the (conditional) probability that a patent changes ownership: the total number of patent claims, the IPC assignments, the number of backward citations, the

Table 5 Correlation matrix for the independent variables in the probit models

Independent variables	1	2	3	4	5	6	7
1. Ln (1 + number of backward citations)	1.000						
2. Ln (1 + number of references to non-patent literature)	0.288	1.000					
3. Ln (1 + number of total backward citations)	0.665	0.863	1.000				
4. Ln (1 + number of forward citations)	0.154	0.075	0.143	1.000			
5. Ln (number of IPC assignments)	0.032	0.084	0.063	0.039	1.000		
6. Ln (number of total claims)	0.151	0.216	0.223	0.109	0.138	1.000	
7. Ln (1 + number of dependent claims)	0.143	0.179	0.191	0.096	0.118	0.955	1.000

number of references to the non-patent literature, the number of forward citations, and a set of ownership dummy variables that account for nationality differences.[12] The probit regression was run two times: first with the Newton-Raphson method (White covariance-heteroskedasticity corrected; see Table 6, Column 1) and second with the Berndt-Hall-Hall-Hausman (BHHH) method (Table 8, Column 5 in the Appendix). The Newton-Raphson method was chosen to correct heteroskedasticity problems detected using the White heteroskedasticity test (see Table 9, in the Appendix).[13] Both estimation methods of Newton-Raphson and BHHH converge to the same results. This indicates that our model is robust.

Table 6 Probit model of ownership change

Independent variable	1 Coefficient (S.E.)	2 Marginal effect (S.E)
Ln (number of total claims)	0.033 (0.020)	0.013 (0.08)
Ln (number of IPC assignments)	0.105** (0.040)	0.041** (0.015)
Ln (1 + number of backward citations)	−0.118*** (0.018)	−0.046*** (0.007)
Ln (1 + number of references to non-patent literature)	0.147*** (0.014)	0.057*** (0.005)
Ln (1 + number of forward citations)	−0.068*** (0.015)	−0.027*** (0.006)
Owner from the USA	0.827*** (0.207)	0.305*** (0.067)
Owner from Europe	0.554** (0.209)	0.217** (0.077)
Owner from Canada	0.676** (0.264)	0.263** (0.091)
Owner from Japan	−0.442* (0.218)	−0.162* (0.070)
Owner from RoW	−1.127* (0.483)	−0.324*** (0.076)
Multiple countries	0.809** (0.277)	0.309*** (0.091)
Constant	−0.996*** (0.204)	
Log likelihood	−426.827	
χ^2	6.827.392	
Probability (χ^2)	0.000	
Pseudo R^2 (%)^a	8.038	

*, **, *** Significant at 0.05, 0.01, and 0.001 levels, respectively
^{a}Likelihood ratio index according to McFadden

---

[12] To account for the skewed distribution of the independent variables (see Table 1), we use a logarithmic transformation on each variable.

[13] Based on the F-statistic (68.776) and the probability values (0.000), the null hypothesis that there is no heteroskedasticity was rejected.

The results for the likelihood of ownership change are summarized in Table 6. We report the probit coefficients and their respective standard errors in Column 1. In Column 2, we present the marginal effects of the independent variables at the sample mean and the respective standard errors.

Estimation results show that the number of total claims, one of the proxies for patent breadth, does not have a statistically significant effect on the incidence of ownership change in our data. Even though its coefficient is positive, indicating that broader patents (patents with more claims) are more likely to be traded, it is not statistically significant. The number of IPC assignments, also a proxy for patent breadth, has a positive and statistically significant (at the 1% confidence level) effect on the likelihood of ownership change. The above imply that broader patents (i.e., patents with more IPC assignments) are more likely to be traded. The marginal effect of the IPC assignments shows that an increase in the number of IPC assignments by one standard deviation (0.778) from its mean (1.894) increases the likelihood of patent ownership change by 4.1% (see Table 1 for mean and standard deviation values).

As discussed earlier, the number of backward citations that refer to patent literature captures both patent breadth (i.e., a high number of backward citations indicate a narrower patent) and the degree of how prone a patent is to litigation and invalidation (i.e., a high number of backward citations indicate a "stronger" patent). The coefficient of the number of backward citations is negative and statistically significant at the 0.1% confidence level. This result implies that the greater the number of backward citations and thus the narrower and "stronger" the patent, the lower the likelihood of ownership change. As was the case with the number of IPC assignments, this variable shows that broader patents are more likely to change hands. The marginal effect of the number of backward citations indicates that an increase in the number of backward citations from the sample mean of 6.768 to 16.706 (a shift of about one standard deviation) decreases the likelihood of ownership change by 4.6%.

The number of references to non-patent literature has a positive and statistically significant (at the 0.1% level of confidence) effect on ownership change. A large number of references to non-patent literature are associated with a greater likelihood of ownership change. As discussed previously, this variable has been interpreted in various ways. Given that a large number of references to the non-patent literature may imply a broader patent, the positive effect of this variable on ownership change suggests that broader patents are more likely to change hands. The marginal effect of the number of references to non-patent literature shows that an increase in the number of references to the non-patent literature from the sample mean of 14.283 to 37.952 increases the likelihood of ownership change by 5.7% points.

The number of forward citations is a measure of patent value. The coefficient of the number of forward citations is negative and statistically significant at the 0.1% confidence level. This result implies that a patent with a large number of forward citations—or, otherwise, a high-value patent—is less prone to ownership change. This variable indicates that more valuable patents are less likely to change hands. The marginal effect is negative and shows that an increase in the number of received citations from 7.381 to 24.602 decreases the likelihood of a patent changing hands by 2.7%.

The nationality of the patent owner seems to play a significant role in the incidence of ownership change as all coefficients of the nationality of ownership variables are highly significant. The results show that the patents most likely to change hands are patents owned by multiple owners of different nationalities. The incidence of ownership change for these patents is 30.9%. Patents owned by US owners face the second-highest incidence of ownership change (30.5%), followed by patents owned by Canadian owners (26.3%) and European owners (21.7%). Patents that are the least likely to change hands—that is, patents whose ownership type has a negative effect on ownership change—are patents owned by RoW owners; these patents face a decrease in the likelihood of ownership change by 32.4%, followed by patents of Japanese owners, which face a decrease in the likelihood of ownership change of 16.2%.[14]

From the above results, the proxies for patent breadth—the number of IPC assignments, the number of backward citations, and references to non-patent literature—indicate that the greater the patent breadth, the greater the likelihood of ownership change. On the other hand, the number of backward citations (an indicator of patent strength) and number of forward citations (an indicator of patent value) show that "strong" and high-value patents are less likely to be traded.

Frequency of Ownership Change

The frequency of ownership change is a polychotomous variable that measures how many times a patent has changed hands. Patents in the dataset changed hands up to three times. Ordered probit regressions were employed to examine the effect of the model covariates (the total number of patent claims, the IPC assignments, the number of backward citations, the number of references to the non-patent literature, the number of forward citations, and a set of ownership dummy variables that account for nationality differences) on the frequency of ownership change. Table 7 summarizes these results. We report the probit coefficients and their respective standard errors in Column 1. Their marginal effects are presented in Columns 2–5. Similar to the ownership change estimation, the ordered probit regression is run twice—first using the Newton-Raphson method (Table 7, Column 1) and second using the BHHH method (Table 10, Column 5 in the Appendix). The Newton-Raphson method is used to correct the heteroskedasticity problems in the data, which were detected by the White heteroskedasticity test (see Table 11 in the Appendix). Similar to the regressions of ownership change, both methods of estimation converge to the same results, indicating that the model is robust.

The estimation results show that the number of total claims has a significant effect in the frequency of ownership change. Its effect is positive, indicating that the greater the number of total claims, and thus the broader the patent, the greater the

---

[14] Note that RoW owners own 0.6%, while Japanese owners own 10.6% of all patents in our dataset.

Table 7 Probit models of the frequency of ownership change

Independent variable (frequency of ownership change)	Coefficient (S.E.)	Marginal effect			
		Fr = 0 (S.E.)	Fr = 1 (S.E.)	Fr = 2 (S.E.)	Fr = 3 (S.E.)
Ln (number of total claims)	0.045* (0.019)	−0.017* (0.007)	0.011* (0.004)	0.005* (0.002)	0.0006* (0.000)
Ln (number of IPC assignments)	0.050 (0.037)	−0.019 (0.014)	0.012 (0.009)	0.006 (0.004)	0.001 (0.000)
Ln (1 + number of backward citations)	−0.121*** (0.017)	0.047*** (0.006)	−0.030*** (0.004)	−0.015*** (0.002)	−0.002*** (0.000)
Ln (1 + number of references to non-patent literature)	0.089*** (0.014)	−0.034*** (0.005)	0.022*** (0.003)	0.011*** (0.001)	0.001*** (0.000)
Ln (1 + number of forward citations)	−0.055*** (0.013)	0.021*** (0.005)	−0.014*** (0.003)	−0.006*** (0.001)	−0.0007** (0.000)
Owner from the USA	0.668** (0.216)	−0.249*** (0.066)	0.167*** (0.044)	0.074*** (0.019)	0.008** (0.002)
Owner from Europe	0.489** (0.218)	−0.192** (0.074)	0.112** (0.037)	0.071* (0.031)	0.009 (0.005)
Owner from Canada	0.473* (0.260)	−0.187* (0.091)	0.098** (0.035)	0.077 (0.048)	0.011 (0.009)
Owner from Japan	−0.621** (0.226)	0.218*** (0.060)	−0.159*** (0.048)	−0.054*** (0.011)	−0.004*** (0.001)
Owner from RoW	−1.268** (0.479)	0.344*** (0.061)	−0.275*** (0.057)	−0.064*** (0.005)	−0.004*** (0.000)
Multiple countries	0.673** (0.271)	−0.262** (0.091)	0.120*** (0.019)	0.120* (0.058)	0.021 (0.015)
γ_1	0.752*** (0.224)				
γ_2	1.989*** (0.226)				
γ_3	3.144*** (0.231)				
Log likelihood	−5.731.606				
χ^2	6.177.150				
Probability (χ^2)	0.000				
Pseudo R^2 (%)[a]	5.388				

*, **, *** Significant at the 0.05, 0.01, and 0.001 levels, respectively

[a]Likelihood ratio index according to McFadden

frequency of ownership change. The results show that an increase from 16.338 to 30.763 (one standard deviation from the mean) increases the likelihood that a patent changes hands for the first time by 1.1%, for the second time by 0.5%, and for the third time by 0.06%.

Contrary to the results for ownership change, the number of the IPC assignments cannot statistically explain the frequency of ownership change. Although the coefficient of this variable is positive (0.050), its statistical significance is very low. Also, its marginal effects (0.012, 0.006 and 0.001) are not statistically significant. The number of backward citations, which is an indicator of both patent breadth and how prone the patent is to litigation and invalidation, is found to be significant at the 0.1% confidence level. Its negative coefficient (-0.121) shows that, as in the case of ownership change, a large number of backward citations (which implies a narrower patent scope and a "stronger" patent) are associated with a lower frequency of ownership change. Its marginal effects indicate that an increase in the number of backward citations by one standard deviation from the mean decreases the likelihood of the patent changing hands for the first time by 3%, for the second time by 1.5%, and for the third time by 0.2%. Clearly, a shift by one standard deviation from the mean affects mostly the first ownership change, and then its effect decreases as the frequency of ownership change increases.

The number of references to non-patent literature has a significant effect on the frequency of ownership change. The coefficient of this variable is positive (0.089) and is highly significant (0.1% level of confidence), indicating that a large number of references to non-patent literature increase the frequency of ownership change. The marginal effects show that an increase of about one standard deviation (23.669) from its mean (14.283) increases the likelihood of ownership change for the first time by 2.2%, for the second time by 1.1%, and for the third time by 0.1%.

Finally, the nationality of the patent owner has similar effects on the frequency of ownership change as on the incidence of ownership change. Patents that are the most likely to change hands for the first time are patents owned by US owners (16.7%), followed by patents owned by multiple owners of different nationalities (12.0%), European owners (11.2%), and Canadian owners (9.8%). However, patents with the highest likelihood of changing hands for a second time are patents owned by multiple owners of different nationalities (12.0%), followed by patents owned by Canadian owners (7.7%). Finally, patents that are more likely to change hands for a third time are those owned by multiple owners of different nationalities (2.1%), followed by patents owned by Canadian owners (1.1%), European owners (0.9%), and US owners (0.8%).

As in the case of occurrence of ownership change, patents owned by RoW owners and Japanese owners are the least likely to change ownership (the effect of these ownership types on the frequency of ownership change is negative). Patents owned by RoW and Japanese owners face a decrease in the likelihood of a first ownership change by 27.5% and 15.9%, of a second change by 6.4% and 5.4%, and of a third change by 0.4% and 0.4%, respectively. Overall, the results show that the greater the patent breadth, the greater the frequency of ownership change. Also, the less valuable and the "weaker" a patent is, the more likely it is that it will be traded more than once.

Conclusions

Intellectual property rights and, most notably, patents are essential assets for firms that compete in globalized markets where innovation is critical for their economic performance. Firms develop their own intellectual properties/technologies, license them from other firms, and/or acquire them through mergers and acquisitions. Control over patent rights played an important role in the consolidation experienced by the agricultural biotechnology sector in the 1980s and 1990s.

Trying to gain insights on the role certain patent qualities may play in the transfer of knowledge and technology that takes place through mergers and acquisitions, this study examined how a patent's breadth/scope, value, and strength affected the occurrence and frequency of patent ownership change that resulted from mergers, acquisitions, and spin-offs in the agricultural biotechnology sector in the 1980s and 1990s. The study used a dataset of private-sector US and non-US agricultural bio-technology patents that were granted by the USPTO during the period of 1976–2000 and a number of patent characteristics as proxies for patent breadth, patent value, and patent strength. Specifically, the number of total claims and the number of IPC assignments were used as proxies for patent breadth; backward citations (references to prior patents) and references to the non-patent literature were used as proxies for both patent breadth and patent strength, while forward citations (citations received from succeeding patents) were used to measure the value of the patent.

The discrete probit model was used to examine the role of patent strength, patent breadth, patent value, and the nationality of the patent owner in the occurrence of patent ownership change; the ordered probit model was used to examine whether and how these characteristics affected the frequency of patent ownership change. The empirical results of the probit model showed that patent breadth indicators such as the number of IPC assignments, the number of backward citations, and refer-ences to non-patent literature suggest that the greater is patent breadth, the greater is the likelihood of patent ownership change. On the other hand, the number of backward citations, which was used as an indicator of patent strength, and the num-ber of forward citations, which was used as an indicator of patent value, suggest that "strong" and high-value patents were less likely to be traded. In addition, patents that were most likely to change hands were those owned by multiple owners of dif-ferent nationalities. Overall, the nationality of the patent holder had the greatest impact on the incidence of ownership change, followed by the number of references to non-patent literature, the number of backward citations, the number of IPC assignments, and the number of forward citations. The results of the ordered probit model suggest a positive relationship between patent breadth and the frequency of ownership change. In addition, the less valuable and the "weaker" is the patent, the more likely it is that the patent will change hands more than once.

It is important to note that accurately measuring or quantifying patent character-istics such as patent breadth, patent strength, and patent value is not an easy task. For instance, it is not just the number of patent claims but also the language in the claims that determine the breadth/scope of protection. However, the interpretation of the language in the claims can be subjective, limiting its use as a measure of patent breadth in empirical research. Recognizing these limitations, we used the insights and findings of a large number of patent studies to identify the proxies that we used as indicators of patent breadth, patent value, and patent strength.

Our results may be of interest to innovators/patent applicants who determine a number of patent characteristics in their patent application and can further refine them during the patent-granting process by helping them understand how their decisions affect the commercial and strategic value of their patents.

Appendix

Table 8 Probit models of the ownership change

Independent variable (ownership change)	Model 1 Coefficient (S.E.)	Model 2 Coefficient (S.E.)	Model 3 Coefficient (S.E.)	Model 4 Coefficient (S.E.)	Final model (BHHH method) Coefficient (S.E.)
Ln (number of total claims)	0.036 (0.020)				0.033 (0.020)
Ln (number of independent claims)		0.012 (0.025)	0.015 (0.025)	0.016 (0.025)	
Ln (1 + number of dependent claims)		0.034 (0.019)	0.034 (0.019)	0.034 (0.019)	
Ln (number of IPC assignments)	0.119** (0.039)	0.102** (0.040)	0.103** (0.040)	0.103** (0.040)	0.105** (0.040)
Ln (1 + number of total backward citations)	0.072*** (0.016)				
Ln (1 + number of backward citations)		−0.118*** (0.018)	−0.119*** (0.018)	−0.119*** (0.018)	−0.118*** (0.018)
Ln (1 + number of references to non-patent literature)		0.147*** (0.014)	0.145*** (0.014)	0.145*** (0.014)	0.147*** (0.014)
Ln (1 + number of forward citations)	−0.082*** (0.014)	−0.067*** (0.015)	−0.069*** (0.015)	−0.069*** (0.015)	−0.068*** (0.015)

(continued)

Table 8 (continued)

Independent variable (ownership change)	Model 1 Coefficient (S.E.)	Model 2 Coefficient (S.E.)	Model 3 Coefficient (S.E.)	Model 4 Coefficient (S.E.)	Final model (BHHH method) Coefficient (S.E.)
Owner from the USA	0.675*** (0.119)	0.669*** (0.121)	0.067 (0.182)	1.977*** (0.432)	0.827*** (0.207)
Owner from Europe	0.349** (0.121)	0.397** (0.124)	−0.205 (0.184)	1.704*** (0.433)	0.554** (0.209)
Owner from Canada	0.495* (0.199)	0.515* (0.204)	−0.085 (0.245)	1.824*** (0.462)	0.676** (0.264)
Owner from Japan	−0.654*** (0.136)	−0.596*** (0.138)	−1.199*** (0.194)	0.709*** (0.437)	−0.442* (0.218)
Owner from Australia and New Zealand			−0.734*** (0.277)	1.175** (0.480)	
Owner from RoW			−1.888*** (0.472)		−1.127* (0.483)
Multiple countries				1.962*** (0.469)	0.809** (0.277)
Constant	−0.890*** (0.132)	−0.840*** (0.130)	−0.234 (0.188)	−2.143*** (0.434)	−0.996*** (0.204)
Log likelihood	−3.969.488	−3.918.605	−3.905.467	−3.904.223	−426.827
χ^2	554.6793	6.564.449	6.827.207	6.852.098	6.827.392
Probability (χ^2)	0.000	0.000	0.000	0.000	0.000
Pseudo R^2 (%)	6.531	7.728	8.038	8.067	8.038

Table 9 White heteroskedasticity test of ownership change models

	F-Statistic	Probability	Obs*R-squared	Probability
Model 1	112.350	0.000	1110.036	0.000
Model 2	62.235	0.000	860.434	0.000
Model 3	61.211	0.000	938.500	0.000
Model 4	61.577	0.000	943.2715	0.000
Final model	68.776	0.000	937.2510	0.000

Table 10 Probit models of the frequency of ownership change

Independent variable (frequency of ownership change)	Model 1 Coefficient (S.E.)	Model 2 Coefficient (S.E.)	Model 3 Coefficient (S.E.)	Model 4 Coefficient (S.E.)	Final model (BHHH method) Coefficient (S.E.)
Ln (number of total claims)	0.046* (0.018)				0.045* (0.019)
Ln (number of independent claims)		−0.025 (0.023)	−0.022 (0.024)	−0.022 (0.024)	
Ln (1 + number of dependent claims)		0.051** (0.017)	0.050** (0.018)	0.050** (0.018)	
Ln (number of IPC assignments)	0.063 (0.037)	0.052 (0.037)	0.052 (0.037)	0.052 (0.037)	0.050 (0.037)
Ln (1 + number of total backward citations)	0.011 (0.015)				
Ln (1 + number of backward citations)		−0.121*** (0.016)	−0.122*** (0.017)	−0.122*** (0.017)	−0.121*** (0.017)
Ln (1 + number of references to non-patent literature)		0.094*** (0.013)	0.092*** (0.014)	0.092*** (0.014)	0.089*** (0.014)
Ln (1 + number of forward citations)	−0.067*** (0.013)	−0.053*** (0.0013)	−0.055*** (0.013)	−0.055*** (0.013)	−0.055*** (0.013)
Owner from the USA	0.575*** (0.121)	0.564*** (0.113)	0.665** (0.217)	1.948*** (0.427)	0.668** (0.216)
Owner from Europe	0.352** (0.124)	0.384*** (0.116)	0.484* (0.218)	1.767*** (0.428)	0.489** (0.218)
Owner from Canada	0.345 (0.184)	0.363 (0.187)	0.465 (0.260)	1.748*** (0.450)	0.473* (0.260)
Owner from Japan	−0.766*** (0.136)	−0.719*** (0.131)	−0.621*** (0.226)	0.661 (0.432)	−0.621** (0.121)
Owner from Australia and New Zealand				1.311** (0.480)	
Owner from RoW			−1.262** (0.482)		−1.268** (0.479)

(continued)

Table 10 (continued)

Independent variable (frequency of ownership change)	Model 1 Coefficient (S.E.)	Model 2 Coefficient (S.E.)	Model 3 Coefficient (S.E.)	Model 4 Coefficient (S.E.)	Final model (BHHH method) Coefficient (S.E.)
Multiple countries				1.948*** (0.457)	0.673** (0.271)
γ_1	0.675*** (0.131)	0.647*** (0.122)	0.741*** (0.223)	2.024*** (0.428)	0.752*** (0.224)
γ_2	1.900*** (0.134)	1.882*** (0.124)	1.979*** (0.225)	3.261*** (0.429)	1.989*** (0.226)
γ_3	2.050*** (0.140)	3.037*** (0.134)	3.135*** (0.230)	4.417*** (0.432)	3.144*** (0.231)
Log likelihood	−57.313.279	−5.731.606	−5.421.495	−5.420.996	−5.731.606
χ^2	5.133.279	5.915.789	6.202.213	6.212.205	6.177.150
Probability (χ^2)	0.000	0.000	0.000	0.000	0.000
Pseudo R^2 (%)	4.478	5.161	5.410	5.419	5.388

Table 11 White heteroskedasticity test of frequency of ownership change models

	F-Statistic	Probability	Obs*R-squared	Probability
Model 1	21.600	0.000	249.336	0.000
Model 2	17.878	0.000	274.205	0.000
Model 3	16.779	0.000	288.897	0.000
Model 4	16.825	0.000	289.644	0.000
Final model	17.854	0.000	273.843	0.000

References

Adelman, D.E., and K. DeAngelis. 2007. Patent Metrics: The Mismeasure of Innovation in the Biotech Patent Debate. *Texas Law Review* 85: 1677–1744.

Brennan, M., C. Pray, A. Naseem, and J.F. Oehmke. 2005. An Innovation Market Approach to Analyzing Impacts of Mergers and Acquisitions in the Plant Biotechnology Industry. *The Journal of Agrobiotechnology Management & Economics* 8 (2&3): Article 5.

Denicolo, V. 1996. Patent Races and Optimal Patent Breadth and Length. *The Journal of Industrial Economics* 44 (3): 249–265.

Gallini, N.T. 1992. Patent Policy and Costly Imitation. *The Rand Journal of Economics* 23 (1): 52–63.

Gilbert, R., and C. Shapiro. 1990. Optimal Patent Length and Breadth. *The Rand Journal of Economics* 21 (1): 106–112.

Graff, G.D., G.C. Rausser, and A.A. Small. 2003. Agricultural Biotechnology's Complementary Intellectual Assets. *The Review of Economics and Statistics* 85 (2): 349–363.

Green, J.R., and S. Schotchmer. 1995. On the Division of Profit in Sequential Innovation. *The Rand Journal of Economics* 26 (1): 20–33.

Hall, B.H., A. Jaffe, and M. Trajtenberg. 2005. Market Value and Patent Citations. *The Rand Journal of Economics* 36 (1): 16–38.

Harhoff, D., and M. Reitzig. 2004. Determinants of Opposition Against EPO Patent Grants-the Case of Biotechnology and Pharmaceuticals. *International Journal of Industrial Organization* 22: 443–480.

Hopenhayn, H.A., and M. Mitchell. 2001. Innovation Variety and Patent Breadth. *The Rand Journal of Economics* 32 (1): 152–166.

Jaffe, A.B., and M. Trajtenberg. 1996. Flows of Knowledge from Universities and Federal Laboratories. *Proceedings of the National Academy of Sciences* 93: 12671–12677.

———. 1999. International Knowledge Flows: Evidence from Patent Citations. *Economics of Innovation and New Technology* 8: 105–136.

Jaffe, A.B., R. Henderson, and M. Trajtenberg. 1993. Geographic Localization of Knowledge Spillovers as Evidenced by Patent Citations. *Quarterly Journal of Economics* 108: 577–598.

Johnson, S.R., and T. Melkonyan. 2003. Strategic Behaviour and Consolidation in the Agricultural Biotechnology Industry. *American Journal of Agricultural Economics* 85 (1): 216–233.

King, J., and D. Schimmelpfennig. 2005. Mergers, Acquisitions and Stocks of Agbiotech Intellectual Property. *The Journal of Agrobiotechnology Management & Economics* 8 (2&3): Article 4.

Lanjouw, J.O., and M. Schankerman. 2001. Characteristics of Patent Litigation: A Window on Competition. *The Rand Journal of Economics* 32 (1): 129–151.

Lerner, J. 1994. The Importance of the Patent Scope: An Empirical Analysis. *The Rand Journal of Economics* 25: 319–333.

Marco, A.C., and G.C. Rausser. 2008. The Role of Patent Rights in Mergers: Consolidation in Plant Biotechnology. *American Journal of Agricultural Economics* 90 (1): 133–151.

Matutes, C., P. Regibeau, and K. Rocket. 1996. Optimal Patent Design and the Diffusion of Innovations. *The Rand Journal of Economics* 27 (1): 60–83.

Merges, R.P., and R.R. Nelson. 1990. On the Complex Economics of Patent Scope. *Columbia Law Review* 90 (4): 839–916.

Miller, A., and M. Davis. 1990. *Intellectual Property, Patents, Trademarks and Copyrights in a Nutshell*. 2nd ed. Eagan, MN: West Publishing Company.

O'Donoghue, T., S. Scotchmer, and J.F. Thisse. 1998. Patent Breadth, Patent Life, and the Pace of Technological Progress. *Journal of Economics & Management Strategy* 7 (1): 1–38.

Rausser, G.C. 1999. Private/Public Research: Knowledge Assets and Future Scenarios. *American Journal of Agricultural Economics* 81: 1011–1027.

Schimmelpfennig, D., J.L. King, and A. Naseem. 2003. Intellectual Capital in a Q-Theory of Ag-Biotech Mergers. *American Journal of Agricultural Economics* 85: 1275–1282.

Schimmelpfennig, D., and J. King. 2006. Mergers, Acquisitions and Flows of Agbiotech Intellectual Property (Chapter 9). In *International trade and policies for genetically modified products*, ed. R.E. Evenson and V. Santeniello. Cambridge, MA: CABI Publishing.

Takalo, T. 2001. On the Optimal Patent Policy. *Finnish Economic Papers, Finnish Society for Economic Research* 14 (1): 33–40.

Trajtenberg, M. 1990. A Penny for Your Quotes: Patent Citations and the Value of Innovations. *The Rand Journal of Economics* 21 (1): 172–187.

US Department of Agriculture, Economic Research Service (USDA ERS). 2006. *Agricultural Biotechnology Intellectual Property [database]*. Washington, DC: Economic Research Service. Available on the World Wide Web: http://webarchives.cdlib.org/sw1m04028n/http://www.ers.usda.gov/data/AgBiotechIP/.

Yiannaka, A., and M. Fulton. 2006. Strategic Patent Breadth and Entry Deterrence with Drastic Product Innovations. *International Journal of Industrial Organization* 24 (1): 177–202.

Innovation and Technology Transfer Among Firms in the Agricultural Input Sector

Nicholas Kalaitzandonakes, Alexandre Magnier, and Christos Kolympiris

Abstract Firms in the agricultural biotech and seed sectors have increased their R&D spending exponentially over the last three decades. The number of patents secured by major integrated biotechnology and seed firms also increased exponentially over this period. We find no evidence of strategic patenting to explain the increase in volume; the increased number of granted patents, therefore, most likely indicates accelerating product innovation in the industry. Technology transfer among private firms in this sector has been increasing as well, as reflected in a large number of licensing and cross-licensing agreements for the commercialization of patented biotech traits and seed germplasm across different suppliers. New product introductions and variety (new biotech traits and hybrids) increased significantly over the last two decades, while the average product life cycle of hybrid seeds declined. All these indicators point to accelerating product innovation and augmented product choices in this market segment.

Introduction

Firms in the US agrifood sector have continued to increase their research and development (R&D) spending over the last several decades and since the 1980s private sector R&D investments have outpaced those of the public sector (Fuglie et al. 2012). Growth in private R&D spending has been particularly significant in the agricultural input sector where investments in biotechnology and improved seeds have expanded quickly in this period.

N. Kalaitzandonakes (✉) • A. Magnier
Department of Agricultural and Applied Economics, University of Missouri, Columbia, MO, USA
e-mail: KalaitzandonakesN@missouri.edu

C. Kolympiris
University of Bath, Bath, UK

Private R&D investments in the agricultural input sector have been motived by increased technical opportunity (Schimmelpfennig et al. 2004; Heisey et al. 2005; Fuglie and Walker 2011), improved appropriability (Alfranca and Huffman 2003; Fuglie and Walker 2011), and the worldwide expansion of input markets (Pray and Fuglie 2001; Shoemaker et al. 2001; Fuglie and Walker 2011). Innovations from private sector R&D investments have been found to raise agricultural productivity and to increase social welfare. For example, private R&D in agricultural biotechnology has produced novel insect-resistant and herbicide-tolerant crops which have been broadly adopted since 1996, when they were first introduced (James 2012). Economists have estimated the annual social benefits from such biotech crops to be in the billions of dollars (Falck-Zepeda et al. 2000; Qaim 2009; Brookes and Barfoot 2010; Alston et al. 2014).

A portion of those benefits have to be captured by the innovating firms in order to finance continuing R&D investments. Thus firms engaged in the development of new genetics, novel biotech traits, or other agricultural input innovations are expected to charge prices that are higher than their marginal costs in order to recoup their fixed R&D costs (Kalaitzandonakes et al. 2010).

Ensuring that firms are able to charge sufficiently high prices is the main function of the patent system. A patent gives the innovating firm a certain amount of market power, in that it confers the exclusive right to control the market supply, and hence the price, of the new product for a given period of time. Without the prospect of earning prices above marginal costs through the exercise of that market power, firms would have no incentive to invest in R&D.

Patents are not an unqualified good, however. Some researchers in this area have noted the potential for overly aggressive patent strategies to produce thickets, a situation where one product is covered by multiple patents. This can go beyond the initial logic of patent awards and inhibit further innovation through fear of patent infringement (Cockburn and MacGarvie 2009; Jaffe and Lerner 2011). In fact, Boldrin and Levine (2008) argued that such inhibition is an unavoidable feature of the patent system. At a minimum patents represent an intentional barrier to the wider adoption of the patented innovation, for the benefit of the innovator. Transferring the patented technology to another firm for some purpose may still be in the innovator's interest, though. Licensing and cross-licensing agreements serve to effect the transfer of patent rights to protected innovations to the benefit of both firms involved in the transaction. Hence, licensing of patented innovation can promote technology transfer across firms and support innovation.

While there is much research on the transfer of technology from the public to the private sector, very little is known about licensing activity between firms. In this chapter we examine recent trends in R&D spending, patent acquisition, and licensing activity involving seeds and biotech traits in the USA. Because time lags between research, discovery, technology patenting, new product development, and commercialization can be rather long in the case of agricultural biotechnologies and crop improvements, all such indicators provide different but complementary windows in the innovative activity and technology transfer in this industry. We focus on the US biotech and seed industries because in the last two decades, they have been the locus of the largest increases in private R&D investments and the most significant structural changes.

The rest of the chapter is organized as follows: In the next section, we provide a brief historical account of the emergence of the integrated biotech/seed industry and review its R&D spending for the period of interest. We then go on to review trends in patent acquisition for biotechnologies and seeds and assess whether strategic patenting might be inhibiting innovation in this industry. In section "Product Licensing", we analyze licensing activity among biotech seed firms and draw conclusions about the factors that drive licensing agreements in the biotech and seed industries as well as about their impacts on innovation. In the last section, we summarize and conclude.

Emergence of the Integrated US Biotech/Seed Industry and its R&D Investments

The development of agricultural biotechnology drastically changed the structure of the US seed industry. In the mid-1970s, fundamental discoveries in molecular biology made it theoretically possible to develop desirable traits in plants and animals through the transfer of DNA from other organisms (Boyd 2003). The new genetic engineering methods provided stimulus for research, while seminal legal decisions made it possible to profit from it. In its 1980 *Diamond v Chakrabarty* case, the Supreme Court ruled that genetically engineered microorganisms could be protected through standard utility patents, and in 1985 it extended such patent protection to genetically engineered plants in *Ex Parte Hibberd*.

Technical opportunity and strengthened intellectual property rights (IPRs) stimulated the interest of both R&D-driven multinationals (e.g., Monsanto, DuPont, American Cyanamid) and venture-funded start-ups (e.g., Agracetus, Agrigenetics, Calgene, Mycogen) and gave rise to a new R&D-minded industry. The new biotechnology firms also developed a parallel interest in seed assets. In the fledgling agricultural biotechnology industry, superior seed genetics (germplasm) were immediately recognized as an essential complementary asset for delivering the new biotechnologies. For the commercial introduction of a new biotech product to be successful, the intellectual property, the biotechnology traits, and the seed germplasm base had to be coordinated. This need for coordination led to a wave of strategic mergers and acquisitions. In the 1980s and early 1990s, leading biotechnology start-ups (e.g., Calgene, BioTechnica International, and Mycogen) acquired a number of firms in the seed industry. In the late 1990s, multinationals DuPont and Monsanto reversed their long-standing strategies of being only technology providers in favor of becoming vertically integrated and acquired the two largest independent seed firms, Pioneer and DeKalb, respectively. Other multinationals such as Dow, Syngenta, and Bayer soon followed, purchasing seed firms such as Northrup King and Golden Harvest. The trend has continued into the most recent decade.

The consolidation of seed and biotech assets has led to a bimodal structure in the US seed industry – a few large multinational integrated seed/biotech firms and 150–200 regional seed firms with markets of different sizes.[1] The large integrated firms are responsible for almost all R&D activity in the industry and have drastically increased their R&D spending since their entry into the industry.

Specifically, we estimate that between 1985 and 2012, R&D spending by major integrated biotech/seed firms and their subsidiaries increased, in nominal terms, 17-fold, from a bit more than $220 million in 1985 to over $3.7 billion in 2012 (Fig. 1).[2] While dedicated biotech start-up firms and some independent seed firms made meaningful investments in R&D during this period, the bulk of the R&D spending in these industries was carried out by the multinational integrated biotech/ seed firms and their subsidiaries. These firms have had the means to invest large sums for sustained periods without the need for parallel revenues; such investment patterns tend to benefit firms with large scale and scope.

While seed/biotech R&D spending increased significantly over the 1985–2012 period, certain R&D costs declined at a fast pace during the same time due to improvements in automation, computation, instrumentation, and other enabling technologies which drastically increased research productivity and reduced unit costs. For instance, the costs of gene sequencing, i.e., the process of identifying the sequence of elementary blocks that form the DNA of plants, plummeted from 2000 on (Wetterstrand 2013). While sequencing was originally a slow and expensive

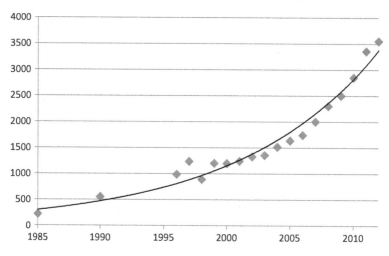

Fig. 1 Nominal R&D spending in Ag-Biotech and seed sectors (in $million) (*Source: Author calculations*)

---

[1] This structure is characteristic of the corn as well as the soybean seed industries. The US rice, cotton, and canola seed markets are generally smaller in size and have fewer firms.

[2] We constructed this series of R&D expenditures through information and data we collected from financial reports of publicly traded companies, financial analyst reports, consulting reports, trade journals, and information provided directly by individual firms. Because our data on licensing agreements in the biotech and seed industries is incomplete from 2013 on, we use R&D investment and other data until 2012, for consistency.

process (Mardis 2011), high-throughput technologies and advances in bioinformatics and related disciplines greatly contributed to reducing its cost (Metzker 2009; Edwards and Batley 2010). Such R&D cost efficiencies and productivity improvements affected most significantly the early stage development of new biotechnology traits, a rather expensive part of R&D in this sector (Phillips McDougall 2011).[3]

Early stage development of biotech traits was not the only part of biotech/crop improvement R&D that saw efficiency improvements in recent years. Traditional breeding programs for major crops have progressively been supplemented by genomics-based technologies that have made crop selection and the introduction of novel traits much more efficient (Fischer and Edmeades 2010). Marker assisted-selection (MAS) has led the way (Tester and Langridge 2010) by using molecular markers (identifiable DNA sequences found at specific locations of the genome) to verify the inheritance of various genes after cultivars are crossed. This approach greatly increased the reliability and effectiveness of the subsequent selection process and significantly reduced the cost of running breeding programs. With the help of MAS technologies, the presence of genes of interest can be verified in plants before they are fully grown, thereby eliminating most of the costs associated with laborious phenotypic selection and field trials (Hoisington and Listman 1998). The development of related tools such as association mapping, marker-aided recurrent selection, bioinformatics, biometrics, robotics, and remote sensing also contributed to improving the efficiency of breeding programs and the introduction of new traits into conventional lines (Fischer and Edmeades 2010). Of course, the cost-effectiveness of such technologies depends on the availability of cheap and reliable marker systems, which were obtained through inexpensive and fast gene sequencing.

The combination of increased R&D spending and declining research unit costs implies that the effective investment on R&D in the biotech/seed industry increased at a quick pace over the 1985–2012 period. A key question, then, is whether the increased level of private R&D spending in the biotech and seed industries translated into a faster rate of innovation. We address this question next by analyzing trends in patent acquisition in the US biotech/seed industry. We also examine whether any patterns of strategic patenting can be detected.

Patenting Trends in the Agricultural Biotechnology Industry

To identify the outcome of the increased amounts of R&D spending, we examine its most visible and immediate product, patented innovations. In the past, most empirical analyses of agricultural biotechnology patenting activity have focused on the

---

[3] Phillips McDougall (2011) also found that in recent years, large integrated biotech/seed firms have been able to increase manyfold the number of genetic constructs they evaluate at their early R&D stages while cutting the time required to do so by almost 20%. These productivity improvements are likely reflective of the same type of efficiency gains in research brought about improvements in sequencing and other enabling technologies.

public sector. Such previous studies have demonstrated the heavy reliance of agricultural biotechnology patenting in the public sector (Graff et al. 2003, 2010); the significant impact of public policies on the growth of agricultural biotechnology patenting (Carew 2005); the university-specific factors, such as quality faculty and infrastructure, which encourage patent production (Foltz et al. 2003); and the complementary relationship between publishing journal articles and patenting in the area of agricultural biotechnology (Kim et al. 2002). It has also been shown that patent quality in agricultural biotechnology, as measured by the number of times a given patent is cited by subsequent patents, has been declining over time (Buccola and Xia 2004). In sum, while our understanding of public sector agricultural biotechnology patenting activities is somewhat well developed, our knowledge of private sector patenting activity in agricultural biotechnology is more limited.

In order to match our measures of R&D investment and patenting activity as closely as possible, we concentrated on the activity of the top six integrated biotech/seed firms, their subsidiaries, and all the firms they acquired over time and examined their US granted patents from 1976 to 2012, effectively from the emergence of the agricultural biotechnology industry on.[4] For this purpose, we procured a database of US granted patents with biotechnology-related International Patent Classification Codes (IPCs) from commercial vendor Thomson Innovation. After consulting with patent experts and practicing patent attorneys, we developed a list of relevant keywords for specific searches in the patent title and claims. The list included both keywords that belonged to agricultural biotechnology patents (e.g., *Solanum*, *Melongena*, aubergine, squash, cabbage, insecticidal, protein, transgenic) and keywords that we used to filter out non-agriculture-related biotechnology patents (e.g., blood, cancer, nervous, cardiovascular, malaria, electronic). To identify the patents belonging to the firms of interest, we employed the assignee information provided in all the patents. Finally, in order to ensure that patents which were not relevant were excluded, we used visual inspection of the individual patents.

These procedures yielded a total of 9441 granted US patents for the period of interest, which are illustrated in Fig. 2. From the illustration we observe four distinct periods of patent production. From 1976 to 1986, as a group the selected biotech/seed firms were producing, on average, 21 patents per year. The corresponding number from 1987 to 1995 increased to 77. From 1996 to 2005, there were significant year-to-year variations, but, on average, the rate of patenting increased to 327 patents per year for the group. Starting in 2006, there was a further increase in the patenting activity with 748 granted patents, on average, procured each year. The exponential trend line in Fig. 2 makes clear the rapid growth in the patenting activity of agricultural biotechnology. It is interesting to note that from 2006 to 2012, the selected firms as a group were granted 5237 patents, which represented 55% of all patents granted to them over the entire 36-year period.

---

[4] There are more than 100 firms in our focal set, and these firms have been the primary locus of our R&D in the agricultural biotechnology and seed industries for the period of analysis. As such, patent acquisition for this set of firms paints a fairly complete industry-wide picture.

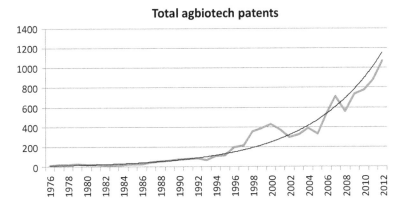

Fig. 2 Agricultural biotechnology patents acquired by selected firms (*Source: Authors' calcula-tions based on data from Thompson Scientific and the USPTO*)

The dramatic increase in the patenting activity of the firms in our sample coincides with a significant growth in the overall patenting activity observed in the USA and elsewhere. The drastic increase in other industries has raised a number of concerns including perhaps the most pertinent one that the patenting system may fail to promote innovation (Shapiro 2003; Jaffe and Lerner 2011). Presumably, the patent system could hinder innovation if patents were increasingly used as strategic tools by firms to block competitors, decrease the odds that patents are disputed, and improve the nego-tiating position of patent holders (Arundel et al. 1995; Cohen et al. 2002). Often, stra-tegic patenting for blocking competition takes the form of a single invention being protected by a large number of patents owned by the same firm, each covering, in the patent claims, part of the invention's novelty and applicability. Whenever such patent walls are created, competitors are typically discouraged from engaging in legal chal-lenges, since disputing multiple patents can become prohibitively expensive.

In order to assess whether strategic patenting could explain the observed increases in agricultural biotechnology patenting activity illustrated in Fig. 2, we derive the average size of the patent family (the number of patents protecting the same or similar inventions) for all patents in our sample,[5] and we illustrate this average for the period 1976–2012 in Fig. 3.

In general, we observe that the average size of the patent family of the US patents granted to the group of selected firms varies significantly from year to year, but it does not meaningfully increase over time, it remains within the range of 15–30 patents for the period of interest, and, at any rate, it does not explain the exponential growth in the patenting activity observed in Fig. 2. Given our single industry focus, the lack of strategic patenting, and the limited expansion of the granted patents of the firms in new industrial fields, we conclude that increased granted patents in our sample are in fact indicators of increased rates of innovation and discovery over the period of our analysis (Kortum and Lerner 1999).

---

[5] Patent families include both patents that protect the same invention across different jurisdictions and patents in the same jurisdiction that cover different parts of the same invention.

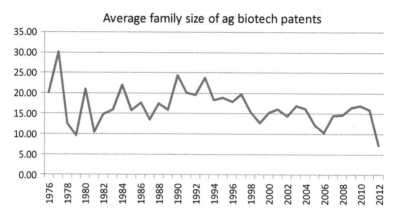

Fig. 3 Average family size of Ag-Biotech patents (*Source: Authors' calculations; data from Thompson Scientific and USPTO*)

Product Licensing

Even though we found no evidence of strategic blocking through patents in the agricultural biotech industry over the period of analysis, issued patents still prevent firms from using other firms' biotech innovations. Broad use of patented discoveries could accelerate commercialization of agricultural biotechnologies. Indeed, in some instances, broad use could be beneficial to the industry as a whole. For instance, the use of different herbicide-tolerant technologies could benefit all firms in the seed and biotech industry. One current problem in agricultural production is growing weed resistance to common herbicides. Plant scientists have been grappling with this issue for nearly as long as herbicides have been in wide use (Retzinger and Mallory-Smith 1997); at last count 443 species of weeds have biotypes that have become resistant to members of 22 different herbicide groups (Heap 2015). Resistance develops most readily when one herbicide, or a group with a common mode of action, is used exclusively and intensively. This can often be the case when a farmer plants one seed line with a single herbicide resistance trait for many years. The key to delaying the development of herbicide resistance in weed populations is using multiple herbicides with different modes of action, either sequentially or in a mixture (Beckie 2011). In order for this strategy to be effective, the crop must be resistant to all herbicides used. Thus the use of resistance traits from various technology suppliers could ensure the longevity of all products. This is true of many other traits as well.

Such broad use of patented agricultural biotechnologies could be achieved through licensing and cross-licensing agreements in the industry. Analyzing such agreements can be challenging, however, as data on the existence of such agreements and their terms are typically confidential and not easily accessible. In order to understand how much licensing and cross-licensing of innovations takes place, in this study we use a unique data set that includes all corn hybrids commercialized in the USA over the 1996–2012 period. The data set includes information about the

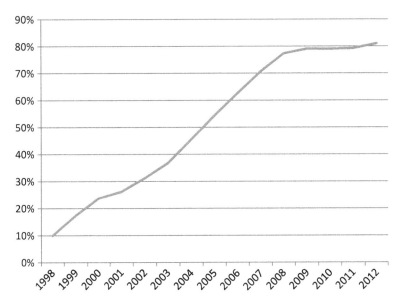

Fig. 4 Percentageof varieties that incorporate at least one trait outsourced from another company (*Source: Authors' calculations*)

individual biotech traits used in each hybrid sold, and as such it provides a complete census of all traits commercialized by each seed firm in the industry.[6] Based on this data, we construct indicators that provide insight on licensing and cross-licensing of biotech innovations in the seed industry.

Figure 4 illustrates the percentage of hybrids sold in a given year in the USA which have been developed through licensing of one or more biotech traits from another company. At the early stages of commercialization of biotechnology traits, only a small share of hybrids was developed with outsourced traits. In contrast, by 2010 more than 70% of hybrids sold included at least one trait developed through a licensing agreement.

As the number of biotech traits and trait providers increased over time, seed firms began incorporating traits licensed from multiple technology suppliers. Figure 5 shows the average number of licensing relationships of firms in the seed industry that used biotech traits in their hybrids over the 1997–2012 period. In the late 1990s and early 2000s, seed firms were licensing traits developed by an average of 1.5 biotech trait suppliers. Since the mid-2000s, this number has grown to over 2.5.

Indeed, over the period of analysis, biotech trait suppliers began to cross-license traits so that their stacks can take advantage of the complementary functionality of their competitors' traits. Figure 6 shows the percentage of firms, relative to the total number of trait providers, which contributed to the development of the various hybrids sold in the market. Initially, most of the biotech hybrids planted in the USA

---

[6]Agricultural biotech traits were first introduced in 1996, so the data set we use for our analysis provides an almost complete picture of the commercial use of the technology.

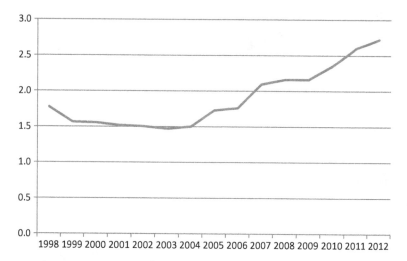

Fig. 5 Average number of licensing relationships of seed companies with biotech providers (*Source: Authors' calculations*)

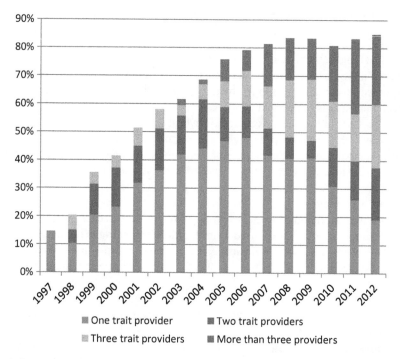

Fig. 6 Percentage of seed companies using multiple trait providers for the development of their hybrids (*Source: Authors' calculations*)

were developed by a single trait provider containing one or two biotech traits. As early as 1998, a few biotech hybrids were developed through the contribution of two trait providers, which mainly combined the European corn borer resistance trait developed by Monsanto and a herbicide tolerance trait developed by either Bayer or BASF. Starting in 2006, the number of hybrids developed with traits from two or more providers began to increase, while single supplier hybrids started to lose market share. During this time period, significant cross-licensing broadened access to new biotechnology traits across the seed industry.

It is worth noting that the increasingly broad licensing activity in the US seed corn industry is somewhat unexpected because such activity tends to occur less in industries that are concentrated (Lieberman 1989; Arora and Gambardella 2010). Since licensing activities are related to the underlying market structure, understanding the causes of the recent licensing trends in agricultural biotechnology traits and germplasm could provide useful insights.

The framework most typically used to analyze the incentives to license is that of transaction costs (Williamson 1991) which posits that technology suppliers will tend to rely on arm's-length contracts to transfer their technology when such costs are low. When transaction costs are high due to incomplete contracts, both the technology supplier and the licensee may be exposed to opportunistic behavior, especially if transaction-specific investments must be made during the transfer. Anderson and Sheldon (2011) proposed that licensing agreements in the biotech/seed industry may have recently increased because of a strengthening of property rights, which implies that transaction costs may be declining. Shi (2009) on the other hand argued that in some situations, vertical integration was preferable; broad licensing of biotech traits in markets where seeds are perfect substitutes would reduce the profits of seed firms to the point where they would not be able to recover negotiation and introgression costs of biotech traits.

The transaction cost framework may nevertheless be too narrow and may not be able to address the broader strategic intent of firms because it abstracts from firm activities that may be important in influencing their licensing decisions. Indeed, Fosfuri (2006) has argued that the effect of licensing decisions on the revenues generated in the product market may take precedence over transaction cost considerations when the technology providers also operate in downstream markets. In such a situation, licensing strategies may have important competitive repercussions since, essentially, technology providers create their own competition when they enable firms in the product market to compete more effectively by granting them access to their own technology.

Fosfuri (2006) has identified the revenue trade-offs that technology providers need to balance when devising their licensing strategies. Holding transaction costs constant, technology providers may on one hand benefit from royalty revenues (or any other forms of compensation for the transfer of the technology), while on the other hand they may lose through indirect dissipation of profits through increased competition in downstream markets. Because of this balance, the structural characteristics of the markets that technology suppliers operate in can influence their licensing decisions.

With respect to such structural considerations, Fosfuri (2006) has made two propositions that are relevant to agricultural biotechnology and seed industries: First, technology suppliers with small market shares in the product market are more likely to resort to licensing than if they were controlling a large share of the downstream product market. Second, when one technology supplier licenses its technology, significant competition in the technology market generally compels other technology providers to license their technology as well (Arora and Fosfuri 2003).[7] These propositions are generally consistent with early developments in the agricultural biotech/seed industries and may explain the broad licensing activities observed in recent years. Specifically, all technology suppliers in the biotech industry (Monsanto, Bayer, and BASF in the early years and Dow and Syngenta more recently) have had small market shares in downstream seed markets and hence an incentive to make their technology available broadly available.[8] The increasing availability of biotech traits and the diminishing differentiation among them may have also encouraged such firms to adopt similar broad licensing strategies.

Motives aside, our analysis shows that biotech innovations have been broadly licensed to seed firms and cross-licensed among agricultural biotechnology developers. Such licensing and cross-licensing activity has, in fact, grown through the commercialization period of agricultural biotechnology. The combined effect of increased R&D spending, lack of strategic patenting, and broad licensing and cross-licensing in the agricultural biotech and seed industries should therefore lead to accelerated product innovation in the marketplace. As a final step in our analysis, we evaluate this last proposition by examining the number of new product introductions and product life cycles in the US seed corn industry over the period of analysis.

Product Introductions and Product Life Cycles

A number of indicators can be used to measure effectiveness at different stages of the innovation process. The one that is most directly experienced by farmers is the rate of new product introductions. We examine here how past R&D expenditures and effort have translated in later years into new seed corn hybrids and new biotech traits marketed in the USA over the 1996–2012 period. Because innovative firms may not always be effective in translating R&D into products or they may not have adequate access to complementary assets, the flow of new products may not be perfectly correlated with firm R&D spending (Gambardella and McGahan 2010).

---

[7] When this domino effect occurs in industries where the technologies offered by the different suppliers are similar, the value of the industry will typically move downward since technology suppliers cannot act strategically upon the technology they possess (Dierickx and Cool 1989; Arora and Gambardella 2010; Gambardella and McGahan 2010). Such distributional effects could continue to encourage biotech firms to vertically integrate through the ownership of seed assets and could encourage entry of new firms into the seed industry.

[8] Monsanto's market share of proprietary seeds was initially limited. It has increased over the years through acquisitions and organic growth.

Still, since technical innovations are embodied in products of newer vintage, the rate of new product introduction can be an effective indicator of the rate of innovation in an industry (Hagedoorn and Cloodt 2003).

To construct appropriate indicators of new product introductions in the agricultural biotechnology and seed industry, we use data collected by a commercial market research company, GFK Kynetecs.[9] Our constructed data set includes all corn hybrids planted in the USA between the years 1998 and 2012 and contains observations at the hybrid level with the corresponding name of the seed firm marketing each hybrid, the type of biotech trait incorporated in the seed (e.g., insect-resistant, herbicide-tolerant hybrid and the name of the technology supplier), and the acres planted to a hybrid in any given year. Using this data set, we develop measures of the rates of new hybrid and new biotech trait introductions, product removals, as well as measures of product life cycles in the industry.

Figure 7 illustrates new hybrid introductions and old hybrid removals in the US seed corn market over the 1998–2012 period and shows that both have increased drastically in the last decade. On average, approximately 1100 new hybrids were introduced each year from 1998 to 2004. After 2005, however, the number of new product introductions increased to 1800 hybrids per year, an increase of more than

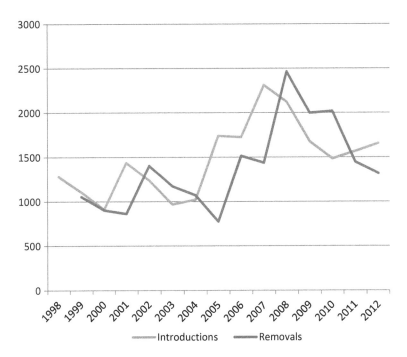

Fig. 7 New hybrid seed introductions and removals in the US corn market (*Source: Authors' calculations based on* GFK Kynetec *data*).

---

[9] The data is collected through annual surveys of corn producers in the USA. There are almost 250,000 farmer responses about annual purchases of seed corn for the period of interest.

60% relative to the first part of the decade, and reached a maximum of 2300 new hybrid introductions in 2007. The number of product removals shared a similar pattern with new product introductions, which is expected since space in the product lines of firms must be made for the new hybrids; otherwise product inventories would become unmanageable. Still, product removals have followed new product introductions with some lag suggesting that firms tend to decide on such removals after the newly introduced products have been assessed for their market fit.

The total number of hybrids sold in the US seed market follows a similar temporal pattern as that observed in the new product introductions (Fig. 8). The total number of hybrids marketed to US corn growers increased by 23%, from about 2700 in 1998 to 3350 in 2001 and stabilized around 3000 hybrids in 2003. The total number of hybrid seeds in the market increased by more than 66% in the next 4 years, however, climbing from 3000 hybrids in 2003 to 5000 hybrids in 2007. After the peak of 2007, the number of hybrids decreased to 3800 by 2010, and since that time it has again grown to more than 4200 hybrids in the subsequent 2 years, indicating a possible third period of product increase in the marketplace.

A somewhat inverse pattern is observed in the duration of the product life cycles of hybrids marketed in the USA, i.e., in the length of time, they remain in the market once introduced. We use the accelerated failure time model proposed by Magnier

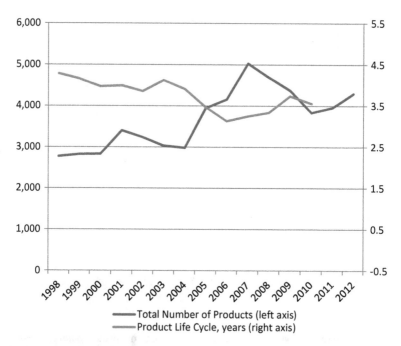

Fig. 8 Total number of products and product life cycle length in the US corn seed market (*Source: Authors' calculations based on* GFK Kynetec *data*)

et al. (2010)[10] to measure the average product life cycle in the US seed corn industry, and we illustrate its values for the 1998–2012 period in Fig. 8. From the illustration it can be readily observed that the life cycle of hybrid seeds in the USA decreased during periods when the number of product introductions and the total number of products in the market increased. Overall, the average product life cycle of hybrids declined from 4.5 years in 1998 to an average of 3.5 years in the last part of the period, which represents a marked decrease of about 20%.

Magnier et al. (2010) observed that new product introductions increased and product life cycles declined in the US seed market during cycles of new biotech trait introductions. As Fig. 9 indicates, there have been three separate waves of new biotech trait introductions between 1997 and 2012, and they seem to coincide with changes in the number of hybrids in the market and the duration of the life cycles. From 1997 to 1999, a period when the number of new hybrid introductions and total number of hybrids increased modestly, a total of ten new biotech traits were introduced, mainly single traits and double stacks (bundles of two biotech traits). From 2003 to 2007, a total of 30 new individual traits and stacks were introduced in the US market, mainly triple stacks and a few quadruple stacks. This period corresponds to the period with the most hybrid introductions and the total number of hybrids in the market. Finally, as more new traits were introduced from 2010 to 2012, the total number of hybrids in the market started to increase again.

The different types of biotech traits and stacks made available to farmers have followed the typical life cycle of adoption, maturity, and decline that are observed for most new technologies and are illustrated in Fig. 10. The single biotech traits that were first introduced in 1996 were quickly adopted and were planted on about one third of all US corn acres by 2004. After that time, their market share started to decline as stacked traits bundling a larger number of biotech traits were placed on the market. Despite their gradual decline in market share, single traits still accounted for about 20% of the market in 2012. Stacks with two biotech traits were introduced

---

[10] Accelerated failure time models are one of the two main types of models used for survival analysis, the branch of statistics dealing with the duration of an event; the other being proportional hazard models. The proportional hazard model is simpler to specify because it is nonparametric model, while a distribution needs to be chosen in the case of the accelerated failure time model. However, the results of accelerated failure time models are often easier to interpret because partial effects represent expected change in duration, while proportional hazard models produce hazard ratios whose partial effects are relative and therefore more difficult to translate into expected life time. Overall, the two types of models produce very similar results.

The accelerated failure time model we use takes the form $\ln(T) = X\beta + \sigma\varepsilon$, where β represents the set of parameters to be estimated, X is a vector of covariates, σ is scale parameter, and ε is a random disturbance term which is normally distributed. The explanatory variables include the average acreage across the lifetime of hybrid, a categorical variable to account for the size of the seed firm marketing the hybrid, trait-specific dummy variables (e.g., insect resistant, herbicide tolerant), and a set of variables which indicate the first year of commercialization of the hybrid. All parameter estimates except a few of the year of introduction dummies were statically significant at the 99% level, and all estimates had the expected sign. While we do not report the statistical results here to keep the manuscript at a manageable size, the results are available from the authors.

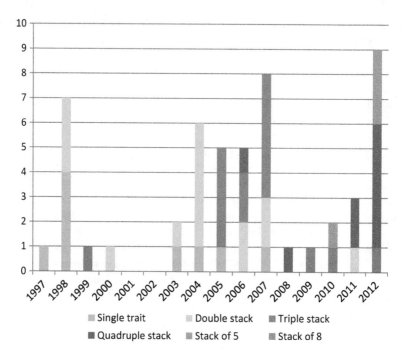

Fig. 9 Number of annual new biotech trait introductions (*Source: Authors' calculations*)

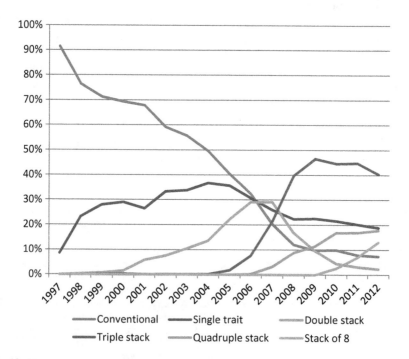

Fig. 10 Market share of different trait combinations (*Source: Authors' calculations based on* GFK Kynetec *data*)

almost in concert with the single traits and reached a maximum penetration by 2006/2007 of roughly 30% of the US corn acres. Nevertheless, their share has quickly declined as "triple stacks" quickly supplanted them to become the most adopted biotech trait bundle in the market. Stacks of four to eight different biotech traits then entered the market and gained market share.

These trends are generally consistent with the characteristics of R&D-driven industries (Bayus and Agarwal 2007), where new products are introduced at a fast rate and older products may still coexist with new ones to satisfy the demand of heterogeneous buyers with different needs (Giannakas 2002). As such, the patterns of new product (hybrids and traits) introductions illustrated in Figs. 7, 8, 9 and 10 are also informative about the ongoing expansion of product variety in the US seed corn market and indicate an increasing pace of innovation over the period of analysis.

Summary and Conclusions

In this chapter we discussed the antecedents to and results of private firm technology transfer in the agricultural biotechnology and seed industry. We examined the innovation process from R&D through product commercialization in order to discern the incentives for technology transfer and its market effects. We focused our analysis on the activities of all major integrated biotech and seed firms, all their subsidiaries, and all the firms they acquired over time. The set, therefore, includes more than 150 firms; collectively, these firms represent the suppliers of a large share of proprietary seeds, all of the commercialized biotech traits, and almost all of the R&D expenditures in these sectors. As we illustrate here, these firms increased their R&D spending at an exponential rate over the 1985–2012 period. Furthermore, since certain R&D costs have declined during this period, their effective R&D spending was likely even higher.

We then examined patterns in patent acquisition by this group of firms over the 1976–2012 period, essentially over the lifetime of the agricultural biotechnology industry. We have found that the number of granted patents secured by the firms in our sample increased exponentially over this period, much like their R&D spending. Since we have found no evidence of strategic patenting to explain the increase in volume, we have concluded that the increased number of granted patents is an indicator of accelerating product innovation in the industry.

We went on to examine the licensing patterns of new biotech traits, once again using the US seed corn/biotech market as a case study, over the 1996–2012 period. In this context, we demonstrated that licensing of biotech traits across technology suppliers and seed marketers expanded over time and represented the dominant strategy in the industry; the number of biotech trait suppliers increased; and the number of hybrid seeds bundling biotech traits from different technology suppliers grew quickly. Taken together, these indicators point to a growing availability of agricultural biotechnologies, increased technology transfer within the industry, and intensified contestability in this technology market.

Finally, we examined the patterns of new product introductions over the period 1996–2012, almost the entire period during which biotech traits have been commercialized. We used the US biotech/seed corn market as a case study due to its leading position in market value and technology development. We found that over the period of the analysis, the rate at which new biotech traits and new hybrids were introduced in the market increased, the total number of hybrids marketed expanded, the total number of biotech traits offered grew while their variety expanded, and the average product life cycle of hybrid seeds declined. All such indicators point to accelerating product innovation and augmented product choices for buyers over the period of the analysis.

Seed and biotech markets are generally fragmented by geography and crop, making it difficult to generalize across such boundaries. Still, information similar to that presented here from seed markets of other crops (e.g., cotton) as well as information from product pipelines (products already in research or development which are expected to be commercialized in the future) suggests accelerating innovation and increased market contestability for new biotech traits and varieties across different crops (e.g., soybeans, cotton, canola) and geographies. As such, we expect that the conclusions we have drawn here are broadly applicable.

References

Alfranca, O., and W.E. Huffman. 2003. Aggregate Private R&D Investments in Agriculture: The Role of Incentives, Public Policies, and Institutions. *Economic Development and Cultural Change* 52 (1): 1–21. https://doi.org/10.1086/380585.

Alston, J.M., N. Kalaitzandonakes, and J. Kruse. 2014. The Size and Distribution of the Benefits from the Adoption of Biotech Soybean Varieties. In *Handbook on Agriculture, Biotechnology, and Development*, ed. S.J. Smyth, P.W.B. Phillips, and D. Castle, 728–751. Cheltenham, UK: Edward Elgar.

Anderson, B., and I.M. Sheldon. 2011. Endogenous R&D Investment and Market Structure: A Case Study of the Agricultural Biotechnology Industry. 2011 Annual Meeting, July 24–26, 2011, Pittsburgh, Pennsylvania, Agricultural and Applied Economics Association.

Arora, A., and A. Fosfuri. 2003. Licensing the Market for Technology. *Journal of Economic Behavior & Organization* 52 (2): 277–295.

Arora, A., and A. Gambardella. 2010. Ideas for Rent: An Overview of Markets for Technology. *Industrial and Corporate Change* 19 (3): 775–803. https://doi.org/10.1093/icc/dtq022.

Arundel, A., G. van de Paal, and L. Soete. 1995. *Innovation Strategies of Europe's Largest Industrial Firms: Results of the Survey for Information Sources, Public Research, Protection of Innovations and Government Programmes*, Maastricht Economic Research Institute on Innovation and Technology, University of Limbourg, Maastricht, PACE Report.

Bayus, B.L., and R. Agarwal. 2007. The Role of Pre-Entry Experience, Entry Timing, and Product Technology Strategies in Explaining Firm Survival. *Management Science* 53 (12): 1887–1902.

Beckie, H.J. 2011. Herbicide-Resistant Weed Management: Focus on Glyphosate. *Pest Management Science* 67 (9): 1037–1048.

Boldrin, M., and D.K. Levine. 2008. *Against Intellectual Monopoly*. New York: Cambridge University Press.

Boyd, W. 2003. Wonderful Potencies? In *Engineering Trouble: Biotechnology and Its Discontents*, ed. R. Schurman and D. Kelso. Princeton, CA: University of California Press.

Brookes, G., and P. Barfoot. 2010. *GM Crops: Global Socio-Economic and Environmental Impacts 1996–2010*. Dorchester, UK: PG Economics Ltd.

Buccola, S., and Y. Xia. 2004. The Rate Of Progress in Agricultural Biotechnology. *Applied Economic Perspectives and Policy* 26 (1): 3–18.

Carew, R. 2005. Science Policy and Agricultural Biotechnology in Canada. *Applied Economic Perspectives and Policy* 27 (3): 300–316.

Cockburn, I.M., and M.J. MacGarvie. 2009. Patents, Thickets and the Financing of Early-Stage Firms: Evidence from the Software Industry. *Journal of Economics & Management Strategy* 18 (3): 729–773.

Cohen, W.M., A. Goto, A. Nagata, R.R. Nelson, and J.P. Walsh. 2002. R&D Spillovers, Patents and the Incentives to Innovate in Japan and the United States. *Research Policy* 31 (8): 1349–1367.

Dierickx, I., and K. Cool. 1989. Asset Stock Accumulation and Sustainability of Competitive Advantage. *Management Science* 35 (12): 1504–1511. http://www.jstor.org/stable/2632235.

Edwards, D., and J. Batley. 2010. Plant Genome Sequencing: Applications for Crop improvement. *Plant Biotechnology Journal* 8 (1): 2–9. https://doi.org/10.1111/j.1467-7652.2009.00459.x.

Falck-Zepeda, J.B., G. Traxler, and R.G. Nelson. 2000. Surplus Distribution from the Introduction of a Biotechnology Innovation. *American Journal of Agricultural Economics* 82 (2): 360–369.

Fischer, R.A., and G.O. Edmeades. 2010. Breeding and Cereal Yield Progress. *Crop Science* 50 (S1): 85–98. https://doi.org/10.2135/cropsci2009.10.0564.

Foltz, J.D., K. Kim, and B. Barham. 2003. A Dynamic Analysis of University Agricultural Biotechnology Patent Production. *American Journal of Agricultural Economics* 85 (1): 187–197.

Fosfuri, A. 2006. The Licensing Dilemma: Understanding the Determinants of the Rate of Technology Licensing. *Strategic Management Journal* 27 (12): 1141–1158.

Fuglie, K., P. Heisey, J. King, C.E. Pray, and D. Schimmelpfennig. 2012. The Contribution of Private Industry to Agricultural Innovation. *Science Magazine* 338 (6110): 1031–1032.

Fuglie, K., and T. Walker. 2011. Economic Incentives and Resource Allocation in US Public and Private Plant Breeding. *Journal of Agricultural and Applied Economics* 33 (3): 225–240.

Gambardella, A., and A.M. McGahan. 2010. Business-Model Innovation: General Purpose Technologies and Their Implications for Industry Structure. *Long Range Planning* 43 (2): 262–271.

Giannakas, K. 2002. Infringement of Intellectual Property Rights: Causes and Consequences. *American Journal of Agricultural Economics* 84 (2): 482–494.

Graff, G.D., S.E. Cullen, K.J. Bradford, D. Zilberman, and A.B. Bennett. 2003. The Public-Private Structure of Intellectual Property Ownership in Agricultural Biotechnology. *Nature Biotechnology* 21 (9): 989–995.

Graff, G.D., D. Zilberman, and A.B. Bennett. 2010. The Commercialization of Biotechnology Traits. *Plant Science* 179 (6): 635–644.

Hagedoorn, J., and M. Cloodt. 2003. Measuring Innovative Performance: Is There an Advantage in Using Multiple Indicators? *Research Policy* 32 (8): 1365–1379.

Heap, I. 2015. "The International Survey of Herbicide Resistant Weeds". Retrieved 27 January 2015, from http://www.weedscience.com/summary/home.aspx.

Heisey, P.W., J.L. King, and K.D. Rubenstein. 2005. Patterns of Public-Sector and Private-Sector Patenting in Agricultural Biotechnology. *AgBioforum* 8 (2 & 3): 89–99.

Hoisington, D., and M. Listman. 1998. Varietal Development: Applied Biotechnology. In *Maize seed Industries in Developing Countries*, ed. M. Morris, 77–102. Boulder, CO: Lynne Rienner Publishers and CIMMYT.

Jaffe, A.B., and J. Lerner. 2011. *Innovation and Its Discontents: How Our Broken Patent System Is Endangering Innovation and Progress, and What to Do About It*. Princeton, NJ: Princeton University Press.

James, C. 2012. *Brief 44. Global Status of Commercialized Biotech/GM Crops: 2012, ISAAA Brief*. New York: Ithaca.

Kalaitzandonakes, N., D. Miller, and A. Magnier. 2010. A Worrisome Crop? *Regulation* 33 (4): 20–26.

Kim, K., J.D. Foltz, and B.L. Barham. 2002. Are There Synergies or Tradeoffs between Articles and Patents in University Ag-Biotech Research. Western Agricultural Economics Association Annual Meetings. Long Beach, California.

Kortum, S., and J. Lerner. 1999. What is Behind the Recent Surge in Patenting? *Research Policy* 28 (1): 1–22.

Lieberman, M.B. 1989. The Learning Curve, Technology Barriers to Entry, and Competitive Survival in the Chemical Processing Industries. *Strategic Management Journal* 10 (5): 431–447.

Magnier, A., N. Kalaitzandonakes, and D. Miller. 2010. Product Life Cycles and Innovation in the US Seed Corn Industry. *International Food and Agribusiness Management Review* 13 (3): 17–36.

Mardis, E.R. 2011. A Decade/'S Perspective on DNA Sequencing Technology. *Nature* 470 (7333): 198–203.

Metzker, M.L. 2009. Sequencing Technologies—The Next Generation. *Nature Reviews Genetics* 11 (1): 31–46.

Phillips. McDougall. 2011. *The Cost and Time Involved in the Discovery, Development and Authorisation of a New Plant Biotechnology Derived Trait. A Consultancy Study for Crop Life International.* Available at: http://croplife.org/wp-content/uploads/pdf_files/Getting-a-Biotech-Crop-to-Market-Phillips-McDougall-Study.pdf.

Pray, C.E., and K.O. Fuglie. 2001. *Private Investment in Agricultural Research and International Technology Transfer in Asia*, United States Department of Agriculture, Economic Research Service, Agricultural Economic Report No. 805.

Qaim, M. 2009. The Economics of Genetically Modified Crops. *The Annual Review of Resource Economics* 1: 665–693.

Retzinger, E.J., and C. Mallory-Smith. 1997. Classification of Herbicides by Site of Action for Weed Resistance Management Strategies. *Weed Technology* 11 (2): 384–393.

Schimmelpfennig, D.E., C.E. Pray, and M.F. Brennan. 2004. The Impact of Seed Industry Concentration on Innovation: A Study of US Biotech Market Leaders. *Agricultural Economics* 30 (2): 157–167.

Shapiro, C. 2003. Antitrust Limits to Patent Settlements. *RAND Journal of Economics* 34 (2): 391–411.

Shi, G. 2009. Bundling and Licensing of Genes in Agricultural Biotechnology. *American Journal of Agricultural Economics* 91 (1): 264–274. https://doi.org/10.1111/j.1467-8276.2008.01174.x.

Shoemaker, R.A., J.L. Harwood, K.A. Day-Rubenstein, T. Dunahay, P.W. Heisey, L.A. Hoffman, C. Klotz-Ingram, W.W. Lin, L. Mitchell, and W.D. McBride. 2001. *Economic Issues in Agricultural Biotechnology*, United States Department of Agriculture, Economic Research Service, Agriculture Information Bulletin No. 762.

Tester, M., and P. Langridge. 2010. Breeding Technologies to Increase Crop Production in a Changing World. *Science* 327 (5967): 818–822. https://doi.org/10.1126/science.1183700.

Wetterstrand, K.A. 2013. "The Cost of Sequencing a Human Genome". National Human Genome Research Institute. Retrieved 15 May 2013, from https://www.genome.gov/sequencingcosts/.

Williamson, O.E. 1991. Comparative Economic Organization: The Analysis of Discrete Structural Alternatives. *Administrative Science Quarterly* 36: 269–296.

Land-Grant University Research as a Driver of Progress in Agriscience

Simon Tripp, Martin Grueber, Alyssa Yetter, and Dylan Yetter

Abstract The agricultural industries of the United States are a vital part of our economy, as are the land-grant universities that are inextricably tied to those industries. Given this importance, NIFA engaged TEConomy Partners, LLC, to categorize and describe the broad range of R&D and associated extension activity undertaken by the land-grant university system and supported by NIFA funding. The analysis in this chapter provides this evaluation and categorization and compares Capacity and Competitive funded research projects to the larger body of published agricultural research. We find that, compared to overall publications, Capacity projects are more focused on production-oriented areas than basic sciences, while Competitively funded research has its largest focus in basic sciences. Additionally, a number of areas that are small or missing from overall publications are present in notably higher concentrations in Capacity projects. The focus areas of both Capacity and Competitively funded research projects follow the goals of the NIFA National Challenge Areas and the 2014 Farm Bill. Finally, we find evidence of substantial return on investment for both forms of funding.

Introduction

The US agricultural sector, together with the social and economic structures that sustain it, is fundamental to national well-being and economic performance.[1] Agriculture and associated industries are part of an economic and social ecosystem that consists of a complex web of actors and activities that serve specific functions

---

[1] In this chapter, for the sake of simplicity, the terms "agriculture," "agricultural sciences," and "agricultural industries" are considered to also embrace forestry, fisheries, and other natural resource-based industries that are of relevance to the work of the USDA, NIFA, and the nation's land-grant universities.

S. Tripp (✉) • M. Grueber • D. Yetter
TEConomy Partners, LLC, Columbus, OH, USA
e-mail: tripps@teconomypartners.com

A. Yetter
Pennsylvania State University, State College, PA, USA

© Springer International Publishing AG 2018   189
N. Kalaitzandonakes et al. (eds.), *From Agriscience to Agribusiness*, Innovation,
Technology, and Knowledge Management, https://doi.org/10.1007/978-3-319-67958-7_10

and make possible the positive outcomes of the system as a whole. Because it is a knowledge-driven and technology-intensive science-based sector, the agricultural system is very much dependent on knowledge advancements, innovations, and the transfer of knowledge and technology from a highly active research and development (R&D) sector.

Agribusiness in the US economy is a high performer in terms of sustained growth in economic output and productivity. The increasing productivity of US agriculture, and the growth of the large-scale value-added industry chain that benefits from it, has not occurred by chance. Rather, it has resulted from the intense and deliberate application of scientific research and technological development across a broad range of disciplines and research challenges.

The ongoing success of US agriculture is a testament both to the sustained work of thousands of American scientists, technologists, and engineers researching and innovating solutions and to the millions of US farmers who deploy the solutions these researchers provide. It is important to recognize that, unlike many other industries, the primary production sector in agriculture, being made up of millions of small and midsize enterprises, has only a limited internal R&D capacity of its own. Instead, innovations and productivity increase predominantly depending on R&D and knowledge transfer from commercial agricultural input suppliers, the US Department of Agriculture (USDA) Agricultural Research Service (ARS), and America's unique system of land-grant universities (LGUs) and Cooperative Extension Services.

The common thread that runs through scientific, technological, and practice advancements, including in agriculture, is research. Basic and applied research in biological sciences, physical sciences, social sciences, and engineering and a broad suite of associated disciplines produce the knowledge and advancements upon which progress is made. Research is the fundamental engine that drives US economic progress and competitiveness, and research funding is the fuel for that engine. While American agriculture is an industry operated by millions (farmers, ranchers, foresters), and sustained by the innovations of thousands (in the R&D sector), it is critically important to note that it is financially supported in its foundational advancement by funding from a select few sources. This select group comprises private-sector industrial companies that develop applied technologies and solutions in terms of farm inputs and agricultural and processing equipment, the US Federal Government (most notably through the USDA and its National Institute of Food and Agriculture [NIFA]), state governments, commodity organizations, and nonprofit foundations.

After the private sector, the federal government is the next largest funder of agricultural and related research by a wide margin and is the primary funder of early-stage, exploratory research and applied agricultural research focused on specialty crops, livestock, and agricultural commodities specific to local geographies and production environments. Importantly, federally funded research also supports work in soils, water, ecological systems, workforce development, rural development, and other elements critical to the sustainability of the agricultural production ecosystem that do not attract significant commercial research.

In 2016 NIFA commissioned TEConomy Partners, LLC (TEConomy), to evaluate Capacity Funding (also known as Formula Funding) to land-grant universities and assess the productivity and impacts of this funding model. The full analysis provided to NIFA[2] assesses the types of basic and applied research programs funded under the Capacity Funding programs, the types of impacts being generated, the relevance of research to current and future national and state needs, and the strengths and weaknesses of the funding model using a set of existing federal and land-grant university datasets and a series of surveys administered to LGU leadership in colleges of agriculture, state experiment station systems, and extension services. This chapter and the one that follows it present a subset of the findings of the NIFA-TEConomy report. In this chapter, we describe the unique industry that is the twenty-first century American agriculture and the mission of the LGU system in support of it. This chapter then describes the methods and results of our analysis of (a) the areas of research output activity (as defined by publications volume and thematic content) in agriculture and related subjects overall and in comparison with NIFA Capacity and NIFA Competitive funding, (b) the fit of these research outputs with NIFA's National Challenge areas and the 2014 Farm Bill Priority Areas, (c) the financial leveraging of Capacity Funding, and (d) the return on investment of Capacity and Competitive Funding in terms of knowledge production.

Agriculture and the US Land-Grant System

Achieving large-scale gains in agricultural output and productivity is no easy task. Unlike almost every other industry, agriculture operates within a production environment that has substantial year-to-year and season-to-season variability. It is largely an outdoor industry dependent on weather and open to the pressures of naturally occurring diseases and pests. Factors both abiotic (rainfall, sunlight, frost, etc.) and biotic (plant and livestock diseases, crop-damaging pests, etc.) are variables that significantly affect production but cannot be assured in advance. New diseases are emerging, and existing diseases and pests are expanding in their geographic range, spurred in part by human activities and the reactions of the biosphere and climate to them. This dynamic production environment, and the challenges associated with it, represents a unique signature of the agricultural industry.

It is also the case, unlike most other manufacturing or technology industry sectors, that agriculture is almost entirely composed of small and midsize business enterprises in terms of primary production. Whereas the global automobile industry, for example, comprises circa two dozen or so major manufacturers, agricultural

---

[2] Simon Tripp, Martin Grueber, Dylan Yetter, Joseph Simkins and Alyssa Yetter. 2017. *"National Evaluation of capacity programs: Quantitative and Qualitative Review of NIFA Capacity Funding."* TEConomy Partners, LLC, for the National Institute of Food and Agriculture (NIFA). March 2017. Available online at https://nifa.usda.gov/sites/default/files/resource/NIFA Capacity Funding Review - TEConomy Final Report.pdf.

output in the United States alone stems from the work of 2.1 million individual farms. The US agricultural industry's national output is the net result of literally hundreds of millions of individual decisions made by farmers across their growing seasons, with those decisions having to take into account an exceptional number of variables, including weather, soil fertility, pathogens, pests, commodity prices, and global competition, among others, and the potential deployment of multiple technologies and solutions, such as specific crop varieties to use, livestock health products to employ, type of tillage to deploy, and capital investments in new farming equipment, to name just some.

The fact that American farmers and the R&D system that supports these farmers have *together* achieved the productivity increases shown on Fig. 1 in the face of the variable production environment and multivariate decision-making environment in which farmers operate is a splendid American success story, but one that goes under-recognized and underappreciated. The success of US agriculture is a testament to the determined and sustained work of many thousands of American scientists, technologists, and engineers developing and innovating solutions and to the millions of US farmers who deploy the solutions these researchers provide.

Because of US scientific research and scientific knowledge translated into practice, the nation's agricultural sector has become expert in doing more with less – working to deploy technologies and research-based solutions to produce increasing output from each existing acre of US agricultural land. Research-driven advancements in animal science, veterinary medicine, genetic marker-assisted livestock breeding, and advanced nutrition formulations, for example, have led to widespread

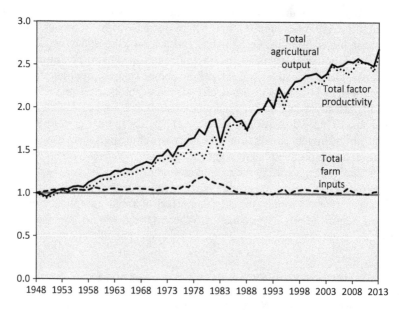

Fig. 1 US agricultural output, inputs, and total factor productivity index, 1948 = 1 (Source: USDA, Economic research service, agricultural productivity in the U.S. data as of December 2015)

gains in the output of the livestock and poultry sectors. Likewise, in crop agriculture, innovations in agronomic techniques, soil science, plant biology and breeding, molecular genetics, pest and disease management technology, and agricultural equipment engineering have led to similarly far-reaching increases in on-farm production. Today, revolutionary new technologies in biotechnology, genomics, precision equipment guidance, robotics, computerized decision support systems, and other technological fields are finding direct application in expanding agricultural production and efficiency. At the same time, rural sociologists, family and consumer science researchers, education and communication specialists, agricultural economists, and other academics and professionals have worked, and are working, to understand and sustain the economic and social fabric of rural, small town, and urban America that supports much of the progress in national farm, forest, and natural resource industries. In other words, research drives increasing productivity in agriculture and associated industries and works to sustain the societal, family, workforce, public policy, and other necessary pillars that support a sustainable agricultural economic ecosystem.

The federal government through the USDA both performs research, through its in-house ARS,[3] and funds research performed by other institutions, primarily academic institutions, across the United States. NIFA Capacity Funding and, to a lesser extent, Competitive Funding support a holistic land-grant-based R&D and extension ecosystem. This ecosystem, depicted in Fig. 2, comprises a complete continuum of R&D activity from basic inquiry, through applied and translational research, to piloting and field demonstration. The innovations and practical knowledge derived from R&D are disseminated through Cooperative Extension and land-grant technology transfer activities to those in production agriculture, industry, and society who can put this knowledge and innovation to work for the betterment of the US economy and society.

Of particular note is that this system is deliberately bidirectional. Communication of needs, challenges, opportunities, and innovations moves from the field to the researcher and from the researcher to the field. This NIFA-supported ecosystem (Fig. 2), rooted in the original vision for land-grant universities and Cooperative Extension, was envisioned, and subsequently evolved and refined, to provide a pragmatic feedback loop – assuring R&D activity is responsive to tangible needs and that novel innovations and findings are not only reported in academic journals but are proactively disseminated by Cooperative Extension activities for use in farms, industries, communities, and beyond.

The universe of potential research inquiry supported by NIFA is extremely diverse. Not surprisingly, there is a robust emphasis on work in support of enhancing and sustaining American production agriculture, forestry, and natural resource industries, but the activities undertaken extend far beyond core areas of agronomy, plant science, and livestock-related animal sciences. NIFA funding supports fundamental basic science inquiry in life sciences of relevance to better understand

---

[3] The USDA Agricultural Research Service (ARS) has more than 2200 permanent scientists working on approximately 1100 research projects at more than 100 locations across the United States.

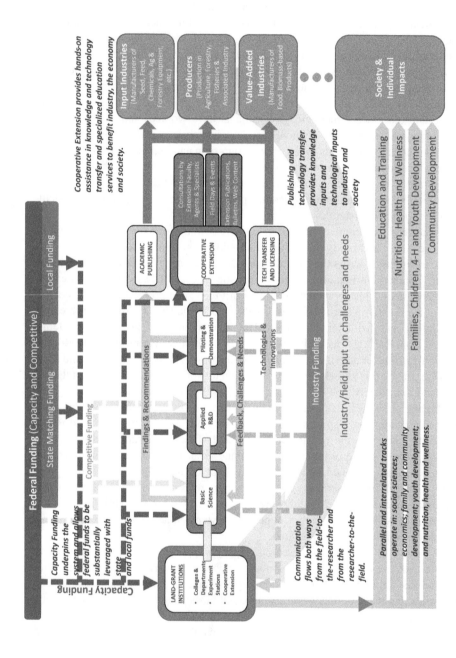

Fig. 2 Federal funding and the land-grant university research and cooperative extension ecosystem

life processes and mechanisms of action. Further, NIFA supports applied work in the value-added industries that work beyond the farm gate, across the supply chain, to provide US residents and global consumers with access to nutritious foods, health products, lumber and wood products, fibers, renewable bio-based fuels, chemical products, and materials. Because of the nationwide nature of agriculture and its associated value chain, the benefits these sectors provide are present in all states and US territories. Furthermore, NIFA supports research and extension activity that is focused on sustaining the rural families and small-town fabric that are crucial to the resiliency of these industry sectors.

Figure 3 depicts core areas of land-grant research activity identified by TEConomy in performance of this project and in previous engagements analyzing land-grant university and extension services impacts. The broad diversity of research activity, noted above, is graphically illustrated in this figure.

Currently, the federally supported land-grant university system is deployed in addressing a large-scale contemporary suite of complex and dynamic challenges and needs. The system is, for example, researching and extending into practice solutions across a range of domains, including, but not limited to, the following:

- Deploying traditional and state-of-the-art modern scientific tools and techniques to protect and improve both the yield and quality of agricultural crops and livestock
- Integrating advanced sensing, precision guidance, and metering technologies to maximize the efficient use of inputs to agriculture (such as water, fertilizers, and pesticides) and limit negative externalities associated with input use
- Developing advanced predictive modeling technologies, big data, and decision support systems to enhance the accuracy of agricultural decision making
- Exploring and developing new and enhanced sustainable biomass-based industries in the production of energy, fuels, materials, chemicals, and fibers
- Leveraging innovations and research findings to achieve rural development and enhanced economic and social opportunities for small towns, rural America, and metro areas engaged in value-added manufacturing using agricultural and natural resources
- Increasing the education, skills, and technical capabilities of the workforce to meet current and projected needs of the high-tech, high-productivity agricultural sector and value-chain industries

It should be recognized that advancements in these and other applied areas are built upon a platform of progress in fundamental, basic science knowledge that is the result of research undertaken predominantly at academic research institutions, including the land-grant universities. While basic sciences, including biological sciences, have experienced an explosion in discovery and knowledge in recent decades, there is still no shortage of fundamental research questions to be explored. Just in plant biology, for example, the American Society of Plant Biologists[4] notes the

---

[4]American Society of Plant Biologists. Unleashing a Decade of Innovation in Plant Sciences: A Vision for 2015–2025.

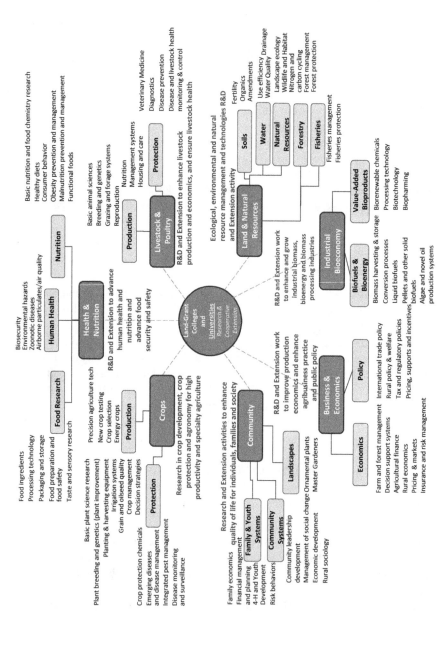

Fig. 3 An illustration of the varied scope of subject matter relevant to research and cooperative extension at land-grant colleges and universities

importance of advancing research in such fundamental areas as predicting plant traits from plant genomes in diverse environments; finding ways to assemble plant traits in different ways to solve specific challenges; discovering, cataloging, and utilizing plant-derived chemicals; and moving plant biology to a predictive science platform based on big data analytics. Basic science and applied science go hand in hand in terms of meeting grand challenges and opportunities in agriculture and associated areas of inquiry.

Our work for NIFA sought to categorize and describe the broad range of R&D and associated extension activity undertaken by the land-grant university system and supported by NIFA funding. It provides an evaluation and categorization of LGU research supported by NIFA Capacity and Competitive Funding in comparison to published agricultural research extant.

Data and Methods

With $0.85 billion currently going to Capacity Funding and $0.7 billion budgeted for NIFA-funded Competitive research,[5] it is important to examine, objectively, what outputs are occurring for the nation via USDA extramural funding of research and associated activities. To address this question, we analyzed data on academic publications and NIFA-funded project summary reports to examine quantitative metrics of research output activity.

Data

First, publication analysis is performed using Clarivate Analytics' (formerly Thomson Reuters) Web of Science™ database. The data used in this analysis include peer-reviewed journal articles, reviews, and conference proceedings papers. The dataset includes documents from 2010 through 2016 in all disciplines associated with agriculture, forestry, fisheries, and natural resources. A total of 123,790 records are included in the analysis. These data include all listed publications and do not provide details on the source of funds used for the research and accordingly are not limited to publications from research funded by NIFA. As such, they provide a baseline of the overall structure of the academic literature in agriculture and related disciplines, to which our subsequent analysis of NIFA-funded projects is compared. Second, for the analysis of NIFA Capacity and Competitive funded

---

[5] Competitive Funding includes the Agriculture and Food Research Initiative (AFRI), plus Mandatory Programs including the Specialty Crops Research Initiative (SCRI), Organic Agriculture Research and Extension Initiative (OREI), Beginning Farmers and Ranchers Development Initiative, Biomass Research and Development Initiative (BRDI), and smaller Competitive Programs.

projects, TEConomy was provided with annual datasets from the Research, Extension, and Education Project Online Reporting Tool (REEport), NIFA's grant reporting system, for the years 2010–2015. This consolidated dataset includes detailed descriptive information regarding the objectives, performance, and ongoing impacts of both Capacity and Competitive funded projects, including financial information regarding both NIFA funding (Capacity or AFRI or NRI Competitive Funding) and related state, local, and industry funding. Separate analyses are run for Capacity ($n = 19{,}791$) and Competitive funded projects ($n = 2299$).

Analysis

A real-text cluster analysis was performed on the full dataset using the OmniViz™ analysis system. The use of OmniViz™ cluster analysis allows the text of titles and abstracts of publications to be analyzed objectively, with no a priori categorization used. OmniViz™ uses real-text pattern-recognition algorithms to analyze the titles and abstracts of research publications, allowing for free association based on the usage of words and phrases rather than forcing clustering based on preselected keywords. Thus, there is no a priori bias to the clusters identified. This analysis also has the advantage of being well suited to identifying multidisciplinary research areas that are often difficult to identify in traditional academic disciplinary classifications. OmniViz™ cluster analysis results produce a classification system with a three-level hierarchy, shown in Fig. 4.

Our analysis is primarily descriptive in nature and details the topic areas of research in agriculture and related areas. The analyses proceed by first presenting the cluster segmentation of overall publications, followed by Capacity funded

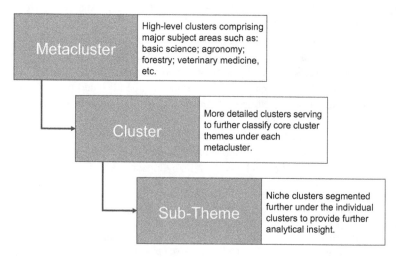

Fig. 4 Three-level hierarchy of OmniViz™ cluster analysis

projects and Competitively funded projects. Second, we compare the segmentation of Capacity projects to overall publications and compare Capacity and Competitively funded projects. Third, we assess the congruence of the clusters identified in Capacity and Competitively funded projects with the six NIFA National Challenge Areas and the six Priority Areas in the 2014 Farm Bill. Fourth, we utilize the REEport data to analyze the leveraging of Capacity Funding in terms of generating and matching other sources of public and private funding across cluster areas. Finally, we examine the return on investment, defined by publications output in the REEport data, across cluster areas.

Results

Publications

To first establish a baseline for the segmentation of agriculture, forestry, fisheries, and natural resources research, TEConomy performed a cluster analysis of the Clarivate Analytics *Web of Science*™ database for journal publications, articles, and conference proceedings papers in relevant disciplines. The cluster analysis produced 70 total clusters comprising 108,180 total publications (with 15,610 publications clustering into an "artifact" cluster not incorporated in the final analysis). The clusters were reviewed and provided with descriptive names for their content in a three-level hierarchy as summarized in Fig. 4. For the publication analysis, OmniViz™ identified 12 meta-clusters, 70 clusters, and 45 subthemes. In addition, Clarivate Analytics assigns a research area classification to each publication, and the percent segmentation for the highest order of this classification system is included herein also.

The results of the cluster analysis of the publications are presented in both graphical (Fig. 5) and tabular (Table 7, see appendix) forms. We find that agronomy and basic science are the largest of the meta-clusters, each with roughly 21% of the publications. For both of these meta-clusters, plant science is the largest cluster. In agronomy, the focus is on plant breeding and improvement, with corn being the single plant variety that makes up the largest subtheme. In basic science, the largest subthemes under the plant science cluster are stress resistance, physiology and morphology, and seeds, each with roughly 20% of the basic plant science publications. The third largest meta-cluster is veterinary medicine (18%), and its largest clusters are canine, infectious diseases, and equine publications.

Clarivate Analytics also assigns a research area classification to each publication, and the segmentation of classifications at the highest order of their classification system is shown in Fig. 6. This classification scheme is more rooted in traditional academic discipline names. Using this more traditional classification, we still see plant science and veterinary medicine as the most frequently published areas in the recent full literature of agriculture and related sciences.

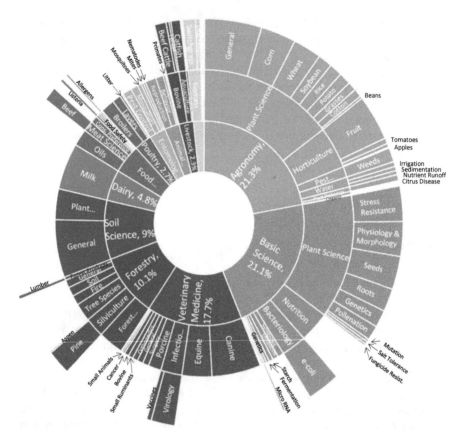

Fig. 5 Percentage segmentation of publications across key disciplines (OmniViz™ Cluster analysis of 108,180 publications)

Capacity Funded Projects

The analysis next turns to describing the segmentation of Capacity funded projects in the NIFA REEport data system. In total, the analysis covers 19,791 distinct Capacity funded projects. The results of the cluster analysis divide these projects into 10 meta-clusters, 55 clusters, and 44 subthemes. The results of the cluster analysis of the Capacity funded projects are presented in both graphical (Fig. 7) and tabular (Table 8, see appendix) forms. As in the overall publication analysis, the largest share of projects is in agronomy (36%), although pest management (27%) has a slightly larger share within this meta-cluster than plant breeding and improvement (25%), which is distinct from the overall patterns, where pest management is a relatively small share (5%). This is indicative of a general pattern in Capacity funded projects. While they are diverse, approximately two-thirds of Capacity funded projects (65.4%) demonstrate focus in "production"-oriented areas of R&D, including agronomy, animal science and livestock, forests and forestry, and fisheries and aquaculture. Other areas addressed include important health and welfare,

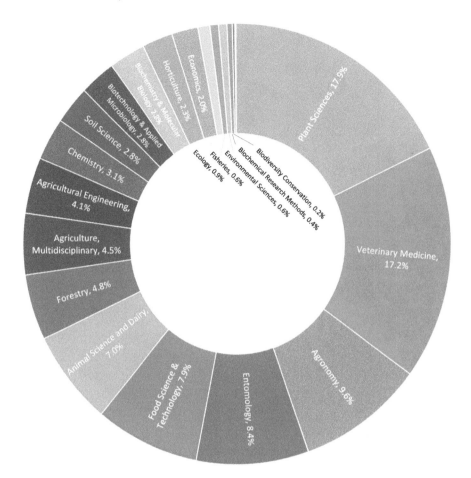

Fig. 6 Percentage segmentation using Web of Science™ classifications

family and youth, community development, and environmental domains. However, Capacity Funding is not only suited to the support of applied and translational research and extension projects. Among the 19,791 funded projects for 2000–2015, fundamental science (basic science) inquiry makes up 12.2% (2414 projects). These are quite focused in basic life sciences, with microbiology (72%) and genetics and genomics (11%) comprising the largest subclusters therein.

Comparison of Capacity Funded Projects and Overall Publications

It is evident that, in comparison to the *Web of Science™* total agbioscience dataset, Capacity funded projects have several "signatures" in terms of focus:

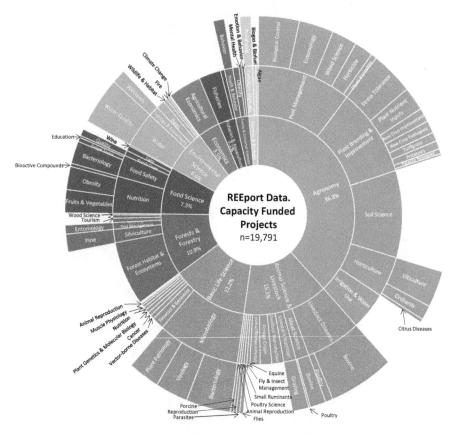

Fig. 7 Percentage segmentation of Capacity funded projects (REEport Data for 2010–2015) across meta-clusters, associated clusters, and subthemes (Data Table 8 in Appendix)

- Less emphasis on basic science projects. Basic science projects are 21.1% of all publications in the *Web of Science*™ dataset, whereas Capacity funded projects see 12.2% of projects clustered as basic science.
- Animal science and livestock research is more focused in the Capacity funded projects on animals used in production agriculture, and a separate veterinary medicine cluster is not evident (as it is in the full *Web of Science*™ dataset).
- A considerably larger emphasis on pest management as a theme, with 9.9% of total records in the Capacity funded analysis, versus just 1.1% in the *Web of Science*™ data.
- There is more emphasis in the Capacity funded projects on water as a research theme (7.7% of records across two clusters), as opposed to a 1% cluster in the *Web of Science*™ data.
- There is more emphasis in the Capacity funded projects on food science (7.3% of records), as opposed to 4.4% in the *Web of Science*™ data.
- A greater emphasis on biomass and biofuels in the Capacity records (3.1%) when compared with the *Web of Science*™ clustering (1.7%).
- A family and consumer science cluster (with 2.1% of records) and an economics cluster (3.5% of records) present under the Capacity Funding analysis that are

not distinct clusters in the *Web of Science*™ analysis. Similarly, fisheries and aquaculture has a Capacity funded cluster (2.8% of records), indicating an importance within Capacity funded activities above that observable in the overall literature.

It is also notable that agricultural engineering does not produce a distinct cluster in either of the cluster analyses, although Fig. 6 shows this discipline makes up 4.1% of the relevant *Web of Science*™ records. It is likely the case that this discipline's research is distributed within the cluster analysis into multiple clusters (e.g., irrigation, pest management, soil science, food science, etc.).

Overall, the comparison between the Capacity funded and *Web of Science*™ datasets illustrates a generally focused inquiry through Capacity projects on applied research – research focused toward current and emerging issues facing agriculture and natural resource sectors and communities.

Competitively Funded Projects

The REEport system also includes data on a total of 2299 NIFA Competitively funded projects. The results of the cluster analysis divide these projects into 9 meta-clusters, 30 clusters, and 11 subthemes (Fig. 8 and Table 9 in appendix). The largest area of Competitively funded projects is basic science, which takes up a quarter of these projects. Of the basic science projects, most are in basic plant science (33%), genetics and genomics (20%), microbiology (17%), and infectious diseases (17%). The prevalence of basic science in the Competitively funded projects is not to the exclusion of applied research projects. The meta-clusters of agronomy (21%), food science (11%), and animal science and livestock (11%) make up a large share of Competitively funded research and address problems including pest management, food safety, and vaccines.

Comparison of Capacity and Competitively Funded Project Meta-Clusters

Figure 9 presents a comparison of the results of the Capacity and Competitive funded projects clustering analysis. As would be expected, given the substantially larger numbers of records in the REEport data for Capacity funded projects (19,791) versus Competitive (2299), the Capacity cluster analysis produces more clusters and subthemes under each meta-cluster. The meta-clusters for each of the funding sources are similar, except for the absence of a fisheries and aquaculture cluster in the Competitive analysis, but they differ considerably in terms of the percent of the total records that each meta-cluster comprises for the respective funding types. The biggest differences can be observed in double the percentage emphasis on basic life science in the Competitively funded project universe when compared with Capacity funded projects and in significantly more Capacity funded projects focused in agronomy, which comprises plant breeding and improvement, pest management,

Fig. 8 Percentage segmentation of Competitive funded projects (REEport data for 2010–2015) across meta-clusters, associated clusters, and subthemes (Data Table 9 in Appendix)

soil science, horticulture, and irrigation and water use management. Animal science and livestock also has a greater emphasis in the Capacity funded portfolio than in the Competitive funded portfolio (15.1% and 10.9%, respectively). Forests and forestry as a percentage of the Competitive portfolio is more than three times smaller than under Capacity Funding, whereas several other meta-clusters show a higher emphasis in terms of Competitive Funding, including food science, environmental science, economics, biomass and biofuels, and family and consumer sciences.

NIFA Capacity and Competitive Funding demonstrate substantially different degrees of emphasis in terms of projects undertaken. Capacity Funding is more likely to focus on production agriculture-oriented research projects in agronomy, animal science and livestock, fisheries and aquaculture, and forests and forestry.

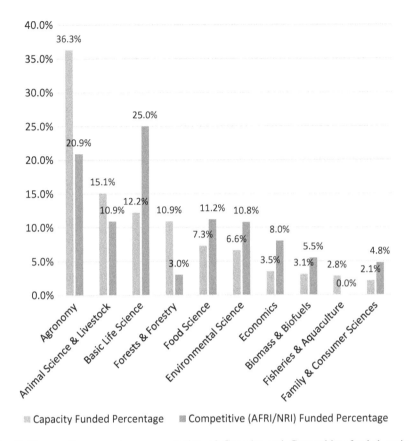

■ Capacity Funded Percentage ■ Competitive (AFRI/NRI) Funded Percentage

Fig. 9 Comparative percentage segmentation of Capacity and Competitive funded projects (REEport Data for 2010–2015)

This is a logical finding, given the ability of Capacity Funding to be focused on the particular needs of agricultural and natural resource industry needs, challenges, and opportunities at a state, regional, or local level. Competitive Funding skews more to an emphasis on basic life sciences, having double the emphasis here as seen in Capacity funded projects, and demonstrates marginally more emphasis on food science, environmental science, biomass and biofuels, economics, and family and consumer sciences.

Comparison of Capacity and Competitively Funded Project Meta-Clusters and Clusters on Six NIFA National Challenge Areas

In reviewing the cluster analysis of the respective portfolios of projects classified as either Capacity funded or Competitive funded, a comparison can be made of the alignment between these project portfolios and the six NIFA National Challenge

Areas. Table 1 lists both the Capacity funded and Competitive funded project meta-clusters and clusters and their relationship, in terms of likely subject matter, to each of the six NIFA National Challenge Areas.

As Table 1 illustrates, the majority of projects in both the Capacity funded (64.2%) and Competitive funded (59.1%) portfolios of work are relevant to the six NIFA National Challenge Areas combined. Capacity Funding shows a higher proportion of projects directed toward two of the challenges: food security, where it makes up almost half of the Capacity funded portfolio, and water. Competitive Funding sees a proportionately higher focus on the themes of climate variability and change, bioenergy, childhood obesity, and food safety. It should be noted that, in absolute project number terms rather than percent of projects, Capacity Funding has the higher total volume of work taking place across all of the National Challenge Areas except for climate variability and change.

Comparison of Capacity and Competitively Funded Project Meta-Clusters and Clusters on Six Priority Areas in the 2014 Farm Bill

The 2014 Farm Bill provides authority to NIFA to pursue programs in support of six congressionally identified priority areas. The Farm Bill priorities are summarized by NIFA as follows (Table 2)[6]:

These six Farm Bill priorities for NIFA can be compared to the results of the Capacity and Competitive NIFA funding REEport cluster analyses in order to produce an estimate of the projects undertaken by the land-grant universities relevant to these priorities. Table 3 lists both the Capacity funded and Competitive funded project meta-clusters and clusters and their relationship, in terms of likely subject matter, to each of the six 2014 Farm Bill priorities for NIFA.

As Table 3 illustrates, both Capacity funded (87.7%) and Competitive grant funded (88.2%) portfolios of work see the majority of projects as relevant to the six priority areas in the 2014 Farm Bill. Capacity Funding shows a higher proportion of projects directed toward the two challenges most directly focused on agricultural production: "animal health, production, and products" (16.4% of Capacity projects versus 10.8% of Competitive projects) and "plant health, production, and products" (36.7% of Capacity projects versus 29.1% of Competitive projects). The Competitive portfolio shows a higher proportion of projects focused on the post farm gate area of "food safety, nutrition, and health" (13.9% of Competitive projects versus 7.6% of Capacity projects). Overall, the Farm Bill priorities are addressed by almost nine out of every ten Capacity and Competitively funded projects.

---

[6] https://nifa.usda.gov/farm-bill-priorities

Table 1 Project meta-clusters and themes as identified in analysis of REEport system data on the six NIFA National Challenge areas

NIFA National Challenge	Capacity funded Meta-clusters (percent of total)	Capacity funded Clusters (percent of total)	Competitive funded Meta-clusters (percent of total)	Competitive funded Clusters (percent of total)
1. Food security	Agronomy (36.3%) Animal science and livestock (15.1%) Fisheries and aquaculture (2.8%)	Pest management (9.9%) Plant improvement (9.2%) Soil science (9%) Horticulture (4.2%) Irrigation and water use (4%) Livestock diseases (5.9%) Meat science (1.4%) Livestock nutrition (1.3%) Livestock reproduction (1.3%) Forage crops (1.2%) Manure management (1.1%)	Agronomy (20.9%) Animal science and livestock (10.9%)	Pest management (3.8%) Plant improvement (4%) Soil science (7.1%) Vaccines (1.3%) Animal nutrition (1.4%) Reproduction (1.2%) Dairy (2.3%) Cattle (2.8%) Bovine genetics (1.8%) Fruit (0.7%) Plant pathology (5.3%)
2. Climate variability and change	Environmental science (6.6%)	Climate change (0.2%)	Environmental science (10.8%)	Agricultural emissions (2.9%)
3. Water	Environmental science (6.6%) Agronomy (36.3%)	Water resources and quality (3.7%) Irrigation and water use (4%)	Environmental science (10.8%)	Water (5.8%)
4. Bioenergy	Biomass and biofuels (3.1%)	Cellulosic biomass (2.5%) Biofuels and biogas (0.3%) Algae and Phycology (0.3%)	Biomass and biofuels (5.5%)	Biomass (4.5%) Conversion processes (1%)
5. Childhood obesity	Food science (7.3%) Family and consumer sciences (2.1%)	Nutrition and obesity (1.8%) Obesity (0.7%)	Family and consumer sciences (4.8%)	Obesity (4.8%)
6. Food safety	Food science (7.3%)	Food safety (2.2%) ⇨	Food science (11.2%)	Food safety (8.4%) ⇨

	Capacity funded (percent of identified clusters focused on this area)	Competitive funded (percent of identified clusters focused on this area)
Food security	48.5%	31.7%
Climate variability and change	0.2%	2.9%[a]
Water	7.7%	5.8%
Bioenergy	3.1%	5.5%
Childhood obesity	2.5%	4.8%
Food safety	2.2%	8.4%
Total	64.2%	59.1%

[a]It should be noted that only some of the agricultural emission work would relate to climate change. Some of the projects under this category also examine odor mitigation or other emission factors (not all of which are gases)

Table 2 2014 Farm Bill priorities for NIFA

2014 Farm Bill priority area	NIFA description
Agricultural economics and rural communities	Prosperity and economic security for individuals and families, farmers and ranchers, business owners, and consumers are vital to a strong economy. The Farm Bill authorizes NIFA to continue to support programs that strengthen rural economies. NIFA's research, education, and extension programs help people make sound financial management decisions, discover new economic opportunities, develop successful agricultural and nonagricultural enterprises, take advantage of new and consumer-driven markets, and understand the implications of public policy on these activities
Agriculture systems and technology	The Farm Bill supports the development of advanced technologies to meet the complex agricultural challenges faced by the United States and countries throughout the world. Agricultural systems – both crop and animal – involve issues such as labor, marketing, finances, natural resources, genetic stock, and equipment. NIFA-supported projects address these issues as a system, rather than on an individual basis, because a holistic approach offers greater management flexibility, safer working conditions, and a sounder economy and environment
Animal health, production, and products	Animals are one of the most important aspects of agriculture in America. NIFA's investments in animal science have found new and better ways to advance animal production technology, enable the industry to respond to consumer demand, and advance human health and nutrition through better animal health and breeding. NIFA's animal-related programs – which include beef, dairy cattle, poultry, swine, sheep, goats, and aquaculture – encourage a multidisciplinary approach to research, education, and extension activities
Bioenergy, natural resources, and environment	NIFA integrates research, education, and extension expertise to address environmental and natural resource priorities. The agency's programs seek to develop the next generation of biofuels that will not only power machines but the American economy as a whole. Furthermore, these programs improve air, soil, and water quality, fish and wildlife management, and sustainable use and management of forests, rangeland, and watersheds and lead to a better understanding of how the changing climate affects agriculture
Food safety, nutrition, and health	Poor dietary choices, unhealthy lifestyles, foodborne illnesses, and the potential for terrorism and other attacks on the US food supply are national concerns. NIFA-funded programs help strengthen the nation's ability to address and reduce the negative effects of these concerns as well as issues related to food security and food science and technology
Plant health, production, and products	NIFA-funded plant and plant product programs provide better understanding of plants: how they grow, how to improve productivity, and how to use them in new ways. These programs reflect the diversity of plants and their uses around the world. NIFA also supports education programs, such as master gardeners and the extension program, which bring science-based information about growing plants to the public

Table 3 Comparing Capacity and Competitive (AFRI/NRI) funded project meta-clusters and clusters as identified in analysis of REEport system data on the six priority areas for NIFA in the 2014 Farm Bill

NIFA 2014 Farm Bill priority	Capacity funded Meta-clusters (percent of total)	Capacity funded Clusters (percent of total)	Competitive funded Meta-clusters (percent of total)	Competitive funded Clusters (percent of total)
1. Agricultural economics and rural communities	Economics (3.5%) Family and consumer sciences (2.1%)	Agricultural economics (3.5%) Youth and behavior (0.9%) Emotion and behavioral management (0.3%) Poverty and mental health (0.3%)	Economics (8.0%)	Agricultural economics (6.7%) Markets and pricing (1.3%)
2. Agriculture systems and technology	Not a specific meta-cluster but elements contained within multiple other meta-clusters and themes	Irrigation and water use (4%) Genetics and genomics (1.3%) Land use (0.4%)	Not a specific meta-cluster but elements contained within multiple other meta-clusters and themes	Agricultural emissions (2.9%) Genetics and genomics (5.0%) Food systems and access (2.0%)
3. Animal health, production, and products	Animal science and livestock (15.1%) Fisheries and aquaculture (2.8%)	Livestock diseases (5.9%) Poultry science (1.6%) Meat science (1.4%) Livestock nutrition (1.3%) Livestock reproduction (1.3%) Manure management (1.1%) Small ruminants (0.6%) Fly/insect management (0.3%) Equine (0.3%) Animal reproduction (0.2%) Fisheries (2.3%) Aquaculture (0.4%)	Animal science and livestock (10.9%)	Cattle (2.8%) Dairy (2.3%) Bovine genetics (1.8%) Nutrition (1.4%) Vaccines (1.3%) Reproduction (1.2%)
4. Bioenergy, natural resources, and environment	Biomass and biofuels (3.1%) Environmental science (6.6%)	Cellulosic biomass (2.5%) Biofuels and biogas (0.3%) Algae and phycology (0.3%) Ecology and ecosystems (1.1%) Climate change (0.2%) Water resources and water quality (3.7%) Fire management 0.3% Bees (0.9%) Wildlife and habitat (0.4%) Forest habitat and ecosystems (6.6%)	Biomass and biofuels (5.5%) Environmental science (10.8%)	Biomass (4.5%) Conversion processes (1.0%) Water (5.8%) Bees (2.2%) Forest ecosystems (3.0%)

(continued)

Table 3 (continued)

5. Food safety, nutrition, and health	Food science (7.3%)	Nutrition (3.8%), Food safety (2.2%), Obesity (0.7%), Dairy (0.5%), Wine (0.1%), Basic nutrition (0.3%)	Food science (11.2%)	Food safety (8.4%), Obesity (4.8%), Lipids (0.7%)
6. Plant health, production, and products	Agronomy (36.3%), Forests and forestry (10.9%)	Pest management (9.9%), Plant breeding and improvement (9.2%), Soil science (9.0%), Horticulture (4.2%), Silviculture (2.7%), Forage crops (1.2%), Wood science (0.2%), Basic plant genetics and molecular biology (0.3%)	Agronomy (20.9%)	Basic plant sciences (8.2%), Soil science (7.1%), Plant pathology (5.3%), Plant breeding and improvement (4.0%), Pest management (3.8%), Fruit (0.7%)

	Capacity funded (percent of identified clusters focused on this area)	Competitive funded (percent of identified clusters focused on this area)
Agricultural economics and rural communities	5.0%	8.0%
Agriculture systems and technology[a]	5.7%	9.9%
Animal health, production, and products	16.4%	10.8%
Bioenergy, natural resources, and environment	16.3%	16.5%
Food safety, nutrition, and health	7.6%	13.9%
Plant health, production, and products	36.7%	29.1%
Total	87.7%	88.2%

[a]Not a specific meta-cluster

Capacity Funding Leverage Identified in REEport Data

An advantage of the regional and local relevance of federal Capacity funded research is that state and local funders observe this local relevance and may then choose to provide additional matching financial support for the research and extension mission serving their state, county, or community. It could also be the case that the applied focus of much of the Capacity funded research portfolio holds appeal to commodity groups, agriscience companies, and other stakeholders to co-invest in land-grant R&D projects. The REEport data allow an evaluation of whether the opinions expressed by land-grant university leaders in a TEConomy survey that "the characteristics of work funded with federal Capacity Funding allows significant further leveraged funding to be raised" hold true.

REEport data indicate that a substantial amount of leveraged funding is indeed occurring and that these funds come from both public (state and local) and private (industry, foundations, commodity groups) funding sources. Table 4 summarizes funding data for the years 2010 through 2015 in aggregate, for each of the meta-cluster areas, identified through the cluster analysis of Capacity funded projects.

These data indicate that, across the ten Capacity funded meta-clusters, NIFA Capacity Funding totaled more than $1.64 billion with additional federal funding support of $3.2 billion over the 6-year period. The projects supported by this combined federal investment received a further $9 billion in funding from nonfederal sources, for a combined funding of activity in the 10 meta-clusters of almost $13.9 billion.

Clearly, this represents a significant overall leverage of federal funding for work in these meta-clusters equivalent to an additional $1.86 in funding being raised for every $1.00 in federal funding (Table 5). The meta-cluster achieving the highest leverage is agronomy with a ratio of $1 in federal funds leveraging an additional $2.30 in nonfederal funding. The lowest leverage is in basic life science, which is still a robust $1 to $1.32. This is to be expected, given the fundamental nature of research here having a less clear or assured path to applied relevance for key external funders like state agencies, industry, or commodity groups. It is important to note that even the nonindustry-oriented meta-clusters of family and consumer sciences achieve a robust level of leveraged external funding, with $1 in federal funding generating an additional $1.76 in external funds. The importance and pragmatic nature of federally funded work at the land-grant universities in agricultural sciences and associated disciplines are reflected in the universities being able to leverage these federal funds to generate significant additional funding.

Comparing Capacity and Competitively Funded Project Publication Return on Investment

Answering return on investment questions for academic research is never simple. There is a significant difference in how "return" might be defined, for example, between a basic science project that elucidates a biological process but produces no

Table 4 Capacity funded projects. NIFA funding and additional funds raised (2010–2015), $ millions

Capacity funded meta-cluster	A. Total NIFA funding	B. Other USDA funding	C. State appropriations	D. Self-generated funds	E. Industry funding	F. Other nonfederal funding	G. Other non-USDA federal funding	H. Total nonfederal funding (C + D + E + F)	I. Total federal funding (A + B + G)	J. Total funding (H + I)
Agronomy	$621.4	$328.9	$2228.2	$318.3	$647.2	$453.5	$635.1	$3647.2	$1585.4	$5232.6
Animal science and livestock	$280.7	$87.4	$917.8	$379.3	$179.1	$169.0	$443.1	$1645.2	$811.2	$2456.4
Basic life science	$176.8	$72.5	$700.8	$100.6	$207.6	$96.1	$590.8	$1105.1	$840.1	$1945.2
Biomass and biofuels	$57.3	$28.4	$180.0	$15.7	$50.1	$31.7	$96.2	$277.5	$181.9	$459.4
Economics	$47.3	$13.0	$138.9	$6.5	$15.5	$21.5	$33.0	$182.4	$93.3	$275.7
Environmental science	$90.0	$46.0	$336.8	$31.1	$62.7	$96.8	$177.7	$527.4	$313.7	$841.1
Family and consumer sciences	$18.3	$1.4	$60.4	$2.1	$8.5	$11.8	$27.4	$82.8	$47.1	$129.9
Fisheries and aquaculture	$49.4	$17.3	$139.3	$13.5	$27.1	$50.7	$86.3	$230.6	$153.0	$383.6
Food science	$117.7	$40.6	$361.3	$41.6	$140.1	$74.6	$168.6	$617.6	$326.9	$944.5
Forests and forestry	$184.8	$109.4	$448.2	$42.9	$80.0	$133.4	$196.2	$704.5	$490.4	$1194.9
Total	$1643.7	$744.9	$5511.7	$951.6	$1417.9	$1139.1	$2454.4	$9020.3	$4843.0	$13,863.3

Table 5 Capacity funded projects. External funds leveraged by federal funding (2010–2015)

Capacity funded meta-cluster	Total NIFA funding	Total nonfederal funding	Total, federal funding	Effective NIFA leverage	Effective federal leverage
Agronomy	$621.4	$3647.2	$1585.4	1 to 7.42	1 to 2.30
Animal science and livestock	$280.7	$1645.2	$811.1	1 to 7.75	1 to 2.03
Basic life science	$176.8	$1105.1	$840.1	1 to 10.00	1 to 1.32
Biomass and biofuels	$57.3	$277.5	$181.9	1 to 7.02	1 to 1.53
Economics	$47.3	$182.4	$93.2	1 to 4.83	1 to 1.96
Environmental science	$90.0	$527.4	$313.7	1 to 8.35	1 to 1.68
Family and consumer sciences	$18.3	$82.7	$47.1	1 to 6.09	1 to 1.76
Fisheries and aquaculture	$49.4	$230.7	$152.9	1 to 6.77	1 to 1.51
Food science	$117.7	$617.6	$326.9	1 to 7.03	1 to 1.89
Forests and forestry	$184.8	$704.5	$490.3	1 to 5.47	1 to 1.44
Total	$1643.6	$9020.4	$4842.7	1 to 7.43	1 to 1.86

commercial technology and say a soybean improvement project that produces a 5% yield increase in certain environmental conditions. Both are important, but they differ in their type of impacts. What both basic and applied research share in common is that research results produced by faculty at universities are likely to be published. Publishing activity may thus provide a baseline surrogate metric for productivity suitable for a high-level evaluation of academic research.

NIFA REEport data contain information on the source and amount of funding for each project. TEConomy's cluster analysis of REEport data for Capacity and Competitive funded projects thus allows for a comparison to be made for the highest-level meta-clusters that are present for both types of funded research. The results of the analysis (Table 6) show that across all areas of research, except forestry, Capacity funded research generates significantly higher volumes of publications per million dollars of federal funding when compared to Competitive Funding. Because of the leverage of Capacity Funds achieved through state and local sources, the federal government, for its share of the funding, receives a high return in terms of knowledge generated and disseminated through land-grant research.

It should be noted, however, that while the majority of all academic disciplines target research toward the generation of peer-reviewed academic publications, the work of the land grants recorded in Table 6 contains publications that are also geared toward agricultural producers, foresters, consumers, etc. that require information in a more concise form than the typical academic paper. For comparison purposes, therefore, care must be taken in comparing the Capacity and Competitive funded research coming via NIFA federally funded research as opposed to some other fed-

Table 6 Publications per $1 million in funding for Capacity and Competitive funded projects (REEport data for 2010–2015) across meta-clusters

	Publications per $1 M total Capacity and leveraged funds	Publications per $1 M in Competitive NIFA-AFRI (and previously NRI) funds	Difference between Capacity and Competitive funded publications per $1 M
Agronomy	12.78	4.90	+7.88
Animal science and livestock	9.96	7.60	+2.35
Basic science	9.14	5.27	+3.87
Biomass and biofuels	11.69	7.42	+4.27
Economics	16.95	4.78	+12.17
Environmental science	12.54	11.03	+1.51
Family and consumer sciences	16.23	3.44	+12.79
Food science	11.45	8.09	+3.35
Forests and forestry	13.08	13.71	−0.63

The same publication may show up multiple times across REEport years for multi-year projects. TEConomy manually removed these duplicates from the data to allow for accurate comparative analysis

eral funding agencies, such as, for example, the National Institutes of Health, where TEConomy's analysis of NIH REEport data finds circa 3.5 peer-reviewed publications generated per $1 million in NIH funding (using the same publication years).

Conclusions

Agriculture and related industries are one of the United States' great success stories. The sustained growth and productivity of these industries are made possible by the strong R&D sector in the United States. While industry is a vital part of this sector, the work of the LGUs and Cooperative Extension Services funded by the federal government through the USDA is critically important. Our evaluation of the Capacity Funding system provides a detailed picture of the ways in which federal funding is developing American science and agriculture.

Our examination of the Web of Science™ database indicates that, in overall publications volume in agriculture and related fields, agronomy, basic science, and veterinary medicine are the largest topic areas, with plant science being an important focus in the first two of these areas. The REEport data on the 20,000 Capacity Funding projects between 2000 and 2015 indicate that these projects are diverse but heavily focused on applied research areas, although not to the exclusion of basic sciences like microbiology. Compared with overall publications, however, Capacity projects are less focused on basic science and more focused on production-oriented areas and downstream value-added activities in food and biomass industries. This is evident in the example of animal research. While overall publications have a heavy focus on veterinary medicine, Capacity research does not have that emphasis but instead has a large focus on livestock health. Additionally, a number of areas that are small or missing from overall publications are present in notably higher concentrations in Capacity projects such as pest management, water, family and consumer sciences, and fisheries and aquaculture.

Competitively funded research in the REEport data has its largest focus area in basic science, which is double the proportion of Competitively funded projects as it is of Capacity funded projects. In comparison, Capacity Funding is much more focused on projects that promote agricultural production. Both Capacity and Competitively funded projects largely fit within the NIFA National Challenge Areas and the 2014 Farm Bill Priority Areas. Capacity funded projects are providing robust coverage of the six NIFA National Challenge Areas, with almost two-thirds of projects so focused. Emphasis, as expected, is not equal across the six, with major focus placed on food security and with 48.5% of projects focused on production agriculture. Water sees the second highest degree of emphasis in the Capacity funded project portfolio. NIFA-AFRI/NRI Competitive funds also see the majority of projects (59.1%) being classified in themes relevant to the six NIFA National Challenge Areas. In the case of Competitive funds, the allocation of projects across the six National Challenge Areas shows less percentage variation in Competitive project allocations. Both NIFA Capacity funded and NIFA Competitively funded portfolios see the vast majority of projects (almost nine out of every ten) being focused in areas specific to the 2014 Farm Bill priorities. Both funding methods therefore seem to be suited to developing research that targets our nation's goals.

Finally, we examined the leveraging of funds and return on investment of NIFA-funded research. All of the meta-cluster areas of Capacity projects leverage external funds. On average, each federal dollar brings an additional $1.86, for a total of almost 9 billion nonfederal dollars spent on Capacity projects between 2010 and 2015. Capacity funded projects have a strong return on investment when measured as publications per $1 million. In all areas but one, Capacity projects produced more publications per $1 million than Competitive projects, with the largest differences in family and consumer sciences, economics, and agronomy.

Appendix

Table 7 Percentage segmentation of publications across key disciplines (OmniViz™ cluster analysis of 108,180 publications)

Meta-cluster.	% of total	Theme	% of meta-cluster	% of total	Subtheme	% of theme	% of total
Agronomy	21.3%	Plant breeding/ improvement	65.5%	14.0%	General	31.8%	4.4%
					Corn	19.6%	2.7%
					Wheat	15.7%	2.2%
					Soybean	8.0%	1.1%
					Rice	7.3%	1.0%
					Potato	6.7%	0.9%
					Grasses	4.9%	0.7%
					Cotton	4.6%	0.6%
					Beans	1.4%	0.2%
		Horticulture	20.6%	4.4%	Fruit	80.2%	3.5%
					Tomatoes	10.0%	0.4%
					Apples	6.5%	0.3%
					Strawberries	1.8%	0.1%
						1.6%	0.1%
		Water	4.8%	1.0%	Irrigation	37.1%	0.4%
					Sedimentation	31.9%	0.3%
					Nutrient runoff	31.1%	0.3%
		Pest management	5.1%	1.1%	Weeds	100.0%	1.1%
		Plant pathology	2.2%	0.5%	Citrus	100.0%	0.5%
		Organic	1.4%	0.3%		100.0%	0.3%
		Mycology	0.4%	0.1%	Mushrooms	100.0%	0.1%
Basic science	21.1%	Plant science	60.3%	12.7%	Stress resistance	21.4%	2.7%
					Physiology and morphology	20.8%	2.6%
					Seeds	20.0%	2.5%
					Roots	13.8%	1.8%
					Genetics	10.5%	1.3%
					Pollination	8.9%	1.1%
					Mutation	1.7%	0.2%
					Salt tolerance	1.7%	0.2%
					Fungicide resistance	1.3%	0.2%
		Nutrition	14.9%	3.1%		100.0%	3.1%
		Bacteriology	12.3%	2.6%	e-coli	100.0%	2.6%
		Symbiosis	2.9%	0.6%		100.0%	0.6%
		Emissions	2.8%	0.6%		100.0%	0.6%
		Starch	2.0%	0.4%		100.0%	0.4%
		Fermentation	1.4%	0.3%		100.0%	0.3%
		Cell biology	1.0%	0.2%		100.0%	0.2%
		Basic genetics	0.8%	0.2%	MicroRNA	100.0%	0.2%
		Algology	0.7%	0.2%		100.0%	0.2%
		Biofilms	0.5%	0.1%		100.0%	0.1%
		Biochemistry	0.3%	0.1%		100.0%	0.1%

(continued)

Table 7 (continued)

Meta-cluster.	% of total	Theme	% of meta-cluster	% of total	Subtheme	% of theme	% of total
Veterinary medicine	17.7%	Canine	29.0%	5.1%		100.0%	5.1%
		Infectious diseases	28.0%	5.0%		54.4%	2.7%
					Virology	38.1%	1.9%
					Vaccines	7.5%	0.4%
		Equine	17.5%	3.1%		100.0%	3.1%
		Porcine	7.7%	1.4%		100.0%	1.4%
		Surgery	3.6%	0.6%		100.0%	0.6%
		General	3.3%	0.6%		100.0%	0.6%
		Orthopedics	3.1%	0.5%		100.0%	0.5%
		Small ruminants	2.8%	0.5%		100.0%	0.5%
		Bovine	2.6%	0.5%		100.0%	0.5%
		Cancer	1.0%	0.2%		100.0%	0.2%
		Small animals	0.9%	0.2%		100.0%	0.2%
		Ophthalmology	0.4%	0.1%		100.0%	`
Forestry	10.1%	Forest management	26.3%	2.7%		100.0%	2.7%
		Silviculture	25.1%	2.5%	Pine	74.6%	1.9%
						20.7%	0.5%
					Aspen	4.7%	0.1%
		Tree species	18.3%	1.9%		100.0%	1.9%
		Fire	9.8%	1.0%		100.0%	1.0%
		Soil	9.4%	0.9%		100.0%	0.9%
		General	7.9%	0.8%		100.0%	0.8%
		Forest products	3.4%	0.3%	Lumber	82.1%	0.3%
					Biofuel	17.9%	0.1%
Soil science	9.0%	General	65.1%	5.9%		100.0%	5.9%
		Plant nutrients	34.9%	3.2%		100.0%	3.2%
Dairy	4.8%	Milk	100.0%	4.8%		100.0%	4.8%
Food science	4.4%	Oils	39.7%	1.7%		100.0%	1.7%
		Meat science	24.6%	1.1%	Beef	100.0%	1.1%
		Consumer preferences	16.5%	0.7%		100.0%	0.7%
		Food safety	5.3%	0.2%	Listeria	100.0%	0.2%
		Food storage	4.3%	0.2%		100.0%	0.2%
		Alkaloids	4.1%	0.2%		100.0%	0.2%
		Peanuts	3.7%	0.2%	Allergens	100.0%	0.2%
		Nutrition	1.7%	0.1%		100.0%	0.1%
Poultry	2.7%	Broilers	53.6%	1.5%		100.0%	1.5%
		Layers	33.2%	0.9%		100.0%	0.9%
		Litter	8.4%	0.2%		100.0%	0.2%
		Turkey	4.8%	0.1%		100.0%	0.1%

(continued)

Table 7 (continued)

Meta-cluster.	% of total	Theme	% of meta-cluster	% of total	Subtheme	% of theme	% of total
Entomology	2.6%	Pest control	36.9%	1.0%		100.0%	1.0%
		Mosquitoes	28.2%	0.7%		100.0%	0.7%
		Mites	15.8%	0.4%		100.0%	0.4%
		Ticks	9.9%	0.3%		100.0%	0.3%
		Nematodes	9.2%	0.2%		100.0%	0.2%
Animal science	2.3%	Reproduction	48.5%	1.1%		100.0%	1.1%
		Behavior	34.5%	0.8%		100.0%	0.8%
		Primates	9.3%	0.2%		100.0%	0.2%
		Wildlife	4.4%	0.1%		100.0%	0.1%
		Nutrition	3.3%	0.1%	Probiotics	100.0%	0.1%
Livestock	2.3%	Bovine	58.1%	1.3%	Beef cattle	70.2%	0.9%
					Forage	18.4%	0.2%
					Grazing	11.4%	0.1%
		Aquaculture	33.0%	0.7%		100.0%	0.7%
		Manure management	8.9%	0.2%		100.0%	0.2%
Biomass and biofuels	1.7%	Biomass	78.6%	1.3%	Switch grass	73.6%	1.0%
					Crop residues	26.4%	0.4%
		Glycerol	7.4%	0.1%		100.0%	0.1%
		Biochar	7.2%	0.1%		100.0%	0.1%
		Anaerobic digestion	6.8%	0.1%		100.0%	0.1%

Table 8 Percentage segmentation of Capacity funded projects (REEport Data for 2010–2015) across meta-clusters, associated clusters, and subthemes

Meta-cluster	% of total	Theme	% of meta-cluster	% of total	Subtheme	% of theme	% of total
Agronomy	36.3%	Pest management	27.3%	9.9%	Biological control	32.3%	3.2%
					Entomology	27.8%	2.8%
					Weed science	20.3%	2.0%
					Herbicide	15.0%	1.5%
					Plant parasites	4.6%	0.5%
		Plant breeding and improvement	25.4%	9.2%	Stress tolerance	37.2%	3.4%
					Plant nutrient inputs	19.9%	1.8%
					Row crop improvement	11.6%	1.1%
					Row crop pathogens	10.6%	1.0%
					Turfgrass	7.6%	0.7%
					Potatoes	7.0%	0.6%
					Parasite resistance	4.0%	0.4%
					Grains	2.0%	0.2%
		Soil science	24.7%	9.0%		100.0%	9.0%
		Horticulture	11.6%	4.2%	Viticulture	67.0%	2.8%
					Orchards	26.6%	1.1%
					Citrus diseases	6.5%	0.3%
		Irrigation and water use	10.9%	4.0%		100.0%	4.0%
Animal science and livestock	15.1%	Livestock diseases	38.7%	5.9%	Bovine	89.8%	5.3%
					Poultry	10.2%	0.6%
		Poultry science	10.4%	1.6%		85.5%	1.3%
					Reproduction	14.5%	0.2%
		Meat science	9.3%	1.4%	Bovine	90.3%	1.3%
					Poultry	9.7%	0.1%
		Livestock nutrition	8.6%	1.3%	Grazing	100.0%	1.3%
		Livestock reproduction	8.2%	1.2%		100.0%	1.2%
		Forage crops	8.0%	1.2%		100.0%	1.2%
		Manure management	7.1%	1.1%		100.0%	1.1%
		Small ruminants	4.1%	0.6%		56.6%	0.3%
					Parasites	43.4%	0.3%
		Equine	2.2%	0.3%		100.0%	0.3%
		Fly and insect management	1.9%	0.3%	Flies	100.0%	0.3%
		Animal reproduction	1.5%	0.2%	Porcine	100.0%	0.2%

(continued)

Table 8 (continued)

Meta-cluster	% of total	Theme	% of meta-cluster	% of total	Subtheme	% of theme	% of total
Basic life science	12.2%	Microbiology	71.7%	8.8%	Bacteriology	40.8%	3.6%
					Virology	30.0%	2.6%
					Plant pathology	28.6%	2.5%
					Phages	0.6%	0.1%
		Genetics and genomics	10.7%	1.3%		100.0%	1.3%
		Vector-borne diseases	3.6%	0.4%		100.0%	0.4%
		Cancer	3.2%	0.4%		100.0%	0.4%
		Plant genetics and molecular biology	3.1%	0.4%		100.0%	0.4%
		Nutrition	2.5%	0.3%		100.0%	0.3%
		Muscle physiology	2.3%	0.3%		100.0%	0.3%
		Animal reproduction	1.5%	0.2%		100.0%	0.2%
		Molecular biology	0.8%	0.1%		100.0%	0.1%
		Biosensors	0.6%	0.1%	Nanotechnology	100.0%	0.1%
Forests and forestry	10.9%	Forest habitat and ecosystems	60.7%	6.6%		100.0%	6.6%
		Silviculture	24.4%	2.7%	Pine	52.0%	1.4%
						48.0%	1.3%
		Pest management	6.3%	0.7%	Entomology	100.0%	0.7%
		Land use	4.0%	0.4%		100.0%	0.4%
		Tourism	3.2%	0.4%		100.0%	0.4%
		Wood science	1.4%	0.2%		100.0%	0.2%
Food science	7.3%	Nutrition	52.5%	3.8%	Fruits and vegetables	46.9%	1.8%
					Obesity	46.5%	1.8%
					Bioactive compounds	6.6%	0.3%
		Food safety	30.7%	2.2%	Bacteriology	78.1%	1.7%
					Fungal toxins	14.7%	0.3%
					Education	7.2%	0.2%
		Starch crops	7.5%	0.5%	Quality	100.0%	0.5%
		Dairy	7.4%	0.5%		100.0%	0.5%
		Wine	1.9%	0.1%		100.0%	0.1%
Environmental science	6.6%	Water	55.9%	3.7%	Water quality	100.0%	3.7%
		Ecology and ecosystems	16.5%	1.1%	Wetlands	100.0%	1.1%
		Bees	13.6%	0.9%		100.0%	0.9%
		Wildlife and habitat	5.8%	0.4%		100.0%	0.4%
		Fire	3.9%	0.3%		100.0%	0.3%
		Climate change	2.9%	0.2%		100.0%	0.2%
		Emissions	0.8%	0.1%		100.0%	0.1%
		Environmental contaminants	0.5%	0.0%	Mercury and metals	100.0%	0.0%
Economics	3.5%	Agricultural economics	100.0%	3.5%		100.0%	3.5%

(continued)

Table 8 (continued)

Meta-cluster	% of total	Theme	% of meta-cluster	% of total	Subtheme	% of theme	% of total
Biomass and biofuels	3.1%	Cellulosic biomass	81.0%	2.5%		65.7%	1.7%
					Processing	34.3%	0.9%
		Biofuel and biogas	11.0%	0.3%		100.0%	0.3%
		Algae and phycology	8.1%	0.3%		100.0%	0.3%
Fisheries and aquaculture	2.8%	Fisheries	84.6%	2.3%		100.0%	2.3%
		Aquaculture	15.4%	0.4%		100.0%	0.4%
Family and consumer sciences	2.1%	Youth and behavior	42.0%	0.9%	Behavior	100.0%	0.9%
		Obesity	31.0%	0.7%		100.0%	0.7%
		Poverty and mental health	14.1%	0.3%		100.0%	0.3%
		Emotion and behavioral management	12.9%	0.3%		100.0%	0.3%

Table 9 Percentage segmentation of Competitive funded projects (REEport Data for 2010–2015) across meta-clusters, associated clusters, and subthemes

Meta-cluster	% of total	Theme	% of meta-cluster	% of total	Subtheme	% of theme	% of total
Basic science	25.0%	Basic plant science	32.7%	8.2%		100.0%	8.2%
		Genetics and genomics	19.8%	5.0%		53.5%	2.7%
						36.0%	1.8%
					Whole genome sequencing	7.0%	0.3%
						3.5%	0.2%
		Microbiology	17.4%	4.3%		100.0%	4.3%
		Infectious diseases	16.7%	4.2%		100.0%	4.2%
		Virology	6.3%	1.6%		100.0%	1.6%
		Inflammation	4.5%	1.1%		100.0%	1.1%
		Mammalian reproduction	2.6%	0.7%		100.0%	0.7%
Agronomy	20.9%	Soil science	34.0%	7.1%		100.0%	7.1%
		Plant pathology	25.2%	5.3%		63.6%	3.3%
					Fungal	36.4%	1.9%
		Plant breeding and improvement	19.0%	4.0%	Genetics	94.5%	3.7%
						5.5%	0.2%
		Pest management	18.3%	3.8%	Insects and insecticides	65.9%	2.5%
					Weed management	19.3%	0.7%
					Aphids	14.8%	0.6%
		Fruit	3.5%	0.7%		100.0%	0.7%

(continued)

Table 9 (continued)

Meta-cluster	% of total	Theme	% of meta-cluster	% of total	Subtheme	% of theme	% of total
Food science	11.2%	Food safety	75.5%	8.4%		71.1%	6.0%
					Poultry	11.3%	1.0%
						10.3%	0.9%
						7.2%	0.6%
		Food systems and access	18.3%	2.0%		100.0%	2.0%
		Lipids	6.2%	0.7%		100.0%	0.7%
Animal science and livestock	10.9%	Cattle	26.0%	2.8%		100.0%	2.8%
		Dairy	20.8%	2.3%		59.6%	1.3%
						40.4%	0.9%
		Bovine genetics	16.8%	1.8%		100.0%	1.8%
		Nutrition	13.2%	1.4%		100.0%	1.4%
		Vaccines	12.0%	1.3%		100.0%	1.3%
		Reproduction	11.2%	1.2%		100.0%	1.2%
Environmental science	10.8%	Water	53.4%	5.8%		100.0%	5.8%
		Agricultural emissions	26.5%	2.9%		100.0%	2.9%
		Bees	20.1%	2.2%		100.0%	2.2%
Economics	8.0%	Agricultural economics	83.6%	6.7%		100.0%	6.7%
		Markets and pricing	16.4%	1.3%		100.0%	1.3%
Biomass and biofuels	5.5%	Biomass	82.5%	4.5%		100.0%	4.5%
		Conversion processes	17.5%	1.0%	Fermentation	54.5%	0.5%
					Enzymes	45.5%	0.4%
Family and consumer sciences	4.8%	Obesity	100.0%	4.8%	Childhood obesity	56.8%	2.7%
					Nutrition	43.2%	2.1%
Forests and forestry	3.0%	Forest ecosystems	100.0%	3.0%		100.0%	3.0%

Agriscience Innovation at Land-Grant Universities, Measured by Patents and Plant Variety Protection Certificates as Proxies

Simon Tripp, Joseph Simkins, Alyssa Yetter, and Dylan Yetter

Abstract One of the major metrics of innovation in agriscience is intellectual property. Land-grant university innovation is documented as intellectual property in two main ways: patents and Plant Variety Protection certificates. To evaluate the innovation generated by NIFA Capacity Funds, TEConomy Partners, LLC, examined the patents and PVP certificates received by LGUs during a 7-year period (2010–2016). The results indicate substantial innovation occurring in LGUs. LGUs generated 4% of total patenting in agriculture and related fields in the study period. When broadened to include patents that cite prior LGU work, LGUs influence up to one in six patents in agbiosciences in the United States. Even higher impacts of LGUs are found in PVP certificates. Between 2010 and 2016, an average of 14% of PVPs were awarded to LGUs. This analysis further demonstrates that LGUs patent in cutting-edge applications of biotechnology and associated life and physical sciences. In PVPs, LGUs generated intellectual property in many crops that were not experiencing IP generation from other sources. Overall, we conclude that university-based research, especially research at LGUs, plays a substantial role in the US agriscience innovation ecosystem.

Introduction

Intellectual property (IP) generation is one important output of federal Capacity and Competitive funded research projects, and thus examining patenting and other IP protection activity is useful for assessing the innovation impact of federally funded research. R&D at universities may result in novel innovations that may be protected

S. Tripp (✉) • J. Simkins • D. Yetter
TEConomy Partners LLC, Columbus, OH, USA
e-mail: tripps@teconomypartners.com

A. Yetter
Pennsylvania State University, State College, PA, USA

© Springer International Publishing AG 2018   223
N. Kalaitzandonakes et al. (eds.), *From Agriscience to Agribusiness*, Innovation,
Technology, and Knowledge Management, https://doi.org/10.1007/978-3-319-67958-7_11

for the university via patenting, administered through the US Patent and Trademark Office or via Plant Variety Protection (PVP) certificates administered by the US Plant Variety Protection Office. Like peer-reviewed scientific publications, the generation of a patent or a PVP certificate is a testament to unique and impactful research results. The National Institute of Food and Agriculture (NIFA) mission areas related to agriculture, food supply, public health, nutrition, natural resources, etc. may be served not only by generating new knowledge and recommendations rooted in research and reported in publications but also by the generation of new innovations that have value when implemented as commercial technologies. Patents and PVP certificates can thus serve as a proxy measure for innovation. It should be noted, however, that these are imperfect measures in that the land-grant service ethos can also result in multiple innovations being released to the field without patent or other IP protections ever being sought. Patent data should be seen, therefore, as underestimating the total universe of technological innovation occurring.

Researchers examining the underpinnings of innovation have demonstrated the use of patents as an intermediary metric that identifies novel innovations with links to federal R&D investment, and thus patents may be used as proxies for "translatable innovation."[1,2] Evaluating innovation impact via patents also allows for the usage of forward citations as a proxy measure for the downstream "forward innovation" that results from new patented innovations generating follow-on advances in related technological areas that effectively build upon the knowledge or technology contained within the referenced patents. Although not all land-grant institution patents or PVP certificates will originate from resources provided through NIFA or other USDA funding, the overall portfolio of innovation activity produced at these institutions can serve as an approximation for the types of innovation being funded by Capacity Programs given their role as major sources of research support at these institutions for agriculture and associated disciplinary work.

Data and Methods

Using patent data published by the US Patent and Trademark Office (USPTO), it is possible to profile the innovation areas that have indirect linkages to NIFA Capacity Funding programs.[3] The indirect impact of Capacity Programs on innovation can be

---

[1] Kalutkiewicz, Michael J., and Richard L. Ehman. 2014. *Patents as proxies: NIH hubs of innovation.* Nature Biotechnology, June 2014.

[2] Grueber, Martin, and Simon Tripp. 2015. *Patents as Proxies Revisited: NIH Innovation 2000 to 2013.* Battelle Technology Partnership Practice. March 2015.

[3] Direct attribution to NIFA Capacity Funding cannot be systematically identified since one of the few ways to capture direct linkages through documentation is the use of the government interest field included on patents that provides any recognition or attribution to government funding support used in creating the IP described in the patent. Patents where the government interest field includes references to funding support from NIFA and other USDA programs demonstrate a direct attribution back to these funding sources, but feedback from land-grant universities indicates that this form of documentation is not used consistently enough for analysis.

profiled through examining the portfolio of IP being generated at land-grant universities, because they are the primary recipients of Capacity Funding. Patents tied to land-grant institutions can be identified by the holders of the IP documented in patents, called assignees. Assignees can include multiple institutions and combinations of private and public entities. Additionally, many patents cite the prior art established in existing patents in documenting new discoveries. Important IP that fundamentally advances the state of technology or science in an area will likely be cited by many other patents which use the initial discovery as the basis for downstream innovation. In examining the scope of land-grant university appearances in cited references for US patents in agbioscience areas, the indirect impact of Capacity Program support for past research at these institutions can be highlighted for its foundational role in follow-on industry and academic innovation. Accordingly, our analysis of patents includes two sets of patents. First, we identify patents based on a land-grant institution being listed as an assignee. Second, we identify patents with a land-grant institution patent cited in prior art references. By using both sets of patents, we capture the downstream innovation of the work in Capacity Funding program areas and the subsequent downstream innovation that may be rooted in original LGU-performed research.

Analysis of patents and forward citation of patents is performed using the Clarivate Analytics "Thomson Innovation" patent database. To capture the innovation activity related specifically to NIFA mission objective areas, detailed patent classes were used to identify relevant technologies and products with applications in agricultural sciences and associated fields. The US Patent and Trademark Office Cooperative Patent Classification (CPC) system assigns each patent a specific numeric major patent "class" as well as supplemental secondary patent classes which detail the primary technology areas being documented by the patented IP. These classes are assigned to patents by dedicated classification staff who examine the documented IP's key focus and end uses. By combining relevant patent classes across the wide array of agricultural science-related activity, these class designations allow for an aggregation scheme that identifies broad technology themes specific to the technology areas that are part of NIFA's key mission. We grouped these relevant US-invented patents into broader agbioscience patent class groups to allow an analysis of innovation trends. The data used in this analysis include all issued US patents from 2010 to 2016 within the set of key patent classes identified by the analysis team at TEConomy Partners LLC (TEConomy). Appendix A provides a listing of the patent classes and class groups that were used in this analysis as "agriculture and related sectors" and how they are grouped into major technology themes.

A second set of data is additionally used to examine the innovative products of capacity funding, via LGUs, Plant Variety Protection (PVP) certificates. Plant breeders may protect their intellectual property not only through patenting but also through PVP certificates, which protect plant varieties for 20 years. Using the USDA Agricultural Marketing Service Scanned Certificates database of issued PVP certificates, we compiled a database of all issued PVPs between 2010 and 2016. The database lists the name of the applicant for the PVP, which allows us to identify which PVPs are the result of research done at a LGU. These data permit us to capture a metric of innovation additional to the analysis of patents.

Results

Dynamics of Land-Grant University Patenting Activity

There were 24,462 total US patents granted in the agriscience class areas shown in Appendix A from 2010 through 2016. Of these patents, 950 (4%) listed land-grant institutions as one of the original assignees and 3911 (16%) listed land-grant institutions in their prior art references. This level of LGU patenting represents a significant component of national innovation activity given the highly concentrated nature of institutions generating innovation in this space. The top five patenting entities in agbiosciences are corporations, and these five together account for almost 26% of all patents generated during this period. In this context, the cumulative patenting impact of land-grant university innovation supported by Capacity Funding can be thought of as roughly equivalent to one of the major agbioscience companies in the United States.

Figure 1 shows growth trends for the analyzed patent groups between 2010 and 2016. Overall US patenting in agbioscience classes (solid line) rose significantly over this period, increasing by 77%. Land-grant university patenting (dashed line), however, increased at a slower rate, growing by 37% over the same period. However, land-grant patenting activity did increase sharply after 2012 and has exhibited consistent annual growth since then, despite declines in overall patenting volume.

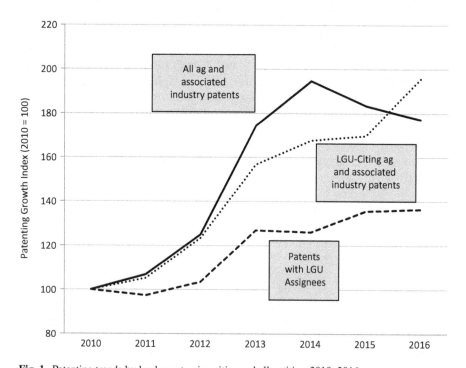

Fig. 1 Patenting trends by land-grant universities and all entities, 2010–2016

Finally, patents citing land-grant patents (dotted line) saw a 95% increase over this period, with no periods of decline. This highlights the benefit of ongoing Capacity Funding support in maintaining a consistent base of innovation despite year-to-year fluctuations in broader trends.

Viewing patent totals solely in terms of their final assignee does not capture the numerous patents where land-grant researchers contributed to technologies that were ultimately assigned to private industry and other institutions besides the land-grant universities. It is challenging to trace all inventors listed on patents back to work produced during their tenure at land-grant or non-land-grant institutions, but it is possible to examine the citation impacts of patents that have been assigned to land-grant institutions as an indication that innovative IP produced there was used as the basis for other downstream technologies.

Figure 2 shows the proportion of total agbioscience patents that cite land-grant-assigned patents in their documentation of new IP from 2010 to 2016. Patents supported by Capacity Funding programs appear to play a significant role in generating downstream innovation by private industry and other institutions. From 2010 to 2016, land-grant university-assigned patents in agriculture and related industry areas were cited by 16% of all US patents generated, with a peak of approximately one in every six patents citing prior land-grant work in 2016.

Capacity Funding programs serve as key supporting mechanisms for innovation activity at land-grant universities, and recent patenting demonstrates a significant impact on the country's stock of associated innovation. Many additional patents, especially those generated as a result of collaborative university and extension inter-

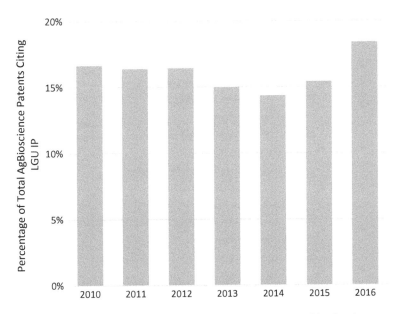

Fig. 2 Percentage of total US agriculture and associated sector patents citing Land-grant university assigned patents, 2010–2016

actions with agriculture industry firms, are not able to be definitively captured through examination of historical patent data, and the innovative footprint of land-grant institutions in the patenting landscape is likely significantly larger. In other words, the data presented herein are likely quite conservative.

Key Areas of Patenting Impact

The patents generated by the land grants display several major innovation focus areas. These serve to highlight the innovation themes across land-grant institutions in terms of driving cutting-edge agricultural science and the importance of continued federal funding support for research. Figure 3 shows the percentages of the land-grant patenting portfolio (blue bars) across broad agriculture and associated sector areas as compared with total US percentages (green bars). The yellow bars indicate the percent of all patents citing LGU-originated patents.

Relative to total US trends (green bars), land-grant university patenting (blue bars) is more concentrated in enzymes, fertilizers, and other agricultural chemicals, genetic engineering, and microbiology. New plant varieties and cultivars make up a large proportion of both the land-grant and national patenting portfolios, which is unsurprising given the end product of much agbioscience innovation is directed toward creating new crops that have improved disease resistance and favorable growth and yield traits. However, technologies that are perceived as more traditionally agriculture centric like agricultural machinery and planting processes and

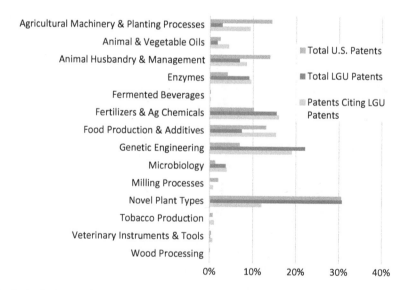

Fig. 3 Agriculture and associated sector patent Portfolio composition of Land-grant institutions and total United States, 2010–2016

animal husbandry and management are more highly concentrated in private industry at the national level, indicating that NIFA funding programs are supporting more cutting-edge science and applications in next-generation agricultural biotechnology as opposed to basic agricultural infrastructure. Land-grant institution patenting appears to be more specialized around the processes and techniques that help form the foundation of key agbioscience technology fields such as genetically engineered organisms, biologically derived agricultural compounds, and chemicals for use in agriculture. Several detailed technology applications of these fields represented in land-grant patenting portfolios are listed in Table 1.

Another way of viewing areas of specialization in land-grant patenting is through their forward innovation impact. As noted above, forward citations from later patents that cite the IP documented in land grants' agriculture and associated areas indicate the impact that the documented technologies have on furthering the pace of innovation. Often, distinct bursts in innovation, as measured by forward citations, can be traced back to critical IP documented in a select few patents that initially documented groundbreaking new research,[4] making forward citation impact a good indicator of the value of a patent's IP. Figure 4 shows both

Table 1 Examples of detailed technology areas represented in specialized agriculture and associated sector patenting areas for land-grant institutions

Broad area	Examples of detailed technology applications present in land-grant patenting activity
Enzymes	More efficient and cost-effective biofuel production Synthesis of bioproducts and organic compounds via enzymes and other hosts Delivery vectors for disease resistance in plants or animals
Fertilizers and other agricultural chemicals	Biorepellents and environmentally compatible pesticides Improved fungicide compounds Biofilm and bacterial growth inhibitors Improved delivery of biocides (via technologies like coated nanoparticles) and antimicrobial coatings and surfaces Toxicity-minimizing fertilizers and growth enhancers Pest insect attractants
Genetic engineering	Transgenic plants and animals Engineered disease/pest resistance and environmental tolerance Precision breeding and improved yields for improved food production Genetically modified organisms for biofuel production and bioreactors
Microbiology	Genetically modified animal disease strains and growth media Livestock stem cell lines and applications in improving animal health Transgenic algae and other beneficial microorganisms

---

[4] Huang, Yi-Hung, Ming-Tat Ko, Chun-Nan Hsu. 2014. "Identifying Transformative Research in Biomedical Sciences," *Technologies and Applications of Artificial Intelligence*, Volume 8916 of the series *Lecture Notes in Computer Science*, November 2014.

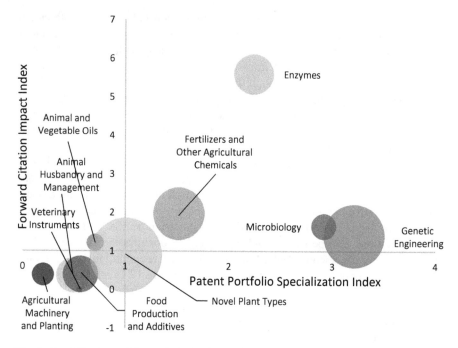

Fig. 4 Specialization and forward citation impact indices of land-grant institution-assigned patents in agriculture and associated areas, 2010–2016, relative to national trends

the specialization and forward citation impact of land-grant institution-assigned patents relative to national patenting trends across broad agricultural and associated science and technology categories.

As seen in Fig. 4, land-grant university agriscience patenting in genetic engineering, microbiology, and enzyme applications is both highly specialized and has high forward citation impact relative to national trends. In particular, patents documenting enzyme applications in agriculture and associated areas had a citation impact almost six times higher than that of the United States, indicating that the IP developed by land-grant institutions in this area has generated significant downstream innovation activity. Fertilizers and other agricultural chemicals also had above-average specialization and forward citation impacts relative to national trends. More traditional agricultural innovation in food production and additives, animal husbandry and management, and veterinary instruments and tools were all below average for land grants relative to total US patenting, with novel plant types being about the same as the wider United States in terms of its role in the land-grant patent portfolio. These areas of specialized and highly innovative impact partially speak to the changing nature of modern agricultural science, where advanced biotechnology serves as much of the basis for new technologies but, more importantly, highlights the advanced nature of land-grant universities' innovation activity supported by federal funding programs. The innovations being generated by land-grant institutions are clearly focused around next-generation applications for agriculture, and the role of Capacity Funds in driving the research activities that produce those outcomes is thus an important piece of the ongoing evolution of the wider US agricultural sciences field.

Land-Grant University PVP Certification

There were a total of 3824 PVP certificates granted between 2010 and 2016, 488 of which were applied for by land-grant institutions. The percentage of PVP certificates granted to LGUs varies year to year, with a peak of 20% in 2016, averaging 14% over 7 years in our data. Together, this places the land-grant institutions as the third largest recipient of PVP certificates in this period, after Pioneer Hi-Bred International, Inc. (with 32% of PVPs), and Monsanto Technology, LLC (with 22% of PVPs). The next largest recipient after LGUs is Syngenta Crop Protection (with 8% of PVPs).

Figure 5 presents the proportion of PVPs granted for each of the 113 types of crops. Crops with less than 1% share of the total are combined in the "Other" category. Of the remaining 14 most prevalent crops, soybeans and field corn have the largest number of protected varieties, each with more than one quarter of the total. Common wheat, potatoes, and cotton are the next three most prevalent varieties.

Figure 6 presents the data split by applicant type. Again, all crop types with less than 1% share are combined in the "Other" category. This comparison indicates that there is both specialization and overlap in the crops developed by LGUs and other institutions and companies. Of the ten most prevalent crops for both groups, five are shared (common wheat, soybean, potato, perennial ryegrass, and Kentucky bluegrass). However, of these shared crops, none make up a similar proportion of PVPs. For example, while soybeans make up almost a third of non-LGU PVP certificates, they are only 3.6% of LGU certificates. It is also notable that there are many plants that are only prevalent in one of the two pie charts. While field corn is almost one third of non-LGU certificates, it is not present in the LGU certificates.

Although some crops have varieties being developed both in and out of the land-grant system, others are more exclusive. Indeed, of the 113 crops in the data, 68 had varieties only developed by non-LGU institutions, and 18 had varieties only developed by LGUs. The remaining 27 crops had varieties developed by both LGUs and others. Table 2 presents all crop types with 50% or more of their PVP certificates received by LGUs. Of these crops, rice, peanuts, and oats have the most protected varieties (all between 30 and 40). These crops represent ones in which LGUs have specialization and a substantial amount of protected varieties. Of the crops that are 100% LGU, none have more than four certified varieties.

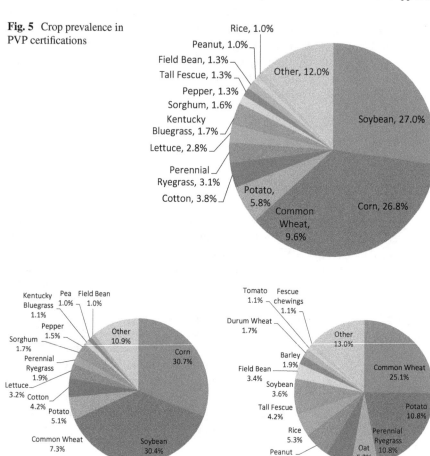

Fig. 5 Crop prevalence in PVP certifications

Fig. 6 Comparison of crop prevalence in LGU and other PVP certifications

Conclusions

Analysis of intellectual property data provide an accepted proxy for evaluating innovation levels occurring at universities. In agriscience, it is land-grant universities that are the primary academic research institutions engaged in research and associated IP development, in part because of their ability to receive and leverage federal NIFA Capacity Funds. Analysis of patents and patent forward citations shows LGUs generating 4% of total patenting in these fields in the 7-year period (2010–2016). However, the impact of land-grant innovation is more wide-ranging, influencing up to one in every six patents (as defined through patent citations) in agbiosciences in the United States. In terms of Plant Variety Protection certificates, the direct impact of the LGUs is even higher than in patenting, with an average of

Table 2 Crops with 50% or more of PVP certifications by land-grant institutions

Crop	Others(%)	LGU(%)
Wheat, durum	50	50
Ryegrass, annual	50	50
Bent grass, creeping	50	50
Flax	50	50
Onion	50	50
Fescue, hard	40	60
Fescue, chewings	38	63
Rice	36	64
Peanut	28	72
Oat	12	88
Bean, lima	0	100
Beet	0	100
Meadow-foam	0	100
Mustard, india	0	100
Bent grass, colonial	0	100
Clover, red	0	100
Clover, white	0	100
Crotalaria, sunn	0	100
Arugula	0	100
Asparagus	0	100
Bahia grass	0	100
Clover, arrowleaf	0	100
Corn, sweet	0	100
Fescue, creeping	0	100
Mustard, white	0	100
Rape, winter	0	100
Switchgrass	0	100
Wheat, club	0	100

14% of PVPs being awarded to LGUs between 2010 and 2016. Patenting in agriculture and associated fields at the LGUs is particularly focused around cutting-edge applications of biotechnology and associated life sciences and physical sciences. Areas that are particularly strong include fertilizers and other agricultural chemicals, genetic engineering, and novel plant types, together with enzymes and microbiology. In PVPs it is found that LGUs demonstrated IP generation in 18 crops that did not generate PVPs from other sources, and the LGUs innovated in 27 crops that others also worked in. Overall, it can be concluded that university-based research, especially research at LGUs, plays a substantial role in the US agriscience innovation ecosystem.

Appendix A: CPC Patent Classes Used in Patent Analysis

Table 3 Mapping of CPC classes to broad agbioscience areas

Broad agbioscience area	CPC class number	Description
Agricultural machinery and planting processes	A01B	Soil working and agricultural machinery
	A01C	Planting, sowing, and fertilizing processes
	A01D	Harvesting and mowing
	A01F	Threshing, baling, cutting, and produce storage
	A01G	Horticulture, forestry, and watering
Animal husbandry and management	A01K	Animal husbandry and breeding
	A01L	Animal shoeing
	A01M	Catching and trapping animals
Veterinary instruments and tools	A61D	Veterinary instruments, tools, or methods
Food production and additives	A01J	Manufacture of dairy products
	A21B	Baking equipment
	A21C	Dough processing
	A21D	Baking additives, products, and preservation
	A22B	Animal slaughtering
	A22C	Meat, poultry, and fish processing
	A23B	Food preservation
	A23C	Downstream dairy products
	A23D	Edible oils and fats
	A23F	Coffee and tea
	A23G	Cocoa products and other candies
	A23J	Protein compositions for foodstuffs
	A23K	Animal feedstocks
	A23L	Foods or foodstuffs not covered by other classes
	A23N	Machines for treating harvested plants
	A23P	Shaping or working of foodstuffs
Fertilizers and other agricultural chemicals	A01N	Preservation, biocides, pest repellants/attractants, growth regulators
	C05B	Phosphatic fertilizers
	C05C	Nitrogenous fertilizers
	C05D	Other inorganic fertilizers
	C05F	Other organic fertilizers
	C05G	Fertilizer mixtures and additives
Animal and vegetable oils	C11B	Producing and refining animal and vegetable oils
	C11C	Secondary fats, oils, or fatty acids obtained from processing
Milling processes	B02B	Preparing grain and fruit for milling
	B02C	Specific milling processes
Novel plant types	A01H	New plants and processes for obtaining them

(continued)

Table 3 (continued)

Broad agbioscience area	CPC class number	Description
Tobacco production	A24B	Manufacture or preparation of tobacco
Wood processing	B27L	Removing bark and splitting wood; manufacture of wood stock, veneer, shavings, fibers, or powder
Fermented beverages	C12C	Beer brewing
	C12G	Preparation of wine and other alcoholic beverages
	C12H	Pasteurization, sterilization, purification, clarification, and aging of alcoholic beverages
Enzymes[a]	C12N (part)	Preparation and compositions of enzymes, proenzymes, or carrier-bound or immobilized cells
Genetic engineering[b]	C12N (part)	Mutation or genetic engineering substances (DNA or RNA), vectors, and host organisms
Microbiology[b]	C12N (part)	Microorganisms, spores, undifferentiated animal or plant cells, tissues, and culture media, viruses, and bacteria

[a]Patent classes that document areas related to microorganisms, plant and animal cell lines, and genetic engineering techniques often do not distinguish between human biomedical and agricultural applications for the end use of the IP listed and many times have multidisciplinary innovation impacts across human and agricultural biotech areas, making attribution of new technologies directly to agricultural biotechnology difficult. For these classes, expert review of all US patents generated for the analysis period was conducted to determine those that had agricultural biotechnology contexts for inclusion

[b]Grueber, Martin, and Simon Tripp. 2015. *Patents as Proxies Revisited: NIH Innovation 2000 to 2013.* Battelle Technology Partnership Practice. March 2015

Part III
Technology Transfer from the Public to the Private Sector

Transfer and Licensing of University Research and Technology in Canadian Agriculture

Stuart J. Smyth

Abstract Reports from the past decade have indicated that Canada is a highly innovative country, but suffers from a bottleneck in technology transfer and commercialization. In fact, many of the reports give Canada a failing grade when it comes to the commercialization of innovation technologies. With substantial investments into public sector research, such a problem would reduce the public good from government funding of innovative research. This chapter assesses Canadian university technology transfer activities from 1998 to 2008, with a particular focus on the transfer of agricultural technologies.

Introduction

Innovation, and the ability to innovate, is a fundamental driver of the knowledge economy. Industrial economies and the Organisation for Economic Co-operation and Development (OECD) in particular have focused on innovative capacity. To measure a nation's innovative capacity, the OECD uses metrics such as gross expenditures on research and development (R&D) as a percentage of gross domestic product, R&D personnel per thousand employed, number of peer-reviewed publications per researcher, and number of patents. In comparing Canada in these four categories within the G8 group of countries, Holguin-Pando et al. (2014) identify that Canada ranks fifth, fourth, third, and third, respectively. By comparison, the Global Innovation Index ranks Canada in 15th position (GII 2016). In this position, Canada leads industrial countries such as Japan and France yet trails countries like the UK, Germany, Sweden, and the USA.

S.J. Smyth (✉)
University of Saskatchewan, Saskatoon, SK, Canada
e-mail: stuart.smyth@usask.ca

© Springer International Publishing AG 2018
N. Kalaitzandonakes et al. (eds.), *From Agriscience to Agribusiness*, Innovation, Technology, and Knowledge Management, https://doi.org/10.1007/978-3-319-67958-7_12

239

While numerous options exist that measure a nation's innovative capacity, assessing the value and economic potential of public sector innovation is perhaps one of the most daunting challenges facing innovation researchers. This is especially the case when trying to assess innovations that have immediate commercial value. Universities routinely advance theories and philosophies for which they are well known. The development of innovation processes, products, and technologies is of key importance, but a lesser known component of universities.

University innovations with commercial potential historically came from the colleges of agriculture, medicine (human, veterinary, and pharmaceutical), and engineering. Agricultural innovations lay in the domain of improvements to plant and animal genetics. Most of the medical innovations have been related to diagnostic tools and occasionally, depending on the institution, new drugs and disease treatment processes. Innovations disseminating from colleges of engineering have been both process and product oriented. A shift occurred in the commercial value of innovation in the late 1970s and early 1980s following the exponential growth in the information technology industry. At this point, departments of computer and computational sciences within universities started to produce software that had commercial appeal to industry. Genomic innovations also facilitated a shift in university innovation, but this shift was different. The genomics shift was a shift away from tangential products to that of knowledge-based innovative processes.

Given the shift that was beginning to occur in public sector innovative research, many universities in Canada followed the American lead and began to establish technology transfer offices (TTOs) within a decade of the 1980 Bayh-Dole Act. There are a variety of terminologies regarding these offices, including technology transfer offices, offices of technology transfer, and industrial liaison offices. For the purposes of this chapter, the term TTO will refer to all potential acronyms referring to the same function. The majority of these offices were established with a "diamonds in the sky" attitude, and the thinking was that these offices would be substantial revenue streams for universities. With the exception of a handful of universities, the revenue streams are but a mere trickle of what was hoped.

Background on University Technology Transfer

Technology transfer has long been an important issue, with the early focus on transfers from the industrial to the developing world, especially during the Green Revolution. Like many streams of literature, there has been a divergence over time as the research and commercialization focus expanded. One stream of literature that has developed focuses on the relationship between innovation and the transfer of the resulting technologies.

While there is abundant literature on the interactions between innovators and commercializers, the literature examined relates to the transfer between public institutions and commercial interests. One of the first to examine the topic was Eisenberg (1996) who identifies a trend that developed in the USA whereby universities have quickly moved to patent innovations resulting from federally funded research. Drawing on qualitative panel data and interviews from American research intensive universities and TTOs, Owen-Smith and Powell (2001, 2003) identify that faculty decisions to submit a patent application are strongly correlated with the perception of accruing benefits and that the stronger the public-private network, the stronger the pool of university patents. However, the authors note that there is a delicate balance to be maintained between technology transfer and academia being co-opted by industry. Finally, Siegel et al. (2004) through similar survey of American research intensive universities identify several barriers to effective and efficient technology transfer.

Several frameworks exist that conceptualize the innovation systems that are used, or have been used, to enable the transfer of public sector innovations. One such framework is that offered by Etzkowitz and Leydesdorff (2000). The authors provide a Triple Helix analysis model of innovation that examines the dynamics occurring between the public sector innovators in academia and government and industrial technology commercializers. Most discussions regarding the Triple Helix model of innovation analysis refer to the third version of this model, or Triple Helix III. The initial model, Triple Helix I, was highly institutionalized, and the relationship between academia, government, and industry was largely controlled or directed by the state. Triple Helix II relationships can be described as distinct innovation agendas with lines of communication between the three stakeholders operating with high levels of mistrust and suspicion.

The Triple Helix III model most realistically represents the existing relationships in industrialized economies. In this model, academia, government, and industry are represented by distinct spheres, but all three spheres overlap each other. The center of this model, where all three spheres overlap, is characterized by trilateral networks and hybrid organizations (Etzkowitz and Leydesdorff 2000). Etzkowitz and Leydesdorff argue that the common objective of this model is "...to realize an innovative environment consisting of university spin-off firms, tri-lateral initiatives for knowledge-based economic development, and strategic alliances among firms (large and small, operating in different areas, and with different levels of technology), government laboratories, and academic research groups" (p. 112).

A second framework is the Contingent Effectiveness Model put forth by Bozeman (2000). Bozeman suggests that the various parties involved in technology transfer have diverse agendas and goals and that these are achieved with varying degrees of effectiveness. The Contingent Effectiveness Model examines numerous factors involved in technology transfer from public institutions, including transfer agents, transfer objects, transfer media, transfer recipients, and the demand environment. The transfer agent is the holder wishing to transfer a technology, such as a university. The transfer object is the particular innovative process or product to be transferred. The transfer medium is the avenue chosen to commercialize the technology, such as a spin-off company or an exclusive license agreement. The transfer recipient is the party (usually a private firm, but not necessarily) that is interested in gaining access to or purchasing the innovative technology. The demand environment includes market and nonmarket factors that will impact the transfer process, such as the price for the technology or the relationship to existing technologies. Bozeman argues that this model shows "that the impacts of technology transfer can be understood in terms of who is doing the transfer, how they are doing it, what is being transferred, and to whom" (p. 637).

A framework that focuses specifically on the transfer of university technologies is found in Bercovitz and Feldmann (2006). These authors argue that there are a variety of motivations and incentives within universities to transfer technology that are affected by economic, social, and political influences. In examining the black box of university technology transfer, the focus is on "factors that enhance or inhibit the creation and transfer of academic science" (p. 176). The University-Industry Relationship Schema provides for an analysis of the dynamics that exist between the four crucial elements of university technology transfer: the individual researcher, the transfer mechanism, the firm characteristics, and the university environment. The dynamics that exist between the four principles of the schema are defined as exogenous shift parameters, behavioral attributes, strategic responses, and policy/legal environments. Bercovitz and Feldmann argue that this framework highlights the "legal, economic, and policy environments that comprise the system of innovation, determine the rate and type of university knowledge production, and thereby influence the rate of technology change" (p. 186).

These frameworks provide some insight into the intricacies and challenges of transferring technologies created in the public sector, especially universities. The Etzkowitz and Leydesdorff framework provides a unique perspective on the interactions between public sector researchers and commercial firms regarding innovations. Bozeman's focus on the factors affecting technology transfer complements Bercovitz and Feldmann's focus on the environmental aspects of technology transfer. Drawing on the strengths of these frameworks provides the opportunity to focus specifically on the ability of technology transfer offices to successfully commercialize genomic innovations.

Much of the literature up to 2005–2006 offers framework assessments for TTOs, while the literature following was considerably more focused on results and impacts of TTO operations. In a comparison of research outcomes in Canada, the UK, and the USA, Heher (2006) observes that Canada had a patent filing rate of 17 per $100 million of adjusted total research expenditure (ATRE) in 2002. This is compared with 21 in the USA and 35 in the UK. In terms of efficiency, the UK leads as this patent filing rate is achieved with US$3.1 billion, while Canada had US$2.5 billion and the USA was more than tenfold above this with US$31.7 billion. The UK also leads in the number of start-up companies created with an average of 5.1 per US$100 million ATRE, whereas Canada has 2.0 and the USA 1.1. License income as a percentage of ATRE is 3% in the USA, 1.3% in Canada, and 1.1% in the UK. Probably the most interesting observation by Heher is that in 2002, the cost of TTO staffing as a percentage of license income was 11% in the USA, 51% in Canada, and 133% in the UK.

Niosi (2006) examines the success of university spin-off firms, identifying that the majority of technologies commercialized in this manner are either in the fields of biotechnology or information technology. Nearly 1200 firms had been established as university spin-offs at the time of this study, but only 65 were listed as publicly traded. Of these 65 firms, Niosi found that 38 of the 65 firms were biotechnology-driven enterprises. In the first few years of the last decade, there were considerable levels of stagnancy in the spin-off firms as barely 40% exhibited signs of growth, in terms of either increased sales or employment, with the most stagnant firms found in biotechnology. Unfortunately, Niosi does not delve into the concerns about a success rate of just over 5% for spin-off companies.

Using data from the Association of University Technology Managers (AUTM) to assess why university TTOs struggle to produce income revenue streams, Swamidass and Vulasa (2008) report that the income from licensing university inventions as a percentage of total research expenditures was 1.7% in 1995 and 2.9% in 2004. To examine this in greater detail, the authors undertook a random survey of 99 American research universities. Three-quarters of the respondents identified the shortage of staff for nonlegal and legal processing as the biggest impediment to greater success rates. Trune and Goslin (1998) argue that TTOs act as significant economic drivers and commercialization success crucially depends on the size and experience of the TTO (Caldera and Debande 2010). Indeed, there would appear to be a contrast between the lack of staff response in the Swamidass and Vulasa survey with the results of Herer, where it is shown that higher TTO staffing does not translate into higher licensing revenues. Regrettably, Swamidass and Vulasa do not examine the correlation between TTO staffing levels in licensing income, thus leaving this question open to some debate. However, Heisey and Adelman (2009) found that increasing the size of a TTO staff increased its ability to patent research and generate licensing revenue. Specifically, the authors relate licensing revenues to the characteristics of TTOs and university research expenditures, suggesting that early initiation of technology transfer programs and staff size increase expected licensing revenues.

In a study on the impacts of the Bayh-Dole Act 30 years after its ascent into law, Grimaldi et al. (2011) conclude that the Act has not resulted in a decrease in basic research and in fact may have actually encouraged the movement toward university spin-off firms. Link et al. (2011) examined the relationship between the Bayh-Dole Act and the US system of national laboratories and determine that while the Bayh-Dole Act was not directly responsible for any noticeable effects in patenting activity, it did have an effect on changes in financial incentives required for technology transfer.

Recent studies indicate that TTOs are earning licensing revenue, albeit at a rate that is lower than hoped for. Part of the challenge to increase this might be found in the staffing levels of TTOs, but this should be cautioned somewhat by the relation between increased staffing and the increased cost of operating TTOs. It should not be taken as a panacea that simply increasing TTO staffing will directly increase licensing revenues and result in greater numbers of university TTOs becoming profitable.

Technology Transfer in Canada

The transfer of university innovation to the private sector grew rapidly beginning in the late 1980s, when universities began to establish offices devoted specifically to transferring intellectual property (IP). By the mid-1990s, most major universities in Canada had established a TTO. Once established, it became possible to gather statistics on TTO operations, raising the question of whether returns to scale existed from public funding of academic research. Ultimately, governments wanted to know if it was possible to establish a correlation between the amount of funding (inputs) and the resulting patents or commercialization agreements (outputs). Whether the TTOs wanted this to develop or not, eventually specific offices were compared to national averages regarding commercialization success.

In October 1998, the Canadian government established the Expert Panel on the Commercialization of University Research. The Panel was established by the Prime Minister's Advisory Council on Science and Technology with the mandate of suggesting a strategy to "… maximize the economic and social returns to Canada from public investments in university research" (Government of Canada 1999; p. v). While the report identifies universities as a crucial part of Canada's innovation capacity, it recommended standardizing operating procedures for TTOs. While the report does not go so far as to suggest that all TTOs should have identical structures and frameworks, thereby recognizing the uniqueness of regional innovation, it does suggest that TTOs should be required to develop and adopt consistent policies. While identifying that developing regulations for TTOs is not practical, the report stresses that technologies should be preferably transferred to Canadian firms or Canadian operations of multinational firms rather than to foreign operations. The report called for greater TTO funding, specifically where the "federal government should invest new and additional resources to strengthen the commercialization capacity of universities in an amount equal to 5 percent of its investment in university research" (p. 28).

The report clearly identifies that universities should not expect the revenues generated from TTOs to provide any relief to the stress that many university operating budgets face. The report observes that in the USA, research universities that have revenue streams from commercialized research indicate that such revenues account for less than one percent of the university budget. The Panel noted that it would not be fiscally feasible for Canadian universities to expect returns at a level greater than this.

The Council of Canadian Academies (2006) released a report on science and technology in Canada, identifying Canada as a world leader in many research areas and increasing research strength in emerging fields. However, Canada does not measure well when it comes to converting strength in basic R&D to commercial activity. The report states that the lack of commercialization success from public sector innovative research is "… a long-standing deficiency in Canada's innovation system…" (p. 25). The findings of this report were reiterated 1 year later when Industry Canada (Government of Canada 2007) released Canada's science and technology strategy. The S&T strategy report acknowledges that Canada is internationally recognized as having a strong research base, but there is considerable room for improvement in the commercialization of innovative research. This perspective held by the federal government has not dissipated and in fact is a constant theme in S&T reports, as the 2012 version observes that "Canada continues to face chronic challenge in knowledge transfer... related to licensing activities and spinoff companies...Canada continues to show disappointing results" (Government of Canada 2012, p. 2).

Is this truly the case? Are Canadian universities really struggling to commercialize technologies through spin-off companies or by licensing IP to private firms? An examination of the data presented below offers a contrasting view. The next section examines Canadian university IP transfer.

Trends in Canadian University Technology Transfer[1]

This section draws upon data from six different surveys on intellectual property at institutions of higher learning, undertaken by Statistics Canada between 1998 and 2008. These surveys were initiated, in part, to respond to the government reports outlined in the previous section as well as to gather data on an important, but not quantified, aspect of the innovation cycle. Unfortunately, this survey series was discontinued after the release of the 2008 data, and further information that is directly comparable to the following is not available.

Statistics Canada (2010) identifies that there are nearly 6,000 issued patents held by universities and research hospitals in Canada. In 1998, a total of 1,250 public institution patents existed, increasing to 3,000 in 2003 and 5,900 by 2008 (Table 1).

If the use of active licenses for existing patents is used as a metric for assessing the transfer of knowledge, then an increase in knowledge transfer is not taking place. The results shown in Fig. 1 reveal that from this perspective, the transfer of knowledge is actually in decline and even the increase in 2008 licensing activity

Table 1 Trends in patents and licensing

Year	Total patents	Total active licenses	Percentage(%)
1998	1,252	788	63
2001	2,133	1,424	67
2003	3,047	1,756	58
2004	3,827	2,022	53
2006	4,784	2,038	43
2008	5,908	3,343	57

Source: Statistics Canada (1999, 2003, 2005, 2006, 2008, 2010)

---

[1] Statistics Canada began a survey series on intellectual property of the higher education sector in 1998. The next study should have been released in late 2012 or early 2013. However, the survey series was discontinued.

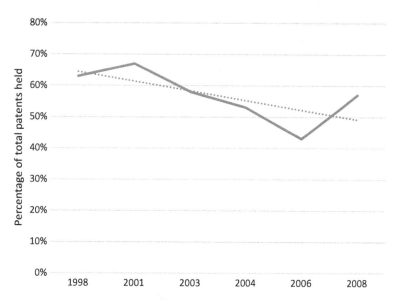

Fig. 1 Trend in patent licensing (% age of total patents held)

does not reverse the decade long downward trend. However, to counter this, at no one point in time has less than 50% of university IP not been licensed to private companies, indicating that at a minimum at least half of the knowledge being generated by universities is being transferred to private firms.

The commercialization of IP has resulted in a total of 1,242 spin-off companies over the 1998–2008 period. The number of spin-off companies rose rapidly starting in the early 1990s, peaking with 359 spin-off firms established between 1995 and 1999. The number of spin-off firms then declined substantially over the period of a few years, with only 142 spin-offs between 2005 and 2008. This is a 4-year comparison, but the trend is downward as only 19 spin-offs were identified in 2008. At the peak, over 70 firms a year were being spin-off, but this has fallen to an average of 35 a year in the 2005 to 2008 period, half of what it was a decade earlier.

The series of surveys found that in 2008 the revenue received (Table 2) by the 121 organizations from commercialized IP was $53.2M.[2] This figure represents a gross return of 2.7% on the $2 billion invested in research. These TTOs identified total operating expenses for managing and transferring IP of $51.1 million (Table 3), making the net return on the investment a negligible 0.1%. Royalty revenue peaked in 2001 and has been trending downward ever since.

Expenses were up dramatically over revenues (Table 3). This has to be of considerable concern to universities, as in 2008 IP management costs were nearly equal to IP revenues. It is worthwhile to note that TTOs began tracking the cost of protecting their IP starting in 2003. Litigation costs ranged from $0.4 to $1.4M which raises

---

[2] All figures are in Canadian dollars.

Table 2 Income from commercialized IP ($millions)

Revenue forms	1998	2001	2003	2004	2006	2008
Royalties	$15.6	$44.4	$40.M	$38.6	$41.2	$35.4
Reimbursements	$0.7	$4.9	$4.4	$5.0	$5.4	$5.9
Others	na	$3.2	$10.3	$7.6	$13.1	$11.9
Total	$16.3	$52.5	$55.5	$51.2	$59.7	$53.2

Source: Statistics Canada (1999, 2003, 2005, 2006, 2008, 2010)

Table 3 Expenses on IP management ($millions)

Expenses	1998	2001	2003	2004	2006	2008
Salaries and benefits	$7.5	$11.9	$16.9	$20.0	$23.9	$28.1
Patent and legal	$5.1	$9.5	$10.4	$10.6	$12.4	$15.3
Litigation	na	na	$1.4	$0.4	$0.6	$0.4
Others	na	$7.1	$7.7	$5.9	$5.6	$7.4
Total	$12.6	$25.7	$36.4	$36.9	$42.5	$51.1

Source: Statistics Canada (1999, 2003, 2005, 2006, 2008, 2010)

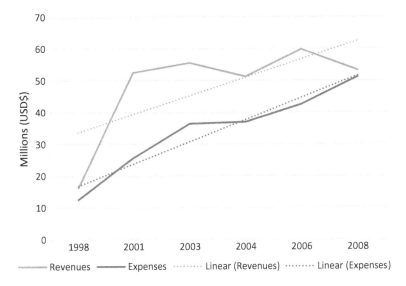

Fig. 2 Trend in revenues and expenses ($millions)

questions of how financially underfunded universities are able to devote financial resources to protection of IP.

Revenues have been in the $50 million range for all of the first decade of the century, while expenses have risen considerably. Figure 2 shows that revenues are trending flatter than expenditures. With TTO revenues and expenses on the verge of intersecting, this should be of concern to university administrators.

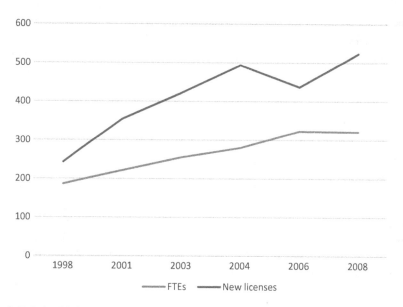

Fig. 3 Relationship between staff and activity

Some of the above cited literature has shown that there is an identifiable correlation in the USA between increased TTO staff and the level of patent activity. Figure 3 examines similar data for Canada. As the number of full-time equivalents (FTEs) increased between 1998 and 2008, so too has the number of new licenses. The early reports revealed that many universities had more than one office for technology transfer and that over time, these activities were consolidated into one office. With the exception of 2006, licensing activity has steadily increased, doubling between 1998 and 2008.

However, it is pertinent to note that even though there was a rise in licensing activity, the rise in TTO operating expenses increased at a faster rate than royalty revenues. To some extent, this places Canadian TTOs in between the proverbial rock and a hard place. For a TTO to be more successful, it has to increase the number of active licenses; however, staff increases are required to accomplish this, which raised operating expenses more than it does royalty revenues. This data suggests that most TTOs are not self-sustaining and require subsidies from university operating budgets.

The federal government has a preference for licensing IP to Canadian firms. Table 4 provides a breakdown of new licenses between 1998 and 2008, including exclusive and non-exclusive as well as domestic and foreign. Exclusive foreign licenses were relatively constant at approximately 11%, while exclusive Canadian licenses varied from 22 to 39%. Non-exclusive foreign licenses dominated the licensing activity, ranging 12–36%, while non-exclusive Canadian licenses ranged from 8 to 20%.

Table 4 Distribution of licenses (percentages)

Year	Non-exclusive Canadian	Exclusive Canadian	Non-exclusive Foreign	Exclusive foreign	Multi-jurisdiction or unknown	Total
1998	32 (13%)	58 (24%)	30 (12%)	24 (10%)	99 (41%)	243
2001	29 (9%)	104 (32%)	82 (26%)	37 (12%)	68 (21%)	320
2003	40 (9%)	108 (26%)	137 (32%)	42 (10%)	95 (22%)	422
2004	41 (8%)	103 (21%)	178 (36%)	55 (11%)	117 (24%)	494
2006	58 (13%)	169 (39%)	156 (36%)	50 (11%)	4 (1%)	437
2008	109 (20%)	120 (22%)	129 (24%)	57 (11%)	123 (23%)	538

Source: Statistics Canada (1999, 2003, 2005, 2006, 2008, 2010)

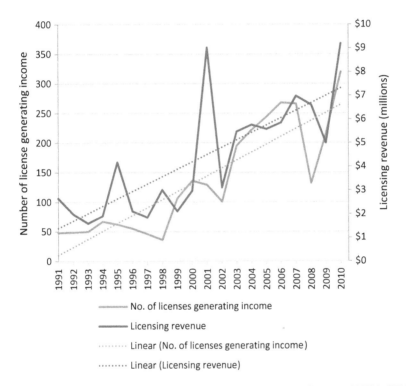

Fig. 4 Licensing revenue and number of licenses, 1991–2010 (Source: AUTM STATT 1991–2010)

On average, non-exclusive licensing leads exclusive licensing. With exclusive foreign licenses at approximately 11%, the concern about the benefits of Canadian innovative research accruing to foreign corporations is minimized.

Figure 4 illustrates that TTO licensing revenue increased significantly between 1994 and 2001, even though the number of licenses generating income declined, suggesting a significant increase in the subscription of high-value licenses by the private sector. In 1994, 67 licenses generated \$2 million in revenues, with the average license value of \$28,500. A similar analysis can be made in 2001, as the number of licenses generating income was 129, with license revenues of \$9 million in 2001. The average value of a license in 2001 was almost \$70,000.

While the Canadian government has identified the transfer of Canadian university IP and knowledge to the private sector as barrier to innovation in Canada, based on this review of the data, this perspective would appear to be misplaced. Certainly, Canadian university TTOs are not highly profitable, but they are transferring nearly two-thirds of patented IP via licenses to the private or, and the average value of these licenses has increased by almost 150%.

Transfer of Agricultural Technology

While some agricultural patent licenses and spin-off companies will be included in the above discussion, agricultural innovation, both plant and livestock based, does not factor heavily into this reporting. There is some information on new plant varieties that can be gleaned from the reports, relating to reporting requirements for plant varieties (Table 5) and ownership (Table 6).

The first thing that stands out from Table 5 is that over half of the institutes of higher education are not involved in the development of new plant varieties. Policies vary in regard to reporting, in that about 20% of institutions always require the

Table 5 Reporting requirements for new plant varieties (percentages)

Year	Always	Sometimes	Never	No policy	No such IP	Total
1998	16	15	47	22	-	81
2001	13	20	8	16	36	85
2003	12	13	7	12	55	121
2004	15	13	5	14	53	119
2006	24	11	7	19	40	101

Source: Statistics Canada (1999, 2003, 2005, 2006, 2008)

Table 6 Ownership of new plant varieties (percentages)

Year	Institution owns	Researcher owns	Shared	No policy	No such IP	Total
1998	12	52	14	22	-	81
2001	12	26	6	26	36	85
2003	7	20	7	8	55	121
2004	8	20	8	11	53	119
2006	6	26	12	28	28	101
2008	8	17	4	-	-	-
Avg.	9%	27%	9%	19%	43%	

Source: Statistics Canada (1999, 2003, 2005, 2006, 2008, 2010)

reporting of new plant varieties, while 15% occasionally have policies of this nature and just under 10% never require the reporting of new plant varieties. Over the decade of reporting, the percentage of institutions requiring the reporting of new plant varieties varied from 25% to 35%.

Table 6 reports on the ownership structure of new plant varieties across the decade in which data was collected. Again, it is readily observable that many institutions are not engaged in agriculture research as 61% of reporting institutions either have no policy on new plant varieties or have no IP in this area. Interestingly, of those institutions reporting new plant varieties, the vast majority of the varieties are solely owned by the plant breeder that developed the variety, meaning that all of the royalties incurred through plant breeders' rights will go directly to the plant breeder. In just 9% of cases, the institution owns the plant variety and in an equal number ownership is shared between the institution and the plant breeder.

In terms of how institutions manage IP, plant varieties are not part of research activities at many institutions of higher learning (Fig. 5). In comparing research ownership of other forms of IP, the number of institutions reporting that they have no plant varieties at their institution is double that of those institutions holding trademarks of industrial designs. Institutional policy favoring the researcher is evident as researchers retain ownership more than any other form. While copyright residing with researchers is logical based on publication practices, it is somewhat surprising that researchers own such a high percentage of IP in terms of patents and industrial designs.

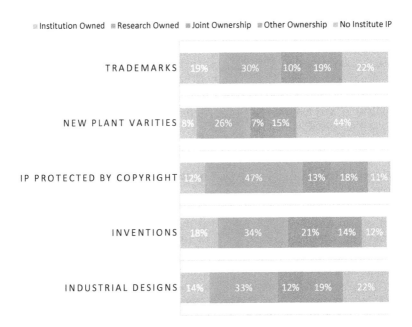

Fig. 5 IP ownership, 1998–2008 (Source: Statistics Canada (1999, 2003, 2005, 2006, 2008, 2010)

In some institutions, the reporting of plant varieties as IP was not required, as agricultural innovations were commonly managed directly by the agricultural colleges. For example, at the University of Saskatchewan, the Crop Development Centre (CDC), housed within the College of Agriculture and Bioresources, manages the commercial release of new plant varieties. As a result of this, for many years, the CDC results were not included in the University of Saskatchewan's IP reporting. The release of new plant varieties by the CDC is now included in the University of Saskatchewan's IP reporting.

Given the disconnect between the reporting of new plant varieties and university TTOs, it is likely that federal government data on agricultural IP is underreported. As a case in point, the CDC at the University of Saskatchewan began in 1971 with the mandate to improve existing crop varieties and develop new crop varieties. Between 1971 and 2016, over 400 new varieties were released. The commercial release of many of these varieties was not captured by surveys of IP and technology transfer, thus inflating the concern that universities are inefficient transfer agents of innovation, knowledge, and technology. Not only was the commercialization of new crop varieties not captured by federal surveys on IP, but in many instances, new plant varieties were not recognized as a form of IP by many universities. When new varieties of fruits, vegetables, and livestock are included in the transfer of IP from universities to the public, the picture looks much different than the one presented by current government reports on the state of public IP transfer in Canada.

Policy Implications

Based on the academic and government studies cited above, the fundamental question that needs to be posed is: Is university IP being transferred to the private sector? A simple response of yes has been shown to be the case based on the above data, but the simplicity of this response fails to delve into the fuller complexity of the issue. The Council of Canadian Academies (CCA) (2006) criticizes universities' abilities to convert basic R&D into commercial success. In fact, this report calls this a "deficiency in Canada's innovation system...." (p.25). But, is it?

Based on Table 1, from 1998 to 2008, the percentage of university IP licensed in any given year has ranged from 43% to 67%, averaging 57%. Given that there are no benchmarks against which to compare, due to the differing governing regimes in the USA and Europe, the fact that Canadian universities have, and are, transferring over 50% of their IP should be seen as a success, not a deficiency. While the trend line in Fig. 1 is downward sloping, Fig. 3 shows there is a positive correlation between the number of FTEs and implemented IP licenses. While the number of active IP licenses had been declining, the 2008 numbers show a sharp increase, from 43% to 57%. If TTOs are able to secure additional operating revenues to hire more staff, it would be expected that this percentage would get back into the range above

60%. If we accept that an IP transfer rate exceeding 60% is successful, then the CCA's referral to the ability of universities to convert basic R&D into commercial success is unsubstantiated and causes one to ponder if the use of the word "deficiency," then, is in reference to fiscal success. This, in turn, raises the crucial research policy question of whether basic public sector R&D has to be profit oriented.

It is quite possible that, given the recent trend toward increased public sector profitability, when the CCA refers to the "deficiency" in Canada's innovation system, they are referring to the fact that TTOs are not lucrative financial revenue generators. If this is what in fact is being referred to, it raises some serious issues for the future of university research. Should universities only be engaging in research that has a high probability of a profitable outcome for the particular university? Should basic scientific research be left to government agencies, encouraging universities to become entrepreneurship oriented?

Without more a detailed survey of Canadian TTOs, it is not possible to state with certainty, but it is reasonable to expect that some IP is not being transferred to the private sector due to research gap concerns. One can hypothesize that some basic R&D is being transferred to the private sector in spite of the evident research gap, which indicates that the private sector values basic university research. Clearly, the private sector will place greater value on IP that is closer to being market ready than IP that requires 3–5 years of further research, but there is still value to the private sector to license IP of this nature.

As part of the effort to narrow this commercialization gap in public sector research, some funding agencies in Canada have reorganized existing grant programs or established new grant programs, requiring matching industry dollars. In these grant programs, industry has to put up a portion of the overall project budget (commonly 50%), and if the project is successfully funded, the government granting agency provides the balance of the funding. The intention of these types of funding programs is to ensure that industry is aware of, and participating in, the design and development of new research programs. The project outcomes are then more in line with the needs of industry, and the gap to commercialization is therefore narrowed.

In the agriculture sector, it is evident that new plant varieties were not considered to be a form of IP by university TTOs or government. That the number of new plant varieties released by universities was not reported and that many universities have no policy on this issue or do not require the reporting of this at the university level indicate the dismissal of agricultural innovation within innovation systems. There is an obvious lack of understanding about how the commercialization of new plant varieties works, since when a new plant variety is given registration approval, it is licensed to a private company to multiply and sell the seed to farmers. The technology of the new plant variety is transferred to the private sector, the same as a patent license would be, but in the case of licensing the production of a new plant variety, IP reporting systems have routinely dismissed plant and livestock agriculture technology transfer.

Conclusions

While it is possible to conclude that knowledge and technologies are indeed being transferred, it is less certain that this occurs cost-effectively. Licensing revenue is marginally above IP management expenses. It has been shown that increasing TTO staffing increases patent licensing activity, but evidence of a corresponding increase in license revenue is lacking. When examining staffing and patent licensing, there is a positive correlation when this is done using new patent licenses implemented during each year, but when this is compared to overall IP management, the correlation becomes negative.

With the leading metric of successful research grants being the number of patents received or patent applications filed, it raises the concern that patent applications are being made with innovative products and processes simply to satisfy reporting requirements. The rate of active patent licenses is declining. The greatest portion of university research is funded by federal granting councils, which raises the issue of whether publicly funded research should be allowed to be patented by the universities and their researchers or instead be made freely accessible.

When universities hold IP and infringement is identified, it can be challenging for universities to protect IP given the limited financial resources available. As identified above, Canadian universities started keeping track of IP litigation costs in 2003; this cost will only rise due to the increasing number of patents and amount of research occurring. Since TTOs are not revenue streams, it raises concerns about university abilities to fund litigation to the detriment of other services and possibly programs. If universities do not have the financial capability to effectively protect their IP in an increasingly litigious society, should universities hold patents?

The above question strikes at the heart of a fundamental policy question regarding public sector research and the IP that flows from the research. The welfare question that rises from university patents is whether there is a greater benefit to the university from the return on the university's IP or from the value of publishing the research in top-ranked peer-review journals. Greater study needs to be given to this important issue.

References

Bercovitz, J., and M. Feldmann. 2006. Entrepreneurial Universities and Technology Transfer: A Conceptual Framework for Understanding Knowledge Based Economic Development. *Journal of Technology Transfer* 31: 175–188.

Bozeman, B. 2000. Technology Transfer and Public Policy: A Review of Research and Theory. *Research Policy* 29: 627–655.

Calderaa, A., and O. Debande. 2010. Performance of Spanish Universities in Technology Transfer: An Empirical Analysis. *Research Policy* 39: 1160–1173.

Council of Canadian Academies. 2006. *The State of Science and Technology in Canada*. Ottawa: Queen's Printer.

Eisenberg, R.S. 1996. Public Research and Private Development: Patents and Technology Transfer in Government-Sponsored Research. *Virginia Law Review* 82 (8): 1663–1727.

Etzkowitz, H., and L. Leydesdorff. 2000. The Dynamics of Innovation: From National Systems and "Mode 2" to A Triple Helix of University-Industry-Government Relations. *Research Policy* 29: 109–123.

Government of Canada. 1999. *Report of the Expert Panel on the Commercialization of University Research*. Ottawa: Queen's Printer.

———. 2007. *Mobilizing Science and Technology to Canada's Advantage*. Ottawa: Queen's Printer.

———. 2012. *Canada's Science, Technology and Innovation System: Aspiring to Global Leadership*. Ottawa: Queen's Printer.

Grimaldi, R., M. Kenney, D.S. Siegel, and M. Wright. 2011. 30 Years After Bayh-Dole: Reassessing Academic Entrepreneurship. *Research Policy* 40: 1045–1057.

Heher, A.D. 2006. Return on Investment in Innovation: Implications for Institutions and National Agencies. *Journal of Technology Transfer* 31: 403–414.

Heisey, P.W., and S.W. Adelman. 2009. Research Expenditures, Technology Transfer Activity, and University Licensing Revenue. *Journal of Technology Transfer* 36: 38–60.

Holguin-Pando, N.C., S.J. Smyth, and P.W.B. Phillips. 2014. Technology Transfer in Transitional Economies: The Case of Mexico. *International Journal of Technology, Policy and Management* 14 (2): 111–132.

Link, A.N., D.S. Siegel, and D.D. Van Fleet. 2011. Public Science and Public Innovation: Assessing the Relationship Between Patenting at U.S. National Laboratories and the Bayh-Dole Act. *Research Policy* 40: 1094–1099.

Noisi, J. 2006. Success Factors in Canadian Academic Spin-Offs. *Journal of Technology Transfer* 31: 451–457.

Owen-Smith, J., and W.W. Powell. 2001. To Patent or not: Faculty Decisions and Institutional Success at Technology Transfer. *Journal of Technology Transfer* 26: 99–114.

———. 2003. The Expanding Role of University Patenting in the Life Sciences: Assessing the Importance of Experience and Connectivity. *Research Policy* 32: 1695–1711.

Siegel, D.S., D.A. Waldman, L.E. Atwater, and A.N. Link. 2004. Toward a Model of the Effective Transfer of Scientific Knowledge from Academicians to Practitioners: Qualitative Evidence from the Commercialization of University Technologies. *Journal of Engineering and Technology Management* 21: 115–142.

Statistics Canada. 1999. *Survey of Intellectual Property Commercialization in the Higher Education Sector, 1998*. Ottawa: Queen's Printer.

———. 2003. *Survey of Intellectual Property Commercialization in the Higher Education Sector, 2001*. Ottawa: Queen's Printer.

———. 2005. *Survey of Intellectual Property Commercialization in the Higher Education Sector, 2003*. Ottawa: Queen's Printer.

———. 2006. *Survey of Intellectual Property Commercialization in the Higher Education Sector, 2004*. Ottawa: Queen's Printer.

———. 2008. *Survey of Intellectual Property Commercialization in the Higher Education Sector, 2006 and 2005*. Ottawa: Queen's Printer.

———. 2010. *Survey of Intellectual Property Commercialization in the Higher Education Sector, 2008*. Ottawa: Queen's Printer.

Swamidass, P.M., and V. Vulasa. 2008. Why University Inventions Rarely Produce Income? Bottlenecks in University Technology Transfer. *Journal of Technology Transfer* 34: 343–363.

The Global Innovation Index. 2016. *Global Innovation Index Rankings*, Available at: https://www.globalinnovationindex.org/gii-2016-report#. Accessed 26 Aug 2017.

Trune, D.R., and L.N. Goslin. 1998. University Technology Transfer Programs: A Profit/Loss Analysis—A Preliminary Model to Measure the Economic Impact of University Licensing. *Technological Forecasting and Social Change* 57 (3): 197–204.

Technology Transfer in Agriculture: The Case of Wageningen University

Sebastian Hoenen, Christos Kolympiris, Emiel Wubben, and Onno Omta

Abstract Even though returns on R&D in agriculture are high, technology transfer from academia to industry is not strong in this field. In this chapter, we study what universities can do to strengthen knowledge transfer from academia to industry, specifically in agriculture. We use Wageningen University and Research (WUR), a leading institution in technology transfer in agriculture science, as a case study. We present a detailed historical account of technology transfer at WUR and follow with a set of interviews conducted with different stakeholders in technology transfer. The results from our interviews highlight that WUR has facilitated technology transfer through four mechanisms: (1) department independence to pursue different forms of technology transfer; (2) implementation of a general legal framework of technology transfer to unburden departments, scientists, and IP staff; (3) embracing a culture where the prime driver for technology transfer is a "responsibility to give back to society" rather than income; and (4) embedding itself in a location where ties with industry are the norm. Our work is timely because technology transfer to industry is increasingly pursued at universities across the globe. The success of those efforts is not always guaranteed. We inform stakeholders and researchers by presenting a better understanding of what works and what does not work in technology transfer in agriculture.

Introduction

Academics, policy makers, and others have systematically studied technology transfer from academia to industry at least since the mid-1900s (Bush 1945). Since then, ample evidence has demonstrated that academic research contributes to economic growth, forms the cornerstone for industrial innovations, leads to

S. Hoenen (✉) • E. Wubben • O. Omta
Wageningen University and Research, Wageningen, Netherlands
e-mail: Sebastian.hoenen@wur.nl

C. Kolympiris
University of Bath, Bath, UK

© Springer International Publishing AG 2018   257
N. Kalaitzandonakes et al. (eds.), *From Agriscience to Agribusiness*, Innovation,
Technology, and Knowledge Management, https://doi.org/10.1007/978-3-319-67958-7_13

improvements in productivity growth, and even sparks the creation of new industries via different forms of technology transfer such as joint projects with industry and academic spin-offs (Mansfield 1991, 1995, 1997; Narin et al. 1997; Tijssen 2002; Toole 2012; Zahringer et al. 2017). Indeed, technology transfer from academia to industry is prevalent in many industries, including the life sciences and information technology, but it is generally not particularly strong in agriculture. While cases of successful technology transfer in agriculture exist, including the Camarosa Strawberry from the University of California and successful spin-offs (Parker et al. 2001; Perez-Ruiz et al. 2013), these cases are hardly the norm despite significant efforts to strengthen technology transfer in the industry (Pray 2001).

This observation calls for attention for two main reasons. One, the returns to investments in research and development (R&D) in agriculture are high (Teece 2000; Fuglie and Toole 2014), and the social welfare benefits of such investments extend both to developed and, perhaps more importantly, to developing economies. Two, universities face increasing pressures to (a) demonstrate the impact of their research and (b) generate income from research conducted *in-house* to cope with decreasing public funds directed toward academia (Henderson et al. 1998; Bulut and Moschini 2009). Strengthening knowledge transfer in agriculture could speak directly to both social welfare and university impact and income considerations.

The challenges of technology transfer in agriculture stem, in large part, from inherent features of the industry itself. As Postlewait et al. (1993) explain "in agriculture, there is just one growing season a year, a limitation to testing that is not imposed on new biopharmaceuticals. Furthermore, crop varieties often need to be adapted to varying local conditions, and agricultural pests, whether insects, bacterial or fungal, tend to be unique and specific by plant." Given such obstacles, and with an eye on the importance of technology transfer, the question we investigate in this paper is what universities can do to strengthen knowledge transfer from academia to industry specifically in agriculture. We explore the drivers, institutional structures, and strategies that can boost technology transfer in agriculture-related academic research.

As our case study, we analyze technology transfer at Wageningen University and Research (WUR) in the Netherlands. WUR is a leading university in the fields of life sciences and agriculture, consistently ranked as the top Dutch university and in the top 3 worldwide in the fields of agriculture and life sciences (Yasmine 2015; Gurney-Read 2016). Importantly, WUR has a long tradition in knowledge transfer in agriculture. For instance, as early as the late 1990s, it has partnered with industry to launch a new pig growth model (Manawatu Standard 1999), in 2005 it signed a research agreement with dairy giant FrieslandCampina (PR Newswire Europe 2005), and in 2010 it started to collaborate with Dow AgroSciences in a project aiming to improve the starch quality of potatoes employing novel technologies (Wireless News 2010). Along the same lines, the Food Valley cluster organization was founded in 2004 in the vicinity of WUR with its member companies collaborating regularly with WUR (Omta and Fortuin 2013). The efforts to strengthen knowledge transfer have increased over the last few years. Since 2015 the WUR campus has hosted a business incubator as well as the R&D labs of FrieslandCampina.

Unilever's R&D labs are also in the process of relocating to the WUR campus (Polish News Bulletin 2016). The existing history of technology transfer combined with the present increased efforts makes WUR a fertile template for our study because they allow us to look at the past, present, and future and therefore analyze the knowledge transfer process instead of deriving our conclusions based solely on cross-sectional observations. Along the same lines, WUR's research covers nearly all agriculture-related fields including entomology, soil science, animal science, plant pathology, and food science. Accordingly, we exploit this feature of WUR so that our conclusions are not limited to a specific sector.

Methodologically, after we present a detailed historical account of technology transfer at Wageningen, we rely on a set of interviews we conducted with different stakeholders in technology transfer at WUR. Specifically, we interviewed three academics employed as faculty members at WUR, two WUR employees engaged in different aspects of technology transfer at the university, and one manager from a large multinational firm with facilities on the WUR campus. We opted to assess the views of different stakeholders after considering that knowledge transfer is a process involving multiple actors. Therefore, we seek to combine and compare insights from different sources.

Our results highlight that WUR has facilitated technology transfer through four mechanisms. First, recognizing that each agriculture-related department within the university is distinctive, WUR has given each department independence to pursue different forms of technology transfer; for instance, some departments specialize in joint projects with industry, while others concentrate on academic spin-offs. Second, within departments, but also on a more aggregate level, WUR implements general legal frameworks of technology transfer that are comprehensive enough to minimize the need to build technology transfer agreements on a deal by deal basis. These frameworks, therefore, free up scientists' time by unburdening them from navigating the institutional environment of WUR. Third, WUR has embraced a culture suggesting that the prime driver for technology transfer is not income but rather a "responsibility to give back to society." This culture is motivating for the majority of scientists while not limiting the potential financial proceeds for WUR. Fourth, WUR is embedded in a location where ties with industry are the norm. As we explain in detail below, the city of Wageningen is home to the Food Valley cluster, a network of colocated firms and R&D labs interacting regularly with WUR. Indeed, in recent years WUR has exploited the benefits of physical proximity even further by placing new industrial R&D labs on its campus.

Our work is timely and has important policy and managerial implications. It is timely because knowledge transfer from academia to industry and other sectors is increasingly pursued at universities across the globe, even within contexts in which academic entrepreneurship and innovation have not received attention (Drivas et al. 2017). The success of those efforts is not always guaranteed (Kolympiris and Klein 2017), and therefore we expect this paper to help us better understand what works and what does not work in technology transfer in agriculture. Along the same lines, a better understanding of knowledge transfer in agriculture can inform policy makers devising measures to boost innovation as well as university administrators who seek new ways of funding in the face of tighter public funds. Indeed, because technology transfer in agriculture represents a largely untapped source of income for most universities, we expect the line of research we explore here to generate valuable insights.

The next section discusses the literature on technology transfer. The section "Technology Transfer at Wageningen University over Time" provides the background of WUR and discusses in detail how technology transfer has unfolded at the university over the years. In section "Methods and Findings" we present the results of the interviews and we conclude in section "Summary and Conclusions".

The Literature on Technology Transfer

Transferring knowledge created at academic institutions to industry is an important driver of economic growth (Etzkowitz 1998; Mansfield 1998; Etzkowitz and Leydesdorff 2000; Hall et al. 2003; Arundel and Geuna 2004), and firms with direct ties to universities improve their innovative performance (Cockburn and Henderson 1998; Fabrizio 2009; Mindruta 2013). Additionally, because the knowledge created at universities is often tacit, it promotes regional growth and development (Jaffe 1989; Acs et al. 1992; Breschi and Lissoni 2001; Feldman and Desrocher 2003).

Interactions with industry can also boost academic productivity, as they help academics in numerous ways. For instance, they can increase academics' ability to develop insights to problems faced by society, grant access to unique data, and provide research funding (Lee 2000; Perkmann and Walsh 2008; Boardman and Ponomariov 2009). Indeed, D'este and Perkmann (2011) and Friedman and Silberman (2003) find that academics engage with industry to further their research rather than to commercialize their knowledge. Despite concerns about shifts in the academic research agenda toward more applied sciences (Callaert et al. 2015), a stream of literature documents that academics who patent or do contract research improve their academic output (Gulbrandsen and Smeby 2005; Van Looy et al. 2006; Azoulay et al. 2007, 2009; Crespi et al. 2011; Callaert et al. 2015). Importantly, even though the publications that derive from industry-funded research are more applied (Gulbrandsen and Smeby 2005; Boardman and Corley 2008), there is some evidence suggesting that the academics' research agenda does not move away from basic science (Van Looy et al. 2004).

Knowledge transfer from academia takes many forms, including patenting and licensing (Jaffe 1989; Henderson et al. 1998; Thursby and Thursby 2003; Shane 2004). For instance, licensed academic innovations have contributed billions to economic activity (Agrawal 2001), and participation of academic inventors in the licensing process is a critical determinant of commercialization success (Markman et al. 2005; Agrawal 2006). However, as Agrawal and Henderson (2002) and Schartinger et al. (2001) argue, patenting and licensing are only minor aspects of knowledge transfer. Hiring university graduates, personnel exchanges, cooperative joint research, contract research, spin-offs, and joint university-industry supervision of PhDs also constitute additional forms of technology transfer (D'Este and Patel 2007; Bekkers and Bodas Freitas 2008; Abrams et al. 2009; Perkmann et al. 2013; Mowery et al. 2015; Schillebeeckx et al. 2016).

The form that technology transfer takes (or is most effective) depends on the target firms (Cohen et al. 2002; Laursen and Salter 2004; Fontana et al. 2006), the type of knowledge that is transmitted (Colyvas et al. 2002; Goh 2002), and characteristics of the transferring party (D'Este and Patel 2007). For instance, D'Este and Patel (2007) find that the researcher's characteristics have a stronger impact than the characteristics of their departments or universities. Looking at motivational aspects, researchers transfer knowledge more efficiently when no commercialization tools (e.g., patents) are used (Landry et al. 2007). Lastly, taking the firm's perspective, Bekkers and Bodas Freitas (2008) argue that firm characteristics such as internal culture can explain the forms of knowledge transfer.

Another aspect that influences the form and intensity of technology transfer is the industry and university field. Firms in scientific fields that require high levels of investment in R&D and other scientific activities have a higher inclination to draw from universities (Meyer-Thurow 1982; Laursen and Salter 2004). Additionally, there is also a difference in how scientific fields contribute to industrial R&D, with some scientific fields influencing more industry sectors than others (Cohen et al. 2002; Kolympiris et al. 2014). To illustrate, Cohen et al. (2002) find that only pharmaceutical firms consider patents to be important, while R&D intensive manufacturing firms prefer collaborative research. By contrast, for industrial fields in which firms interact less with universities, contract research becomes more important (Schartinger et al. 2002).

Increasingly, technology transfer is organized via Technology Transfer Offices (TTOs). When the first TTOs were launched at Stanford (1970) and Leuven (1973), their operation and communication with industry were based mainly on their private contacts, and the offices acted as advisors and problem solvers on a personal basis (Geuna and Muscio 2009). Since then, to encourage technology transfer and to support researchers through the formal and administrative aspects of technology commercialization, the popularity of the TTO has spread throughout the rest of the United States and Europe (Siegel et al. 2003b; O'Gorman et al. 2008). Entering the new millennium, TTOs generally act as knowledge brokers who position themselves between academia and industry (Powers and McDougall 2005; Rothaermel et al. 2007; O'Kane et al. 2015), support academics in the commercialization process, and help attract resources (Colombo and Delmastro 2002; Siegel et al. 2003a; Clarysse and Moray 2004).

However, not all TTOs are created equal; there are differences in the way they manage the commercialization process (Bercovitz et al. 2001; Feldman et al. 2002; Siegel et al. 2003b). Institutional and organizational resources (Hewitt-Dundas 2012) and scientific fields (Bekkers and Bodas Freitas 2008), as well as characteristics of individual researchers shape how different TTOs manage technology transfer. For instance, Colyvas et al. (2002) show that researchers with strong network ties to industry will not benefit from TTO marketing activities. Other studies on

TTO management have shown that monetary incentives to faculty tend to be ineffective in spurring entrepreneurial activity (Friedman and Silberman 2003; Markman et al. 2004), and this informs TTO management. In fact, critics have raised concerns about the role of TTOs in universities and society, with a focus on the TTO goal of revenue generation (Siegel et al. 2007; Thursby and Thursby 2007; Abrams et al. 2009). But as Siegel and Wright (2015) recently argued, it has never been the stated objective of any TTO they are aware of to maximize profits. That note aside, others have cautioned that TTOs impede commercialization and academic entrepreneurship since they act as bottlenecks in the flow of information (Litan et al. 2007; Kenney and Patton 2009). As a result, there is evidence that many academics bypass their university's TTO and IP regulation by not disclosing inventions (Markman et al. 2008; Thursby et al. 2009; Huyghe et al. 2016).

All in all, the literature on technology transfer has demonstrated not only that industry benefits from it but also that technology transfer takes many forms, some more controversial than others, and that participation in it is more often than not beneficial for academics. Importantly, the lack of literature on agriculture indicates that indeed technology transfer is not particularly strong in the industry. Against this background, the next section outlines how WUR has managed to be actively engaged in technology transfer in agriculture-related technologies.

Technology Transfer at Wageningen University over Time

In 2017 WUR is to appoint a director for value creation and commercialization. This appointment is the outcome of a larger movement in which WUR places technology transfer next to its two traditional missions (in WUR language, "pillar") of research and teaching. This new pillar can be interpreted as the second round of systematically organizing the commercialization of academic knowledge. The first round of management of commercialization at WUR started around two decades earlier. Major commercialization initiatives, which took place at different points in time, during this first round included, among others, (a) the creation of Food Valley NL, an organization representing and connecting a network of high-technology agrifood companies; (b) the Wageningen Business Generator (WBG), the first attempt for a formal TTO at WUR; (c) DAFNE, the Dutch Agro-Food Network of Entrepreneurship, which was a consortium of organizations that support entrepreneurship; (d) the incubator BioPartner Center Wageningen; and (e) StartLife, a food and agriculture incubator which, as we elaborate below, succeeded WBG and conducts some of the functions of a TTO.

As early as 2001, Michael E. Porter, a preeminent Harvard strategy professor, praised WUR in public for being an exception to the rule in the Netherlands, with its substantial linkages with the very strong Dutch agrifood cluster (Porter 2001). This section presents items on this timeline in commercialization practices at WUR. The listing illustrates a very diverse and evolving spectrum of commercialization activities at WUR in the Netherlands.

WUR has grown substantially over the years. In 2017 it is home to roughly 11,000 students and 5000 FTE employees (50:50 employed in research institutes versus the university). The equivalent figures in 2002 are 5000 students and 6000 employees (60:40).

In the 1990s both agrifood research and education were in a poor state, with rather bleak expectations. The established innovation system at the time was the linear top-down Research, Education, and Extension-triptych (in Dutch: *OVO-drieluik*) that had worked very well as a farmer-oriented knowledge trickle-down system, bringing enormous productivity increases in agrifood commodities such as dairy, meat, flowers, vegetables, beer, and fisheries. However, incentives for incremental process innovations harmed competitive advantages in a wealthier, integrating European Union market, where consumers increasingly appreciated original and high-quality products. Agrifood businesses, and by extension research, had to change from knowledge-driven toward demand-driven research; more multidisciplinary arrangements and major investments in technologies were needed in an increasingly privatized and globalized research market (Peper 1996). A sense of urgency was felt to privatize and consolidate the involved institutes for applied research and experimental field stations (Beemer 2006).

Around the turn of the century, a complex array of established organizations in agrifood research and education merged in a complex organization. In 1997, it was decided to form Wageningen UR (Peper 1996). The DLO strategic research institutes and various other institutes for applied research were privatized or set at distance from the government. They combined, legally, with the Agricultural University to form Wageningen UR, in a new organizational format with five integrated science groups (see Fig. 1). In 2004, the Van Hall Larenstein University of Applied Agrifood Sciences linked up with WUR.

On the one hand, the academic fundamental research was complemented with strategic and applied research in the specialized research institutes. On the other hand, one may distinguish between contract research, collective/private research, publicly funded research, policy support research, and legally allocated research tasks (Beemer 2006). The fragmentation of governance and funding had to be reduced to reach more efficient scales in innovation-oriented activities. As the government set up a tight financial regime for public research, WUR was forced to go through a series of consolidations, raising the external orientation for funds and customer demands. Stakeholder involvement has become a more common practice, and WUR was successful in raising co-funding from companies for research projects. Consequently, the university moved from a linear knowledge diffusion paradigm to a network perspective with consortia of public and private partners. The research assessments of the institutes were very positive in their conclusions. In sum, a 2006 external evaluation concluded that customers acknowledge and appreciate the application-orientation and usefulness of WUR research (Beemer 2006).

Also initiated in 1997 was the genesis of Food Valley (Hulsink and Dons 2008). Food Valley was a locally oriented initiative to "reinforce synergies between the business community, knowledge institutes, and government in Wageningen and its surrounding areas" (Hulsink and Dons 2008). Within a short time period, over 40

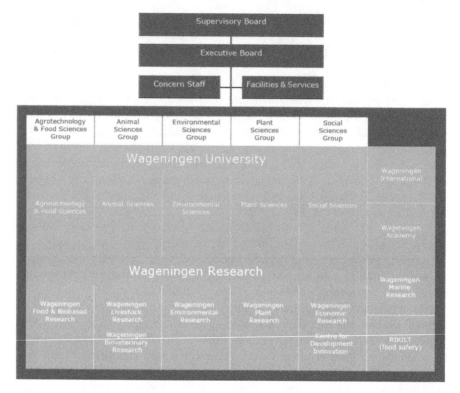

Fig. 1 Legal and organization chart of Wageningen University and Research

companies in the region supported the initiative. One of the outcomes was the creation of an incubator, later known as the BioPartner Center Wageningen. The relocation to Wageningen of a new high-technology research institute Numico (a dairy firm that focused on baby and cattle feed, later acquired by Danone) and the foundation of the Wageningen Centre for Food Sciences, later the Top Institute Food and Nutrition (TIFN), by large food companies helped to broaden the mindset and horizon of key stakeholders from Dutch farmer-oriented agriculture to the international agrifood industry.

Evidently, the recognition of the substantial, top-notch, and very diverse cluster with research organizations, companies, start-ups, and joint ventures was helped by both the association with Silicon Valley and the unexpected support from Professor Michael Porter, a recognized expert on industry competitiveness and clusters (Hulsink and Dons 2008). He was praised both the Dutch agrifood cluster in general and Wageningen UR in particular. The fast recognition was supported by extensive media coverage in both national (e.g., Omta and Wubben (2004)) and international arenas (*Nature, New Food*), culminating in the statement by the European commissioner Busquin identifying the Wageningen-based knowledge and innovation cluster as the Netherlands' strongest competitive edge (Crombach et al. 2008).

By 2003 a business plan was accepted by four neighboring municipalities, Wageningen UR, Synthens, and the development agency Oost NV. The Food Valley organization was set up, active in the international promotion of Food Valley innovation cluster and directly linked to the agrifood research organizations in the region, creating joint innovation projects. Two of the early projects were (a) the Milk Genome project, which analyzed which genes contribute to milk that is suitable for the production of cheese or milk with a favorable fatty acid composition, and (b) the Restaurant of the Future, a restaurant located on the WUR campus that presents and tests innovations in food science to its customers. Food Valley NL has some 150 members, and the annual Food Valley conference and expo attracts some 800 participants, primarily SMEs. All in all, Food Valley has become a strong cluster and a sectoral brand for the Dutch agrifood sector.

The consolidation of different institutions into what is now known as WUR materialized as a way to address a number of trends (Beemer 2006). The critical mass created there helped further a wide range of initiatives directed at private and societal value creation and knowledge commercialization. One such initiative is the creation, in 2004, of the Wageningen Business Generator (WBG), aimed at commercializing the rich knowledge base and patent portfolio of WUR, searching and selecting high potential spin-offs in agrifood and life sciences, and stimulating employees to be more commercially active. WBS provided support with IP expertise, legal knowledge, financial and commercial knowledge, and housing. On behalf of WUR, WBG exploited windmill and other equity participations (Versluis 2006). WBG, in many respects the first TTO at WUR, was supposed to be cash flow neutral, with revenues from licenses and participation in spin-offs combining to generate €3 M/year. However, the revenues did not exceed €1 M/year. As discussed in the next section, there was also a clear preference among companies, faculty, and the specialized research institutes alike to continue dealing with IP issues through direct contacts with consortium or outsourcing partners instead of via WBG, the formal, centralized TTO of WUR. By 2008 it was clear that WBG could not profit sufficiently from the different types of commercialization. It was dismantled and knowledge commercialization was again a matter of decentralized decision making (Hulsink et al. 2014).

The 2008–2012 economic crisis impacted WUR and Food Valley, as governments and firms were unable to keep up their innovation budgets. Nevertheless, WUR continued to act as a crystallization point for a variety of services. For example, at the time WUR was able to fund a network of five international account managers, focused on creating international projects. It also has some 40 patent applications up for sale, from a portfolio that contains more than 100 patented inventions, dealt with by an IP manager.

With 58 granted patents during 2000–2010, the number of patents for WUR is lower than for the other technical universities. On the other hand, agrifood companies may not patent for a purpose or may not be able to patent, as one may deal with native traits instead of inventions. The former cannot be patented. On the other hand, WUR clearly went above the 2.13 average number of spin-offs per €100 M revenues in university research (Agentschap and Octrooicentrum 2013). A signal confirming the quality of the Food Valley knowledge cluster is the consolidation and establishment of the FrieslandCampina Innovation Centre, with 350 researchers, on the Wageningen Campus in 2013.

Dutch universities are generally less commercially oriented than those in other countries. But the drive for societal impact triggered WUR in actively promoting collaborative partnerships between private companies, universities, and research institutes. This is in line with views on so-called Industry Science Links to create and transfer scientific knowledge and technologies to companies (Debackere and Veugelers 2005; Cassiman et al. 2008). Examples of high-profile collaborative partnerships of WUR are AlgaePARC, a major facility for microalgae research; Wetsus, a center for sustainable water technologies; and CAT AgroFood, the Centre for Advanced Technology AgroFood, which utilizes facility sharing to give private and public researchers access to the latest research facilities in, for example, sequencing, microscopy and imaging, and spectrometry.

When it comes to start-ups, WBG has been succeeded by StartLife, with the mission to foster entrepreneurship in agrifood and support entrepreneurs. StartLife realizes its mission by running a thriving community consisting of more than 179 contracted and supported start-ups, who have created approximately 815 jobs. Over a period of 10 years since inception, StartLife has invested some €68 M as pre-seed capital and has offered intensive mentoring trajectories. StartLife has helped various academic start-ups grow into fully fledged businesses, such as Plant-E, a start-up that develops electronic products in which electricity is generated from living plants; PhenoVation, a start-up that develops camera systems that can analyze the chlorophyll fluorescence from plants; and TripleT Biosciences, a start-up that provides biotech companies with gene design services. Along the same lines, StartLife offers mentoring services and workspace for students with entrepreneurial intentions.

Despite the vibrant environment, recent years show a need to find new tracks to enhance value creation and knowledge commercialization. To start, Foodcase, a company that develops methods to create fresh meals with extended shelf-life without freezing, started in the local incubator and was able to contract with Swiss Gate Gourmet to create dedicated food concepts and deliver non-frozen airplane meals (Broekhuizen 2016). But in 2015 merely seven out of 499 agrifood companies around the world that raised capital are from the Netherlands (Zeemeijer and Verbeek 2016). Wageningen showcase company Noldus Information Technology, with 45 of its 150 employees in research and development in biomimicry-based software, cautions that research funding has become scarce. StartupDelta's inventory of over 1500 start-ups shows that only 3.3% are agrifood companies (Zeemeijer and Verbeek 2016). The maturity of the agrifood industry and its long time-to-market trajectories could explain part of the story. But how would that reconcile with the fact that twelve of the largest agrifood companies in the world have major research facilities in the Netherlands, such as Cargill and Mars? In Wageningen, the first round in stimulating knowledge transfer has come to a negative turning point when there were no academic spin-offs in Wageningen in 2015. These negative recent trends forced key stakeholders to reflect and change practices. For example, both in 2011 and 2013, it was recognized that the supra-regional contacts (so-called global pipelines) by companies in the Food Valley region could complement the benefits derived from regional contacts (*local buzz*) (Wubben and Batterink 2011).

As one result, the four technical universities in the Netherlands initiated the independent Innovation Industries fund to enable investments up to €8 M in a spin-off. It may overcome shortages of valley-of-death funding. Then, 2016 gave birth to the annual F&A Next conference, the first European platform for start-ups in the food and agriculture, bringing together the largest group of international agrifood investors in the Netherlands. Twenty-five international venture capital and corporate venture funds, such as global leaders Anterra Capital and Syngenta Ventures, respectively, were present at F&A Next. The best news was the 2016 press release by Unilever to relocate all of Unilever Foods R&D organizations from Vlaardingen (the Netherlands), Heilbronn (Germany), and Poznan (Poland) to a new food innovation center in Wageningen, adding up to some 550 researchers (Unilever 2016).

As stated above, the 2017 appointment of a WUR director for value creation and commercialization to promote a commercialization pillar that complements the pillars of teaching and research signals a second round of systematically organizing the commercialization of academic knowledge. The first round brought about an unexpected boost in agrifood innovation and reputation that started around two decades earlier; early signs for this second round of value creation and commercialization are very promising.

Methods and Findings

The Interviews

Given the rich history of technology transfer at WUR, in early 2017 one of the authors conducted face-to-face interviews with three academics employed as faculty members at WUR, two WUR employees engaged in different aspects of technology transfer at the university, and one manager from a large multinational firm with facilities on the WUR campus. The interviews lasted between 20 and 35 min; were semi-structured, allowing the interviewer to target topics for discussion while permitting interviewees scope to provide their individually preferred responses; and centered around two broad themes: (a) how technology transfer takes places at WUR and (b) whether new institutional structures (i.e., a Technology Transfer Office) could facilitate the process or not.

The interviewed academics responded positively to interview requests sent to 20 randomly selected academics at WUR. One of the technology transfer specialists we interviewed specializes in spin-offs and the other specializes in patents and other forms of intellectual protection. Besides technology transfer specialists hired ad hoc or employed part time within departments at WUR, the two specialists we interviewed are the "go-to" individuals when it comes to technology transfer at WUR. Due to confidentiality, we cannot disclose information on the interviewee from the multinational corporation.

Main Findings

We structure the discussion below according to the five main findings we derived from the interviews. Three main findings refer to how technology transfer is taking place at present at WUR and to a large degree how it has been taking place in the past. Two main findings are informed by the past but relate more to the future of technology transfer at WUR.

The first main finding was that each department is autonomous in the way it pursues (or not) technology transfer. This autonomy may be reflected in the forms of technology transfer (e.g., licensing versus joint projects with industry), the way the deals are structured, the overall attitude of the department toward technology transfer, and the like. To demonstrate, one of the academics we interviewed explained how the department employs its own intellectual property lawyer. The second academic stressed that the department sets important goals for technology transfer and facilitates them. Toward this end, he highlighted that the use of a public-private collaboration platform is the main tool used by many faculty members in the department. The platform is called Top Institute for Food and Nutrition (TiFN, http://www.tifn.nl/partners/) which focuses on food and nutrition, and industrial participants include some of the world's largest food companies such as Unilever, Nestle, and PepsiCo. Further stressing the autonomy of each department, one of the technology transfer specialists stated that "there is no best way to conduct technology transfer. It completely depends on the situation to see what the best approach is or what is most attainable." He also commented that "What we currently have, and what the schools prefer is a bottom-up design where departments or science groups can set their own rules based on their needs and cultures." Along the same lines, the second technology transfer specialist noted that "Bottom-up is required here because you have different types of knowledge and different types of audiences. If it's very practical, hands-on, then you use licencing. We noticed that for the real disruptive technologies and radical innovations, start-ups are the best way to spread the knowledge, because integrated market parties are 'scared' to do the investments that are needed compared to the risks, or may see it as cannibalism of their current core business. Then it becomes interesting to provide targeted services to start-ups in niche markets to eventually create a change in the main market."

The second main finding was that WUR has implemented strategies to minimize the need for scientists to navigate through the formal institutional channels when engaging in technology transfer. These strategies can be partitioned to informal and formal. With regard to informal, technology transfer specialists often take the required steps of completing a technology transfer contract once the initial agreement between the WUR scientist and the industrial partner has materialized. To illustrate, in the case of a patent, this would mean that the scientist would have substantial assistance in the process of searching for prior art, filling out the application form, communicating with the patent examiner, and the like. As it pertains to formal strategies, WUR has formed a general agreement which serves as a basis for specific deals. The following quote from one of the interviewed academics describe the benefits of the agreement with precision "[The basic agreement] makes life much easier, I'm actually very happy with these general agreements because then you don't have to negotiate every time how to exactly deal with technology transfer. So, in my perspective these general agreements with companies that I frequently collaborate with are the core, and then the individual contract for the individual project is limited to one or two pages. It's prepared very quickly and takes away a lot of bureaucracy."

The third main finding is that WUR has promoted a culture among faculty and staff that considers technology transfer to be not so much a vehicle to generate revenues, but more of a means for academics to give back to society. This culture does not present obstacles to generating income, but it does incentivize academics to pursue technology transfer as in essence they still maintain their academic identity (Stern 2004). As a result, it is not uncommon for WUR academics to leverage their own industry contacts (developed over many years) to initiate knowledge transfer activities. To illustrate one of the interviewed scientists stated the following: "I always contact the [department's] lawyer myself, I tell him I want to make a collaboration with this company, doing this work. I give him a project plan and tell him the budget and a time frame and then he just fills the standard contract in and sends it back to me - I send it to the company and it is done." The initiation of the contact from the scientist is a point worth emphasizing, as it relates back to the autonomy given to WUR departments discussed above. It appears that such autonomy also extends to individual researchers. As one of the interviewed academics put it "… I've stopped 'advertising' my research to large companies because it just did not work. Right now, I mainly look at the smaller firms, who seem more eager to acquire my research or knowledge."

The forth main finding was that physical proximity between industrial partners and WUR has facilitated technology transfer. As explained above, a number of companies have R&D labs in the Food Valley cluster, and the proximity to the WUR campus has proven beneficial. The following quote from one of the interviewed academics demonstrates the benefit of minimized spatial distance: "Being able to actually walk by to someone helps. That is not only externally, because in the past I worked quite frequently with Animal Sciences, but we didn't meet each other frequently because we were both on two different sides of Wageningen. Now they are over there [points to building], I walk to them three times more often than I did drive to them in the past." He continues: "So being within walking distance of each other really makes a difference. Some people talk about video conferencing and that it doesn't matter if they are in Singapore or Wageningen. I don't believe that." To illustrate, he gives another example: "I also work together with a Chinese dairy company, and they also have a small office in Wageningen with a few people for that specific reason. They want to be able to physically sit together with people without having to fly all the way to Europe. I do believe that physical distance makes a difference in the quality of the collaboration." Similarly, one of the technology transfer specialists noted that "…an increasing mix of different types of institutions and firms, bringing R&D labs together, allowing researchers to meet each other, these things all adds up. The idea of 'splendid isolation', high levels of secrecy in R&D

have become almost impossible for complex innovations. Combining forces has become a necessity." The importance of physical proximity has been shown in the literature (e.g., Kolympiris et al. 2011; Kolympiris and Kalaitzandonakes 2013), and in fact the present expansion of the WUR campus to host a business incubator and R&D labs of leading corporations suggests that the colocation of academia and industry is a key ingredient in promoting technology transfer at Wageningen.

The fifth main finding relates more to the future of technology transfer at WUR, which as discussed above is at crossroads. Given (a) the new landscape with new industrial players coming into the picture, (b) the previous WUR efforts for a full-blown TTO, and (c) the fact that TTOs are the norm among US universities who are world leaders in technology transfer, we inquired the following: would WUR benefit from adopting a structure in which a central organization such as a TTO would be responsible for every aspect of technology transfer at WUR? Here, we uncovered opposing views. Academics do not see a need for a TTO as was the case with WGB. When asked specifically about the TTO, one of the academics expressed concerns and noted that "…I do believe that technology transfer starts with the individual scientist being able to collaborate with another individual somewhere else. And then these two people can go do something together." Another academic stressed that the independence of departments is an effective mechanism that does not need to be changed. Toward this end, he stated that "Within the division there are contracts and a very clear framework in which we have to work." On the other side, the manager expressed a different view: "I believe the director of Valorisation still has to start – in March – which is when we will **finally** start up a TTO." (bold added). Reflecting the independence of departments, he also commented that "It is difficult to 'go shopping' at ten different research groups to find the right place for your research. It's never the feeling 'we are talking with Wageningen University' but rather Chair of X or School of Y. In the commercial world, we can sort of enter a partnership walking into the CEO's room and talk business. We miss that here; it's always dealing with many small stakeholders."

All in all, we find that WUR has facilitated technology transfer in agriculture by providing independence to each department, reducing bureaucracy, embracing a culture that considers technology transfer as a means for academics to give back to society, and by exploiting the advantages of physical proximity. Regarding the future, the creation of a TTO is under consideration, but the scientists we interviewed expressed concerns about such plans.

Summary and Conclusions

In this paper, we examine how technology transfer from academia to industry can become stronger in agriculture. Methodologically, we opt to study technology transfer at Wageningen University and Research as our case study. WUR is one of the leading institutions in technology transfer in agriculture, and it has been so for a number of years, making it a fertile template for our research. After we describe in detail how technology transfer has taken place over time at WUR, we present the findings of interviews we conducted with different stakeholders involved in technology transfer at WUR: academics, technology transfer specialists, and representatives of industry.

We find that WUR has embraced a view of technology transfer as a means to contribute to society, has given independence to different departments to pursue knowledge transfer, has benefited from physical proximity to industrial actors, and has implemented policies that minimize the involvement of inventors in the bureaucratic aspects of technology transfer. The question is whether these strategies are replicable at other universities and, therefore, what lessons interested parties might derive from this study.

In terms of considering technology transfer as a means to contribute to society, we posit that this view can adopted with ease. In fact, the finding at hand highlights the fact that WUR researchers are not driven primarily by profit considerations when transferring technology, and as such they appear to be similar to scientists elsewhere. Pertaining to the independence of each department, as explained above, this is about to change also at WUR, so the takeaway message here is that the idiosyncrasies of each institution will dictate the best organizational form. Physical proximity to industry is of course difficult to achieve overnight, but we do note that WUR has, in more recent years, pulled industrial actors to its campus. Such pull is, again, challenging but, as the case at hand demonstrates, feasible. The key factor for pull of this kind is to develop the long-term contacts that the university as a whole and the individual researchers have formed with the industrial sector. Therefore, contacts matter. Lastly, when it comes to bureaucracy, there is very little doubt that minimizing it has been a key ingredient for technology transfer success at WUR. Less bureaucracy provides incentives to academics to engage in technology transfer without strong concerns of having to spend time and effort in navigating the formal institutional channels.

We close with the main limitations of our work. First and foremost, as in most case studies, extrapolating the findings to other contexts should be done with caution as idiosyncratic factors may limit generalization. For our application, this means that our findings should not be used as a roadmap for every university aspiring to strengthen technology transfer in agriculture but rather as a starting point in deriving strategies and devising specific policies. Second, while we expect our interviewees to be representative of the population of WUR employees, it is likely that WUR scientists opposed to technology transfer did not respond to our interview requests. Our findings, therefore, may be subject to such bias.

References

Abrams, I., G. Leung, and A.J. Stevens. 2009. How Are US Technology Transfer Offices Tasked and Motivated-Is It All About the Money. *Research Management Review* 17 (1): 1–34.

Acs, Z.J., D.B. Audretsch, and M.P. Feldman. 1992. Real Effects of Academic Research: Comment. *The American Economic Review* 82 (1): 363–367.

Agentschap, N., and D.N. Octrooicentrum. 2013. *Regionale Innovatie Systemen (Ris) En Ip-Based Entrepreneurschip in De Economische Regio's Rondom Nederlandse Universiteiten.* Agentschap NL: Divisie NL Octrooicentrum.

Agrawal, A. 2006. Engaging the Inventor: Exploring Licensing Strategies for University Inventions and the Role of Latent Knowledge. *Strategic Management Journal* 27 (1): 63–79.

Agrawal, A., and R. Henderson. 2002. Putting Patents in Context: Exploring Knowledge Transfer from Mit. *Management Science* 48 (1): 44–60.

Agrawal, A.K. 2001. University-to-Industry Knowledge Transfer: Literature Review and Unanswered Questions. *International Journal of Management Reviews* 3 (4): 285–302. https://doi.org/10.1111/1468-2370.00069.

Arundel, A., and A. Geuna. 2004. Proximity and the Use of Public Science by Innovative European Firms. *Economics of Innovation and New Technology* 13 (6): 559–580.

Azoulay, P., W. Ding, and T. Stuart. 2007. The Determinants of Faculty Patenting Behavior: Demographics or Opportunities? *Journal of Economic Behavior and Organization* 63 (4): 599–623. https://doi.org/10.1016/j.jebo.2006.05.015.

———. 2009. The Impact of Academic Patenting on the Rate, Quality and Direction of (Public) Research Output. *Journal of Industrial Economics* 57 (4): 637–676. https://doi.org/10.1111/j.1467-6451.2009.00395.x.

Beemer, F. 2006. Groene Kennis (De) Centraal?: Evaluatie Van De Wijzigingen in Het Landbouwkundig Onderzoek, Berenschot, Utrecht. http://www.minlnv.nl/cdlpub/servlet/CDLServlet.

Bekkers, R., and I.M. Bodas Freitas. 2008. Analysing Knowledge Transfer Channels between Universities and iIndustry: To What Degree Do Sectors Also Matter? *Research Policy* 37 (10): 1837–1853. https://doi.org/10.1016/j.respol.2008.07.007.

Bercovitz, J., M. Feldman, I. Feller, and R. Burton. 2001. Organizational Structure as a Determinant of Academic Patent and Licensing Behavior: An Exploratory Study of Duke, Johns Hopkins, and Pennsylvania State Universities. *The Journal of Technology Transfer* 26 (1): 21–35. https://doi.org/10.1023/a:1007828026904.

Boardman, P.C., and E.A. Corley. 2008. University Research Centers and the Composition of Research Collaborations. *Research Policy* 37 (5): 900–913.

Boardman, P.C., and B.L. Ponomariov. 2009. University Researchers Working with Private Companies. *Technovation* 29 (2): 142–153.

Breschi, S., and F. Lissoni. 2001. Knowledge Spillovers and Local Innovation Systems: A Critical Survey. *Industrial and Corporate Change* 10 (4): 975–1005.

Broekhuizen, K. 2016. Grote Bedrijven Moeten Zich Ook Weer Als Starter Gaan Gedragen. Het Financieel Dagblad. from https://fd.nl/blogs/1177701/grote-bedrijven-moeten-zich-ook-weer-als-starter-gaan-gedragen.

Bulut, H., and G. Moschini. 2009. US Universities' Net Returns from Patenting and Licensing: A Quantile Regression Analysis. *Economics of Innovation and New Technology* 18 (2): 123–137.

Bush, V. 1945. Science: The Endless Frontier. *Transactions of the Kansas Academy of Science (1903-)* 48 (3): 231–264.

Callaert, J., P. Landoni, B. Van Looy, and R. Verganti. 2015. Scientific Yield from Collaboration with Industry: The Relevance of Researchers' Strategic Approaches. *Research Policy* 44 (4): 990–998. https://doi.org/10.1016/j.respol.2015.02.003.

Cassiman, B., R. Veugelers, and P. Zuniga. 2008. In Search of Performance Effects of (in) Direct Industry Science Links. *Industrial and Corporate Change* 17 (4): 611–646.

Clarysse, B., and N. Moray. 2004. A Process Study of Entrepreneurial Team Formation: The Case of a Research-Based Spin-Off. *Journal of Business Venturing* 19 (1): 55–79. https://doi.org/10.1016/s0883-9026(02)00113-1.

Cockburn, I.M., and R.M. Henderson. 1998. Absorptive Capacity, Coauthoring Behavior, and the Organization of Research in Drug Discovery. *The Journal of Industrial Economics* 46 (2): 157–182.

Cohen, W.M., R.R. Nelson, and J.P. Walsh. 2002. Links and Impacts: The Influence of Public Research on Industrial R&D. *Management Science* 48 (1): 1–23.

Colombo, M.G., and M. Delmastro. 2002. How Effective Are Technology Incubators? Evidence from Italy. *Research Policy* 31 (7): 1103–1122.

Colyvas, J., M. Crow, A. Gelijns, R. Mazzoleni, R.R. Nelson, N. Rosenberg, and B.N. Sampat. 2002. How Do University Inventions Get into Practice? *Management Science* 48 (1): 61–72.

Crespi, G., P. D'Este, R. Fontana, and A. Geuna. 2011. The Impact of Academic Patenting on University Research and Its Transfer. *Research Policy* 40 (1): 55–68. https://doi.org/10.1016/j.respol.2010.09.010.

Crombach, C., and J. Koene. 2008. From 'Wageningen City of Life Sciences'to 'Food Valley'. *Pathways to High-Tech Valleys and Research Triangles: Innovative Entrepreneurship, Knowledge Transfer and Cluster and Cluster Formation in Europe and the United States* 24: 293.

D'Este, P., and P. Patel. 2007. University-Industry Linkages in the Uk: What Are the Factors Underlying the Variety of Interactions with Industry? *Research Policy* 36 (9): 1295–1313. https://doi.org/10.1016/j.respol.2007.05.002.

D'este, P., and M. Perkmann. 2011. Why Do Academics Engage with Industry? The Entrepreneurial University and Individual Motivations. *The Journal of Technology Transfer* 36 (3): 316–339.

Debackere, K., and R. Veugelers. 2005. The Role of Academic Technology Transfer Organizations in Improving Industry Science Links. *Research Policy* 34 (3): 321–342.

Drivas, K., A. Panagopoulos, and S. Rozakis. 2016. Instigating Entrepreneurship to a University in an Adverse Entrepreneurial Landscape. *The Journal of Technology Transfer* 41: 1–20.

Etzkowitz, H. 1998. The Norms of Entrepreneurial Science: Cognitive Effects of the New University-Industry Linkages. *Research Policy* 27 (8): 823–833.

Etzkowitz, H., and L. Leydesdorff. 2000. The Dynamics of Innovation: From National Systems and "Mode 2" to a Triple Helix of University-Industry-Government Relations. *Research Policy* 29 (2): 109–123.

Fabrizio, K.R. 2009. Absorptive Capacity and the Search for Innovation. *Research Policy* 38 (2): 255–267.

Feldman, M., and P. Desrochers. 2003. Research Universities and Local Economic Development: Lessons from the History of the Johns Hopkins University. *Industry and Innovation* 10 (1): 5–24.

Feldman, M., I. Feller, J. Bercovitz, and R. Burton. 2002. Equity and the Technology Transfer Strategies of American Research Universities. *Management Science* 48 (1): 105–121.

Fontana, R., A. Geuna, and M. Matt. 2006. Factors Affecting University–Industry R&D Projects: The Importance of Searching, Screening and Signalling. *Research Policy* 35 (2): 309–323.

Friedman, J., and J. Silberman. 2003. University Technology Transfer: Do Incentives, Management, and Location Matter? *The Journal of Technology Transfer* 28 (1): 17–30. https://doi.org/10.1023/a:1021674618658.

Fuglie, K.O., and A.A. Toole. 2014. The Evolving Institutional Structure of Public and Private Agricultural Research. *American Journal of Agricultural Economics* 96 (3): 862–883. https://doi.org/10.1093/ajae/aat107.

Geuna, A., and A. Muscio. 2009. The Governance of University Knowledge Transfer: A Critical Review of the Literature. *Minerva* 47 (1): 93–114. https://doi.org/10.1007/s11024-009-9118-2.

Goh, S.C. 2002. Managing Effective Knowledge Transfer: An Integrative Framework and Some Practice Implications. *Journal of Knowledge Management* 6 (1): 23–30.

Gulbrandsen, M., and J.C. Smeby. 2005. Industry Funding and University Professors' Research Performance. *Research Policy* 34 (6): 932–950. https://doi.org/10.1016/j.respol.2005.05.004.

Gurney-Read, J. 2016. The World's Top Universities by Subject. The Telegraph, 12:01AM GMT 22 Mar 2016. from http://www.telegraph.co.uk/education/universityeducation/12200078/The-worlds-top-universities-by-subject.html.

Hall, B.H., A.N. Link, and J.T. Scott. 2003. Universities as Research Partners. *The Review of Economics and Statistics* 85 (2): 485–491.

Henderson, R., A.B. Jaffe, and M. Trajtenberg. 1998. Universities as a Source of Commercial Technology: A Detailed Analysis of University Patenting, 1965–1988. *The Review of Economics and Statistics* 80 (1): 119–127.

Hewitt-Dundas, N. 2012. Research Intensity and Knowledge Transfer Activity in Uk Universities. *Research Policy* 41 (2): 262–275. https://doi.org/10.1016/j.respol.2011.10.010.

Hulsink, W., H. Dons, T. Lans, and V. Blok. 2014. Boosting Entrepreneurship Education within the Knowledge Network of the Dutch Agri-Food Sciences: The New Wageningen' Approach. In *Handbook on the Entrepreneurial University*, 248–278. Cheltenham: Edward Elgar Publishing.

Hulsink, W., and J. Dons. 2008. *Pathways to High-Tech Valleys and Research Triangles: Innovative Entrepreneurship, Knowledge Transfer and Cluster Formation in Europe and the United States*. Dordrecht: Springer Science & Business Media.

Huyghe, A., M. Knockaert, E. Piva, and M. Wright. 2016. Are Researchers Deliberately Bypassing the Technology Transfer Office? An Analysis of Tto Awareness. *Small Business Economics* 47 (3): 589–607. https://doi.org/10.1007/s11187-016-9757-2.

Jaffe, A.B. 1989. Real Effects of Academic Research. *The American Economic Review* 5: 957–970.

Kenney, M., and D. Patton. 2009. Reconsidering the Bayh-Dole Act and the Current University Invention Ownership Model. *Research Policy* 38 (9): 1407–1422. https://doi.org/10.1016/j.respol.2009.07.007.

Kolympiris, C., and N. Kalaitzandonakes. 2013. Geographic Scope of Proximity Effects among Small Life Sciences Firms. *Small Business Economics* 40 (4): 1059–1086.

Kolympiris, C., N. Kalaitzandonakes, and D. Miller. 2011. Spatial Collocation and Venture Capital in the US Biotechnology Industry. *Research Policy* 40 (9): 1188–1199.

———. 2014. Public Funds and Local Biotechnology Firm Creation. *Research Policy* 43 (1): 121–137.

Kolympiris, C., and P.G. Klein. 2017. The Effects of Academic Incubators on University Innovation. *Strategic Entrepreneurship Journal* 11: 145–170.

Landry, R., N. Amara, and M. Ouimet. 2007. Determinants of Knowledge Transfer: Evidence from Canadian University Researchers in Natural Sciences and Engineering. *Journal of Technology Transfer* 32 (6): 561–592. https://doi.org/10.1007/s10961-006-0017-5.

Laursen, K., and A. Salter. 2004. Searching High and Low: What Types of Firms Use Universities as a Source of Innovation? *Research Policy* 33 (8): 1201–1215.

Lee, Y.S. 2000. The Sustainability of University-Industry Research Collaboration: An Empirical Assessment. *The Journal of Technology Transfer* 25 (2): 111–133.

Litan, R.E., L. Mitchell, and E. Reedy. 2007. Commercializing University Innovations: Alternative Approaches. *Innovation policy and the economy* 8: 31–57.

Manawatu Standard. 1999. Lecturer Launching a Pig Growth Model. Manawatu Standard (New Zealand). from.

Mansfield, E. 1991. Academic Research and Industrial Innovation. *Research Policy* 20 (1): 1–12.

———. 1995. Academic Research Underlying Industrial Innovations: Sources, Characteristics, and Financing. *The Review of Economics and Statistics* 77: 55–65.

———. 1997. Academic Research and Industrial Innovation: An Update of Empirical Findings. *Research Policy* 26 (7): 773–776.

———. 1998. Academic Research and Industrial Innovation: An Update of Empirical Findings. *Research Policy* 26 (7–8): 773–776.

Markman, G.D., P.T. Gianiodis, and P.H. Phan. 2008. Full-Time Faculty or Part-Time Entrepreneurs. *IEEE Transactions on Engineering Management* 55 (1): 29–36.

Markman, G.D., P.T. Gianiodis, P.H. Phan, and D.B. Balkin. 2004. Entrepreneurship from the Ivory Tower: Do Incentive Systems Matter? *The Journal of Technology Transfer* 29 (3): 353–364. https://doi.org/10.1023/b:jott.0000034127.01889.86.

———. 2005. Innovation Speed: Transferring University Technology to Market. *Research Policy* 34 (7): 1058–1075. https://doi.org/10.1016/j.respol.2005.05.007.

Meyer-Thurow, G. 1982. The Industrialization of Invention: A Case Study from the German Chemical Industry. *Isis* 73 (3): 363–381.

Mindruta, D. 2013. Value Creation in University-Firm Research Collaborations: A Matching Approach. *Strategic Management Journal* 34 (6): 644–665.

Mowery, D., R. Nelson, B. Sampat, and A. Ziedonis. 2015. *Ivory Tower and Industrial Innovation: University-Industry Technology Transfer before and after the Bayh-Dole Act*. Redwood City: Stanford University Press.

Narin, F., K.S. Hamilton, and D. Olivastro. 1997. The Increasing Linkage between US Technology and ublic Science. *Research Policy* 26 (3): 317–330.

O'Gorman, C., O. Byrne, and D. Pandya. 2008. How Scientists Commercialise New Knowledge Via Entrepreneurship. *The Journal of Technology Transfer* 33 (1): 23–43. https://doi.org/10.1007/s10961-006-9010-2.

O'Kane, C., V. Mangematin, W. Geoghegan, and C. Fitzgerald. 2015. University Technology Transfer Offices: The Search for Identity to Build Legitimacy. *Research Policy* 44 (2): 421–437. https://doi.org/10.1016/j.respol.2014.08.003.

Omta, O., and F. Fortuin. 2013. *Effectiveness of Cluster Organizations in Facilitating Open Innovation in Regional Innovation Systems: The Case of Food Valley in the Netherlands*. in *Open Innovation in the Food and Beverage Industry*, ed. G. M. Martiner. Oxford: Woodhead Publishing.

Omta, O., and E. Wubben. 2004. Agrosector Verdient Navolging. Het Financeele Dagblad, 27 November 2004. In *from*.

Parker, D., F. Castillo, and D. Zilberman. 2001. Public-Private Sector Linkages in Research and Development: The Case of U.S. Agriculture. *American Journal of Agricultural Economics* 83 (3): 736–741.

Peper, B. 1996. Duurzame Kennis, Duurzame Landbouw. *Gemeente Rotterdam* 43.

Perez-Ruiz, M., J. Carballido, and J. Agüera Vega. 2013. University Spin-Off Creation by Spanish Researchers in Agricultural Engineering. *Journal of Technology Management & Innovation* 8 (3): 152–159.

Perkmann, M., V. Tartari, M. McKelvey, E. Autio, A. Broström, P. D'Este, R. Fini, A. Geuna, R. Grimaldi, A. Hughes, S. Krabel, M. Kitson, P. Llerena, F. Lissoni, A. Salter, and M. Sobrero. 2013. Academic Engagement and Commercialisation: A Review of the Literature on University–Industry Relations. *Research Policy* 42 (2): 423–442. https://doi.org/10.1016/j.respol.2012.09.007.

Perkmann, M., and K. Walsh. 2008. Engaging the Scholar: Three Types of Academic Consulting and Their Impact on Universities and Industry. *Research Policy* 37 (10): 1884–1891.

Polish News Bulletin. 2016. *Unilever Relocates Its Polish R&D Centre to the Netherlands*. Polish News Bulletin, BUSINESS. from.

Porter, M. 2001. *Innovation and Competitiveness: Findings on the Netherlands: Innovation Lecture 2001 Organizing Innovation in the Knowledge-Based Economy, the Hague, the Netherlands, December 3, 2001*. The Hague: Ministry of Economic Affairs.

Postlewait, A., D.D. Parker, and D. Zilberman. 1993. The Advent of Biotechnology and Technology Transfer in Agriculture. *Technological Forecasting and Social Change* 43 (3–4): 271–287.

Powers, J.B., and P.P. McDougall. 2005. University Start-up Formation and Technology Licensing with Firms That Go Public: A Resource-Based View of Academic Entrepreneurship. *Journal of Business Venturing* 20 (3): 291–311. https://doi.org/10.1016/j.jbusvent.2003.12.008.

PR Newswire Europe. 2005. Campina and Wageningen University Sign Research Agreement. PR Newswire Europe. from.

Pray, C.E. 2001. Public-Private Sector Linkages in Research and Development: Biotechnology and the Seed Industry in Brazil, China and India. *American Journal of Agricultural Economics* 83 (3): 742–747.

Rothaermel, F.T., S.D. Agung, and L. Jiang. 2007. University Entrepreneurship: A Taxonomy of the Literature. *Industrial and Corporate Change* 16 (4): 691–791. https://doi.org/10.1093/icc/dtm023.

Schartinger, D., C. Rammer, M.M. Fischer, and J. Fröhlich. 2002. Knowledge Interactions between Universities and Industry in Austria: Sectoral Patterns and Determinants. *Research Policy* 31 (3): 303–328.

Schartinger, D., A. Schibany, and H. Gassler. 2001. Interactive Relations between Universities and Firms: Empirical Evidence for Austria. *Journal of Technology Transfer* 26 (3): 255–268.

Schillebeeckx, S.J.D., S. Chaturvedi, G. George, and Z. King. 2016. What Do I Want? The Effects of Individual Aspiration and Relational Capability on Collaboration Preferences. *Strategic Management Journal* 37 (7): 1493–1506. https://doi.org/10.1002/smj.2396.

Shane, S. 2004. Encouraging University Entrepreneurship? The Effect of the Bayh-Dole Act on University Patenting in the United States. *Journal of Business Venturing* 19 (1): 127–151.

Siegel, D.S., R. Veugelers, and M. Wright. 2007. Technology Transfer Offices and Commercialization of University Intellectual Property: Performance and Policy Implications. *Oxford Review of Economic Policy* 23 (4): 640–660.

Siegel, D.S., D. Waldman, and A. Link. 2003b. Assessing the Impact of Organizational Practices on the Relative Productivity of University Technology Transfer Offices: An Exploratory Study. *Research Policy* 32 (1): 27–48.

Siegel, D.S., D.A. Waldman, L.E. Atwater, and A.N. Link. 2003a. Commercial Knowledge Transfers from Universities to Firms: Improving the Effectiveness of University–Industry Collaboration. *The Journal of High Technology Management Research* 14 (1): 111–133. https://doi.org/10.1016/S1047-8310(03)00007-5.

Siegel, D.S., and M. Wright. 2015. Academic Entrepreneurship: Time for a Rethink? *British Journal of Management* 26 (4): 582–595.

Stern, S. 2004. Do Scientists Pay to Be Scientists? *Management Science* 50 (6): 835–853.

Teece, D.J. 2000. Strategies for Managing Knowledge Assets: The Role of Firm Structure and Industrial Context. *Long Range Planning* 33 (1): 35–54.

Thursby, J., A.W. Fuller, and M. Thursby. 2009. US Faculty Patenting: Inside and Outside the University. *Research Policy* 38 (1): 14–25.

Thursby, J.G., and M.C. Thursby. 2003. University Licensing and the Bayh-Dole Act. *Science* 301 (5636): 1052–1052.

———. 2007. University Licensing. *Oxford Review of Economic Policy* 23 (4): 620–639.

Tijssen, R.J. 2002. Science Dependence of Technologies:Evidence from Inventions and Their Inventors. *Research Policy* 31 (4): 509–526.

Toole, A.A. 2012. The Impact of Public Basic Research on Industrial Innovation: Evidence from the Pharmaceutical Industry. *Research Policy* 41 (1): 1–12.

Unilever. 2016. Unilever Intends to Build a Foods Innovation Centre in Wageningen. London/Rotterdam.

Van Looy, B., J. Callaert, and K. Debackere. 2006. Publication and patent Behavior of Academic Researchers: Conflicting, Reinforcing or Merely Co-Existing? *Research Policy* 35 (4): 596–608. https://doi.org/10.1016/j.respol.2006.02.003.

Van Looy, B., M. Ranga, J. Callaert, K. Debackere, and E. Zimmermann. 2004. Combining Entrepreneurial and Scientific Performance in Academia: Towards a Compounded and Reciprocal Matthew-Effect? *Research Policy* 33 (3): 425–441.

Versluis, K. 2006. Weekblad Voor Wageningen Ur. Resource. Wageningen, Cereales. from http://edepot.wur.nl/402476.

Wireless News. 2010. Dow Agrosciences and Wageningen Ur Sign Agreement.

Wubben, E., and M. Batterink. 2011. Food Valley Als Ondernemend Kenniscluster. *ESB Economisch Statistische Berichten* 96 (4609S): 40–46.

Yasmine. 2015. Spotlight: Wageningen Ur. Institute of Food Science and Technology, 01/12/2015. from http://www.fstjournal.org/features/29-4/wageningen-ur.

Zahringer, K., C. Kolympiris, and N. Kalaitzandonakes. 2017. Academic Knowledge Quality Differentials and the Quality of Firm Innovation. *Industrial and Corporate Change* 26 (5): 821–844.

Zeemeijer, I. and J. Verbeek. 2016. Investeringen in 'Groene' Start-Ups Zijn Booming. Het Financieel Dagblad. from https://fd.nl/economie-politiek/1152856/investeringen-in-groene-start-ups-zijn-booming.

The Evaluation Process of Research Commercialization Proposals and its Links to University Technology Transfer (TT) Strategy: A Case Study

Odysseas Cartalos, Alexander N. Svoronos, and Elias G. Carayannis

Abstract Open innovation and continuously evolving collaborative schemes of key actors along the innovation chain increase the complexity of technology transfer. University TTOs need to adapt to new challenges and therefore move from their traditional role of facilitating patenting and licensing activities to one of active engagement and deep involvement in supporting the different stages of research commercialization. Building successful TTO business models requires aligning the TTO service offerings with the characteristics of research produced in the parent institution and to the various forms of assistance needed by academic staff to commercially exploit their research results.

This work presents a method to assess and support commercialization proposals by university researchers. Although the intention is to choose projects with the highest exploitation potential, the objective is not to just have the top projects of an innovation contest, but rather select projects together with the support services and corresponding resources needed to enable them to reach their commercialization objectives. Moreover, it is shown that when available TTO resources are not enough to handle all projects with merit, a more formal approach can be adopted, involving the solution of a decision problem that may also serve as a planning tool for future TTO staffing.

Applied in an academic environment with limited technology transfer experience, the proposed assessment framework is used to develop a longer-term TTO strategy.

The original version of this chapter was revised.
An erratum to this chapter can be found at https://doi.org/10.1007/978-3-319-67958-7_25

O. Cartalos (✉) • A.N. Svoronos
Logotech, Ltd., Athens, Greece
e-mail: cartalos@logotech.gr

E.G. Carayannis
George Washington University, Washington, DC, USA

Introduction

In recent years scientific knowledge became a key factor to consider when dealing with entrepreneurship, competitiveness, and prosperity. This was one of the reasons pushing academic institutions and other knowledge producers of the public sector to develop the so-called third mission of economic and societal impact in addition to research and teaching (Florida and Cohen 1999; Etzkowitz et al. 2000; Gulbrandsen and Slipersæter 2007; Acs and Audretsch 2010; OECD 2011). But for nonacademic actors to benefit from this form of knowledge, the results of scientific research would still need to be brought from the university[1] to society, a process involving knowledge transfer and research commercialization.

Knowledge is recognized as a valuable commodity (Arnesse and Cohendet 2001). Knowledge transfer takes place between university actors and other stakeholders for the purpose of further development and commercialization (Lundquist 2003) through different channels, the most common being joint research (Cockburn and Henderson 1998; Veugelers and Cassiman 2005; Belderbos et al. 2006), academic consulting (Thursby et al. 2009), and licensing contracts (Jensen and Thursby 2001; Thursby and Kemp 2002). In this context, Perkmann et al. (2013) drew attention to "academic engagement," defined as knowledge-related collaboration by academic researchers with nonacademic organizations, which represents an important pathway through which academic knowledge can be directed into the industrial domain.[2] Research commercialization usually denotes the act of turning scientific results into marketable products and services in the form of selling, contracting, or licensing of technology-based services, intellectual assets, and related knowledge and know-how (Bradley et al. 2013a).

The spillover of knowledge and the commercial exploitation of university research have been largely facilitated by the creation of technology transfer (TT)[3] structures in public academic and research institutions, with a mission to develop and strengthen the links between science and areas/applications of industrial, commercial, or societal relevance (Audretsch 2014). Such structures comprise university technology transfer offices or organizations[4] (TTOs), proof of concept centers (Gulbranson and Audretsch 2008; Bradley et al. 2013b), incubators, and science/technology parks. Of these, TTOs have received special attention and are recognized as the institutional bridges between universities and industry, due to their

---

[1] In this text we use "university" as shorthand for public research organizations (PROs) that include higher education institutions, as well as research centers funded by public sources.

[2] The related topic of distinguishing between formal and informal knowledge transfer is discussed in Link et al. (2007) and Grimpe and Fier (2010).

[3] One important reason for keeping with the TT terminology at a time where many such activities may exceed the classical meaning of technology is that TT is by now well embedded in the professional innovation community (Debackere 2012). Technology is used throughout this text in its wider, knowledge-based sense.

[4] TTO standing for technology transfer organization is more frequently used by European authors (e.g., Debackere 2012).

significant contribution in generating economic and social impact from university research (Siegel et al. 2003; Debackere 2012).

TTOs were originally conceived as administrative structures facilitating the processes of patenting and licensing intellectual property, but have progressively moved to cover other forms of commercial exploitation of research (Bradley et al. 2013a, b). The growth of external collaborations and the variety of their forms led to complex knowledge transfer schemes, where TTOs interact with other TT structures to shape university-led innovation environments (Trueman et al. 2014) or liaise with external actors as active members of high-tech clusters contributing to regional development (Carayannis et al. 2015). The marked increase over the last 20 years of professional staff employed in TTOs (Bradley et al. 2013a, b) should be linked to the growth and diversification of TTO service delivery that, in addition to intellectual property (IP) and license management, has been extended to include active marketing of university research results, as well as various forms of mentoring and counseling support to the research teams (Conti and Gaule 2008; Weckowska 2015).

The successful operation of TTOs primarily depends on the long-term commitment of the parent institutions to support technology transfer while ensuring governance autonomy, strategic flexibility, and financial sustainability within the university structures (Debackere and Veugelers 2005; Young 2007; Debackere 2012). According to Young (2007), key factors that should be taken into account when a university decides to launch a TTO are "internal" characteristics, such as the quality of the research produced, its volume, as well as its focus on applications of economic/societal relevance together with the university culture toward entrepreneurship. Related studies also draw attention to external characteristics, such as the regional entrepreneurial environment, the concentration of high-tech firms, and the university links with industry, together with supporting measures at the public policy level (Friedman and Silberman 2003; Heinzl et al. 2008; Hayter 2013). These internal and external characteristics should be carefully considered when delineating the strategic approach of a university in the area of technology transfer and, therefore, the strategic objectives and operational design of the TTOs, taking into account that the way TTOs operate should mirror the broader societal and academic mission of the parent institution to mobilize innovative research and knowledge for the benefits of the economy and society (Campbell 2007; Baglieri et al. 2015).

There still exist other motivations for public research organizations to develop TTOs; an important one relates to reduced academic budgets that push universities and research centers to concentrate their efforts on the productive use of research achievements through technology transfer in addition to competitive funding for research. This is particularly true for Greek universities that have suffered drastic budget cuts since 2010, when a severe economic crisis hit the country, but also for academic and research institutions in other European countries and regions with reduced innovation performance (Veugelers 2014, 2016).

A common difficulty in most such cases is that technology transfer is attempted in environments that have very little experience in this field,[5] which means that limited know-how and evaluative evidence are available to support the development of adequate TT strategies, or to efficiently handle critical operational aspects, such as how to assess the commercialization potential of research results. Other operational issues of significant importance deal with defining the services that should be provided to the research teams, taking into account that the target audience has a rather poor entrepreneurial background,[6] as well as ensuring that adequately skilled resources are available in sufficient numbers to provide such services.

The present work was motivated by a two-year project with objective to enhance and support the research commercialization in the Agricultural University of Athens (AUA). The AUA Entrepreneurship and Innovation project was part of a broader regional development program managed by the Municipality of Athens, aiming to promote the participation of universities located in the capital region of Greece in initiatives that stimulate competitiveness and economic growth.[7] The focus of the presentation that follows is on the methods used to evaluate research commercialization proposals[8] and then organize counseling schemes for a number of these proposals on their way to reach the market. Our objective is to show how this combined process can be used to develop a longer-term TTO strategy in an academic environment that, despite servicing scientific and technological fields related to agriculture and agrifood, both being vital sectors of the regional and national economy, had not attempted so far to commercially exploit its research, with the exception of a very small number of individual initiatives of its academic staff.

Our approach contributes to a topic that appears to have received limited attention in the technology transfer literature so far, namely, the links that may exist between the assessment of research commercialization proposals and the support that researchers should receive, in order to successfully move through the different steps of exploitation. In this way, the assessment process is used to develop strategic guidelines for the TTO service provision, by adapting it to the main characteristics of research conducted in the parent institution and to the forms of technology transfer assistance needed by its academic community.

---

[5] The reduced TT experience of Greek universities and research centers is discussed in Karra and Tolias (2012). Evidence of limited TT activity in EU countries with moderate to poor innovation performance can be found in European Commission (2016).

[6] In such cases the TTO offer would need to go well beyond IP appraisal by also including a range of business and management consulting services.

[7] This regional development program was based on "smart specialization," a key ingredient of growth policies in most European Union countries for the current programming period 2014–2020 (Foray et al. 2009; JRC 2014).

[8] "Research commercialization proposals" can be synonymous with "invention disclosures," but it has a broader meaning as it also encompasses proposals that may lead to joint actions with industrial or business partners.

The proposed assessment framework may be sufficient for choosing the proposals to be pursued further, except for cases of congestion, i.e., when requirements for supporting research exploitation proposals largely exceed available resources in terms of budget and/or expertise, implying that hard choices need to be made. Simply put, when available resources are not sufficient to develop all the proposals with merit, it does not suffice to simply evaluate each proposal independently of the others, as choosing to pursue one proposal exhausts the supply of limited resources available for the rest. In such cases, the situation may be better served by an explicit mathematical formulation of the underlying decision problem: the optimal allocation of the limited resources available for proposal development. In this work we present such a formulation and discuss how it can be used as an alternative method for selecting research commercialization proposals.

The background section that follows is a review of previous work examining the evolving role of TTOs and the implications for their service offer, along with the methods used for appraising research commercialization proposals. These aspects are crucial for the design and organization of a TTO, especially in environments with modest prior experience in academic entrepreneurship. The proposed assessment framework is presented next, followed by an overview of the innovation and entrepreneurship project in AUA and the key findings when applying our assessment methodology in this context.[9] As shown, the assessment outcome can be used to develop strategic guidelines for the TTO operation. Still, compromises have to be made to address the shortage of resources to support the research commercialization proposals, so we formulate an alternative approach where commercialization proposal selection is treated as a solution to an optimization problem with constraints linked to resource availability. The final section presents conclusions together with suggestions for follow-up research.

Background

The Evolving Role of TTO

The Bayh–Dole Act[10] of 1980 is considered to have opened the way for American universities to engage in technology transfer and to have initiated the subsequent substantial increase in the commercialization of university inventions (Shane 2004). According to Colyvas et al. (2002), the principal effect of Bayh–Dole was to accelerate and strengthen trends that already were occurring with the development of new concepts and techniques in molecular biology, genetic engineering, and computer science that were not only particularly relevant to industrial applications, but have fueled disruptive innovations and entirely new business paradigms. This

---

[9] More detailed presentation of the AUA project and the commercialization proposals can be found in Cartalos et al. (2016).

[10] Public Law 96–517, Patent and Trademark Act Amendments of 1980

increased emphasis on university technology transfer led most universities in the USA to establish TTOs (Friedman and Silberman 2003). Bayh–Dole-type legislation implemented in many European countries in the following years and the increased interest in the university "third mission" pushed academic and research institutions in these countries to implement research commercialization policies and develop TTOs, very often by extending the role of existing industry liaison offices (European Commission 2008 and 2009).

A prevailing view for TTOs' core role is that of assisting their parent institutions in managing their intellectual assets in ways that facilitate their transformation into benefits for the university and society, bridging the gap between research and innovation (OECD 2003, European Commission 2009). Earlier literature has studied TTO productivity and effectiveness as measured by TTO outputs such as the number of patents and licenses, as well as revenue generated from these activities (Thursby et al. 2001; Siegel et al. 2003; Lockett et al. 2003; Degroof and Roberts 2004; Chapple et al. 2005; Phan et al. 2005; Siegel et al. 2007a; Belenzon and Schankerman 2007; Djokovic and Souitaris 2008; Lach and Schankerman 2008; O'Shea et al. 2008). Other studies pointed to the need to take a broader view of technology transfer and, in addition to characteristics related to patenting and licensing, include indicators measuring the effects of TT forms like research collaboration with industrial and business partners (European Commission 2009) or contract research and consulting that are important components of academic engagement (Perkman et al. 2013).

In this context, Bozeman presented the contingent effectiveness model of technology transfer (Bozeman 2000) and its revised version (Bozeman et al. 2015). The model defines different dimensions of technology transfer effectiveness that should be understood in terms of a number of determinants. The effectiveness dimensions comprise the "out-the-door"[11] (looking at direct TT outputs such as patenting results or licensing revenues), the market impact/economic development (encompassing commercial success of transferred technology and effects on regional/national economic growth), the political advantage (effects on the reputation and image of the technology provider), the development of scientific and technical human capital (referring to capacities, networks, and careers), the opportunity cost (cost–benefit analysis of alternative uses of available scientific and technical resources), and public value (linked to broader societal benefits, including sustainable development and quality of life). The determinants comprise characteristics describing the initiators of TT or transfer agents, the way TT is being conducted, the TT object, and the recipient. Bozeman's in-depth analysis highlights the need for adequate logic models to interpret results, raising attention to the issue of attributing the observed effects to their actual sources. It also indicates that a key issue of concern in studying

---

[11] This dimension comprises three subcategories: (a) the "pure out-the-door" where no indication is available that anything has occurred with research except for its transfer, (b) "out-the-door with transfer agent impacts" where evidence is collected on benefits from the activity for the university, (c) "out-the-door with transfer partner impacts," where the benefits to the parties acquiring the technology are examined.

the different dimensions of effects is data availability, as in most cases it is only TTO direct output data that are readily available, which is the case for the earlier studies mentioned above.

More recent studies have examined the effects of the underlying objectives of universities on TTO performance (Warren et al. 2008; Conti and Gaule 2011; Baglieri et al. 2015; Curi et al. 2015). The analysis of Baglieri et al. (2015) shows that different business modes may govern TTO operation depending on the interplay of "third mission" objectives that either push for patenting and licensing agreements or give a stronger focus on serving society. The business model is meant to describe the value proposition of the TTO offer for the two main sets of key actors, the ones involved in value exploration (the internal stakeholders, i.e., the faculty researchers) and those in value exploitation (the external stakeholders, including enterprises and existing and new entrepreneurs). An adequate TTO business model should be the result of a balance between these two stakeholder groups. The study identifies four types of university TTO business models, within a framework defined by the level of targeting external TT recipients from global to local on the one hand and the level of faculty engagement from less to more selective, on the other. Selectivity refers to the quality and prospective value of patents and licenses to which the TTO gives priority. This work highlights the increasing role of university in addressing societal needs, in addition to optimizing research commercialization, and also the fact that such a role will have a strong influence on TTO operational directives and its targets and performance measurement criteria.

Technology transfer is a dynamic process that continuously adapts to new trends in the ways the key innovation actors involved interact, considering that innovation communities are continuously changing networks taking resources from academia, government, and industry (Etzkowitz and Leydesdorff 2000; Carayannis and Campbell 2005, 2009, 2010). Bradley et al. (2013a, b) point out that the traditional linear model of technology transfer needs to be reviewed, taking into account non-linear technology transfer mechanisms that have been developed in recent years. Their work gives thorough descriptions and related literature around such nonlinear mechanisms, including (a) reciprocal relationships among university–industry and government actors (Etzkowitz and Leydesdorff 2000); (b) "multiversity" approaches, in which many subunits and programs of the university interact with companies in many different ways (Kerr, 2001); (c) open innovation approaches, where innovators integrate their ideas, expertise, and skills with those of others outside their organization to deliver commercial products and services using the most effective means possible (Chesbrough 2003); and (d) the collaborative view mechanism developed on the basis of legal and technical infrastructures, allowing participants to engage in knowledge and idea sharing as a joint effort, where the TTO could assume a broker role.[12]

---

[12] Creative Commons is one example of the collaborative view mechanism.

TTO Service Provision

With the development of new technology transfer mechanisms, the TTO has moved from an operational model targeted at collecting royalties and license fees from industry to one of active engagement in the strategic management of IP and deeper involvement in the commercialization process, by assisting the research teams in determining the potential of their discoveries and going through the different stages of business development. The assistance may range from help with applications for external funds to specialized advice in the different stages of business planning (Clarysse et al. 2005), including recruitment of human and financial resources required to create start-up firms and provide company formation expertise (O'Shea et al. 2005).

The above trends in TTOs' increased role are frequently observed in certain European countries, like the UK, the Netherlands, Belgium, and Germany (Aykut and Laffite 2011). A similar trend is also developing in the USA, with the multiplication of proof of concept centers (Bradley et al. 2013b). This evolution has affected key services provided by TTOs to university researchers in ways discussed next, taking into account observations and examples presented in different studies (Campbell 2007; Debackere 2012; Trueman et al. 2014).

Encouraging researchers to disclose inventions or obtaining advice on the different forms to commercially exploit their research receives a high priority in many TTOs, since the sooner an opportunity is identified, the more time the TTO has to assess its potential and develop exploitation plans. Therefore, TTO professionals spend time to inform researchers and incite them to engage into TT actions. The interaction of TTO with academic staff can be largely facilitated by clear rules regarding royalty sharing (Baldini 2010), policies supporting self-licensing (Panagopoulos and Carayannis 2013), and those enabling to link academic promotion to achievements in the area of technology transfer or foreseeing faculty reward systems (Siegel et al. 2007b; Anderson et al. 2007).

IP management involves assessment of research commercialization proposals along several dimensions before deciding which IPR strategy to follow.[13] On the one hand, the assessment should look at the ownership of the proposed technology on the basis of background IPR, persons and organizations involved in the development, and sources of funding. A key question to be addressed is the freedom to operate in the market place without infringing any existing patent rights (Lockett and Wright 2005). On the other hand, a technological assessment should examine the stage of development with respect to the requirements of industrial and business exploitation (Ndonzuau et al. 2002). A precondition for this aspect is having access to appropriate technical expertise; that may be a critical issue, in view of the high degree of specialization in the scientific and technological fields in the different areas of university research and the limited resources of TTOs.

---

[13] TTOs are traditionally involved in patenting, but they may also be called to support other non-patent IP actions, like copyright registration for creative works and industrial design registration.

The TTO should also be in position to assess the market potential of the research exploitation project and estimate its potential commercial value. On this subject, selecting the form of commercialization is a key decision for the research exploitation project. A frequent dilemma for researchers is choosing between licensing the technology to other entrepreneurs and venturing in a start-up firm. According to Gans and Stern (2003), the most appropriate commercialization strategy comes as the result of interactions between the degree to which the technology can be protected from expropriation and the importance of complementary assets needed to have a successful market presence. The two extreme situations are (a) when technology is adequately protected, but other assets that are needed, like production capacity, sales networks, or brand name, require substantial investments, in which case the best strategy is licensing to incumbents; and (b) when the technology is not or cannot be protected, and barriers to market entry are low, in which case it would be preferable to challenge competition by launching a new business. The intermediate situations require further analysis and more refined strategic approaches, taking into account the specific characteristics of the markets and their key players, including their attitudes toward adopting innovative technologies and entering into new partnership schemes.

The TTO should be in position to assist researchers in making the right strategic decisions, which often requires thorough market assessments, identification and analysis of complementary specialized assets needed, and support in the different stages of negotiations in view of creating alliances. Efficiently supporting researchers in these directions also requires the TTO to build links with relevant industry, business, and community stakeholders to facilitate circulation of the university knowledge assets and enhance knowledge co-production with formal and informal research cooperation schemes. In this sense, it might be very useful for TTOs to engage with technology incubators to support spin-offs and research-based firms. There are many examples of TTOs located next to other TT intermediaries like incubators, accelerators, and science or technology parks (Trueman et al. 2014).

The final point in this brief overview of TTO service provision concerns staff skills that are considered to largely contribute to TTO operational efficiency (Lockett and Wright 2005; Bruneel et al. 2010; Bradley et al. 2013a, b; Weckowska 2015). TTO staff should be in position to adapt to the culture and function of academia and industry, especially when working on licensing deals (Powers and McDougall, 2005). Siegel et al. (2003) found that employing staff with experience in the industry sector is beneficial because it enables the TTO to better understand the needs and values of private companies. Siegel et al. (2004) point to the requirement for TTO staff to have marketing, technical, and negotiation skills. Conti and Gaule (2008) report that personnel with a PhD in science facilitate communication between academics and the TTO. Other relevant staff skills include those related to evaluating technological discoveries and inventions, identifying and proposing ways to protect intellectual property rights (IPRs), initiating and maintaining contacts with commercial partners, and establishing new ventures for commercial exploitation of research results (Weckowska 2015). These observations, together with the changing focus of TTO services discussed in the previous section, show that TTO staffing skills related to assessing, disseminating, and commercializing new technologies should be prioritized at least at the same level as those dealing with intellectual property protection.

Assessment of Research Commercialization Proposals

The need to develop an ex ante evaluation framework together with specific criteria to assess the commercialization potential of university research prior to any technology transfer action was pointed out by Heslop et al. (2001). Such a need is linked to assessing the potential of new ideas, ensuring that important opportunities are not missed out, and also obtaining solid evidence for IP management decisions. These aspects are highly relevant to overall TTO performance and efficient use of TTO resources (Bradley et al. 2013a, b). Other early papers on this subject were the ones by Thursby et al. (2001) and Thursby and Thursby (2003), who examined the likelihood of licensing and commercialization of university research from the perspective of the two main actors involved, the producers, i.e., the research teams, and the buyers, i.e., the firms investing in the technologies. An assessment model for emerging environmental technologies was proposed by Jain et al. (2003). Assessment frameworks of university research have been proposed more recently by Rahal and Rabelo (2006) and Mohannak and Samtani (2014).

A common denominator of most of these ex ante assessment studies referred to above was the development of core categories, structured to include criteria and decision factors that are more frequently used by professionals involved in technology transfer. The cloverleaf model of technology transfer, proposed by Heslop et al. (2001), comprises four categories, namely, market readiness, technology readiness, commercial readiness, and management readiness. The model of Mohannak and Samtani (2014) is built along similar lines, a key difference being the replacement of management readiness by social benefits and impacts. The Strategic Technology Evaluation Program (STEP) described in Jaine et al. (2003) is formulated as a synthesis of six evaluation dimensions: technical, process, economic, market, perception, and regulatory/policy. The model developed by Rahal et al. distinguishes the following determinants of technology licensing: institutional, inventor related, technology related, market and commercialization related, and intellectual property related.

From these studies it can be concluded that ex ante assessment of research exploitation prospects should look at different aspects of the technology transfer process. Furthermore, the assessment dimensions can be grouped in the broad categories of (a) technology, (b) market and broader environment conditions, and (c) people and skills available for the commercialization project. The assessment model presented in the next section is based on this high-level grouping of assessment criteria.

TTOs implement different methods to evaluate research commercialization proposals, but only a few of them use a standard evaluation process (Hallam et al.

2011). Different studies report that research commercialization proposals receiving positive evaluations by TTOs are very often the ones considered to be commercially viable, potentially competitive in the market place, and profitable for the university (Jensen and Thursby 2001; Thursby et al. 2001; Thursby and Thursby 2002; Siegel et al. 2003; Litan et al. 2007). However, we could not find any reference on how the evaluation process relates to the TTO service provision, other than indications that the evaluation process can be negatively affected when TTOs have limited resources available (Litan, et al. 2007).

In summary, past studies reveal a range of criteria to be used to assess research commercialization proposals but not if and how such methods may shape TTO working methods and practices. This aspect is important when considering the many different forms of technology transfer that TTOs may currently be engaged in, as discussed in the previous subsections, which can only be determined after due assessment of the commercialization proposal. According to Bradley et al. (2013a, b), serious bottlenecks can be created by the TTO, if the incorrect assumption is made "...(that) the technology transfer process is the same for all innovations and as such, all innovations should be treated the same on their path to market." Put simply, providing advice to a university researcher to create a start-up calls for different qualifications and skills for the TTO than the ones required when assisting a research team to launch university–industry cooperation through research contracts, clustering, or other forms of interaction that facilitate open innovation approaches. Our study contributes to the literature on university TTO by presenting a framework for using the assessment of commercialization proposals to establish the most promising form of commercialization and then the corresponding needs in terms of exploitation support that should guide TTO service provision, as discussed next.

Assessment Methodology

Assessment Criteria

The method used to assess the exploitation potential of research results in this work distinguishes two major assessment dimensions, one for the technology and innovation prospects and one for the commercialization prospects. The latter is made of two groups of criteria, one characterizing the market opportunity and the other the team that manages the commercialization project. The three groups of criteria are shown in Table 1. The model was developed by selecting criteria that are more frequently used in the ex ante evaluation studies referred to in prior sections.

The technology–innovation dimension examines if the technology used enables to reach the goal of the commercial exploitation project. Technology maturity (criterion I.1) relates to how close the project is to being market-ready; this can be

Table 1 The dimensions and criteria used to assess the exploitation potential of research

Dimension of assessment	Group of criteria	Criteria
Technology prospects	I. Technology–innovation	I.1 level of technology maturity
		I.2 added value of proposed innovation
		I.3 relevance to societal/economic needs
		I.4 degree of IP protection
Commercial prospects	II. Market opportunities	II.1 clarity of exploitation objective: Products/services and market segment
		II.2 competitive advantage
		II.3 expected benefits against development effort
	III. Exploitation team	III.1 clarity of the exploitation scheme
		III.2 degree to which key competencies are covered
		III.3 degree of commitment of key research staff

Table 2 The technology readiness levels used in the present work

Technology readiness level	Description
9	Actual system proven in operational environment
8	System complete and qualified
7	System prototype demonstration in operational environment
6	Prototype validation in relevant environment
5	Technology validation in relevant environment
4	Laboratory testing and validation
3	Experimental proof of concept established
2	Applied research: Technology concept and/or application formulated
1	Basic research: Basic principles are observed and reported

determined with technology readiness levels (TRL).[14,15] As shown in Table 2, one of the levels corresponds to the existence of a validated prototype (TRL 6), which is considered to largely increase the commercialization potential (Thursby et al. 2001; Rahal and Rabelo 2006). The innovation added value (criterion I.2) relates to innovativeness in the sense of patentability, by looking to aspects such as originality, non-obviousness as perceived by a domain specialist, and potential usefulness. The question of relevance to concrete societal and economic needs (criterion I.3) is used to assess the level of demand for the expected commercial outcome, as an initial viability check. The degree of IP protection (criterion I.4) examines the existence

---

[14] TRL was introduced by NASA in the 1980s and subsequently adopted by other research institutions (EARTO 2014). The form presented in Table 3 follows the one in European Commission (2015).

[15] A detailed description of how TRL can be used to guide an inventor's strategy in the different steps of the innovation process is presented in Vekinis (2014).

and effectiveness of IPR strategies[16] and in particular the "expropriation" dimension of the framework introduced by Gans and Stern (2003) to select the most appropriate exploitation strategy referred to above.

The *market opportunity* dimension is constructed in correspondence with the assessment criteria of the market group in Heslop et al. (2001) and Mohannak and Samtani (2014). Proposals are assessed for the clarity of their focus in terms of products/services and target groups (criterion II.1) and their competitive advantage compared to existing practices (criterion II.2). A qualitative cost–benefit analysis (criterion II.3) looks into market size and expected benefits, comparing them to the remaining effort in terms of time and resources required for commercialization.

The importance of including the exploitation team in the assessment was stressed in Heslop et al. (2001) and Rahal and Rabelo (2006). The first criterion deals with the degree to which the management scheme has been defined, including the identification and involvement of strategic external partners (criterion III.1). Two further key aspects are assessed: if all necessary business skills are available or, alternatively, if concrete plans in this direction have been formulated (criterion III.2), as well as if the key research personnel assume a role that will safeguard the technological competitiveness of the venture (criterion III.3).

Scoring for each criterion is done with a four-level Likert-type scale (1, to a low, very low extent; 2, to some extent; 3, to a considerable extent; 4, to a high/very high extent), except for criterion I.1, which is marked using the TRL scale of Table 3.

The following indicators can be used to assess overall performance across the two major assessment dimensions:

- Technology Performance Indicator (T): average of normalized scores to criteria related to technology–innovation (Group I)
- Commercialization Performance Indicator (C): average of normalized scores related to market opportunity (Group II) and exploitation team (Group III)

The Assessment Method

The proposed method comprises a technology and a commercialization assessment, followed by a combined analysis that leads to the design of the support to be provided to the research teams. The main steps of the assessment method are presented in Table 3.

The technology assessment is conducted by experts with relevant technical background. The commercialization assessment is made by business experts with experience in technology–innovation financing. All experts produce evaluation

---

[16] In view of the very limited patenting activity in AUA, it was decided not to include criterion I.4 in the technology assessment of research commercialization proposals in the AUA project. All the same, the assessment took into account qualitative aspects concerning IPR and other legal/environmental aspects and formulated recommendations for actions in these fields, as discussed above.

Table 3 Overview of the assessment method

Step	Analysis	Data collection	Outcome
1	Technology assessment by experts – Internal/external – with relevant technical background	Research teams fill in form describing the research result, the exploitation objective, and a roadmap for subsequent actions	Technology assessment report, with summary of findings and scores for technology–innovation criteria
2	Commercialization assessment by experts with business background and experience in innovation financing	Meetings of assessors with research teams to elaborate on the exploitation strategy and roadmap	Commercialization assessment report, with summary of findings, scores for commercialization criteria, and recommendations for next steps, including the areas where support is mostly needed
3	Combined analysis	The TTO collects and examines the evaluation reports produced in steps 1 and 2	Strategy and roadmap for the support to be provided to the research teams

reports using a predefined template with narrative parts providing justification for the scores given in the different criteria, as well as comments and recommendations on other relevant topics.

In their reports, the experts in charge of the technological assessment provide their opinion on the applicability of the proposed technology and the distance still to be covered for the technology to reach the market, followed by estimations on the corresponding time frame and required resources. They further report on current or foreseeable developments in the legal and regulatory environment that may push or hinder the market uptake of the proposed technology, including their judgment on how to best approach IPR protection.

The experts in charge of the commercialization assessment give recommendations on the exploitation strategy to be adopted as well as on the way to proceed with IPR issues, building on the observations made in the technology assessment report. Their recommendations also include the areas of consulting support that should be provided to the research teams.

The combined analysis involves the examination of information and data collected during the previous steps of the assessment in order to determine the kind, direction, and extent of support that the research teams should receive from the TTO. The overall approach takes into account the broader objectives of technology transfer within the parent institution that may lead to different TTO strategies as illustrated in the AUA case study in the following sections.

The AUA Case Study

The Innovation and Entrepreneurship Project in AUA

Founded in 1920, the Agricultural University of Athens has a long track record of scientific contributions in agricultural and economic development. Current research topics include biotechnological applications in agriculture, biological farming, food quality and safety, water resource conservation, and alternative energy sources.

The research community counts 429 members as of May 2014, of which 179 are permanent staff, organized in 6 departments and 42 laboratories. In the period from 2008 to 2012, the research output was 1203 papers in peer-reviewed journals,[17] with an annual production of about 300 papers per year. During this period, the relative citation impact accounting for all university publications in their respective fields was equal to 1.00. The major fields with the highest relative citation impact were engineering and technology (1.23) and agricultural sciences (1.09).[18] An extensive patent search revealed that in the period from 2002 to 2013, there have been 28 patent applications, corresponding to 0.0145 applications per researcher per year (Drivas et al. 2016), which shows very little involvement of research staff in patenting activities.

The innovation and entrepreneurship (I&E) project referred to in the introduction had the objective to enhance commercial exploitation of the research produced in AUA. The project objective was in fact synonymous with testing the prospects of an ad hoc TTO; prior to this initiative, there was no organized approach to technology transfer in AUA. The project followed a staged approach, comprising:

- An internal promotion campaign to generate commercialization proposals from the different research teams
- The assessment of these proposals with regard to their commercialization potential
- The design and provision of customized support for the researchers to pursue their attempts until the launch of a commercial operation

The project ran from December 2013 to November 2015. During the first 6 months, the research teams were informed of the project-specific objectives. Researchers, both permanent and nonpermanent staff, were invited to prepare proposals for the exploitation of their work, which would be evaluated. They would then receive training and consulting support through the different stages leading to commercialization.

The information sessions were attended by 80% of the permanent staff, which indicates a high degree of interest of the research community in the topics of

---

[17] In this period there have been 1, 69, and 130 papers from AUA in, respectively, the top 1%, 10%, and 25% most influential.

[18] Data on number of publications, number of citations, and relative citation impact are taken from Sahini (2014).

innovation and entrepreneurship. At the set deadline, 42 proposals were submitted.[19] Overall, 23% of permanent staff participated in at least one proposal. To put this number into perspective, in their study of disclosures at six US universities over 17 years, Thursby and Thursby (2007) find that on average just 7% of faculty members disclosed per year, whereas 80% of faculty either never disclosed or disclosed only once in the seventeen year period. The much higher number of proposals created conditions of congestion, considering the limited funds and time available for the project. Therefore, choosing a robust method to assess the commercialization potential of proposals and organizing efficient training and consulting for the most promising cases turned out to be critical conditions of success for the project.

The average size of the teams was 2.4 researchers, whereas exploitation teams with more than two members were recorded in just about three cases out of 10. In only three cases, proposals came from collaborations involving more than one of the 42 laboratories, indicating limited interactions across different thematic fields. A distinctive feature of research staff that submitted exploitation proposals was that they had 1.6 times more research contracts than the university average, indicating that participants of the I&E project were much more active, and/or more efficient, in obtaining research funding. This is consistent with the observation in Colyvas et al. (2002) that researchers involved in successful technology transfer cases are in general those actively involved in scientific or business networks and collaborations.

Organization of Technology and Commercialization Assessments

In view of the limited experience of AUA in the field of research commercialization, special attention was given to the following organizational aspects:

Supporting Researchers to Prepare Application Forms The researchers had on average about 3–4 months to obtain information about the program and prepare their applications. This was a compromise between (a) offering sufficient time for researchers to prepare comprehensive proposals and (b) ensuring later on a long enough period of time for the support to be provided to the selected proposals within the fixed, two-year duration of the project. To further facilitate the process, researchers had access to full support by the project team that provided comments and suggested additions to be made to submitted drafts.

Choosing the Evaluators The technology assessors were experts who, on the grounds of their long involvement in similar thematic fields in industry and/or

---

[19] In two cases, researchers that each submitted two proposals with overlapping commercial targets followed the recommendation of the technology evaluators to merge their submissions into one giving a stronger commercialization potential. As a result, the number of proposals that followed the complete assessment cycle came to a total of 40.

academia, had the capacity to formulate expert opinion and judgment on the criteria involved in the technological assessment. Each research team was asked to provide up to three potential experts for this purpose. The final choice on which expert to involve for each project was made by the project management, taking into account specific profiles and availability, in an effort to have a balanced representation of internal/external and university–industry experts. The commercial assessors were experts with a combined business and technology background and substantial experience in high-tech and innovation financing. The three experts that undertook the commercial assessment had also previously worked with university teams in research exploitation projects in Greece and in other European countries.

Optimizing the Interaction of Assessors with the Research Teams The technology assessment was conducted on the basis of information provided in the application forms. The possibility existed for the experts to ask for additional information through email. Similarly, the researchers could ask for clarifications on the conclusions of the evaluation reports. In most such cases, consensus was reached prior to the conclusion of the assessment. The commercial assessment was actually an interactive process, as during the assessment meetings the research team and the assessor examined together different strategic options, as well as the different ways that the research results could be exploited. An important outcome of these meetings was the identification of the areas of support that would be required for the commercialization project to succeed. The underlying objective of the whole assessment process was to give concrete feedback and ideas to the researchers as to how they could benefit by including commercialization aspects in their research.

Technology and Commercialization Assessment Results

A brief overview of the assessment results is provided in this section. A more detailed presentation can be found in Cartalos et al. (2016). The proposals covered different forms of commercial exploitation that can be grouped into the following main categories:

- Research and development (R&D) services for private and public organizations, meaning services that can enhance process, product, and service deliveries of their recipients
- Services related to methods, techniques, and tools for accreditation and certification (A&C)
- Products and services in the form of commercial offers to enterprises (B2B) and consumers (B2C)

Indicative results of the technology assessment for the different forms of exploitation are presented in Table 4. Put together, proposals that intend to commercialize R&D and A&C services account for more than 60% of total proposals submitted. Such proposals were generally based on more mature technologies, as indicated by

Table 4 Characteristics of technology assessment for the proposed exploitation forms

	R&D services	Accreditation–certification	Products	Services
Number of proposals	18	9	7	8
Average time from project initiation (years)	4.88	4.63	5.43	7.38
Average TRL	6.00	5.78	5.71	5.50
Proposals with the highest innovation added value	10	3	3	4
Proposals responding to economic and societal challenges to a high extent	8	5	5	6

their higher average TRL compared to the one for proposals for products and services, although these TRL levels were reached in shorter development times than the ones for commercial products and services. But projects leading to commercial products and services presented a higher innovation added value and were assessed to better adapt to economic and societal challenges, suggesting increased commercial exploitation prospects. However, the development effort still needed for products and services to reach the market was substantially higher than that for R&D and A&C services. Put together, these observations tend to show that the general research approach in AUA leads more naturally to exploitation forms through R&D and A&C services, and the fewer teams that engage in research leading to commercial products or services have a longer and more resource-intensive road to follow.

The average scores for the commercialization prospects criteria shown in Fig. 1 imply the following general characteristics for the research exploitation proposals:

- The exploitation objective and corresponding target groups have been clearly defined in most cases (high score in criterion II.1: clarity of the exploitation objective).
- Very often the research teams plan to be heavily involved in the commercial exploitation (high score in criterion III.3: degree of commitment of key research staff).
- Key competencies needed for the exploitation project are generally available (high score in criterion III.2: degree to which key competencies are covered).

However, most research teams have not worked out in sufficient detail the scheme that will undertake the exploitation project (low score in criterion III.1: clarity of the exploitation scheme), which, in many cases, means that business collaborations have still to be identified and/or developed with external partners.

The characteristics of the commercial assessment vary across the different forms of commercial exploitation. The proposals for developing products obtain higher scores in the market (Group II) criteria when based on advanced technologies, but obtain lower marks in the team (Group III) criteria because in most cases complementary business skills are needed, especially in everyday management, commercial and operation planning, product promotion, and customer service. The proposals

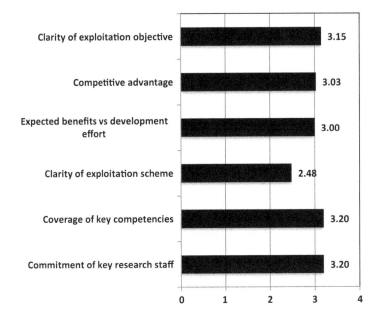

Fig. 1 Average scores for the commercialization criteria (Groups II and III of Table 1)

for services have a weaker competitive advantage and lower expected commercial benefits due to limited knowledge of commercial practices in the target markets. In both cases, considerable marketing investment would be needed. For example, some proposed software applications that can be offered as products or services related to monitoring the health and well-being of individuals have a strong scientific background and are backed up by extensive validation studies. A key challenge is to convince potential clients of their increased capabilities and scientific and technological added value compared to existing competitive services that have largely invested in obtaining large market shares with emphasis on user friendliness and reputation.

The projects offering R&D services are based on competitive, state-of-the-art technologies. A major difficulty is that firms that could ask for these services usually adopt cost reduction policies, especially in sectors such as farming, aquaculture, and horticulture, under the current adverse economic situation in Greece. Such business strategies give very little priority to the development of value-added products, which seriously reduces the demand for value-added R&D services. In a number of such cases, the teams were advised to consider international markets with appropriate strategic alliances. Proposals for A&C services have average market prospects due to the additional cost that these services create for industries and businesses. In many cases, relevant legislation would be needed to enforce or give incentive to firms to seek for such services. Examples of such legislation would include measures to control the origin, hygiene, and sanitary conditions of raw material used in commercial products.

A common characteristic for R&D and A&C services was the lower level of commitment for researchers to be involved in commercialization, due to unclear market prospects, but also because research teams often gave higher priority to their academic work. The scores for coverage of necessary skills were, on the contrary, higher than those for commercial products and services due to the fact that R&D and A&C services were actually very close to the research work of the teams. In most cases it was proposed that the R&D and A&C services be provided through contracts between interested parties and the university, but it was pointed out that the existing framework needed to be adapted to allow for increased operational flexibility and a client-centric approach in the different aspects of service provision.

Combined Analysis: Organization of Commercialization Support

The combined analysis of the technology and commercialization assessments was used to define and streamline the support to be provided to the research teams. As already mentioned, the key aspects of the exercise concerned determining the kind, direction, and extent of support.

The kind of support depends on the main needs to be addressed, as these were identified during the assessment. In the case of AUA, two broad categories of exploitation emerged, R&D and A&C services on the one hand and commercial products and services on the other, each having its own support requirements. The characteristics of the TTO service offerings discussed earlier were taken into account, but they had to be adapted to each case as discussed next.

For proposals targeting the exploitation of R&D and A&C services, the main need for support was in identifying the most suitable business and industrial sectors for each commercialization proposal and the ways these sectors could be best approached. The emphasis was on the different modes of cooperation with external partners, taking into account opportunities for contract research, joint technological developments, or strategic research partnerships with enterprises and technology-intensive clusters. In this context, it was very useful to examine potential synergistic effects of combining the service offers of different proposals and work out suitable schemes in cooperation with the research teams. The other area of support concerned increasing the efficiency of service provision within the current institutional environment of the university.

For proposals that developed commercial products and services, the support primarily concerned conducting the competition analysis and picking the best strategies with regard to prevailing market conditions, in accordance with the framework developed by Gans and Stern (2003). Having made such choices, the support was then directed toward covering operational matters related to licensing or setting up a new firm. For the latter, the TTO undertook the development of business plans, together with associated staffing and marketing plans.

In all cases, special attention was given to provide consulting on legal matters to researchers, with seminars and on-the-job training essentially on knowledge protection issues. Legal advice was organized around fundamental aspects, such as scientific integrity or explaining the criterion of non-obviousness in patent law, and specialized services, such as patentability prerequisites, ability to streamline prior art, defining a patent strategy and claims, and patenting strategy.

From an operational point of view, consulting was organized around the following areas:

- Strategy consulting, encompassing strategic planning, marketing strategy, partner search, alliances, and funding sources
- Business consulting, having as components business mentoring, feasibility studies, market research, financial analysis, and preparation of detailed business plans
- Legal consulting, with emphasis on defining and implementing adequate IP protection strategies

Accordingly, a pool of experts was created following an open call for expression of interest, specifying skills and experience of consultants in each category of services. Additional criteria were used to distinguish consultant backgrounds that would better fit to the requirements of each of the above commercialization routes.

As previously indicated, due to the increased participation of AUA researchers in the I&E project, a much higher than expected number of proposals were received, creating a problem of resource availability for the provision of support. In fact, as shown in Table 8, the required volume of support largely exceeded the budgeted amount (expressed in person-months) for all three consulting areas.

The situation called for a compromise that took account of the following considerations. The overall objective of the I&E project was to instigate a new, more entrepreneurial approach in AUA, in line with the "third mission." One way to reach this objective would be to concentrate the limited resources available on the projects with the highest commercialization prospects, in order to produce "quick wins," meaning cases of successful research commercialization serving as prominent examples showing the way to other research teams. Another approach would be to distribute resources more evenly, so that a larger part of the academic community could have hands-on experience with research commercialization.

Under these circumstances, it was decided to adopt an intermediate solution consisting of providing support in proportion to the overall commercialization potential of each proposal. The way to proceed was determined by examining the diagram shown in Fig. 2, where the commercial performance indicator is plotted against the technology performance indicator.[20]

The horizontal and vertical lines that cross the median values of the two indicators form four quartiles that group proposals with the following characteristics:

---

[20] The numerical values for the technology and commercial performance indicators for each proposal are given in Table 8 in the annex, together with the support needed for the exploitation in the three broad categories of consulting services presented above.

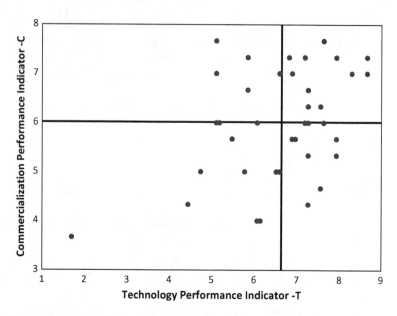

Fig. 2 Plot of commercialization versus technology performance indicator for the proposals assessed in the AUA program

- High technological and commercialization prospects (HT-HC): the 17 proposals in the upper right section
- High technological and low commercialization prospects (HT-LC): the seven proposals in the lower right section
- Low technological and high commercialization prospects (LT-HC): the seven proposals in the upper left section
- Low technological and commercialization prospects (LT-LC): the nine proposals in the lower left section

The direction and extent of support were developed taking into account the positioning of proposals in the different quartiles. The proposals in the HT – HC quartile having the highest exploitation potential for short-medium term results received the required support in full.[21] For the other cases, the support was organized in a way to reach intermediate objectives on the way to commercialization with the remaining available resources, as follows:

- The proposals in the HT-LC quartile needed to strengthen their commercialization prospects. The support that was offered essentially comprised business mentoring and market research to better understand market needs and therefore adapt

---

[21] It should be mentioned that although proposals for commercial products and services corresponded to a small fraction of the total number, their share in the HT-HC quartile was the largest among the other forms. This means that despite the general research approach of AUA pushing for commercialization of R&D and A&C services, the few research teams that work on applications leading to commercial products and services had stronger chances of success.

the commercialization project accordingly. Support also comprised creating links with potential business and industrial partners, in order to promote the technologies, but also to enable the research teams to come closer to actual market needs, so as to test alternative areas of application for their technological solutions.

- The proposals in the LT-HC quartile had good prospects of commercial exploitation, but it was necessary to further develop technology readiness. In a number of cases, the proposals required additional investment in R&D. The support was organized toward obtaining funding for this purpose through different channels, including recommending and promoting a search of industrial partners willing to participate in joint development.
- The proposals in the LT-LC quartile did not show any clear exploitation potential. The recommendation to researchers was to follow the general purpose seminars on research commercialization of the I&E project and to interact with the other research teams, giving them the opportunity to investigate new ideas with commercialization prospects.

By the end of the project, five research teams were in the process of launching concrete research commercialization actions.[22] It may be argued that with a different support strategy, for instance, concentrating only on the highest-ranking proposals, more projects could have increased their readiness to commercialization, but at the same time, a smaller number of AUA staff would have received some kind of assistance that could in turn initiate future innovation projects. These questions are linked to decisions made at a higher level and dealing with the broader position of the university with regard to encouraging staff involvement in technology transfer. The work of Baglieri et al. (2015) that examined the influence of faculty engagement on TTO performance shows that, depending on such decisions, very different TTO business models are put in place, leading to very different performance characteristics.

The proposed quartile approach is an empirical method enabling a compromise to be made among the competing objectives of (1) concentrating on the best proposals and (2) addressing a larger number of researchers. Applying it to the AUA case study illustrates the usefulness of such a formal analytical framework for evaluating the different research commercialization proposals, as it allows the TTO to adapt its services to the actual needs of the research community. At the same time, it also demonstrates that resource availability is a significant parameter for TTO service provision, especially when it comes to deciding the direction and extent of support to be provided.

---

[22] The work of Vinig and Lips (2015) provides grounds to claim that the performance of the ad hoc TTO of the I&E project was within the research exploitation potential of the University. Vinig and Lips (2015) state that technology transfer performance of a university should be measured against the potential for technology transfer, which they propose to link to the organization's research output. In their method, the actual valorization output (AVP), being the sum of patents, spin-offs, and licensing agreements on a yearly basis, is compared to the potential valorization projects (PVP), taken to be equal to the total number of journal publications times a valorization coefficient that is assumed to range from 1% to 3%. Technology transfer performance is good (poor), if AVP is larger (lower) than PVP. In view of the current journal publication figures of AUA, the PVP would range from 3 to 9 projects achieving their exploitation target.

Optimization as an Aid for Selecting, Prioritizing, and Planning Support for Research Exploitation Proposals

TTO resource availability is an issue to consider in its own right, given that TTOs operate on budgeting assumptions that may underestimate their service demand. The AUA project is a particular example of a more general case, where a university may decide to raise the importance of its "third mission" that is very likely to increase the demand for technology transfer services and therefore create situations of TTO resource shortage.

In this section we develop a more rigorous approach designed to specifically address resource constraints when designing the TTO service offer. We first present a formal optimization framework for selecting proposals without exceeding the limited resources currently at hand and also illustrate its use as an aid in planning for future resource procurement and prioritizing the proposals selected for further development. We then illustrate its use by applying it to the AUA case study.

The General Optimization Framework

Let each Proposal P_i, $i = 1, \ldots, N$ be defined by the estimate $P_i = \left(c_i, R_i^k\right)$, where:
c_i = The objective function weight for proposal P_i, $c_i \geq 0$ and
R_i^k = The kth ($k = 1, \ldots, K$) resource needed to develop proposal $P_i, R_i^k \geq 0$
and let:
R^k = The total k^{th} resource ($k = 1, \ldots, K$) available for all proposals
Then, our resource allocation problem becomes the integer (binary) programming problem, BINRA.

$$\text{BINRA} : \max_{x_i} \sum c_i x_i$$

subject to $\sum R_i^k x_i \leq R^k, k = 1, \ldots, K$ (k^{th} resource constraint)
$x_i \in \{0, 1\}$ (0 = proposal not selected, 1 = proposal selected)
Relaxing the binary constraints to $0 \leq x_i \leq 1$ yields a closely related linear program approximation LPRA.

$$\text{LPRA} : \max_{x_i} \sum c_i x_i$$

subject to $\sum R_i^k x_i \leq R^k, k = 1, \ldots, K$ (k^{th} resource constraint)
$0 \leq x_i \leq 1$ (0 = proposal not selected, 1 = proposal selected)

Note that fractional solutions $0 \leq x_i \leq 1$ correspond to proposals on the cusp, and these may be selected or not based on proximity to 0 or 1 or other considerations.

While the binary problem formulation is a more precise representation of the decision problem we face, linear programs (LPs) present some significant advantages: they are inherently easier to solve (LPRA is in fact a weighted distribution LP, a subclass for which there are particularly efficient algorithms readily available), and additionally, standard LP duality theory may be used to provide useful insights for the decision makers through a sensitivity analysis.

For example, at an optimal solution, the resulting dual multipliers allow us to rank all the proposals according to relative desirability, taking into account their marginal contribution to the objective function, adjusted by the cost of resources they are expected to consume. For each proposal P_i, we compute D_i, the critical value of the objective function coefficient i at an optimal solution, as $D_i = c_i - \sum_k \lambda_k R_i^k$, where λ_k = optimal dual multiplier for the kth resource constraint. Note that:

$D_i \geq 0 \; \forall \; i$ where $x_i = 1$
$D_i \leq 0 \; \forall \; i$ where $x_i = 0$
$D_i = 0 \; \forall \; i$ where $0 < x_i < 1$

And also:

$x_i = 1 \; \forall \; i$ where $D_i > 0$
$x_i = 0 \; \forall \; i$ where $D_i < 0$

Alternatively, whenever x_i is positive at an optimal solution, D_i may also be interpreted as the amount by which the corresponding objective function weight c_i can be reduced before x_i is forced to zero at the new solution (while all other parameters remain unchanged). Similarly, whenever x_i is zero at an optimal solution, the corresponding D_i may be interpreted as the amount by which the corresponding objective function weight c_i has to be increased before x_i is forced to become positive at the new solution (while all other parameters remain unchanged).

Furthermore, at an optimal solution, the resulting dual multipliers of the tight constraints, $\lambda_k > 0$, may be used to identify the most costly resource shortages; the higher the multiplier, the more costly the shortage.

Finally, since all the parameters defining our problems are estimates and cannot be determined exactly, stochastic extensions to LPRA would be a natural way to deal with this uncertainty. For example, when many experts evaluate each of the proposals under consideration, one could use the variance in the experts' assessments to define probability distributions. Stochastic extensions are beyond our current scope, but it should be noted that the LP structure lends itself rather readily to addressing such considerations in a computationally amenable setting.

The AUA Case Study as an Optimization Problem

We now illustrate the optimization approach by applying it to the AUA case study. We identify three different types of consulting services in the TTO offer:

$S=$ total strategic consultant person-months available for all proposals
$B=$ total business consultant person-months available for all proposals
$L=$ total legal consultant person-months available for all proposals

We further denote each proposal P_i, $i = 1, ..., N$ by the following estimates:

$$P_i = (T_i, C_i, S_i, B_i, L_i),$$

where: $T_i=$ average technology performance index for proposal i, $T_i \geq 0$

$C_i=$ average commercialization performance index for proposal i, $C_i \geq 0$
$S_i=$ total strategic consultant person-months to develop proposal i, $S_i \geq 0$
$B_i=$ total business consultant person-months to develop proposal i, $B_i \geq 0$
$L_i=$ total legal consultant person-months to develop proposal i, $L_i \geq 0$

Finally, let's say that «b» units of the technology performance index are judged roughly equivalent to «a» units of the commercialization performance index (where a, b $\geq$ 0). Our resource allocation problem then becomes the integer (binary) programming problem, BINAU(a,b):

$$\text{BINAU}(a,b): \max_{x_i} a\sum T_i x_i + b\sum C_i x_i = \sum (aT_i + bC_i) x_i$$

subject to:

$\sum S_i x_i \leq S$ (strategic consultant constraint)
$\sum B_i x_i \leq B$ (business consultant constraint)
$\sum L_i x_i \leq L$ (legal consultant constraint)
$x_i \in \{0, 1\}$ (0 = proposal not selected; 1 = proposal selected)

Relaxing the binary constraints to $0 \leq x_i \leq 1$ yields a closely related linear program approximation, LPAU(a,b).

$$\text{LPAU}(a,b): \max_{x_i} a\sum T_i x_i + b\sum C_i x_i = \sum (aT_i + bC_i) x_i$$

subject to:

$\sum S_i x_i \leq S$ (strategic consultant constraint)
$\sum B_i x_i \leq B$ (business consultant constraint)
$\sum L_i x_i \leq L$ (legal consultant constraint)
$0 \leq x_i \leq 1$ (0 = proposal not selected; 1 = proposal selected)

For illustration purposes, we chose a = b = 1/2 depicting the case where technology and commercialization were valued equally. The values shown in Table 8 for the technology and commercialization performance indicators and those for strategic, business, and legal consultant effort are taken for each proposal. The values used for the constraints are those corresponding to total resources available for each consulting area.

The resulting integer programming problem was solved using a variant of the branch-and-bound algorithm readily available in many optimization packages; for a general description and examples, see Clausen (1999). Table 5 presents the results of solving BINAU(1/2,1/2).

It is worthwhile pointing out that the optimal solution is largely in agreement with the choices made using the quartile approach: proposals located in the HT-HC quartile were selected at a significantly higher rate than those located in the LT-HC quartile, which in turn were selected at a higher rate than those located in the HT-LC quartile; proposals located in the LT-LC quartile were not selected at all. However, the solution to BINAU(1/2,1/2) is not identical to the choices made using the quartile approach: certain proposals located in the HT-HC quartile (x01, x20, x26, and x16) were not selected despite their having relatively high commercialization and technology indices; they simply were expected to consume comparatively too many costly resources. In their place it was deemed more beneficial to exploit certain proposals from the LT-HC quartile (x33, x38, x41 and x02) and also the HT-LC quartile (x04 and x30).

Next we turn our attention to the closely related LPAU(1/2,1/2). The linear program was solved using a variant of the simplex method, again readily available in many optimization packages. For a complete description, see, for example, Dantzig (1963). Table 6 presents the optimal solution.

Comparing the solution of LPAU(1/2,1/2) to the closely related BINAU(1/2,1/2), it should be apparent that the two optimal solutions are practically identical. Note also that, at the optimum, the value of the optimal objective function of BINAU(1/2,1/2) is slightly lower than that of LPAU(1/2,1/2); that is to be expected as the LP constraints represent a relaxation of the integer constraints. As far as the non-integer decision variables go, at the LPAU(1/2,1/2) optimal, x10, x13, and x11 are the proposals on the cusp, but most of the proposals selected at the optimum of BINAU(1/2,1/2) are identical to those selected at the optimum of LPAU(1/2,1/2). Once again proposals located in the HT-HC quartile were selected at a significantly higher rate than those located in the LT-HC quartile, which in turn were selected at a higher rate than those located in the HT-LC quartile; proposals located in the LT-LC quartile were not selected at all.

But the real value of the LP lies in the sensitivity analysis and the insights it offers for TTO resource planning. The dual multipliers for the three resource constraints calculated at the optimal solution take the following values:

- Strategic consultant month constraint $S = 0.238$
- Business consultant month constraint $B = 0.885$
- Legal consultant month constraint $L = 2.359$

First, we note that all three constraints are tight, with multipliers larger than 0. It is therefore clear that all three resources, strategic, business, and legal consulting,

Table 5 Results obtained by solving problem BINAU(1/2,1/2): optimal solution 130.148

Proposal	x_i	Quartile	Quartile pick %
x23_24	1.000	HT-HC	76.47%
x05	1.000		
x01	0.000		
x07_08	1.000		
x20	0.000		
x26	0.000		
x10	1.000		
x32	1.000		
x13	1.000		
x40	1.000		
x19	1.000		
x37	1.000		
x16	0.000		
x36	1.000		
x14	1.000		
x42	1.000		
x28	1.000		
x02	1.000	LT-HC	57.14%
x38	1.000		
x41	1.000		
x15	0.000		
x33	1.000		
x39	0.000		
x11	0.000		
x22	0.000	HT-LC	28.57%
x30	1.000		
x17	0.000		
x03	0.000		
x27	0.000		
x04	1.000		
x34	0.000		
x06	0.000	LT-LC	0.00%
x21	0.000		
x12	0.000		
x09	0.000		
x18	0.000		
x25	0.000		
x31	0.000		
x35	0.000		
x29	0.000		
Proposals to be developed	19.000		

Table 6 Results obtained by solving problem LNPU(1/2,1/2): optimal solution 133.679

Proposal	x_i	Quartile	Quartile pick %
x23_24	1.000	HT-HC	75.70%
x05	1.000		
x01	0.000		
x07_08	1.000		
x20	0.000		
x26	0.000		
x10	0.947		
x32	1.000		
x13	0.921		
x40	1.000		
x19	1.000		
x37	1.000		
x16	0.000		
x36	1.000		
x14	1.000		
x42	1.000		
x28	1.000		
x02	1.000	LT-HC	60.15%
x38	1.000		
x41	1.000		
x15	0.000		
x33	1.000		
x39	0.000		
x11	0.211		
x22	0.000	HT-LC	28.57%
x30	1.000		
x17	0.000		
x03	0.000		
x27	0.000		
x04	1.000		
x34	0.000		
x06	0.000	LT-LC	0.00%
x21	0.000		
x12	0.000		
x09	0.000		
x18	0.000		
x25	0.000		
x31	0.000		
x35	0.000		
x29	0.000		
Proposals to be developed	19.079		

Table 7 Critical values of the objective function coefficient Di at the optimal solution

Proposal	x_i	D_i	Quartile
x23_24	1.000	2.035	HT-HC
x05	1.000	4.465	
x01	0.000	−1.085	
x07_08	1.000	3.395	
x20	0.000	−0.932	
x26	0.000	−1.341	
x10	0.947	0.000	
x32	1.000	2.821	
x13	0.921	0.000	
x40	1.000	1.865	
x19	1.000	3.225	
x37	1.000	1.326	
x16	0.000	−0.291	
x36	1.000	1.716	
x14	1.000	2.910	
x42	1.000	2.673	
x28	1.000	3.462	
x02	1.000	0.039	LT-HC
x38	1.000	0.662	
x41	1.000	0.532	
x15	0.000	−1.621	
x33	1.000	1.195	
x39	0.000	−1.257	
x11	0.211	0.000	
x22	0.000	−1.527	HT-LC
x30	1.000	1.901	
x17	0.000	−2.305	
x03	0.000	−0.791	
x27	0.000	−2.284	
x04	1.000	2.267	
x34	0.000	−1.054	
x06	0.000	−3.650	LT-LC
x21	0.000	−5.582	
x12	0.000	−0.040	
x09	0.000	−2.174	
x18	0.000	−2.014	
x25	0.000	−4.943	
x31	0.000	−2.217	
x35	0.000	−6.477	
x29	0.000	−4.403	

are in short supply, and increasing any of the three is expected to have a positive impact on the overall objective of supporting the highest number of good proposals.

Comparing the relative size of the corresponding multipliers, it also becomes immediately apparent that the most costly shortage, by far, is in legal consulting, followed by business consulting. Increasing the available supply of legal consultant time is expected to have the most pronounced effect in increasing the number of commercialization projects that can be supported and should therefore be a focal point for concerted effort in the future. Conversely, increasing the supply of strategic consulting, while still helpful, is expected to have a much smaller relative impact. The analysis can, therefore, be used to find the mix of consulting resources that enables the TTO to support the highest number of good proposals at a fixed consulting budget.

In Table 7, the above values of the dual multipliers calculated at the optimal solution have been used to compute the critical values of the objective function coefficient i at the optimal solution, D_i, described above. These values may be of practical use, as they allow for ranking and therefore setting priorities for the proposals being evaluated. They are based on the objective value estimate of each proposal, but they also reflect the scarcity and implied cost of the resources they consume. Thus, for example, x05 is the most desirable proposal to be exploited, followed by x28, x07_08, and x19; all of them are located in the HT-HC quartile. Conversely, x35, x21, x25, x29, and x06 are the least desirable proposals to be exploited, all located in the LT-LC quartile.

The critical values also provide deeper insight for the proposals located in the HT-HC quartile (x01, x20, x26, and x16) that were not selected in lieu of certain proposals selected to be exploited despite belonging to the LT-HC quartile (x33, x38, x41, and x02) and also the HT-LC quartile (x04 and x30). In some of these cases, the critical value differences of those substituted were actually significantly higher than those chosen to be omitted – compare, for example, the difference in the critical values of x33, x30, and x04 (selected from the LT-HC and HT-LC quartile) to those of x01, x26, and x20 (from the HT-HC quartile, but chosen to be omitted).

Conclusions

Technology transfer creates research connections between university and external stakeholders that lead into research commercialization, innovation, and broader economic and societal benefits. TTOs are instrumental in shaping and enhancing these connections within the frame of the university's "third mission." TTOs can be developed in a variety of ways depending on the broader strategic objectives of their parent institutions, but in all cases it is essential to align their service offer to the needs of the academic community they intend to serve.

In our work, we developed a framework to assess and support commercialization proposals of university researchers and then tested it in an academic environment with very limited prior experience with research commercialization. The assessment method used jointly looked at the technological and commercial prospects of the projects. With the proposed framework, it was possible to address different aspects relating to the design and operation of a technology transfer structure.

As shown, the TTO should be in position to support two broad commercialization routes, one comprising R&D services to external organizations, including those relating to accreditation and certification, and the other dealing with developing commercial products and services. Each commercialization route has its own requirements in terms of support that need to be addressed by the TTO service offer. For the former, the support should focus on the different modes of cooperation with external partners, exploiting opportunities for contract research, joint technological developments, or strategic research partnerships with enterprises and technology-intensive clusters. Another important direction is increasing the efficiency of service provision within the current institutional environment of the university. For the latter, the service offer should include developing business strategies together with operational matters related to licensing or setting up a new firm. In all cases there is a need for legal consulting with a focus on selecting and implementing suitable knowledge protection strategies.

The proposed framework can be used to define the kind and extent of support the research commercialization projects should receive. However, a situation that may frequently occur is the one where there are not enough available resources to support all projects, requiring straightforward methods to resolve the problem of allocating these limited resources. Such methods can be elaborated by referring to broader policies of the parent institution with regard to technology transfer and in particular those related to faculty engagement in technology transfer, provided such policies exist. In the particular case considered, an empirical method was developed as a compromise between two objectives with opposite effects, namely, choosing to support the best projects on the one hand and providing support to the largest possible number of researchers, on the other. The projects having the highest scores in the technology and commercialization assessments have allocated all resources needed. For the others, intermediate objectives have been defined that could be reached with assistance from remaining resources. In this way it was possible to concentrate on the potential exploitation champions, but also to offer guidance to proposals with lower market prospects and/or less mature technology basis. The broader information and motives provided to an enlarged population of researchers, not just those who have developed concrete exploitation plans, in order for them to take into account innovative entrepreneurship approaches in their work was felt to be one of the major benefits of the I&E project.

As the resource shortage can be encountered in many situations of practical importance, a more rigorous approach was designed, involving the explicit mathematical formulation of a decision problem subject to constraints, reflecting the limited number of resources available to cover the different areas of consulting support.

To our knowledge, optimization techniques have not been used so far in the context of TTO service organization and resource planning. The solution to this optimization problem gives choices for the projects to be fully supported that are very close to the ones of the empirical approach. The advantage of the optimization approach is that it can be used to further examine the effect each constraint has on the optimal solution. Such sensitivity analysis can be very useful for developing TTO staffing plans.

Our work is particularly relevant for inexperienced TT structures that are likely to be developed as a response to academic budget cuts, quite frequently in environments with reduced prior knowledge and practice in technology transfer. The proposed method enables TTO management to develop evidence-based guidelines to organize the TTO offerings and in particular the kind of services and the extent of support that are needed. More experienced TTOs can also benefit from the proposed framework, as new technology transfer practices are being developed, involving novel public–private contractual research schemes, clustering, and joint ventures of public research organizations with external parties. One topic for future research concerns the kind of support required for researchers to better engage in these new forms of technology transfer that may lead TTOs to redefine their role and their service offer accordingly.

Another topic relates to using optimization problems as a decision tool to address TTO resource shortage. With this approach, preference is given to proposals with merit that consume less resources, implying that more proposals with merit could be supported, by eliminating the ones that are very resource demanding. While the optimization problem is shown to give results that are very similar to the empirical model, there is a need to validate the usefulness of the approach in practice. An interesting variant would be to restate the mathematical formulation explicitly in financial terms. This would require introducing budget constraints needed for proof of concept phases, as well as restating the objective function to reflect expected financial benefits stemming from the commercialization projects. Both aspects are currently being taken into account in a qualitative way, as components to consider in the assessment criteria. Including them explicitly in the formulation of the mathematical problem is not a trivial task, especially for the benefits, as it would require quantifying very different types of effects (such as revenues for the university, the TTO, or for new or existing enterprises that are directly affected by the commercialization project) that, moreover, may occur at different time scales.

Annex: Data from the Assessment of Research Commercialization Proposals

Table 8 provides the data used for the quartile method in Fig. 2 and the solution of the optimization problem.

Table 8 Values taken for T, C, S, B, and L for each commercialization proposal

Proposal	T	C	S	B	L	Quartile
x23_24	8.67	7.33	4.00	3.00	1.00	HT-HC
x05	8.67	7.00	3.00	3.00	0.00	
x01	8.30	7.00	2.00	4.00	2.00	
x07_08	7.63	7.67	3.00	4.00	0.00	
x20	7.93	7.33	5.00	3.00	2.00	
x26	7.93	7.33	3.00	4.00	2.00	
x10	7.19	7.33	2.00	5.00	1.00	
x32	6.81	7.33	3.00	4.00	0.00	
x13	7.26	6.67	2.00	2.00	2.00	
x40	6.89	7.00	4.00	2.00	1.00	
x19	7.56	6.33	2.00	1.00	1.00	
x37	7.63	6.00	2.00	3.00	1.00	
x16	7.26	6.33	5.00	4.00	1.00	
x36	6.59	7.00	4.00	2.00	1.00	
x14	7.26	6.00	2.00	1.00	1.00	
x42	7.26	6.00	3.00	1.00	1.00	
x28	7.19	6.00	2.00	3.00	0.00	
x02	5.85	7.33	4.00	1.00	2.00	Lt-HC
x38	5.11	7.67	3.00	3.00	1.00	
x41	5.85	6.67	3.00	3.00	1.00	
x15	5.11	7.00	5.00	2.00	2.00	
x33	6.07	6.00	3.00	2.00	1.00	
x39	5.19	6.00	4.00	4.00	1.00	
x11	5.11	6.00	6.00	2.00	1.00	
x22	7.93	5.67	4.00	3.00	2.00	HT-LC
x30	7.93	5.33	5.00	4.00	0.00	
x17	6.96	5.67	4.00	6.00	1.00	
x03	7.26	5.33	5.00	4.00	1.00	
x27	6.89	5.67	5.00	3.00	2.00	
x04	7.56	4.67	5.00	3.00	0.00	
x34	7.26	4.33	4.00	4.00	1.00	
x06	6.59	5.00	5.00	4.00	2.00	Lt-LC
x21	6.52	5.00	8.00	8.00	1.00	
x12	5.48	5.67	5.00	5.00	0.00	
x09	5.78	5.00	7.00	4.00	1.00	
x18	6.15	4.00	5.00	4.00	1.00	
x25	6.07	4.00	6.00	7.00	1.00	
x31	4.74	5.00	5.00	4.00	1.00	
x35	4.44	4.33	6.00	8.00	1.00	
x29	1.70	3.67	5.00	4.00	1.00	
Total resources available			60.00	50.00	15.00	
Total resources demanded			163.00	141.00	42.00	

References

Acs, Z.J., and D.B. Audretsch. 2010. Knowledge Spillover Entrepreneurship. In *Handbook of Entrepreneurship Research*, International Handbook Series on Entrepreneurship, vol. 5, ed. Z.J. Acs and D.B. Audretsch. Boston: Kluwer Academic Publishers. https://doi.org/10.1007/978-1-4419-1191-9_11.

Anderson, R., U. Daim, and F. Lavoie. 2007. Measuring the Efficiency of University Technology Transfer. *Technovation* 27: 306–318.

Arnesse, F., and A. Cohendet. 2001. Technology Transfer Revisited from the Perspective of the Knowledge-Based Economy. *Research Policy* 30: 1459–1478.

Audretsch, D.B. 2014. From the Entrepreneurial University to the University for the Entrepreneurial Society. *Journal of Technology Transfer* 39: 313–321.

Aykut, S., and Laffite, N.B. (2011). Technology Transfer Offices. Policy Brief, The Innovation Policy Platform https://www.innovationpolicyplatform.org/sites/default/files/Technology%20transfer%20offices_0_0.pdf.

Baglieri, D., Baldi, F., and Tucci, C. (2015). University Technology Transfer Office Business Models: One Size does NOT Fit All. Paper presented at the DRUID Society Conference 2015, Rome, June 15–17 http://druid8.sit.aau.dk/acc_papers/159889emvut56oldvoc5eps4a9jp.pdf.

Baldini, N. 2010. Do Royalties Really Foster University Patenting Activity? An Answer from Italy. *Technovation* 30: 109–116.

Belderbos, R., M. Carree, and B. Lokshin. 2006. Complementarity in R&D Cooperation Strategies. *Review of Industrial Organization* 28: 401–426.

Belenzon, S., and Schankerman, M. 2007. Harnessing Success: Determinants of University Technology Licensing Performance. EI/44. Suntory and Toyota International Centres for Economics and Related Disciplines, London School of Economics and Political Science, London, UK. http://eprints.lse.ac.uk/3726/.

Bozeman, B. 2000. Technology Transfer and Public Policy: A Review of Research and Theory. *Research Policy* 29: 627–655.

Bozeman, B., H. Rimes, and J. Youtie. 2015. The Evolving State-of-the-art in Technology Transfer Research: Revisiting the Contingent Effectiveness Model. *Research Policy* 44: 34–49.

Bradley, S.R., C.S. Hayter, and A.N. Link. 2013a. Models and Methods of University Technology Transfer. *Foundations and Trends® in Entrepreneurship* 9 (6): 571–650.

———. 2013b. Proof of Concept Centers in the United States: An Exploratory Look. *Journal of Technology Transfer* 38: 349–381.

Bruneel, J., P. d'Este, and A. Salter. 2010. Investigating the Factors that Diminish the Barriers to University–Industry Collaboration. *Research Policy* 39 (7): 858–868.

Campbell, A.F. 2007. How to Set Up a Technology Transfer Office: Experiences from Europe. In *Intellectual Property Management in Health and Agricultural Innovation: A Handbook of Best Practices*, ed. A. Krattiger, R.T. Mahoney, L. Nelsen, et al. Oxford/Davis: MIHR, PIPRA. Available at: www.ipHandbook.org.

Carayannis, E.G., and D. Campbell. 2005. 'Mode 3': Meaning and implications from a knowledge systems perspective. In *In Knowledge creation, diffusion, and use in innovation networks and knowledge clusters*. Westport, CT: Praeger.

———. 2009. 'Mode 3' and 'Quadruple Helix': Toward a 21st Century Fractal Innovation Ecosystem. *International Journal of Technology Management* 46: 201–234.

———. 2010. Triple Helix, Quadruple Helix, and Quintuple Helix and How do Knowledge, Innovation, and the Environment Related to Each Other: A Proposed Framework for Transdisciplinary Analysis of Sustainable Development and Social Ecology. *International Journal of Social Ecology and Sustainable Development* 1 (1): 41–69.

Carayannis, E.G., D. Meissner, and A. Edelkina. 2015. Targeted Innovation Policy and Practice Intelligence (TIP2E): Concepts and Implications for Theory, Policy and Practice. *Journal of Technology Transfer*. https://doi.org/10.1007/s10961-015-9433-8.

Cartalos, O., S. Rozakis, and D. Tsiouki. 2016. A Method to Assess and Support Exploitation Projects of University Researchers. *Journal of Technology Transfer*. https://doi.org/10.1007/s10961-016-9519-y.

Chapple, W., A. Lockett, D.S. Siegel, and M. Wright. 2005. Assessing the Relative Performance of University TTOs in the UK. *Research Policy* 34: 369–384.

Chesbrough, H. 2003. *Open Innovation: The New Imperative for Creating and Profiting from Technology*. Boston: Harvard Business School Press.

Clarysse, B., M. Wright, A. Lockett, E. VandeVelde, and A. Vohora. 2005. Spinning Out New Ventures: A Typology of Incubation Strategies from European Research Institutions. *Journal of Business Venturing* 20: 183–216.

Clausen, J. (1999). Branch and Bound Algorithms–Principles and Examples. Technical Report, Copenhagen, Denmark: University of Copenhagen.

Cockburn, I.M., and R.M. Henderson. 1998. Absorptive Capacity, Coauthoring Behavior, and the Organization of Research in Drug Discovery. *Journal of Industrial Economics* 46 (2): 157–182.

Colyvas, J., M. Crow, A. Gelijns, R. Mazzoleni, R.R. Nelson, N. Rosenberg, and B.N. Sampat. 2002. How Do University Inventions Get into Practice? *Management Science* 48: 61–72.

Conti, A., and P. Gaule. 2008. *The CEMI Survey of University Technology Transfer Offices in Europe*. Lausanne: Ecole Polytechnique Federale de Lausanne. http://cemi.epfl.ch/page-30722-en.html.

Conti, A., and P. Gaule. 2011. Is the US Outperforming Europe in University Technology Licensing? A new Perspective on the European Paradox. *Research Policy* 40(1): 123–135.

Curi, C., C.C. Daraio, and P. Llerena. 2015. The Productivity of French Technology Transfer Offices after Government Reforms. *Applied Economics* 47: 3008–3019.

Dantzig, G. B. The Rand Corporation, and University of California, Berkeley 1963. Linear Programming and Extensions, Princeton University Press, Princeton, New Jersey.

Debackere, K., and R. Veugelers. 2005. The Role of Academic Technology Transfer Organizations in Improving Industry Science Links. *Research Policy* 34: 321–342.

Debackere, K. 2012. The TTO, A University Engine Transforming Science into Innovation. League of European Research Universities (LERU), Advice Paper No 10 http://www.leru.org/files/publications/TTO_paper_final.pdf.

Degroof, J.J., and E.B. Roberts. 2004. Overcoming Weak Entrepreneurial Infrastructures for Academic Spin-off Ventures. *Journal of Technology Transfer* 29: 327–352.

Djokovic, D., and V. Souitaris. 2008. Spinouts from Academic Institutions: A Literature Review with Suggestions for Further Research. *Journal of Technology Transfer* 33: 225–247.

Drivas, K., Balafoutis, A.T., and Rozakis S. 2016. Research Funding and Academic Output: Evidence from the Agricultural University of Athens, Prometheus (United Kingdom): 1-22, DOI: https://doi.org/10.1080/08109028.2016.1150575.

Etzkowitz, H., and L. Leydesdorff. 2000. The Dynamics of Innovation: From National Systems and Mode 2 to a Triple Helix of University–Industry–Government Relations. *Research Policy* 29: 109–123.

Etzkowitz, H., A. Webster, C. Gebhardt, and B.R.C. Terra. 2000. The Future of the University and the University of the Future: Evolution of Ivory Tower to Entrepreneurial Paradigm. *Research Policy* 29: 313–330.

EARTO. 2014. The TRL Scale as a Research and Innovation Policy Tool. EARTO Recommendations. European Association of Research and Technology Organisations http://www.earto.eu/fileadmin/content/03_Publications/The_TRL_Scale_as_a_R_I_Policy_Tool_-_EARTO_Recommendations_-_Final.pdf.

European Commission. 2008. Commission Recommendation on the Management of Intellectual Property in Knowledge Transfer Activities and Code Practice for Universities and Other Public Research Organizations, Office for Official Publications of the European Communities, Luxemburg http://ec.europa.eu/invest-in-research/pdf/download_en/ip_recommendation.pdf.

———. 2009. Metrics for Knowledge Transfer from Public Research Organisations in Europe. Report from the European Commission's Expert Group on Knowledge Transfer Metrics. European Commission-DG Research, Brussels http://ec.europa.eu/invest-in-research/pdf/download_en/knowledge_transfer_web.pdf.

———. 2015. Horizon 2020 Work Programme 2016-2017, Annex G. European Commission Decision C 6776 of 13 Oct 2015 http://ec.europa.eu/research/participants/data/ref/h2020/other/wp/2016-2017/annexes/h2020-wp1617-annex-ga_en.pdf.

———. 2016. *Science, Research and Innovation Performance of the EU*. Luxembourg: Publications Office of the European Union.

Florida, R., and W.M. Cohen. 1999. Engine or Infrastructure? The university Role in Economic Development. In *Industrializing Knowledge: University–Industry Linkages in Japan and the United States*, ed. L.M. Branscomb, F. Kodama, and R. Florida, 589–610. Cambridge: MIT Press.

Foray, D., David, P. A., and Hall, B. 2009. Smart Specialisation – The Concept. Knowledge Economists Policy Brief No. 9.

Gans, J.S., and S. Stern. 2003. The Product Market and the Market for "Ideas": Commercialization Strategies for Technology Entrepreneurs. *Research Policy* 32: 333–350.

Grimpe, C., and H. Fier. 2010. Informal University Technology Transfer: A Comparison Between the United States and Germany. *Journal of Technology Transfer* 35: 637–650.

Gulbrandsen, M., and S. Slipersæter. 2007. The Third Mission and the Entrepreneurial University Model. In *Universities and Strategic Knowledge Creation: Specialization and Performance in Europe*, ed. A. Bonaccorsi and C. Daraio, 112–143. Cheltenham: Edward Elgar.

Gulbranson, C.A., and D.B. Audretsch. 2008. Proof of Concept Centers: Accelerating the Commercialization of University Innovation. *Journal of Technology Transfer* 33: 249–258.

Friedman, J., and J. Silberman. 2003. University Technology Transfer: Do Incentives, Management, and Location Matter? *The Journal of Technology Transfer* 28(1): 17–30.

Hallam, C., A. Leffel, and B. Garcia. 2011. Early Phase Technology Valuation in Intellectual Property Portfolios and its Impact on the Management and Commercialization of University-Derived Technologies. Proceedings, PICMET Conference 2011.

Hayter, C. 2013. Harnessing University Entrepreneurship for Economic Growth: Factors of Success among University Spinoffs. *Economic Development Quarterly* 27 (1): 18–28.

Heslop, L.A., E. McGregor, and M. Griffith. 2001. Development of a Technology Readiness Assessment Measure: The Cloverleaf Model of Technology Transfer. *Journal of Technology Transfer* 26: 369–384.

Heinzl, J., Kor, A., Orange, G., and Kaufmann, H. 2008. Technology Transfer Model for Austrian Higher Education Institutions. Paper presented at the European and Mediterranean Conference on Information Systems, May 25–26, 2008.

Jain, R.K., A.O. Martyniuk, M.M. Harris, R.N. Niermann, and K. Woldmann. 2003. Evaluating the Commercial Potential of Emerging Technologies. *International Journal of Technology Transfer and Commercialisation* 2: 32–50.

Jensen, R.A., and M.C. Thursby. 2001. Proofs and Prototypes for Sale: The Licensing of University Inventions. *American Economic Review* 91: 240–259.

JRC. 2014. RIS3 Implementation and Policy Mixes. S3 Policy Brief Series No. 07. Brussels, European Commission Joint Research Centre http://s3platform.jrc.ec.europa.eu/documents/20182/114990/JRC91917_RIS3_implementation_and_policy_mixes_final.pdf/e56f2977-f217-475c-95c2-649c55d83b40.

Karra, S.C., and Tolias, Y.A. 2012. Greek Universities and Knowledge Transfer Performance: Assessment, Implications and Prospects. Paper appeared in the proceedings of the 12th International Conference of the Economic Society of Thessaloniki, Thessaloniki, Oct. 11–12 http://www.innovatiasystems.eu/docs/Karra_and_Tolias_2012.pdf.

Kerr, C. 2001. *The Uses of the University*. Cambridge, MA: Harvard University Press.

Lach, S., and M. Schankerman. 2008. Incentives and Inventions in Universities. *The Rand Journal of Economics* 39: 403–433.

Link, A.N., D.S. Siegel, and B. Bozeman. 2007. An Empirical Analysis of the Propensity of Academics to Engage in Informal University Technology Transfer. *Industrial and Corporate Change* 16: 641–655.

Litan, R., L. Mitchell, and E. Reedy. 2007. The University as Innovator: Bumps in the Road. *Issues in Science and Technology* 23: 57–66.

Lockett, A., M. Wright, and S. Franklin. 2003. Technology Transfer and Universities' Spin-out Strategies. *Small Business Economics* 20 (2): 185–201.

Lockett, A., and M. Wright. 2005. Resources, Capabilities, Risk Capital and the Creation of University Spin-out Companies. *Research Policy* 34: 1043–1057.

Lundquist, G. 2003. A Rich Vision of Technology Transfer–Technology Value Management. *Journal of Technology Transfer* 28: 265–284.

Mohannak, K., and Samtani, L. (2014). A Criteria-based Approach for Evaluating Innovation Commercialisation. Paper Presented at the DRUID Society Conference 2014, CBS,

Copenhagen, June 16–18 http://druid8.sit.aau.dk/acc_papers/i1xk9l9pli4jnefryvacrvpjdy22. pdf.

Ndonzuau, F.N., F. Pirnay, and B. Surlemont. 2002. A Stage Model of Academic Spin-off Creation. *Technovation* 22: 281–289.

OECD. 2003. *Turning Science into Business: Patenting and Licensing at Public Research Organizations.* Paris: OECD Publishing.

———. 2011. Reviews of Regional Innovation: Regions and Innovation Policy. Organisation for Economic Co-operation and Development. Publication Date: 04/05/2011 http://www.oecd.org/gov/regional-policy/oecdreviewsofregionalinnovationregionsandinnovationpolicy.htm.

O'Shea, R.P., T.J. Allen, K.L. Morse, C. O'Gorman, and F. Roche. 2005. Entrepreneurial Orientation, Technology Transfer and Spin-off Performance of US Universities. *Research Policy* 34: 994–1009.

O'Shea, R.P., H. Chugh, and T.J. Allen. 2008. Determinants and Consequences of University Spinoff Activity: A Conceptual Framework. *Journal of Technology Transfer* 33: 653–666.

Panagopoulos, A., and E.G. Carayannis. 2013. A Policy for Enhancing the Disclosure of University Faculty Invention. *Journal of Technology Transfer* 38: 341–347.

Phan, P., D. Siegel, and M. Wright. 2005. Science Parks and Incubators: Observations, Synthesis and Future Research. *Journal of Business Venturing* 20 (2): 165–182.

Perkmann, M., V. Tartari, M. McKelvey, E. Autio, A. Broström, P. D'Este, R. Fini, A. Geuna, R. Grimaldi, A. Hughes, S. Krabel, M. Kitson, P. Llerena, F. Lissoni, A. Salter, and M. Sobrero. 2013. Academic Engagement and Commercialisation: A review of the Literature on University – Industry Relations. *Research Policy* 42: 423–442.

Powers, J.B., and P.P. McDougall. 2005. University Start-up Formation and Technology Licensing with Firms that Go Public: A Resource-based View of Academic Entrepreneurship. *Journal of Business Venturing* 20: 291–311.

Rahal, A.D., and L.C. Rabelo. 2006. Assessment Framework for the Evaluation and Prioritization of University Inventions for Licencing and Commercialization. *Engineering Management Journal* 18: 28–36.

Sahini, E. 2014. Bibliometric Analysis of Greek Publications in International Scientific Journals. National Documentation Centre. Publication date: 15 Dec 2014 http://report04.metrics.ekt.gr/.

Shane, S. 2004. Encouraging University Entrepreneurship? The Effect of the Bayh-Dole Act on University Patenting in the United States. *Journal of Business Venturing* 19: 127–151.

Siegel, D.S., D.A. Waldman, and A.N. Link. 2003. Assessing the Impact of Organizational Practices on the Productivity of University Technology Transfer Offices: An Exploratory Study. *Research Policy* 32 (1): 27–48.

Siegel, D.S., D.A. Waldman, L. Atwater, and A.N. Link. 2004. Toward a Model of the Effective Transfer of Scientific Knowledge from Academicians to Practitioners: Qualitative Evidence from the Commercialization of University Technologies. *Journal of Engineering and Technology Management* 21: 115–142.

Siegel, D.S., R. Veugelers, and M. Wright. 2007a. Technology Transfer Offices and Commercialization of University Intellectual Property: Performance and Policy Implications. *Oxford Review of Economic Policy* 23 (4): 640–660.

Siegel, D.S., M. Wright, and A. Lockett. 2007b. The Rise of Entrepreneurial Activity at Universities: Organizational and Societal Implications. *Industrial and Corporate Change* 16: 489–504.

Thursby, J.G., R. Jensen, and M.C. Thursby. 2001. Objectives, Characteristics and Outcomes of University Licensing: A Survey of Major US Universities. *Journal of Technology Transfer* 26: 59–72.

Thursby, J.C., and M.C. Thursby. 2002. Who is Selling the Ivory Tower? Sources of Growth in University Licensing. *Management Science* 48: 90–104.

Thursby, J.G., and S. Kemp. 2002. Growth and Productive Efficiency of University Intellectual Property Licensing. *Research Policy* 31: 109–124.

Thursby, J., and M. Thursby. 2007. Patterns of Research and Licensing Activity of Science and Engineering Faculty. In *Science and the University*, ed. P. Stephan and R. Ehrenberg. Madison: University of Wisconsin Press.

Thursby, J.G., A.W. Fuller, and M.C. Thursby. 2009. US Faculty Patenting: Inside and Outside the University. *Research Policy* 38: 14–25.

Thursby, J.G., and M.C. Thursby. 2003. Industry/University Licensing: Characteristics, Concerns and Issues from the Perspective of the Buyer. *The Journal of Technology Transfer* 28(3/4): 207–213.

Trueman, S., Borrell-Damian, L., and Smith, J. H. 2014. The Evolution of University-based Knowledge Transfer Structures, The EUIMA Collaborative Research Project Papers http://www.eua.be/Libraries/Publications/Stephen_Trueman_Final.sflb.ashx.

Vekinis, G. 2014. Technology Transfer in Practice: From Invention to Innovation. Presstime, Athens (eBook ISBN 978-960-93-5996-2 and Paperback ISBN 978-960-93-5855-2).

Veugelers, R. 2014. Undercutting the Future? European Research Spending in Times of Fiscal Consolidation. Policy Contribution 2014/06, Bruegel http://bruegel.org/wp-content/uploads/imported/publications/pc_2014_06_.pdf.

———. 2016. The European Union Growing Innovation Divide. Policy Contribution 2016/08, Bruegel http://bruegel.org/wp-content/uploads/2016/04/pc_2016_08.pdf.

Veugelers, R., and B. Cassiman. 2005. R&D Cooperation Between Firms and Universities. Some Empirical Evidence from Belgian Manufacturing. *International Journal of Industrial Organization* 23 (5–6): 355–379.

Vinig, T., and D. Lips. 2015. Measuring the Performance of University Technology Transfer Using Meta Data Approach: The Case of Dutch Universities. *Journal of Technology Transfer* 40 (6): 1034–1049.

Warren, A., R. Hanke, and D. Trotzer. 2008. Models for University Technology Transfer: Resolving Conflicts Between Mission and Methods and the Dependency on Geographic Location. *Cambridge Journal of Regions, Economy and Society* 1 (2): 219–232.

Weckowska, D.M. 2015. Learning in University Technology Transfer Offices: Transactions-Focused and Relations-Focused Approaches to Commercialization of Academic Research. *Technovation* 41 (42): 62–74.

Young, T.A. 2007. Establishing a Technology Transfer Office. In *Intellectual Property Management in Health and Agricultural Innovation: A Handbook of Best Practices*, ed. A. Krattiger, R.T. Mahoney, L. Nelsen, et al. Oxford/Davis: MIHR, PIPRA. Available at: www.ipHandbook.org.

The Technology Cycle and Technology Transfer Strategies

Kenneth A. Zahringer, Christos Kolympiris, and Nicholas Kalaitzandonakes

Abstract University technology transfer offices (TTOs) must make decisions about whether and how to commercialize university innovations and do so with little or no information about the ultimate market value of the products that might eventually be derived from those innovations. Using technology life cycle theory, we derive and assess the usefulness of metrics that could provide additional information to assist in TTO decision making. We find that being able to locate a given innovation along a life cycle progression can decrease the uncertainty inherent in technology transfer decisions.

Introduction

University technology transfer offices (TTOs) face a daunting task. Acting as the agent both of the individual faculty member that produced a given invention and of the university as a whole, the TTO is responsible for assessing the potential value of a nascent, patented technology in final product markets. Based on that assessment, the TTO must then decide whether to commercialize the invention and what the optimal means, from the university's point of view, might be for doing so. This generally involves entering into some sort of agreement with a private firm to do the necessary follow-on research and development to turn the invention into a marketable product. Even under the best of conditions, the valuation process is largely a matter of entrepreneurial judgment; both the original inventors and their prospective firm partners find it difficult to arrive at an accurate estimate (Siegel et al. 2007). A primary reason for this difficulty is the high degree of uncertainty

K.A. Zahringer (✉) • N. Kalaitzandonakes
Department of Agricultural and Applied Economics, University of Missouri, Columbia, MO, USA
e-mail: ZahringerK@missouri.edu

C. Kolympiris
University of Bath, Bath, UK

© Springer International Publishing AG 2018
N. Kalaitzandonakes et al. (eds.), *From Agriscience to Agribusiness*, Innovation,
Technology, and Knowledge Management, https://doi.org/10.1007/978-3-319-67958-7_15

surrounding that value. New inventions often require considerable development to transform them into an innovative product. The relative costs and possible outcomes of alternative development paths are not clear at the outset. In addition, it is virtually impossible to foresee all possible applications, and thus formulate a realistic valuation, of a new invention at such an early stage. The closer a given invention is to basic research, the greater is the degree of uncertainty surrounding its potential value (Bercovitz and Feldman 2006). Since the bulk of university research involves basic science, TTOs must contend with a large amount of uncertainty in their decision making about structuring technology transfer agreements with private industry.

In this paper we propose a simple method for generating additional information that TTOs may find valuable and helpful in intellectual property (IP) valuation and refining their technology transfer strategy. By using some fairly simple, easily obtained patent data, it is possible to arrive at a reasonably accurate view of the current state of the life cycle of the technology area in which a particular invention resides. We propose that the indicators we develop here can capture information regarding how the value of an invention, as well as uncertainty about its value, is influenced by the developmental stage of the overall technology, as reflected in the technology life cycle (TLC) progression. Thus, placing a particular invention in its life cycle context can give a TTO valuable information as to its likely value and how accurate that valuation might be. We illustrate this process within the context of a technology that has been essential to the development of all of biotechnology, including agricultural, the polymerase chain reaction (PCR).

The importance of the TTO's task, and thus our contribution to its successful completion, goes far beyond the potential income to the university from any given transfer agreement. The interaction between a university and a private firm may begin with a specific, isolated transaction regarding technology transfer, but it often progresses beyond that to a long-term relationship that is highly beneficial to both parties. In addition to subsequent technology transfer, this relationship may take the form of firm-sponsored research at the university, students becoming a source of quality personnel for the firm, and the creation of additional spin-off firms. How the relationship develops, and its ultimate value to both parties, can be strongly influenced by the quality of the initial transactions (Bercovitz and Feldman 2006). It is thus critical that individual technology transfer agreements be viewed as valuable and equitable by both parties.

The rest of the paper proceeds as follows: in the next section, we give an overview of our current study, its position within the TLC literature, and why the TLC concept might be valuable in TTO decision making. In two subsequent sections we discuss the TLC literature and describe PCR technology. Following that, we report our data selection process, describe the dataset and relate our empirical findings. The final section concludes.

Overview

Innovative technologies evolve over time. They often follow a path by which their scope of usage and technological advancement proceed in distinct periods: an introduction stage is followed by a growth stage until maturity and eventual decline are reached (Taylor and Taylor 2012). This so-called technology life cycle (TLC) is generally difficult to describe analytically as the observable characteristics of technologies may not adequately capture the beginning and/or end of a stage. As a result, a large body of work has employed various indices based on patent documents and bibliometrics in an attempt to capture and, ultimately, measure the TLC for a number of innovative technologies (e.g., Kayal and Waters 1999; Chang et al. 2010; Huang and Yan 2011).

While most of the existing literature has focused on the description and measurement of the TLC of various technologies, we are more interested gaining a more generalized understanding of how key features of a new technology change over its life cycle. That is, we want to know whether and how (a) the value of the technology, (b) its complexity, (c) the speed it progresses within the intellectual property (IP) system, and (d) the pace of technological progress change as the technology moves from the introduction to the maturity phase. We do so by empirically mapping the TLC of a fundamental discovery in the life sciences, the PCR process, and examining the evolution of such features during the lifecycle of this technology.

Theoretically, we expect changes over the life cycle of any new technology. We build this expectation on the notion that the breakthroughs of most innovative technologies tend to happen early in the life cycle and the marginal contribution of subsequent developments is diminishing over time. If that proposition holds, we expect all the abovementioned features of a given technology to differ over the life cycle. For instance, we expect the more valuable and original forms of the technology in the early stages of the TLC.

Our case study is interesting for, among other reasons, its broad applicability in the life sciences. PCR was developed by scientists at Cetus Corp. in the early and mid-1980s. PCR is a method of rapidly producing large quantities of DNA from an initially small sample. The innovation that PCR became is now a standard piece of equipment in molecular biology laboratories and in a wide range of disciplines. By 2002 over 3% of all articles cited in PubMed referred to it (Bartlett and Stirling 2003). From a technical standpoint, as we explain in detail in the following section, PCR follows an identifiable life cycle with a long history which makes it a suitable template for studying changes in a TLC.

We use patent data as a primary input for our empirical analysis. A technology, any technology, is not merely a specific product. Rather, a technology is a set of knowledge and skills needed to produce, manipulate, and improve upon the design that is embodied in that tangible product (Lundquist 2003). The patent record provides a means of tracking the spread of the technological knowledge and the industry's response to it in the form of further related innovation. To implement the analysis, then, we rely on patent data of the PCR technology sourced by commercial vendor Thomson Innovation. We have obtained data from 2414 US utility patents applied for from 1985 to 2008 and granted through 2012. These data allow us to identify the life cycle of the technology as well as to estimate how its value and other key features changed over time.

Our results show that the majority of the technology characteristics we study do change during the life cycle. For instance, individual innovations within a given technology are potentially much more valuable during the early stages of the life cycle when compared to later stages. Of course, this is also when the value is most uncertain. This study is strictly retrospective; we know that PCR became a tremendously successful innovation. Many other inventions did not turn out so well. We also see how the progression of the TLC reflects the valuation of the overall technology by the wider market. As the TLC progresses and market actors become more familiar with the technology, the potential value of any given new invention becomes less uncertain. Thus, information concerning the current state of a TLC could aid TTO decision making.

Technology Life Cycle Theory

Innovation is one of the more visible categories of human action. Economic actors are engaged in a more or less continuous process of seeking out and choosing means that they believe will achieve their desired ends (Mises 1998). As part of this process, actors develop new means that differ to varying degrees from what has gone before. Some of these inventions are substantially novel, representing what Ayres (1988) calls a technological discontinuity and the beginning of a technology cycle. In Ayres' model the discontinuity provides a means of overcoming a technological barrier and opens up new technological opportunities. Over time, knowledge of the discontinuity diffuses, and actors exploit the new opportunities with incremental improvements to the original innovation. Gradually, innovation in the new area experiences diminishing returns as opportunities are realized and new constraints become binding. At some point a new discontinuity solves these constraints and signals the end of the old technology cycle and the beginning of a new one.

While the foregoing outlines TLC conceptually, in practice the process can be considerably more complicated. Innovation is always characterized by a great deal of uncertainty as to its ultimate market acceptance and value. Different technology areas are often characterized by particular timeframes between early research and market impact. Biotechnology, the general area within which PCR falls, often develops radically new products for markets that have yet to exist. Often these products are regulated, which adds to development costs and increases the time needed to bring them to a marketable state. This is especially true for pharmaceutical inventions (DiMasi and Grabowski 2007; Kalaitzandonakes et al. 2007). Thus the impacts of such technologies may take some time to develop (Powell and Moris 2004). In fact, our results indicate that PCR followed this basic pattern. The constraints which constitute barriers to innovation are not only technological but also economic and social and include raw material availability, production capabilities, and customer acceptance, among others (Kline and Rosenberg 1986). Ayres (1988) also emphasized that the barriers to innovation may not be located in the technology area where the invention originates.

In fact, the technology area that provides the context for our study, PCR technology, offers an example of this. The research that led directly to PCR (Mullis et al. 1986) was presaged by earlier work (Kleppe et al. 1971). This research was plagued by the same issue that hampered Mullis' initial attempts at implementing his idea – the lack of a polymerase enzyme that was not denatured and rendered inert by the high temperatures involved in the PCR process. It was only the discovery and isolation, in the intervening years, of a DNA polymerase from the thermophilic bacteria *Thermus aquaticus* (Chien et al. 1976), which came to be known as Taq polymerase, that enabled the research team to turn PCR from a laboratory invention into a useful innovation and a subsequent torrent of products (Saiki et al. 1988).

Thus, the technology life cycle is characterized not only by uncertainty but also by change. As the example suggests, each new discovery or innovation, whether a novel discontinuity or a small incremental improvement, changes the opportunities and incentives faced by subsequent innovators. It is these changes that lead to the changing character of innovations over the course of the life cycle. There are two basic, complementary theoretical perspectives for describing the changes that occur over a technology life cycle (Taylor and Taylor 2012).

Building on Ayres' concept of technological discontinuity, Anderson and Tushman (1990) put forth a three-stage model of the technology life cycle. The cycle begins with the introduction of a discontinuous innovation. During this introductory period, often characterized as the fuzzy front end of innovation, uncertainty is at a very high level. Not only is the innovating firm, as well as others in the industry, assessing the full potential of the innovation, but it is also bringing resources together to enable further development. Often this entails explaining and selling the concept to others, sometimes in order to secure outside investment funding. The firm's relative success in this effort can be a significant factor in determining the length of the introductory phase and whether the innovation progresses beyond it (Schoonmaker et al. 2012). If successful, the discontinuity engenders a period of ferment when many variations on and improvements of the original invention are generated. Out of this period of ferment comes a dominant design that becomes the industry standard. The emergence of a dominant design marks the boundary between the period of ferment and that of incremental change. Innovators continue to make incremental improvements to the dominant design until another discontinuity occurs and begins its own cycle. Anderson and Tushman (1990) construct a model whose predictions are validated with historical data from glass, cement, and minicomputer manufacturing technology. Among other results, they find that most new designs and most of the total performance improvement in the innovation occur during the period of ferment. Also, they found that a dominant design is more likely to appear in a regime of low appropriability of the rents that accrue to the innovation. Taylor and Taylor (2012) term this the "macro view" of the technology life cycle. They also point out that this model implies a shift in emphasis from innovation concerning product design (product innovation) during the ferment period to innovation concerning producing the product more efficiently (process innovation) during the period of incremental improvement.

A somewhat more quantitative, yet complementary, perspective is represented by what Taylor and Taylor (2012) term the "S-curve view" of the life cycle. This model is more widely used than the macro view and with greater diversity in parameters. Here different measures of patents awarded, units sold, performance improvements, or other characteristics are usually plotted against time, resulting in S-shaped, logistic style curves. Generally, this type of curve represents the pace of change in some sense; in this lies the complementarity with the macro view. During the introduction period immediately following the discontinuity, the rate of innovation is slower as knowledge of the discontinuity begins to diffuse and others come to understand its implications. This corresponds to the flatter initial portion of the curve. During the period of ferment, the pace of change increases, corresponding to the steeper central portion. As the technological opportunities come to be more fully exploited, the cycle enters the period of incremental improvement, and the pace of change slows again, which corresponds to the later, again flatter portion of the curve. In this study we employ concepts from both models to better understand the changes in the character of innovations that take place over the course of the technology life cycle.

Polymerase Chain Reaction Technology

The technique of polymerase chain reaction (PCR), a method allowing rapid production of large quantities of DNA from a small sample, was developed by scientists at Cetus Corp. in the early and mid-1980s. The basic idea of PCR was conceived by Cetus scientist Kary Mullis in 1983, and Mullis and Cetus applied for the first patent on this invention in 1985. Ultimately, the invention earned Mullis the 1993 Nobel Prize in chemistry. Initially, however, few of his colleagues saw the potential of the idea (Mullis 1990). The first attempts at implementing the idea were inefficient and inaccurate. It took another few years of work, including the adaptation of a special enzyme (Taq polymerase) that was instrumental to the process, by a team of Cetus scientists to bring PCR largely into the form we see today (Rabinow 1996). The innovation that PCR became is now a standard piece of equipment in molecular biology laboratories in a wide range of disciplines; as already discussed, in 2002, over 3% of all articles cited in PubMed referred to PCR (Bartlett and Stirling 2003).

In the PCR process, the initial sample of DNA is heated, causing the two strands of the double helix to separate. Also in the solution with the DNA are smaller molecules made of nucleotides, the same building blocks from which DNA is made, called oligonucleotide primers or simply primers. These primers are constructed so as to bind with specific spots in the unraveled DNA. The solution contains two different primers which, when attached to the DNA strand, bracket the area to be replicated. After the solution cools a bit, a special enzyme called a polymerase (hence the name) builds a complementary strand of DNA between the primers. The solution is again heated, again separating the DNA strands. The newly constructed DNA strands become patterns for new sequences, along with the original sample. Thus with each cycle the amount of the target DNA sequence in the sample doubles in a sort of chain reaction (hence the rest of the name). The amount of DNA produced is limited only by the amount of ingredients in the original solution. This exponential progression allowed the original PCR process to multiply a given DNA sample a billion-fold in a matter of a few hours. More recent advances in the process have cut this time to 30 minutes or less with some techniques and equipment (Wittwer 2001).

The basic concept of PCR is straightforward and has proven to be highly adaptable. The needs of the different areas of research and analysis which use PCR technology have given rise to a host of different techniques. These involve differences in, for example, temperatures used, timing, primer design, or catalysts included in the solution (Hayashi 1994). PCR's simplicity and adaptability have added two main features that have made it a particularly interesting technology to study. First, since the basic technology is so adaptable and thus so powerful, a dominant design emerged in an environment where theory would not necessarily have predicted. We commonly see dominant designs in realms of low appropriability, where innovations are more likely to remain in the public domain (Anderson and Tushman 1990). Biotechnology, however, is generally a high appropriability regime; patents play an important role in maintaining these firms' ability to safeguard the rewards from innovation (Ko 1992). In this type of environment, we would expect to see multiple competing proprietary designs, but here we do not. It is likely that the simplicity of PCR made it difficult to invent around. Second, the dominant design emerged very early in the life cycle. TLC theory predicts that the dominant design would emerge during the growth phase or period of ferment (Anderson and Tushman 1990). Yet, with the adaptation of Taq polymerase (Saiki et al. 1988), the basic structure of the technology and the standard complement of ingredients were essentially standardized less than 2 years after the original patent was granted and before any significant adoption of the innovation by the scientific community. Later innovations enhanced the speed and decreased the cost of the process and broadened its range of applications, as described above, but did not change its basic characteristics. All in all, these unique features of PCR make it an interesting and instructive context for technology life cycle research. In addition, PCR technology has a well-defined starting point (Mullis 1990; Rabinow 1996) and represents what could be termed a significant competence-destroying technological discontinuity (Anderson and Tushman 1990); nothing like it had been available before. In the terminology of Taylor and Taylor (2012), for the technology application of amplifying DNA samples, PCR is the only extant paradigm. For the most part, later developments have broadened the range of research areas using PCR rather than replacing older versions of the technology. Thus we do not have several generations of PCR technology complicating the development of the life cycle. This gives us an opportunity, in a fairly simple context, to see how the path of development progressed during the lifecycle of this technology.

Data and Variables

Data Selection and Description

For our empirical analysis, we used patent data. To source a relevant patent dataset, we proceeded in two parallel directions. The one direction involved the identification of all biotechnology patents[1] in which the term "polymerase chain reaction" was included either in the title or in the abstract of a patent. Out of the total 155,985 biotechnology patents granted through 2012, 2059 included the term in question. The second direction was to directly identify the basic group of PCR patents awarded to Cetus Corp. (Carroll and Casimir 2003). The original PCR patent was heavily cited, garnering well over 3000 citations from follow-on patents. Under the premise that (some) citing patents may also represent PCR technologies, we included all patents that cited the original PCR patent as long as they were assigned the same primary four-digit IPC code. Removing patents already selected during the first direction we described above, we identified 434 additional patents, bringing the total dataset to 2493 PCR patents. As a final adjustment, we eliminated patents applied for after 2008. Given that the current median pendency time at the USPTO is in excess of 3 years (Mitra-Kahn et al. 2013), including issued patents applied for after 2008 would likely result in a sample selection bias toward short pendency patents at the end of the sample period. The final dataset includes 2414 US utility patents applied for 1985–2008 that meet our search criteria. All patents and features of the technology we are interested in were sourced from Thomson Innovation.

Study Design

To map the progression of the technology over the life cycle, we follow convention and chart the numbers of patents over time. Figure 1 shows the numbers of granted patents, grouped by the year each respective application was filed. Given the generally long time it takes for a patent application to be granted, we use the application date rather than publication date under the premise that it should better capture the time that the innovation was created. In order to smooth the curve and chart the underlying trends more clearly, we also include the 3-year moving average of the number of annual applications. The graph shows that PCR technology had an introductory period of approximately 8 years during which there were comparatively few patents filed each year. The growth phase lasted until 2002, after which the number of annual applications dropped dramatically, signaling entry into the

[1] To identify biotechnology patents, we employed the list of International Patent Classification (IPC) codes that belong to biotechnology compiled by OECD (2014). The IPC categories were A01H(1/00, 4/00), A61K(38/00, 39/00, 48/00), C02F3/34, C07G(11/00,13/00,15/00), C07K (4/00, 14/00, 16/00, 17/00, 19/00), C12M, C12N, C12P, C12Q, C12S, G01 N27/327, and G01 N33/ (53*, 54*, 55*, 57*, 68, 74, 76, 78, 88, 92).

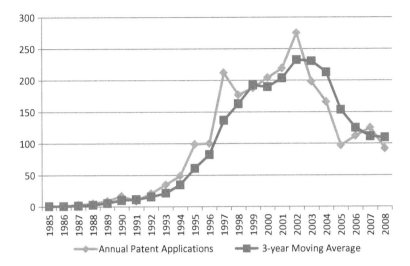

Fig. 1 Annual PCR-related patent applications

maturity phase. It appears that the innovation rate may have leveled off in the last 3 or 4 years of our sample. Thus we have the full spectrum of a technology life cycle in this sample, with each of the three phases represented.

As noted above, once we map the life cycle of the technology, we are interested in studying if and how key features of the technology change across time. The first feature we examine is the value of the technology which we approximate with patent value. We measure patent value with the number of times a given patent has been cited by later patents (forward citations) and with the size of the group of patents that describe a given technology (patent family). We use these measures based on evidence that they correlate with the market value of a technology as well as with importance, impact, and other measures of value (Harhoff et al. 2003; Gambardella et al. 2008; Sneed and Johnson 2009; Fischer and Leidinger 2014; Odasso et al. 2015).

The second feature we analyze is patent pendency, defined as the length of time that elapses between the application date of a given patent and its grant date. Patent pendency can be influenced by a host of factors including the strategic behavior of applicants which may favor long or short pendency time (Lanjouw and Schankerman 2004; Berger et al. 2012), patent value (Régibeau and Rockett 2010), work load at the patent office (Harhoff and Wagner 2009), familiarity of the patent examiner with the technology (Lemley and Sampat 2012), and so on. All these factors may drive patent pendency in different ways, and here we are interested to see the final outcome of the interplay of these factors over time.

The third feature we analyze is the pace of technological change. Following previous works (Kayal 1999; Kayal and Waters 1999; Haupt et al. 2007), we employ the technology cycle time (TCT) index to measure technological change. TCT is defined as the average age of the patents cited by the focal patent, and it is calculated as the elapsed time (in months) between the publication dates[2] of the two patents. Once the elapsed time is measured for all the patents in questions, we calculate TCT by averaging out the figures for all patents. Formally, TCT is defined as $\text{TCT}_f = n^{-1} \sum_{r=0}^{n} \frac{(p_f - p_r)}{30}$ for each focal patent f, where n is the number of prior art patents referenced by the focal patent, p_f is the publication date of the focal patent, and p_r is the publication date of the referenced patent. To be clear, the shorter the cycle time, the smaller the index and the faster the pace of technological advancement.

The fourth feature we study is the originality of the technology. To measure originality we follow Harhoff and Wagner (2009) in constructing the originality measure first pioneered by Trajtenberg et al. (1997). This index measures the degree of commonality between the technology area of the focal patent and those of the patents it references as prior art. The rationale is that more fundamental patents will draw on a wider technological base than those that are more incremental improvements. Patents that reference patents from many different technology areas earn a higher score on this index, while those that draw on only a few areas earn lower scores. This index is a Herfindahl-type measure that measures the degree of similarity between the technology area of the focal patent and the technology areas of the patents referenced as prior art. Formally, the measure is calculated as $ORIGINAL_i = 1 - \sum_{N_k}^{k=1} \left(\frac{Refs_{ik}}{Refs_i} \right)^2$, where patent i references patents from k technology classes. Thus $Refs_i$ is the total number of referenced patents for focal patent i, and $Refs_{ik}$ is the number of referenced patents from focal patent i that fall into technology class k. Importantly, N_k is the total number of technology areas represented in the list of referenced patents, not the total number of technology areas in the classification system.[3] To calculate this index, we first converted the primary IPC code of the focal patent and all of its referenced patents to the ISI-OST-INPI classification system, which more accurately reflects technological relatedness than does the IPC coding system (Schmoch 2008).[4] Each term in the summation, then, is the number of patent references belonging to a particular technology class divided by the total number of patent references for the focal patent. The index ranges from 0 for the least original patents to 1 for the most original patents.

---

[2] Application dates could capture elapsed time more accurately. However, the vast majority of applications do not include any prior art when they are originally submitted; these are commonly provided later in a document known as an Information Disclosure Statement (IDS) (USPTO 2015). Accordingly, this limits the use of application dates.

[3] The index assigns a score of 0 for any patent without any or with only 1 reference included as previous art. As a result, the first patents, which have no antecedents, would receive a score of 0. This is not consistent with the theoretical expectation that the first patents are also among the most original. As such, any patent with no references was assigned an originality score of 1. For patents with 1 reference, if the patent and its reference were of the same technology class, the patent scored 0. If they were of different classes, the patent scored 1.

[4] This classification scheme collapses a total of 550 unique four-digit IPC codes into 35 technology classes.

The fifth feature we study is the complexity of the technology. We measure complexity via patent scope (Van Zeebroeck 2007), defined as the number of different four-digit IPC codes assigned to a patent during the examination process (Lerner 1994; Gans et al. 2008). The main rationale behind that measure is that more complex technologies span across multiple field boundaries. IPCs indicate the industrial field(s) a patent belongs to and as such the higher the number of IPC codes for a patent, the greater the complexity.

Results

Technology Value

Figure 2 plots the average values of forward citations and patent family size for each year of the technology cycle. Both values are at their maximum during the introduction phase before declining and maintaining a relatively constant level during growth and maturity. The outlier year of 2001 in the family size plot is due to one large family, with over 2000 members, consisting of patents related to a particular area of cancer diagnosis and therapy. Seven members of this family, having to do with PCR techniques, are included in our dataset. In this technology cycle, then, high value patents are very strongly clustered in the introductory phase, consistent with previous evidence (Haupt et al. 2007; Régibeau and Rockett 2010). This is an important observation in that it suggests that, when dealing with very new inventions, TTOs should position the university to be able to benefit strongly from a highly valuable invention. However, this is also when the value is most uncertain,

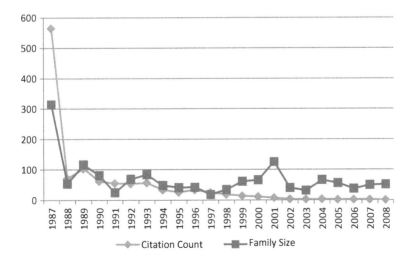

Fig. 2 Average annual patent value

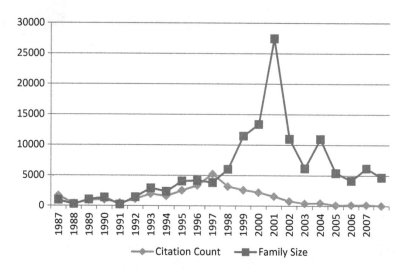

Fig. 3 Annual total patent value

and it is the potential licensee firm that bears most of that uncertainty. Its R&D investment in the invention could come to naught. Thus, in order to make a technology transfer agreement attractive to the firm, the university may need to be willing to share some portion of the uncertainty and the associated risk of low or no return on the invention.

Also relevant to questions of value are predictions that most of the improvements in quality and performance, and by extension added value, of a given technology will occur during the growth phase (Kline and Rosenberg 1986; Anderson and Tushman 1990). As a rough approximation of this, we summed each of our value measures for each year. As Fig. 3 shows, both forward citations and family size peak during the growth phase, although in different years. Citations peak in 1997, during the early portion of the growth phase, while family size is at its maximum in the latter part, in 2001. Although the height of the family size peak is affected by the outlier discussed above, the location of the peak is consistent with surrounding years. The increase in annual patent applications and grants that signals the beginning of the growth phase, then, is an indication that the wider technology community has decided that development of the technology is worth pursuing. Thus the level of uncertainty about the value of a given follow-on invention is reduced, along with the risk of that invention being of extremely low value. By the time the maturity phase is reached, and the annual flow of patents begins to taper off, there is even more market data available that further reduces the uncertainty of the valuation of a particular new invention in the technology field. We see that the probability of both extremes of value, very high and very low, is much lower than in the introductory phase of the TLC.

Patent Pendency

Figure 4 depicts the average pendency time of the PCR patents in the life cycle. In line with Haupt et al. (2007), the figure reveals a roughly inversely U-shaped relationship: pendency times increase during the early phases, it then decreases with a minimum value of 30 months, and then it increases again until it eventually flattens out. While there is a wealth of literature on patent pendency (Popp et al. 2004; Batabyal and Nijkamp 2008; Harhoff and Wagner 2009; Henkel and Jell 2010; Van Zeebroeck 2011; Xie and Giles 2011), only Haupt et al. (2007) and Régibeau and Rockett (2010) study pendency in the life cycle. The two studies reach slightly different conclusions with regard to how pendency might change over time. Still, they both provide explanations of pendency revolving around patent complexity and learning at the patent office.[5] A major issue is that these explanations find it difficult to account for the short pendency of the earliest patents, an observation that holds in our sample. Even beyond the scope of our work, a possible explanation for that trend is that because novelty and nonobviousness are patentability requirements, it may be straightforward to recognize a highly original invention even if the patent examiner does not fully understand the technology at the time. That understanding may become more important later on, when more patent applications related to the

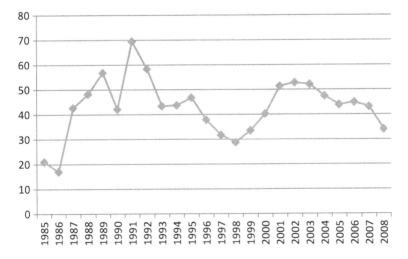

Fig. 4 Average patent pendency in months

---

[5] Régibeau and Rockett (2010) expected that pendency time would steadily decrease throughout the technology cycle, due to decreasing technological uncertainty in the examination process as the patent office learned more about the new technology. Their results were generally consistent with this expectation. Haupt et al. (2007), on the other hand, expected pendency time to decrease during the growth phase due to learning at the patent office, but then to extend again during the maturity phase since "then the applications have to be compared to a higher technological standard" (p. 393).

new technology are filed. At this point finer judgments would have to be made, and
the learning curve at the patent office would become a more important factor.

Pace of Technological Change

Figure 5 plots the TCT over time and it documents that it varies over the technology
cycle. TCT is higher (the cycle is longer and the technology progresses more slowly)
during the early and later stages, but the pace, as expected, increases during the
growth phase. Interestingly, this U-shaped pattern is strikingly similar to that of
pendency time in Fig. 4. It therefore implies that pendency and the pace of technological change move together. It is likely that when technology advances faster, the
actions of applicants promote speedier patent process times, and/or the patent office
responds in the same manner. These two indicators can give additional information
as to the current state of the TLC. Since the TTO will be examining the TLC in real
time, as it were, comparing TCT with the flow of applications and grants may allow
a more accurate judgment regarding the TLC stage and its impact on patent value.

Complexity

In Fig. 6 we see that patent scope, our measure of complexity, does not vary in any
regular fashion over the course of the technology life cycle; the slope of the trend
line is essentially zero. This, then, is one area that the TTO may be able to safely

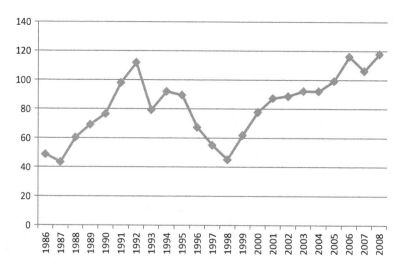

Fig. 5 Technology cycle time

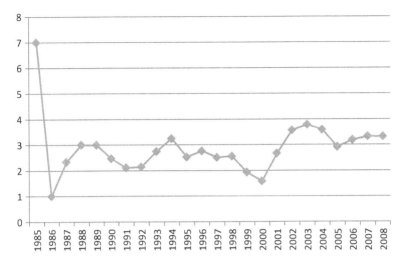

Fig. 6 Average patent scope

ignore in its valuation decision. More complex inventions are not necessarily any more or less valuable; other factors are more important.

Conclusion

One fundamental purpose of a university TTO is to maximize the future income streams from university IP holdings. In order to do this successfully, the TTO must estimate the market value of a patented invention as accurately as possible and formulate a technology transfer agreement with a private firm to develop the invention into a marketable innovation. This is a difficult task, always undertaken in conditions of uncertainty and insufficient information. In this study we have proposed that indicators drawn from patent data, specifically the annual flow of granted patents and TCT, can be used to position a given invention within the context of a progressing technology life cycle. Using the real-world example of PCR, we demonstrated that these indicators vary predictably over the TLC and thus are potentially useful in charting the current state of a specific life cycle. Further, we have shown how these indicators relate to the potential value of a patented invention and the uncertainty of that value. These indicators can be calculated from readily available patent data and can inform TTO decisions about the optimal form for a particular technology transfer agreement.

More specifically, our results shed some light on the relative merits of equity holdings versus traditional licensing as remuneration to the university for technology transfer. Under conditions of high uncertainty, as pertain early in a TLC, by accepting an equity stake in the firm, the university bears some of the uncertainty surrounding a new invention, making the agreement more attractive to the firm, which may be a relatively new startup with limited resources. At the same time, equity may be more attractive to the university as its fortunes are tied to overall firm performance rather than the potential of just one invention (Feldman et al. 2002). Late in the TLC, when the prospective value of an invention is both more moderate and more certain, a traditional licensing agreement may be more effective in maximizing university income and maintaining the relationship with the private firm.

We must also keep in mind that income stream maximization is not the only goal for university TTOs. In some cases it may not even be the primary goal, taking a back seat to the mission of ensuring research results are used to benefit society at large (OECD 2003). This is often especially true in agriculture, as the founding principles of land grant universities include a mandate to share the results of agricultural research through their cooperative extension services. Even in these cases, though, the TTO may be in a position of allocating scarce resources to numerous technology transfer projects, as described by Cartalos in another chapter in this volume, and would need to assess their relative values to society in order to ensure the best use of TTO capabilities. Our results here might be helpful in decreasing the uncertainty surrounding the potential value of these types of agricultural innovations and thus promote economically optimal TTO decisions.

This is admittedly a preliminary investigation. While our results agree in large part with previous work in this area (e.g., Kayal and Waters 1999; Haupt et al. 2007), more research using other technology areas is definitely needed in order to demonstrate the general applicability of the concepts advanced here.

References

Anderson, P., and M.L. Tushman. 1990. Technological Discontinuities and Dominant Designs: A Cyclical Model of Technological Change. *Administrative Science Quarterly* 35 (4): 604–633.

Ayres, R.U. 1988. Barriers and Breakthroughs: An "Expanding Frontiers" Model of the Technology-Industry Life Cycle. *Technovation* 7 (2): 87–115.

Bartlett, J.M., and D. Stirling. 2003. A Short History of the Polymerase Chain Reaction. In *PCR Protocols*, ed. J.M. Bartlett and D. Stirling, vol. 226, 3–6. Totowa, NJ: Humana Press.

Batabyal, A.A., and P. Nijkamp. 2008. Is There a Tradeoff between Average Patent Pendency and Examination Errors? *International Review of Economics & Finance* 17 (1): 150–158.

Bercovitz, J., and M.P. Feldman. 2006. Entrepreneurial Universities and Technology Transfer: A Conceptual Framework for Understanding Knowledge-Based Economic Development. *Journal of Technology Transfer* 31 (1): 175–188.

Berger, F., K. Blind, and N. Thumm. 2012. Filing Behaviour Regarding Essential Patents in Industry Standards. *Research Policy* 41 (1): 216–225.

Carroll, P., and D. Casimir. 2003. PCR Patent Issues. In *PCR Protocols*, ed. J.M. Bartlett and D. Stirling, vol. 226, 7–14. Totowa, NJ: Humana Press.

Chang, P.-L., C.-C. Wu, and H.-J. Leu. 2010. Using Patent Analyses to Monitor the Technological Trends in an Emerging Field of Technology: A Case of Carbon Nanotube Field Emission Display. *Scientometrics* 82 (1): 5–19.

Chien, A., D.B. Edgar, and J.M. Trela. 1976. Deoxyribonucleic Acid Polymerase from the Extreme Thermophile *Thermus aquaticus*. *Journal of Bacteriology* 127 (3): 1550–1557.

DiMasi, J.A., and H.G. Grabowski. 2007. The Cost of Biopharmaceutical R&D: Is Biotech Different? *Managerial and Decision Economics* 28 (4–5): 469–479.

Feldman, M.P., I. Feller, J. Bercovitz, and R. Burton. 2002. Equity and the Technology Transfer Strategies of American Research Universities. *Management Science* 48 (1): 105–121.

Fischer, T., and J. Leidinger. 2014. Testing Patent Value Indicators on Directly Observed Patent Value—An Empirical Analysis of Ocean Tomo Patent Auctions. *Research Policy* 43 (3): 519–529. https://doi.org/10.1016/j.respol.2013.07.013.

Gambardella, A., D. Harhoff, and B. Verspagen. 2008. The Value of European Patents. *European Management Review* 5 (2): 69–84.

Gans, J.S., D.H. Hsu, and S. Stern. 2008. The Impact of Uncertainty Intellectual Property Rights on the Market for Ideas: Evidence from Patent Grant Delays. *Management Science* 54 (5): 982–997.

Harhoff, D., F.M. Scherer, and K. Vopel. 2003. Citations, Family Size, Opposition and the Value of Patent Rights. *Research Policy* 32 (8): 1343–1363.

Harhoff, D., and S. Wagner. 2009. The Duration of Patent Examination at the European Patent Office. *Management Science* 55 (12): 1969–1984.

Haupt, R., M. Kloyer, and M. Lange. 2007. Patent Indicators for the Technology Life Cycle Development. *Research Policy* 36 (3): 387–398.

Hayashi, K. 1994. Manipulation of DNA by PCR. In *The Polymerase Chain Reaction*, ed. K.B. Mullis, F. Ferre, and R.A. Gibbs, 3–13. Boston: Birkhauser.

Henkel, J., and F. Jell. 2010. Patent Pending–Why Faster Isn't Always Better. Available at SSRN 1738912.

Huang, L.-C., and L. Yan 2011. Research on Technological Trajectories Based on Patent Documents and Related Empirical Study. 2011 International Conference on Management Science and Engineering (ICMSE), IEEE.

Kalaitzandonakes, N., J.M. Alston, and K.J. Bradford. 2007. Compliance Costs for Regulatory Approval of New Biotech Crops. *Nature Biotechnology* 25 (5): 509–511.

Kayal, A. 1999. Measuring the Pace of Technological Progress: Implications for Technological Forecasting. *Technological Forecasting and Social Change* 60 (3): 237–245.

Kayal, A.A., and R.C. Waters. 1999. An Empirical Evaluation of the Technology Cycle Time Indicator as a Measure of the Pace of Technological Progress in Superconductor Technology. *IEEE Transactions on Engineering Management* 46 (2): 127–131.

Kleppe, K., E. Ohtsuka, R. Kleppe, I. Molineux, and H. Khorana. 1971. Studies on Polynucleotides: Xcvi. Repair Replication of Short Synthetic Dna's as Catalyzed by DNA Polymerases. *Journal of Molecular Biology* 56 (2): 341–361.

Kline, S.J., and N. Rosenberg. 1986. An Overview of Innovation. In *The Positive Sum Strategy: Harnessing Technology for Economic Growth*, 275–305. Washington, DC: National Academy Press.

Ko, Y. 1992. An Economic Analysis of Biotechnology Patent Protection. *The Yale Law Journal* 102 (3): 777–804.

Lanjouw, J.O., and M. Schankerman. 2004. Protecting Intellectual Property Rights: Are Small Firms Handicapped? *Journal of Law and Economics* 47 (1): 45–74.

Lemley, M., and B. Sampat. 2012. Examiner Characteristics and Patent Office Outcomes. *The Review of Economics and Statistics* 94 (3): 817–827.

Lerner, J. 1994. The Importance of Patent Scope: An Empirical Analysis. *The Rand Journal of Economics* 25 (2): 319–333.

Lundquist, G. 2003. A Rich Vision of Technology Transfer Technology Value Management. *The Journal of Technology Transfer* 28 (3): 265–284. https://doi.org/10.1023/a:1024949029313.

Mises, L.v. 1998. *Human Action: A Treatise on Economics*. Auburn, AL: Ludwig von Mises Institute.

Mitra-Kahn, B., A. Marco, M. Carley, P. D'Agostino, P. Evans, C. Frey, and N. Sultan. 2013. Patent Backlogs, Inventories and Pendency: An International Framework. London, UKIPO-USPTO

Joint Report, available at: https://www.gov.uk/government/uploads/system/uploads/attachment_data/file/311239/ipresearch-uspatlog-201306.pdf.

Mullis, K.B. 1990. The Unusual Origin of the Polymerase Chain Reaction. *Scientific American* 262 (4): 56–61.

Mullis, K.B., F.A. Faloona, S.J. Scharf, R.K. Saiki, G.T. Horn, and H.A. Erlich. 1986. Specific Enzymatic Amplification of DNA in Vitro: The Polymerase Chain Reaction. *Cold Spring Harbor Symposia on Quantitative Biology* 51: 263–273.

Odasso, C., G. Scellato, and E. Ughetto. 2015. Selling Patents at Auction: An Empirical Analysis of Patent Value. *Industrial and Corporate Change* 24 (2): 417–438. https://doi.org/10.1093/icc/dtu015.

OECD. 2003. *Turning Science into Business. Patenting and Licensing at Public Research Organizations*. Paris: OECD Publications.

———. 2014. OECD Patent Databases: Identifying Technology Areas for Patents. Organization for Economic Cooperation and Development. www.oecd.org/sti/inno/40807441.pdf.

Popp, D., T. Juhl, and D. Johnson. 2004. Time in Purgatory: Examining the Grant Lag for US Patent Applications. *Topics in Economic Analysis & Policy* 4 (1): 1–43.

Powell, J., and F. Moris. 2004. Different Timelines for Different Technologies. *The Journal of Technology Transfer* 29 (2): 125–152. https://doi.org/10.1023/b:jott.0000019535.77467.68.

Rabinow, P. 1996. *Making PCR: A Story of Biotechnology*. Chicago, IL: University of Chicago Press.

Régibeau, P., and K. Rockett. 2010. Innovation Cycles and Learning at the Patent Office: Does the Early Patent Get the Delay? *The Journal of Industrial Economics* 58 (2): 222–246.

Saiki, R.K., D.H. Gelfand, S. Stoffel, S.J. Scharf, R. Higuchi, G.T. Horn, K.B. Mullis, and H.A. Erlich. 1988. Primer-Directed Enzymatic Amplification of DNA with a Thermostable DNA Polymerase. *Science* 239 (4839): 487–491.

Schmoch, U. 2008. *Concept of a Technology Classification for Country Comparisons: Final Report to the World Intellectual Property Organization (WIPO)*. Fraunhofer Institute for Systems and Innovation Research: Karlsruhe, Germany.

Schoonmaker, M., E. Carayannis, and P. Rau. 2012. The Role of Marketing Activities in the Fuzzy Front End of Innovation: A Study of the Biotech Industry. *The Journal of Technology Transfer* 38 (6): 850–872. https://doi.org/10.1007/s10961-012-9296-1.

Siegel, D.S., R. Veugelers, and M. Wright. 2007. Technology Transfer Offices and Commercialization of University Intellectual Property: Performance and Policy Implications. *Oxford Review of Economic Policy* 23 (4): 640–660.

Sneed, K.A., and D.K. Johnson. 2009. Selling Ideas: The Determinants of Patent Value in an Auction Environment. *R&D Management* 39 (1): 87–94.

Taylor, M., and A. Taylor. 2012. The Technology Life Cycle: Conceptualization and Managerial Implications. *International Journal of Production Economics* 140 (1): 541–553.

Trajtenberg, M., R. Henderson, and A. Jaffe. 1997. University Versus Corporate Patents: A Window on the Basicness of Invention. *Economics of Innovation and New Technology* 5 (1): 19–50.

USPTO. 2015. 609 – Information Disclosure Statement. Retrieved 25 April 2017, from https://www.uspto.gov/web/offices/pac/mpep/s609.html.

Van Zeebroeck, N. 2007. Patents Only Live Twice: A Patent Survival Analysis in Europe. CEB Working Paper No. 07/028. Brussells, Belgium, Centre Emile Bernheim, Solvay Business School, Universite Libre de Bruxelles. Available at: https://ideas.repec.org/p/sol/wpaper/07-028.html.

———. 2011. Long Live Patents: The Increasing Life Expectancy of Patent Applications and Its Determinants. *Review of Economics and Institutions* 2 (3): 1–37.

Wittwer, C. 2001. Rapid Cycle Real-Time PCR: Methods and Applications. In *Rapid Cycle Real-Time PCR: Methods and Applications*, ed. S. Meuer, C. Wittwer, and K. Nakagawara, 1–8. Berlin: Springer.

Xie, Y., and D.E. Giles. 2011. A Survival Analysis of the Approval of US Patent Applications. *Applied Economics* 43 (11): 1375–1384.

Part IV
Technology Transfer to Agricultural Producers

Role of Extension in Agricultural Technology Transfer: A Critical Review

Alex Koutsouris

Abstract Technology transfer (TT), or transfer of technology (TOT), is an integral part of the extension process involving the transfer and spread of technical innovation and know-how to the farming population. The TOT model of the research-extension-farmer linkage is based on the tenets of DOI theory, in particular on a description of the diffusion process as a normal bell-shaped curve with farmers being placed in one of five categories according to their appearance on the curve. However, this linear model has limitations and has been severely criticized on a number of grounds, especially its assumptions about the dissemination process which raise the "issue of equality" and contribute to the "agricultural treadmill."

Furthermore, despite being dominant in agricultural development, on a worldwide basis, TOT has lost utility in understanding the sources of and thus the solutions to highly complex contemporary problems. As a result, alternative proposals have emerged, prominent among which have been systemic approaches such as systems of innovations (SoI). Therefore, there has been a shift of conceptual frameworks in the study of agriculture-related policy, research, technology, and rural development toward agricultural innovation systems (AIS) focusing on processes relevant to innovation networks as formed by heterogeneous actors with particular attention being given to social coordination. In this respect, a new species emerges, that of "intermediaries" (innovation facilitators/brokers) who take an independent systemic role in process facilitation rather than in the production or dissemination of innovation. New systemic extension approaches thus emerge, aiming at the role of co-learning facilitators to stimulate innovations.

Introduction

Technology transfer (TT), or transfer of technology (TOT), is the process of transferring or disseminating technology from the places/groups where it was generated to users in wider audiences in other places. Despite their different interpretations, different views seem to share the basic idea of TT as "a movement of

A. Koutsouris (✉)
Agricultural University of Athens, Athens, Greece
e-mail: koutsouris@aua.gr

know-how, technical knowledge, and/or technology from one or more donor sources to another, recipient entity" (Roxas et al. 2011: 7). In agriculture, TT/TOT is thus an integral part of the extension process involving the transfer and spread of technical innovation and know-how from technology developers through extension communicators to the farming population (Blackburn and Vist 1984).

The term "extension education" was coined by Cambridge University to describe the effort to take the educational advantages of the universities to ordinary people; starting in 1873, it created a movement which adapted to meet the needs of the people, the place, and the time (Maunder 1972: 1; see also Jones and Garforth 1997; Leeuwis 2004). Therefore, extension is broadly defined by Maunder (1972: 2) as "The extending of, or a service or system which extends, the educational advantages of an institution to persons unable to avail themselves of them in a normal manner."

In this vein, Maunder (op. cit.: 3) defines agricultural extension as "[A] service or system which assists farm people, through educational procedures, in improving farming methods and techniques, increasing production efficiency and income, bettering their levels of living, and lifting the social and educational standards of rural life." According to Coombs and Ahmed (1974), various kinds of extension activities and short-term training constitute nonformal agricultural education. However, "extension means different things to different people" (Röling 1982: 87) since it is "organized in different ways to accomplish a wide variety of objectives" (Swanson and Claar 1984: 1) and has evolving definitions (Leeuwis 2004: 22–29); in parallel, extension services have experienced severe changes and transformations over time, especially since the 1980s, and continue to be in transition (Rivera and Qamar 2013; Cristóvão et al. 2012).

Nevertheless, "[M]ost people see extension as a government instrument to promote techniques for improving agricultural production…" (Röling op. cit.), or, as Nagel (1997) argues, traditionally extension has been conceived of as the appropriate means for transferring "modern" research results to the "traditional" farmer. In sum, it can be argued that extension is, more or less, on a worldwide basis, identified with TOT and the diffusion of innovations (DOI) theory.

The TOT model of the research-extension-farmer linkage was based on a combination of a general faith in science and commitment to modernization (Nagel op. cit.; Röling 1988) and the tenets of DOI theory. As Lamble (1984: 32) asserts, in order to be able to facilitate the adoption of innovations by farmers (i.e., to fulfill their major function), extension practitioners must have a good understanding of the processes involved in DOI which, in turn, provides the basis for the development of effective strategies for extension programs.

Diffusion of Innovations (DOI)

For the purposes of this work, there is no need to go into detail about the description and analysis of DOI. Therefore, the basic concepts, i.e., innovation, diffusion, and adoption, will be briefly dealt with, along with the main components of DOI, i.e., (a) the model of adoption as a sequential process of five stages, (b) a classification of innovations according to five characteristics, and (c) a description of the diffusion process as a normal bell-shaped curve with farmers being placed in one of five categories according to their appearance on the curve.

According to Rogers (1983: 134–162), the innovation-development process consists of six stages: recognizing a problem/need, research (basic/applied), development, commercialization, diffusion and adoption, and consequences.

"[A]n *innovation* is an idea, practice, or object perceived as new by an individual or other unit of adoption" (Rogers 1983: 11) to which Van den Ban and Hawkins (1988: 100) add the phrase "…but which is not always the result of recent research." This addition is very important in agriculture due to the heterogeneity of biophysical environments, farms, and farmers as well as the scattering of farm holdings over large spaces implying that something that is known in one area may be an innovation when introduced in another area of the same region/country.

Then, "*[D]iffusion* is the process by which an innovation is communicated through certain channels over time among the members of a social system" (Rogers 1983: 5). Diffusion is "a special type of communication" (Lamble op. cit.: 33) with the latter being "a process in which participants create and share information with one another to reach a mutual understanding" (Rogers op. cit.). In the diffusion process, information flows through networks. The nature of networks and the roles opinion leaders play in them influence the likelihood that the innovation will be adopted.

The individual decision-making process that occurs when individuals consider adopting a new idea, product, or practice can be described as follows (Rogers 1962: 81–86):

Awareness: The individual is exposed to the innovation; awareness is usually driven by sources outside the community.

Interest: The individual is interested and actively seeks out more/new information.

Evaluation: The individual mentally examines the innovation (mentally applies the innovation) using the available information.

Trial: The individual actually tests the innovation to see if reality matches expectations, usually with small-scale, experimental efforts.

Adoption: The individual adopts (decides to continue the full use of) the innovation.

Rogers and Shoemaker (1971: 99–133) presented an alternative adoption model of four steps (knowledge-persuasion-decision-confirmation) to which later Rogers added a fifth one, "implementation" (Rogers 1983: 174). Therefore, the adoption process was formed as follows (Rogers 1983: 163–209):

Knowledge: The individual is exposed to the new innovation.

Persuasion: The individual shows more interest in the innovation (becomes more psychologically involved), seeks more information about it, and forms a favorable or unfavorable attitude toward the innovation (affective domain).

Decision: The individual evaluates the positive and negative aspects of the innovation, decides whether to accept or reject the innovation, and engages in activities that lead to a choice to adopt or reject the innovation, including a trial if the innovation is trialable.

Implementation: The individual puts an innovation into use.

Confirmation: The decision to adopt or reject is not the final stage of the process; the individual seeks reinforcement of an innovation decision that has already been made but may reverse this previous decision if exposed to conflicting messages about the innovation.

The speed with which each individual passes through these five stages varies depending on the particular innovation's characteristics which influence its adoption, i.e., relative advantage (the degree to which it is superior to ideas it supersedes), compatibility (the degree to which it is consistent with existing values and past experiences of the adopter), complexity (the degree to which it is relatively difficult to understand and use), divisibility (the degree to which it may be tried on a limited basis), and communicability (the degree to which the results may be diffused to others) (Rogers 1983: 210–240). Furthermore, the communication channels used in the various stages of the adoption process are differentiated (op. cit. 197–201).

Innovation diffusion research has attempted to explain the variables that influence how and why users adopt an innovation. Based on innovativeness (i.e., earliness or lateness of adoption; Rogers 1983: 242) and the fact that "adopter distributions closely approach normality" (Rogers op. cit.: 246), five ideals of adopter categories are recognized, as follows: (1) innovators (venturesome), the first ones to try out a new idea accounting for 2.5% of the adopters; (2) early adopters (respected), who adopt a little later making up for 13.5%; some time later (3) the early (deliberate) and (4) the late majority (skeptical) follow one after the other, accounting for 34% each; and finally (5) laggards (traditional), who make up for 16% and are the last ones to adopt. Moreover, these categories differ systematically in a number of ways, i.e., in the characteristics of individuals that make them likely to adopt an innovation (Rogers op. cit.). For example, innovators have been found to be relatively young, to be better educated, to have more land, and to be specialized, as well as to have multiple information sources and to be more cosmopolitan; laggards tend to lie at the opposite extremes with respect to the aforementioned characteristics, with the other categories ranking between the two extremes (Rogers op. cit.: 240–270).

Given that extension agents are not able to work closely with all farmers in their districts (as they are outnumbered by farmers), they can increase their impact by cooperating with opinion leaders (Van den Ban and Hawkins 1988: 115) since following Rogers (1983: 331) "Change agent success is positively related to the extent that he or she works through opinion leaders." This is so as, on the one hand, the two parties are similar in certain attributes, which increases the effectiveness of their communication contact (Rogers op. cit.: 321–322). On the other hand, opinion leaders fulfill important functions with regard to innovations: they pass on and interpret information on the basis of own opinions and experience, set an example for others to follow, and give their approval or disapproval to changes (Van den Ban and Hawkins op. cit.: 113–114). Therefore the so-called progressive farmer strategy followed within the classical, centralized TOT model can be depicted as a trickle-down process, as follows:

Research → Extension → Progressive Farmers → Other Farmers

Progressive farmers coincide with opinion leaders, who in turn largely coincide with early adopters, given that they adopt many innovations but usually are not the first to adopt them, are well educated, enjoy sound financial positions in their communities, lead an active social life, have many contacts outside their immediate surroundings, and have a special interest in their subject (Van den Ban and Hawkins op. cit.).

Critique of the TOT Model/DOI Theory

According to Rogers et al. (1976, in Nitsch 1982: 7), there is a reciprocal relationship between extension and DOI: extension provides the empirical material and DOI the concepts and models. As mentioned earlier, classical DOI claims that innovations originate from scientists, are transferred by extension agents, and are applied by farmers. Agricultural research and extension based on this TOT model have a long history of successfully transferred innovations and increased efficiency in food production. However, this linear model has limitations and has been severely criticized on a number of grounds; Nitch (1982: 6) summarizes the critiques of DOI in terms of its three basic assumptions: assumptions about content, assumptions about the dissemination process, and assumptions about learning (see also Rogers 1976a).

In particular, diffusion is seen as information dissemination through a trickle-down process from individual early innovators to other farmers. This assumption takes as a given that information is relevant and applicable for a majority of farmers as well as that interaction and communication between farmers actually takes place. Therefore, the model is open to criticism for being oversimplified, ignoring the complexity of multiple situational and individual factors and the increasing stratification of social interaction (op. cit.). Röling et al. (1976: 69) underline the fact that "differences in resources endowment ... may imply great differences among farm households in their capacity to benefit from innovations." In this respect, Röling (1982: 95) underscores "the untenability of the assumption that farmers are homogeneous in basic attributes so that a uniform innovation is relevant to all farmers"; later Röling (1988: 70) demarcated the heterogeneity of the farming population in terms of psychological characteristics, life cycle differences, access to resources, and access to information. It follows that "small producers are not necessarily 'laggards', but will respond rationally and favorably to realistic opportunities" (Ascroft et al. 1973, in Röling 1982: 90). As Garforth (1982: 44) argues "bias arises because the information offered by extension services is more appropriate to larger farmers and richer members of the community."

DOI has been found to strongly suffer from pro-change, pro-innovation, and pro-technology bias (Nitch 1982; Röling 1988).

Moreover, Ascroft et al. (1973, in Röling 1982: 90) stress that in our times "innovations come in rapid succession" which along with the fact that "early adopters reap 'windfall profits'" implies a self-reinforcing process (Röling 1988: 75), resulting in the widening of gaps between early and late adopters. This is known in DOI as the "issue of equality" (Rogers 1983: 133); i.e., "diffusion processes lead to inequitable development" (Röling et al. 1976: 71). Rogers (1976b: 137) recognizes the "propensity for diffusion to widen socioeconomic gaps in a rural audience" and argues that, on the one hand, new ideas (1983: 382) and technological innovations (1983: 264) and, on the other hand, change agents in the extension service tend to widen the gaps between advantaged and disadvantaged groups of farmers (1983: 391). In this respect, DOI "unfortunately tends to contribute to inequality by providing reinforcement of this current practice on the part of the development agencies" (Rogers 1976c: 11), thus his call to view communication as a total process rather than "just a one-way, direct, communicator-to-passive-receiver activity" and the questioning of the "components approach" which "fails to capture the systemic nature of the communication process" (Rogers op. cit.: 13).

Despite such criticisms, especially Rogers' revision of his initial classical, centralized DOI and the "growing awareness that traditional extension methods are inherently biased toward the more progressive and better-off elements of the rural population" (Garforth 1982: 43), Röling et al. (1976: 65–66) argue that "the diffusion generalizations often become normative for the practice of change agencies." This, in turn, implies that "extension services focus on progressive farmers ... [since DOI insures that] innovations do trickle down from progressive farmers," thus resulting in "a multiplier effect for the efforts of the change agent." This way extension indeed contributes to widening the gap between progressive farmers who are opinion leaders and less-advantaged, resource-poor ones.

In the same vein, diffusion is an integral element of the agricultural treadmill theory (Cochrane 1958). According to the treadmill, many farmers produce the same product and produce as much as possible at the going price, which they cannot affect. Early adopters make profits for a short while due to the adoption of a new technological innovation. After some time, other farmers follow (diffusion); as more farmers adopt the technology/innovation production and/or efficiency increases and prices go down, thus profits are no longer possible. Laggards are lost in the price squeeze and must either adopt or leave the scene, leaving room to more successful farmers to expand (scale enlargement).

From Transfer to Cogeneration

As already mentioned, the diffusion of innovations model, also known as the transfer of technology or knowledge (TOT/TOK) model, which is dominant in agricultural development, has been based on the understanding that innovations originate from scientists, are transferred by extension agents, and are adopted and applied by farmers. On the other hand, the agrarian sciences that support TOT have been dominated by instrumental rationalist knowledge (Habermas 1984) or the paradigm of experimental, reductionist science (Packham and Sriskandarajah 2005). This, in turn, resulted in a "culture of technical control" (Bawden 2005), implying reliance upon scientific experimentation to create solutions for agricultural problems (Nerbonne and Lentz 2003).

However, as stressed by Hubert et al. (2000: 17), "The dominant linear paradigm of agricultural innovation based on delivery to, and diffusion among, farmers of technologies developed by science, has lost utility as an explanation of what happens." There are two reasons for this. First, despite reductionism's dazzling achievements, alternative proposals have flourished since the 1970s based on the realization of the inadequacy of linear, mechanistic thinking in understanding the sources of and thus the solutions to problems (Hjorth and Bagheri 2006). Prominent among these alternatives have been systemic approaches (see Ison 2010). Such approaches look at a potential system as a whole (holistically) and focus on the important causal relationships among a system's parts and on system dynamics, rather than on the parts themselves. Second, its long history of innovations and increased effectiveness in food production notwithstanding the diffusion of innovations model has been heavily criticized for failing to respond to complex challenges and rapidly changing contexts (see below).

A leap in this respect has been, in both theoretical and practical terms (Byerlee et al. 1982, Simmonds 1986), the emergence of farming systems research/extension (FSR/E) approaches. Inspired by ecology and general systems theory (Schiere et al. 1999), FSR/E approaches have, on the one hand, demonstrated that local farming systems are complex adaptive systems that have coevolved with human societies to fit local ecological conditions and satisfy human needs. On the other hand, through FSR/E, vast experience has been accumulated in terms of understanding farmers, eliciting information, and developing relevant tools and methods. FSR/E contributed substantially to the recognition of different actors in development and helped to create awareness about the need for new ways to conduct research and extension, taking into account context and relations (see Collinson 2000; Darnhofer et al. 2012).

A further important evolution has been, within the FSR/E tradition, the turn from Rapid Rural Appraisal (RRA) to Participatory Rural Appraisal (PRA) (Chambers 1992, 1994; Pretty 1995; Webber 1995), which "tends to favor facilitation of a non-interventionist variety" (Robinson, 2002). A suite of participatory approaches and methods relating to agricultural and rural development has thus been developed, including Farmer Participatory Research, Participatory Action Research, Participatory Rural Appraisal, Participatory Technology Development, etc. (see Pretty 1995). This shift underlines the need for interaction and dialogue between different actors and networks (Chambers 1993; Scoones and Thompson 1994) or the interpenetration of actors' lifeworlds and projects (Long 1992), based on the realization that communication flows and exchange between different actors are extremely important for existing knowledge to be either reinforced or somehow transformed or deconstructed, thus leading to the emergence of new forms and a "fusion of horizons" (Leeuwis et al. 1990).

Therefore, the question of how to go about generating innovation and development in agriculture does not concern solely technical issues. For Leeuwis (2000), it is important to consider farmers' views regarding new technical solutions' compatibility with prevailing management demands and wider social-organizational conditions. This, in turn, implies that farmers must be able to set their own strategic goals, participate actively, and build upon their own experiences and knowledge within a co-learning process which does justice to individual differences and qualities of people.

Subsequently, the emphasis has gradually shifted toward learning, i.e., the processes of human interaction from which learning emerges (LEARN Group 2000; Röling and Wagemakers 1998). The epistemological point of departure is that learning is an active knowledge construction process rather than the passive reception and absorption of knowledge. In this respect, learning is seen as a social process in which participants interact and negotiate to determine what is socially known (Koutsouris and Papadopoulos 2003). Thus the emphasis currently given to the principles of experiential learning (Kolb 1984) and its advances, such as participatory learning and action research, stressing, among others, the importance of reflection and dialogue.

The Sustainability Era

In general, the attempts to solve current, increasingly complex problems with a view to sustainability make it clear that this is a particularly complicated task since there is no single, privileged analytical point of view. Besides, when dealing with such problems sustainably, there may be little useable science, high levels of inherent uncertainty, and severe potential consequences from decisions that have to be made. Moreover, the realization that real-world problems do not come in disciplinary boxes calls for the cooperation of diverse academic experts and practitioners. Such a problematique, in turn, reinforces new forms of learning and problem-solving integrating a variety of perspectives and insights. As a result, new, multidisciplinary forms of learning and research strive to take into account the complexity of an issue and challenge the fragmentation of knowledge; they accept local contexts and uncertainties, address both science's and society's diverse perceptions of an issue through communicative action, and work to produce practically relevant knowledge. New concepts, theoretical contributions, and metaphors are thus flourishing nowadays to help understand and predict the links between social, ecological, and economic systems, meet real-world challenges, and address sustainability, as well as to organize various forms of cross-disciplinarity into a coherent framework (see Koutsouris 2008).

With the sustainability era having in general favored "multi-stakeholder processes" thinking (Dalal-Clayton and Bass 2002; Hemmati 2002), such considerations have been further enhanced in agricultural literature and practice since, in addition to the ecologically, agronomically, and socioeconomically complex nature of farming systems, sustainable agricultural practices are per se complex and nonprescriptive.

According to Röling and Jiggins (1998), ecologically sound agriculture, focusing on holistic farm and resource management, is observation, knowledge, and learning intensive; it is also technology intensive, due to its reliance on sophisticated technologies for production and resources, energy, and quality management. Additionally, sustainable agricultural systems require tailor-made interventions, adapted to local conditions (Leeuwis 2004) while paying attention to higher system levels as well. In this respect, Deugd et al. (1998) underline the importance of discovery and experiential learning. Indeed, participatory approaches, involving farmers, extension workers, and researchers in group work and joint experimentation, are deemed suitable for the development and adaptation of site-specific knowledge (Röling and van de Fliert 1994; Somers 1998; Leeuwis 2004).

Crucially, according to Röling and Jiggins (1998), the shift to sustainable agriculture concerns a systemic change requiring double loop learning, i.e., a profound change in assumptions and strategies underlying subsequent actions (Argyris and Schön 1974) or a move from traditional, first-order practice to second-order change, i.e., a change in perspective or level (Ison and Russel 2000). Moreover, Röling and Jiggins (1998) argue that the move toward an ecological knowledge system and away from the conventional knowledge system means the need to move from a praxeology (i.e., theory informing practice and practices feeding new theory) of transfer of knowledge to one of facilitating knowledge, focusing "on enhancing the farmers' capacity to observe, experiment, discuss, evaluate and plan ahead" (Deugd et al. 1998: 269; see also Röling and van de Fliert 1994; Röling and Jiggins 1998; Somers 1998). The new praxeology, i.e., facilitation of learning processes, thus calls for an alternative extension pedagogy entailing stakeholders' participation in experiential learning and knowledge exchange (Woodhill and Röling 1998).

Social learning (SL) lies at the heart of such multi-stakeholder processes. It refers to the collective action and reflection that occurs among stakeholders as they work toward mutually acceptable solution to a problem pertaining to the management of human and environmental interrelationships (Keen et al. 2005; Wals 2007). SL thus concerns an interactive, participatory style of problem-solving, with outside intervention taking the form of facilitation (Leeuwis and Pyburn 2002: 11), and supports multiple-loop learning (Argyris and Schön 1974) or adaptive learning (Webler et al. 1995).

Furthermore, SL emerges as a policy option – a relevant framework for processes of social change vis-à-vis the main coordination mechanisms, i.e., hierarchy and market (SLIM 2004). SL implies an actor-oriented approach focusing on participatory processes of social change which are defined as nonlinear and nondeterministic. SL denotes a form of network seen as an active, transformative process allowing stakeholders to engage in concerted actions that lead to sustainable development. For Röling (2002: 35) "social learning can best be described as a move from multiple to collective and/or distributed cognition." That is, through SL, stakeholders, each with their own cognition, may develop distributed cognition, a situation where ideas, values, and aspirations need not be shared but overlap or are mutually supportive (Leeuwis 2004: 145).

Extension for sustainable agriculture therefore implies a social mechanism for facilitating SL (Allahyari et al. 2009), i.e., participatory processes of social change through shared learning, collaboration, and the development of consensus about the action to be taken. Consequently, a new extension approach aiming at participatory group learning and networking with extension agents acting as facilitators is required (see Garforth and Lawrence 1997).

All in all, the transition toward more sustainable forms of agriculture requires the reinvention of extension (Leeuwis 2004), that is, the engagement of a wide range of stakeholders in networks allowing for and promoting social learning and the cogeneration, dissemination, and use of innovations (Klerkx et al. 2010, 2012; Cristóvão et al. 2012; Brunori et al. 2013; Hermans et al. 2013; Moschitz et al. 2015). Thus, the emergence, both in theory and practice, of a wide variety of approaches to collaborative-participatory development (see Koutsouris 2008), especially in sustainable natural resources management and integrated, sustainable agricultural and rural development, entails new configurations including learning partnerships, group extension, farmer-field schools, communities of practice, study circles, and farmer networks (see Cristóvão et al. 2012).

Agricultural Innovation Systems

During the last few decades, a number of new systems of innovations (SoI) approaches have emerged in the nonagricultural literature, including the national SoI approach (e.g., Edquist 1997; Lundvall 1992), the technological systems approaches (e.g., Hughes 1987; Carlsson 1995), and the sociotechnical systems approach (e.g., Bijker 1995; Geels 2004). Such approaches emphasize the multiplicity of determinants which influence the development, diffusion, and use of innovations. They also stress that innovation emerges from networks of actors involving interactive learning process; therefore, contemporary interactive approaches emphasize the iterative, adaptive nature of innovation. Additionally, for SoI, innovations concern not only new technological arrangements but new social and organizational arrangements as well.

In this respect, there has been a shift of conceptual frameworks in the study of agriculture-related policy, research, technology, and rural development from TOT and the strengthening of National Agricultural Research Systems (NARS) to network and systems approaches such as the agricultural knowledge and information systems (AKIS) and, more recently, toward agricultural innovation systems (AIS) (see Röling and Engel 1991; Rivera and Zijp 2002; Klerkx and Leeuwis 2008a; Klerkx et al. 2010; Leeuwis 2004, Rivera et al. 2005; World Bank 2006; EU-SCAR 2012). Contra TOT, these approaches claim that the process of innovation is messy and complex; new ideas are developed and implemented by people who engage in networks and make adjustments in order to achieve desired outcomes (Van de Ven et al. 1999).

The NARS framework, espousing the linear TOT model which assumes a pipeline where innovations are developed by research and handed over to extension who then pass the innovation onto farmers, aimed at investments in agricultural research institutes and higher education institutions in order to strengthen research supply. Subsequently, the agricultural knowledge systems (AKS) framework brought attention to demand side factors. It aimed at integrating farmers, education, research, and extension and has been depicted as a knowledge triangle, with the farmer being placed at the center of this arrangement.

Its successor, agricultural knowledge and information systems (AKIS), broadened the scope of the system and included actors beyond research, extension, and education. More recently, agricultural innovation systems (AIS) embrace all actors involved in innovation and their interactions and extend beyond the creation of knowledge to include the factors affecting demand for and use of knowledge. AIS, in line with SoI, claims that the process of innovation is messy and complex with new ideas being developed and implemented by actors who engage in networks and make adjustments in order to achieve desired outcomes. Nowadays, as aforementioned, innovation studies increasingly focus on learning itself, with emphasis on facilitation and the processes of human interaction from which learning emerges.

The Intermediation Era

As already pointed out, SoI approaches build on networks as social processes encouraging the sharing of knowledge and, notably, as preconditions for innovation. Networks, as "sets of formal and informal social relationships that shape collaborative action" between heterogeneous actors "that transcend organizational structures and boundaries" (Dredge 2006: 270), have attracted increased interest from quite a number of disciplines.

Network theory, in short, implies that individuals are not isolated but connected to others, i.e., that there is some connectedness (ties; Granovetter 1973) between actors which may both facilitate and constrain their actions (embeddedness; Granovetter 1985). While actors interact within existing constraints and opportunities, they also act upon and restructure them. A social network thus concerns a populace of individual and/or organizational actors who act, intervene, exchange, and make decisions. In this sense, such groupings provide the appropriate interactive structure which allows for the definition and redefinition of their members' interpretative frameworks and supports the process of structuring and empowering their identity. The actors assimilate the multiple interactions, elaborate them, give meaning, and finally shape their perceptions and preferences; it follows that the actors' individual decisions and actions are shaped, at least partially, by interactions among network members and may in turn lead to the undertaking of collective action (Oliver and Myers 2003).

Importantly, networks are not limited to tangible resource coordination and actor collaboration; they evolve into collective learning processes, utilizing, empowering, and developing local knowledge, thus also fostering the development of innovations (Dredge 2006). Especially, the establishment and enhancement of cross-sectoral networks broadens the number of cooperating actors, stretches the boundaries of their collaboration beyond conventional arrangements, and opens wider windows of opportunity for the generation of innovations. According to Fadeeva (2005), cross-sectoral networks respond to the increased complexity of the issues to be dealt with, as well as the need to balance the power of the actors involved and augment the legitimacy of such partnerships as processes aiming at sustainable development practices.

SoI concepts/approaches, therefore, focus on processes relevant to innovation networks as formed by heterogeneous actors (see Corsaro et al. 2012) with particular attention being given to social coordination. Particularly, in order to avoid or overcome gaps (cognitive, information, managerial, or system) resulting in network and institutional failures (for a review, see Klerkx and Leeuwis 2009; Klerkx et al. 2012), growing attention is given to various types of process intermediaries and facilitators. For example, Davenport and Prusak (1998) claim that one of the characteristics of successful knowledge networks is neutral facilitation; Van Lente et al. (2003) distinguish "systemic intermediaries" as actors working mainly at the system or network level to facilitate actor interactions; Haga (2009) argues for the need to orchestrate networking enablers and thus for mediators or brokers as independent players in networks aiming at (a) acting as points of passage to external actors outside the network, bringing in experience and expertise, and (b) building internal network resources and structures upon which network governance and processes depend (see also Dhanaraj and Parkhe 2006).

Such intermediaries are increasingly found in literature as third parties: knowledge or technology brokers, bridging organizations, intermediaries, boundary organizations, and so on (see Howells 2006). Such a flourishing dialogue in the network literature on intermediaries stems, according to Kirkels and Duysters (2010: 376), "from the concept of social capital which is seen as the value that arises from the way a person is connected to others." Extensive reviews on the topic of various types of intermediaries, mainly found in the industrial dynamics, technology policy, and firm strategy sectors (see, inter alia, Howells 2006; Bakici et al. 2013) and increasingly in the healthcare literature (see, inter alia, Shea 2011; Knight and Lyall 2013), however, show that the field is still theoretically fragmented, not well grounded, and largely practice oriented. Therefore, Howells (2006: 720) prefers to employ the broad term "innovation intermediary" according to the following working definition:

> An organization or body that acts as an agent or broker in any aspect of the innovation process between two or more parties. Such intermediary activities include: helping to provide information about potential collaborators; brokering a transaction between two or more parties; acting as a mediator, or go-between, bodies or organizations that are already collaborating; and helping find advice, funding and support for the innovation outcomes of such collaborations.

It is thus quite clear that such intermediaries take an independent systemic role in process facilitation rather than in the production (i.e., source) or dissemination (i.e., carrier) of innovation (Van Lente et al. 2003). Or, according to Haga (2005), they are involved in indirect innovation processes (i.e., in enabling individuals and enterprises) rather than direct ones (i.e., in actual innovation projects).

Furthermore, Howells (2006) discriminates between intermediaries as organizations and intermediaries as processes and identifies the following functions of intermediaries: foresight and diagnostics, scanning and information processing, knowledge processing and combination/recombination, gatekeeping and brokering, testing and validation, accreditation, validation and regulation, protecting the results, commercialization, and evaluation of outcomes (see also Katzy et al. 2013). The author also states that such functions are dependent on the context, the development stage, and the composition of the innovation network and the system aggregate levels of the innovation system.

In terms of extension, pluralistic extension advisory services (Birner et al. 2009) hold a central position within or are an integral part of AIS (Klerkx et al. 2010; Faure et al. 2011). Yet, in terms of AIS, a new extension approach aiming at participatory and group learning and networking with extension agents acting as intermediaries is required. Conventional extension, identified with the linear model of innovation/TOT, has to do with exploitation, i.e., with the capture, transfer, and deployment of knowledge in other similar situations. On the contrary, new extension approaches are emerging, operating on systemic perspectives and aiming at enhancing the interaction among a variety of actors; they thus focus on exploration, i.e., on sharing and synthesizing and thus the creation of new knowledge. A major role in the new extension is that of the co-learning facilitator, usually found in literature as facilitators or brokers, aiming at the development of shared meaning and language between dialogue partners in order to stimulate change and develop innovative solutions. The engagement of stakeholders in dialogue, despite its difficulties and its time-consuming nature (since social learning and change are gradual), is necessary for achieving critical self-inquiry and collaboration. According to Sriskandarajah et al. (2006: 27), "[L]earning among heterogeneous groups of stakeholders, and among different epistemologies has become one of the most central issues today."

Facilitation has a rather long history (see Hogan 2002). According to Auvine et al. (2002) facilitation "is designed to help make groups perform more effectively" and that "a facilitator's job is to focus on how well people work together." Facilitation also relates to "providing opportunities to end-users for adoption of technology by educating them, distributing resources and setting local rules" (Theodorakopoulos et al. 2014: 648). For agriculture extension, Leeuwis (2004) summarizes the facilitator's tasks as (a) to facilitate the group process, (b) to teach, and (c) to be an expert on technical aspects of farming.

On the other hand, brokerage is new, particularly innovation brokerage. Brokers, in general, span structural holes, i.e., gaps in the social structure between groups of people or organizations (Burt 2005), either by introducing disconnected people, organizations, and networks or by facilitating new coordination between already connected ones (see also Boari and Riboldazzi 2014). Especially an innovation broker is defined as "an organization acting as a member of a network ... that is focused neither on the organization nor the implementation of innovations, but on enabling other organizations to innovate" (Winch and Courtney 2007: 751) or "a type of boundary organization that specializes in brokering or facilitating innovation processes involving several other parties, but does not itself engage in the innovation process" (Devaux et al. 2010), i.e., as a facilitator of innovation (see Winch and Courtney 2007; Van Lente et al. 2003). Innovation brokers are generally seen as beneficial to the innovation process by closing system gaps and acting as animators or catalysts.

Despite Hekkert et al.'s (2007) argument that innovation brokers contribute to several of the innovation system's functions, the topic has not been extensively embraced by the agricultural academic and research community, with the notable exception of the Dutch agricultural sector. In parallel, Klerkx and Leeuwis (2009) note that, thus far, the emergence of innovation brokers in the Dutch agricultural sector is not the result of coherent policy and maintain that, despite dilemmas, government should play the role of innovation system coordinator and mediator and thus provide funding for innovation brokers. Furthermore, Klerkx and Leeuwis (op. cit.) identify three major functions of an innovation broker: (a) demand articulation, (b) network formation, and (c) innovation process management (see Kilelu et al. 2011).

A number of examples of innovation brokering are also found in Nederlof et al. (2011) in which, within the framework of innovation platforms, Heemskerk et al. (2011) identify and discuss a number of brokering functions: facilitation, linking and strategic networking, technical backstopping, mediation, advocacy, capacity building, management, documenting learning, and championing. Brokers thus provide three lines of support: developing a common vision and articulating related demands; scoping, scanning, filtering, and strategic networking; and innovation process management (see also Swaans et al. 2014). The authors stress that, in the identification of a number of training instances for brokers notwithstanding, a good broker goes beyond training and it takes time and interaction for brokers to develop their skills. They also underline that brokering is a time-demanding and costly job, concluding that brokering is "[E]asier said than done" (p. 52). Furthermore, Klerkx and Gildemacher (2012) provide a typology of innovation brokers while also identifying key policy issues and providing a number of recommendations for practitioners, policymakers, and project leaders. Nevertheless, it is quite clear that the broker role is still very new.

Despite the overall positive intermediation functions of facilitators in knowledge diffusion and interactive innovation generation, some points of concern also emerge. For example, the experience of Landcare groups has shown that (Campbell 1997:147) (a) in many instances "[L]andcare facilitation often looks anything but strategic, and its purpose is often lost"; (b) although the key premise is that facilitators and brokers hold an impartial, independent position, "there is no such thing as a neutral, detached, value-free facilitator" (see also Drennon and Cervero 2002; Devaux et al. 2010; Klerkx and Leeuwis 2009); and (c) a facilitator should have both facilitation skills and appropriate technical background (i.e., be a social agronomist; Leeuwis 2000, 2004).

Furthermore, the issue of sustainability is also of crucial importance. Despite Oakley et al.'s (1991) argument that the withdrawal dimension implies a conscious move on the part of the facilitator/change agent along with the empowerment of local actors to undertake the role, as shown by Ljung and Emmelin (2000) and Cristóvão et al. (2008), the withdrawal of external, project-supported facilitators results in the end of such work in the localities concerned. Finally, the dilemma of "top-down" vs. "bottom-up" roles of an intermediary should be pointed out. This theme is extensively dealt with in the participation literature dealing with obstacles to participation, especially the expert syndrome (see, e.g., Botes and van Rensburg 2000; Cooke and Kothari 2001; Leal 2007; Quaghebeur et al. 2004). In the specific case of process facilitators, Savage and Hilton (2001) also take notice of the need that sometimes arises for facilitators to steer processes toward consensus, an action which the authors perceive as desirable. Similarly, Harvey et al. (2002), although favoring the enabling approach, argue that under certain circumstances the task-oriented, practical approach is also effective, while for Stetler et al. (2006), depending on the projects, specific sites, related progress, and individuals involved, the flexible facilitator may take either a directive or a nondirective style.

Conclusion

Currently there is concern about a number of issues pertaining to the generation, dissemination, and use of innovations in agriculture such as (see EU-SCAR 2012, 2014; World Bank 2012):

(a) Research is insufficiently related to practice, so science-driven innovations remain on the shelf due to little or no dissemination activities.
(b) Farmers' needs are not sufficiently addressed during innovation generation; hence, innovations are not relevant enough.
(c) Innovative ideas from practice are not captured and spread, so local or practice-generated innovations with strong potential for dissemination are not recognized or diffused.
(d) A shift from science-driven to innovation-driven research has not yet taken place; the institutional, methodological, and behavioral changes that are required for such a shift are not yet comprehensively explored, and findings and experiences are not systematically documented and assessed.

Such tasks were more or less included in the mandate of publicly funded bodies aiming at bridging the gap between agronomy science and farming practice, i.e., mainstream or conventional extension. However, as since the 1980s public extension has been found to suffer from a number of shortcomings, many countries have started experimenting with and implementing different processes (decentralization, contracting/outsourcing, public-private partnerships, privatization, etc.) in the provision of extension services, resulting in pluralistic advisory services (see Alexopoulos et al. 2009; Cristóvão et al. 2012; Birner et al. 2009).

Within such a transition framework and despite the fact that ideas about innovation and change have evolved considerably over the years, classical DOI/TOT, and thus conventional extension, is still dominant. In parallel, though, owing to the changing conceptions of innovation and extension that have been previously outlined, a "new extension approach aiming at participatory, group learning and networking with extension agents acting as facilitators" (Cristóvão et al. 2012: 214) is also sought. In responding to the aforementioned challenges, new mechanisms are put in place, or old ideas are reinvented, both in terms of transfer (e.g., knowledge brokers (Ye and Kankanhalli 2013), knowledge and technology transfer organizations (KTTOs) (Landry et al. 2013), TT brokers (Roxas et al. 2011), technology-transaction services (Parker and Hine 2014), incubators (Suvinen et al. 2010), and university TT offices (Hoppe and Ozdenoren 2005)) and intermediation, in particular innovation brokerage.

For example, in the framework of the EU common agricultural policy, measures addressing both, known as transfer and cooperation, respectively, are included. Nevertheless, the interest of the EU innovation policy for rural development currently focuses on the establishment of the European Innovation Partnership (EIP-AGRI). This policy instrument relies on partnerships and "bottom-up" initiatives, mainly through operational groups, in order to bridge the gap between actors across the value chain, especially between research and practice, and facilitate the cogeneration of innovations through the employment of facilitators or innovation brokers (Regulation (EC) No. 1305/2013; see also EU-SCAR 2012, 2014).

As already noticed, contrary to the classical DOI/TOT model, intermediation and facilitation have yet to be thoroughly described, operationally defined, or evaluated well (Stetler et al. 2006). Therefore, on the one hand, there is a need for conceptual clarity since the current abundance of terminology and the use of the same terms with different meanings complicate the scene. Explicit attention should be given to theoretical developments; without a nuanced understanding of the concepts, terminology, and controversies, study findings will be difficult to interpret, and guidance for practice change may become untenable. In the same vein, Klerkx and Leeuwis (2009) state that further research is needed along two lines: the position of innovation brokers in relation to the different stages of the innovation process, including their specific competencies needed to successfully carry out their tasks, and the emergent types of brokers and their fit in the innovation system. On the other hand, Klerkx and Leeuwis (2008b) underline that, despite inherent difficulties, there is a need to become able to measure the added value of intermediaries. This way their contribution will become explicit and thus recognized in the knowledge infrastructure. Such an agenda will help in further highlighting gaps in our knowledge as well as strategies to address such gaps and, thus, in building a solid knowledge base which will be valuable for policymakers, academics and researchers, and practitioners. In this respect, the role of policy and institutions of higher education in fostering intermediation thinking and practice remains an open question.

References

Alexopoulos, G., A. Koutsouris, and E. Tzouramani. 2009. The Financing of Extension Services: a Survey Among Rural Youth in Greece. *The Journal of Agricultural Education & Extension* 15: 175–188.

Allahyari, M., M. Chizari, and S. Mirdamadi. 2009. Extension-Education Methods to Facilitate Learning in Sustainable Agriculture. *Journal of Agriculture & Social Sciences* 5: 27–30.

Argyris, C., and D. Schön. 1974. *Theory in Practice: Increasing Professional Effectiveness*. San Fransisco: Josey-Bass.

Ascroft, J.R., N. Röling, J. Kariuki, and F. Shege. 1973. *Extension and the Forgotten Farmer. Bulletin van de Afdelingen Sociale Wetenschappen*. Wageningen: Agricultural University of Wageningen.

Auvine, B., B. Densmore, M. Extrom, S. Poole, and M. Shanklin. 2002. What Do We Mean by Facilitation. *Group Facilitation: A Research and Applications Journal* 4: 53–55.

Bakici, T., E. Almirall, and J. Wareham. 2013. The Role of Public Open Innovation Intermediaries in Local Government and the Public Sector. *Technology Analysis & Strategic Management* 25: 311–327.

Bawden, R. 2005. Systemic Development at Hawkesbury: Some Personal Lessons from Experience. *Systems Research and Behavioral Science* 22: 151–164.

Bijker, W.E. 1995. *Of Bicycles, Bakelites, and Bulbs: Toward a Theory of Sociotechnical Change*. Cambridge: The MIT Press.

Birner, R., K. Davis, J. Pender, E. Nkonya, P. Anandajayasekeram, J. Ekboir, A. Mbabu, D.J. Spielman, D. Horna, S. Benin, and M. Cohen. 2009. From Best Practice to Best Fit: A Framework for Designing and Analyzing Pluralistic Agricultural Advisory Services Worldwide. *The Journal of Agricultural Education and Extension* 15: 341–355.

Blackburn, D., and D. Vist. 1984. Historical Roots and Philosophy of Extension. In *Extension Handbook*, ed. D. Blackbourn, 1–10. Guelf: University of Guelf.

Boari, C., and F. Riboldazzi. 2014. How Knowledge Brokers Emerge and Evolve: The Role of Actors' Behaviour. *Research Policy* 43: 683–695.

Botes, L., and D. van Rensburg. 2000. Community Participation in Development: Nine Plagues and Twelve Commandments. *Community Development Journal* 35: 41–58.

Brunori, G., D. Barjolle, A.C. Dockes, S. Helmle, J. Ingram, L. Klerkx, H. Moschitz, G. Nemes, and T. Tisenkopfs. 2013. CAP Reform and Innovation: The Role of Learning and Innovation Networks. *EuroChoices* 12: 27–33.

Burt, R.S. 2005. *Brokerage and Closure*. New York: Oxford University Press.

Byerlee, D., L. Harrington, and D.L. Winkelmann. 1982. Farming Systems Research: Issues in Research Strategy and Technology Design. *American Journal of Agricultural Economics* 64: 897–904.

Campbell, A. 1997. Facilitating Landcare: Conceptual and Practical Dilemmas. In *Critical Landcare*, ed. S. Lockie and F. Vanclay, 143–152. Wagga Wagga: Centre for Rural Social Research, Charles Stuart University.

Carlsson, B., ed. 1995. *Technological Systems and Economic Performance: The Case of Factory Automation*. Dordrecht: Kluwer Academic Publishers.

Chambers, R. 1992. Rural Appraisal: Rapid, Relaxed and Participatory. In *IDS Discussion Paper 311*. Brighton: IDS.

———. 1993. *Challenging the Professions: Frontiers for Rural Development*. London: Intermediate Technology Publications.

———. 1994. The Origins and Practice of Participatory Rural Appraisal. *World Development* 22: 953–969.

Cochrane, W.W. 1958. *Farm Prices: Myth and Reality*. St. Paul: University of Minnesota Press.

Collinson, M., ed. 2000. *A History of Farming Systems Research*. Wallingford: FAO, IFSA and CABI.

Cooke, B., and U. Kothari, eds. 2001. *Participation: The New Tyranny?* London: Zed-Books.

Coombs, P.H., and M. Ahmed. 1974. *Attacking Rural Poverty: How Non-Formal Education Can Help*. Baltimore: Johns Hopkins University Press.

Corsaro, D., C. Cantù, and A. Tunisini. 2012. Actors' Heterogeneity in Innovation Networks. *Industrial Marketing Management* 41: 780–789.

Cristóvão, A., P. Ferrao, R. Madeira, M.L. Tibério, M.J. Rainho, and M.S. Teixeira. 2008. Circles and Communities, Sharing Practices and Learning: Looking at Old and New Extension Education Approaches. In *Empowerment of Rural Actors: A Renewal of Farming Systems Perspectives*, ed. B. Didieu and S. Zasser-Bedoya, 797–807. Montpellier: INRA-SAD.

Cristóvão, A., A. Koutsouris, and M. Kügler. 2012. Extension Systems and Change Facilitation for Agricultural and Rural Development. In *Farming Systems Research into the 21st Century: The New Dynamic*, ed. I. Darnhofer, D. Gibbon, and B. Dedieu, 201–227. Dordrecht: Springer Science.

Dalal-Clayton, B., and S. Bass. 2002. *Sustainable Development Strategies*. London: Earthscan (OECD and UNDP).

Darnhofer, I., D. Gibbon, and B. Dedieu, eds. 2012. *Farming systems research into the 21st century: The new dynamic*. Dordrecht: Springer.

Davenport, T., and L. Prusak. 1998. *Working Knowledge: How Organizations Manage What They Know*. Cambridge: Harvard Business School Press.

Deugd, M., N. Röling, and E.M.A. Smaling. 1998. A New Praxeology for Integrated Nutrient Management, Facilitating Innovation with and by Farmers. *Agriculture, Ecosystems and Environment* 71: 269–283.

Devaux, A., J. Andrade-Piedra, D. Horton, M. Ordinola, G. Thiele, A. Thomann, and C. Velasco. 2010. *Brokering Innovation for Sustainable Development: The Papa Andina Case*. ILAC Working Paper 12. Rome: Institutional Learning and Change (ILAC) Initiative.

Dhanaraj, C., and A. Parkhe. 2006. Orchestrating Innovation Networks. *The Academy of Management Review* 31: 659–669.

Dredge, D. 2006. Policy Networks and the Local Organisation of Tourism. *Tourism Management* 27: 269–280.

Drennon, C., and R. Cervero. 2002. The Politics of Facilitation in Practitioner Inquiry Groups. *Adult Education Quarterly* 52: 193–209.

Edquist, C., ed. 1997. *Systems of Innovation: Technologies, Institutions and Organizations*. London: Pinter Publishers.

EU-SCAR. 2012. *Agricultural Knowledge and Innovation Systems in Transition - a reflection paper*. Brussels: Standing Committee on Agricultural Research (SCAR), Collaborative Working Group AKIS.

———. 2014. *Agricultural knowledge and innovation systems towards 2020*. Brussels: Standing Committee on Agricultural Research (SCAR), Collaborative Working Group AKIS-2.

Fadeeva, Z. 2005. Translation of Sustainability Ideas in Tourism Networks: Some Roles of Cross-Sectoral Networks in Change Towards Sustainable Development. *Journal of Cleaner Production* 13: 175–189.

Faure, G., P. Rebuffel, and D. Violas. 2011. Systemic Evaluation of Advisory Services to Family Farms in West Africa. *The Journal of Agricultural Education and Extension* 17: 325–339.

Garforth, C. 1982. Reaching the Poor: A Review of Extension Strategies and Methods. In *Progress in Rural Extension and Community Development*, ed. G. Jones and M. Rolls, vol. 1, 43–70. Chichester: Wiley.

Garforth, C., and A. Lawrence. 1997. *Supporting Sustainable Agriculture Through Extension in Asia*. Natural Resources Perspectives 21. London: ODI.

Geels, F. 2004. From Sectoral Systems of Innovation to Socio-Technical Systems. Insights About Dynamics and Change from Sociology and Institutional Theory. *Research Policy* 33: 897–920.

Granovetter, M. 1973. The Strength of Weak Ties. *American Journal of Sociology* 78: 1360–1380.

———. 1985. Economic Action and Social Structure: The Problem of Embeddedness. *American Journal of Sociology* 91: 481–510.

Habermas, J. 1984. *The Theory of Communicative Action: Reason and the Rationalization of Society*. Cambridge: Polity Press.

Haga, T. 2005. Action Research and Innovation in Networks, Dilemmas and Challenges: Two Cases. *Artificial Intelligence & Society* 19: 362–383.

———. 2009. Orchestration of Network Instruments: A Way to De-Emphasize the Partition Between Incremental Change and Innovation? *Artificial Intelligence & Society* 23: 17–31.

Harvey, G., A. Loftus-Hills, J. Rycroft-Malone, A. Titchen, A. Kitson, B. McCormack, and K. Seers. 2002. Getting Evidence into Practice: The Role and Function of Facilitation. *Journal of Advanced Nursing* 37: 577–588.

Heemskerk, W., L. Klerkx, and J. Sitima. 2011. Brokering Innovation. In *Putting Heads Together: Agricultural Innovation Platforms in Practice*, ed. S. Nederlof, M. Wongtschowksi, and F. van der Lee, 43–54. Amsterdam: KIT Publishers.

Hekkert, M.P., R.A.A. Suurs, S.O. Negro, S. Kuhlmann, and R.E.H.M. Smits. 2007. Functions of Innovation Systems: A New Approach for Analysing Technological Change. *Technological Forecasting and Social Change* 74: 413–432.

Hemmati, M. 2002. *Multi-stakeholder Processes for Governance and Sustainability - Beyond Deadlock and Conflict*. London: Earthscan.

Hermans, F., M. Stuiver, P.J. Beers, and K. Kok. 2013. The Distribution of Roles and Functions for Upscaling and Outscaling Innovations in Agricultural Innovation Systems. *Agricultural Systems* 115: 117–128.

Hjorth, P., and A. Bagheri. 2006. Navigating Towards Sustainable Development: A System Dynamics Approach. *Futures* 38: 74–92.

Hogan, C. 2002. *Understanding Facilitation: Theory and Practice*. London: Kogan Page Limited.

Hoppe, H., and E. Ozdenoren. 2005. Intermediation in Innovation. *International Journal of Industrial Organization* 23: 483–503.

Howells, J. 2006. Intermediation and the Role of Intermediaries in Innovation. *Research Policy* 35: 715–728.

Hubert, B., R. Ison, and N. Röling. 2000. The "Problematique" with Respect to Industrialised Country Agricultures. In *Cow Up a Tree, Knowing and Learning for Change in Agriculture – Case Studies from Industrialised Countries*, ed. LEARN Group, 13–30. Paris: INRA.

Hughes, T.P. 1987. The Evolution of Large Technological Systems. In *The Social construction of Technological Systems: New Directions in the Sociology and History of Technology*, ed. W.E. Bijker, T.P. Hughes, and T.J. Pinch, 51–82. Cambridge: The MIT Press.

Ison, R. 2010. *Systems Practice: How to Act in a Climate-Change World*. London: Springer and The Open University.

Ison, R., and D. Russel, eds. 2000. *Agricultural Extension and Rural Development: Breaking Out of Traditions*. Cambridge: Cambridge University Press.

Jones, G., and C. Garforth. 1997. The History, Development, and Future of Agricultural Extension. In *Improving Agricultural Extension A Reference Manual*, ed. E. Burton, R. Swanson, A. Bentz, and J. Sofranko, 2–12. Rome: FAO.

Katzy, B., E. Turgut, T. Holzmann, and K. Sailer. 2013. Innovation Intermediaries: A Process View on Open Innovation Coordination. *Technology Analysis & Strategic Management* 25: 295–309.

Keen, M., V. Brown, and R. Dyball. 2005. Social Learning: A New Approach to Environmental Management. In *Social Learning in Environmental Management – Towards a Sustainable Future*, ed. M. Keen, V. Brown, and R. Dyball, 3–21. London: Earthscan.

Kilelu, K., L. Klerkx, C. Leeuwis, and A. Hall. 2011. *Beyond Knowledge Brokerage: An Exploratory Study of Innovation Intermediaries in an Evolving Smallholder agricultural System in Kenya*. RIU Discussion Paper 13. London: DFID.

Kirkels, Y., and G. Duysters. 2010. Brokerage in SME Networks. *Research Policy* 39: 375–385.

Klerkx, L., and P. Gildemacher. 2012. The Role of Innovation Brokers in Agricultural Innovation Systems. In *Agricultural Innovation systems: An investment sourcebook*, 221–230. Washington: The World Bank.

Klerkx, L., and C. Leeuwis. 2008a. Balancing Multiple Interests: Embedding Innovation Intermediation in the Agricultural Knowledge Infrastructure. *Technovation* 28: 364–378.

———. 2008b. Matching Demand and Supply in the Agricultural Knowledge Infrastructure: Experiences with Innovation Intermediaries. *Food Policy* 33: 260–276.

———. 2009. Establishment and Embedding of Innovation Brokers at Different Innovation System Levels: Insights from the Dutch Agricultural Sector. *Technological Forecasting and Social Change* 76: 849–860.

Klerkx, L., N. Aarts, and C. Leeuwis. 2010. Adaptive Management in Agricultural Innovation Systems: The Interactions Between Innovation Networks and their Environment. *Agricultural Systems* 103: 390–400.

Klerkx, L., B. Van Mierlo, and C. Leeuwis. 2012. Evolution of System Approaches to Agricultural Innovations: Concepts, Analysis and Interventions. In *Farming Systems Research into the 21st Century: The New Dynamic*, ed. I. Darnhofer, D. Gibbon, and B. Dedieu, 457–483. Dordrecht: Springer Science.

Knight, C., and C. Lyall. 2013. Knowledge Brokers: the Role of Intermediaries in Producing Research Impact. *Evidence & Policy* 9: 309–316.

Kolb, D. 1984. *Experiential Learning: Experience as the Source of Learning and Development.* N. Jersey: Prentice-Hall.

Koutsouris, A. 2008. Higher Education Facing Sustainability: The Case of Agronomy. *International Journal of Learning* 15: 269–276.

Koutsouris, A., and D. Papadopoulos. 2003. What is 'Social' about Social Learning? *The Journal of Agricultural Education & Extension* 9: 75–82.

Lamble, W. 1984. Diffusion and Adoption of Innovations. In *Extension Handbook*, ed. D. Blackbourn, 32–41. Guelf: University of Guelf.

Landry, R., N. Amara, J.S. Cloutier, and N. Halilem. 2013. Technology Transfer Organizations: Services and Business Models. *Technovation* 33: 431–449.

LEARN Group. 2000. *Cow up a Tree: Learning and Knowing Processes for Change in Agriculture; Case Studies from Industrialised Countries*. Paris: INRA Editions.

Leal, P. 2007. Participation: The Ascendancy of a Buzzword in the neo-Liberal Era. *Development in Practice* 17: 539–548.

Leeuwis, C. 2000. Learning to be Sustainable. *The Journal of Agricultural Education & Extension* 7: 79–92.

———. 2004. *Communication for Rural Innovation: Rethinking Agricultural Extension*. Oxford: Blackwell.

Leeuwis, C., and R. Pyburn, eds. 2002. *Wheelbarrows full of Frogs – Social Learning in Rural Resource Management: International Research and Reflections*. Assen: Van Gorcum.

Leeuwis, C., N. Long, and M. Villareal. 1990. Equivocations on Knowledge Systems Theory: An Actor-Oriented Critique. *Knowledge, Technology and Policy* 3: 19–27.

Ljung, M., and A. Emmelin. 2000. The Development of Farmers; Dialogue: The Decision Making Process Behind a Facilitated Learning Process in Swedish Agriculture. In *European Farming and Rural Systems Research and Extension into the Next Millennium: Environmental, Agricultural and Socio-economic Issues*, ed. A. Koutsouris and L. Omodei-Zorini, 336–357. Athens: Papazisis Editions.

Long, N. 1992. Conclusion. In *Battlefields of Knowledge*, ed. N. Long and A. Long, 268–277. London: Routledge.

Lundvall, B.-Å., ed. 1992. *National Systems of Innovation: Toward a Theory of Innovation and Interactive Learning*. London: Pinter Publishers.

Maunder, A.H. 1972. *Agricultural Extension: A Reference Manual*. Rome: FAO.

Moschitz, H., G. Brunori, D. Roep, and T. Tisenkofs, (guest eds). 2015. Learning and Innovation Networks for Sustainable Agriculture: Processes of Co-Evolution, Joint Reflection and Facilitation. *Journal of Agricultural Education and Extension* 21: 1–89.

Nagel, U.J. 1997. Alternative Approaches to Organizing Extension. In *Improving Agricultural Extension A Reference Manual*, ed. E. Burton, R. Swanson, A. Bentz, and J. Sofranko, 13–24. Rome: FAO.

Nederlof, S., M. Wongtschowksi, and F. van der Lee, eds. 2011. *Putting Heads Together: Agricultural Innovation Platforms in Practice*. Amsterdam: KIT Publishers.

Nerbonne, J.F., and R. Lentz. 2003. Rooted in Grass: Challenging Patterns of Knowledge Exchange as a Means of Fostering Social Change in a Southeast Minnesota Farm Community. *Agriculture and Human Values* 20: 65–78.

Nitsch, U. 1982. *Farmers' Perceptions of and Preferences Concerning Agricultural Extension Programs*. Uppsala: Swedish University of Agricultural Sciences, Dept. of Economics and Science.

Oakley, P., et al. 1991. *Projects with People: The Practice of Participation in Rural Development*. Geneva: ILO.

Oliver, P., and J. Myers. 2003. *Networks, Diffusion, and Cycles of Collective Action*. Oxford: Oxford University Press.

Packham, R., and N. Sriskandarajah. 2005. Systemic Action Research for Postgraduate Education in Agriculture and Rural Development. *Systems Research and Behavioral Science* 22: 119–130.

Parker, R., and D. Hine. 2014. The Role of Knowledge Intermediaries in Developing Firm Learning Capabilities. *European Planning Studies* 22: 1048–1061.

Pretty, J. 1995. *Regenerating Agriculture: Policies and Practice for Sustainability and Self-reliance*. London: Earthscan.

Quaghebeur, K., J. Masschelein, and H. Nguyen. 2004. Paradox of Participation: Giving or Taking Part? *Journal of Community & Applied Social Psychology* 14: 154–165.

Rivera, W., and M.K. Qamar. 2013. *Agricultural Extension, Rural Development and the Food Security Challenge*. Rome: FAO.

Rivera, W., and W. Zijp. 2002. *Contracting for Agricultural Extension. International Case Studies and Emerging Practices*. Washington D.C: CABI Publishing.

Rivera, W.M., M.K. Qamar, and H.K. Mwandemere. 2005. *Enhancing Coordination Among AKIS/RD Actors: An Analytical And Comparative Review of Country Studies on Agricultural Knowledge and Information Systems for Rural Development (AKIS/RD)*. Rome: FAO.

Robinson, L. 2002. Participatory Rural Appraisal: A brief introduction. *Group Facilitation: A Research & Applications Journal* 4: 45–52.

Rogers, E.M., ed. 1976a. *Communication and Development: Critical Perspectives*. Beverly Hills: Sage Publ.

———. 1976b. Communication and Development: The Passing of the Dominant Paradigm. In *Communication and Development: Critical Perspectives*, ed. E. Rogers, 121–148. Beverly Hills: Sage Publ.

———. 1976c. New Perspectives on Communication and Development: Overview. In *Communication and Development: Critical Perspectives*, ed. E.M. Rogers, 7–15. Beverly Hills: Sage Publ.

———. 1962, 1983. *Diffusion of Innovations*. New York: Free Press.

Rogers, E.M., and F.F. Shoemaker. 1971. *Communication of Innovations: A Cross-Cultural Approach*. New York: The Free Press.

Rogers, E.M., J.D. Eveland, and A.S. Bean. 1976. *Extending the Agricultural Extension Model*. Stanford: Sanford University, Institute for Communication Research.

Röling, N. 1982. Alternative Approaches to Extension. In *Progress in Rural Extension and Community Development*, ed. G. Jones and M. Rolls, vol. 1, 87–115. Chichester: Wiley.

———. 1988. *Extension Science*. Cambridge: Cambridge University Press.

Roling, N. 2002. Beyond the Aggregation of Individual Preferences. Moving from Multiple to Distributed Cognition in Resource Dilemmas. In *Wheelbarrows full of Frogs – Social Learning in Rural Resource Management: International Research and Reflections*, ed. C. Leeuwis and R. Pyburn, 25–47. Assen: Van Gorcum.

Röling, N., and P. Engel. 1991. The Development of the Concept of Agricultural Knowledge and Information Systems (AKIS): Implications for Extension. In *Agricultural Extension: Worldwide Institutional Evolution and Forces for Change*, ed. W. Rivera and D. Gustafson, 125–139. Amsterdam: Elsevier.

Röling, N., and J. Jiggins. 1998. The Ecological Knowledge System. In *Facilitating Sustainable Agriculture: Participatory Learning and Adaptive Management in Times of Environmental Uncertainty*, ed. N. Röling and M.A.E. Wagemakers, 283–311. Cambridge: Cambridge University Press.

Röling, N., and E. van de Fliert. 1994. Transforming Extension for Sustainable Agriculture: the Case of Integrated Pest Management in Rice in Indonesia. *Agriculture & Human Values* 11: 96–108.

Röling, N., and M.A.E. Wagemakers, eds. 1998. *Facilitating Sustainable Agriculture: Participatory Learning and Adaptive Management in times of Environmental Uncertainty*. Cambridge: Cambridge University Press.

Röling, N., J. Ascroft, and F.W. Chege. 1976. The Diffusion of Innovations and the Issue of Equity in Rural Development. In *Communication and Development: Critical Perspectives*, ed. E. Rogers, 63–79. Beverly Hills: Sage Publ.

Roxas, S.A., G. Piroli, and M. Sorrentino. 2011. Efficiency and Evaluation Analysis of a Network of Technology Transfer Brokers. *Technology Analysis & Strategic Management* 23: 7–24.

Savage, G., and C. Hilton. 2001. A Critical View of Facilitating Labor-Management Collaboration. *Group Facilitation: A Research & Applications Journal* 3: 47–55.

Schiere, J.B., J. Lyklema, J. Schakel, and K.G. Rickert. 1999. Evolution of Farming Systems and System Philosophy. *Systems Research and Behavioral Science* 16: 375–390.

Scoones, I., and J. Thompson, eds. 1994. *Beyond Farmer First*. London: Intermediate Technology Publications.

Shea, B. 2011. A Decade of Knowledge Translation Research - What has Changed? *Journal of Clinical Epidemiology* 64: 3–5.

Simmonds, N.W. 1986. A Short Review of Farming Systems Research in the Tropics. *Experimental Agriculture* 22: 1–13.

SLIM. 2004. Facilitation in policy processes: developing new professional skills, Policy Briefing, no. 4, http://slim.open.ac.uk.

Somers, N. 1998. Learning About Sustainable Agriculture: the case of Dutch Arable Farmers. In *Facilitating Sustainable Agriculture: Participatory Learning and Adaptive Management in Times of Environmental Uncertainty*, ed. N. Röling and M.A.E. Wagemakers, 125–134. Cambridge: Cambridge University Press.

Sriskandarajah, N., M. Cerf, and E. Noe. 2006. Learning as a Process: Understanding One's Role in the New Learning Demands of Multifunctional Land Use Systems, Working with Different Actors, Tools and Scales. In *Changing European Farming Systems for a Better Future: New Visions for Rural Areas*, ed. H. Langeveld and N. Röling, 27–28. Wageningen: Wageningen Academic Press.

Stetler, C.B., M.W. Legro, J. Rycroft-Malone, C. Bowman, G. Curran, M. Guihan, H. Hagedorn, S. Pineros, and C.M. Wallace. 2006. Role of "External Facilitation" in Implementation of Research Findings: A Qualitative Evaluation of Facilitation Experiences in the Veterans Health Administration. *Implementation Science*. https://doi.org/10.1186/1748-5908-1-23.

Suvinen, N., J. Konttinen, and M. Nieminen. 2010. How Necessary are Intermediary Organizations in the Commercialization of Research? *European Planning Studies* 18: 1365–1389.

Swaans, K., B. Boogaard, R. Bendapudi, H. Taye, S. Hendrickx, and L. Klerkx. 2014. Operationalizing Inclusive Innovation: Lessons from Innovation Platforms in Livestock Value Chains in India and Mozambique. *Innovation and Development* 4: 239–257.

Swanson, B., and J. Claar. 1984. The History and Development of Agricultural Extension. In *Agricultural Extension: A Reference Manual*, ed. B. Swanson, 1–19. Rome: FAO.

Theodorakopoulos, N., D. Bennett, and D.J.S. Preciado. 2014. Intermediation for Technology Diffusion and User Innovation in a Developing Rural Economy: A Social Learning Perspective. *Entrepreneurship & Regional Development: An International Journal* 26: 645–662.

Van de Ban, A.W., and H.S. Hawkins. 1988. *Agricultural Extension*. Harlow: Longman Scientific and Technical.

Van de Ven, A.H., D.E. Polley, R. Garud, and S. Venkataraman. 1999. *The Innovation Journey*. Oxford: Oxford University Press.

Van Lente, H., M. Hekkert, R. Smits, and B. Van Waveren. 2003. Roles of Systemic Intermediaries in Transition Processes. *International Journal of Innovation Management* 7: 1–33.

Wals, A., ed. 2007. *Social Learning Towards a Sustainable World*. Wageningen: Wageningen Academic Publishers.

Webber, L. 1995. Participatory Rural Appraisal Design: Conceptual and Process Issues. *Agricultural Systems* 17: 107–131.

Webler, T., H. Kastenholz, and O. Renn. 1995. Public Participation in Impact Assessment: A Social Learning Perspective. *Environmental Impact Assessment Review* 15: 443–463.

Winch, G., and R. Courtney. 2007. The Organisation of Innovation Brokers: An International Review. *Technology Analysis and Strategic Management* 19: 747–763.

Woodhill, J., and N. Röling. 1998. The second Wing of the Eagle: The Human Dimension in Learning Our Way to More Sustainable Futures. In *Facilitating Sustainable Agriculture: Participatory Learning and Adaptive Management in Times of Environmental Uncertainty*, ed. N. Röling and M.A.E. Wagemakers, 46–71. Cambridge: Cambridge University Press.

World Bank. 2006. *Enhancing Agricultural Innovation: How to go Beyond the Strengthening of Research Systems*. Washington DC: The World Bank.

———. 2012. *Agricultural Innovation Systems: An Investment Source Book*. Washington: World Bank.

Ye, J., and A. Kankanhalli. 2013. Exploring Innovation Through Open Networks: A Review and Initial Research Questions. *IIMB Management Review* 25: 69–82.

Technology Adoption by Agricultural Producers: A Review of the Literature

Albert I. Ugochukwu and Peter W.B. Phillips

Abstract The increasing rate of technological advancement across various disciplines, and in particular the agricultural sector, has resulted in increased efficiency and productivity. Recent advances in biotechnology research and development offer new prospects for increased food production and security in various jurisdictions. However, adoption and commercialization of existing and emerging technologies both at the farm and industry levels have been of great concern to governments and the food industry. This chapter provides a review existing literature on technology adoption in agriculture, explores different dimensions of technologies and factors influencing their adoption, and examines returns on investment in technological research and development.

Introduction

Technology plays a pivotal role as a vehicle for change in many disciplines. While development economists advocate for technology transfer from developed to developing economies to achieve economic growth (Feder et al. 1985), agriculture and food economists are interested in how emerging technologies could improve food production and enhance food safety and authenticity. On the other hand, natural and environmental economists are concerned with how new technologies could be employed for efficient resource and environmental management (Tietenberg 2000), while firms and industries advocate for technologies that will reduce production costs and enhance overall efficiency, effectiveness, and individual and collective reputations.

In past decades, considerable progress has been made in technological innovation globally. Development of a new technology occurs at a particular point in time, while

This work was undertaken as part of the research in two Genome Canada projects administered by Genome Prairie: Application of Genomics to Innovation in the Lentil Economy (AGILE) and Reverse Vaccinology Approach for the Prevention of Mycobacterial Disease in Cattle (MyVAMP).

A.I. Ugochukwu • P.W.B. Phillips (✉)
University of Saskatchewan, Saskatoon, SK, Canada
e-mail: peter.phillips@usask.ca

© Springer International Publishing AG 2018   361
N. Kalaitzandonakes et al. (eds.), *From Agriscience to Agribusiness*, Innovation,
Technology, and Knowledge Management, https://doi.org/10.1007/978-3-319-67958-7_17

the awareness and use of the technology takes place over a long period of time. The impact or intended purpose (e.g. productivity growth) of a new technology can only be felt after adoption and use by the target end users (e.g. individuals, firms, industries). However, the magnitude of the impact is determined by the rate of adoption, following the diffusion and learning about the technology or innovation over time. Several studies using different models of technology diffusion and adoption in different fields, including agriculture, information technology, and medicine, among others, have investigated factors influencing the acceptance and/or rejection of new technologies. Of these studies and models, Everett Rogers' model of *diffusion of innovations* is the most widely used to date. Rogers' model became more popular and widely applied as he used the concept of innovation, which he described not only as technology but any idea, object, or practice that is absolutely new, thereby bringing commonality and encompassing diverse fields. However, the newness of an innovation depends on the time it gets to a particular place or population. For example, a new plant cultivar already in use in North America may be new in Africa some years after its development.

Adoption of a new technology follows diffusion, which Rogers (1983, p.5) described as the "process by which an innovation is communicated through certain channels over time among the members of the social system". This also involves individual valuation of the undetermined benefits of the innovation relative to the costs (Hall and Khan 2002). Rogers (2003, p.172) describes the adoption decision process as "an information-seeking and information-processing activity, where an individual is motivated to reduce uncertainty about the advantages and disadvantages of an innovation". Upon introduction of a new technology, it can either be adopted if found to be beneficial and profitable relative to existing alternatives or rejected if found unprofitable (Dinar and Yaron 1992).

A growing number of studies that cut across many disciplines have identified several factors, including personal, cultural, social, and economic attributes, as well as characteristics of the technology, which influence technology adoption (Pannell et al. 2006). For example, while Sunding and Zilberman (2001) emphasize personal characteristics such as human capital, age, or risk preferences of potential adopters, Miller and Tolley (1989) found that market intervention by regulators, through a price support programme for example, could enhance the adoption of new technologies. In the social science literature, several adoption studies focus on the influence of social norms, values, and beliefs on technology adoption. In the area of agricultural production, for example, scale of operation, education, specialization, social networks, peer group influence, extension services, complexity, and the cost of acquiring the technology, among others, have been found to affect technology adoption (Batz et al. 1999; El-Osta and Morehart 2002; Garforth et al. 2003; Saurer and Zilberman 2010; Millar 2010).

One important consideration in technology adoption, which previous studies have not explored in modelling adoption decision processes, is the issue of transaction costs. Standard economic theories are based on the assumption of perfect information, which is essential for efficiency in resource allocation, making informed choices, full employment of resources, and uniform commodity prices. Looking at this presumption from the lens of technology adoption, perfect information may not be a reality in practice, as access to available information concerning a new technology is associated with transaction costs. Information asymmetry problems have affected peoples' perception of risks; hence, some potential adopters may not rely on available information, particularly concerning the benefits of a new technology, and therefore would prefer to test and confirm the results themselves in order to make informed decisions or optimal choices.

Development of new innovations or technologies requires huge investments in research and development (R&D) activities. However, intellectual property rights (IPRs) have been a contentious issue regarding incentives for technology innovation development. IPRs give innovators and technology developers the opportunity to appropriate a sizable part of the returns arising from their R&D investment or activities. It also grants innovators the exclusive right to sell the products of their R&D above marginal cost, thereby increasing their return on investment (Légér 2007). However, the inability of innovators to capture the gains of their research output has been a disincentive for private investment in R&D (Gray and Malla 2007). The call for stronger IPRs for inventors increased following the establishment of the Trade-Related Aspects of Intellectual Property Rights (TRIPS) Agreement, which came into force on January 1, 1995. Although weak IPRs could enhance knowledge spillover, Falvey et al. (2006) argue that strong IPRs have potential implications in terms of both costs and benefits for technology development, diffusion, and adoption, particularly in developing countries with insufficient innovative capacity and factor endowments; this suggests a need for a balance in policy choices. Cohen and Levinthal (1989) argue that excessively strong IPR protection negatively affects technology innovation development as it will not be possible for researchers, in most cases, to improve an existing technology without violating the rights of patent holders on the technology. Several studies (e.g. Scherer et al. 1959; Taylor and Silberston 1973; Mansfield et al. 1981; Cohen et al. 1997) conclude that patent protection is a major determinant of the introduction of new technological innovations. A prime example is the establishment of the International Union for the Protection of New Varieties of Plants (UPOV 78). Ratification of UPOV by Canada in 1991 is believed to have enhanced plant breeding in Canada (e.g. the pulse industry).

In the adoption literature, several studies list factors that influence the adoption of new technologies. However, an important element that affects adoption, consumer resistance, has not been widely explored. This was recognized in the uptake of agricultural biotechnology (GM foods) by Anderson et al. (2001), Barkeley (2002), and Haggui (2004) and was identified to have impacted the acceptance of GM food in Europe and Japan over food safety and environmental concerns. Consumer perception of GM food was adduced as the reason for the low rates of diffusion and adoption of GM crops in Europe, Japan, and other parts of the world in 2000 (Hanf and Bocker 2002). Many consumers, particularly in developing countries, despite the benefits of biotechnology, perceive GM products to have some health risks and negative effects on the environment following media reports. This would serve as a disincentive to adopt GM crops by farmers, which would affect food production, especially in developing countries with a weak technological base and high population growth.

This chapter provides a review of the relevant literature on technology adoption and introduces other important influencing factors into the existing standard model of technology adoption developed by Everett Rogers. Several studies are reviewed to ascertain factors that influence adoption of different technological innovations. Given the scope of this chapter, technology is examined from the general perspective, with emphasis on the adoption of agricultural technologies.

The Adoption-Decision Process

The economic decision literature suggests that the decision to adopt a new technology or innovation is determined by four important factors: the recognition of competitive stance among firms in an industry, awareness of the existence of an alternative innovation following market conditions, motivation and/or incentive to explore alternatives, and the resource availability to implement the decision (Chen 1996). Following Rogers (2003), the decision to adopt a new technology involves five stages including: knowledge (awareness); persuasion, potentially by gaining sufficient information on the characteristics, benefits, and costs of a new technology; decision; implementation; and confirmation. To better understand the role a new technology plays, there is a need for an understanding of the adoption decision process and the important factors that could affect adoption of the technology. The process is shown in Fig. 1.

Figure 1 describes the steps and/or process an individual, a farmer, a firm, or a group passes through in making a technology adoption decision. The adoption process starts with getting information (awareness) about the new technology, whether through media advertisement, extension agents, or social networks. This is followed by a careful review of the perceived attributes of the technology and the potential benefits and costs of acquiring the technology. After examining the characteristics and weighing the benefits, costs, and trade-offs associated with the new technology, the decision to either adopt or reject the technology, the most critical stage, is made.

Some factors including opposition,[1] the time of introducing the technology, location of introduction, or social networks, in which the opinions of technical leaders drive adoption in most cases, could trigger rejection. There could be continued rejection of a technology over time or a decision to adopt later. If at first the poten-

---

[1] These are people who would reject a new technology based on experience of others, presumably early adopters, or perceived risks associated with the output of the technology. A prime example is consumer rejection of GM food products arising from biotechnology in some parts of the world, particularly developing countries. In addition, the Consumer Association of Canada (CAC) vehemently opposed the food irradiation technology proposed by Health Canada as a food safety measure against *E. coli*, *Salmonella*, listeria, and other pathogens following an *E. coli* outbreak in Europe that killed more than 42 people and left about 4000 sick in 2011 (Powell 2011). CAC argued that irradiation removes essential nutrients in food, alters the molecular structure, and is associated with uncertain health risks.

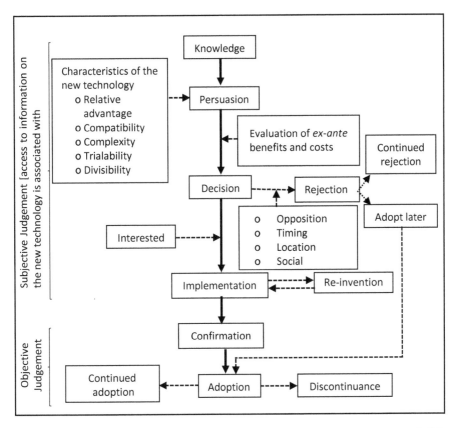

Fig. 1 Model of technology adoption decision process (Source: Adapted from Rogers (2003) Diffusion of Innovation, 3rd Edition (p. 165), with some additions)

tial adopter develops interest in the new technology, he or she will put it into practice, potentially with the help of experts to reduce uncertainty about the full effects of the technology. At this stage, there could be continued evaluation of the technology to ensure that it meets expectations. This could lead to *reinvention*, a modification of the technology to suit individual needs.[2] It should be noted that from the knowledge stage through implementation, the potential adopter continuously seeks more information about the technology and therefore incurs transaction costs. Adoption decisions made prior to the implementation stage of the adoption decision process could be driven by subjective judgement. After implementation and reinvention, the implementer seeks factual evidence, considering attributes of the technology (objective judgement), to support his/her adoption decision. If the implementer is satisfied, he/she would objectively adopt the technology.[3]

---

[2] Reinvention may involve exploring uses of the technology outside its main purpose.

[3] Rejection can also occur at this stage if the implementer does not have robust evidence to convince him that the new technology would meet expectations.

There could be continuous use of the technology depending on the outcome. Alternatively, the technology may be discontinued if there is a newer version for replacement or if the technology no longer meets expectations or has a perceived relative disadvantage.

Adoption and Diffusion of Technological Innovations

Several technology adoption studies in the literature examine adoption at different levels, such as household, firm, industry, or nation, using different methodologies and sometimes with conflicting results. A common result of technology adoption studies in the literature (e.g. Bohlen and Beal 1955; Griliches 1957; Hildebrand and Partenheimer 1958; Mansfield 1961, 1963) is that adoption pathway follows an S-shaped (sigmoid) curve, suggesting that adoption of a new technology starts slowly at first with few adopters. The number of adopters increases as knowledge about the technology spreads and then slows down as a greater proportion of potential end users adopt the technology. Figure 2 shows timing of adoption and diffusion of innovations (i.e. the relationship between the number of users of a new technology and the time of adoption).

However, despite the perceived benefits of a new technology, some agents will not adopt, owing to reasons including: attributes of the technology, such as relative advantage, complexity, compatibility, or divisibility; consumer opposition, as in the case for agricultural biotechnology; farm size; costs relative to benefits; profitability; socio-economic characteristics of decision-makers; and location, as the impact of some technologies could vary from one region to another. Mansfield's (1961) adoption model attributed the S-shape to interfirm or interindustry differences and hypothesized that "the probability that a firm will introduce a new technique is an

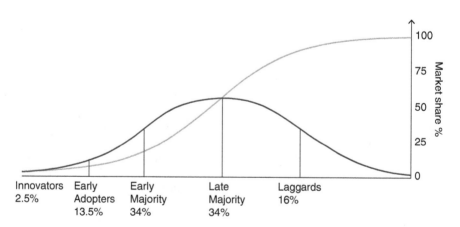

Fig. 2 Timing of adoption of technological innovations (adopter categorization) (Source: Rogers' diffusion of innovations theory (2003))

increasing function of the proportion of firms already using it, ... but a decreasing function of the size of the investment required" (p. 672–763). On the other hand, Stoneman (1981) in his "Bayesian theory of learning" model of adoption interprets the S-shape as an intrafirm diffusion path and hypothesized that a firm changes its level or rate of adoption of a new technology as it learns more about it and accordingly adjusts its expectations.

The size and distribution of the benefits from a new technology to the adopters are determined by the timing of adoption (Rubas 2004). Potentially, early adopters would have the greatest share of the benefits of a new technology relative to later adopters. For some technologies, the incentive to adopt would be reduced as the adoption rate increases and may go to zero shortly before everyone adopts. A prime example is the adoption of diagnostic technologies, such as the DNA barcoding technology used for fish species identification and authentication (see Ugochukwu 2015). For this technology, early adopters would enjoy the market benefit of a price premium, while laggards may enjoy little or no profit.

As mentioned earlier, a number of previous studies in different fields identified factors affecting the adoption of new technologies. Rogers and Stanfield (1968) reviewed several empirical adoption studies in 14 disciplines and summarized the relationships between the factors and adoption. These are shown in Table 1.

Some previous studies (e.g. Wozniak 1987; Lleras-Muney and Lichtenberg 2002) have shown that education and experience play positive roles in technology adoption. Highly educated people could enhance diffusion of innovations and potentially would adopt new technologies earlier than the less educated as they have more knowledge and can easily access information necessary to make an early adoption decision. For example, the results of the farm financial survey carried out by Statistics Canada (AAFC 2016, p.59) show that 91% of farmers adopt and implement new technological innovation following their "own experience", while about 68% make adoption decision based on information obtained from colleagues in a networking effect. Results of the same study show the influence of "timing of adop-

Table 1 Factors influencing adoption of a new technology

Factor	Relationship
Education	+
Income	+
Knowledge (awareness) about the technology	+
Attitude towards change	+
Group participation (networks)	+
Interpersonal communication	+
Contact with change agencies	+
Compatibility of the technology	+
Opinion leadership	+
Fulfilment of felt need	+

Source: Rogers and Stanfield (1968, p. 249–250)

tion" and "age" on the speed of technology adoption. It indicates that 32% of the farmers usually wait until a new technology is properly tested before they adopt, while 43% (out of which 51% are young farmers) often wait for a few farmers to try the technology before deciding whether to adopt or not. This result confirms the limitation of the perfect rationality and complete information assumptions of economic theory and underscores that the cognitive attitude of potential adopters influences their behavioural decisions to adopt a new technology.

Adoption of Agricultural Technologies

The history and economics of diffusion and adoption of agricultural technologies began with the pioneering study of Griliches (1957). The process and models of adoption have been studied by different scholars, with the most popular and widely used being that of Everett Rogers, titled *diffusion of innovations* (Sherry and Gibson 2002), which spans the disciplines of economics, technology, education, political science, public health, history, and communications (Dooley 1999).

In the literature, technology and innovation are sometimes used interchangeably. While the process by which a new technology or innovation is transmitted through certain media over time to members of society is referred to as diffusion, the rate at which a new or emerging technology is adopted depends on some important attributes of the technology including the perceived advantages relative to existing ones and its compatibility with existing needs and values of the society or potential adopter, simplicity (ease of understanding and use), trialability for potential adjustment, and observability (ease of visualizing the results) (Rogers 2003).

Adoption of improved agricultural technologies has been traced to the success of the Green Revolution initiated by an American scientist, Norman Borlaug, in Mexico in the 1940s (Dethier and Effenberger 2012). The Green Revolution enhanced the adoption of high-yielding crop cultivars and inputs such as fertilizer and irrigation, which resulted in increased food production. Improved high-yielding crop varieties developed during the revolution produced high yields with the help of fertilizers and irrigation systems, which provide water for farming in areas with little or no rainfall, thereby putting more land to use for food production (Briney 2015).

In the context of agriculture, technology has been described as a:

> ...factor that changes the production function and regarding which there exists some uncertainty, whether perceived or objection (or both). The uncertainty diminishes over time through the acquisition of experience and information, and the production function itself may change as adopters become more efficient in the application of the technology. (Gershon and Umali 1993, p.216)

In agricultural production, given the different actors, sizes of technologies, timing, and scale of operation, Feder et al. (1982) classified adoption into three categories including: individual, farm-level versus aggregate-level adoption; single (e.g.

fertilizer) versus package (e.g. fertilizer + improved seed variety + good management practices) adoption; and divisible (e.g. new crop cultivar) versus indivisible (e.g. harvester) adoption. Several studies in the literature (e.g. Feder et al. 1982; Belsey and Case 1993; Adesina and Baidu-Forson 1995; Zeller et al. 1997; Fuglie and Kascak 2001; Arellanes and Lee 2003; Moser and Barrett 2003; among others) examined adoption of agricultural technologies and found common factors that influence adoption. These include farm size, land tenure arrangements, access to credit and extension services, land and labour availability, human capital (education, gender, demographics), and farmer attitude towards risks and uncertainty. Notwithstanding the availability of these factors, adoption of improved agricultural technologies usually increases at a slow rate initially and rapidly thereafter to a maximum level resulting in increased productivity (Griliches 1957). Results of some empirical studies (e.g. Marra et al. 2002; Moshini et al. 2000) underscore the potential of improved agricultural technologies in enhancing productivity, income, and overall economic growth.

The potential benefits of a new technology can only be realized when it is adopted and used; the adoption decision involves a critical comparison of perceived benefits and costs associated with the technology (Uaiene 2011). A better understanding of the diffusion, adoption, and impact of improved technologies will guide producer groups, research institutions, and policy makers in making prudent and informed decisions about allocating resources for technology development.

Crop Production Technologies

Some studies that examine agricultural technology adoption have been carried out, particularly in developing countries. Abera (2008) used xtprobit and random effect models to examine the influence of farmer learning and risk on the likelihood and intensity of adopting improved *tef* and wheat technologies in northern and western Shewa zones of Ethiopia. The study underscores the importance of learning and experience as drivers of continued technology adoption. Results indicate that awareness, timely availability, and profitability of new *tef* and wheat varieties enhanced farmers' learning and experience. This positively influenced adoption of the new technologies.

Dibba et al. (2012) employed an average treatment estimation (ATE) framework to examine the adoption rate and determinants of adoption of new rice variety for Africa (NERICA) in Gambia. Results of the study show that the adoption rate stood at 40% against anticipated rate of 83% due to lack of information about and access to NERICA, thereby suggesting the need for the supply and distribution of more NERICA to farmers for easy access, experience, and adoption. In another study carried out in Africa, Uaiene (2011) looked at the factors influencing agricultural technology adoption by rural households in Mozambique. The results of the study show that rural farmers who have access to credit and extension advisory services, attended a higher level of education, and are members of agricultural associations have a higher probability of adopting new agricultural technologies.

Learning through networks has been identified as a factor that influences technology adoption. For example, Bandiera and Rasul (2006) examined the role of social networks and how the adoption choices of network members influence a farmer's adoption decision in Northern Mozambique. They found that farmers who discuss and/or learn about new technologies within their social network have a greater tendency to adopt. However, this result cannot be generalized. As stated earlier, the technical opinion of social network leaders on a particular technology affects adoption by members of the social network. If the leader's opinion is not in favour of the new technology, members may not adopt. Zavale et al. (2005) used a probit model to show that level of education; access to credit, extension, and seed stores; household size; and off-farm employment influence farmer adoption of improved maize seed. While the result for off-farm income is consistent with that of Feder et al. (1985), who opined that earned off-farm income will provide financial resources used to acquire new technologies, Besley and Case (1993) argue that farmers who have the financial resources to acquire new technologies, particularly those in which the benefits are undetermined, must first learn about the technology over time, examine the number of people in their networks who have adopted or used the technology, and care about having first-mover advantage; these farmers are more likely to adopt the technology.

Zero (no-till) Technology

Zero tillage (ZT) refers to a new resource conserving method of cultivation that enhances efficient water and fertilizer use and reduces the cost of cultivation and weed infestation (Malik and Singh 1995; Hobbs et al. 1997). Several studies have reported the yield and cost-saving benefits of zero-tillage technology. For example, Igbal et al. (2002) and Erentein et al. (2007) carried out studies on the effect of zero-tillage technology on farm profits of rice-wheat cropping system in Punjab. Results of the studies show that ZT gave higher yield and reduced cost of production per hectare, which resulted in widespread adoption of the technology.

Awada et al. (2015) studied adoption of ZT in the Canadian Prairies. The study identified some economic factors that enhanced the adoption of ZT technology in western Canada including reduction in the market price of glyphosate herbicide relative to gasoline used in machines for tillage operations, increased yield of crops under ZT technology system, reduction in interest rate from 13% in 1989 to 7% in 1999 and further to 5% in 2011 (Saskatchewan Ministry of Agriculture 1990–2012), and information dissemination on the benefits of ZT through extension services (Lafond et al. 1996). In a related study, factors including neighbourhood effect; farmer characteristics such as level of education, farm ownership, and size; and high risk of soil erosion were identified to have a positive influence on ZT technology adoption (Awada 2012).

Quality Verification and Authenticity Diagnosis Technologies

Several quality verification and authenticity technologies have recently emerged, given the many avenues for food fraud. However, the incentive to adopt these technologies, particularly by the private sector, remains a big question. Underinvestment in agricultural research and development by the private sector has been attributed to their inability to capture the benefits of their research activities (Gray and Malla 2007). Therefore, the incentive for the private sector to adopt these technologies depends on the size of private benefits relative to public benefits (Hobbs et al. 2009). Several studies (e.g. Alston et al. 2008; Falck-Zepeda and Traxler 2000; Mensah and Wohlgenant 2009) have shown that technology adoption in the agri-food sector is associated with increased yield and social welfare benefits. Ugochukwu (2015) identified the costs associated with a technology, the size of the private market benefits relative to market opportunity costs, and the number of people using the technology at a particular point in time as important factors that affect adoption of diagnostic technologies, such as the International Barcode of Life (DNA Barcoding) technology. Processors and retailers would be willing to adopt this technology if the perceived benefits exceed the costs and the profit margin with the technology is high enough.

Livestock Health and Breeding Technologies

There have been an increasing number of technological innovations within the livestock industry globally. A number of studies have examined the factors that influence the adoption of technologies ranging from animal health, disease prevention, and management practices to breeding, genetics, and genomics innovations due to recent advances in computational biology and DNA sequencing. In the area of animal health, different types of vaccines have been produced to protect animals from different diseases. Studies have examined the efficacy of these vaccines and levels and determinants of adoption by livestock farmers. For instance, Ochieng and Hobbs (2016) examined *E. coli* vaccine and the incentives for cattle producers to adopt the vaccine in Canada. Results of the study show that there has been low level of adoption of *E. coli* vaccines owing to absence of market premiums for *E. coli*-vaccinated cattle to offset the additional cost associated with vaccination. Farmers argue that the benefits are enjoyed by other supply chain actors, primarily consumers and beef processors. Other reasons for low adoption identified by the study include scepticism regarding the efficacy of the vaccine; absence of regulatory and market pressure to adopt the vaccine, which is consistent with the findings of Ellis-Iversen et al. (2010); absence of reputational and/or liability penalties if a farmer's herd is the source of spread; and uncertainty of adoption by downstream feedlots.

Adoption of animal breeding technologies such as artificial insemination, embryo transplants, and sexed semen has been widely explored in the agricultural technology literature, given their economic benefits, in terms of productivity, to the live-stock industry. Several factors have been identified to influence adoption of these technologies. For example, Kaaya et al. (2005) showed that highly educated, young, and specialized dairy farmers have a higher tendency to adopt animal breeding tech-nologies in the United States. In addition, Khanal and Gillespie (2011) found that herd size, farm-level costs, breed of animal, age of farmer, and quality of extension services influence adoption of artificial insemination (AI) in the Ugandan dairy sec-tor. The results of Howley et al. (2012) indicate that the type of farm system (i.e. sheep, goat, cattle), experience with AI, and farm factors like gross margin and stocking rate affect adoption of AI among dairy farmers in Ireland. The study fur-ther shows that dairy farmers use AI more widely than sheep and goat farmers. This is consistent with the findings of Vishwanath (2003), who opined that dairy herd cows are usually confined, thereby making it possible to observe when they are in oestrus for insemination.

Technology Adoption and Return on R&D Investment

Endogenous growth theory views technological innovation as a nonrival good (Romer 1990). However, the theory fails to take into consideration non-R&D activi-ties carried out sometimes by nontechnical personnel that are associated with some costs (Clark and Fujimoto 1991; Alston et al. 2000). These activities, such as exten-sion services that promote awareness and enhance implementation and adoption of new technologies, are associated with some costs and time elements that are rele-vant in accurately determining the return on R&D investments.[4] Measurement of adoption costs has not been widely explored in the literature; this would be relevant for R&D policy analysis and investment optimization, particularly for private firms (Jonanovic 1997; Bessen 2000). A review of previous studies that did not consider adoption costs shows higher rates of return for R&D investment. For example, the review by Nadiri (1993) showed rates of return on investment between 20 and 40%. Alston et al. (2000) reviewed 294 studies that examined 1854 rates of return to R&D investments. The results show an overall average rate of return of 64.6%. Disaggregating the rates of return, research has an average return of 79.6%, and extension shows an 80.1% return, while activities that combine extension and research give an average 46.6% rate of return. This highlights the importance of extension as a post-R&D activity.

An extension service is an important component of adoption that motivates potential adopters to be profitable. Phillips McDougall (2011) estimated the time and costs involved in the process of developing a new plant biotechnology from discovery to authorization by regulatory authorities, fuelling the debate as to whether the time and costs associated with the development of a new technology

---

[4] For the purpose of this chapter, these costs are referred to as adoption costs, which should be a component of R&D expenditures when calculating return on investment (ROI).

exceed that of post-R&D activities. In order to illuminate this issue, further studies are needed to determine the magnitude of costs and duration of post-R&D activities that involve extension services and adoption. Inclusion of adoption costs in the calculation of return on investment (ROI) will give a robust estimate that will inform policy decision and help determine the distributional effects of gains from research.

Conclusions

Technological advancement and adoption are relevant for improvements in every sector. In recent years, there has been an increase in funding for agricultural research and development in technological innovations, particularly by the private sector. This has yielded positive returns on investment. However, significant adoption and commercialization of emerging technologies has not been achieved, particularly in less-developed countries, due to a combination of cultural beliefs, ethical concerns, regulatory delays, and lack of information and understanding of the science and technology being used. This has put consumers and producers in a dilemma. Although significant improvements have been made in technological advancement, more is needed to better understand the root causes of low adoption rates, especially in developing countries. Greater understanding would serve as a guide for technology developers to develop better strategies.

References

Abera, H.B. 2008. Adoption of Improved tef and Wheat Production Technologies in Crop-Livestock Mixed Systems in Northern Shewa Zones of Ethiopia. Unpublished Ph.D Dissertation, University of Pretoria.

Adesina, A.A., and J. Baidu-Forson. 1995. Farmers' Perceptions and Adoption of New Agricultural Technology: Evidence from Analysis in Burkina Faso and Guinea, West Africa. *Agricultural Economics* 13 (1): 1–9.

Agriculture and Agri-food Canada (AAFC). 2016. An Overview of the Canadian Agriculture and Agri-Food System. April 2016. Available at: https://caes.usask.ca/members/_pdf/Overview%20 2016-Final_eng.pdf. Accessed 1 June 2016.

Alston, J.M., M.C. Marra, P.G. Pardey, and T.J. Wyatt. 2000. Research Returns Redux: A Meta-Analysis of the Returns to Agricultural R&D. *Australian Journal of Agricultural and Resource Economics* 44 (2): 185–215.

Alston, J., G. Edwards, and J. Freebairn. 2008. Market Distortions and Benefits from Research. *American Journal of Agricultural Economics* 70: 281–288.

Anderson, K., C.P. Nielson, S. Robinson, and K. Thierfelder. 2001. Estimating the Global Effects of GMOs. In *The Future of Food: Biotechnology Markets and Policies in an International Setting*, ed. P.G. Pardey, 49–74. Washington, DC: International Food Policy Institute.

Arellanes, P., and D.R. Lee. 2003. The Determinants of Adoption of Sustainable Agricultural Technologies: Evidence from the Hillsides of Honduras. Paper Presented at XXV Conference of International Association of Agricultural Economists, Durban, August 2003.

Awada, L. 2012. The Adoption of Conservation Tillage on the Canadian Prairies. Unpublished Ph.D Dissertation, University of Saskatchewan.

Awada, L., S.R. Gray, and C. Nagy. 2015. The Benefits and Costs of Zero Tillage RD & E on the Canadian Prairies. *Canadian Journal of Agricultural Economics* 64 (3): 417–438. https://doi.org/10.1111/cjag.12080.

Bandiera, O., and I. Rasul. 2006. Social Networks and Technology Adoption in Northern Mozambique. *The Economic Journal* 116 (514): 869–902.

Barkley, A.P. 2002. The Economic Impacts of Agricultural Biotechnology on International Trade, Consumers and Producers: The Case of Corn and Soybeans in the U.S.A. 6th International ICABR Conference, Ravello.

Bassen, J. 2000. Adoption Costs and the Rate of Return to Research and Development. Working Paper 1/00, Research on Innovation, Wallingford. Available at: www.researchoninnovation.org/rdadopt.pdf.

Batz, F.J., K.J. Peters, and W. Janssen. 1999. The Influence of Technology Characteristics on the Rate and Speed of Adoption. *Agricultural Economics* 21 (4): 121–130.

Besley, T., and A. Case. 1993. Modelling Technology Adoption in Developing Countries. *The American Economic Review* 83 (2): 396–402.

Bohlen, J., and G. Beal. 1955. How Farm People Accept New Ideas. Special Report No. 15, Agricultural Extension Service, Iowa State College, Ames.

Briney, A. 2015. History and Development of Green Revolution. Available at: http://geography.about.com/od/globalproblemsandissues/a/greenrevolution.htm. Accessed 5 May 2016.

Chen, M. 1996. Competitor Analysis and Interfirm Rivalry: Toward a Theoretical Integration. *The Academy of Management Review* 21 (1): 100–134.

Clark, K., and T. Fujimoto. 1991. *Product Development Performance: Strategy, Organization, and Management in the World Auto Industry*. Boston: Harvard Business School Press.

Cohen, W.M., and D.A. Levinthal. 1989. Innovation and Learning: The Two faces of R&D. *The Economic Journal* 99: 569–596.

Cohen, W.M., Nelson, R.R. and Walsh, J. (1997). Appropriability Conditions and Why Firms Patent and Why They Do not in the U.S. Manufacturing Sector. Working Paper. Pittsburgh: Carnegie Mellon University.

Dethier, J.-J., and A. Effenberger. 2012. Agriculture and Development: A Brief Review of the Literature. *Economic Systems* 36: 175–205.

Dibba, L., S.C. Fialor, A. Diagne, and F. Nimoh. 2012. The Impact of NERICA Adoption on Productivity and Poverty of the Small-Scale Rice Farmers in the Gambia. *Food Security* 4 (2): 253–265.

Dinar, A., and D. Yaron. 1992. Adoption and Abandonment of Irrigated Technologies. *Agricultural Economics* 6: 315–332.

Dooley, K.E. 1999. Towards a Holistic Model for the Diffusion of Educational Technologies: An Integrative Review of Educational Innovation Studies. *Educational Technology & Society* 2 (4): 35–45.

Ellis-Iversen, J., A.J.C. Cook, E. Watson, M. Nielen, L. Larkin, M. Wooldridge, and H. Hogeveen. 2010. Perceptions, Circumstances and Motivators that Influence Implementation of Zoonotic Control Programs on Cattle Farms. *Preventive Veterinary Medicine* 93 (4): 276–285.

El-Osta, H.S., and M.J. Morehart. 2002. Technology Adoption and Its Impact on Production Performance of Dairy Operations. *Review of Agricultural Economics* 22 (2): 477–498.

Erenstein, O., U. Farook, R.K. Malik, and M. Sharif. 2007. Adoption and Impacts of Zero Tillage as a Resource Conserving Technology in the Irrigated Plains of South Asia. Comprehensive Assessment Research Report No. 19, International Water Management Institute, Colombo. Available at: www.impact.cgiar.org/sites/default/files/pdf/59.pdf.

Falck-Zepeda, J.B., and G. Traxler. 2000. Rent Creation and Distribution from Transgenic Cotton in the United States. *American Journal of Agricultural Economics* 82: 360–369.

Feder, G., R.E. Just, and D. Zilberman. 1982. Adoption of Agricultural Innovation in Developing Countries: A Survey. World Bank Staff Working Papers No. 542, 1982.

———. 1985. Adoption of Agricultural Innovation in Developing Countries: A Survey. *Economic Development and Cultural Change* 33: 255–298.

Felvey, R., N. Foster, and O. Memedovic. 2006. *The Role of Intellectual Property Rights in Technology Transfer and Economic Growth: Theory and Evidence*. Vienna: United Nations Industrial Development Organization.

Fuglie, K.O., and C.A. Kascak. 2001. Adoption and Diffusion of Natural-Resource-Conserving Agricultural Technology. *Review of Agricultural Economics* 23 (2): 386–403.

Garforth, C., B. Angell, J. Archer, and K. Green. 2003. Fragmentation or Creative Diversity? Options in the Provision of Land Management Advisory Services. *Land Use Policy* 20 (4): 323–333.

Gershon, F., and D.L. Umali. 1993. The Adoption of Agricultural Innovations: A Review. *Technological Forecasting and Social Change* 43 (3–4): 215–239.

Gray, R., and S. Malla. 2007. The Rate of Return to Agricultural Research in Canada. CAIRN Policy Brief. Canadian Agricultural Innovation Research Network. Available at: www.ag-innovation.usask.ca/finalpolicybriefs/mallaGray_11.pdf.

Griliches, Z. 1957. Hybrid Corn: An Exploration in the Economics of Technology Change. *Econometrica* 25: 501–522.

Haggui, F. 2004. Cost of EU Opposition to Genetically Modified Wheat in Terms of Global Food Security. Unpublished Ph.D. Dissertation, University of Saskatchewan.

Hall, B.H., and B. Khan. 2002. Adoption of New Technology. New Economy Handbook, 38. University of California Berkeley.

Hanf, C.H., and A. Bocker. 2002. Is European Consumers' Refusal of GM Food a Serious Obstacle or a Transient Fashion? In *Market Development for Genetically Modified Foods*, ed. R.E. Evenson, V. Santaniello, and D. Zilberman, 49–52. Wallingford: CABI Publishing.

Hildebrand, P.E., and E.J. Partenheimer. 1958. Socioeconomic Characteristics of Innovators. *Journal of Farm Economics* 40 (2): 446–449.

Hobbs, P.R., G.S. Giri, and P. Grace. 1997. *Reduced and Zero Tillage Options for the Establishment of Wheat After Rice in South Asia*, Rice-Wheat Consortium Paper Series, vol. 2. New Delhi: RWC.

Hobbs, J.E., W.A. Kerr, and M.T Yeung. 2009. Public and Private Goods: The Canadian Livestock and Poultry Traceability Program. Agriculture and Agri-Food Canada, CAT: A34-13/2009E-PDF, 31 August, 39 pp. ISBN: 978-1-1000-14090-2.

Howley, P., C.O. Donoghue, and K. Heanue. 2012. Factors Affecting Farmers' Adoption of Agricultural Innovations: A Panel Data Analysis of the Use of Artificial Insemination Among Dairy Farmers in Ireland. *Journal of Agricultural Science* 4 (6): 171–179.

Igbal, M., M.A. Khan, and M.Z. Anwar. 2002. Zero -Tillage Technology and Farm Profits: A Case Study of Wheat Growers in the Rice Zone of Punjab. *The Pakistan Development Review* 41 (4 part II): 665–682.

Jonanovic, B. 1997. Learning and Growth. In *Advances in Economics and Econometrics: Theory and Applications*, ed. Kreps and Wallis, vol. 2, 318. Econometric Society Monograph. Cambridge, UK: Cambridge University Press.

Kaaya, H., B. Bashaasha, and D. Mutetikka. 2005. Determinants of Utilisation of Artificial Insemination (AI) Services Among Ugandan Dairy Farmers. *African Crop Science Conference Proceedings* 7: 561–567.

Khanal, A.R., and J.M. Gillespie. 2011. Adoption and Profitability of Breeding Technologies on United States Dairy Farms, Southern Agricultural Economics Association Annual Meeting, Corpus Christi, TX, 5–8 Feb 2011.

Lafond, G.P., S.M. Boyetchko, S.A. Brandt, G.W. Clayton, and M.H. Entz. 1996. Influence of Changing Tillage Practices on Crop Production. *Canadian Journal of Plant Science* 76: 641–649.

Léger, A. 2007. Intellectual Property Rights and Innovation Around the World: Evidence from Panel Data. Discussion Paper 696, German Institute for Economic Research, Berlin.

Lleras-Muney, Adriana, and Frank Lichtenberg. 2002. The Effect of Education on Medical Technology Adoption: Are the More Educated More Likely to Use New Drugs? NBER Working Paper #9185.

Malik, R.K., and S. Singh. 1995. Littleseed Canarygrass Resistance to Isoproturon in India. *Weed Technology* 9: 419–425.

Mansfield, E. 1961. Technical Change and the Rate of Imitation. *Econometrica* 29 (4): 741–766.

———. 1963. The Speed of Response of Firms to New Techniques. *The Quarterly Journal of Economics* 77 (2): 290–311.

Mansfield, E., M. Schwartz, and S. Wagner. 1981. Imitation Costs and Patenting: An Empirical Study. *The Economic Journal* 91: 907–918.

Marra, M., Pardey, P.G. and Alston, J.M. (2002). The Payoffs to Agricultural Biotechnology: An Assessment of Evidence. EPDT Discussion Paper No. 87, International Food Policy Research Institute, Washington, DC.

Mensah, C.C., and M.K. Wohlgenant. 2009. A Market Impact Analysis of Soybean Technology Adoption. *Research in Business and Economics Journal* 2: 2009.

Millar, J. 2010. The Role of Extension for Improving Natural Resource Management: The Australian Experience. In *Shaping Change: Natural Resource Management, Agriculture and the Role of Extension*, ed. J. Jennings, R. Packham, and D. Woodside, 102–110. Wodonga: Australasia-Pacific Extension Network (APEN).

Miller, T., and G. Tolley. 1989. Technology Adoption and Agricultural Price Policy. *American Journal of Agricultural Economics* 71 (4): 847–857.

Moser, C.M., and C.B. Barrett. 2003. The Disappointing Adoption Dynamics of a Yield-Increasing, Low External-Input Technology: The Case of SRI in Madagascar. *Agricultural Systems* 76 (3): 1085–1100.

Moshini, G., H. Lapan, and A. Sobolevsky. 2000. Roundup Ready Soybeans and Welfare Effects in the Soybean Complex. *Agribusiness* 16 (1): 33–55.

Nadiri, M.I. 1993. *Innovation and Technological Spillovers*. NBER Working Paper No. 4423. Washington, DC: NBER.

Ochieng, B.J., and J.E. Hobbs. 2016. Incentives for Cattle Producers to Adopt an E.Coli Vaccine: An Application of Best-Worst Scaling. *Food Policy* 59: 78–87.

Pannell, D.J., G.R. Marshall, N. Barr, A. Curtis, F. Vanclay, and R. Wilkinson. 2006. Understanding and Promoting Adoption of Conservation Practices by Rural Landholders. *Australian Journal of Experimental Agriculture* 46 (11): 1407–1424.

Phillips-McDougall. 2011. The Cost and Time Involved In The Discovery, Development and Authorization of a New Plant Biotechnology Derived Trait. A Consultancy Study for Crop Life International, September 2011. Available at: https://croplife.org/wp-content/uploads/pdf_files/Getting-a-Biotech-Crop-to-Market-Phillips-McDougall-Study.pdf.

Powell, C. 2011. Irradiation is Back on the Table. Canadian Grocer. Available at: http://www.canadiangrocer.com/top-stories/irradiation-is-back-on-the-table-12160. Accessed 9 June 2016.

Rogers, E.M. 1983. *Diffusion of Innovation*. 3rd ed, 236. New York: The Free Press.

———. 2003. *Diffusion of Innovations*. 5th ed. New York: The Free Press.

Rogers, E.M., and J.D. Stanfield. 1968. Adoption and Diffusion of New Products: Emerging Generalizations and Hypotheses. In *Applications of the Sciences in Marketing*, ed. Frank M. Bass, Charles W. King, and Edgar A. Pessemier, 227–250. New York: Wiley.

Romer, P. 1990. Endogenous Technological Change. *Journal of Political Economy* 98: S71.

Rubas, D. 2004. Technology Adoption: Who is likely to Adopt and How Does the Timing Affect Benefits. Unpublished Ph.D. Dissertation submitted to the Office of Graduate Studies of the Texas A & M University, August 2004.

Saskatchewan Ministry of Agriculture. 1990–2012. Farm Machinery Custom and Rental Rate Guide, Published Yearly. Government of Saskatchewan.

Sauer, J., and D. Zilberman. 2010. Innovation Behaviour at Farm Level – Selection and Identification, 114th EAAE Seminar 'Structural Change in Agriculture', Berlin, 15–16 April 2010.

Scherer, F.M., S.E. Herzstein, A.W. Dreyfoos, W.G. Whitney, O.J. Bachman, C.P. Pesek, C.J. Scott, T.G. Kelly, and J.J. Galvin. 1959. *Patents and the Corporation: A Report on Industrial Technology Under Changing Public Policy*. Cambridge: Harvard University.

Sherry, L., and D. Gibson. 2002. The Path to Teacher Leadership in Educational Technology. *Contemporary Issues in Technology and Teacher Education [Online serial]* 2(2). Retrieved from http://www.citejournal.org/volume-2/issue-2-02/general/the-path-to-teacher-leadership-ineducational-Technology.

Stoneman, P. 1981. Intra-Firm Diffusion, Bayesian Learning and Profitability. *The Economic Journal* 91 (362): 375–388.

Sunding, D., and D. Zilberman. 2001. The Agricultural Innovation Process: Research and Technology Adoption in a Changing Agricultural Sector. In *Handbook of Agricultural Economics*, vol. 1, ed. B. Gardner and G. Rausser. Amsterdam: Elsevier Science B.V.

Taylor, C.T., and Z.A. Silberston. 1973. *The Economic Impact of the Patent System*. Cambridge: Cambridge University Press.

Tietenberg, T.H. 2000. *Environmental and Natural Resource Economics*. 5th ed. Reading: Addison-Wesley.

Uaiene, R.N. 2011. Determinants of Agricultural Technology Adoption in Mozambique. Paper Presented at "Dialogue on Promoting Agricultural Growth in Mozambique." International Food Policy Research Institute, July, 2011.

Ugochukwu, A.I. 2015. Essays on Collective Reputation and Authenticity in Agri-Food Markets. Unpublished Ph.D. Dissertation, University of Saskatchewan.

Vishwanath, R. 2003. Artificial Insemination: The State of the Art. *Theriogenology* 59 (2): 571–584.

Wozniak, Gregory D. 1987. Human Capital, Information, and the Early Adoption of New Technology. *Journal of Human Resources* 22 (1): 101–112.

Zavale, H., E. Mabaya, and R. Christy. 2005. Adoption of Improved Maize Seed by Smallholder Farmers in Mozambique. Staff Papers, Department of Applied Economics and Management, Cornell University, Ithaca.

Zeller, M., A. Diagne, and C. Mataya. 1997. Market Access by Smallholder Farmers in Malawi: Implications for Technology Adoption, Agricultural Productivity, and Crop Income. International Food Policy Research Institute: FCND Discussion Paper No. 35, September 1997.

Commercialization Mechanisms for New Plant Varieties

Sherzod B. Akhundjanov, R. Karina Gallardo, Jill J. McCluskey, and Bradley J. Rickard

Abstract Developing and marketing new varieties is essential for the long-term profitability of US crop producers. The ultimate goal of university breeding programs is to release improved plant varieties, either with superior quality or more efficient production management. For certain horticultural products, notably apples, plant breeders have developed several new differentiated varieties that have the capacity to be marketed with premium prices and that can compete on world markets. If these innovations are not commercialized or are commercialized in a suboptimal way, then the benefits of the research are greatly reduced. In this chapter, we use game theoretic analysis and an experimental auction to investigate the effects of contract exclusivity and payment structure on innovator and producer profits from a hypothetical new apple variety.

Introduction

Developing and marketing new varieties is essential for the long-term profitability of US crop producers. Responding to this need, there has been a rapid increase in the number of patented fruit varieties released by university breeding programs (Brown and Maloney 2009; Bareuther 2011; Gallardo et al. 2012). The ultimate goal of these programs is to release improved plant varieties, either with superior quality or more efficient production management. For some grain and oilseed crops, we have observed a number of new varieties that aim to reduce per acre costs through improvements in yields. There are many examples of new specialty crop

S.B. Akhundjanov
Utah State University, Logan, UT, USA

R.K. Gallardo
Puyallup Research and Extension Center, Washington State University, Puyallup, WA, USA

J.J. McCluskey (✉)
Washington State University, Pullman, WA, USA
e-mail: mccluskey@wsu.edu

B.J. Rickard
Cornell University, Ithaca, NY, USA

© Springer International Publishing AG 2018
N. Kalaitzandonakes et al. (eds.), *From Agriscience to Agribusiness*, Innovation, Technology, and Knowledge Management, https://doi.org/10.1007/978-3-319-67958-7_18

varieties that were developed specifically to increase quality, some of which command a large premium in the market. For certain horticultural products, notably apples, plant breeders have developed several new differentiated varieties that have the capacity to be marketed with premium prices and that can compete on world markets. Once these new varieties are developed, they must be commercialized. If the innovations are not commercialized or commercialized in a suboptimal way, then the benefits of the research are greatly reduced.

Federal and state support for research and development (R&D) at public universities had been down over the last few decades prior to 2010 (Alston et al. 2010). This general trend has also been occurring for horticultural crops (Cahoon 2007; Alston and Pardey 2008), but it has been moderated to some degree by the introduction of new federal funding (e.g., the Specialty Crop Research Initiative) that began in 2008. Decreasing government support creates strong incentives to develop alternative ways to fund R&D activities at public universities (Huffman and Just 1999; Just and Huffman 2009), including the use of intellectual property rights (IPRs) and patents for innovations introduced by public universities, made possible by the passage of the Bayh-Dole Act in 1980. The Bayh-Dole Act gave universities the ability to claim IPRs for federally funded, university-conducted research, where the revenue flows from the patents are used to support the universities' R&D efforts. However, the use of patents by universities and the subsequent licensing issues raise questions about the best mechanism for funding research investments and maximizing industry revenues.

The traditional arguments for public funding of research are that knowledge spillovers and imperfect IPR protection cause innovators to not realize the economic value of their discoveries, leading to private sector underinvestment in basic research. Public land grant universities are a special case of government funding of academic research. The US land grant mission of research and extension faculty is to deliver and apply research and new knowledge to positively impact communities. US land grant university agricultural research is funded in many ways, sometimes including mandatory assessments on growers. In the case of mandatory assessments, growers have paid a portion of the R&D costs and thus expect to benefit from the research. In the case of new varieties introduced by public universities, there are many economic issues to resolve in order to maximize the long-run revenues to the overall industry and to universities' research programs. An open research question is then, given the political and funding constraints surrounding the development of new fruit varieties, what is the optimal way to commercialize publically developed innovations?

Commercialization Mechanisms of University Innovations

There are several factors to consider in a commercialization process. One factor is the exclusivity of the commercialization. The question is whether all growers should have access to innovations that are developed at public universities, often accomplished with funds from mandatory grower assessments. The University of Minnesota has developed licensing schemes wherein a cooperative of growers is able to obtain exclusive access to a variety – a "managed variety" – for a fee that is levied both on the initial planting (a fixed fee) and percentage of sales on every box sold thereafter (a per-unit royalty). This approach is extremely controversial; other states are committed to providing the industry with equal access to new crop varieties for all growers or providing access through a lottery that allocates trees. Indeed, growers who were denied full access to a patented apple variety released by the University of Minnesota instigated legal action (see Lehnert 2010; Milkovich 2011). As a result of this litigation, administrators at other land grant universities are reluctant to employ exclusive contracts. Cornell University introduced two patented apple varieties in 2015 and made them available to all growers in New York State; they also levied a two-part fee on both the trees (a fixed fee) and the fruit that was marketed each year (a per-unit royalty). In terms of the economics, if the innovation results in product differentiation, then market power can exist. If the innovator limits the quantity made available to growers, the selected growers will receive a higher price in the market. Alternatively, if all growers have unlimited access, it will drive the final product price down.

A second factor is the structure of the contracts. Proprietary innovations, whether in agriculture or elsewhere, are utilized under licenses issued by the innovator, which are typically paid for using either fixed fees or per-unit royalties, where the total royalty payment depends on the number of units used. New institutional arrangements have arisen for the transfer of new plant varieties from research universities to consortia or cooperatives of growers willing to pay for licenses for new varieties (Cahoon 2007), but pricing mechanisms in these markets have been inefficient and not conducive to the rapid growth of R&D in new fruit varieties.

Licensing mechanisms for patented fruit varieties are typically established via negotiations between a technology transfer office (TTO) and grower-based licensees. These negotiations typically begin with a request for bids from potential licensees. The bids are evaluated based on financial and management considerations by the TTO with a focus on initial payments, annual payments, quality control issues, contracts with individual growers, and marketing plans. A successful bid for a new variety may allow the licensee the first right of refusal on subsequent varietal introductions. The licensees may include growers or grower-packers, a grower-owned cooperative, or a management company acting on behalf of a group of growers.

In practice, varieties are licensed to individual growers and the licensing mechanisms involve some combination of upfront fixed fees and output royalties that require annual payments based on the quantity of fruit that is marketed. In the case of perennial fruit crops, we consider the upfront fees to include the one-time charges applied per unit of land or per tree. Ad valorem or per-unit output royalties have not been widely used for patented fruit varieties but are becoming more common (Brown and Maloney 2009).

Previous literature has explored innovator profits under fees and royalty schemes. In particular, Arrow (1962) showed that it is profit-maximizing if the innovator is perfectly competitive. In the context of imperfect competition, Kamien and Tauman

(1986), Katz and Shapiro (1986), and Kamien et al. (1992), studying oligopolistic innovators, showed that a fixed fee generates higher revenue for an innovator (new entrant) than a royalty scheme. In contrast, royalties, or a combination of fees and royalties, have been found to yield the greatest profits for innovators in empirical applications (Sen and Taumann 2007).

In order to reconcile theoretical predictions with real-life observations, subsequent research has incorporated more realistic institutional settings and characteristics in modeling frameworks, including product differentiation (Muto 1993; Fauli-Oller and Sandonis 2002), risk aversion (Bousquet et al. 1998), asymmetric information (Gallini and Wright 1990; Sen 2005), moral hazard (Choi 2001), strategic delegation (Saracho 2002), and incumbency (Shapiro 1985; Kamien and Tauman 2002; Sen and Tauman 2007), among others. Such detailed characterization of various attributes of market stakeholders and interactions allowed the researchers to reconcile theory with empirical evidence. A key distinguishing feature of all of these studies, however, is that they primarily focus on cost-reducing innovation, which is certainly of interest to some industries. However, for the horticultural industry, the interest primarily lies in quality-improving innovation rather than cost-reducing.

Li and Wang (2010) examine the profits an inventor can realize by using an exclusive or a nonexclusive contract (under different licensing schemes). They focus on a vertical quality innovation, which is the type of innovation that describes new fruit varieties with better eating qualities. Their nonexclusive case has two licensees. They show that, in the case of a duopoly, licensing by means of a two-part tariff (i.e., a combination of fixed fee and per-unit royalty) generates greater profits for the innovator compared to licenses that are financed through royalties or fees alone. By setting the license price such that both downstream firms license an improved product, the licensee is able to raise industry profit and then extract much of the resulting surplus via a fixed fee. Rickard et al. (2016) examine the fee-versus-royalty decision with more than two potential licensees; they collect data from an experiment that captures many of the important conditions facing fruit growers considering an investment in patented varieties. Their results suggest that the profits for the innovator (the university in this case) will be maximized with the use of royalties on the annual production of fruit in a nonexclusive contract when a new variety is introduced. We argue that the innovator has multiple objectives and multiple licensees. Specifically, the innovator wishes to maximize the weighted sum of its own revenues and the licensees' revenues. We consider a range of weights assigned to the innovator and hence the producers, to provide a more complete understanding of how the licensing decision will affect the joint economic outcome. This scenario corresponds to the case of a US land grant university (the innovator) and its stakeholder growers (the licensees). We discuss results from experimental auctions with apple growers and simulations.

Evaluation of Commercialization Mechanisms

Theory of Innovation, Licensing, and Market Competition

This section makes an argument based on the theoretical model developed in Akhundjanov et al. (2017). In particular, the model is designed to examine contracts for an innovator who owns a patent for a new technology and whose objective is to maximize the weighted sum of its own profits and the licensees' profits. This objective is consistent with the mission of US land grant universities, which is to provide research in agricultural and related sciences that is designed to improve information and technologies for US producers. In this context, the land grant university is the innovator and the growers are the licensees. This is different from previous literature where the innovator only cares about its own profits.

In order to study, the effect of market competition on profits, we do not limit the number of firms in the market ex ante. Firms are assumed to produce a homogenous product, with constant unit production costs, and compete in the market as Cournot oligopolists. The innovation introduced by the innovator is vertical, meaning that a new technology enables licensees to produce a better quality product (i.e., a vertically differentiated product) than those produced using the old technology. Thus, the firms must decide whether or not to compete for the acquisition of an IPR for such new technology. Consumers are assumed to have Mussa and Rosen (1978) type of utility, which depends on the quality level of a product and the product market price. We model the quality of a product as a function of the degree of vertical product innovation (i.e., the level of quality improvement), which allows us to explore the impact of quality improvement on market demand, and consequently the returns to firms and the innovator.

We examine the innovator and firm profits under different licensing arrangements using a game theoretic framework, by first analyzing the innovator's decision problem (i.e., the licensing decision), then the problem of the firm(s) that adopt a new technology, and finally the remaining firms in the industry that continue using old technology. We consider three types of licensing contracts through which the innovator can release its innovation: a fixed fee, a per-box royalty, and a two-part tariff, which is essentially the combination of fixed fee and per-box royalty. These contracts come in two forms: exclusive or nonexclusive contracts. Further, we set the weighting parameters such that the innovator places equal weights on its own and the licensees' profits.

The results from numerical simulations indicate that, under an exclusive contract, the innovator generates the greatest profits with the two-part tariff, followed by the fixed fee and then the per-box royalty. On the other hand, with nonexclusive contract, the innovator's profits are the greatest with the two-part tariff, followed by the per-box royalty and then the fixed fee. Moreover, the innovator's profits are largely unaffected by the industry size under exclusive contracts, while the profits become sensitive to the size of the industry under nonexclusive contracts, which makes an intuitive sense. In general, from the innovator's perspective, a nonexclusive contract with either a two-part tariff or a per-box royalty, depending on the level of innovation, is always preferred. The two-part tariff dominates other commercialization mechanisms at higher levels of innovation, while the per-box royalty contract is dominant at relatively lower levels of innovation.

The analysis of the firm (the licensee) profits demonstrates that, under exclusive contracts, the firm receives the greatest profits with the per-unit royalty, followed by the fixed fee and then the two-part tariff. In contrast, with nonexclusive contracts, the firm's profits are the largest with the fixed fee, which holds true across different industry structures and levels of innovation, followed by the per-box royalty and then the two-part tariff. However, if the level of innovation is low and/or the industry size is large, then the profit-ranking under nonexclusive contract becomes the fixed fee, followed by the two-part tariff and then the per-box royalty. Overall, from the firm's (the licensee's) perspective, an exclusive contract with per-box royalty is beneficial. Since US land grant universities emphasize a broad impact of their research and extension work, then focusing more on nonexclusive licensing arrangements in the analysis would be more appropriate. The predictions from the theoretical model are tested with data that we collected in an experiment, and we will discuss the details in the following section.

Experiments with Washington Apple Growers

In order to understand firm (licensee) preferences for different commercialization mechanisms, and also to evaluate innovator and licensee profits under these schemes, we conducted experimental auctions with Washington apple growers during the Washington State Horticultural Association Annual Meeting in December 2014. In particular, we had 32 apple growers participating in the experiment, who collectively operated 26,080 acres (or 16% of all apple acreage in Washington) and had on average 23 years of experience in apple production. See Akhundjanov et al. (2017) for the details of the experiment and other statistics.

We conducted Becker-DeGroot-Marschak (BDM) auctions (Becker et al. 1964), where the participants bid on hypothetical access to growing a promising new apple variety using licensing schemes distinguished by contract type (fixed fee, per-box royalty, and two-part tariff) and the degree of contract exclusivity (exclusive and nonexclusive). The participants submitted a bid to obtain access to grow 1450 trees, which is the conventional number of trees that can be grown on one acre of land. The experiment was designed to closely mimic the actual situation that growers find themselves in while deciding whether or not to adopt a new fruit variety.

Figure 1 provides the distribution of all growers' bids (in $) under different licensing arrangements. It is apparent that the growers in general are willing to pay more under fixed fee, per-box royalty, and two-part tariff (combination) when the contract is exclusive. This makes an intuitive sense as the grower who is able to have a sole access to an IPR is also willing to pay an extra premium for it. Further, since a two-part tariff combines both fixed fee and per-box royalty in a single contract, we

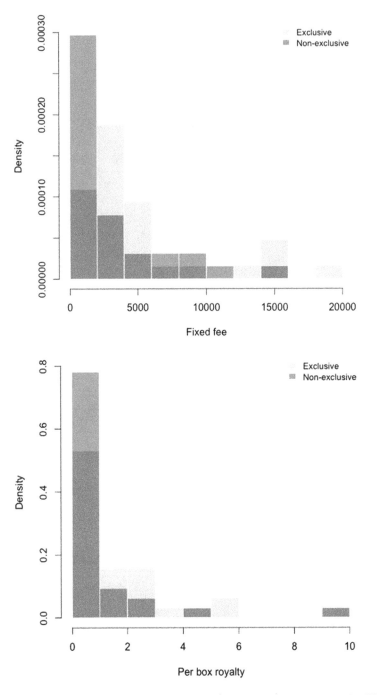

Fig. 1 The empirical distributions of growers' bids (in $) for a new apple variety under different commercialization mechanisms

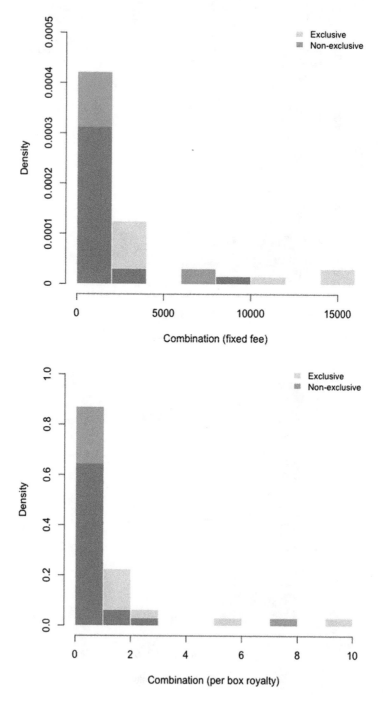

Fig. 1 (continued)

can observe that most of the weights for fixed fee and per-box royalty under two-part tariff, i.e., combination (fixed fee) and combination (per-box royalty), respectively, fall to the lower tail relative to stand-alone fixed fee and per-box royalty contracts, which is intuitive.

In order to compare the relative profitability of different licensing arrangements, we compute the innovator's and licensee's costs and profits for eligible bids. We use the "Honeycrisp" cost-of-production study as the reference for understanding the likely costs of growing the new varieties (Galinato and Gallardo 2012). Eligible bids are determined based on the BDM auction approach using the binding licensing schemes and whether or not the grower's bid is greater than or equal to a randomly drawn market clearing price. We calculate 10-, 15-, and 20-year present values of profits based on production of the new apple variety on either 10% of grower's total apple land or 10 acres of land, whichever is higher.

Figure 2 depicts the variation in estimated grower profits arising from six different licensing arrangements. It is clear that the grower's profits are the greatest across three contract types (fixed fee, per-box royalty, and two-part tariff) and different time horizons when the contract is exclusive. This makes sense as the contract

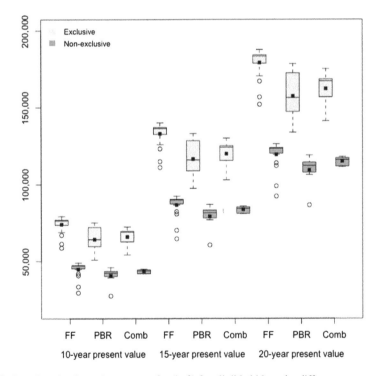

Fig. 2 Boxplot of estimated grower profits (in $) for eligible bids under different commercialization mechanisms and time horizons. Note: The bottom and the top of the box correspond to the 25th and 75th percentiles, respectively. The horizontal line inside the box represents the median (the 50th percentile), while the small black box denotes the mean. Whiskers indicate variability outside the upper and lower quartiles. Circles denote outliers

exclusivity is the largest statistically significant nonconstant factor that affects grower bids under all three contract types. Furthermore, under both exclusive and nonexclusive contracts, the grower obtains the largest profits with the fixed fee, followed by the two-part tariff and then the per-box royalty. Our empirical findings for nonexclusive contracts support those from theoretical analysis, while the results for exclusive contracts provide partial support. In particular, for exclusive contracts, theoretical and empirical results agree on the ranking for fixed fee and two-part tariff but disagree on the ranking of per-box royalty.

The estimated innovator profits under six commercialization mechanisms are reported in Fig. 3. It is apparent that exclusive contracts are beneficial to innovators as well, a finding that is line with the literature (Sen and Taumann 2007). Moreover, under the exclusive contract, the innovator's profits are highest with the per-box royalty, followed by the two-part tariff and then the fixed fee. The profit-ranking under a nonexclusive contract remains largely the same, with the only change being in the relative position of the two-part tariff and the fixed fee for some periods. Generally, the empirical findings for nonexclusive contracts are in line with those from theoretical analysis, whereas those for exclusive contracts are in partial agreement with the theoretical predictions. Specifically, for exclusive contracts, theoretical

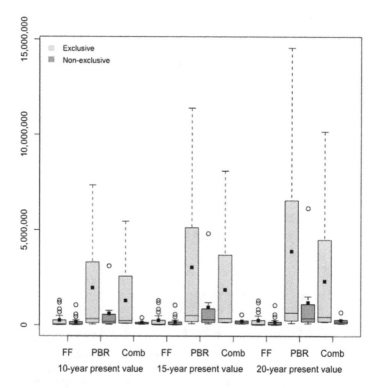

Fig. 3 Boxplot of estimated innovator profits (in $) for eligible bids under different commercialization mechanisms and time horizons

and empirical results agree on the rankings for two-part tariff and the fixed fee but disagree on the ranking of per-box royalty.

Conclusions and Discussion

This chapter considers the economic implications of how university plant breeding programs commercialize the new plant cultivars that they develop. New horticultural varieties are often developed by public universities that receive public funding in addition to funding from producers directly through commodity commissions. As a result, university administrators are increasingly pressed to optimize the way that they commercialize new varieties and how these decisions affect growers in their state. The real-world nuances related to these sensitivities need to be fully considered in the economic analysis of the optimal licensing strategy.

Several insights can be drawn from our work. The results provide evidence that the fixed-fee exclusive contract is the most profitable for growers. Of the nonexclusive contracts, the fixed fee contract also performs the best from the growers' perspective. For the innovator, the most preferable licensing scheme is the per-box royalty contract for both exclusive and the nonexclusive versions of the contracts. Our findings on potential profits for both adopters and innovators signal that exclusive contracts outperform the nonexclusive licensing schemes. However, there are distributional effects and fairness concerns.

The political and institutional limitations to the contracts that can be used to license new varieties being released by public universities, especially when plant breeding programs have a stated objective to make new varieties available to all growers, may make a suboptimal outcome necessary. From an economic point of view, it may be possible for the growers who benefit from exclusive access to compensate the growers who do not have access with all parties being better off relative to providing open access to all growers. Findings from our research warrant further in-depth research of this complex and contrasting situation.

References

Akhundjanov, S.B., K.R. Gallardo, J.J. McCluskey, and B.J. Rickard. 2017. Optimal Licensing of Plant Variety Patents: Benefiting both the Public University and the Industry. Working Paper, Washington State University.

Alston, J.M., and P.G. Pardey. 2008. Public Funding for Research into Specialty Crops. *HortScience* 43 (5): 1461–1470.

Alston, J.M., M.A. Andersen, J.S. James, and P.G. Pardey. 2010. *Persistence Pays: US Agricultural Productivity Growth and the Benefits from Public R&D Spending*. New York: Springer. Available at: http://www.springerlink.com/content/978-1-4419-0657-1.

Arrow, K.J. 1962. Economic Welfare and the Allocation of Resources for Inventions. In *The Rate and Direction of Inventive Activity: Economic and Social Factors*, ed. R.R. Nelson. Princeton: Princeton University Press.

Bareuther, C.M. 2011. Washington Apples: Variety Report. *Produce Business* 27 (8): 42–50.

Becker, G.M., M.H. DeGroot, and J. Marschak. 1964. Measuring Utility by a Single-Response Sequential Method. *Behavioral Science* 9 (3): 226–232.

Bousquet, A., H. Cremer, M. Ivaldi, and M. Wolkowicz. 1998. Risk Sharing in Licensing. *International Journal of Industrial Organization* 16 (5): 535–554.

Brown, S.K., and K.E. Maloney. 2009. Making Sense of New Apple Varieties, Trademarks and Clubs: Current Status. *New York Fruit Quarterly* 17 (3): 9–12.

Cahoon, R.S. 2007. Licensing Agreements in Agricultural Biotechnology. In *Intellectual Property Management in Health and Agricultural Innovation: A Handbook of Best Practices*, ed. A. Krattiger, R.T. Mahoney, L. Nelsen, J.A. Thomson, A.B. Bennett, K. Satyanarayana, G.D. Graff, C. Fernandez, and S.P. Kowalski. Ithaca: Bio Developments-International Institute.

Choi, J.P. 2001. Technology Transfer with Moral Hazard. *International Journal of Industrial Organization* 19 (1–2): 249–266.

Fauli-Oller, R., and J. Sandonis. 2002. Welfare Reducing Licensing. *Games and Economic Behavior* 41 (2): 192–205.

Galinato, S., and R.K. Gallardo. 2012. 2011 Cost Estimates of Establishing, Producing, and Packing Honeycrisp Apples in Washington. Washington State University Extension Factsheet FS062E.

Gallardo, R.K., D. Nguyen, V. McCracken, C. Yue, J. Luby, and J.R. McFerson. 2012. An Investigation of Trait Prioritization in Rosaceous Fruit Breeding Programs. *Hortscience* 47 (6): 771–776.

Gallini, N.T., and B.D. Wright. 1990. Technology Transfer Under Asymmetric Information. *RAND Journal of Economics* 21 (1): 147–160.

Huffman, W.E., and R.E. Just. 1999. The Organization of Agricultural Research in Western Developed Countries. *Agricultural Economics* 21 (1): 1–18.

Just, R.E., and W.E. Huffman. 2009. The Economics of Universities in a New Age of Funding Options. *Research Policy* 38 (7): 1102–1116.

Kamien, M.I., and Y. Tauman. 1986. Fees Versus Royalties and the Private Value of a Patent. *Quarterly Journal of Economics* 101 (3): 471–492.

Kamien, M.I., and Y. Tauman. 2002. Patent Licensing: The Inside Story. *The Manchester School* 70(1): 7–15.

Kamien, M.I., S.S. Oren, and Y. Tauman. 1992. Optimal Licensing of a Cost Reducing Innovation. *Journal of Mathematical Economics* 21 (5): 483–508.

Katz, M.L., and C. Shapiro. 1986. How to License Intangible Property. *The Quarterly Journal of Economics* 101 (3): 567–589.

Lehnert, R. 2010. Not so sweet tangle: Minnesota growers sue over club agreement. Good Fruit Grower (August 2010): 8–9. Available at: http://www.goodfruit.com/Good-Fruit-Grower/August-2010/Not-so-sweet-shytangle/.

Li, C., and J. Wang. 2010. Licensing a Vertical Product Innovation. *The Economic Record* 86 (275): 517–527.

Milkovich, M. 2011. Litigants Settle SweeTango Dispute. *Fruit Grower News* (November 2011).

Mussa, M., and S. Rosen. 1978. Monopoly and Product Quality. *Journal of Economic Theory* 18 (2): 301–317.

Muto, S. 1993. On Licensing Policies in Bertrand Competition. *Games and Economic Behavior* 5 (2): 257–267.

Rickard, B.J., T.J. Richards, and J. Yan. 2016. University Licensing of Patents for Varietal Innovations in Agriculture. *Agricultural Economics* 4: 3–14.

Saracho, A.I. 2002. Patent Licensing Under Strategic Delegation. *Journal of Economics and Management Strategy* 11 (2): 225–251.

Sen, D. 2005. On the Coexistence of Different Licensing Schemes. *International Review of Economics and Finance* 14 (4): 393–413.

Sen, D., and Y. Tauman. 2007. General Licensing Schemes for Cost-Reducing Innovation. *Games and Economic Behavior* 69: 163–186.

Shapiro, C. 1985. Patent Licensing and R&D Rivalry. *American Economic Review* 75(2): 25–30.

Water Efficient Maize for Africa: A Public-Private Partnership in Technology Transfer to Smallholder Farmers in Sub-Saharan Africa

Mark Edge, Sylvester O. Oikeh, Denis Kyetere, Stephen Mugo, and Kingstone Mashingaidze

Abstract Water Efficient Maize for Africa (WEMA) is a public-private partnership working to improve food security and rural livelihoods among smallholder farmers and their families in sub-Saharan Africa by developing and deploying new drought-tolerant and insect-pest-protected hybrid maize (corn) varieties. Maize is the most widely grown staple crop in Africa, where more than 300 million people depend on it as their main food source. Droughts, foliar diseases, and insect pests are intensifying food production problems in Africa, which makes for a vulnerable food security situation. Smallholder farmers in Africa, like farmers everywhere, want the choice to use the best tools and technologies available to minimize their risks and improve their lives.

Introduction

At the time of writing, the WEMA project is in its ninth year of operations and an ongoing work in progress. There is much to be gained by combining the strengths and core competencies of the public sector with the private sector; however, it's neither simple nor straightforward to establish this type of collaboration. Additionally, public-private partnerships should not be construed as an automatic

M. Edge (✉)
Monsanto Company, St. Louis, MO, USA
e-mail: mark.edge@monsanto.com

S.O. Oikeh • D. Kyetere
African Agricultural Technology Foundation, Nairobi, Kenya

S. Mugo
International Maize and Wheat Improvement Center (CYMMT), Nairobi, Kenya

K. Mashingaidze
Agricultural Research Council Grain Crops Institute, Potchefstroom, South Africa

© Springer International Publishing AG 2018
N. Kalaitzandonakes et al. (eds.), *From Agriscience to Agribusiness*, Innovation, Technology, and Knowledge Management, https://doi.org/10.1007/978-3-319-67958-7_19

formula for success. Our hope is that after reading this case study on the WEMA partnership, you gain insights and additional understanding of the key challenges and factors for success of public-private partnerships in agricultural development for smallholder farmers.

Water Efficient Maize for Africa (WEMA) is a public-private partnership (PPP) project started in 2008 and led by the Kenyan-based African Agricultural Technology Foundation (AATF), involving Monsanto Company, the International Maize and Wheat Improvement Center (CIMMYT), and five National Agricultural Research Systems (NARS) in Uganda, Kenya, Tanzania, Mozambique, and South Africa. The objective of the project is to improve food security and rural livelihoods among smallholder maize producers in sub-Saharan Africa (SSA) by developing new drought-tolerant and insect-pest-protected maize hybrids and providing the technology royalty-free to African seed companies for distribution and sale to smallholder farmers. The partnership helps build technical breeding and biotechnology capacity as well as seed systems in Africa. WEMA is funded by the Bill and Melinda Gates Foundation, the Howard G. Buffett Foundation, and the United States Agency for International Development (USAID).

The project's goals are to increase maize yield stability and reduce risk under drought conditions in sub-Saharan Africa (SSA) through plant breeding and biotechnology. Specific targets are to increase yields by 20–35% in 10 years, promote adoption of drought-tolerant maize hybrids, and deliver biotech insect-pest protected and drought-tolerant maize hybrids to smallholder farmers in SSA.

Deciding who to engage as partners and defining what we want to accomplish are the easy parts. Implementing the plans, overcoming barriers, and actually making a positive impact on smallholder farmers are more complicated and challenging than what you might imagine. However, it's a big challenge to do the initial steps we just called the "easy parts." Getting started, establishing the right framework, and agreeing on common goals are a lot of hard work and critical to do well if the PPP is to have a reasonable chance to tackle the "hard parts" of implementing the technology and delivering it to the smallholder farmers.

A Brief History of WEMA

Officially, the WEMA partnership started in 2008; however, to get to the "real" starting point, we need to go several years earlier and look at the various partners and interests that came together in order to formalize the idea into a funded project.

African Agricultural Technology Foundation (AATF)

The African Agricultural Technology Foundation (AATF) was set up in 2003 after 2 years of consultations, facilitated by the Rockefeller Foundation, among a wide range of stakeholders from Africa, North America, and Europe to determine an operational model for AATF to address food security and poverty reduction challenges. AATF's mission is to access, develop, adapt, and deliver appropriate agricultural technologies for sustainable use and improve the livelihoods of smallholder farmers in SSA through innovative partnerships and effective stewardship along the entire value chain.

AATF develops and manages public-private partnership projects and became a central player in WEMA in 2007, when asked by Monsanto to take the lead in preparing an investment plan to the Bill and Melinda Gates Foundation to develop drought-tolerant maize in Africa.

International Maize and Wheat Improvement Center (CIMMYT)

The International Maize and Wheat Improvement Center (commonly called by its Spanish acronym CIMMYT for *Centro Internacional de Mejoramiento de Maíz y Trigo*) is a nonprofit research and training institution dedicated to maize and wheat science for improved livelihoods. CIMMYT works throughout the developing world to improve livelihoods and foster more productive, sustainable maize and wheat farming. Its portfolio squarely targets critical challenges, including food insecurity and malnutrition, climate change, and environmental degradation. Through collaborative research, partnerships, and training, the center helps to build and strengthen a new generation of national agricultural research and extension services in maize- and wheat-growing nations. As a member of the CGIAR Consortium of 15 agricultural research centers, CIMMYT leads the CGIAR Research Programs on Maize and Wheat, which align and add value to the efforts of more than 500 partners.

CIMMYT grew out of a pilot program sponsored by the Mexican government and the Rockefeller Foundation in the 1940s–1950s to raise Mexico's farm productivity.

Wheat varieties bred by Norman Borlaug, Ph.D., as part of the program helped Mexico attain self-sufficiency for wheat in the 1950s and were imported by India and Pakistan in the 1960s to stave off famine, soon bringing those countries record harvests. This led to the widespread adoption of improved varieties and farming practices called the "Green Revolution."

CIMMYT was formally launched in 1966. Dr. Borlaug received the 1970 Nobel Peace Prize for his contributions to the Green Revolution. He worked as a CIMMYT wheat scientist and research leader through 1979 and remained a distinguished consultant for the center until his death in 2009 (CIMMYT 2016).

Building on the legacy of the Green Revolution and the Nobel Peace Prize, CIMMYT's maize breeding program in Africa collaborates with NARS, nongovernment organizations (NGOs) and community-based organizations (CBOs), seed sector organizations, regional research networks, other CGIAR centers, private seed companies, and advanced research institutions to provide diverse, high-yielding maize varieties that withstand infertile soils, drought, pests, and diseases.

CIMMYT worked to develop drought-tolerant varieties of both wheat and maize for several decades, making modest gains with wheat but finding considerable success with maize, thanks in part to the wider range of natural genetic variation in maize. They developed a stress-breeding procedure in Africa to help effectively select for improved drought tolerance. By 2002, CIMMYT had been able to develop maize hybrids with yields under drought conditions averaging 20 percent above local hybrids not improved through stress breeding.

With such progress being made at low cost through the use of conventional breeding methods in Africa, there was a legitimate question of why anyone should use the more expensive approach of genetic engineering. Genetic engineering offered the promise to add still greater drought tolerance to the already improved CIMMYT hybrids, resulting in an even more substantial gains for drought-tolerant maize. Scientifically, the optimal approach was to use both techniques together. It was less clear if it would be the optimal political approach in Africa.

CIMMYT had seen burdensome regulations slow down other genetic engineering projects in Africa, including a Kenya Agricultural Research Institute (KARI)-CIMMYT project to introduce insect-resistant genetically modified (GM) varieties of Bt maize. The project was launched in 2000, but Kenya's National Biosafety Committee did not allow a first set of field trials until 2005 (Paarlberg 2008). It wasn't clear to CIMMYT in 2007 whether the scientifically justified approach using genetic engineering to develop drought-tolerant maize was sufficient to overcome the potential political barriers. That's how things stood when the AATF invitation to participate in WEMA funded by the Bill and Melinda Gates Foundation landed on CIMMYT's doorstep.

National Agricultural Research Systems (NARS)

Governments play a vital role in food security and policy for the well-being of their citizens and typically have an organization (collectively referred to as the NARS) within the Ministry of Agriculture to focus on research for the purpose of crop improvement of key local staple crops. Maize is the main local staple crop for most countries in East and Southern Africa and consequently most have maize breeding programs. The NARS have a tradition of working together with CIMMYT to develop improved maize varieties for farmers in each of their countries.

As WEMA was forming in 2007, a central question for those developing the project concept was "Which governments in East and Southern Africa have, or are supportive of developing, biosafety laws for the commercial cultivation of genetically modified crops?" Governmental support and the political will to introduce biotechnology for smallholder farmers in Africa were seen as critical components for the success of the WEMA project. It is often asked how it was decided which NARS joined the WEMA partnership project and the simple answer is, at the time in 2007, the countries with an affirmative response to the question were Kenya, Mozambique, South Africa, Tanzania, and Uganda. The respective NARS within these five countries are officially known as the following:

- Kenya Agricultural and Livestock Research Organization (KALRO)
- Instituto de Investigação Agrária de Moçambique (IIAM)
- Agricultural Research Council of South Africa (ARC)
- Tanzania Commission for Science and Technology (COSTECH)
- National Agricultural Research Organization (NARO) in Uganda

The NARS have maize breeding programs that use unique genetic resources to develop maize hybrids, which are made available to farmers in their country for the greater public good. In 2007, none of the NARS had experience with the unique challenges of integrating biotechnology into their programs, but they had the desire to learn and the willingness to try.

Bill and Melinda Gates Foundation (BMGF)

Based in Seattle, Washington, and guided by the belief that every life has equal value, the Bill and Melinda Gates Foundation (BMGF) works to help all people lead healthy, productive lives. In developing countries, it focuses on improving people's health and giving them the chance to lift themselves out of hunger and extreme poverty. In the United States, it seeks to ensure that all people—especially those with the fewest resources—have access to the opportunities they need to succeed in school and life (Bill and Melinda Gates Foundation 2016).

Prior to 2006, the only grants for agriculture given by the foundation were indirect and made through the global health window in the form of various projects to develop food crops with enhanced vitamin, iron, or zinc content, called "biofortified" crops. After years of quiet study, it made a significant move into the agricultural sector and created a separate agricultural development division. Its first large grant in 2006 was a $100 million gift to support a partnership with the Rockefeller Foundation called the Alliance for a Green Revolution in Africa (AGRA), a project based in Nairobi, Kenya, and focused on crop science. When Kofi Annan agreed in 2007 to become the chair of the AGRA initiative, he explained that the plan at first was not to rely on GM seeds, but nothing was ruled out for the future (Paarlberg 2008).

Drought tolerance was identified by BMGF officers as one of the most important crop improvement goals for helping smallholder farmers in Africa. They brought in several high-level scientific experts as new staff at the foundation, tasked with improving crop yields in SSA via the best and most appropriate science and technology, including biotechnology (Paarlberg 2008). In 2007, the foundation didn't have a specific strategy to embrace genetically engineered crops for Africa, but the stage was set to support crop improvement projects that used technologies most likely to address the ravages of drought in Africa.

Monsanto Company

Over the past 20 years, Monsanto has evolved into a business focused on being a sustainable agriculture company, delivering products that support farmers around the world. Its success depends on empowering farmers—large and small—to produce more from their land while conserving more of our world's natural resources, such as water and energy. Its leading seed brands in crops like corn, cotton, oilseeds, and vegetables produce in-the-seed trait technologies for farmers, which are intended to protect crop yield, support on-farm efficiency, and reduce on-farm costs. Monsanto strives to make its products available to farmers throughout the world by broadly licensing its seed and trait technologies to other companies. In addition to its seeds and traits business, Monsanto also manufactures Roundup® and other herbicides used by farmers, consumers, and lawn-and-garden professionals (Monsanto 2016).

An important early indication of broad stakeholder interest in a GM drought-tolerant (DT) crop project for Africa was provided in 2004–2005, when Monsanto took the initiative and offered to share its newly discovered DT traits for humanitarian purposes. Monsanto was motivated by genuine humanitarian concern, knowledge of how technology can transform agriculture, business interests, and corporate social responsibility. In 2004, Monsanto hired Don S. Doering, Ph.D.—a respected private consultant previously a senior associate at the World Resources Institute (WRI)—to approach donors with the suggestion we could be willing to share the new DT technology if someone was willing to pay most of the cost. Dr. Doering convened an ad hoc meeting that brought together representatives from eight different public-sector or nonprofit organizations.

The result of the first meeting was the formation of an 11-member international exploratory committee that received enough money from USAID and the Rockefeller Foundation to schedule a larger strategy and planning meeting in 2005. Doering's plan was to use this second meeting to forge a multi-stakeholder consensus and secure donor commitments to form and finance a PPP with Monsanto playing a partnering but not a leading role. The donors attending this meeting in May 2005 in Arlington, Virginia, did not open their check books.

There were a number of challenging obstacles, some of which seemed intractable, standing in the way of getting donors on board.

Monsanto had new DT technology, but it was still in the development pipeline and intended for commercial use in the USA and elsewhere, so there were a number of intellectual property considerations limiting Monsanto's ability to share details about its research results. Monsanto's commercial intentions with the technology in the USA precluded it from making an unrestricted donation for Africa; instead it would need to offer the DT technology under a royalty-free license for limited use in some countries. Donors naturally were concerned about what a license rather than a donation of the technology would mean.

Most African countries did not have well-established biosafety regulations in place, and for the few that did, the regulatory process seemed slow and cumbersome due to local political considerations and misunderstandings about GMOs. However, even if all the regulatory and political challenges could be addressed, it wasn't clear how GM hybrid seed would be extended to smallholder farmers in Africa. When private companies license GM technology, they typically require a number of stewardship and quality control assurances in return, to protect against lawsuits and potential damage to their reputation. How would that work with smallholder farmers in Africa?

Despite the intrinsic benefit of hybrid vigor providing at least a 15 percent yield increase in maize, many local institutions in Africa that deliver improved maize seed to farmers have trouble working with hybrids. There are a number of technical steps to maintain the basic parental seed which make it difficult to maintain purity and quality, and the production of the hybrid seed itself requires vigilant management, especially during the critical step of crossing the male parent to the female parent during the seed production growing season. Due to these challenges, much of the maize seed market in Africa is still planted to the less-productive but easier-to-produce, open-pollinated varieties (OPVs) which do not have hybrid vigor. If a farmer saves grain as seed from an OPV—a common occurrence in Africa—the resulting seed planted will yield similar to the original seed. If a farmer saves grain to be used as seed from a hybrid, the resulting seed planted does not have the hybrid genetic purity and will not deliver as much yield as the original seed. The farmer is not actually restricted from saving the grain from hybrid maize to be used as seed; it's just a poor choice for biological reasons related to how hybrid vigor works.

A royalty-free license would require the DT technology to only be made available in hybrid maize seed; OPVs would not be an option due to stewardship and quality control concerns. The debate about the merits of hybrids vs. OPVs has been going on for decades, but this project for DT maize in Africa wasn't going to engage in the debate. That felt uncomfortable to a number of the potential public-sector donors.

These numerous concerns contributed to the end result at the 2005 meeting in Arlington that the participants failed to agree on how they could move forward. Monsanto's effort to get public-sector donors to fund the proposed public-private partnership for drought-tolerant maize for Africa failed. But the idea did not die; it simply needed to find a new route to market. Monsanto realized the political and bureaucratic barriers holding back the public-sector donors might be surmountable with a more corporate-friendly private foundation—for example, the Bill and Melinda Gates Foundation.

Monsanto found a supportive advocate and partner when AATF agreed to take the lead. An AATF proposal went to the BMGF in 2007, asking for an initial $45 million over 5 years to develop—in partnership with CIMMYT and the five NARS—improved hybrids of tropical white maize with greater drought tolerance. WEMA was born and started operating in 2008 (Paarlberg 2008).

Making It Work

Project Structure

One of the interesting opportunities and advantages of a PPP is the business acumen that can be brought to the partnership and applied to the project goals and processes. At its core, the WEMA project is like a new product launch at a business, but without the usual business drivers of revenues and profit. The success of WEMA is measured by how well it empowers farmers in Africa to produce more from their land while conserving more resources such as water. Led by and formulated by AATF and other partners, the project developed its goals, processes, and metrics with many similarities to how a business would approach a new product development and introduction. The ultimate goal in mind is that farmers need to purchase and plant the seed and get an unambiguous yield advantage benefit to create a scalable and sustainable adoption of the technology.

New business development and product introductions in the seed business follow a predictable path to market that can be categorized into five basic phases or functions as follows: product development, regulatory, deployment, legal, and communications. If you're starting from scratch, the sequence of phases generally follows in the order already listed, but the seed business requires new product introductions yearly, so in practicality the functions all end up working simultaneously. It's critical they work in a highly integrated and cross-functional matrix to manage the complexity effectively. To manage the complexity, facilitate the cross-functional connectivity, and keep everyone focused on the common goal, a good project management leadership structure is required.

When partners worked to develop the project proposal for the Gates Foundation, they started with this basic structure and approach in mind. They formed teams for each of the five functions made up of representatives from each of the partners with expertise for that particular function, with each team being led by an expert from AATF, except for the product development team that is co-lead by CIMMYT and Monsanto. They also developed clear goals and metrics to guide and measure progress toward success. The teams meet regularly by phone and in person, working collaboratively within the team, engaging all partners, and also working across teams to enhance cross-functional connectivity.

Product Development Team (PDT)

The product development team is made up of maize breeding experts from CIMMYT, the five NARS, and Monsanto all working together with a common set of goals and objectives. This team digs into the details to work through specifics on how to implement best practices and improve the efficiency of their breeding programs. They don't just meet in conference rooms and discuss things at a theoretical level, but they arrange PDT joint site visits to breeding stations of each of the partners to share insights and offer constructive critique on how to improve by implementing best practices. This team has tangible metrics to evaluate their success; they count the number of rows planted per year, the number of new hybrids in national performance testing (NPT), and the number of new hybrids registered for commercial release and compare the yield data on their newest hybrids to the best alternative standard checks currently in the market.

The scope of their work is to develop and test:

- Drought-tolerant maize germplasm (source populations, inbred lines, and hybrids) through:

  - Conventional breeding (including doubled haploid (DH) technology) and
  - Molecular breeding technology

- Drought-tolerant and insect-pest-resistant maize germplasm through:

  - Transgenic trait technology

Regulatory Team (RT)

The regulatory team brings together scientists from each of the partners who engage with the competent authorities in each of the WEMA countries to build capacity and develop functioning regulatory systems. Each country and each product need to be handled on a case-by-case basis because there is so much variability in the circumstances of each country.

The main objective for the RT in WEMA is to support multi-site testing and commercial release of transgenic drought-tolerant and insect-pest-resistant maize hybrids in the WEMA partner countries.

They measure progress based on the number of applications submitted and approved as well as based on the project's compliance with regulations for monitoring confined field trials. It's quite difficult to effectively measure the progress made to help build regulatory capacity, but they have regular interaction with the responsible government agencies involved in regulating biotechnology.

Deployment Team (DEPT)

The deployment team is made up of seed system specialists from each of the partners. They serve as the interface between the breeders and the African seed companies who license the WEMA products. Deployment encompasses everything involved in the steps from hand-off of breeder seed by the PDT through getting the farmers to plant improved hybrids.

The DEPT goals are to:

- Facilitate production and distribution of drought-tolerant and insect-pest-resistant maize seeds for end users.
- Ensure the stewardship of drought-tolerant and insect-pest-resistant maize inbred lines, hybrids, and traits throughout the value chain.

Progress or success for DEPT is measured by parameters like number of seed companies licensed, amount of basic and commercial seed produced, brand awareness, and ultimately the amount of seed sold and planted by smallholder farmers.

Legal and Licensing Team (LLT)

Licensing the improved varieties to seed companies in Africa is a unique approach introduced for the first time in Africa by WEMA because although the technology is royalty-free, it does come with certain obligations. The LLT has lawyers from each of the partner organizations with knowledge and experience in seed laws and intellectual property management.

The goals for the LLT are to develop and implement appropriate sub-licensing and intellectual property protection mechanisms for WEMA products. They measure success based on the number of seed companies and products licensed, but they also make many other tangible contributions as the WEMA partners work through any issues that arise among the various partners, who each have proprietary intellectual property to consider.

Communications Team (CT)

The CT brings together media and communications experts from each of the partner organizations with experience reaching out to various stakeholders (media, government officials, academics, seed industry, and general society) who want to know more about the WEMA project in general and GMOs specifically.

The objectives for CT are to support testing, dissemination, commercialization, adoption, and stewardship of conventional and transgenic drought-tolerant and insect-pest-resistant hybrids in the five target countries. It can be a challenge to establish good ways to measure the impact of their efforts, but by tracking media coverage and cataloging interactions with various stakeholders, they are able to monitor progress and gauge success.

Project Management (PM)

The goal of project management is to ensure effective coordination, management, and scientific leadership of the WEMA project. The way WEMA is set up delegates the responsibility for achieving this goal across the project manager, an Operations Committee (OPSCOM), and the Executive Advisory Board (EAB).

The project manager employed by AATF manages across all the functions and teams to ensure all the partners stay on track to hit key milestones. The project manager is responsible for setting agendas, facilitating communications and partner relations, managing budget issues, addressing barriers, as well as tracking and compiling the progress reports.

The Operations Committee (OPSCOM) is a team made up of the lead representatives from each of the partner organizations. AATF, CIMMYT, and Monsanto each have a person designated as the lead from their organization, while the five NARS elect one delegate as their representative on an annual rotational basis. The OPSCOM meets monthly to review progress and make administrative decisions that require consensus among the partners.

The Executive Advisory Board (EAB) is made up of executives from each of the partner organizations, including the donors. The EAB meets annually when the WEMA project convenes for an annual review and planning. They evaluate progress, give feedback, and provide recommendations and suggestions to ensure the project stays on track to meet the commitments made in the original project proposal.

Building a Basic Model for Scalable Sustainability

A central element to ensure the various WEMA functional teams work well and stay focused on success is creating a shared vision of how the improved seed we create actually gets to the farmers and improves their livelihoods. With the ultimate goal in mind that farmers need to purchase and plant the seed and get an unambiguous yield advantage, the question is what is the shared vision of how we make it happen?

Through extensive team dialogue incorporating practical knowledge at the local level about how seed systems work in Africa, the WEMA partners have devised a basic working model to get improved seed to farmers through African seed companies already doing business. The partners recognize as a fundamental concept that a sustainable and scalable model needs to be profitable for seed companies, distributors, and farmers. The basic structure of the model is as follows:

- WEMA breeders develop and test the new hybrids (both conventional and transgenic) (PDT and RT).
- NARS and AATF get the new hybrids officially registered for commercial release (PDT and DEPT).
- AATF licenses the hybrids royalty-free to seed companies in Africa (DEPT and LLT).
- Seed companies produce, package, and distribute the licensed hybrids.
    - WEMA helps seed companies with seed production and promotion (DEPT and CT).
- Competitive market prices for the seed prevail.
    - Each seed company has its own brand and unique selling proposition based on:
        - Product performance
        - Production costs
        - Seed quality
        - Distribution strategy
        - Customer service

It is important to recognize that the increased competition among the seed companies will mean farmers have more choices to buy improved seed and demand better services. The new technology in the seeds is made available to seed companies royalty-free, but they must cover expenses and be profit driven and deliver value to the farmer to earn repeat sales in the next season.

Successes and Lessons Learned

Product Development: Research and Development

The first 5 years of WEMA were focused primarily on building the partnership, functional teams, and research and development aspects for maize breeding systems to create a steady pipeline of new drought-tolerant maize hybrids. The improved conventional hybrids would be licensed to seed companies and also used for introgression of the biotech traits for drought tolerance and insect-pest protection.

Each of the WEMA partner organizations, except AATF, already had maize breeding programs, but the project meant starting a new collaborative effort, which required working through many details about what things would be done jointly and which work remained a separate responsibility for each partner organization. Monsanto had a unique challenge to start up the WEMA-Monsanto breeding program from scratch, keeping a firewall between its existing commercial breeding and the new WEMA-Monsanto breeding program. The WEMA breeding programs of CIMMYT, NARS, and Monsanto agreed on ways to share germplasm, testing sites, equipment, data, new breeding techniques, and decision-making processes to create a collaborative maize breeding program with a common set of goals and objectives. The collaborative spirit of the teamwork led to sharing of doubled haploid (DH) technology, marker-assisted recurrent selection (MARS) technology, and best practices for high-throughput data generation, all of which have already had an enduring positive impact on the research and development capabilities for each of the partner organizations. Monsanto provided DH lines that are likely the first significant DH products in public maize breeding in Africa, and WEMA conducted the largest MARS project in public-sector breeding and showed the benefit of MARS to select for drought tolerance.

There were many challenges the partners needed to address throughout this process, because fundamentally some issues are seen quite differently depending on if your perspective is that of a public institution or a private business. Sometimes, we had to agree to disagree and then find a compromise approach that would be acceptable to both the public and private sensibilities. Most issues could be addressed through mindful dialogue which was established as a valued attribute among the partners from the beginning by the way the rules of engagement were established in the structure and objectives of the project. Some issues, however, can be more intractable. We have been fortunate on the WEMA project that top-level management from all of the partners have been engaged and committed to making it work. It's important for PPPs to have executive-level commitments among all the partners because the few intractable issues inevitably end up on executives' desks to decide. It is also important to recognize the value of not allowing the perfect to get in the way of the good. There is a lot of value in being pragmatic and recognizing the trade-off value of deciding one way will be sufficient even if it could be done better another way "if only things were different." The PDT did a very good job on keeping the focus on results.

Product Introductions

The first new hybrid from WEMA to test the basic model for scalable sustainability was introduced in 2013 in Kenya. It was a conventional white maize hybrid with improved drought tolerance. To help get the licensing model up and going quickly, the WEMA project undertook the initial seed production of 74 tons of good-quality seed of the hybrid designated as WE1101. In the initial introduction, six seed companies licensed the hybrid, purchased the seed from AATF, and began sales to farmers in Kenya.

At the time of writing this in 2016, there has been significant progress to get additional hybrids registered for commercial release. WEMA now has more than 60 conventional drought-tolerant white maize hybrids registered across the five WEMA countries. These hybrids are available for licensing royalty-free to all seed companies in SSA, and seed companies have started seed production of the new hybrids for introduction and sales in Kenya, Uganda, Tanzania, and South Africa. Mozambique is expected to get started with new product introductions in 2016.

Insect-pest-resistant transgenic maize hybrids are on track for royalty-free introduction in South Africa for the 2016 planting season and in Kenya in 2017.

Branding

The hybrid licensing strategy for WEMA provided a unique opportunity to incorporate a product branding strategy to facilitate communication to famers about the unique benefits they would get from the WEMA products. The Deployment (DEPT) and Communication (CT) teams together developed the brand *Drought*TEGO™ or more simply TEGO™. Each seed company would carry it on their seed bag as a secondary brand to their own primary seed brand. TEGO™ came from the *Latin* word *contego* meaning "shield," but more importantly, it was phonetically easy to say in all local African languages and didn't have any unintended negative connotations. A simple logo of an African shield with an ear of maize on the shield was created to help build the brand communications. DEPT and CT worked together with the seed companies to get the word out to farmers in Kenya about the new hybrid being sold under the brand of TEGO™, and it wasn't long before many farmers were asking where they could buy the new TEGO™ hybrids.

DroughtTEGO™ and TEGO™ are registered trademarks of the African Agricultural Technology Foundation (AATF) in Nairobi, Kenya.

Innovation and protection for a better harvest

Farmer Experiences

The introduction of the first hybrid under the TEGO™ brand went exceptionally well. The seed had excellent quality, and together with the new improved genetics, it was no surprise farmers had much better yields than normal. Data collected from 13 different maize farming communities had an average yield of 4.5 tons/hectare. The farmers didn't do anything different in their fields from what they normally do except plant the TEGO™ seed. Unfortunately, it wasn't possible to do side-by-side comparisons, but if you compare the 4.5 tons/hectare average against the national average yield of 1.8 tons/hectare, it was obvious to see yield gains using improved seed can be substantial and impactful. Farmers in Kenya started talking to their neighbors about TEGO™ branded seed and demand for the first hybrid increased rapidly. Seed companies realized the demand was there, but now they needed more supply. We all learned quickly that farmers value and demand quality seed with good genetic potential, but delivering large volumes of it consistently requires a professional seed system infrastructure with capacity built to match the demand.

Regulatory Progress

Steady progress has been made building regulatory capacity in each of the WEMA countries to lay the foundation for commercial introduction of the drought-tolerant and insect-pest-protected biotech traits. The PDT and RT have worked together to generate the data and prepare the regulatory dossiers to make applications to the competent authorities for commercial release approvals in South Africa and Kenya. Applications for confined field trials (CFTs) have been made to allow for testing and data collection in all five WEMA countries. All these applications were approved, and testing was done in full compliance with conditions set for various applications, except in Tanzania and Mozambique where the applications are still under consideration by the regulatory authorities.

South Africa already has established regulatory systems, and biotech traits have been planted by commercial farmers for many years. The introduction of the biotech drought trait in South Africa will be the first cultivation approval of the trait outside of the United States, where it was first commercialized in 2013. WEMA did the regulatory trials for the drought trait in Africa and during that process realized that drought-tolerant maize without protection from insect pests is too vulnerable to serious losses from insect pressure. Therefore, the decision was made to only make the drought trait available to smallholder farmers stacked together with the insect-pest-protected trait. The regulatory process in South Africa uses a sequential approach for stacked approvals which requires first getting the approval for the single trait alone and then subsequently for the stack of two traits together. The application for the single drought trait was made in 2014 and received approval in South Africa in 2015. The next step in the process has been to generate the data for the stacked traits and then submit the application to the regulators which the RT is targeting to be completed by 2017. Royalty-free, drought-tolerant stacked with insect-pest-protected transgenic hybrids are on track to be planted by smallholder farmers in South Africa by 2017.

Significant progress has been made in Kenya with the February 2016 first approval of a biotech trait by the Kenya National Biosafety Authority for the MON810 Bt (insect-pest-protected) maize submitted by the WEMA partnership. The WEMA RT and CT worked diligently since the project started in 2008 to help build the capacity of the regulatory system in Kenya to make the approval possible. Multiple stakeholders were engaged through a special Bt outreach taskforce. Many organizations and people played significant roles to build the consensus among academics, scientists, seed companies, health professionals, economists, farmers, politicians, professional and trade associations, and the general society regarding the safety and benefits of the technology to be an additional tool for farmers to help address food security issues in Kenya. A few final steps remain in the regulatory process before the hybrids can be planted in Kenya, but royalty-free insect-pest-protected transgenic hybrids are on track to be sold to smallholder farmers in Kenya by 2017.

The regulatory approvals to do CFTs in all five WEMA countries plus the progress toward commercial release in South Africa and Kenya are significant accomplishments and signs of progress toward the WEMA goals to increase maize yield stability and reduce risk under drought conditions in sub-Saharan Africa through plant breeding and biotechnology. We have learned in the process the importance of transparency and engagement with multiple stakeholders and society to earn the trust and approval for new technologies based on the principles of sound science.

Tackling Barriers

The seed business can seem deceptively simple. After all, who can't understand the basic premise that the breeders select the best variety and then you simply grow it, harvest the seed, put it in a bag, and sell it? If only it were so simple!

As mentioned previously, there are a number of technical steps for producing good-quality hybrid maize seed. It's difficult to maintain the purity and quality of the basic parental seed, and the production of the hybrid seed itself requires vigilant management, especially during the critical step of crossing the male parent to the female parent during the seed growing season. It all requires a lot of advance planning, technical expertise, and understanding of where mistakes happen and how to avoid them.

Let's start with a basic review of how the process requires advance planning. In Africa, most hybrid maize sold is actually a three-way cross, meaning it has three inbred parents [(A × B) × C] instead of just two (A × B) typical for a single-cross hybrid. The main reason three-way crosses are used is because the cost to produce the seed in a three-way cross is less because the female parent (A × B) will yield substantially more seed than the female inbred parent (A) in the single-cross. As a consequence, there is this extra complexity for the seed company to manage for the three-way cross hybrids. A quick summary of the process is as follows:

- Three seasons before commercial sales: Seed production of inbred lines A, B, and C

  Inbred lines are the homozygous or "true breeding" lines that go into making up the hybrid, so each one has to be grown in isolation and strict quality guidelines must be followed to maintain the genetic purity of each inbred line. If genetic purity is compromised, the result will be a hybrid that doesn't have as much hybrid vigor and the farmer loses yield potential.

- Two seasons before commercial sales: Production of the female parent (A × B) of the three-way cross [(A × B) × C]

  This step is exactly the same as for creating the single-cross hybrid, except that the resulting hybrid seed is going to be used as a female parent in the next step rather than as seed for sale.

  To produce the (A × B) hybrid seed requires planting three rows of female "A" for each one row of male "B" and then at flowering time to remove all the pollen tassels (detasseling) from the three female rows so they are only fertilized by the pollen from the male "B" plants. The process of detasseling to produce high-quality hybrid seed requires a crew of people who know what, how, and when to do it properly. Missing the timing by 1 day can ruin the entire field. Leaving a few tassels by mistake on the female parent can ruin seed purity. There are many ways to make mistakes that diminish final seed quality.

- One season before commercial sales: Production of the three-way cross [(A × B) × C] to produce the seed to be sold to farmers

  The process is the same as for producing the single-cross hybrid except you plant three rows of female (A × B) and one row of male "C." Detasseling is still the key step, but this time your female parent (A × B) will be vigorous and highly productive because it's a single-cross with hybrid vigor. The male "C" parent is, however, inbred and can present a problem due to its shortness and poor pollen yield compared to the female single-cross hybrid.

  At each step along the way, quality tests must be done for genetic purity and germination. The purity and germination of the seed harvested to sell to farmers at this stage will be highly dependent on how well you have done all the steps in the previous three seasons.

  During these three seasons of preparation for making the seed, you have relied on the expertise of:

- Lab technicians who know how to test genetic purity and germination
- Field production experts who know everything from best agronomic practices, irrigation, fertilization, planting, detasseling, and harvest techniques
- Plant managers who know all the best practices to handle seed and maintain good quality through drying, shelling, sorting, treating, and bagging

Although the WEMA partners had gone through all of these steps to get the first 74 tons of WE1101 hybrid seed produced and ready for sale, we hadn't been able to adequately prepare the licensed seed companies to be as ready as they needed to be when the strong demand for the TEGO™ branded seed took them by surprise. Demand outstripped supply, and there are no quick fixes when the process takes three seasons of advance planning. In addition to the many challenges mentioned, seed production is also highly regulated by government authorities.

The DEPT had a lot of work to do to help build capacity for the advance planning required in the hybrid maize seed business. The steps in the process before commercialization were clearly identified as significant barriers for most seed companies in Africa. It's one of the main reasons good-quality hybrid seed hasn't been making it the last mile to farmers at scale.

We have learned through experience the importance and value of addressing barriers faced by seed companies so they can focus on their core strengths and deliver value to their customer, the farmers. One strategy is to help the seed companies build capacity to manage the technical aspects for each step of the complex process. However, another strategy being developed is to aggregate the early steps in the process of producing the basic parental seed to improve quality and capitalize on economies of scale.

AATF has contracted production of the basic parental seed with Monsanto Company and other seed companies with the capacity and know-how to produce good-quality basic parental seed which AATF then sells to the licensed seed companies, while maintaining confidentiality of the producer and licensed seed companies. With this approach, the seed company only needs to manage the final step in the process one season before commercial sales. Currently, in 2016, multiple seed companies across the different WEMA countries are producing several new commercially registered conventional hybrids using basic parental seed produced under contract by AATF. Additional TEGO™ branded hybrids from licensed seed companies will give more and better choices for smallholder farmers to plant in Africa in 2017.

The Next Phase

Scaling up

Taking any product to scale in any market requires a few fundamentals. Scaling requires a reliable and sustainable supply of good-quality product to meet growing demand and value (profit) for each component (user, distributor, and producer) of the product value chain. To scale seed is no different. The next phase of WEMA will therefore focus on deployment issues to address the barriers to creating a reliable and sustainable supply of good-quality seed. Helping to build capacity at seed companies will be an important focus for the WEMA partners to enable scaling up.

Equally or perhaps more important will be the challenge to keep the focus on delivering real and tangible value to the customer—the smallholder farmers. Farming depends on a complex and interdependent ecological system. Quality seed with improved genetic potential is vitally important, but most often this alone is not enough to address the challenges farmers face. Agronomic practices (tillage, fertilization, weed, pest, and disease control) all work together with the genetic potential of the seed in a system unique for each farm and field to determine the final yield. We will not only need to help seed companies provide good agronomic advice but also reach out to multiple stakeholders (extension, distributors, and NGOs) who play vital roles to help farmers in Africa improve their farming practices in a way appropriate to their local conditions.

To become a truly sustainable and scalable endeavor, farmers also need to have dependable markets where they can sell their excess grain at a fair price with assurance of prompt payment so they can use their profits to make investments in the next crop cycle. It's beyond the scope of the WEMA project to address all the elements of the value chain that drive farmer profit, but the need to reach out to multiple stakeholders and develop effective collaborations to enable the development of sustainable value chains for smallholder farmers in Africa is well understood. Seed companies interested in growing their businesses in Africa can and will play a vital role in helping make the connections with other players in the value chain to develop markets and create sustainable value for scaling up.

Introducing Transgenic Hybrids

On the one hand, transgenic seeds are exactly like conventional seeds, and all the steps and challenges to get a new hybrid into the market are the same. Conversely, regulatory requirements and perceptions and misunderstandings about GMOs make the introduction of transgenic seed an exceptionally more complicated process.

For insect-pest-protected hybrids, the biggest difference is to manage the product stewardship requirements with the farmers. To help prevent insect-pest resistance from developing, a structured refuge using non-transgenic maize needs to be planted near the insect-pest-protected maize. The basic idea is that many susceptible insects survive on the refuge maize and then mate with the few resistant insects that may survive on the insect-pest-protected maize. If there isn't a refuge, then those few resistant insects that survive will mate with each other (rather than with susceptible insects) and create a bigger population of resistant insects. The refuge field produces many more susceptible insects than the number of resistant insects that survive in the insect-pest-protected field so when they mate, most offspring will be susceptible. This is a difficult concept to communicate effectively to farmers, especially if the transgenic maize yields substantially more than the conventional refuge maize. Consequently, introduction of insect-pest-protected maize requires additional stewardship and communication efforts to inform farmers of the value and benefit of planting a refuge to help maintain durability and thus the value of the transgenic insect-pest-protected seed.

Quality controls for transgenic seed production also require additional processes and tests to assure genetic purity. Stewardship training for seed companies to help them manage effectively the additional complexities with transgenic seed is an important part of the deployment team's work.

Summary

Key Elements for Successful Public-Private Partnerships (PPP)

We don't pretend that WEMA has found a fail-safe formula for making a PPP successful, and success is a subjective concept often dependent on the eye of the beholder. We do, however, think the WEMA PPP is delivering on its stated objectives and has potential to make a significant impact to improve the livelihood of smallholder farmers in Africa. We've listed below the main elements we think have been instrumental to help WEMA succeed. It isn't meant to be an exhaustive list because each PPP has its unique circumstances which may require different or additional elements to be successful. However, we think these are the attributes to look for when evaluating the potential of any new PPP project (*in no particular order of importance*).

Agreement on the Key Objective

Having all partners start with the same vision of the end in mind is a critical first step. It's not enough to have a general generic objective to eliminate poverty or improve the livelihood of farmers. It needs to be specific about how and which tools or products will be developed and deployed with a clear understanding of how the target end user will access and benefit from whatever is developed.

It helps if the objective has a target to create a long-term sustainable improvement that will live beyond donor funding. All partners need to see a path to realize the goal and see the value of their contribution to the goal.

Alignment with Core Competencies

All organizations, institutions, and businesses have a few things they do best that make them who they are and sustain their reason for being. We call these the core competencies and think it's generally a mistake when we try to venture into doing things that aren't central to who we are. For example, Monsanto isn't a finance company, so it shouldn't try to lead the way in fixing smallholder finance challenges, even though this is an issue critical for the farmer's and WEMA's success.

Partners in the PPP need to bring their core competencies to the table to contribute however they can to the agreed-upon objectives. If the core competencies don't match up with the objectives, it's going to be difficult to maintain and persevere through the challenges of contributing to a PPP.

Compromise, Patience, and Acknowledgment of Cultural Differences

Mind-set and flexibility matter. Each partner contributes more effectively by acknowledging the cultural differences inherent between the public and private sectors. Each one brings a unique and valid perspective to the table, and both can be right even if they are different. Candid recognition of the cultural differences and perspectives helps bridge to common understanding. You may need to agree to disagree, but the spirit of partnership and shared objectives helps achieve necessary compromises as you work through barriers to progress.

Unwavering Support from Top Management

For those doing the day-to-day work making the partnership function effectively, it matters that the top managers within their respective organizations recognize and value the work they are doing. If it's not important to your manager, it's not long before it's no longer important to you.

Engagement of, and support from, top managers sends an important message that what you are doing matters, but it also can be critical for the partners to be able to work through what may seem like intractable issues. Unfortunately, some compromise decisions can be so fundamental that only top management can decide.

Structure and Management

Most PPPs are formed to take on complex and vexing problems with no simple solutions. To achieve the goals set out at the initiation of the project requires some careful thought to break it down into manageable components which can then be delegated to teams with expertise to tackle the specific challenges in each component. It takes good management with experience and vision to understand how best to structure the partnership and tap into the talents and skills of each individual to contribute to the success of the project. Spend the time up front to agree on a structure and operating process which is tailored to the unique challenges of the project.

Milestones and Accountability

Inertia is hard to overcome and momentum is hard to create. The goals of the project need to be broken down into steps or milestones along the project road map to measure progress toward the ultimate goal. Clear action items to be done by specific teams or individuals should be summarized at the end of meetings with follow-up at the next meeting. Holding people accountable for delivering on work to achieve each milestone and putting consequences in place for failure to meet the targets is important to overcome inertia, create momentum, and build team spirit.

What Matters

Fortunately for WEMA, all the partners agree that what really matters is for the better seed we develop to be planted by smallholder farmers throughout the WEMA countries and for those farmers to achieve sustainable increased yields, giving them more profit and improved lives. It's simple to say but hard to do. The difficulty and complexity of achieving our goal combined with the spirit of partnership and contribution from each partner make it exceptionally gratifying to be part of a public-private partnership making an impact like WEMA.

References

Bill and Melinda Gates Foundation. 2016. Who We Are. http://www.gatesfoundation.org/Who-We-Are.

Centro Internacional de Mejoramiento de Maiz y Trigo (CIMMYT). 2016. About Us, Our History. http://www.cimmyt.org/organization/.

Monsanto Company. 2016. Who We Are. http://www.monsanto.com/whoweare/pages/default.aspx.

Paarlberg, Robert. 2008. Starved for Science: How Biotechnology Is Being Kept Out of Africa. Harvard University Press, Cambridge, MA. ISBN 9780674033474. 149–177.

Part V
Benefits from Agricultural Research and Innovation

Public Research and Technology Transfer in US Agriculture: The Role of USDA

Steven R. Shafer and Michael S. Strauss

Abstract Agriculture has been of fundamental and growing importance from the earliest days of human society. Over millennia, farmers have domesticated and improved a wide array of crops and livestock and passed their knowledge and experience down over generations. As the challenge to feed an ever-growing world population has increased, however, so has the need for ever greater levels of production. The latest science and technological advances undergird the success of modern agriculture. Virtually every item in a typical meal is available, at least in part, because of scientific and technological advances that have led to increased production, protection from pests or disease, or enhancements to their nutritional value. This vast array of research activities can be clearly seen in the story behind the daily Western breakfast table.

When the United States was young, agriculture was the major part of its economy, engaging the vast majority of the nation's people. Crops were grown repeatedly on a plot of land until the soil was exhausted, making it essential to move west in search of new land. But as the Civil War closed in, it was President Abraham Lincoln, himself the son of a farmer, who sought to formalize the growth, development, and science of agriculture. The act of the 37th Congress signed into law by Lincoln on May 15, 1862, established agriculture as the purpose of a federal government department without Cabinet rank (Grover Cleveland raised it to the Cabinet in 1889). The act charged the Commissioner of Agriculture to:

> "…acquire and preserve in his Department all information concerning agriculture which he can obtain by means of books and correspondence, and <u>by practical and scientific experiments</u> *[emphasis added]*, (accurate records of which experiments shall be kept in his office,) by the collection of statistics, and by any other appropriate means within his power;…."

S.R. Shafer (✉)
Soil Health Institute, Morrisville, NC, USA
e-mail: sshafer@soilhealthinstitute.org

M.S. Strauss
USDA Agricultural Research Service, Washington, DC, USA

© Springer International Publishing AG 2018   415
N. Kalaitzandonakes et al. (eds.), *From Agriscience to Agribusiness*, Innovation, Technology, and Knowledge Management, https://doi.org/10.1007/978-3-319-67958-7_20

Subsequently, the Morrill Acts (1862, 1890) created land-grant colleges (one of Lincoln's other priorities); the Hatch Act (1887) funded state agricultural experiment stations; and the Smith Lever Act (1914) funded each state's Cooperative Extension Service. Thus, Lincoln's vision grew and developed, and today, scientific innovation is integral to a vibrant and productive US agriculture.

USDA's modern research operations span multiple agencies and billions of dollars in congressional appropriations. But within all of USDA's congressionally authorized budget ($139.7 billion in Fiscal Year 2015), the largest investment in agricultural research occurs in the agencies that comprise the research, education, and economics mission area, including (in Fiscal Year 2015) the Agricultural Research Service (ARS) ($1.1 billion) and the Economic Research Service (ERS) ($0.1 billion), which are intramural agencies; the National Institute of Food and Agriculture (NIFA) ($1.5 billion), funding state programs and extramural programs (including competitive research); and the National Agricultural Statistics Service (NASS) ($0.2 billion), which conducts surveys and issues reports on agricultural production, economics, demographics, and the environment (e.g., the Census of Agriculture). Other USDA agencies, such as the US Forest Service (USFS) and the Animal and Plant Health Inspection Service (APHIS), conduct research in specific areas.

Today, research across these many agencies encompasses hundreds of locations and thousands of scientists and technicians. With today's scope, it is fortunate indeed that the modern Secretary of Agriculture no longer is held to the requirement of that first Commissioner of Agriculture (the interestingly named Isaac Newton; USDA 1969) that records of research "…be kept in his office…."

The combination of department-centered intramural research and largely university-centered extramurally funded research is a hallmark of publicly funded agricultural research in the United States. The highly complementary nature of the intramural and extramural programs promotes research within government (through intramural programs) and in academia and the private sector (through NIFA's extramural research support). The impact of over 150 years of these scientific investments is impossible to document in one place. Even a rudimentary, highly selective, simple listing of accomplishments is extraordinary in its length (http://www.ars. usda.gov/oc/timeline/comp/, accessed October 11, 2016). A visual impact of this sustained public investment in agricultural science can be seen in a walk down the aisles of any modern American supermarket.

But perhaps an even better way for an individual to realize the impact of USDA science is at the breakfast table. Most, if not all, food found there have been improved or protected in some way through the efforts of USDA and USDA-funded researchers.

Everyone eats breakfast of some sort, if not by time of day, or food type, then only by definition. Breakfast food items vary tremendously around the world, and there is great diversity in the quantities and varieties of foods on breakfast tables every morning across the United States as well. A big family breakfast, or a well-stocked breakfast buffet in a hotel, may offer dozens of fresh, processed, or cooked items. Few people would eat some of everything in such a setting (although therein lies the introduction to a potential discussion of the obesity epidemic in America and elsewhere). But considering even a handful of items that might be on a typical American breakfast table illustrates the breadth and impact of USDA's scientific endeavors.

For many of us, the day begins with a glass of orange juice. During World War II, USDA researchers, along with members of the Florida Citrus Commission, developed the processes that led to frozen concentrated orange juice (Liu et al 2012; Kelley 1993), helping establish key aspects of the modern orange juice industry and making it almost synonymous with breakfast. But today, orange juice production faces one of the most potentially disastrous threats it has ever encountered in a disease called citrus greening (technically, Huanglongbing or HLB), for which there is no cure. This disease has virtually eliminated commercial citrus production everywhere it has become established and is probably the most difficult plant disease to control in any modern crop (Gottwald 2010). There is no cure for HLB, and until recently, all commercial citrus varieties were susceptible to its devastating effects. Infected trees produce fruits that are green, misshapen, bitter, and unsuitable for juice. Most trees, if they do not die within a few years, must be destroyed to prevent further spread of the disease.

The annual economic loss to Florida from HLB has been estimated to be just over $1 billion (Farnsworth et al. 2014). It has reduced citrus production in Florida by over 70% since the disease was first recognized in 2005 (Bouffard 2016). However, USDA scientists and partners who are studying the presumed bacterial pathogen (*Candidatus Liberibacter asiaticus*; CLas) and the Asian citrus psyllid (*Diaphorina citri*) that transmits it from infected trees are pursuing multiple approaches. These include insecticides to control the psyllid; removal of infected trees; antimicrobials as therapy in an attempt to "cure" infected trees or reduce the symptoms that make them unproductive (Yang et al. 2016; Zhang et al. 2014); use of tolerant rootstocks and scion cultivars (sweet orange, mandarin, etc.) that are being developed by the USDA-ARS, the University of Florida, and the University of California (Bowman et al. 2016); thermotherapy (Doud et al. 2012); and a diverse set of early detection methods for the CLas itself or other signs of infection based on specific tree responses (Hartung and Levy 2006). Even dogs have been trained to detect non-symptomatic infected trees – under controlled conditions – with great accuracy (Berger 2014; Mittelman 2016), but they remain to be fully tested under field conditions where the infection status of trees is unknown. For the long term, USDA scientists are developing resistant varieties by conventional breeding (Bowman et al. 2016) and, for the future, are pursuing biotechnological solutions that might control the insect, block transmission, or introduce novel genes to combat the disease.

Aside from orange juice, fresh fruit is part of many breakfasts. However, breeding new varieties of fruits with better flavor, size, color, or disease resistance can be a lengthy process that takes many years. The plants must be grown from seed to maturity, often taking 3–10 years, then the most promising are selected and bred, and the offspring, in turn, are grown another 3–10 years to produce seed. The plants from this seed are bred to still others with needed traits, which are again selected and bred over yet another lengthy period. Only after several such multiyear cycles does a new and improved variety begin to emerge. Thus, a plant breeder may be able to produce only a handful of new varieties in his or her entire career.

A new technology called FasTrack, developed by ARS scientist for plums (a common fresh or dried fruit on the breakfast table), speeds all that up (Yao 2011). A gene originally found in poplar trees produces almost immediate and continuous flowering and fruit production in plums, thus eliminating the years of growth to maturity. As a result, the time between successive breeding events is greatly reduced, and the finished variety emerges much sooner. Once the desired variety is achieved, the poplar gene is eliminated through traditional breeding methods. The resulting new plum variety lacks that foreign gene, which was used only to speed up the breeding process, so regulatory or other issues related to release of genetically modified organisms are not a concern. Best of all, what was originally up to 10 years between each cross is reduced to just 1 year. Improved varieties can be developed five to six times (or more) faster than pre-FasTrack breeding methods (Scorza et al. 2012; Yao 2011; van Nocker and Gardiner 2014). Applications to species other than plum are being developed.

The FasTrack technology also illustrates how USDA research can have benefits and applications not imagined during the original project. The National Aeronautics and Space Administration (NASA) is cooperating with USDA to examine developing FasTrack applications for future interplanetary missions where having a plant that could rapidly produce nutritious fruit would be a major benefit to astronauts facing months or years away from Earth (Graham et al. 2015).

Newly emerging technologies, such as the gene-editing CRISPR/Cas methods, coupled with FasTrack, promise a further enhanced ability to create new varieties without the need for either foreign genes or lengthy breeding cycles (Xiong et al. 2015). So we can expect a variety of fresh fruit to remain an integral part of the breakfast table.

A breakfast omelet literally folds in several ingredients. It contains eggs, of course, and probably some cheese, maybe tomato or peppers, and perhaps some fresh vegetables such as broccoli. All have been improved in some way through USDA research. Poultry, eggs, and other livestock can carry serious pathogens, however, including *Salmonella*, *Campylobacter*, and *E. coli*, that can place consumers at risk of illness or even death (Doyle and Erickson 2006; Koluman and Dikici 2013).

In the past, a variety of antibiotics were used to reduce and control the incidence of such pathogens in agricultural animals, as well as to stimulate growth. In recent years, there has been increasing concern that widespread use of antibiotics both in livestock and humans is leading to development of pathogens that are able to resist their effects and survive. Scientists within USDA as well as those funded by USDA's NIFA, the National Institutes of Health, and others are working to find alternatives to antibiotics. Several look promising.

Selenium in its organic form can inhibit bacterial growth in the chicken gastrointestinal tract (Xu et al. 2015). Such compounds can be found in a variety of plant extracts such as those from chili peppers, garlic, cinnamon, and green teas (Diaz-

Sanchez 2015). This could reduce the need for the antibiotics which can suppress bacteria but which also can slow growth of treated birds. Prebiotic and probiotic bacteria common to the environment can produce a similar effect when fed to chickens (Patterson and Burkholder 2003).

Still other research seeks to use the birds' own immune system to develop and pass along resistance to a parasite (Yun et al. 2000). Intestinal parasites are fed to chickens with the intent to induce a protective immune response. These birds then pass some factors related to that immune response into their eggs. When powdered yolk from those eggs is fed to day-old chicks, the young birds exhibit enhanced immunity to the original parasite. These kinds of advances enhance poultry health and egg safety while reducing the use of antibiotics.

The peppers that may be in the omelet have been the subjects of a variety of scientific efforts. Peppers have considerable variation in sweet and hot flavors and aromas, and they may exhibit variation in their susceptibility to different diseases and in shelf life. Such characteristics are based on the extensive genetic variability among peppers. Breeding programs, including those taking advantage of known molecular markers in the plants' genome, have enabled USDA scientists to develop breeding lines and varieties of peppers with many desirable traits, not only for food but also as ornamentals, highly valued for their leaf shapes, growth form, vivid colors, and interesting shapes of the fruit (Stommel et al. 2014, Stommel et al. 2015; Nimakayala et al. 2016). Any omelet that contains peppers – hot, sweet, tangy, red, yellow, green, purple, disease resistant or not – carries the fruit, so to speak, of USDA research, along with the benefits of research for the eggs and most other ingredients.

Another of the ingredients in an omelet may be bacon. Pigs are among the animals that are very susceptible to foot and mouth disease, or FMD, which is caused by a virus and is extremely easily spread; indeed, as Bob Dylan, had he been an agricultural scientist, might have said, it can even be found "blowin' in the wind." The symptoms are highly unpleasant to the animals, which also include beef and dairy cattle, as well as other important livestock species. There has not been an outbreak of FMD in the United States since 1929, and USDA's Animal and Plant Health Inspection Service (APHIS) keeps stringent quarantine procedures in place to keep it out. There was a major epidemic in the United Kingdom in 2007; thousands of cases occurred, and many livestock animals had to be destroyed. The potential economic impact (in terms of farm income losses) of a similar FMD outbreak, were it to occur, in the United States has been estimated at $14 billion or more (Paarlberg et al. 2008).

There is a vaccine for FMD, but it is made with a live virus, and the US vaccine bank is dependent on overseas sources (USDA-APHIS 2007). Serious headway is being made to protect American livestock from FMD, however. USDA scientists have developed a vaccine that lacks a segment of the viral DNA that prevents it from increasing in the animal and causing infectious disease while stimulating the animal's immune system. Importantly, genetic markers in the vaccine enable discrimination of vaccinated animals from infected ones, something not possible with a vaccine produced with unmodified virus. The new vaccine can be produced safely in the United States and can be modified if new FMD strains arise. Once regulatory reviews and approvals have been obtained, the vaccine can be produced for widespread inoculation of livestock in a future FMD outbreak.

Some people may prefer poultry-based breakfast meats, such as turkey sausage. USDA made its mark on turkey production many years ago, but until the 1940s, turkeys were not an everyday item consumed on the dinner table, let alone at breakfast. Many people did not like the flavor, the birds had many pinfeathers that had to be removed, and they were so big that they often did not fit in the typical kitchen oven of the day. ARS scientists developed a small white turkey with a lot of white meat and white pin feathers that were easy to remove. The Beltsville Small White turkey became the standard at holidays and, due to the improvements, for other occasions as well. Today, not many of this kind of turkey are served, but their genetics are the foundation of most turkeys that are consumed in a variety of ways, including turkey sausage at breakfast (The Livestock Conservancy, no date).

Potatoes are served at many meals, and breakfast is no exception, as hash browns or other fried potatoes, for instance. Potatoes have long been a focus of research aimed at improving them and protecting them from disease, such as the potato late blight (*Phytophthora infestans*) pathogen, which caused the European, Irish, and Scottish Highland potato famines in the mid-1800s and led to more than a million deaths through starvation and which can still be a problem for potato farmers today. Growing potatoes remains a challenge even with the absence of disease threats, with a wide variety of factors that spell the difference between success and failure. In the state of Maine, where potato is an important crop, USDA researchers combined the results of many research projects to give producers the Potato Systems Planner Decision Support tool. The tool builds on the findings that the other crops grown in a field in rotation with the potato crop influence the various microbes in the soil, pest and pathogen populations, nutrients, and other beneficial and detrimental influences on potato plants.

The Potato Systems Planner Decision Support tool allows Maine potato growers to track and record a variety of information, such as the crops in a rotation, the kind of soil, the fertilizer used, incidence of disease in years past, and so forth, and make projections of the kinds of yields they can anticipate when they plant potatoes (Honeycutt et al. 2007; Peabody 2005).

Growers know which crops should precede and follow potatoes in their fields and when it is best to grow them. Growing potatoes every year in the same field, it turns out, is ill-advised (Peabody 2005). This decision aid can help farmers prevent crop failures and support farm income, a key feature of agricultural sustainability.

Milk and milk products are almost certain to be on many breakfast tables in some form, whether as a beverage, poured on cereal, or served as yogurt or cheese. Dairy cows and processing have been a major focus for USDA scientists for more than a century. Research on animal production and health, genetics, waste management, and product development and safety all have contributed to the dairy products found at breakfast. Nevertheless, the challenge remains to produce more milk with fewer cows and thereby reduce environmental and financial costs while increasing production.

USDA scientists and their industry partners have been particularly effective at increasing milk production. Some of this has been due to improvements in feeding (O'Brien 2016a, b). In addition, however, with new and emerging genetic and molecular technologies, further advances have been possible. Before 1994, the traits considered important in breeding highly productive dairy cows included milk produced per cow and the protein and fat content of the milk. Breeding programs depended on extensive record keeping and pedigree analysis. Selection of bulls for breeding programs often did not occur until the animals reached reproductive age and their offspring could be evaluated…an expensive endeavor. Today, through the use of molecular genetic markers and genomic analyses, breeding dairy cows has been improved tremendously. Additional traits such as animal longevity, disease resistance, conformation, ease of calving, and risk of stillbirths – all traits that may have low heritability and may have formerly been difficult or impossible to track – have become part of the breeding program. These allow animals possessing desirable genetic traits to be identified at birth rather than waiting to analyze their offspring. Such technologies provide an incremental boost to milk production and quality (McGinnis et al. 2008; Xu et al. 2014). The result is that the nation's dairies produce more milk with fewer cows and, thus, produce benefits that ripple through the economy, down to the breakfast table.

And for those 30–50 million American consumers who cannot digest milk sugar, USDA scientists conducted microbial enzyme and processing research that resulted in lactose-reduced and lactose-free dairy products (Holsinger 1997; Stanley 1995) available in nearly every grocery store across the country. Thus, dairy products are available on the breakfast tables of the lactose intolerant, like they are for everyone else.

For many people, some sort of bread item – toast, muffin, or biscuit, for example – may be their entire breakfast or at least an important part of it. If so, it's very likely that wheat was the main ingredient, a crop that has been improved and cultivated for many centuries. Despite all that effort, the diseases that have accompanied and threatened wheat for centuries are still a threat with the potential to cause serious famines in parts of the world. One of the oldest wheat diseases is the fungus that causes wheat stem rust, *Puccinia graminis f.* sp. *tritici.* Once one of the most feared of wheat pathogens, this fungus can destroy the crop on a widespread scale if environmental conditions favor the disease and plants lack resistance to it. The fungus is constantly changing through new genetic combinations, and a particularly threatening strain called Ug99 (for Uganda 1999, the place and year it was first discovered) has drawn the attention of plant pathologists and wheat breeders. It is not yet present in the United States, but USDA scientists have developed methods for detecting it quickly, and they are screening all new domestic wheat and barley breeding lines (about 2000 per year) annually in Kenya, where the disease is present and where new germplasm can be evaluated for genes that will confer resistance to it. With the aid of molecular genetic markers, the wild relatives of wheat growing in the eastern hemisphere are being screened for additional new sources of resistance genes (Olivera et al. 2012; Rahmatov et al. 2016; Yu et al. 2015). With this kind of effort, USDA scientists and their global partners continue to stay ahead of Ug99 stem rust and have kept it from entering the United States. Results of this and similar research on other diseases of our major grain crops are used worldwide in the effort to control this and other dangerous diseases and to keep bread and cereal products on the breakfast table.

Bread and other breakfast foods such as pancakes or oatmeal may be topped with honey, the most obvious manifestation of the importance of bees and other pollinators to the first meal of the day. Their importance goes far beyond just honey, however. Without pollinators, breakfast probably would be foods developed only from crops that are wind pollinated, so the meal might consist of bread, a porridge or gruel, and perhaps ale, a sort of breakfast of medieval champions. Many breakfast items, including melons, blueberries, strawberries, almonds, raisins, and coffee, come from crops that are pollinated by insects. In recent years, however, the farming, food production, and research communities have been alerted to serious problems about the health of pollinator populations.

The most notable are health declines seen in honeybees, including colony collapse disorder (CCD), which affects honeybees. In CCD-affected hives, the worker bees leave the hive seemingly in search of pollen, but do not return, so the hive gradually dies (Kaplan 2012). No single cause for honeybee decline has been identified, but most evidence suggests that a confluence of stressors is involved, including possibly pathogenic microbes, tiny parasitic mites, exposure to certain pesticides, poor nutrition in managed hives, and increasing weather variability (Goulson et al. 2015; Kaplan 2012). In 2014–2015, about 40 percent of the hives on which agriculture depends for pollination of a wide array of crops were lost (Seitz et al. 2015). While some loss each winter is expected, these levels are alarming.

These losses can be offset by beekeepers' efforts to establish new colonies in support of the demand for bees to crop pollination, and this has led to a stabilizing of the number of colonies in production in the United States. This comes at a significant cost. Reproducing new colonies to replace those that are dying is both expensive and labor intensive and, if done too frequently, leads to smaller colonies that cannot pollinate as many flowers, do not produce as much honey, and may not survive the winter.

Pollinator health and decline is of such national importance to both agriculture and natural ecosystems that Federal agencies were directed to develop a Pollinator Research Action Plan (Pollinator Health Task Force 2015) to counter continuing threats to pollinators, including honeybees. By engaging in systems research supporting Integrated Bee Management, USDA scientists are responding to the Action Plan with an emphasis on the "5 Ps":

- Parasites – Developing bees with genes that make them resistant to parasitic mites
- Pathogens – Developing and getting regulatory approval for chemicals that kill microbes that cause bee diseases
- Pests – Developing lures and traps that prevent hive invaders from getting in
- Pesticides – Determining the proper role of pesticides, balancing their ability to control pests versus the impacts on the bees themselves

- Poor nutrition – Developing the best forages and diets to keep bees healthy and resistant to other stresses

CCD and pollinator health is a very complex issue, and much has been accomplished, but we have a long way to go to understand and control it. It will require a coordinated effort of the research community, including USDA scientists.

Yet another topping for breakfast pancakes is syrup, and the most notable is maple syrup, which comes through a generations-old process from maple trees growing in forests of the Northeastern United States. A beetle native to China and Korea, the Asian longhorn beetle, ALB (*Anoplophora glabripennis*), could remove that once commonplace item (Hu et al. 2009; Smith and Wu 2008). To date, the only control methods are to detect the presence of the beetles or their larvae and to remove and destroy infected trees. Research has focused on improving methods to more rapidly detect the presence of adult beetles before they are able to infect trees. The work involves cooperation between multiple Federal and State agencies, scientists, industries (such as maple syrup producers), and the general public (through campaigns to prevent the movement of firewood that may spread the beetle larvae). All of this helps to preserve Northern hardwood forests and to keep one more item on your breakfast table.

When agricultural scientists start their research day, many of them, like many others, have a cup of coffee. For many of us, coffee is the essential part of the morning. The coffee berry borer, the most damaging pest of coffee worldwide, threatens the crop. Adults are small black beetles just a few millimeters long. The females drill into the coffee berries (often called coffee beans) and lay their eggs. The larvae that hatch from the eggs eat within the berry and destroy it (Vega et al. 2015).

Coffee production in Hawaii and Puerto Rico, two significant sources of coffee, is on small farms, but many of them are certified for organic production, so they cannot use insecticides to control such insect pests. USDA scientists are helping the farmers develop methods to manage and possibly eradicate this pest, which can destroy not only the quantity of coffee harvested but the quality of the coffee as well (Kawabata et al. 2015). Researchers have launched a multipronged attack against the beetle, including removal of berries left in the field after harvest, which can continue to host the insect; using repellents that ward off the insect; replacing coffee plants with other plants the insect cannot eat; minimizing pesticide sprays where they are allowed to minimize the development of pesticide-resistant borers; using native organisms that prey on the borers; using geographic information systems to help predict invasions based on where the insects have been found; and interfering with microbes in the insect gut that are involved with digestion, including detoxifying caffeine in the insects' diet (Ceja-Navarro et al. 2015). Implementing this variety of actions in what are termed "area-wide pest control programs" involving many growers in a large geographic zone is making headway toward eliminating this devastating pest from the islands it invaded about 10 years ago.

USDA science doesn't stop with research on the crops and livestock. It takes more than attention to what makes up the final products on the table. All of agricultural production rests on a foundation of natural resources – soil, water, and air –

that must be cared for if agricultural systems are to be sustained for future production.

Many people refer to animal manure as "waste," and if it is simply discarded, it is indeed a wasted resource. For thousands of years, farmers have used manure on their fields with great benefits for crop production. Animal manures contain nutrients that were in the feed and forage but not absorbed by the animal. Dumping these nutrients back into the air or water degrades the quality of the environment, and the nutrient value of that manure for crops is lost. That translates to lost potential income for the farmer.

USDA scientists are developing technologies to recover nutrients and more from manure produced by the hogs that are the source of the bacon on the breakfast table. In a systematic approach, bacteria are used to remove nitrogen that would be lost as ammonia gas to the atmosphere, thus reducing the amount of bioactive nitrogen pollutants released back into the environment. These can also contaminate water and lead to algal blooms and hypoxia in surface waters, as well as combine with other gases and create the unpleasant odors associated with hog farms. Controlled chemical reactions can recover phosphorus that also has adverse effects on surface waters. This technology is highly efficient: it can remove nearly 100% of the ammonia and more than 90% of the phosphorus, copper, and zinc (which hogs require but absorb poorly from their feed) and almost all of the harmful coliform bacteria that occur in swine manure and can contaminate surface water and soil. Nearly all of the solids are removed, too, and can be composted. All these nutrients and solids can be recovered and reused or marketed by the farmer. Important for everyone, the water coming out of the system meets environmental standards in the state where the research is evaluated and is considered clean enough to release back into the environment (Sharpley et al. 2006; Szogi et al. 2006; Vanotti et al. 2005). Applications for dairy operations and even municipal wastewater are being considered.

Another aspect of putting food on the breakfast table that may escape consideration by many people is how very safe their food is. Research on food safety, and the technologies and methods to keep it that way, is an important part of USDA research. One example is the use of cold plasma, which is generated by passing high-voltage electricity through air. The cloud of charged atoms, stripped of their electrons, can kill disease-causing microorganisms on the surface of foods such as fruits and nuts without damaging them (Niemira 2012). Other researchers seek new ways to detect contamination in and on foods, such as using different wavelengths of light and imaging technologies to detect microbes invisible to the naked eye on poultry or on the conveyor belts used in handling and processing a wide variety of commodities and foods (Bhunia et al. 2015, Chao 2010, Chao et al. 2007, Kim et al. 2006, Heitschmidt et al. 2007). Every American's health, and the health of many people around the world, benefits from food safety research conducted by USDA.

And then there is a product of USDA research that so many use so routinely that they forget where it originated, namely, the USDA Plant Hardiness Zone Map (http://planthardiness.ars.usda.gov/PHZMWeb/) developed by USDA and Oregon State University's PRISM Climate Group (http://www.prism.oregonstate.edu). This map helps farmers and home gardeners decide which varieties to plant for their environment to get the best-adapted vegetable varieties and other crops. For those people who grow their own, the breakfast table owes much of its bounty to good varietal selection decisions gleaned from this map, one of the most popular tools developed by USDA.

On most mornings, most of us make our way to the kitchen, eat something quickly, gulp down some orange juice and coffee, and rush out to begin our day. We rarely think about the quantity and quality of food or beverage we just consumed, or the work that goes into assuring that it is safe, or the natural resources that were essential to producing it. We just know it was there, and off we go.

On occasion, we have the pleasure of a breakfast that includes a greater portion of the diversity of foods available to us and the time to enjoy them. Taking time to survey the food on the table is an entry point to realizing a sense of all the science that goes into keeping all of it on the table: research on crop and livestock productivity and health, the quality and safety of the foods, the protection of the environment, the availability of information, technologies, and methods available to producers, processors, and consumers. It's doubtful whether the 37th Congress and President Abraham Lincoln envisioned the bounty of foods that would be available in the twenty-first century, as a result in very large part to the "practical and scientific experiments" tasked to Lincoln's new Department of Agriculture. Continuing this tradition of research and technology transfer, started more than 150 years ago, will ensure that not just Americans but people around the world will have food that is diverse, of high quality, nutritious, and safe… not just at breakfast, but at every meal of the day.

Acknowledgements The vast array of advances we profile result from the efforts of hundreds (thousands?) of researchers and for their many efforts we are grateful. We also thank an array of individuals who provided guidance, edits, and information to this chapter, including ARS National Program Leaders Peter Bretting, José Costa, Rosalind James, James Lindsay, Sally Schneider, and Gail Wisler, and ARS Center Director Marisa Wall. This chapter is based on a presentation at the 2016 USDA Agricultural Outlook Forum, February 25–26, 2016.

References

Berger, L. 2014. Canine Detection of Citrus Canker may Show HLB Application Promise. *Citrograph, Citrus Research Board, Fall* 2014: 22–27.

Bhunia, A.K., M.S. Kim, and C.R. Taitt, eds. 2015. *High Throughput Screening for Food Safety Assessment. Biosensor Technologies, Hyperspectral Imaging and Practical Applications.* 1st ed, 523pp. Amsterdam: Woodhead Publishing.

Bouffard, K. 2016. Turmoil Expected from Projected 26 Percent Orange Crop Drop. The Ledger, Lakeland, Florida. August 10, 2016. http://www.theledger.com/article/20160810/NEWS/160819987.

Bowman, K.D., L. Faulkner, and M. Kesinger. 2016. New Citrus Rootstocks Released by USDA 2001–2010: Field Performance and Nursery Characteristics. *Hortscience* 51 (10): 1208–1214. 10.21273/HORTSC10970-16.

Ceja-Navarro, J.A., F.E. Vega, U. Karaoz, Z. Hao, S. Jenkins, H.C. Lim, P. Kosina, F. Infante, T.R. Northen, and E.L. Brodie. 2015. Gut Microbiota Mediate Caffeine Detoxification in the Primary Insect Pest of Coffee. *Nature Communications* 6: 7618. https://doi.org/10.1038/ncomms8618.

Chao, K. 2010. Automated Poultry Carcass Inspection by a Hyperspectral-Multispectral Line-Scan Imaging System. In *Hyperspectral Imaging for Food Quality Analysis and Control*, ed. D.-W. Sun, 241–272. London: Academic Press/Elsevier.

Chao, K., C.C. Yang, Y.R. Chen, M.S. Kim, and D.E. Chan. 2007. Hyperspectral-Multispectral Line-Scan Imaging System for Automated Poultry Carcass Inspection Applications for Food Safety. *Poultry Science* 86: 2450–2460. https://doi.org/10.3382/ps.2006-00467.

Diaz-Sanchez, S., D. D'Souza, D. Biswas, and I. Hanning. 2015. Botanical Alternatives to Antibiotics for Use in Organic Poultry Production. *Poultry Science* 94 (6): 1419–1430. https://doi.org/10.3382/ps/pev014.

Doud, M.S., M.T. Hoffman, M.-Q. Zhang, E. Stover, D. Hall, S. Zhang, and Y.P. Duan. 2012. Thermal Treatments Eliminate or Suppress the Bacterial Pathogen in Huanglongbing-Affected Citrus. *Phytopathology* 102 (7): 3340.

Doyle, M.P., and M.C. Erickson. 2006. Reducing the Carriage of Foodborne Pathogens in Livestock and Poultry. *Poultry Science* 85: 960–973. Downloaded from http://ps.oxfordjournals.org/ at DigiTop USDA's Digital Desktop Library on December 2, 2016.

Farnsworth, D., K. A. Grogan, A. H.C. van Bruggen, and C. B. Moss. 2014. The Potential Economic Cost and Response to Greening in Florida Citrus. Choices. Quarter 3. Available online: http://choicesmagazine.org/choices-magazine/submitted-articles/the-potential-economic-cost-and-response-to-greening-in-florida-citrus   -   http://www.choicesmagazine.org/choices-magazine/submitted-articles/the-potential-economic-cost-and-response-to-greening-in-florida-citrus#sthash.xXA2riSY.dpuf.

Gottwald, T.R. 2010. Current Epidemiological Understanding of Citrus Huanglongbing. *Annual Review of Phytopathology* 48 (1): 119–139. https://doi.org/10.1146/annurev-phyto-073009-114418.

Goulson, D., E. Nicholls, C. Botias, and E.L. Rotheray. 2015. Bee Declines Driven by Combined Stress from Parasites, Pesticides, and Lack of Flowers. *Science* 347 (6229): 1255957. https://doi.org/10.1126/science.1255957.

Graham, T., R. Scorza, R. Wheeler, B. Smith, C. Dardick, A. Dixit, D. Raines, A. Callahan, C. Srinivasan, L. Spencer, J. Richards, and G. Stutte. 2015. Over-Expression of FT1 in Plum (*Prunus domestica*) Results in Phenotypes Compatible with Spaceflight: A Potential New Candidate Crop for Bio-regenerative Life-Support Systems. *Gravitational and Space Research* 3 (1): 39–50.

Hartung, L.W., and J.S. Levy L. 2006. Quantitative Real-Time PCR for Detection and Identification of Candidatus Liberibacter Species Associated with Citrus Huanglongbing. *Journal of Microbiological Methods* 66 (1): 104–115. https://doi.org/10.1016/j.mimet.2005.10.018 pmid:16414133.

Heitschmidt, G.W., B. Park, K.C. Lawrence, W.R. Windham, and D.P. Smith. 2007. Improved Hyperspectral Imaging System for Fecal Detection on Poultry Carcasses. *Transactions of the ASABE* 50 (4): 1427–1432.

Holsinger, V.H. 1997. Physical and Chemical Properties of Lactose. In *Advanced Dairy Chemistry, Volume 3. Lactose Water, Salts, and Vitamins*, ed. P.F. Fox, 2nd ed., 1–38. London: Chapman & Hall.

Honeycutt, C.W., Larkin, R.P., Halloran, J.M., Griffin, T.S. 2007. The Potato Systems Planner: A successful Decision Support Tool for Growers. Symposium Proceedings. 2007: pp. 87–88.

Hu, J., S. Angeli, S. Schuetz, Y. Luo, and A.E. Hajek. 2009. Ecology and Management of Exotic and Endemic Asian Longhorned Beetle Anoplophora Glabripennis. *Agricultural and Forest Entomology* 11: 359–375. https://doi.org/10.1111/j.1461-9563.2009.00443.x.

Kaplan, J.K. 2012. Colony Collapse Disorder. An Incomplete Puzzle. *Agricultural Research* 60 (6): 4–8.

Kawabata, A.M., S.T. Nakamoto, and R.T. Curtiss (Eds.). 2015. Proceedings: 2015 Coffee Berry Borer Summit. College of Tropical Agric. and Human Resources, University of Hawaii. http://www.ctahr.hawaii.edu/oc/freepubs/pdf/CBB_Summit_2015_Proceedings.pdf.

Kelly, H.W. 1993. Always Something New. A Cavalcade of Scientific Discovery. USDA Agricultural Research Service Misc. Pub. 1507. 150pp. Washington, DC: USDA

Kim, M.S., Y.R. Chen, S. Kang, I. Kim, A.M. Lefcourt, and M. Kim. 2006. Fluorescence Characteristics of Wholesome and Unwholesome Chicken Carcasses. *Applied Spectroscopy* 60 (10): 1210–1216.

Koluman, A., and A. Dikici. 2013. Antimicrobial Resistance of Emerging Foodborne Pathogens: Status Quo and Global Trends. *Critical Reviews in Microbiology* 39 (1): 57–69.

Liu, Y., E. Heying, and S.A. Tanumihardjo. 2012. History, Global Distribution, and Nutritional Importance of Citrus Fruits. *Comprehensive Reviews in Food Science and Food Safety* 11: 530–545. https://doi.org/10.1111/j.1541-4337.2012.00201.x.

McGinnis, L., S. Durham, A. Perry, J. Suszkiw, and D. Comis. 2008. Genomics, Phenomics Research Paves the Way for Improve Animal Health and Productivity. *Agricultural Research* 57 (7): 12–16.

Mittelman, M. 2016. Meet the Canines Sniffing Out Trouble in Florida's Orange Groves. Bloomberg, March 3, 2016. https://www.bloomberg.com/news/articles/2016-03-03/meet-the-canines-sniffing-out-trouble-in-florida-s-orange-groves.

Niemira, B.A. 2012. Cold Plasma Decontamination of Foods. *Annual Review of Food Science and Technology* 3: 125–142.

Nimakayala, P., V. Abburi, T. Saminathan, S. Alaparthi, A. Almeida, B. Davenport, J. Davidson, G. Vajja, C. Reddy, Y. Tomason, M. Nadimi, G. Hankins, D. Choi, J. Stommel, and U. Reddy. 2016. Genome-Wide Divergence and Linkage Disequilibrium Analyses for *Capsicum baccatum* Revealed by Genome-Anchored Single Nucleotide Polymorphisms. *Frontiers in Plant Science* 7: 1646. https://doi.org/10.3389/fpls.2016.01646.

O'Brien, D. 2016a. Canola: Good Protein Source for Dairy Cattle. AgResearch February 2016. https://agresearchmag.ars.usda.gov/2016/feb/canola/.

———. 2016b. Finger Millet Shows Promise as Cattle Feed. AgResearch June, 2016. https://agresearchmag.ars.usda.gov/2016/jun/fingermillet/.

Olivera, P.D., A. Badebo, S. Xu, D. Klindworth, and Y. Jin. 2012. Resistance to Race TTKSK of *Puccinia graminis f. sp. tritici* in emmer Wheat (*Triticum turgidum ssp. dicoccum*). *Crop Science* 52: 2234–2242.

Patterson, J.A., and K.M. Burkholder. 2003. Application of Prebiotics and Probiotics in Poultry Production. *Poultry Science* 82 (4): 627–631.

Paarlberg, P.L., A.H. Seitzinger, J.G. Lee, and K.H. Matthews, Jr. 2008. Economic Impacts of Foreign Animal Disease. Economic Research Report No. 57. 71pp. Washington, DC: USDA, Economic Research Service. https://www.ers.usda.gov/publications/pub-details/?pubid=45991

Peabody, E. 2005. Playing the Field. New Resource Helps Potato Farmers Decide on the Right Crop Rotations. *Agricultural Research* 53 (12): 19–21.

Pollinator Health Task Force. 2015. Pollinator Research Action Plan. The White House, Washington, D.C. 85pp. https://www.whitehouse.gov/sites/default/files/microsites/ostp/Pollinator%20Research%20Action%20Plan%202015.pdf.

Rahmatov, M., M.N. Rouse, B.J. Steffenson, S.C. Andersson, R. Wanyera, Z.A. Pretorius, A. Houben, N. Kumarse, S. Bhavani, and E. Hohansson. 2016. Sources of Stem Rust Resistance in Wheat-Alien Introgression Lines. *Plant Disease* 100: 1101–1109. https://www.ars.usda.gov/ARSUserFiles/45739/Rahmatov%20Plant%20Disease%202016.pdf.

Scorza, R., C. Dardick, A. Callahan, C. Srinivasan, T. Delong, J. Harper, C. Raines, S. Castro. 2012. 'FasTrack'—A Revolutionary Approach to Long-Generation Cycle Specialty Crop Breeding. [abstract]. Xth International Symposium Plum and Prune Genetics. Paper No. 101. https://www.ars.usda.gov/research/publications/publication/?seqNo115=279906.

Seitz, N., K.S. Traynor, N. Steinhauer, K. Rennich, M.E. Wilson, J.D. Ellis, R. Rose, D.R. Tarpy, R.R. Sagli, D.M. Caron, K.S. Delaplane, J. Rangel, K. Lee, K. Baylis, J.T. Wilkes, J.A. Skinner, J.S. Pettis, and D. vanEngelsdorp. 2015. A National Survey of Managed Honey Bee 2014–2015 Annual Colony Losses in the USA. *Journal of Apicultural Research* 54 (4): 292–304. https://doi.org/10.1080/00218839.2016.1153294.

Sharpley, A.N., T. Daniel, G. Gibson, L. Bundy, M. Cabrera, T. Sims, R. Stevens, J. Lemunyon, P. Kleinman, and R. Parry. 2006. Best Management Practices to Minimize Agricultural Phosphorous Impacts on Water Quality. U.S. Department of Agriculture, Agricultural Research Service, ARS—163, 50pp.

Smith, M.T., and J. Wu. 2008. Asian Longhorned Beetle: Renewed Threat to Northeastern USA and Implications Worldwide. *International Pest Control* 50 (6): 311–316.

Stanley, D. 1995. Dairy Science to the Defense. *Agricultural Research* 43 (10): 10.

Stommel, J., M. Camp, Y. Luo, and A.M. Welten. 2015. Genetic Diversity Provides Opportunities for Improvement of Fresh-Cut Pepper Quality. *Plant Genetic Resources: Characterization and Utilization* 14 (2): 112–120.

Stommel, J., M. Pushko, K. Haynes, and B. Whitaker. 2014. Differential Inheritance of Pepper (Capsicum annum) Fruit Pigments Results in Black to Violet Fruit Color. *Plant Breeding* 133: 788–793. https://doi.org/10.1111/PBR.12209.

Szogi, A.A., M.B. Vanotti, and A.E. Stansbery. 2006. Reduction of Ammonia Emissions from Treated Anaerobic Swine Lagoons. *Transactions of the ASABE* 49 (1): 217–225. 10.13031/2013.20241.

United States Department of Agriculture, Animal and Plant Health Inspection Service. 2007. Foot-and-Mouth Disease Vaccine. APHIS Factsheet, Veterinary Services, March 2007. 2pp.

USDA. 1969. The Story of U.S. Agricultural Estimates. Miscellaneous Publication No. 1088. Statistical Reporting Service, Washington, D.C. 137pp.

Vanotti, M.B., P.D. Millner, P.G. Hunt, and A.Q. Ellison. 2005. Removal of Pathogen and Indicator Microorganisms from Liquid Swine Manure in Multi-Step Biological and Chemical Treatment. *Bioresource Technology* 96 (2): 209–214.

van Nocker, S., and S.E. Gardiner. 2014. Breeding Better Cultivars, Faster: Applications of New Technologies for the Rapid Deployment of Superior Horticultural Tree Crops. *Horticulture Research* 1: 14022. https://doi.org/10.1038/hortres.2014.22.

Vega, F.E., F. Infante, and A.J. Johnson. 2015. The Genus *Hypothenemus*, with Emphasis on *H. hampei*, the Coffee Berry Borer. In *Bark Beetles, Biology and Ecology of Native and Invasive Species*, ed. F.E. Vega and R.W. Hofstetter, First ed., 427–494. London: Elsevier.

Xiong, J.-S., J. Ding, and Y. Li. 2015. Genome-Editing Technologies and Their Potential Application in Horticultural Crop Breeding. *Horticulture Research* 2: 15019. https://doi.org/10.1038/hortres.2015.19.

Xu, L., J.B. Cole, D.M. Bickhart, Y. Hou, J. Song, P.M. vanRaden, T.S. Sonstegard, C.P. Van Tassell, and G.E. Liu. 2014. Genome Wide CNV Analysis Reveals Additional Variants Associated With Milk Production Traits in Holsteins. *BMC Genomics* 15: 683–693. http://www.biomedcentral.com/1471-2164/15/683.

Xu, S., S.H. Lee, H.S. Lillehoj, Y.H. Hong, and D. Bravo. 2015. Effects of Dietary Selenium on Host Response to Necrotic Enteritis in Young Broilers. *Research in Veterinary Science* 98: 66–73. https://doi.org/10.1016/j.rvsc.2014.12.004.

Yang, C., C.A. Powell, Y. Duan, R.G. Shatters, Y. Lin, and M. Zhang. 2016. Mitigating Citrus Huanglongbing via Effective Application of Antimicrobial Compounds and Thermotherapy. *Crop Protection* 84: 150–158. https://doi.org/10.1016/j.cropro.2016.03.013.

Yao, S. 2011. "FasTracking" Plum Breeding. *Agricultural Research* 59 (3): 16–17.

Yu, G., D.L. Klindworth, T.L. Friesen, J.D. Faris, S. Zhong, J.B. Rasmussen, and S.S. Xu. 2015. Development of a Diagnostic Co-Dominant Marker for Stem Rust Resistance Gene Sr47 Introgressed from *Aegilops speltoides* into Durum Wheat. *Theoretical and Applied Genetics* 128: 2367–2374.

Yun, C.H., H.S. Lillehoj, and E.P. Lillehoj. 2000. Intestinal Immune Responses to Coccidiosis. *Developmental & Comparative Immunology* 24 (2–3): 303–324.

Zhang, M., Y. Guo, C.A. Powell, M.S. Doud, C. Yang, and Y. Duan. 2014. Effective Antibiotics against 'Candidatus Liberibacter asiaticus' in HLB-Affected Citrus Plants Identified via the Graft-Based Evaluation. *PLoS One* 9 (11): e111032. https://doi.org/10.1371/journal.pone.0111032.

The Role and Impact of Public Research and Technology Transfer in Brazilian Agriculture

Geraldo B. Martha Jr and Eliseu Alves

Abstract The public sector played a pivotal role in transforming a traditional agriculture in Brazil into a modern one by leading the agricultural research and development (R&D) network in the country and by providing the majority of funds to R&D activities. The spillover effects arising from agricultural R&D were not restricted to the primary sector. A vibrant agricultural sector creates sizable markets for industrial and service sectors if they can deliver quality products at competitive prices. More broadly, the success of this science-based agriculture in Brazil provided the means for ample improvements in food and nutritional security; expanded opportunities for employment and income generation in agricultural (and associated) value chains; a more positive balance of trade; and a substantial attenuation of inflationary pressures. In the coming decades, the value of Brazilian agriculture to society will eventually be even bigger, as the so-called bio-economy gets strengthened. However, it is imperative to encourage a more intense engagement of the private sector in agricultural R&D activities in Brazil.

Successful technological scaling-up will depend upon multi-stakeholder approaches. Knowledge exchange, capacity development and strengthening, technology transfer, extension services, and well-functioning input and market chains, to minimize detrimental effects of market imperfections on technology adoption, are key components to foster the adoption of technologies. In particular, a more widespread and inclusiveness technological adoption in Brazilian agriculture will depend on successful approaches to minimize market imperfections' effects.

Introduction

The importance of the agricultural sector to the Brazilian economy has been demonstrated since the first ventures in colonial times. Despite the role of agriculture in Brazilian history, until the 1960s the country systematically received food donations from abroad, and until the 1980s it was one of the world's largest food importers.

G.B. Martha Jr (✉) • E. Alves
Embrapa, Brasilia, Brazil
e-mail: geraldo.martha@embrapa.br

© Springer International Publishing AG 2018
N. Kalaitzandonakes et al. (eds.), *From Agriscience to Agribusiness*, Innovation, Technology, and Knowledge Management, https://doi.org/10.1007/978-3-319-67958-7_21

429

The traditional agriculture that prevailed in the country until the 1970s, based on the extensive margin, was progressively and significantly transformed in the following decades. A modern and vibrant agriculture, strongly based on science, emerged.

Several factors played a decisive role in this process of transforming Brazilian agriculture. To cite a few, consider (1) the entrepreneurship of Brazilian farmers; (2) the commitment of the Government; (3) the availability of basic infrastructure; (4) the favorable climatic conditions for a productive agriculture; (5) the availability of land suitable for mechanization; (6) the suitable physical characteristics of tropical soils (e.g., oxisols, ultisols, alfisols) and the supply of mineral resources such as limestone and phosphorus; and (7) the recognition of the need and importance of a science-based agriculture, with an ample and solid research system focusing on the adaptation and development of technologies for the tropical environment, in order to make such a transformation a reality (see, e.g., Albuquerque and Silva 2008a, b; Cunha et al. 1994; Martha and Alves 2017).

The achievements in Brazilian agriculture prove that it is possible to produce food, feed, and other agricultural products in tropical environments in efficient, sustainable, and competitive ways. The results of the Brazilian science-based agriculture, such as new varieties adapted to the tropics and agricultural practices tailored to new production environments, such as the Cerrado, among other technologies and innovations avidly adopted in farms, eventually allowed Brazil to become an agricultural power in the period of only one generation.

In this chapter we bring insights into the role of the public sector to Brazilian agriculture, with an emphasis on agricultural research. In the first section, we provide a short introduction to the dynamics of Brazilian agriculture transformation. Then, in the second section, we highlight the importance of research and development (R&D) in supporting these achievements. In the third section, examples of the impacts of public agricultural R&D and associated technology transfer activities on society are provided. In that section we also emphasize key challenges to a more widespread adoption of technologies, stressing the critical role of market imperfections. Finally, in the fourth section, a few thoughts on future possibilities and challenges are discussed.

Agriculture in Brazil

Brazil's Geographic Characteristics

Brazil's geographic area is one of the largest in the world and totals 8,515,767 km^2 distributed among 5570 municipalities (IBGE 2016). Brazil provides vital environmental services to the world through its large availability of land (ca. 13.2% of the world's potential arable land (FAO 2000)) and water (ca. 15.2% of the world's water resources (WRI 2008)).

Table 1 Area covered with native vegetation in Brazilian biomes

Biomes	Total area (km²)[a]	% Remaining (natural cover)[b]
Caatinga (2011)	844,453	53.2
Cerrado (2013)[c]	2,036,448	51.1
Pantanal (2009)	150,355	35.9
Pampa (2009)	176,496	83.1
Amazônia (2014)[d]	4,196,943	82.4
Mata Atlântica (2011)	1,110,182	54.5
Total (Brazil)	8,514,877	61[e]

[a]Area of Brazilian biomes (available at http://brasilemsintese.ibge.gov.br/territorio.html); further information at http://www.ibge.gov.br/home/geociencias/areaterritorial/historico.shtm and http://www.ibge.gov.br/home/geociencias/cartografia/default_territ_area.shtm
[b]Control and prevention of deforestation in Brazilian biomes (available at http://www.mma.gov.br/florestas/controle-e-preven%C3%A7%C3%A3o-do-desmatamento)
[c]TerraClass Cerrado (available at http://www.dpi.inpe.br/tccerrado/index.php?mais=1)
[d]TerraClass Amazônia (available at http://www.inpe.br/cra/projetos_pesquisas/arquivos/TerraClass_2014_v3.pdf)
[e]Brazilian agriculture overview (available at https://polcms.secure.europarl.europa.eu/cmsdata/upload/f312ee34-a6e1-4cf1-8a21-d21040a321fd/Brazilian%20Minister_Presentation.pdf).   All the above mentioned information were accessed on April 24th, 2017

The country's diverse climatic regimes (from tropical to subtropical), combined with such natural capital, have evolved over the ages to create six diverse biomes, from semiarid to Amazon rainforest. As of today, over 60% of the Brazilian territory is still covered with native vegetation (Table 1). Brazil's biodiversity potential is outstanding: among the world's 250,000 species of higher plants, nearly 60,000 are native to Brazil (Lopes 2012; MMA 2017).

Agriculture in Brazil: From Colony up to Mid-Twentieth Century

Brazil was a colony from Portugal from 1500 to 1822. And since colonial times, agriculture was important to the country. In the sixteenth and seventeenth centuries, sugar exports were prominent and peaked during the 1650s, with profitability declining shortly thereafter, owing to the decline in international prices and competition imposed by the colonies in the Caribbean (Furtado 2005). Due to the collapse of the gold cycle in the country by the end of the eighteenth century, by 1822, at the time of Brazil's independence from Portugal, exports of agricultural products – cotton, sugar, and coffee – once again represented the main source of income to the country (Maddison 2011).

From mid-nineteenth century until the 1920s, coffee production was by and large the main economic activity in the country (Bacha 2004). Coffee and some other agricultural commodities (rubber, cocoa, and cotton) destined for foreign markets accounted for over 55% of exports until the 1960s (Thorp 1998). Because of this economic model, Brazil repeatedly faced volatile economic growth and considerable external vulnerability for much of its history (Baer 2008; Gremaud et al. 2004).

Up to late 1960s, Brazilian agriculture was still trapped in cycles of low productivity and was heavily dependent on area expansion as a strategy to increase food production. The shift toward the modernization of Brazilian agriculture had its origins in the import substitution industrialization strategy adopted after the 1950s and 1960s up to the early 1980s. Nevertheless, in that period the industrial sector was granted a series of advantages that strongly discriminated against agriculture.

The persistent food supply crisis throughout the 1960s and early 1970s led to several hypotheses being formulated to explain the lack of a more substantial increase in agricultural productivity. Three policies turned out to play a central role in Brazilian agricultural modernization process: (a) rural credit, mainly for capital goods and purchasing of modern inputs; (b) rural extension; and (c) support to agricultural research.

The role of rural credit in the modernization of Brazilian agriculture was of pivotal importance in the 1970s and the 1980s, by boosting the production and adoption of modern inputs (seeds, fertilizers, etc.), machinery, and equipment. Interest rates were subsidized, particularly from late 1960s to 1985 (Coelho 2001). Martha and Alves (2017) estimated that rural credit in Brazil, in 2016 Brazilian reals, averaged R\$ 154.53 billion per year, from 1969 to 1985; R\$ 76.40 billion per year, from 1986 to 2000; and R\$ 113.60 billion per year, from 2001 to 2015.[1]

Until the early 1970s, Brazilian policy makers emphasized rural extension and neglected efforts in agricultural research. As discussed by Martha and Alves (2017):

> ... The belief that strengthening human capital was key to better utilize available resources and to increase the impact of the investments made in capital goods and modern inputs was, of course, in the right direction. The flaw emerged in not recognizing that agricultural problems – and the demands posed to the sector – were not static, they were actually quite dynamic. A successful strategy would inevitably embrace a robust research system to continuously generate knowledge and technology to be transferred to extension services that, in turn, would be better positioned to support a sustained innovation process at the farm level.

Major developments in agricultural research only got traction in the post-WWII period and especially in the 1970s. The research-driven approach in Brazilian agriculture experienced a very important milestone in 1973, when the Brazilian Ministry of Agriculture boldly established its agricultural research arm – the Brazilian

---

[1] Despite those incentives, it is important to note that the overall level of incentives to Brazilian agriculture has been low compared to other countries. For example, considering the metric provided by the Organization for Economic Cooperation and Development (OECD), the producer support estimate (PSE), Brazilian farmers received incentives averaging only 1.6% of total gross farm receipts from 1995 to 2014. The corresponding values to the farmers in the USA and Europe in the same period were 13.5% and 28.3% of the total gross farm receipts, respectively (data available at https://www.oecd.org/tad/agricultural-policies/producerandconsumersupportestimatesdatabase.htm)

Agricultural Research Corporation (Embrapa)[2] – to strengthen agricultural research in the country.

This overall broad picture was summarized by Martha and Alves (2017) as follows:

> … the development of a modern agriculture in Brazil was initially prompted by the import substitution industrialization policy from late 1960s to mid-1980s. The accelerated growth in population, urbanization, and per capita income at that time posed a clear and strong demand for the agricultural sector. The expansion of agricultural output enabled larger export volumes, as well as more diverse exports, which in turn provided the means to finance imports of technology and capital goods for the emerging national industry. The increased opportunity cost of labor for farmers, and the sustained migration from rural areas to cities additionally led to a favorable environment for agricultural growth and modernization … A science-based approach, based on the continuous generation of new knowledge and technologies, played a crucial role in transforming Brazilian agriculture from mid-1970s on.

A Few Highlights on Brazil's Agricultural R&D

Innovation activities take different forms (technology embedded in capital goods, "hardware," "software," licenses, technology training, other forms of services, OECD 2005) and, of course, are not restricted to R&D activities. Nevertheless, in targeting Brazil's science-based agriculture, R&D activities have been playing a central role in increasing the sector's sustainability and competitiveness over the past few decades.

There are no alternative means to sustain this knowledge generation flow but to support both basic (fundamental) and problem-solving (applied) research. To that end, continuously improving and strengthening human capital plays a central role to overall innovation goals. Giving up on this approach – e.g., to quit playing a key role in basic and applied research and to quit investing in a highly qualified human capital to run those activities which boost the innovation process over time – will inevitably result in losing the national capacity to design directions to be pursued by key sectors in the economy over the medium and long run.

From the mid-1970s on, Brazil improved its research structure and capacity substantially by developing a two-tier system of federal and state-based agencies, called the "National Agricultural Research System (SNPA) (Lopes 2012). The Brazilian SNPA includes state agricultural research organizations, university agricultural colleges, and Embrapa, which coordinates the SNPA.

Embrapa has a nationwide mandate, is decentralized in the territorial dimension, and is organized into product, resource, and theme research centers. The successful

---

[2] More precisely, Embrapa was created by the federal law 5851, from December 1972, and effectively installed on April 26, 1973. When Embrapa was created, it incorporated the former research structure of the Brazilian Ministry of Agriculture, the "Departamento Nacional de Pesquisa Agropecuária."

Embrapa model centers heavily on continued strengthening of human resource capacity and on excellence research centers (Alves 2010; Martha and Alves 2017).

As of 2013, Embrapa represented 42% of the SNPA's research capacity, followed by state research organizations (29%), agricultural colleges (26%), and nonprofit organizations (3%). The full-time research equivalents in 2013 (FTE – 5869.4) were composed by 72.5% of researchers with PhD, 21.5% with MSc, and 6.0% with BSc (Flaherty et al. 2016). At Embrapa, as of 2015 only 0.7% of researchers had a BSc degree and 13.5% had an MSc degree. The share of researchers with a PhD was 85.8% (Martha and Alves 2017).

Public funds have traditionally accounted for more than 90% of Brazil's agricultural research effort. Thus, the financial support of the Brazilian government to SNPA – and, thus, to the agricultural sector – has been of overwhelming importance. The level of investment in public agricultural R&D, from 1981 to 2013, has averaged USD 1.9 billion per year. This was translated into an average intensity of agricultural R&D expenditures of 1.2% of the agricultural gross domestic product (GDP), in the 1980s, and ca. 1.85% in the 1990s and 2000s.[3]

The support to Embrapa, which has traditionally accounted for ca. 55% of public agricultural R&D expenditures in Brazil, has been of paramount importance. In absolute terms, and considering 2016 constant Brazilian real values, Embrapa's budget progressively increased from 1973 onwards to reach R$ 2.44 billion in 1982; then it sharply decreased to R$ 1.58 billion (1984), to gradually increase again and reach R$ 2.77 billion in 1996. Embrapa's budget progressively dropped (again) to R$ 1.77 billion in 2003. After a couple of years around this budget level, Embrapa's budget resumed a positive trend and progressively increased in the following decade to peak at R$ 3.37 billion in 2015. In 2016, it totaled R$ 3.2 billion. This later amount would be equivalent to approximately USD 940 million, or perhaps, more correctly, to ca. USD 1.75 billion, when appropriate expenditures are expressed as USD purchasing power parity.

From an institutional point of view, Brazil operates with a R&D model of responsibilities that converges to the ones practiced in developed countries. Universities tend to focus on basic research, although not exclusively. Research organizations are more engaged in problem-solving (applied) research, although in strategic areas they play a key role in basic research and in development efforts as well. Private companies concentrate their efforts in development, but sometimes present initiatives in research, occasionally even in basic research.

Brazil has maintained an appropriate path in balancing expenditures in basic and problem-solving research. And the justification for that is simple: one type of research nourishes the other. Basic/fundamental research expands the pool of knowledge necessary for problem-solving/applied research to respond to more specific real-world opportunities and challenges. At the same time, such feedbacks from perceived sectoral opportunities and challenges provide relevant signals and demands for knowledge expansion on fundamental questions, the object of basic research.

---

[3] Based on ASTI-IFPRI's database on agricultural research (available at www.asti.cgiar.org/data). Values based on constant 2011 PPP dollars

R&D and Technology Transfer Impacts

Once the technology, process, or agricultural practice has been generated by the research system, it needs to be properly "decoded" (e.g., "the transfer of technology phase"). In a subsequent stage typically represented by public and private rural extension/consultancy activities, end users get to understand the technology, process, or agricultural practice and are thus better positioned to analyze advantages and disadvantages among available options and decide toward adopting (or not) any given innovation.

In other words, research and technology transfers are components of the innovation flow, and their impacts on society will inevitably be linked to each other's success. Ultimately, perceived outputs and outcomes will be influenced by end users' ability to understand and successfully implement novel methods, tools, and courses of action in a desirable direction and in a timely manner.

Public Research-Driven Impacts

The choice of a technology will vary according to the priority problem to be solved. Hayami and Ruttan (1985) indicated that agricultural technologies can broadly focus on land- and/or labor-saving technologies. In the first group are biological and chemical technologies, while the latter includes mechanical technologies. The so-called product-saving technologies, linked to reduced losses along the food chain, are additionally perceived as crucial to the agricultural sector's outcomes for society.

The research model adopted by Embrapa facilitates the interaction between researchers and farmers (and more broadly with society) by establishing an interesting way to identify research priorities – a typical case of induced innovation. Among the strategies used to accomplish that end is the direct researcher-farmer interaction (field days, on-farm research, etc.), as well as connections through permanent and temporary committees and councils, in which stakeholders' and overall society's needs and demands might be captured and translated into problems to be solved by the research system (Martha and Alves 2017). Present and future challenges can then be timely identified and thus incorporated into research activities that properly provide for adaptation and/or generation of technologies. Thus, for public research, the market influence is indirect, since to a great extent, it is derived from farmers' and/or society's lens. For the private research market, it acts directly; otherwise the technology developed would not find buyers (Hayami and Ruttan 1985).

Over the past four decades, Brazilian public agricultural research, in many instances led by Embrapa, decisively contributed to sizable achievements in agriculture, whether in land-, labor-, or product-saving technologies. There is little doubt that the payoffs to agricultural R&D have been high over the past 60 years (Alston et al. 1998; Pardey et al. 2006, Avila et al. 2010).

The internal rates of return (IRR) to investments at Embrapa have averaged 25%–30% over recent decades, ranging from 20% to 74% in the studies reported by Avila and Souza (2002). From 1997 to 2015, Embrapa's aggregated IRR was estimated at 39.1%.[4] While such high IRR values are thrilling, in a recent reassessment encompassing more than 2000 evaluations from 1958 to 2011, Hurley et al. (2014) indicated that a median of around 10% (versus a median of ca. 40% previously reported) was perhaps a more reasonable estimate to agricultural R&D's IRR. However, an IRR of 10% is still substantial enough to justify massive investments in public agricultural R&D.

Another metric commonly used to evaluate the impacts of public agricultural R&D is the benefit/cost ratio (Avila et al. 2008). Over the past two decades, where annual impact evaluations are available, Embrapa has shown a benefit/cost ratio to society's investment ranging from 7.5:1 to 14.8:1. On average, Embrapa's benefit/cost ratio is 11:1 – that is, for each dollar invested at Embrapa, Brazilian society has received 11 dollars back in the form of knowledge and technologies fueling the innovation process.

Over the past 19 years (1998–2016), the net accumulated benefit (e.g., the sum of benefits minus the sum of expenditures) of Embrapa's research was approximately R$ 460 billion in 2016 values[5] (Fig. 1). After a decrease in R&D funding, a decreased return (benefit) to society is expected within a few years. However, if R&D funding is resumed relatively shortly, the flow of R&D benefits to society is expected to resume a positive trend within a few years (Fig. 2).

On the "cost side" of benefit/cost analyses, no major value change is expected. However, one must keep in mind that on the "benefit side," such values are a fraction of Embrapa's contribution to society. The 11:1 ratio considered around 100 technologies and some 150–200 plant cultivars, whereas in fact over the past 45 years, Embrapa has contributed with considerably more knowledge and technologies than those. The point to note here is that there is imprecise evidence regarding the impacts of agricultural research over an ample array of technologies. In part this reflects the difficulties in attributing adequate weights to benefits and costs among different agents involved in the process.

Another impact metric that might be considered is, of course, the direct economic benefit (Avila et al. 2008). Taking the seed market as an example, Embrapa was a major player in Brazil up to the mid-1990s. This happened because at that time the private sector, in the country and also abroad, was not sufficiently developed to meet Brazilian farmers' needs. As exemplified in Embrapa's 1998 social balance report,[6] in the 1995/1996 season, Embrapa's seeds held sizable market shares: 8.1%

---

[4] Please see Embrapa's 2015 social balance, available at http://bs.sede.embrapa.br/destaques.html (information accessed on April 10th, 2017).

[5] Such a social return is very impressive to the overall Brazilian economy. For example, in 2016, the gross value of agricultural (crops + livestock) production totaled ca. R$ 552 billion, according to Brazil's Agriculture and Livestock Confederation (CNA 2017). Thus, Ceteris paribus, Embrapa's returns to society would potentially generate such an innovation flow that would eventually be translated into doubling the size of agriculture's annual gross value of production every quarter of a century.

[6] Available at http://bs.sede.embrapa.br/1998/tdtsoc4.htm (information accessed on April 10, 2017)

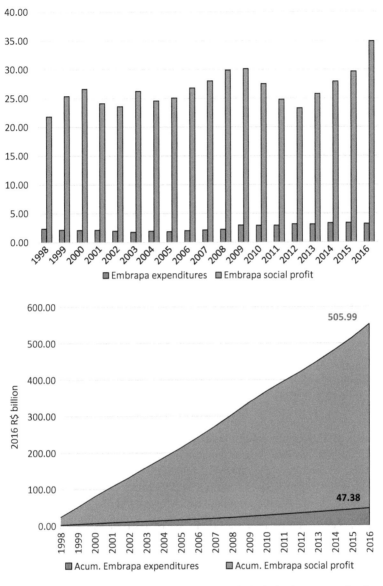

Fig. 1 Embrapa expenditures and social profits, on a yearly basis (top) or accumulated over the 1998–2016 period (bottom). Values are in 2016 Brazilian reals (Source: Expenditure values from Embrapa-DAF database. Social profits from Embrapa's social balances (data available at http:// bs.sede.embrapa.br//2015/). Authors' calculations and elaboration)

for cotton, 63.23% for irrigated rice, 98.04% for upland rice, 38.68% for common beans, 21.07% for corn, 55.01% for soybeans, and 58.04% for wheat. In that harvest season, 44% of Brazilian cropland was estimated to be planted with Embrapa's seed.

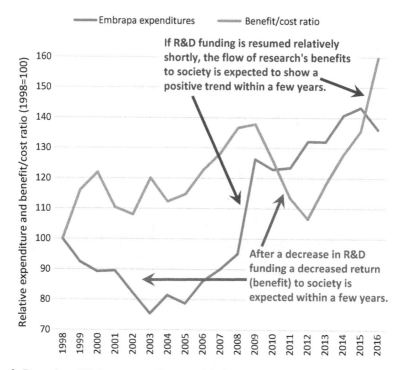

Fig. 2 Dynamics of Embrapa expenditures and benefit/cost ratios over the 1998–2016 period (Source: Expenditure values from Embrapa-DAF database. Social profits from Embrapa's social balances (data available at http://bs.sede.embrapa.br//2015/). Authors' calculations and elaboration)

Pardey et al. (2006) presented a study aiming to evaluate the impact of soybean, dry beans, and rice varietal improvement at Embrapa as compared to non-Embrapa investments. In the aggregate, varietal improvement in these crops from 1981 to 2003 yielded benefits of US$ 14.8 billion at 1999 prices. Attributing all the benefits to Embrapa, the benefit/cost ratio would be 27 for upland rice, 15 for dry beans, and 149 for soybeans. Under alternative distribution rules, which indicate Embrapa was given partial credit for the varieties developed jointly with other partners, the ratios would drop to 5, 3, and 31, respectively. Despite of the alternative distribution rule considered, the role of public research to Brazilian agriculture is obviously enormous.

Another example comes from the forage seed market, where Embrapa plays a very important role up to today. Three of the most adopted forage cultivars in the country – *Panicum maximum* cv. Mombaça, *P. maximum* cv. Tanzania, and *Brachiaria brizantha* cv. Marandu – are directly linked to Embrapa's research. Embrapa's returns to society in this case have provided an estimated economic benefit of R$ 6.67 billion in 2015 alone. In 2014, the estimated contribution was even higher – R$ 10.89 billion.[6]

Other tangible inputs generated by the agricultural research system might be considered. For example, soybean varieties that require no nitrogen have been selected for use in Brazil (Dobereiner 1997), and production contests have recently recorded potential yields exceeding 6 metric tonnes/hectare. Such achievement reflects important R&D contributions on biological nitrogen fixation (BNF) led by public agricultural research especially after the 1970s. In 2016, the soybean area with BNF was estimated to be 33.25 million hectares. In 2016, Embrapa's returns to society considering solely this technology were estimated at R$ 14.7 billion.[6]

It is worth of noting that a research organization such as Embrapa provides society not only with tangible deliverables (say, "crystalized knowledge"), such as seeds and other inputs. Embrapa and other research organizations benefit society with non-tangible contributions – the "non-crystalized forms of knowledge."

Non-tangible products may represent a considerable portion of public agricultural R&D organizations' benefits to society. However, they are more difficult to be adequately estimated. For example, what are the private (e.g., to farmer) and social (e.g., to other stakeholders and to society as whole) value and costs of knowing how to properly manage any given input, solely or in combination with other inputs? What are the private and social value and costs of knowing how to adequately implement agricultural practices for a better resource use efficiency, improved water quality, reduced erosion and runoff, smaller environmental pollution, and higher economic return? Definitely, there is no easily quantifiable metric to those questions.

Tentatively, the total factor productivity (TFP) may provide a few insights on that matter. The TFP is a productivity measure taking into account the partial productivities of land, labor, and capital; it is thus defined as a ratio of output to inputs. Put simply, TFP is the portion of the product not explained by the inputs.

Over the past four or five decades, the yearly TFP growth of Brazilian agriculture has been estimated at 2.24% (Gasques et al. 2010) and 2.31%.[7] Considering that a 1% increase in Embrapa's research spending would increase Brazilian agricultural TFP an estimated 0.2% (Gasques et al. 2009), one could probably say that over the long-run, public research, in this case represented by Embrapa, has been associated with at least 10% of overall agricultural sector productivity.

The Increasing Role of Technology to Inclusiveness, Sustainability, and Competitiveness Goals

The future, by definition, brings uncertain outcomes. However, if one was to bet on the most influential factor for future agriculture, it would probably be technology. Alves et al. (2013), working with data from the 1995/1996 and 2006 agricultural

---

[7] These estimates were based on the USDA-Economic Research Service's database, assumptions, and methods. This work is led by USDA-ERS's researchers Keith Fuglie and Nicholas Rada. Data available at www.ers.usda.gov/data-products/international-agriculture-productivity

census, found that in the first period, land and labor accounted for about 50% of the variation in gross income in agriculture; the other half was the result of technology. That is, technology was already important to Brazilian agriculture in the 1990s.

In just one decade, according to the 2006 agricultural census data, the contribution of technology grew by about 35% and accounted for roughly two-thirds of the gross income variation in Brazilian agriculture. Of course technology does not occur in an "empty space," so farmer entrepreneurship, public policies, and available stocks of knowledge and technologies all contributed to that outcome. It is worth of noting, however, that given the long maturation period inherent to agricultural research, such a result was only possible because of persistent and focused agricultural R&D efforts toward innovation that have been actively developed in Brazil since the 1970s.

Furthermore, it is important to note that the contribution of land to income variation dropped by 50% (from around 18% to 9%) between the agricultural censuses of 1995/1996 and 2006. Similarly, the contribution of labor to income in agriculture dropped by ca. 30% (from 31% to 22%) in this period. Those facts highlight that in a science-based agriculture, such as was established in Brazil, land and labor progressively lose their power to explain income over time. Technology, for at least two decades, has been the main factor explaining income in Brazilian agriculture. In addition, technology, together with market imperfections, is a key factor to be looked at when targeting inclusiveness, sustainability, and competitiveness policies and regional development approaches.

Put a bit differently, a more widespread dissemination and effective adoption of modern technologies by a more significant number of farmers in Brazil may represent a disruptive, but substantially positive, contribution to agricultural product in the coming decades. Alves et al. (2012) estimated that 44% of the 4.4 million farms that have declared income in the 2006 agricultural census (out of a total of 5.2 million farms) were able to pay for all inputs. Nevertheless, only about 500,000 farms had a monthly income of more than 10 minimum wages. There were approximately 2 million farms with monthly incomes of up to 10 minimum wages, which may have a solution in the agricultural sector.

As emphasized above, the success of such a strategy would depend on the adoption of modern technologies, which reinforces the importance of effectively minimizing market imperfections. For the purpose of this discussion, we understand market imperfection not only as a market power concentration (monopoly, oligopoly, monopsony, and oligopsony). It also refers to non-technological asymmetries (such as the availability of infrastructure and education) that restrict a more widespread assimilation and adoption of modern technologies (for additional details, please see Alves and Silva 2013; Martha and Alves 2017). Therefore, market imperfection, given its several channels of interference in the overall decision-making process and its influence in altering the relative prices to farmers and thus the return to investment in technologies, needs to be reduced to increase the effectiveness of policies targeting technology adoption by the farmers and to allow agricultural production to expand in a more inclusive way (Martha and Alves 2017).

Final Thoughts

Spillover effects of agricultural R&D and on-farm agricultural innovations are, of course, not restricted to the primary sector – they are much bigger and can benefit other countries as well.

A sustainable and competitive science-based agriculture can provide transformation industries with a continuous flow of quality raw materials at declining real prices, potentially increasing its own competitiveness over time. The data provided by CEPEA ("Center for Advanced Studies on Applied Economics"), hosted at the University of São Paulo (USP), "Luiz de Queiroz" College of Agriculture (ESALQ), provides unique insights on that matter. In 2015, Brazilian agribusiness gross domestic product (GDP) totaled R$ 1.267 billion (2015 Brazilian reals). The agro-industry accounted for 27.5% of agribusiness GDP, contributing R$ 348.149 million to the Brazilian economy.[8]

In addition, such a competitive and sustainable science-based agriculture demands modern inputs with high technological content, which are provided by urban activities. Thus, a vibrant agricultural sector creates sizable markets for industrial and services sectors if they can deliver quality products at competitive prices. Calculations by CEPEA, at ESALQ/USP, have showed that in 2015 the input industry in agribusiness contributed R$ 151.133 million to the Brazilian economy.

Brazil's benefits from agriculture are not only due to expanding opportunities for employment and income generation in the sector but also to the effects of increased production in attenuating inflationary pressures. In addition, agriculture in Brazil has generated income effects of demand which brings positive spillovers to other sectors in the economy and especially benefits the low-income population (Martha and Alves 2017). The country has also gained from substantial surpluses in the agricultural balance of trade over the past two decades. Among other things, a trade balance surplus contributes to government funds and in this way might play a role in implementing and maintaining social and development programs in Brazil.

In the coming decades, the value to society of Brazilian agriculture and its research and innovation system will eventually be even bigger, as the so-called bio-economy gets strengthened. The ample variety in the supply of biomass in the country offers real opportunities for the development of value chains based on high value-added materials and substances targeted for food, feed, flavors, and non-food uses. Chemical biocatalytic processes lead to the development and use of microbial catalysts that directly convert raw materials into a range of products and chemical intermediates that can be subsequently converted into new products with a high value-added potential (Embrapa 2014). Such a bio-economy strategy may eventually boost the growth of associated capital goods industries, engineering services, and biomass suppliers in food, feed, chemistry, and pharmaceutical value chains, among others, creating opportunities for expanding higher value-added exports (Lopes and Martha 2016; Martha and Alves 2017).

---

[8] http://www.cepea.esalq.usp.br/br/pib-do-agronegocio-brasileiro.aspx

However, such thrilling outcomes from agriculture are constantly being challenged by biotic and abiotic pressures and, increasingly, by an intricate economic, political, and legal framework. Ultimately, there are no alternative means to an inclusive, sustainable, and competitive agriculture but strengthening the agricultural research system.

In addition to increasing research investments in agriculture to ensure the continuity of past decades' virtuous cycles on innovation, it is imperative to encourage a more intense engagement of the private sector in agricultural R&D activities in Brazil. Coordinated and expanded public, public-private, and private efforts are necessary to increase our current ability to understand and respond to present and future risks and challenges in diverse areas of knowledge and to more fully meet Brazil's potential in agriculture and bio-economy in the coming decades.

Successful technological scaling-up will depend upon multi-stakeholder approaches. Knowledge exchange, capacity development, technology transfer, extensions services, and well-functioning input and market chains, to minimize detrimental effects of market imperfections on technology adoption, are key components to foster the adoption of technologies.

In order to make such views a reality, it is key to expand investments in human resources training at all levels (Martha and Alves 2017). As pointed out by Alves (2008), the most severe restriction in boosting the production capacity of the agricultural sector is human capital, and that requires time to be removed. Capital restrictions embodied by the new technology are an outstanding deficiency, but they can be solved by credit policies, while access to more complex machinery and equipment can be solved by amending leasing legislation (Alves 2008).

References

Albuquerque, A.C.S., and A.G. Silva, eds. 2008a. *Agricultura tropical: quatro décadas de inovações tecnológicas, institucionais e políticas.* Vol. 1, 1337p. Brasília: Embrapa.
———, eds. 2008b. *Agricultura tropical: quatro décadas de inovações tecnológicas, institucionais e políticas.* Vol. 2, 700p. Brasília: Embrapa.
Alston, J.M., G.W. Norton, and P.G. Pardey. 1998. *Science Under Scarcity: Principles and Practice for Agricultural Research Evaluation and Priority Setting,* 585p. Wallingford: CABI Publishing.
Alves, E. Alguns desafios que a Embrapa enfrentará. Seminário Fertbio, Londrina, 17 de setembro de 2008.
———. 2010. Embrapa: A Successful Case of Institutional Innovation. *Revista de Política Agrícola* 19 (special issue): 64–72.
Alves, E.R.A., and R.C. Silva. 2013. Qual é o problema de transferência de tecnologia do Brasil e da Embrapa? In *Contribuições da Embrapa para o desenvolvimento da agricultura no Brasil,* ed. E.R.A. Alves, G.S. Souza, and E.G. Gomes, 279–291. Brasília: Embrapa.
Alves, E., G.S. Souza, and D.P. Rocha. 2012. Lucratividade da agricultura. *Revista de Política Agrícola* 21 (2): 45–63.
Alves, E.R.A., G.S. Souza, D.P. Rocha, and R. Marra. 2013. Fatos marcantes da agricultura brasileira. In *Contribuições da Embrapa para o desenvolvimento da agricultura no Brasil,* ed. E.R.A. Alves, G.S. Souza, and E.G. Gomes, 13–45. Brasília: Embrapa.

Ávila, A.F.D.; Souza, G.S. 2002. The Importance of Impact Assessment Studies for the Brazilian Agricultural Research System. Paper presented at the "International Conference on Impacts of Agricultural Research and Development: Why has impact assessment research not made more a difference?" San José (Costa Rica), February 4–7, 2002.

Ávila, A.F.D., G. Stachetti, and G.L.V. Rodrigues. 2008. *Avaliação dos impactos de tecnologias geradas pela Embrapa: metodologia de referência*, 189p. Embrapa Informação Tecnológica: Brasília.

Ávila, A.F.D., L. Romano, and F. Garagorry. 2010. Agricultural Productivity in Latin America and the Caribbean and Sources of Growth. In *Handbook of Agricultural Economics*, vol. 4, ed. P.L. Pingali and R.E. Evenson, 3713–3768. Amsterdam: Elsevier.

Bacha, C.J.C. 2004. *Economia e política agrícola no Brasil*, 226p. São Paulo: Atlas.

Baer, W. 2008. *The Brazilian economy*. 6th ed, 443p. Boulder: Lynne Rienner Publishers.

CNA. 2017. Confederação da Agricultura e Pecuária do Brasil. Boletim VBP. Edição 24, abril de 2017. Brasília: CNA. 3p.

Coelho, C. N. 2001. 70 anos de política agrícola no Brasil (1931–2001). *Revista de Política Agrícola* 10, edição especial, 2001.

Cunha, A.S., C.C. Mueller, E.R.A. Alves, and J.E. Silva. 1994. *Uma avaliação da sustentabilidade da agricultura nos cerrados*, 256 p. IPEA: Brasília.

Dobereiner J. Biological Nitrogen Fixation in the Tropics: Social and Economic Contributions. Soil Biology and Biochemistry, v. 29, p. 771–774, 1997.

Embrapa. 2014. *Visão 2014–2034: o futuro do desenvolvimento tecnológico da agricultura brasileira*, 194. Brasília: Embrapa.

Flaherty, K., Guiducci, R.C.N., Torres, D.P., Vedovoto, G.L., Ávila, A.F., and Perez, S. Brazil: Agricultural R&D Factsheet, 2016. Available at www.asti.cgiar.org/brazil.

Food and Agriculture Organization (FAO). 2000. *Land Resource Potential and Constraints at Regional and Country Levels*. World Soil Resources Report, 90. Rome: FAO.

Furtado, C. 2005. *Formação econômica do Brasil*. 32nd ed, 256p. São Paulo: Companhia Editora Nacional.

Gasques, J.G.; Bastos, E. T.; Bacchi, M. R. P. 2009. *Produtividade e Fontes de Crescimento da Agricultura*. Seminário IPEA, Brasília, 08 de junho de 2009.

Gasques, J.G., E.T. Bastos, M.R.P. Bacchi, and C. Valdes. 2010. Produtividade total dos fatores e transformações da agricultura brasileira: análise dos dados dos Censos Agropecuários. In *Agricultura Brasileira: Desempenho, Desafios e Perspectivas*, ed. J.G. Gasques, J.E.R. Vieira Filho, and Z. Navarro, 19–44. Brasília: IPEA.

Gremaud, A., M.A.S. Vasconcellos, and R. Toneto Jr. 2004. *Economia Brasileira Contemporânea*. 5th ed. Editora Atlas: São Paulo.

Hayami, Y., and V.W. Ruttan. 1985. *Agricultural Development: An International Perspective*. 2nd ed. Baltimore and London: John Hopkins Press.

Hurley, T.M., X. Rao, and P.G. Pardey. 2014. Reexamining the Reported Rates of Return to Food and Agricultural Research and Development. *American Journal of Agricultural Economics* 96: 1492–1504.

IBGE. Instituto Brasileiro de Geografia e Estatística. Área territorial brasileira. Available at < http://www.ibge.gov.br/home/geociencias/cartografia/default_territ_area.shtm >. Accessed on November 29th, 2016.

Lopes, M.A. 2012. The Brazilian Agricultural Research for Development (ARD) System. In *Improving Agricultural Knowledge and Innovation Systems: OECD Conference Proceedings*, 323–338. Paris: OECD.

Lopes, M.A., and G.B. Martha Jr. 2016. Embrapa: Development of Brazilian Agriculture. In *The Arab World and Latin America: Economic and Political Relations in the 21st Century*, ed. F. Saddy, 305–329. London: IB Tauris.

Maddison, A. 2011. Brazilian Development Experience from 1500 to 1929. Available at http://www.ggdc.net/maddison/ARTICLES/Brazil_1500-1929.pdf. Accessed on 15 Nov 2011.

Martha Jr., G.B., and E. Alves. 2017, forthcoming. Brazil's Agriculture Modernization and Embrapa. In *The Oxford Handbook of the Brazilian Economy*, ed. W. Baer, E. Amann, and C.R. Azzoni. New York: Oxford University Press.

Ministério do Meio Ambiente (MMA). 2017. Biomas. Available at http://www.mma.gov.br/biomas. Accessed on 24 Apr 2017.

OECD. 2005. *Oslo Manual: Guidelines for Collecting and Interpreting Innovation Data*. 3rd ed, 168p. Paris: OECD.

Pardey, P.G., J.M. Alston, C. Chan-Kang, E.C. Magalhães, and S.A. Vosti. 2006. International and Institutional R&D Spillovers: Attribution of Benefits Among Sources for Brazil's New Crop Varieties. *American Journal of Agricultural Economics* 88: 104–123.

Thorp, R. 1998. *Progress, Poverty and Exclusion: An Economic History of Latin America in the 20th Century*. Washington, DC: Inter-American Development Bank.

World Resource Institute (WRI). 2008. *World Resources 2008: The Roots of Resilience – Growing the Wealth of the Poor*. Washington, DC: WRI.

Public Agricultural Research and Its Contributions to Agricultural Productivity

Wallace E. Huffman

Abstract There is broad agreement about the importance of investments in public agricultural research and extension in the United States, but there is less agreement about the exact methods to be used in data collection, variable definitions, econometric model specification, and benefit-cost comparisons. This chapter reviews these issues and presents a summary and comparison of recent estimates of the rate of return to investments in US public agricultural research and extension. This chapter will be useful to graduate students, researchers, university administrators, and agricultural science policy advisors.

Introduction

In order to feed the growing population of the world, expected to reach 9.6 billion people by 2050—a 29% increase over 2013—without causing immense environmental damage and human hunger, society must increase agricultural productivity. Two ways of achieving this are to invest in public agricultural research and extension. The importance of investing in agricultural research worldwide is explicitly cited as a target of Goal 2 in the recently released United Nations Sustainable Development Goals (United Nations 2015). However, increased investments in public agricultural research have not always been forthcoming. Although agricultural extension frequently draws upon research results in communicating with farmers and agribusinesses, agricultural research and extension might be complements or substitutes for increasing agricultural productivity.

Developed countries like the United States have been leaders in science-based agricultural productivity increases since the middle of the twentieth century. Public, productivity-oriented agricultural research investment in the United States grew rapidly from 1960 to 1982 (see Fig. 1) but then declined over 1995–1998 by 20%. The trend then turned around, showing some growth to 2006 before declining again during the recent Great Recession. In contrast, since 2002 China has been rapidly

W.E. Huffman (✉)
Iowa State University, Ames, IA, USA
e-mail: whuffman@iastate.edu

© Springer International Publishing AG 2018

N. Kalaitzandonakes et al. (eds.), *From Agriscience to Agribusiness*, Innovation, Technology, and Knowledge Management, https://doi.org/10.1007/978-3-319-67958-7_22

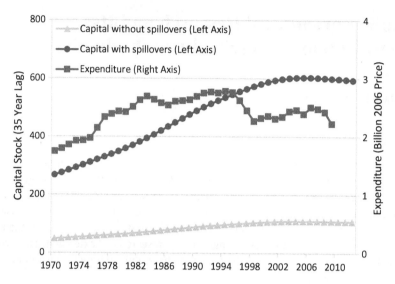

Fig. 1 Total public agricultural, productivity-oriented research expenditures, research capital, with and without spillovers, 48 US states, 1970–2011 (billion 2006 dollars)

increasing and Western Europe more modestly increasing its investments in agricultural research relative to the United States (OECD 2016, p. 216). These investments threaten to put future international competitiveness of US agricultural exports at risk. Furthermore, consumers worldwide will be worse off if future investments in public and private agricultural research and extension are not large enough to deliver declining real-world food prices in the twenty-first century.

The objective of this paper is to provide a review and assessment of the recent literature on the contributions of public agricultural research to US agricultural productivity. A number of important decisions underlie the agricultural productivity analysis and benefit-cost comparisons for public agricultural research and extension investments. They include identifying separate investments in agricultural research, which produce discoveries and inventions, and extension, which disseminates information to farmers and others; identifying investments that contribute to agricultural productivity growth and separating them from investments that promote other worthy causes but not TFP in agriculture; accounting for the benefits of investment in one location or farm practice, i.e., spillovers appropriate to the geo-climatic sensitivity of most agricultural technologies; identifying the separate lag lengths for public agricultural research and extension going into research and extension stock variables that explain state agricultural productivity; and employing the most appropriate metric for summarizing the payoffs to these investments. To produce high-quality information for those engaged in agricultural research and extension policy and administration, it is important that scholars guard against conceptual and measurement errors that distort estimates of returns to public agricultural research and extension.

Major Institutions that Undertake US Public Agricultural Research

In the United States, agricultural research and cooperative extension are separate public programs, each jointly funded primarily by the federal and state governments. Public agricultural research is undertaken primarily by state institutions—state agricultural experiment stations (SAESs) and colleges/schools of veterinary medicine. Federal institutions engaged in this activity are the US Department of Agriculture (USDA)'s Agricultural Research Service (ARS) and Economic Research Service (ERS). In addition, public agricultural research receives a small amount of funding from the private sector and from nongovernmental organizations, and pubic extension receives significant funding from county governments.

SAESs were established to conduct original research on agriculture, and the breadth of the research undertaken has increased over time. Although the early focus was on plant and animal diseases and insects and agricultural production, more recent research has included efforts to improve the rural home and rural life (starting in 1925), on agricultural marketing and resource conservation (starting in 1935), on forestry and wildlife habitat (starting in 1962), and on rural development (starting 1972) (Huffman and Evenson 1993). In addition, the veterinary medical colleges of the land-grant universities are state institutions that also conduct agricultural research, especially on the health of animals.

The breadth of research undertaken by the USDA also expanded over time, and new institutions to shepherd this work have been developed. For example, the Bureau of Home Economics was established (1924) to undertake home economics research. It was later named the Bureau of Human Nutrition and Home Economics (1943). In 1957, the Home Economics Division and Utilization Division, which focused on post-harvest agricultural research, were combined into one Nutrition, Consumer, and Industrial Uses Division (Huffman and Evenson 1993, p. 33). In addition, in 1940–1941, the USDA established four regional utilization laboratories or centers (Western in Albany, CA; Midwest in Peoria, IL; Southeastern in New Orleans, LA; and Northeastern in Wyndmoor, PA) to undertake research to develop new uses and new and extended markets and outlets for farm commodities and products. The goal was to increase demand for farm-produced products. Initially they were independent agencies, but in 1953 the USDA placed these labs under the administration of the ARS (USDA 2015). Currently, the research enterprise of the USDA is concentrated in the ARS and the ERS.

Since 1914, the USDA and land-grant universities have worked together to provide cooperative extension activities (Huffman and Evenson 2006b). Extension is primarily adult education for immediate decision-making by farmers, households, and communities and youth activities (Ahearn et al. 2003; Wang 2014; USDA 2016). Broadly, the goal has been to provide information for better farm, agribusiness, and home decision-making. The youth activities are comprised of "boy" and "girl" clubs, called "4-H" clubs, where members undertake practical projects in agriculture, home economics, and related subjects. In the 1960s, extension added programs in community development and natural resources.

Critical Measurement Issues

In developing measures of returns to investments in public agricultural research and extension delivery, economists address a variety of issues about data and methods. Four critical issues include (i) separating investments in research and extension that contribute to agricultural productivity growth from those that do not, (ii) accounting for the benefits of research undertaken in one location on farm practices that also get transferred to others, (iii) identifying the lagged effects of an annual investment in research and extension over multiple years, and (iv) employing the most appropriate metric for calculating returns to investments. In addition, it is important to think carefully about and identify defensible measures of benefits and costs. In particular, scholars should guard against creating measures of costs and benefits that contain obvious measurement errors.

Agricultural Productivity Investments

Since 1900, the USDA has provided gross measures of federal funding of its own agricultural research enterprise and that of the state agricultural experiment stations, which are under the control of the land-grant universities.[1] These aggregate data have been heavily used by Alston et al. (2010, 2011) and Anderson and Song (2013) in their state agricultural productivity analysis. However, data on investment in research by the colleges/schools of veterinary medicine only became available in the late 1960s.

As suggested in the previous section, by 1970, the intramural research of the USDA and the research of the SAES were much broader than in the first half of the twentieth century. In fact, it was much broader than what could reasonably be expected to impact US agricultural productivity. Hence, overestimates of costs and major measurement errors occur if gross expenditures on research of the federal and state agricultural research systems are used as the investments that contribute to agricultural productivity at the farm level.

In 1967, the USDA started to implement a new data collection system for detailed information on research projects of scientists working for the USDA in ARS and ERS, SAES, veterinary medical colleges, and affiliated institutions (Huffman and Evenson 1993).[2] The collected data include a description of each new project by the principal investigator—the commodity or resource (land, water, people) that is the target of the research and the research problem areas (RPAs), more recently labeled knowledge areas (KA)—and the state location of the research (USDA 2005, 2013). The range of research topics span traditional crop and livestock production, includ-

---

[1] However, two state agricultural experiment stations operate independently of the local land-grant universities. These are the ones at Geneva, NY, and New Haven, CT.

[2] This change was facilitated by major advances in computer storage and software.

ing biological efficiency, diseases, pests, and resources, but also forestry research, post-harvest research (food processing, agricultural marketing, and agricultural policy), rural and community development research, and home economics and human nutrition research (Huffman 2010, 2015).[3] These data were entered into the Current Research Information System (CRIS) along with annual funding of each project by source, summarized in the annual Inventory of Agricultural Research (USDA, 1971–2012).

Huffman and Evenson (1993) worked closely with representatives of the USDA and the Cooperative States Research Service in selecting among CRIS research problem areas and research commodities to obtain those that were likely to lead to discoveries that would increase agricultural productivity. Updated details on Huffman's work to revise, extend backward, and update the data on US productivity-oriented public agricultural research are summarized in Huffman (2010, 2015). Huffman (2010, 2015) estimated that in 1970, 70% of the US total expenditures on public agricultural research reported to CRIS were on agricultural productivity-oriented research. However, by 1990 the share invested in agricultural productivity-oriented public agricultural research had declined to 59% and in 2010 to only 50%. Hence, the gross measure of investments in public agricultural research is an over-estimate of the costs of advancing agricultural productivity. The difference and measurement error are large in 1970 and also growing over 1970–2010.

The federal, state, and county governments fund US public extension activities. Gross measures of resources going into cooperative extension extend back to 1915 and of agent and specialist time by major activity since 1924. Alston et al. (2010, 2011) have used gross expenditures on extension in their state agricultural productivity analysis. In contrast, Huffman and Evenson (1993, 2006a, b) and Jin and Huffman (2016) have used the adjusted measure of agricultural and resource extension in their state agricultural productivity analysis. This requires netting out resources allocated to other types of extension activities, such as home economics, community development, and 4-H. Over 1977–1992, only 55% of the gross investments in extension were for agricultural and natural resource extension.[4] In 2012, only 39% of cooperative extension expenditures were on agricultural and natural resource extension. Hence, gross expenditures on cooperative extension represent an overestimate of the costs of agricultural and natural resource extension that has an agricultural productivity focus. The measurement error from using the gross measure of extension is large and growing over time.

Should investments in public agricultural research and extension expenditures be aggregated together in each year and then converted into one R&E stock variable to explain agricultural productivity? Agricultural research and extension use different types of skilled labor and produce different products. Academic research requires

---

[3] In the United States, forestry is a minor activity on farms and ranches and generally excluded from agricultural productivity measures.

[4] In addition, in 1977, 30% of the gross investments in extension were allocated to 4-H (youth activities), but this share declined to 23% in 1992 and seemingly leveled off. The investment in these youth activities seems unlikely to contribute much to agricultural productivity.

Ph.D. degree level training to make scientific discoveries that increase agricultural productivity with a lag. In contrast, extension requires largely a BS or MS degree signifying the ability to interpret research results and complex food, resource, and environmental policies and then effectively communicate this information in bulletins, videos, and direct communication with nonscientists—farmers, agribusinesses, households, and others. Since the information environment of farmers' decision-making often changes rapidly, extension information has a short useful life compared to research discoveries reported in refereed publications and patents (Huffman and Evenson 1993; Ahearn et al. 2003; Wang 2014). Although extension frequently builds on research results, it is important to be able to estimate their separate but possibly interactive contribution to agricultural productivity, maintaining separate research and extension variables permitting separate benefit-cost analyses. The question of whether research and extension are complements or substitutes is important for public policy decision-making.

Should the research undertaken by state institutions and the USDA in the states be aggregated together or treated separately? Over 1920–1972, the USDA moved much of its intramural research out of the Washington, DC, area into field stations and research centers in various states. Many are located near land-grant university campuses. This close proximity of federal and state researchers has frequently facilitated joint research on locally and regionally important agricultural topics and problems. Hence, it makes little sense to try to estimate the separate impact of the USDA's own research and state-institution-administered public agricultural research on state agricultural productivity; this is the route taken by Huffman and Evenson (1993), Huffman and Evenson (2006b), and Huffman (2010, 2015). In contrast, Alston et al. (2010, 2011) and Anderson and Song (2013) create separate measures of intramural USDA research and SAES research.

Lags

As suggested above, public agricultural research and extension are inherently different types of activities. The goal of original research is discovery and invention followed by the development, testing, and marketing of new products and processes. This is a long-drawn-out process. In contrast, cooperative extension is primarily the dissemination of information about products, processes, markets, and policies that is an input into decision-making of farmers and others. This is an enterprise with a relatively short time lag from initiation to impact on farmers. Hence, public agricultural research and extension should not be aggregated together, and they should have different lag patterns. Huffman and Evenson (1993, 2006a, b) and Jin and Huffman (2016) are best known for making these distinctions. In contrast, Alston et al. (2010, 2011) aggregate gross expenditures on public agricultural and extension together in each year and then apply the same lag pattern to this heterogeneous aggregate.

It is widely accepted that the impact of public agricultural research on state agricultural productivity has a gestation period where the initial impact is negligible, then blossoms to full marginal impact, and later becomes obsolete. Jin and Huffman (2016) and Huffman and Evenson (2006a, b) approximate this pattern with a gestation period of 2 years, during which the impacts and timing weights are zero; the next 7 years, during which impacts and timing weights are rising; followed by 6 years of maturity, during which timing weights are high and constant; and then 20 years, during which impacts and timing weights decline and fade away to zero by the end of the period. Across this 35-year period, the timing weights sum to one (see Huffman and Evenson (2006b, p. 271)). This weighting pattern is known as trapezoidal-shaped timing weights, and it is used to translate real public agricultural research expenditures into a stock of public agricultural research capital for each state.[5]

In contrast, Alston et al. (2010, 2011) combine the gross measures of SAES research and extension within a state into one variable, creating a heterogeneous mixture of science and information, which they then convert into and label as "knowledge stocks." Hence, they apply the same long lag length of 50 years and pattern/timing weights (gamma distribution) to the combination of agricultural research and extension.[6] The gamma distribution that they use for converting flows into stocks is smoother than the pattern used by Huffman and Evenson (1993, 2006a, b) and Jin and Huffman (2016), but they have a similar shape with a gestation lag followed by increasing weights that peak more or less in the middle of the distribution and then fade away. However, the tail of the distribution is much longer in the Alston et al. (2010, 2011) and Anderson and Song (2013) weights.

Trends in Productivity-Oriented Public Research and Extension Capital

In Fig. 1, the green line shows that the total public, productivity-oriented agricultural research capital across the 48 US states—without spillovers—increased slowly from $47 billion in 1970 to $105 billion in 2006, an average rate of increase of 2.2% per year. The smooth path for research capital (green line) relative to research expenditures (purple line) is due to the long lags used to construct the research capital variable. After 2006, the US total public agricultural research capital began to decline slowly, being dragged down by the major break in total public agricultural research expenditures a decade earlier (See Fig. 1, red line). The US total public

---

[5] Since extension is largely information for current decision-making, 50% of its impacts—or timing weight—occurs within the year undertaken, and then the impact and weights decline to zero with obsolescence (See Huffman and Evenson 2006b, p. 272).

[6] In addition, they separate the USDA's own research, which is largely conducted in the states, from that of the state institutions. Also, they ignore the livestock research undertaken by the colleges of veterinary medicine.

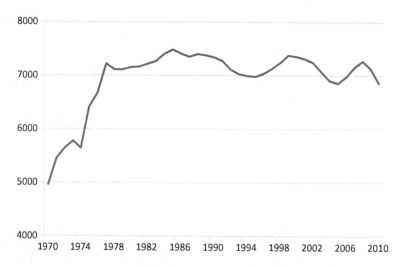

Fig. 2 Total public agricultural extension capital, 48 US states, 1970–2011 (full-time-equivalent staff-years per 1000 farms)

agricultural research capital across the 48 states, including each state's spillover component, is about five times larger than each state's own contribution (See Fig. 1, purple line). Hence, if public agricultural research expenditures in one state are increased by one dollar, on average, it increases the US total public agricultural research expenditures by an additional five dollars. With a lag, the effects of a long-term change in the growth rates of public agricultural research expenditures over time are revealed in public agricultural research capital, e.g., Fig. 1. Given the long research lags for public agricultural research capital and the major break in expenditures in public agricultural research that occurred in the mid-1990s and continuing, the public agricultural research capital will continue to decline well into the twenty-first century.

The US total public agricultural extension capital per farm grew very rapidly over 1970–1978 at 4.5% per year (Fig. 2).[7] Over the next 33 years, there is no net growth, although there have been short periods when the capital was increasing, for example, 1980–1986, 1996–2000, and 2005–2008. However, each of these short periods of growth has been offset by an almost equal decline. With total lag length being only 5 years for measuring public agricultural extension capital (vs. 35 for public agricultural research capital), downturns in agricultural extension capital can fairly quickly be reversed by increased expenditures on agricultural extension per farm.

---

[7] Of course there are differences across states. Jin and Huffman (2016) report trends for California, Iowa, North Carolina, and Texas.

Spillovers

Public agricultural research undertaken in one state produces discoveries that also spill over to the public and private agricultural research efforts in other states and to technologies available to farms and agribusinesses in other areas, i.e., that are an impure public good (Cornes and Sandler 1996). They can be represented by (1) similarity of agroecological zones, (2) output-mix similarities, or (3) geographical proximity. Agroecological zones are relatively homogeneous in geo-climates and ecology, but don't necessarily follow political boundaries. For example, in *Soils: The 1957 Yearbook of Agriculture*, Barnes (USDA, 1957, pp. 452–455) reports that US soils and climate follow definite regional patterns. Furthermore, geo-climates are a major factor in soil formations. Differences across regions are due to latitude, elevation, and worldwide movement of air masses. Major differences in soils across regions result from the climate under which the soils developed, the parent materials from which the soils developed, and the slope and drainage potential. Hence, across regions of the United States, major differences exist in climates, soils, and ecology. Since crop and livestock production are primarily open-air and open-field activities using the earth's surface, agricultural production and its associated problems are very much affected by local agroecological zones, such as in Fig. 3, which has 16

Legend:
1. Northeast Dairy Region
2. Middle Atlantic Coastal Plain
3. Florida and Coastal Flatwoods
4. Southern Uplands

5. East-Central Uplands
6. Midland Feed Region
7. Mississippi Delta
8. Northern Lake States

9. Northern Great Plains
10. Winter Wheat and Grazing Region
11. Coastal Prairies
12. Southern Plains

13. Grazing-Irrigated Region
14. Pacific Northwest Wheat Region
15. North Pacific Valleys
16. Dry Western Mild-Winter Region

Fig. 3 Geo-climatic region map (Source: Huffman and Evenson 1993)

geo-climatic regions and a number of subregions. This is the map used to define the potential for public agricultural research spillovers by Huffman and Evenson (2006a, b) and Jin and Huffman (2016).

Different producers of the same commodity frequently face similar technologies and some of the same production problems. For private manufacturing companies, Jaffe (1986) developed a spillover weight that is based on similarity of private-sector patent-based technology clusters, which are not strictly commodity based, to gauge interfirm private R&D spillovers on profits. However, all of his firms are engaged in enclosed and environmentally controlled environments, so the nature of the technology and production problems is relatively similar. A commodity similarity index for effects of public agricultural research conducted in one state on other states' agricultural productivity has been used by Alston et al. (2010, 2011) and Anderson and Song (2013). Because of the open-air, earth-surface-using nature of agricultural production, technology choice and production problems may follow geo-climates more closely than commodity-mix attributes. For example, consider milk production on dairy farms in Wisconsin under relatively small-scale silage-grazing herds versus large-scale hay-based confined desert milk production on large dairy farms of California and Arizona. Although they are producing a similar product and using dairy cows to do this, their production problems are quite different.

When areas are close to one another, geographical proximity, as in shared state boundaries, reduces the physical distance that discoveries and information must travel before they can be used by farmers and agribusiness in another area. This reduces one dimension of the costs of information transfers. For example, discoveries made by public agricultural research in Iowa on corn can easily travel to agribusinesses and farmers in Illinois and southern Minnesota. This is the type of method for measuring public agricultural research spillovers used by Plastina and Fulginiti (2012). However, this type of spillover effect would most likely exclude the benefits of public corn research conducted in Iowa on Indiana and Ohio farms and agribusinesses, even though these states have a large area in the same geo-climatic zone (Fig. 3). Hence, across these three methods of measuring spillover benefits of public agricultural research, the use of agroecological zones represents a middle-ground solution between geographical proximity, as in shared state boundaries, and commodity-mix similarity, irrespective of distance and similar geo-climatic region. Hence, we prefer the one using agroecological zones.

Typical Empirical TFP-Research Stock Relationship

In the field of state agricultural productivity analysis, a log-log productivity function is widely used (Huffman and Evenson 1993, 2006a, b; Alston et al. 2011; Andersen and Song 2013).[8] For example, consider the model in the latest

---

[8] The other primary approach is a cost function model, e.g., Yee et al. (2002), Plastina and Fulginiti (2012), and Wang et al. (2012).

study—Jin and Huffman (2016). Agricultural productivity in state i and year t is represented as follows:

$$\ln\left(\mathrm{TFP}\right)_{it} = \beta_1 + \beta_2 \ln R\left(m\right)_{it} + \beta_3 \ln S\left(m,r\right)_{it} + \beta_4 \ln \mathrm{EXT}\left(q\right)_{it}$$

$$+\beta_5 \left[\ln R\left(m\right)_{it}^{*} \ln \mathrm{EXT}\left(q\right)_{it}\right] + \sum_{K}^{k=1} \delta_k D_k + \tau t + \mu_{it}, \mu_{it} \qquad (1)$$

$$= \rho \mu_{it} + \varepsilon_{it}, \, i = 1,\ldots,n, t = 1,\ldots,T,$$

where total factor productivity, TFP, is a ratio of the quantity index for farm outputs divided by a quantity index for farm inputs under the control of farmers, $R(m)_i$ is the within-state public agricultural research capital with a lag length of m, and $S(m,r)_i$ is the interregional public agricultural research spill-in capital of (S).[9] Hence, lag lengths for R and S are assumed to be the same, i.e., we use the stock of public agricultural research capital for each state in a geo-climatic region to construct the regional research stock spillover/spill-in variable.[10] The agricultural extension capital is represented by $EXT(q)_i$ with lag length q.[11]

To capture unmeasured effects of private R&D, a time trend is included in (1). It also effectively de-trends the dependent variable and all of the explanatory variables or regressors (Enders 2010; Wooldridge 2013). This is necessary to be able to draw causal inference.[12] In addition, de-trended time series have less autocorrelation and are more likely to be trend stationary (Enders 2010). Other controls in (1) are dummy variables for regions composed of groups of states, D_k. They reflect some of the regional nature in ARS decision-making on projects and regional nature of some of the formula funding for state agricultural research institutions. A variable representing the stock of private agricultural research would be included if a reliable one were available at the state level. Huffman and Evenson (2006a) found that a private agricultural research stock variable created from the state-level patent data of Johnson and Brown (2002) was not statistically significant once a linear trend was included in the ln(TFP) econometric model. This made the estimates in Huffman and Evenson (2006b) somewhat obsolete. Hence, private R&D capital was not

---

[9] With lags of significant length, including expenditures rather than capital as regressors leads to estimated coefficients on successive lags that tend to oscillate in sign and be statistically weak and are impossible to rationalize. Griliches (2000) suggests that it is useful in these situations to impose some structure on the lag pattern. Since we do not know the "true" lag pattern, we are involved in constructing plausible proxy variables for stocks (Greene 2003).

[10] One could use different lag lengths for constructing within-state and spillover research stock variables. That issue might be useful to pursue in the future.

[11] Due to the very applied nature and high rate of obsolescence of agricultural extension information, Huffman and Evenson (2006a, 2006b) and Jin and Huffman (2016) ignore any interstate spillovers for agricultural extension.

[12] Ignoring the fact that two series are trending in the same or opposite directions can lead to a false conclusion that changes in one variable are actually caused by changes in another variable (Wooldridge 2013; Enders 2010). In many cases, two time series processes appear to be correlated, only because they are both trending over time for reasons related to other unobserved factors.

included in Huffman's research on agricultural productivity going forward. Other factors are included in the random disturbance term, μ_{it}.[13] As is common with annual time series data, the random disturbance term follows a first-order autoregressive process, with $0 < \rho < 1$.[14] However, Jin and Huffman (2016) also estimate Eq. (1) permitting each state to have a separate estimate for ρ.

The elasticity of productivity with respect to R, S, and EXT is useful in computing the marginal product and rate of return to investments in these activities. Starting with Eq. (1), they are summarized in Eqs. (2)–(4):

$$\partial \ln(\text{TFP})/\partial \ln(R) = \beta_2 + \beta_5 \ln(\text{EXT}) \tag{2}$$

$$\partial \ln(\text{TFP})/\partial \ln(S) = \beta_3 \tag{3}$$

$$\partial \ln(\text{TFP})/\partial \ln(\text{EXT}) = \beta_4 + \beta_5 \ln(R) \tag{4}$$

The total impact of public agricultural research on state agricultural productivity is obtained by substituting (2) and (3) into Eq. (5):

$$d\ln(\text{TFP}) = \left[\partial \ln(\text{TFP})/\partial \ln(R)\right] d\ln(R) + \left[\partial \ln(\text{TFP})/\partial \ln(S)\right] d\ln(S) \tag{5}$$

For a 1% increase in R and S, Eq. (5) reduces to the summation of the two elasticities in Eqs. (2) and (3).

Research by Huffman and Evenson (2006a) and Jin and Huffman (2016) show that the logarithm of stocks of public agricultural research and extension explains significantly the logarithm of state agricultural productivity over 1970–1999 and 1970–2004, respectively. In addition, they find strong statistical evidence that public, productivity-oriented agricultural research and extension are substitutes and not complements. Other US studies, e.g., Alston et al. (2010, 2011), Plastina and Fulginiti (2012), and Anderson and Song (2013), do not provide any empirical evidence on this latter issue. The estimate of the coefficient of trend reported by Jin and Huffman (2016) is 0.011, once autocorrelation of disturbances is permitted, i.e., trended factors contribute an average of 1.1% per year to TFP growth over 1970–2004. They suggest that private agricultural R&D, which is an excluded variable but

---

[13] This model does not include a measure of stochastic spatial correlation of spillovers. In private communication, Wayne Fuller suggested to me that spillover effects and stochastic spatial effects are most likely related. For example, an error in defining spillover regions could make the disturbances appear to be spatially correlated. More likely, however, is that plausible spillover measures dramatically reduce and perhaps eliminate significant stochastic spatial correlation.

[14] With 33 (or even 50) observations per state, Wayne Fuller does not recommend unit root tests for short time series (Dickey and Fuller 1979) because the test statistic has only good large sample properties and 33 or 50 observations are not large. Moreover, in small samples, he suggests that these unit root tests are unreliable, tending to create confusion.

crudely represented by a linear trend, may be a major contributor to state agricultural productivity.[15]

The Metric for Cost-Benefit Analysis

Social cost-benefit analysis provides important metrics for comparing alternative public investments. Potential methods include summarizing projects by the real, inflation-adjusted social internal rates of return and the net present values or benefit-cost (B/C) ratio. To compute the net present value and B/C ratio, additional arbitrary information is needed beyond that which is needed for an internal rate of return (IRR) computation. This information is the social opportunity costs of public funds, i.e., the interest or discount rate, in each year of the life of the investment project. Moreover, there is no reason to believe that these interest/discount rates are the same in each year of the project (Harberger 1972, pp. 29–30; Just et al. 2004, pp. 580–581). Hence, the B/C ratio is very sensitive to the choice of the discount rate.[16] In addition, Evenson (2001, pp. 605–606) discusses common problems in interpreting B/C ratios for public agricultural research.

In ln(TFP) linear econometric models, the value of the marginal product can be evaluated at the sample mean and then distributed over time using the timing weights—determined by the research lag length and pattern—and then discount benefits back to the current period, e.g., see Yee et al. (2002).[17]

However, Alston et al. (2011) argued that there are conceptual problems in this calculation because the benefits really could not be invested in another project, but most surprising is that they do not consider additional investments in public agricultural research and extension, which would lead them to estimate the traditional IRR. In addition, their concerns vanish once we take a slightly different perspective on the IRR computation. Given Eq. (1), including the timing weights $\omega_i s$, where $0 \leq \omega_i < 1$, $\sum_m^{i=0} \omega_i = 1$, and spillover patterns, e.g., Fig. 3, the IRR to an incremental investment in public agricultural research, say $1 million, can also be obtained by solving Eq. (6) for r:

---

[15] Another interpretation is that it is just a summary indicator of the differences in the trend in the dependent variable less the contribution of trend in the explanatory variables in Eq. (1). See Enders (2010) and Wooldridge (2013).

[16] In developing countries where rates of inflation may be high and variable and government budget constraints are severe, it becomes difficult to obtain a defensible measure of the real discount rates for evaluating investments in public agricultural research and extension.

[17] Because the relevant productivity elasticities used in these computations have their narrowest confidence interval at the sample mean of the data, this is an advantageous place to perform the evaluation. Evaluations of marginal products at each point of the data set suffer from the fact that the confidence interval differs for each point, being generally much larger at the beginning and end of the series. This type of evaluation seems unnecessary in a linear model of state agricultural productivity.

$$-1\left[\sum_{m}^{i=0}\omega_i/(1+r)^i\right]^{-1}+\left[\left(\overline{\partial\ln\left(\text{TFP}\right)}/\partial\ln\left(R\right)\right)\frac{\overline{Q}}{\overline{R}}+\left(N-1\right)\left(\overline{\partial\ln\left(\text{TFP}\right)}/\partial\ln\left(S\right)\right)\frac{\overline{Q}}{\overline{S}}\right]=0$$

(6)

$\overline{Q}$ is the mean annual value of gross agricultural output at the state level, $\overline{R}$ is mean within-state stock of public agricultural research, and $(N-1)$ is the average number of states into which public agricultural research spillover benefits flow. $\overline{S}$ is mean public agricultural research capital spillovers. In Eq. (6), r is the uniform interest rate that the project could pay on the distribution of repayments of the investment of $1 billion distributed over the next m years, given the timing weights, and as represented by the first set of terms in brackets in Eq. (6). This repayment supports the marginal payoff at $t=0$, i.e., the second set of terms in the bracket to the right of the plus (+) sign in Eq. (6). Hence, r is the interest rate that the project could pay and still have a net present value of zero (Harberger 1972). When costs and benefits are in constant dollars, and benefits include interstate spillover effects, a real social IRR obtains.[18,19]

For computing the real IRR for a $1 million investment in agricultural extension distributed over m' years, the computation is simpler because there is no interstate spillover effect included in (1):

$$-1\left[\sum_{m'}^{i=0}\omega_i'/(1+r)^i\right]^{-1}+\left[\left(\overline{\partial\ln\left(\text{TFP}\right)}/\partial\ln\left(\text{EXT}\right)\right)\frac{\overline{Q}}{\overline{\text{EXT}}}\right]=0$$

(7)

where $\overline{\text{EXT}}$ is the sample mean value of EXT and r' is the IRR to an incremental investment in agricultural extension. The ω_i' s are the usual time weight for benefits. Eqs. (6) and (7) show that the current payoff to public agricultural research (extension) can only be obtained by having an ongoing long-term public agricultural research (extension) program.

---

[18] Even though politicians may like sound bites that B/C ratios can generate, they are more problematic than IRR estimates. In computing the B/C ratio, one must have an estimate of the social opportunity costs of funds (interest rate) in each year of the project. Harberger (1972, pp. 29–30) discusses how it is difficult to do this accurately. Moreover, it is extremely arbitrary to assign a single value to this social opportunity funds for every year of the project, e.g., 3%, and it would make a big difference if the rate were twice this large for more distant dates. Evenson (2001, pp. 605–606) discusses some common problems in interpreting B/C ratios, including the gross misinterpretation of Griliches (1958) estimate of the B/C ratio for hybrid corn research.

[19] The use of Eq (6) above or Eq. (7) in Huffman and Evenson (2006a) leads to the same IRR.

Comparisons of Payoffs to Public Agricultural Research in Recent US Studies

It is useful to compare the payoff to public agricultural research. We chose studies for the United States published between 2006 and 2016. The most common metric is the IRR, and this is the one that I will focus on. Table 1 summarizes six such studies, ordered from most recent date published to earlier ones. Among the information provided is the type of analysis undertaken (TFP vs. variable cost), unit of observation (states vs. national level), time period covered in the statistical analysis, whether a gross or net measure of public agricultural research is used, the lag length for creating stocks of public research and extension, and an estimate of the IRR from investing in public agricultural research and extension.

The Plastina and Fulginiti (2012) study uses gross measures of public agricultural research and obtains real social IRR estimates of 29%. They do not include extension as an explanatory variable, which would tend to bias their estimates

Table 1 Estimates of real internal rates of return (IRR) to public agricultural research and extension in the United States

Source (year)	Type of analysis	Unit of obs	Time period covered	Public ag research		Public ag extension		Real social IRR	
				Type	Lag length	Type	Lag length	Ag research	Ag extension
Jin and Huffman (2016)	TFP	States	1970–2004	Net	35 yrs	Net	4 yrs	67%	> 100%
Andersen and song (2013)	TFP	United States	1949–2002	Gross	50 yrs	Gross	50 yrs	21%	Mix[a]
Wang et al. (2012)	Var cost	States	1980–2004	Net	35 yrs	Gross	None	45%	No Est[b]
Alston et al. (2011)	TFP	States	1949–2002	Gross	50 yrs	Gross	50 yrs	23%	Mix[a]
Plastina and Fulginiti (2012)	Var cost	States	1949–1991	Gross	31 yrs	None included		29%[c]	None
Huffman and Evenson (2006b)	TFP	States	1970–1999	Net	35 yrs	Net	4 yrs	49%	> 100%

[a]Expenditures on public agricultural research and extension are aggregated together in each year before creating one single stock variable. Hence, separate estimates of the IRR to public agricultural research and extension are impossible
[b]No estimate of IRR is computed
[c]The range of IRR estimates across the 48 states is 8–37%

upward, but not likely as much as the downward bias caused by using a gross rather than net measure of public agricultural research. In these studies, the gross measure of agricultural research likely overestimates the cost by roughly 30%.

In contrast, Wang et al. (2012), Huffman and Evenson (2006a), and Jin and Huffman (2016) use net measures of agricultural productivity-oriented public agricultural research to explain TFP or variable cost, and they obtain IRR estimates to public agricultural research of 45%, 49%, and 67%, respectively, which are significantly larger than the Plastina and Fulginite (2010).[20]

Huffman and Evenson (2006a) and Jin and Huffman (2016) use a net measure of agricultural extension investment and assume that 50% of the impact occurs in the current period and the other 50% is distributed over the following 4 years. Evidence for a very short lag includes the impact of extension on farmers' adoption decisions (Huffman 1974, 1977, 1981; Rahm and Huffman 1984). They report an estimate of the IRR to agricultural and natural resource extension of over 100%. Wang et al. (2012) use a gross measure of extension and assume that all of the impact of this extension on agricultural productivity occurs in the year that it is invested. Although they find that agricultural extension significantly reduces variable cost, they do not provide an estimate of the rate of return to public extension.

In contrast, Alston et al. (2011) and Andersen and Song (2013) have chosen a gross unadjusted measure of public agricultural research and extension, but to further complicate B/C analysis comparisons, they also attempt to estimate separate impacts of the USDA's intramural agricultural research, which is largely conducted in the various states, and SAES research. In addition, they exclude the livestock research undertaken by the state colleges/schools of veterinary medicine from their public agricultural research stock variable. Their methods for defining "Knowledge Stocks" were described above, including that they add together expenditures of SAES research and extension in each state before applying a 50-year time lag with weights distributed as a gamma distribution. The result is that they cannot produce separate estimates of the IRR to public agricultural research and extension.

Although Alston et al. (2011) report a number of estimates of the IRR and B/C ratios, their IRR that is most comparable to those reported by Huffman and Evenson (2006a) and Jin and Huffman (2016), except that it is for a heterogeneous mixture of SAES research and extension, is 22.7% (Table 1).[21] Compared to studies that used net measures of public agricultural research of federal and state institutions, this IRR is significantly lower as expected, as it overestimates costs and underesti-

---

[20] The difference in the estimate of the IRR to productivity-oriented public agricultural research reported in Huffman and Evenson (2006a) and Jin and Huffman (2016) is due to a significant revision of the public agricultural research expenditure data set occurring over 2009–2010 (see Huffman 2010, 2015). The largest change came about in the methods used to extend public agricultural research expenditures backward over 1935–1970. This revision most likely reduced measurement error, which increased the estimated impact of public agricultural research on agricultural productivity. The panel of states was also extended 5 years to include 2000–2004.

[21] They also report what they call a marginal IRR of 10%, but it arbitrarily includes only 3% of the estimated benefits; the argument for doing this is not convincing, as mentioned above.

mates benefits.[22] Hence, differences in estimates of the IRR to investments in public agricultural research arise because of the use of different measurement and methods used to construct the public agricultural research and extension stock variables. The low estimates reported in Table 1 seem to be the result of overestimating the costs and underestimating the benefits due, especially due to attenuation bias in estimated TFP models caused by measurement errors (Fuller 1987).

However, all of the IRRs reported in Table 1 are largely relative to a 2–5% long-term real rate of return on stocks and bonds traded in major financial markets.

Conclusions

Given the long time lags between costs and benefits for public agricultural research, the decline in US public agricultural research capital starting in the mid-1990s will be a drag on US agricultural productivity for more than the first quarter of the twenty-first century. While the potential losses from that past decline in public research investment cannot be recovered, it is uplifting to recognize that more immediate productivity gains can be obtained from investing in agricultural extension. The importance of investment in agricultural research is widely recognized. Given this unusually large degree of agreement on a public policy issue, perhaps the United States is poised to increase its investment in public agricultural research and extension and thereby ensure a prosperous agricultural sector and continued low food prices for consumers in the future while reducing soil, water, and air pollution.

Future scholars undertaking studies of the estimates of the rate of return to public investments in agricultural research and extension can benefit from measurement issues discussed in this paper. First, it is important to think carefully about and identify plausible benefits and costs of each of these activities. In particular, one should guard against creating variables that contain obvious forms of measurement error, such as inaccurately measuring the costs and/or benefits or aggregating public agricultural research and extension together. Second, econometric analysis should be used where possible to estimate the impact of public agricultural research and extension stocks on aggregate TFP or variable cost. Since successful estimation of coefficients of logarithmic TFP models requires considerable variation in TFP and of the research and extension stocks, a sample size of most likely more than 300 observations is required. Hence, econometric analysis of national aggregate TFP data is not likely to be fruitful.[23] Furthermore, when research and extension are separate explanatory variables in these studies, it is possible to test whether they are

---

[22] Another complication is that they provide a separate estimate of the IRR from investing in intramural research of the USDA. In Alston et al. (2010, p. 1274), they report an estimate of 18.7%.

[23] Some of the limitations of a small sample can be seen by comparing the estimated model of ln(*TFP*) using national aggregate data by Wang et al. (2013) relative to those using state-level data (Alston et al. 2010, 2011; Huffman and Evenson 2006a; Jin and Huffman 2016).

complements or substitutes. Third, the benefit-cost ratio is not a reliable summary statistic for summarizing the economic payoff to investment in public agricultural research and extension.

References

Ahearn, M., Yee, J., and Bottom, J. 2003. Regional Trends in Extension System Resources. USDA, ERS Agricultural Information Bulletin No. 781, April.

Alston, J.M., M.A. Anderson, J.S. James, and P.G. Pardey. 2010. *Persistence Pays: U.S. Agricultural Productivity Growth and the Benefits from Public R&D Spending*. New York: Springer.

———. 2011. The Economic Returns to U.S. Public Agricultural Research. *American Journal of Agricultural Economics* 93: 1257–1277.

Anderson, M.A., and W. Song. 2013. The Economic Impact of Public Agricultural Research and Development in the United States. *Agricultural Economics* 44: 287–295.

Cornes, R., and T. Sandler. 1996. *The Theory of Externalities, Public Goods and Club Goods*. New York: Cambridge University Press.

Dickey, D., and W.A. Fuller. 1979. Distribution of the Estimates for Autoregressive Time Series with a Unit Root. *Journal of the American Statistical Association*. 74: 427–431.

Enders, W. 2010. *Applied Econometric Time Series*. 3rd ed. New York: Wiley.

Evenson, R.E. 2001. The Impacts of Agricultural Research and Extension. In *Handbook of Agricultural Economics, Vol 1A (Agricultural Production)*, ed. B.L. Gardner and G.C. Rausser, 574–628. New York: Elsevier.

Fuller, W.A. 1987. *Measurement Error Models*. New York: Wiley.

Greene, W.H. 2003. *Econometric Analysis*. 5th ed. Upper Saddle River: Prentice Hall.

Griliches, Z. 1958. Research Costs and Social Returns: Hybrid Corn and Related Innovations. *Journal of Political Economy* 66: 419–431.

———. 2000. *R&D, Education and Productivity*. Cambridge, MA: Harvard University Press.

Harberger, A.C. 1972. *Project Evaluation*. Chicago: Markham Publishing Co.

Huffman, W.E. 1974. Decision Making: The Role of Education. *American Journal of Agricultural Economics* 56: 85–97.

———. 1977. Allocative Efficiency: The Role of Human Capital. *Quarterly Journal of Economics* 91: 59–80.

———. 1981. Black-White Human Capital Differences: Impact on Agricultural Productivity in the U.S. South. *American Economic Review* 71: 104–118.

———. 2010. Measuring Public Agricultural Research Capital and Its Contribution to State Agricultural Productivity. Iowa State University, Department of Economics Working Paper #09022, August.

———. 2015. Measuring Public Agricultural Research Capital and Its Contributions to State Agricultural Productivity. In *Innovations, Technology and Economic Development: Essays in Honor of Robert E. Evenson*, ed. K.J. Joseph, D. Johnson, and L. Singh, 107–146. New Delhi/Thousand Oaks: SAGE Publications India Pvt Ltd.

Huffman, W.E., and R.E. Evenson. 1993. *Science for Agriculture: A Long-Term Perspective*. Ames: Iowa State University Press.

———. 2006a. Do Formula or Competitive Grant Funds have Greater Impacts on State Agricultural Productivity? *American Journal of Agricultural Economics*. 88: 783–798.

———. 2006b. *Science for Agriculture: A Long-Term Perspective*. Ames: Blackwell Publishing.

Jaffe, A.B. 1986. Technology Opportunity and Spillovers of R&D: Evidence from Firm's Patents, Profits, and Market Value. *American Economic Review* 76: 984–1001.

Jin, Y., and W.E. Huffman. 2016. Measuring Public Agricultural Research and Extension and Estimating their Impacts on Agricultural Productivity: New Insights from U.S. Evidence. *Agricultural Economics* 47: 15–31.

Johnson, D.K.N., and A. Brown. 2002. Patents Granted in U.S. for Agricultural SOV, by State of Inventor, 1963-1999. In *Wellesley College*. Wellesley: Department of Economics Working Paper.

Just, R.E., D.L. Hueth, and A. Schmitz. 2004. *The Welfare Economics of Public Policy*. Northampton: Edward Elgar

OECD. 2016. Innovation, Agricultural Productivity and Sustainability in the United States. OECD Food and Agricultural Reviews. OECD Paris.

Plastina, A., and L. Fulginiti. 2012. Rates of Return to Public Agricultural Research in 48 US States. *Journal of Productivity Analysis*. 37: 95–113.

Rahm, M., and W.E. Huffman. 1984. The Adoption of Reduced Tillage: The Role of Human Capital and Other Variables. *American Journal of Agricultural Economics* 66: 405–413.

United Nations. 2015. The 2030 Agenda for Sustainable Development. Available online: https://sustainabledevelopment.un.org/sdg2.

USDA. 1957. *Soils: the 1957 Yearbook of Agriculture*. Washington, DC: U.S. Government Printing Office.

———. 1971–2012. *CSRS/CRIS Inventory of Agricultural Research, Fiscal Years 1970–2011*. Beltsville: USDA-CSRS.

———. 2005. *Manual of Classification of Agricultural and Forestry Research*. Revision VII. Beltsville: USDA-NIFA.

———. 2013. *Manual of Classification of Agricultural and Forestry Research*. Revision VIII. Beltsville: USDA-NIFA.

———. 2015. ARS Utilization Centers' 75th Anniversary. Ag Research Magazine. Oct. Available at: http://agresearchmag.ars.usda.gov/2015/oct/anniversary

———. 2016. *USDA Research, Education, and Economic Information System, 4-H Overview*. Available at: https://reeis.usda.gov/reports-anddocuments/4-h-reports/overview.

Wang, S.L. 2014. Cooperative Extension System: Trends and Economic Impacts on U.S. Agriculture. Choices. Quarter 1. Available online: http://choicesmagazine.org/choices-magazine/submitted-article/cooperative-extension-system-tend-and-economic-impacts-on-us-agriculture

Wang, S.L., V.E. Ball, L.E. Fulginiti, and L.E. Plastina. 2012. Accounting for the Impact of Local and Spill-in Public Research, Extension and Roads on U.S. Regional Agricultural Productivity, 1980-2004. In *Productivity Growth in Agriculture: An International Perspective*, ed. K.O. Fuglie, S.L. Wang, and V.E. Ball, 13–32. Cambridge, MA: CABI.

Wang, S.L., P.W. Heisey, W.E. Huffman, and K.O. Fuglie. 2013. Public R&D, Private R&D, and US Agricultural Productivity Growth: Dynamic and Long-Run Relationships. *American Journal of Agricultural Economics* 95: 157–185.

———. 2013. *Introductory Econometrics: A Modern Approach*. 5th ed. Mason: South-Western Cengage Learning.

Yee, J., W.E. Huffman, M. Ahearn, and D. Newton. 2002. Sources of Agricultural Productivity Growth at the State Level, 1960-1993. In *Agricultural Productivity: Measurement and Sources of Growth*, ed. V.E. Ball and G.W. Norton, 187–209. Norwell: Kluwer Academic Publishers.

A Bayesian Measure of Research Productivity

Lin Qin and Steven T. Buccola

Abstract We use Bayesian probability theory to develop a new way of measuring research productivity. The metric accommodates a wide variety of project types and productivity sources and accounts for the contributions of "failed" as well as "successful" investigations. Employing a mean-absolute-deviation loss functional form with this new metric allows decomposition of knowledge gain into an outcome probability shift (mean surprise) and outcome variance reduction (statistical precision), a useful distinction, because projects scoring well on one often score poorly on the other. In an international aquacultural research program, we find laboratory size to moderately boost mean surprise but have no effect on precision, while scientist education improves precision but has no effect on mean surprise. Returns to research scale are decreasing in the size dimension but increasing when size and education are taken together, suggesting the importance of measuring human capital at both the quantitative and qualitative margin.

Introduction

The centrality of research to economic growth begs for rigorous, practical methods of assessing scientific knowledge. Now occupying 2.8% of US gross domestic product, R&D is nearly universally regarded to be essential to continued economic health (Industrial Research Institute 2016). At country, institution, program, and scientist levels, however, research administrators are continually asked to demonstrate R&D's benefits over costs. That would require understanding not only the net

This chapter is an abbreviated and edited version of the article entitled "Knowledge Measurement and Productivity in a Research Program" published in the *American Journal of Agricultural Economics* 99 (4): 932–951.

L. Qin
comScore, Inc., Reston, VA, USA

S.T. Buccola (✉)
Oregon State University, Corvallis, OR, USA
e-mail: sbuccola@oregonstate.edu

© Springer International Publishing AG 2018   465
N. Kalaitzandonakes et al. (eds.), *From Agriscience to Agribusiness*, Innovation,
Technology, and Knowledge Management, https://doi.org/10.1007/978-3-319-67958-7_23

Fig. 1 Stages of the research and dissemination process

benefits themselves but how they are influenced by research goals, analytical strategies, scientist recruitment, and management.

The cost side of R&D assessment follows much the same protocol as in any other enterprise. The main problem is with the knowledge outputs, which are resistive of statistical simplification, difficult to track once released, and only indirectly observable. Research effort and productivity response, furthermore, begin well before and continue well after the easily observable research activities and include problem inception and funding; observations and testing; writing and presenting; and the scientific, administrative, and industrial uses to which the research will be put. Because each phase represents a certain "production," each can be the object of productivity evaluation. Figure 1 depicts a simplified schema of these production stages, emphasizing applied research.[1] The first is the research project itself, the second its communication, and the third its economic impacts.

Although distinctions among the three are ambiguous in actual situations, they are valuable for understanding the differences among research evaluation methods. Economic surplus methods focus on the economic impact stage, examining the net relationships between research expenditures and subsequent industry productivity. A virtue of the surplus approach is that because expenditures are dual to and therefore reflect research design, management, and communication, they afford an efficient, statistically unbiased focus on the bottom line – economic gains (White and Havlicek 1982; Alston et al. 1995; Huffman and Evenson 2006; Alston et al. 2011; Hurley et al. 2014). A largely separate bibliometric literature concentrates on the communication phase, especially on relationships between research funding and directly observable outputs – patent counts and citations if intellectual property markets are present (Hall et al. 2005; Fontana et al. 2013), publication counts and citations they are if not (Pardey 1989; Adams and Griliches 1996; Oettl 2012). The bibliometric approach offers a more refined view of the transmission of scientific ideas than economic surplus can.

Despite their analytical power in the purposes for which they were designed, neither of these two approaches is positioned to look very far into the laboratory itself. Neither therefore is very suitable for assessing individual projects nor the factors like research topic, laboratory resources, and management policies affecting the research programs under which they are organized. It would be useful then to

---

[1] Basic research cannot as easily be divided into Fig. 1's steps or into any regular steps at all. We note below the important differences between basic research and the applied research that motivates our present approach.

examine the possibility of a research output metric helpful for that purpose. Like a case study, the metric would require insights and data from the principal investigators (Polanyi 1974; Schimmelpfennig and Norton 2003; Shapira et al. 2006). Unlike a case study, it would be expressible in a manner that can be readily compared across projects and programs. The metric must, in particular, be flexible enough to accommodate a variety of project topics, methods, and settings, while suitable for pooling into an econometric model of research outputs and inputs. It must, for example, overcome the problems of distinguishing program from nonprogram influences on research success.

We develop such a metric here by deriving a scientific knowledge measure reflective of individual laboratory, treatment, and control conditions but useful for the administration of heterogeneous applied research projects in a variety of technical and institutional settings. We use the approach to investigate the knowledge returns to an international aquacultural research program involving, over a 4-year span, 55 studies in 16 nations, showing how returns vary by research team characteristics, scale, topic area, analytical approach, and outcome dimension. To be useful for these purposes, the metric must be capable of comparison with the factors hypothesized to influence it. Much of our effort therefore is devoted to accommodating and exploiting cross-study heterogeneity in a research program.

A Direct Approach to Scientific Knowledge Measurement

A knowledge metric accounting adequately for research program discovery would satisfy at least three requirements. It should be (a) ratio-scale comparable across the studies investigated (i.e., contain a meaningful zero point); (b) ex-ante in the sense of conditional on the anticipation of future significant R&D events; and (c) reflective of all new knowledge a study provides, regardless of whether it achieved its most ambitious goals or outperformed an earlier study in some positive respect. The ratio-scale cardinality in criterion (a) assures that statements such as "Project A provided twice as much knowledge as Project B" will be valid. Criterion (b) assures that findings will be evaluated in a way conformable to their usefulness in specific future applications. Criterion (c) assures that research "failures" be counted with potentially the same weight as "successes." A treatment's failure to outperform an old one does not imply efforts have been wasted: the disappointment was potentially valuable in pointing to more fruitful research directions (CGIAR Science Council 2009). Sufficient for satisfying these criteria is that research success should be evaluated in terms of the information it offers about the probabilities of treatment outcomes, expressed as a shifting or narrowing of the outcome probability distribution in the face of alternative settings.

Bayesian reasoning is well-suited to criterion (b) as well as (c) because it considers knowledge in terms of improvements in the predictability of unknown future outcomes (Lindley 1956; Winkler 1986, 1994). A valid experiment or survey can never reduce our forecast ability and generally will improve it. To see this, consider the prospective user, a fish farmer say, of a clinical study to predict the efficacy of a fish vaccine. We want to know how much the farmer would gain from vaccination decisions or regime based on research forecasts of their effect on fish mortality and, therefore, eventual harvest, as opposed to those that use no research information. To do so we use the Bayesian notion of a loss function: the expected utility of the vaccination regime unsupported by a study from the research program in question, less the expected utility of a regime that does take advantage of the program information.

The negative of that loss is the value K of the research information itself. If we let d be the vaccination decision or regime, Y the mortality or harvest outcome, and Z the study forecast of that outcome, our measure of research knowledge gain K (viz., the expected value of sample information EVSI) therefore is:

$$K \overset{\text{def}}{=} \text{EVSI} = EU\big[d|;Z|;p(Y|Z)\big] - EU\big[d;p(Y|Z)\big] \tag{1}$$

(Winkler 1972, p. 311; Berger 1985, p. 60). Here p ($Y|Z$) is the probability that outcome Y will occur given that we know its forecast Z. Its presence in both the first and second right-hand term of K indicates only that the utility of research-informed decision $d|Z$ and the research-uninformed decision d is each being evaluated with the use of the research forecast model from which forecasts Z have been drawn. This is valid because the research studies we are investigating have already been conducted, so the forecasts are already known. Including these forecasts in both right-hand terms of the knowledge equation therefore is necessary as well as possible, because it is the only way to compute the expected utility the farmer foregoes by declining to use the research information that the program has made available.

Our principal interest is in determining how the research program's purview, resources, and management policies – including the topics it takes up, the research disciplines involved, its budgets, and the training of its scientists – affect the knowledge it produces. Many of these factors, which we indicate by the vector **X**, are observed at the research project level, such as the research discipline, human and physical research capital, study methods and materials, research treatments, and the type and difficulty of the topic addressed. Others are observed at the program rather than project level, such as the physical environment spanning a number of projects.[2]

We model an applied research program's economic value in terms of its improvement to decision makers' forecast accuracy. Thus, we must adopt a functional form for utility U or equivalently for the loss incurred when outcome Y (such as harvest volume) diverges from its forecast Z. For that purpose, we use the mean absolute deviation (MAD) functional form $U(d, Y) = -|d - Y|$, so that loss is proportionate to the absolute difference between decision, and hence prediction, and outcome

---

[2] Basic research in contrast could be argued to lack any concrete outcomes or probabilities, being a matter more of discrete realizations than incremental steps. Probit models might in future be useful in representing that kind of discrete space.

(Robert 2001). Research utility and knowledge K improve, in other words, to the extent forecasts come closer to outcomes, whether overshooting or undershooting them.

In this case, it is not too difficult to show that Eq. (1) should depend to a high degree of accuracy on two terms. The first is the difference the research has made in the scientist's outcome prediction Z. That is, it is the difference between the prior forecast M_{prior} and the posterior forecast M_{post}, defined as the shift in the location of the outcome's probability distribution, which we call the study *mean surprise*. The greater the mean surprise, the more knowledge the research has provided. The second is the sample variation of the research outcomes, or in a regression context the standard deviation of the model error σ_{post}, which we will call the study's *imprecision*. The lower the imprecision, the greater the study's knowledge contribution. In sum, our own regression model of a research program's knowledge production is

$$K = g\left(\left|M_{prior} - M_{post}\right|, -\sigma_{post}\right) = f\left(\mathbf{X}, \varepsilon\right). \tag{2}$$

Knowledge contribution is greater to the extent of its mean surprise and lower to the extent of its precision, and this contribution depends on the research program characteristics $\mathbf{X}$.

Application to Research Assessment

As an illustration, we apply this framework to a pond fisheries research program funded by the US Agency for International Development (USAID), which during the 2007–2011 period comprised 55 studies managed under seven subprograms in 16 nations.[3] It combined the resources of 17 US universities and 31 foreign universities and institutes. Twenty-five of the studies were completed during the program's 2007–2009 phase, examined here. Data are drawn from a research input and output questionnaire administered to the 25 2007–2009 investigators, plus associated interviews. In each controlled experiment study, an output observation consisted of a pair of prior and posterior probability distributions for each major treatment and for each dimension if the treatment involved multiple outcome dimensions. In each survey study, an output observation consisted of such a probability distribution pair for each major survey question posed. Study expenditure data were obtained from the study proposals and their subsequent quarterly, annual, and final reports. Sample size from the 25 studies was 415.

---

[3] Feed-the-Future Innovation Lab for Collaborative Research on Aquaculture and Fisheries, Oregon State University, sponsored by US Agency for International Development. The countries are Bangladesh, Cambodia, China, Ghana, Guyana, Indonesia, Kenya, Mexico, Nepal, Nicaragua, the Philippines, South Africa, Tanzania, Thailand, Uganda, and Vietnam.

Research Problem Type

Research topic can affect knowledge output because some topics are more easily exploitable than others – requiring fewer scarce resources, of more recent interest and thus fewer scientific competitors, or benefiting from earlier discoveries that enhanced the likelihood of new ones (Alston et al. 2000). Program administrators would have intuitions about which areas will conduce to the greatest study output with a given budget. Ex post however, the productivity of a topic area is empirical and can be determined only by comparing topic research performance when costs are held constant. In a highly diversified program like this aquacultural one, categorizing problem types is difficult because "topic" can refer to a scientific discipline like biology, a subdiscipline like developmental biology, or a problem area like mutation. Topic areas in are here aggregated into four groups: development biology, human health science, economic science, and environmental science.

Research outcome dimensions, too, have implications for research performance because, for example, water microcystin problems may be less familiar and so costlier than water phosphorus problems. At the same time, relative unfamiliarity can bring greater breakthrough opportunities in the sense of shifting the expected outcome away from the literature's current one. Similarly, some outcome dimensions are more easily measured than others and hence more amenable to predictive precision, a disease's immunity rate more predictable, for example, than its duration. A typical study in our data focused on five or six separate outcome dimensions. For parsimony, they are aggregated here into four categories: mortality and growth, demand and price, species diversity, and water quality. Outcome dimensions crosscut topic areas. Developmental biology and environmental science studies, for instance, frequently consisted of mortality/growth and water quality dimensions.

A crucial element of problem difficulty is the analytical approach required to address it. Experiments are usually more expensive than surveys. But the difficulty of managing a controlled experiment depends on the lead investigator's training and experience and the topic at hand. Because experimental controls are designed to reduce random noise, we expect them to bring lower unexplained sample variance, that is, greater precision, than surveys do. On the other hand, science's normal preference for a controlled setting suggests surveys are used only when a problem's conceptual frame is too poorly understood to formulate an incisive experiment. That absence of a strong a priori likely brings large and frequent distribution shifts – a substantial amount of mean surprise – in statistical surveys.

Research Cost

The potentially best indicator of a project's resources is its budget, encapsulating its physical and human capital and material costs. Research budgets in our data often included administrative support and lab space costs but rarely equipment. In either case their service flows to the given project were unreliable because they were based on local accounting conventions, which vary by country. A reliable measure of project scale, however, was budgeted principal investigator and research assistant time: project FTE.

Researcher quality might be as important as size: education has been widely shown to lift labor productivity. This would be especially true in a knowledge-intensive activity like research (Cohen and Levinthal 1989; Rynes et al. 2001; Schulze and Hoegl 2008). A valuable proxy for unobserved infrastructure can be researcher travel cost because most program study sites were far from the home institution. Travel consumes resources – the scientist's time and energy as well as cash cost – otherwise devotable to analysis. Education and travel time therefore were included in our model in addition to laboratory assistant FTE. Research material and training expenses were unavailable. Table 1 lists the knowledge measures

Table 1 Summary statistics, aquaculture and fisheries research, 2007–2009 ($N = 415$)

Variable	Unit	Mean	Standard deviation	Coefficient of variation
Knowledge generated				
Value of sample information (K)	Proportion	0.123	0.212	1.723
Mean surprise (distribution shift)	"	0.224	0.278	1.241
Imprecision (error st. deviation)	"	0.380	0.653	1.718
Laboratory human capital				
Lab size (FTE)	Years	4.8	2.9	0.604
Mean lab education	Years/person	17.1	1.2	0.070
Mean lab age	Years/person	33	6.1	0.185
Research problem type				
Topic area category				
Development biology	Category	0.51	0.50	0.98
Human health science	"	0.12	0.32	2.67
Economic science	"	0.11	0.31	2.82
Environmental science	"	0.27	0.44	1.63
Research outcome dimension				
Mortality and growth	Category	0.68	0.47	0.69
Demand and price	"	0.14	0.37	2.64
Species diversity	"	0.002	0.05	25.00
Water quality	"	0.18	0.39	2.17
Analytical approach				
Experiment vs survey	Category	0.70	0.46	0.657
Public infrastructure				
Site proximity	Kilometers	843	891	1.06
Region of world				
Asia	Category	0.78	0.41	0.53
Africa	"	0.05	0.22	4.40
Latin America	"	0.17	0.37	2.18

and relevant productivity factors for which we have data: laboratory human capital, topic area category, research outcome dimension, analytical approach, and public infrastructure proxies.

Data Construction and Econometric Specification

In sum, research program analysis involves eliciting investigators' prior and posterior density functions and formulating and estimating the associated loss function.

Eliciting Prior and Posterior Densities

The director of each *controlled experiment study* was asked to identify the three most important experimental controls to be used in her research. For each control, and each major outcome dimension of that control, she then was asked to state her prior probabilities that a respectively low, medium, and high outcome level would be observed. These stated probabilities were used to compute that control's and dimension's prior mean M_{prior}. When the experimental results were later obtained for that control and dimension, she was asked to provide its mean outcome M_{post}. The corresponding research precision measure σ_{post} was obtained as the standard deviation of the ANOVA model's residual error. The director of each *survey study* was asked to name the three most important survey questions to be enumerated. For each, we asked him to identify his prior probability that the respondent would give a respectively low, medium, and high answer, giving us the expected survey question outcome M_{prior}. The corresponding precision measure was the residual standard deviation of the investigator's multiple regression analysis of the responses (Winkler 1972).

At two international program meetings and several other workshops, we trained principal investigators in the process of quantitatively expressing their prior probabilities, together with the kinds of information, such as the scientific literature and earlier experience with related projects, admissible in priors. Among the experimental studies, the 14 investigators each reported an average of 8 treatments and 3 outcome dimensions per treatment. In the statistical survey studies, the 11 investigators reported an average of 4 respondent subgroups and three survey questions per subgroup.

Data

Key sample statistics are shown in Table 1. In the average study, research control, and outcome dimension, the prior outcome expectation was 22.4% greater or less than the mean outcome in the subsequent experiment or survey. That is, research outcome expectations tended to be 22.4% of what eventually happened, creating a 22.4% mean surprise. Study precision is reflected in the sample mean posterior standard deviation (0.380) in Table 1 – measuring the average spread of unexplained research outcomes around their unity-normalized experimental or survey means. Research utility lost, that is, on account of prediction or estimation noise was 38% of the typical outcome mean. The mean expected value of sample information – our knowledge metric K – was 12.3% of the typical outcome mean.

The knowledge density functions provide a broader picture. The distribution of mean surprises (Figs. 2 and 3) is skewed strongly to the right, most observations lying just above zero. Mean surprise appears to be a tournament: the greater the outcome distribution shift, the fewer that achieve it. Something of a reverse tournament is evidenced in study precision, the worst performances being the least likely. The bulk of investigators, that is, maintain a relatively low error variance. Aggregating mean surprise and precision together, the new knowledge distribution appears to be dominated by its mean-surprise component. Most projects bunch near the low end of the new knowledge range, a phenomenon often noticed in competitive outcomes (Hausman et al. 1984; Griliches 1990; Lanjouw and Schankerman 2004). Logs of mean surprise and precision (Fig. 2) are rather symmetrically distributed. But especially in knowledge K (Fig. 2c), left-tail outliers are evident, representing mean surprises near zero and hence with large negative logs.

As Table 1 shows, the average lab assistant had 17 years of education – about 1 year of postgraduate work. Seventy percent of the projects were controlled experiments and the remaining 30% surveys. Fifty-one percent of topics were in development biology, 27% in environmental science, 12% in human health science, and 11% in economics. Crosscutting these areas, 68% of treatment outcomes were on mortality and growth, 18% on water quality, and about 14% on demand and price. Seventy-eight percent of the studies were in Asia, 17% Latin America, and 5% Africa. Coefficients of variation (CV) of explanatory variables, reflecting adequacy of variation for statistical inference, varied widely. Education's relative variability (CV = 0.07) is the lowest, as expected on a research team. None of these factors were correlated to an extent creating inference problems.

Results

A way to think of basic research is that it is an effort to find a "whole new approach" to the problem in question, shifting the entire probability distribution of predicted outcomes. That is, if successful, it will generate a substantial mean surprise $|M_{prior} - M_{post}|$.

One expects to see statistical surveys used most frequently in these situations, when the problem's stochastic structure is poorly understood. Survey approaches, that is, might be expected to bring greater mean surprise than experiments do. Conversely, experimental controls would be used when the structure is better known and so have greater success in achieving research precision.

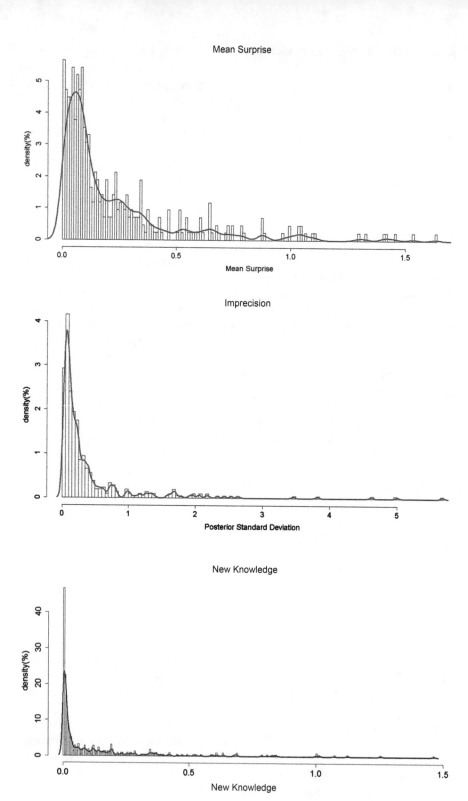

Fig. 2 Histograms of (a) Mean Surprise $|M_{prior} - M_{post}|$, Imprecision (posterior standard deviation σ_{post}), and (c) New Knowledge K

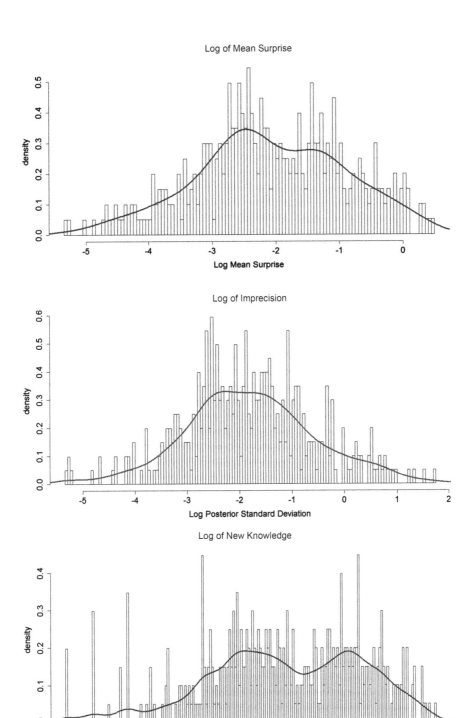

Fig. 3 Histograms of (a) Log Mean Surprise (ln $|M_{prior} - M_{post}|$), (b) Log Imprecision (log posterior standard deviation ln σ_{post}), and (c) Log New Knowledge (ln K)

At the same time, because structural shifts are more poorly observable to the econometrician and hence harder to model than are the more marginal scientific efforts to reduce prediction variance, mean surprise should be more difficult for research evaluators to assess than research precision is. Explaining surprise would require deeper attention to the nature of the subject and its institutional and intellectual constraints, modeled here in only a summary way by analytical approach, topic area, and outcome dimension. Explaining precision therefore would involve greater attention to the more numerate factors like budget, laboratory equipment, and the number, experience, and education of the research assistants.

Factor Effects on Mean Surprise and Predictive Precision

The first step in our own evaluation of the USAID program is to regress mean surprise on the associated project inputs and program features. We then separately regress the study outcome residual (i.e., unexplained) variances on these same project inputs and program features. The results are shown in Tables 2 and 3. Several factors not included in these tables – research assistant numbers and age and travel mode to study site – were consistently nonsignificant in earlier regressions and dropped. R-squares, 0.26 in the mean surprise and 0.44 in the research precision model, are reasonably high considering the sample's cross-sectional structure and the variety of research problems, methods, treatments, outcome types, institutional settings, and cultural settings it contains.

Topic area category and research outcome dimension each help explain mean surprise (Table 2). Developmental biology studies bring 0.47 [i.e., $0.266 - (-0.204)$] percentage points more mean surprise than economics studies do, a difference 2.24 times as large as the average (0.21) of the associated standard errors. Human health science work similarly brings 0.35% points more mean surprise than economics work does, 1.45 times the average (0.24) standard error. Mean-surprise differences between the remaining topic-area pairs are small. Among outcome dimensions, demand and species diversity each bring significantly more mean surprise than water quality does (t-statistics 1.9 and 1.6, respectively).

Topic area and outcome dimension have even more striking influences on research precision (Table 3) than they do on mean surprise. Predictive precision averages 48% higher in development biology, 48% lower in human health, and 73% lower in economics than in environmental science. The low associated standard errors make clear that the precision differences among biology, human health, and economic science are also statistically significant at normal confidence levels. Among outcome dimensions, mortality/growth predictions carry 78% greater precision, and demand/price predictions 67% greater precision, than do water quality predictions. Separately, and consistent with our hypothesis, statistical surveys produce the greater probability distribution shifts, and controlled experiments produce the more precise predictions. All else equal, surveys bring an average 105% greater mean surprise than controlled experiments do (Table 2) and experiment an average 75% lower posterior outcome error than surveys do (Table 3).

Table 2 Input effects on absolute difference between prior and posterior mean finding (mean surprise)

Research input	Estimate	Standard error
Intercept	0.171	3.790
Continuous inputs		
Lab size (FTE)	0.206	0.097
Mean education	−0.353	1.333
Site proximity	0.107	0.025
Topic area category		
Development biology	0.226	0.196
Human health science	0.143	0.252
Economic science	−0.204	0.232
(Base: Environmental science)		
Research outcome dimension		
Mortality and growth	−0.087	0.200
Demand and price	0.568	0.300
Species diversity	1.836	1.140
(Base: Water quality)		
Analytical approach		
Experiment vs survey	−1.051	0.248
(Base: Statistical surveys)		
Region of world		
Asia	−0.667	0.163
Africa	0.576	0.303
(Base: Latin America)		
Notes:		
Dependent variable:	Absolute difference between prior expectation and posterior sample mean of experimental finding or survey response. Estimation linear in logs	
Residual standard error:	1.091	
Sample size:	415	
Multiple *R*-square:	0.26	

Laboratory size (proxied by employment) does turn out to significantly boost mean surprise, lifting it 0.21% for every 1.0% lab size increment (Table 2). It has no significant effect however on predictive precision (Table 3).[4] Study site proximity to the research center enhances mean surprise only moderately (elasticity 0.11 in Table 2) and statistical precision even less.

---

[4] If laboratory expansion did impair precision, we would be unlikely to observe any expansion unless the mean-surprise advantage more than compensated for the precision loss.

Table 3 Input effects on negative of standard deviation of unexplained finding (precision)

Research input	Estimate	Standard error
Intercept	−11.543	3.302
Continuous inputs		
Lab size (FTE)	−0.112	0.085
Mean education	4.263	1.161
Site proximity	0.033	0.021
Topic area category		
Development biology	0.481	0.171
Human health science	−0.476	0.219
Economic science	−0.735	0.202
(Base: Environmental science)		
Research outcome dimension		
Mortality and growth	0.797	0.174
Demand and price	0.670	0.261
Species diversity	1.614	0.993
(Base: Water quality)		
Analytical approach		
Experiment vs survey	0.752	0.216
(Base: Statistical surveys)		
Region of world		
Asia	0.370	0.142
Africa	−0.516	0.264
(Base: Latin America)		
Notes:		
Dependent variable:	Negative of standard deviation of unexplained experimental finding or survey response. Estimation linear in logs	
Residual standard error:	0.9508	
Sample size:	415	
Multiple R-square:	0.44	

Implications for Knowledge Production

The second step in our evaluation is to decompose total knowledge production into its mean surprise and unexplained error variance components. Our regression fit to the 415 sample observations ($R^2 = 0.97$) is, with t-statistics in parentheses:

$$\ln K = -1.188 + 1.76 \ln \left| M_{prior} - M_{post} \right| + \left(-0.71 \ln STD_{post} \right)$$
$$(-30.97) \; (122.08) \qquad (-50.79) \tag{3}$$

Three conclusions can be drawn from this estimate. (a) The high R^2 suggests mean surprise and unexplained posterior variance together virtually exhaust the knowledge generated. In other words, EVSI in a MAD functional form is very successfully decomposed into mean surprise and statistical precision. (b) Surprise and

Table 4 Decomposition of input effects on new knowledge, continuous variables

Research input	Knowledge contribution via research mean surprise	Knowledge contribution via research precision	Total knowledge contribution
Lab size (FTE)	0.363	0	0.363
Mean education	0	3.027	3.027
Site proximity	0.189	0.023	0.212

Notes:
Contributions in the first column are Table 2 elasticities multiplied by mean surprise's marginal knowledge contribution, and in the second column, the Table 3 elasticities multiplied by precision's marginal knowledge contribution
Third column numbers are the sums of those in the first and second columns
Continuous input effects are percentage changes induced by a 1% change in the indicated input
Analytical approach effects are the percentage changes associated with switching from the reference group to the group indicated

precision are each positive contributors to new knowledge K. (c) Surprise does turn out, in both an elasticity and goodness-of-fit sense, to be the more powerful knowledge factor, and precision the less powerful: the mean-surprise knowledge elasticity is $1.76/0.71 = 2.5$ times greater than precision.

We now use the above regression weights 1.76 and 0.71 in conjunction with the research output elasticities in Tables 2 and 3 to compute in Table 4 how each selected research input affects new knowledge output K. The contribution of lab size to scientific knowledge is, by way of its effect on mean surprise, $(1.76)(0.206) = 0.36\%$ and, by way of its effect on research precision, statistically nonsignificant. Scaling-up lab size 1% thus lifts knowledge output by 0.36%. Decreasing returns to lab scale are evident; the average project's ability to produce new findings with its observable physical resources is tightly constrained by, presumably, not only unaccounted for missing inputs but breakthrough opportunities in the research field.

On the other hand, research scale economies can be considered in a qualitative as well as physical or quantitative direction. In particular, we might want to know how knowledge output is affected by a simultaneous expansion of research lab size and quality. An elasticity at the combined quantitative and qualitative margins can, to the degree that quality is reflected in formal training, be obtained by adding the elasticity with respect to size together with the elasticity with respect to education. We have found that team education has essentially no mean-surprise effect (Table 2), although a precision elasticity of 4.263 (Table 3). Weighting the latter by precision's 0.71 knowledge, weight in Eq. (3) says a 1.0% education improvement boosts knowledge production by a very strong 3.027% (Table 4). Combining this with the lab size elasticity discussed above implies that expanding research capacity, 1.0% in both quantitative and qualitative dimensions lifts knowledge output by $0.363 + 3.027 = 3.39\%$. That is, taking input quality as well as quantity into account, increasing rather than decreasing returns to research scale is evident. Kocher et al. (2006) and Wang and Huang (2007) also find increasing returns to research scale, although with bibliometric methods and in situations much different than examined here.

Conclusions

We have outlined a method of estimating research productivity at program, project, and scientific control level, permitting, in turn, direct comparisons with the associated research inputs and costs. New knowledge is modeled as the Bayesian expected value of sample information. The mean absolute deviation (MAD) utility form used here for that metric enables decomposing knowledge into mean surprise (outcome probability density shift) and research precision (density compactness), permitting independent examination of how each moment is influenced by the research settings.

In an application to an international research program, we find that (i) mean surprise and precision explain nearly the entire variation in research productivity, surprise more so than precision; (ii) greater laboratory size brings decreasing scale returns in the mean-surprise dimension and insignificant returns in the precision dimension; and (iii) researcher education powerfully improves precision, to the extent that, if expanded along with laboratory size, it brings increasing returns to scale in aggregate scientific knowledge. Furthermore, gains at the qualitative margin are much greater than at the quantitative margin.

Despite efforts to quantify the sources of research productivity, many lie beneath the surface even in as comparatively detailed a model as the present one. We have been able to match treatment- and dimension-specific research outcome statistics, hidden to most outside viewers, to many of the factors affecting them. But, for instance, we have not controlled for a research assistant's allocation across treatments and trials, which would affect the number of trials per treatment and the quality of effort per trial and hence research productivity. Although our model suggests they might be valuable, program accountants rarely record that kind of data.

Just as importantly, the present work points to the advantage of requiring scientists to specify their quantitative expectations of research outcomes. Priors have three virtues in a proposal. They encapsulate intuitions about previous work and about the scientist's own ideas, resources, and objectives that will differ from it. They require the proposer to specify precisely what the study controls or treatments are expected to be. And finally, they give managers and funders a more precise basis for judging the study's eventual success.

References

Adams, J., and Z. Griliches. 1996. Measuring Science: An Exploration. *Proceedings of the National Academy of Science* 93: 12664–12670.

Alston, J.M., G.W. Norton, and P.G. Pardey. 1995. *Science Under Scarcity: Principles and Practices for Agricultural Research Evaluation and Priority Setting*. Ithaca: Cornell University Press and ISNAR.

Alston, J.M., M.C. Marra, P.G. Pardey, and T.J. Wyatt. 2000. Research Returns Redux: A Meta-Analysis of the Returns to Agricultural R&D. *Australian Journal of Agricultural and Resource Economics* 44 (2): 185–215.

Alston, J.M., M.A. Andersen, J.S. James, and P.G. Pardey. 2011. The Economic Returns to US Public Agricultural Research. *American Journal of Agricultural Economics* 93 (5): 1257–1277.

Berger, J.O. 1985. *Statistical Decision Theory and Bayesian Analysis*. 2nd ed. New York: Springer.

CGIAR Science Council. 2009. *Defining and Refining Good Practice in Ex-Post Impact Assessment – Synthesis Report*. Rome: CGIAR Science Council Secretariat.

Cohen, W.M., and D.A. Levinthal. 1989. Innovation and Learning: The Two Faces of R&D. *Economic Journal* 99: 569–596.

Fontana, R., A. Nuvolari, H. Shimizu, and A. Vezzulli. 2013. Reassessing Patent Propensity: Evidence from a Dataset of R&D Awards, 1977–2004. *Research Policy* 42 (10): 1780–1792.

Griliches, Z. 1990. Patent Statistics as Economic Indicators: A Survey. *Journal of Economic Literature* 27: 1661–1707.

Hall, B.H., A.B. Jaffe, and M. Trajtenberg. 2005. Market Value and Patent Citations. *RAND Journal of Economics* 36: 16–38.

Hausman, J.A., B.H. Hall, and Z. Griliches. 1984. Econometric Models for Count Data with an Application to the Patents-R&D Relationship. *Econometrica* 52 (4): 909–938.

Huffman, W.E., and R.E. Evenson. 2006. Do Formula or Competitive Grant Funds Have Greater Impacts on State Agricultural Productivity? *American Journal of Agricultural Economics* 88 (4): 783–798.

Hurley, T.M., X. Rao, and P.G. Pardey. 2014. Re-Examining the Reported Rates of Return to Food and Agricultural Research and Development. *American Journal of Agricultural Economics* 96 (5): 1492–1504.

Industrial Research Institute. 2016. 2016 Global Funding Forecast. *R&D Magazine* (Winter 2016 Supplement), 3–34.

Kocher, M.G., M. Luptacik, and M. Sutter. 2006. Measuring Productivity of Research in Economics: A Cross-Country Study Using DEA. *Socio-Economic Planning Sciences* 40: 314–332.

Lanjouw, J.O., and M. Schankerman. 2004. Patent Quality and Research Productivity: Measuring Innovation with Multiple Indicators. *Economic Journal* 114 (495): 441–465.

Lindley, D.V. 1956. On a Measure of the Information Provided by an Experiment. *Annals of Mathematical Statistics* 27: 986–1005.

Oettl, A. 2012. Reconceptualizing Stars: Scientist Helpfulness and Peer Performance. *Management Science* 58 (6): 1122–1140.

Pardey, P.G. 1989. The Agricultural Knowledge Production Function: An Empirical Look. *The Review of Economics and Statistics* 71: 453–461.

Polanyi, M. 1974. *Personal Knowledge*. Chicago: University of Chicago Press.

Robert, C.P. 2001. *The Bayesian Choice*. 2nd ed. New York: Springer.

Rynes, S.L., J.M. Bartunek, and R.L. Daft. 2001. Across the Great Divide: Knowledge Creation and Transfer between Practitioners and Academics. *Academy of Management Journal* 44 (2): 340–355.

Schimmelpfennig, D.E., and G.W. Norton. 2003. What is the Value of Agricultural Economics Research? *American Journal of Agricultural Economics* 85: 81–94.

Schulze, A., and M. Hoegl. 2008. Organizational Knowledge Creation and the Generation of New Product Ideas: A Behavioral Approach. *Research Policy* 37 (10): 1742–1750.

Shapira, P., J. Youtie, K. Yogeesvaran, and Z. Jaafar. 2006. Knowledge Economy Measurement: Methods, Results, and Insights from the Malaysian Knowledge Content Study. *Research Policy* 35 (10): 1522–1537.

Wang, E.C., and W. Huang. 2007. Relative Efficiency of R&D Activities: A Cross-Country Study Accounting for Environmental Factors in the DEA Approach. *Research Policy* 36: 260–273.

White, F.C., and J. Havlicek. 1982. Optimal Expenditures for Agricultural Research and Extension: Implications of Underfunding. *American Journal of Agricultural Economics* 64 (1): 47–55.

Winkler, R.L. 1972. *An Introduction to Bayesian Inference and Decision*. New York: Holt, Rinehart and Winston.

———. 1986. Expert Resolution. *Management Science* 32 (3): 298–303.

———. 1994. Evaluating Probabilities: Asymmetric Scoring Rules. *Management Science* 40 (11): 1395–1405.

Innovation and Technology Transfer in Agriculture: Concluding Comments

Nicholas Kalaitzandonakes, Elias G. Carayannis, Evangelos Grigoroudis, and Stelios Rozakis

Abstract The authors in this book have described and analyzed a complex, dynamic system of agricultural innovation and technology transfer that has produced food in unprecedented quantity and quality, enhancing economic and food security worldwide. The agricultural innovation system has been in a near constant state of flux as fundamental technical discoveries, institutional adjustments, and increasing public and private investments have fueled the ongoing transformation. If societies are to meet the challenges of the future and promote both food security and environmental sustainability, they will need to adopt long-term approaches to building and maintaining innovation systems that can nurture innovations from original concept through development to the end user. Given the changes that we have seen and the further change that the future likely holds, research into the effective transformation of agriscience into agribusiness will continue to be important for many years to come.

Over the last 100 years, the process of agricultural innovation has been radically changed. At the turn of the last century, most new plant varieties, farm implements, or production processes were still the result of the efforts of individual farmers, naturalists, or tinkerers attempting to solve specific problems. Since that time, organized scientific investigation has taken a progressively larger role, until in our present day innovation is almost exclusively the domain of formalized, sophisticated, large-scale R&D programs in universities, government laboratories and research stations, and, increasingly, private firms. As government R&D funding expanded

N. Kalaitzandonakes (✉)
Department of Agricultural and Applied Economics, University of Missouri, Columbia, MO, USA
e-mail: KalaitzandonakesN@missouri.edu

E.G. Carayannis
George Washington University, Washington, DC, USA

E. Grigoroudis
School of Production Engineering & Management, Technical University of Crete, Chania, Crete, Greece

S. Rozakis
Institute of Soil Science and Plant Cultivation, IUNG-PIB, Pulawy, Poland

© Springer International Publishing AG 2018
N. Kalaitzandonakes et al. (eds.), *From Agriscience to Agribusiness*, Innovation, Technology, and Knowledge Management, https://doi.org/10.1007/978-3-319-67958-7_24

483

after WWII, public research institutions devoted more resources to both basic and applied research as well as to improving their capacity to transfer the results of that research to potential developers and users. The resulting stream of innovation transformed the agriculture industry through increased productivity and accelerated substitution of capital for labor and land. The increased capital investment aided broad economic development by releasing labor for other pursuits and the increased farm productivity improved food security around the world.

Countries around the world have also introduced institutional changes in order to encourage private R&D investment and provide market signals to direct agricultural innovation in general. Intellectual property rights (IPRs), and the protection they afford, were introduced to help firms recover R&D costs and thereby fund future research efforts. As IPR laws were progressively strengthened over the years, private sector R&D expenditures increased apace and a division of labor between public and private R&D emerged. Public research institutions tend to concentrate on more basic scientific research, while private firms tend to specialize in more applied research projects that have the potential to lead directly to new products. The modern IPR regime also worked to encourage technology transfer from the public to the private sector in that it allows public institutions to benefit from their discoveries and preserves the value of the inventions, giving private firms more of an incentive to develop them into market-ready products. The practice of cross-licensing IP facilitates cooperation and technology transfer among private firms as well. Other institutional arrangements were also put in place to encourage transfer of technology and knowledge from the public to the private sector including the cooperative extension services, academic publishing, collaborative public-private research, and many others.

Society in general has benefitted from agricultural R&D investments and the institutional arrangements that support them. The return on investment (ROI) of public R&D has been estimated to be high in all studies, including the ones reported in this volume. Private firms across the agrifood supply chain have experienced significant growth based on their investment in R&D and innovation, creating employment and wealth that has spread far beyond the agriculture sector. At the same time, political actors have continued to strengthen controls in the legal system in an attempt to minimize societal costs and increase the net benefits from innovation. Efficient regulations can mitigate risks that might accompany some innovations, and refinements to IP laws as well as antitrust laws have been used to curb excessive market power that could result from overuse of IPR.

The accelerating pace of scientific discovery produced by our modern R&D system and the global institutional, structural, and economic adaptations that have followed have created a dynamic environment of near constant change. In this book we have provided a comprehensive review of the key elements of the agricultural innovation process, from agriscience to agribusiness. Our discussion has centered on a few questions that are critical in such a rapidly changing environment.

What Is the Status and What Are Important Emerging Trends in Public and Private Agricultural R&D Investment and Innovation?

Investments in R&D made today will have effects that extend far into the future. It is therefore important to understand the changes in the pattern of R&D spending that are underway in both the public and the private sectors. In our opening chapter, *Pardey et al.* describe the changing face of global agricultural R&D. They find that while high-income countries still do the lion's share of agricultural R&D, the overall growth rate in expenditures has slowed over the recent years. Middle-income countries, on the other hand, have accelerated their overall R&D spending. One result of this is an increasing gap in R&D between higher- and lower-income countries. These trends imply that high-income countries, like the USA, must focus on increasing the efficiency of R&D, to get more results with less spending. This also emphasizes the importance of effective technology transfer to low-income countries, who stand to gain the most from innovation. The agricultural R&D landscape has been changing in other ways as well. *Fuglie, Clancy, and Heisey* document the trend toward increased private R&D funding over the past 25 years. This trend entails changes in the nature of agricultural R&D; private efforts tend to be more oriented toward product development, while public R&D tends to emphasize basic research. Given that division of labor, public and private research are largely complementary. They find minimal crowding out of private research by public R&D. Complementarity also opens up opportunities for public-private collaboration, which has been encouraged by recent policy changes. Private spending decisions are also more sensitive to costs of and returns to research, so public policy affecting those, such as IPRs and regulatory requirements, have a stronger effect on what types of projects are undertaken. This further emphasizes the importance of striking the right balance in public policy.

Phillips also emphasizes the complementary relationship of public and private R&D as he recounts the development of canola as the oilseed crop of Canada, which was achieved through both public and private R&D investments and innovation. In the early days, when the uncertainty about the market potential of the crop was quite high, research and breeding was almost completely publicly funded. As the potential became clearer, seed firms increased their R&D activity and formed an association to pool resources and spread risk. Now canola R&D is strictly privately funded and canola continues to become a major oilseed crop. The early support of public R&D and the free flow of knowledge from it was instrumental in canola's ultimate success.

As the private sector has taken on a larger role in agricultural R&D, the concept of private R&D has evolved and impacted the basic business model of R&D-based firms. *Kalaitzandonakes and Zahringer* describe an expansive integrated technology platform that is being developed in the agricultural input sector. This innovation model both is made possible by and drives the current trend of consolidation in this sector. Firms have integrated vertically in order to decrease transaction costs and ensure access to the wide range of complementary assets necessary to produce an integrated product line and have consolidated horizontally in a quest to pump up sales volume to the level necessary to support the prodigious R&D expenditures that this strategy requires. Their analysis also clarifies how institutional arrangements (regulation and IPR) shape private sector innovation strategies, R&D spending, and industry structure.

Do Institutional Arrangements Provide Appropriate Incentives to Foster Agricultural Innovation?

The institutional environment can have a big impact on the direction and amount of innovation in agriculture. Among the most significant aspects of that environment is the patent law regime under which the innovation takes place. *Smith and Kurtz* document the dramatic increase in corn yields in the USA over the last 150 years with the development of hybrid and, later, biotech varieties. They emphasize the role of the institutional environment, especially effective IPR protection, in creating the incentives for innovators to continue developing new cultivars. They also stress the role of international treaties in making that environment globally uniform, and especially in striking the proper balance between IPR protection and the free flow of public information.

The matter of balance can be very important. IPR protections that are too weak or too strong can distort incentives and hamper innovation. One concern often expressed concerning patenting is that patents may function to block, rather than facilitate, technology transfer by creating an "anticommons" of fragmented property rights and high transaction costs. *Lesser* investigates this possibility in depth. He finds that patent holders usually restrict infringement suits to commercial use, presumably those cases where the potential damage avoided would justify the expense of legal action. He finds no significant anticommons in research use of IP, especially for basic research, where such damage would not likely be forthcoming. He also finds that IP owners have generally allowed free use of patented technology in the development of charitable products as well, citing the example of Golden Rice. Thus market incentives seem to be sufficient to prevent any substantial anticommons situation. A robust market for patents and firms may also indicate a more competitive environment. *Gjonca and Yiannaka* analyze patent characteristics that are related to whether and how often patents, and the firms that hold them, change hands by merger or acquisition. They find that less valuable and less enforceable patents and those with more fragmented ownership are more often bought and sold and overall find an active market for patents.

Kalaitzandonakes, Magnier, and Kolympiris also find an active market for IPR as well as a direct link between R&D spending and the level of innovation achieved. In the context of the agricultural input sector, they show that private R&D expenditures have increased dramatically since 1990, but also that direct research costs have dropped, which has enhanced R&D efficiency. The increased spending has resulted in a greatly increased number of agricultural patents awarded each year as well as faster new product introductions. Their analysis of awarded patents indicates that for the most part disclosures and awards represent real innovation, not strategic firm patenting to limit competition. They also find that there is broad licensing and cross-licensing activity as firms find it is in their interest to share technology to develop more valuable products. Overall, these chapters suggest that in well-functioning markets with clear property rights, rules play an essential role in encouraging innovation.

Institutions of higher education, especially land-grant universities (LGUs) in the USA, are an important part of the agricultural innovation system. *Tripp, Grueber, Yetter, and Yetter* investigate one of the key public knowledge products of LGU research supported by federal funding – journal articles. They find that USDA funding to LGUs supports both basic and applied research and such federal research funding induces an even larger amount of non-federal funding for research at LGUs. *Tripp, Simkins, Yetter, and Yetter* further examine the intellectual property output of LGUs, in the form of patents and plant variety protection (PVP) certificates. Here they find that LGU patents are highly influential in stimulating follow-on innovation and that LGU and private PVPs are largely complementary. Their findings imply the importance of balance in federal programs, to support both basic and applied work, and of maintaining the flexibility of LGUs to take on research projects of high relevance that will attract other funds and influence later innovation.

Do Institutional Arrangements Provide Appropriate Incentives to Encourage Technology Transfer from the Public to the Private Sector?

As patenting of university innovations has become more common, institutional arrangements have been put in place to encourage transfer of knowledge and technology to product developers and users. As a result, TTOs have become a common feature at universities worldwide. TTOs offer the twin benefits of facilitating the flow of innovations to the public and augmenting university income. However, they have achieved variable, and sometimes only modest, success in the latter. *Smyth* examines the performance of TTOs in Canadian universities and offers evidence of a strong link between staffing levels and licensing rates and also notes a change underway in research funding to ensure research is more readily commercializable. *Hoenen, Kolympiris, Wubben, and Omta* present a case study of a successful TT system. They attribute the effectiveness of the system at Wageningen University to a balance of central and decentralized decisions and support; individual departments can implement the specific mode of technology transfer that best suits their discipline and personnel, while the central university provides general legal frameworks for different modes, thus reducing transaction costs. They also credit a corporate culture that places high value on producing long-term social value and ongoing industry cooperation.

A common view of the mission of a university TTO is to manage the institution's patent portfolio, particularly with respect to licensing agreements. In a case study of the technology transfer activity at the Agricultural University of Athens, *Cartalos, Svoronos, and Carayannis* offer a broader view of how a TTO can facilitate commercialization. The TTO there offers a range of services to both faculty researchers and licensee firms, including business planning and securing follow-on venture funding. They also offer two measures for identifying higher potential innovations, ones worth the allocation of scarce resources. *Zahringer, Kolympiris, and Kalaitzandonakes* discuss how the stage of the technology life cycle can influence the optimal licensing strategy and efficient resource allocation of TTOs.

These chapters highlight one area of ongoing change in university agricultural innovation and technology transfer programs. TTOs were originally conceived as patent portfolio management offices, but they have progressively assumed the broader mission of facilitating transfer and further development of university innovations.

Do Institutional Arrangements Provide Appropriate Incentives to Encourage Technology Transfer from Innovators to Agricultural Producers?

Extension is also a critical factor in enhancing agricultural productivity through effective technology transfer because, in the end, for an innovation to be successful, farmers must adopt and use it. *Koutsouris* reviews the dominant paradigms used in extension research and practice. Early research focused on a linear model of transfer that somewhat overlooked the participation of the farmer. He concludes that public research should be linked even closer to practice in order to ensure that innovations are relevant to farmer needs and that the extension system should be able to capture and spread innovations originating in production agriculture as well as academic research. *Ugochukwu and Phillips* focus their analysis on the conditions that improve farmer adoption of agricultural innovation. They identify several factors that influence the adoption of many different types of innovations, including land tenure, access to credit, extension services, human and physical capital resources, and farmer risk aversion. They also note the importance of informal networks in diffusing information and experience about innovations. A better understanding of the adoption process can inform upstream decision-making about R&D and technology transfer resource allocation.

Effective contracts are also an important factor in transferring innovative technology to producers. Contract structure strongly affects how the benefits of new agricultural technologies are shared between the technology developers and agricultural producers and whether commercializing the technology is in the best interest of each. *Akhundjanov, Gallardo, McCluskey, and Rickard* investigate the relative attractiveness of different license contracts to producers considering purchasing a new variety of apple tree. They find that the economic interests of producers and innovators do not necessarily coincide on all dimensions of contract provisions. Also, non-economic factors can play a significant role in determining the overall attractiveness of different contracts. They emphasize the need for patent owners to be sensitive to a wide range of considerations when negotiating license contracts.

Large technology development and transfer projects can require a high level of institutional support to be successful. *Edge, Oikeh, Kyetere, Mugo, and Mashingaidze* offer a study of a current and ongoing project, Water Efficient Maize for Africa (WEMA). Similar to canola, WEMA is a successful public-private partnership. In this account, though, the authors emphasize how the unique characteristics of the individual organizations involved in the project contributed to its success. They stress the importance of getting the division of labor right, where each participating organization contributes from its strengths, ensuring that all participants, especially their top management, commit to the goals and structure of the project from the beginning, holding all participants accountable, and maintaining a spirit of patience and compromise that is critical in an international project.

Are the Levels of Public and Private R&D Investments Appropriate to the Societal Returns, and how Should we Measure Those Returns?

Social benefits from innovation are multidimensional, and not all can be measured precisely. Several contributors in this volume explain the varied types of benefits offered by agricultural innovation. *Shafer and Strauss* describe the extent of internal and extramural USDA-sponsored research and its contribution to society. Nearly every food item present in US homes has been impacted by plant varieties, production processes, or management systems developed at least in part by research performed or funded by USDA and passed on to producers through the cooperative extension system. The impact of a higher-quality diet produced at lower cost is difficult to fully define and measure. It is safe to say, though, that it likely impacts every aspect of our quality of life, including health, longevity, productivity at work, enjoyment of leisure, and many others. In Brazil, *Martha and Alves* discuss and demonstrate some of the more quantifiable impacts of agricultural research and innovation. The Brazilian agricultural research organization Embrapa is the major player in R&D there. Through policy initiatives and programs not only in research but also in rural extension and improved access to farm credit, Embrapa has significantly contributed to an annual growth in agriculture total factor productivity (TFP) of 2.2–2.3% since the 1980s. This high rate of TFP growth is a direct antecedent to increasing real income and wealth, due to a lower cost and greater availability of food, and broader economic growth through the release of labor to other sectors of the economy.

When exploring the question of societal benefits, the way we study this area becomes an important consideration. How investigators operationally define basic concepts like research expenditures, returns, and productivity, to name just a few, can have a significant impact on the results obtained. *Huffman* reviews recent research that quantifies productivity gains from basic agricultural research and notes a few areas where such research could be improved, including a more rigorous differentiation among basic research aimed at productivity gains, other types of research, and extension activities. He also emphasized the importance of using realistic time lags for the effects of new research and extension knowledge and choosing accurate measures for calculating net benefits. He also emphasizes that extension is a different sort of activity from research and uses different resources. Thus it should be kept conceptually separate and studied on its own terms. He shows how studies that conflate research and extension expenditures have distorted estimates of the returns to R&D. The dollar impact of an innovation on farm profit is an extremely important metric and also fairly readily quantifiable, but it is not the only dimension of adoption decision-making nor the only effect of innovation on farm operations. Many innovations can be used to decrease the uncertainty of future outcomes, improving decision-making and reducing risk. *Qin and Buccola* discuss two novel metrics aimed at quantifying these benefits in a way that would be comparable across research projects. In their system, mean surprise measures the shift in the probability distribution of predicted future outcomes, while precision measures the decrease in the error of those predictions. They relate the two metrics to characteristics of the research enterprise in a way that could help researchers and planners alike.

Final Thoughts

Our authors have described and analyzed a complex, dynamic system of agricultural innovation and technology transfer that has produced food in unprecedented quantity and quality, enhancing economic and food security worldwide. The agricultural innovation system has been in a near constant state of flux as fundamental technical discoveries, institutional adjustments, and increasing public and private investments have fueled the ongoing transformation. Investments in agricultural research still give ROIs estimated to be significantly greater than those in other sectors of production.

Such high returns on R&D investments will continue to be crucial in the future. Population growth, climate change, and pressure on critical natural resources make the need for effective and efficient public and private agricultural innovations systems urgent. Higher than usual ROIs suggest that additional investment in agricultural research and investment may be in order. If societies are to meet the challenges of the future and promote both food security and environmental sustainability, they will need to adopt long-term approaches to building and maintaining innovation systems that recognize the long time horizons over which innovations move from original concept through development and into the life span of a marketed product. Given the changes that we have seen and the further change that the future likely holds, research into the effective transformation of agriscience into agribusiness will continue to be important for many years to come.

Erratum to: The Evaluation Process of Research Commercialization Proposals and its Links to University Technology Transfer (TT) Strategy: A Case Study

Odysseas Cartalos, Alexander N. Svoronos, and Elias G. Carayannis

Erratum to:
Chapter 14 in: N. Kalaitzandonakes et al. (eds.),
From Agriscience to Agribusiness, **Innovation,**
Technology, and Knowledge Management,
https://doi.org/10.1007/978-3-319-67958-7_14

Chapter 14 titled **"The Evaluation Process of Research Commercialization Proposals and its Links to University Technology Transfer (TT) Strategy: A Case Study"**, the equations in page no. 300 were corrected to read as:

$$\text{BINRA} : \max_{x_i} \sum c_i x_i$$

$$\text{LPRA} : \max_{x_.} \sum c_i x_i$$

The updated online version of this chapter can be found at
https://doi.org/10.1007/978-3-319-67958-7_14

© Springer International Publishing AG 2018   E1
N. Kalaitzandonakes et al. (eds.), *From Agriscience to Agribusiness*, Innovation,
Technology, and Knowledge Management, https://doi.org/10.1007/978-3-319-67958-7_25

CPSIA information can be obtained
at www.ICGtesting.com
Printed in the USA
BVHW052035161218
535393BV00006B/111/P